W9-BCM-508

CLASSICS
OF
INTERNATIONAL
RELATIONS

CLASSICS
OF
INTERNATIONAL
RELATIONS

Third Edition

Edited by

John A. Vasquez
Vanderbilt University

PRENTICE HALL, Upper Saddle River, New Jersey 07458

Library of Congress Cataloging-in-Publication Data

Classics of international relations / edited by John A. Vasquez.—
   3rd ed.
      p.   cm.
   Includes bibliographical references.
   ISBN 0–13–146648–8
   1. International relations.   I. Vasquez, John A.
JX1308.C63 1996
327—dc20

                                                      95–34432
                                                      CIP

Acquisitions editor: Michael Bickerstaff
Editorial assistant: Anita Castro
Editorial/production supervision
   and interior design: Darrin Kiessling
Copy editor: Larry Feinberg
Cover director: Jayne Conte
Buyer: Bob Anderson

©1996, 1990, 1986 by Prentice-Hall, Inc.
Simon & Schuster/A Viacom Company
Upper Saddle River, New Jersey 07458

All rights reserved. No part of this book may
be reproduced, in any form or by any means,
without written permission from the publisher.

Printed in the United States of America
10 9 8 7 6 5 4 3 2 1

ISBN 0-13-146648-8

Prentice-Hall International (UK) Limited, *London*
Prentice-Hall of Australia Pty. Limited, *Sydney*
Prentice-Hall Canada Inc., *Toronto*
Prentice-Hall Hispanoamericana, S.A., *Mexico*
Prentice-Hall of India Private Limited, *New Delhi*
Prentice-Hall of Japan, Inc., *Tokyo*
Simon & Schuster Asia Pte. Ltd., *Singapore*
Editora Prentice-Hall do Brasil, Ltda., *Rio de Janeiro*

In memory of

Sean Henehan Vasquez

d.
b. October 12, 1982

Contents (Topical)

Part I   Morality and Politics

Part II   Debates over Methods and Theory

Part III   Foreign Policy and Global Conflict

Contents (Chronological)

The Western Heritage

Reactions to World War, 1914–1948

The 1950s

The 1960s

The 1970s

The 1980s

The 1990s

Preface

My purpose in editing this book has been to present some of the best analyses of the most enduring questions of international relations. In doing so, I hope to capture the essence of what the field has to say to humanity. I have chosen to do this by bringing together the reflections of the great thinkers and the analyses of twentieth-century scholars on a common set of problems. In selecting the works of the great thinkers, I have tried to select those works that are regarded as classics of Western civilization and essential to a liberal education. In selecting more recent works, I have tried to select classics of the discipline—representatives of the most influential work published on international relations in each of the last five decades. The resulting volume, I believe, constitutes one of the most efficient and comprehensive sources through which the student or general reader can gain an overview of international relations inquiry. Hence, the volume is meant to stand by itself and does not need a supplemental textbook. For those who feel the need for further treatment of the topics and thinkers in this book, I have co-authored with Marie T. Henehan a *Companion to International Relations: Major Concepts, Terms, and Thinkers*, published by Prentice Hall. It is organized in a format that allows students to answer their own questions quickly and easily.

The book is divided into four parts, each of which is devoted to a central issue. Part I focuses on the perennial question of whether morality should or can govern political behavior. Chapters on how the realist, just-war, idealist, and radical traditions have addressed this question in different historical contexts are included. Part II treats questions of how international relations should be studied—whether knowledge about the subject can be acquired, whether a science of international relations is possible, and whether a new theoretical approach is needed to comprehend world politics. Chapter 4 treats debates over how international relations inquiry should be defined and studied. Chapter 5 presents some of the analyses of those who argue that an alternative to realism or power politics would provide a more valid perspective on the subject. Part III is devoted to the primary empirical concerns of the field—the conduct of foreign policy and its relationship to global conflict. The chapters on foreign policy, crisis, war, and imperialism provide a distillation of the most important theories and research on each of these questions. Part IV reflects the main purpose of the field—how peace can be achieved and maintained. Chapters on the balance of power, nuclear deterrence, world order, the democratic security community, and international law and world government present and evaluate the major proposals for the mitigation or elimination of war. Chapter 12 includes selections on how conflict has been mitigated in the world political economy.

Although this book is lengthy, there were still many important pieces that could not be included because of space limitation. Among the works of the great thinkers, only classics from the Western tradition have been included; a separate volume would be needed to do justice to the rich tradition of non-Western thought. The only exception has been the inclusion of Gandhi, whose ideas have had a tremendous impact in the West, particularly upon peace movements. As for more recent scholarship, the emphasis has been placed on the Anglo-American tradition, or on works that have directly affected that tradition. But even after applying these rather restrictive selection criteria, many significant thinkers who met them could not be included; their works have been recommended for further reading in the introduction to each section.

In the third edition I have made a number of changes as a result of the end of the Cold War and the collapse of the Soviet Union. In particular, the emphasis in Part IV, The Search for Peace, has shifted away from an avoidance of nuclear war to an analysis of how to build and maintain peace in the post–Cold War era. I have added a chapter on global leadership and world order that provides critical analyses by Richard Rosecrance and by Inis Claude of the possibilities for peace provided by a concert of power and by collective security. A recommendation for a concert system as a framework for peace among the strongest states had been advocated in the first edition (1986), and I am glad to see that the new international situation has made scholars give a concert of power more serious attention. As in the earlier edition, world order is treated in the context of possibilities raised by the world political economy.

If peace among the former Cold War rivals has been one of the major sources for rethinking international relations theory, the second has been the widespread discussion of the hypothesis that democratic states do not fight each other. I have added a chapter on what I call "the democratic security community," with selections by Kant, Karl Deutsch, Dean Babst, and Maoz and Russett. I have included Deutsch's analysis in this chapter because the theoretical rationale and prediction he made for the rise of security communities seem now to be clearly applicable to advanced industrial democracies.

In addition to these major chapters, I have updated the collection by selecting some of the classics of the discipline in the 1980s and 1990s. These reflect three major intellectual currents that are having profound effects on the discipline—post-positivism and post-modernism, feminism, and the new attention to conflict resolution. While I could have included a chapter on each of these, space limitations forced me to add only one or two representative selections of the best of these approaches. In Chapter 4, I have added Yosef Lapid on "the third debate" and Richard Ashley and R. B. J. Walker on "dissident thought." In Chapter 5, I have excerpted Dean Pruitt and Jeffrey Rubin's analysis of the problem-solving approach in conflict resolution. Chapter 11 presents Carol Cohn's seminal feminist analysis and deconstruction of nuclear thinking. I have also added two new empirical studies on war to Chapter 8—one by Stuart Bremer and one by Frank Wayman, J. David Singer, and Gary Goertz.

I have also, due to popular demand by students, used the more modern translation of Thucydides by Rex Warner, and I have updated the English in Hobbes' *Leviathan*. I have still kept the J. J. Gramhan translation of Clausewitz, which is quite readable. I am reluctant to use the more recent translation by Michael Howard and Peter Paret, mostly because I feel it is overly influenced by post–World War II thinking on deterrence.

My greatest debt in preparing this volume is to my former students in my introductory course on Global Peace and War and in my graduate core course on Theories of International Relations. Both of these courses have challenged me to present, at different levels, the most important work in the field within the constraint of a single semester. My students' reactions to my various efforts have had a major impact on the content of this volume. As has become increasingly common in my work, my colleague and partner Marie T. Henehan has shared in both the burden and the pleasure of preparing this book. Her advice, encouragement, patience, and criticism have had a major impact on my selection and my commentary. My thanks to the reviewers of this edition, Lisa Brandes and Randy Siverson, for valuable suggestions. My thanks, as always, to the exceptional editorial staff at Prentice Hall. Of course, despite the aid of all these people, I accept the final responsibility for the volume.

Lastly, as I wrote in the first edition, this book is dedicated to our stillborn son. In a world in which millions can lie only a few minutes away from annihilation, his death has reminded us of the fragility and miracle of human life.

John A. Vasquez
Block Island, Rhode Island

About the Editor

John A. Vasquez is Professor of Political Science at Vanderbilt University and a specialist in international relations theory and peace research. He has published ten books and numerous articles including *The War Puzzle; The Power of Power Politics: A Critique; In Search of Theory: A New Paradigm for Global Politics* (co-authored with Richard W. Mansbach); *The Scientific Study of Peace and War: A Text-Reader* (co-edited with Marie T. Henehan); and *A Companion to International Relations: Major Concepts, Terms, and Thinkers* (co-authored with Marie T. Henehan).

I

MORALITY AND POLITICS

THE TOPIC

The most persistent philosophical question that has plagued those who have thought about international relations has been whether the foreign policy of a state ought to be based on the norms and principles of moral conduct. While there are few who would say that the individual should not be bound by moral rules in his or her everyday life, or even that the government should not follow basic standards of decency in the way it treats its citizens, many would say that in questions of international affairs, the state should do whatever is in its interest without the hindrance of ethical strictures. This position is often referred to as *raison d'état* or "reason of state." Whether reason of state should take precedence over moral rules has been an issue from the time of ancient Greece to our own day.

THE SELECTIONS

The tension between political self-interest and morality is explored in "The Melian Dialogue" of **Thucydides** (ca. 460–ca. 400 BC). It is a debate taking place against the backdrop of the Peloponnesian War between the weak Melians and the strong Athenians. The Dialogue is taken by realists as an immutable lesson that morality in and of itself is not sufficient against power; the selection can also be interpreted as making a similar point against reason in the face of action. An alternative reading sees it as a morality play criticizing Athens' abuse of power.

Perhaps even more influential than Thucydides in shaping realism is the Italian Renaissance thinker **Machiavelli** (1469–1527). The selection from *The Prince* (1513) makes the case that self-interest should be the prince's main goal, and that nothing, particularly morality, should stand in its way. Indeed, Machiavelli goes so far as to argue that morality should be used by the prince as a facade to gain support and to deceive fools.

The notions that power is the key to international politics and that self-interest, not morality, is the prime motivation of leaders are the hallmarks of the approach to international relations known as *realism* or *realpolitik*. In the twentieth century, realism has been a direct reaction to the failure of Wilson

and other idealists to prevent World War II. Their use of reason was seen as
utopian because they underestimated the role of power in enforcing a new
order and preventing war. In addition, idealists were perceived as exaggerating the influence of reason by assuming a fundamental harmony of interests,
when in fact, according to the realists, there are often profound conflicts of interest that can only be resolved by a struggle for power. The ways in which these
insights percolated through the inter-war generation that had to deal with
Hitler are demonstrated in the selection by **Reinhold Niebuhr** (1940), who
makes the case for Christian realism against those within the Church taking a
more pacifistic and/or isolationist position. Niebuhr's work in the United
States and E. H. Carr's work in Britain the year before were critical in setting
the stage for the idealist-realist debate of the 1940s, which resulted in the ascendancy of realism.

The definitive contemporary statement on realism, and the work that is usually credited with converting the field from idealist advocacy to realist analysis, is **Hans Morgenthau's** (1948) *Politics among Nations*. In the selection
reprinted here, Morgenthau defines international politics in terms of power,
makes the case against idealism, and argues for the primacy of realpolitik over
morality in affairs of the state.

George Kennan (1951) takes up many of the insights of Morgenthau and
the other realists to analyze the failure of an American diplomacy based on the
legalistic-moralistic approach. He points out that the emphasis on moral goals
rather than self-interest makes foreign policy more dangerous and more prone
to wars that seek total victory. In a more theoretical vein, Morgenthau (1952;
see selection 20) makes the case for basing foreign policy solely on national
interest. In the same year, **Arnold Wolfers** (1952; see selection 21) in a prescient essay, points out the dangers inherent in this concept.

Those who have rejected the idea of self-interest have usually maintained
that moral precepts must guide foreign policy, or at least must not be violated
in the pursuit of self-interest. This stance raises several questions: Is it possible
for a state to follow moral rules in its global conduct? What would a moral foreign policy look like? Would it work? Historically, there have been two approaches toward developing a guideline for a moral foreign policy. The first
argues that a foreign policy is moral so long as no immoral acts are committed. Elements of this approach can be found in the just war tradition, which is
based on a Judeo-Christian ethic and is illustrated in the selection by Saint
Thomas Aquinas. The second approach goes a step further, maintaining that
the goal of foreign policy should be to promote the Good. This is the approach
of idealism and is illustrated in the selection by Woodrow Wilson.

In the West, the just war tradition has been primarily a religious one. Faced
with the ethical requirements outlined both in the Old and in the New
Testament and the political demands first of pagan Rome and then of Christian
Rome and Medieval Europe, Christian theologians attempted to develop a set
of rules for determining when, if ever, killing for political purposes could be
justified. The work of **Thomas Aquinas** (ca. 1225–1274) was pivotal in this
process, because he systematized previous thought on the question and laid
the foundation for all subsequent doctrine on just war within the Roman
Catholic Church. He addressed the question from the perspective of how
Christians should behave on earth in order to insure eternal salvation.

Machiavelli was reacting against the idea that, in fact, a prince can follow Christian precepts and still be successful in politics. Protestant positions on morality and politics have been more varied than those of Roman Catholics, ranging from absolute pacifism to acquiescence and obedience to state demands.

Toward the end of World War I, **Woodrow Wilson** promulgated a different approach to morality and politics derived from liberalism and that placed the blame for the war on power politics, the machinations of secret diplomacy, and the sinister interests of undemocratic leaders (see also Kant, selection 48). If these things could be changed, war could be ended, because war is fundamentally irrational. By this he meant that war is not in the interests of most people, and most conflicts are resolvable through the use of reason. Wilson believed that, by spreading democracy (through the creation of the Weimar Republic in Germany and of new states in Eastern Europe) and creating a League of Nations to inhibit aggression and peacefully resolve disputes, a revolution in the conduct of world politics would be brought about. It was in this context that the contemporary academic discipline of international relations was born, breaking away from diplomatic history, theology, and philosophy, upon which it had been previously based. These scholars, who were later labeled idealists and utopians by the realists, pursued and advanced many of the ideas initially suggested by Wilson and have been the main advocates for some form of world government (see Clark and Sohn, selection 53).

The critics of these two moral approaches have taken a reason-of-state position, which maintains not only that the state is exempt from morality, but also that if the state does rely on morality, morality will fail to protect it, as it failed to protect the Melians (see Thucydides, selection 1). Some critics have even gone on to argue that attempts to promote the Good can actually create more suffering in the world than there would be if everyone simply followed their selfish interests (Morgenthau, selection 4; Kennan, selection 5).

The realists were very successful in dominating both the academic discipline and policy-making circles in the United States and Great Britain in the fifties and sixties. This domination was due in part to the fact that realism was a natural ideology for an ascending status-quo power like the United States. With the onset of the Vietnam War, however, it became increasingly clear to Americans outside the intellectual and policy-making establishment that the realist argument—that morality has no place in international politics, and that power and interest are all that are important—was too facile and convenient. Instead of looking back to Thucydides and Machiavelli, these scholars reexamined the just war tradition, and looked at a radical tradition that emphasized the interests of the common person rather than the interests of the prince or decision-making elite.

It is the strong tendency of analysts and students of international relations to do as Machiavelli did—to pretend that we are princes or decision makers, define problems through those eyes, and then recommend accordingly. Most of us are not decision makers, however, and it is not very clear that their interests are ours, or that the way they define the world should be the way we define it; this is one of the starting points of the radical critique of realism. This critique then goes on to insist that moral rules serve the interests of common people, particularly on the question of war, and that intellectuals, all too often, instead of helping people to see this truth, help the elite to deceive people into becoming cannon fodder. As Noam Chomsky says, "It is the responsibility of intellectuals to speak the truth and to expose lies."

The selections from the essays of **Leo Tolstoy** (1828–1910) highlight the moral responsibilities of all individuals in the face of the power of the state. Steeped in the traditions of Christian pacifism and political anarchy, his message to citizens and common soldiers everywhere is: It is not only wrong to kill, but there is also no need to kill, because wars serve only the interests of the state, and not people. His emphasis of this message is one of the reasons Tolstoy, like other antiwar thinkers such as Thoreau and Mark Twain, was read widely in the United States in the late 1960s.

Even more influential has been the work of **Gandhi** (1869–1948). Gandhi insisted, particularly through his example, that the means by which a goal is sought has an effect on what is obtained. Political means, especially violent ones, produce a number of consequences, only one of which is attainment of a goal. The other consequences may undermine, or even destroy, the value of the original goal. From this perspective, violence is not simply a means; it is evil. To engage in violence, no matter what the reason, is to lose the battle, to become corrupted, to become part of the problem. To believe that the end can justify the means is to become deluded into thinking that the immediate goal is more important than the ultimate goal, the Good. Our actions as we attempt to attain a goal determine what we attain, because our behavior in political action shapes who we are (that is, our moral character). For Gandhi, a true revolution must not only achieve political independence but also free people from the evils of violence and hatred. For many Americans involved in the civil rights and antiwar movements of the 1960s, nonviolence was not only a technique but also a strategy designed to change the spirit that had given rise to oppression of American blacks at home and support of counter-revolutionary dictatorships abroad. Gandhi's prophecy loomed as a final warning in the nuclear age, as billions were spent in the United States and in the Soviet Union on the weapons of complete destruction, and as more and more nations sought nuclear capability.

The essay by **Howard Zinn** (1966) is an attempt to apply the insights of the radical tradition to an ongoing Vietnam War. It was highly influential at the time, and continues to be an important statement about the role of morality in guiding both foreign policy and intellectual inquiry about international politics. The essay demonstrates the limits of realism for an important segment of a generation of Americans.

Underlying many of the arguments in this section is the question of the relationship between the individual and the state. Must the state serve the interests of the individual? Must it serve the interests of all or just some? Is an individual obliged to meet the demands of the state or the larger community? Can the state morally require individuals or certain groups to risk their lives in a war? For Aquinas and for many others within the just war tradition, obligation to the moral principles of God and the Church clearly takes precedence over the demands of the state or the individual, both of which had little status within medieval Christendom. For liberal idealists like Wilson, the individual has an obligation not only to defend the community but also to fight for the Good. For realists, individuals are often seen as resources for the state, much like coal and steel. The feelings of individuals are handled more from the perspective of morale than morality. For some radicals, particularly those who are anarchists rather than collectivists, individuals not only have no obligations to the state, but also must come to realize that the state is an enemy of the individual.

AN ANALYSIS OF THE TOPIC

The selections in Part I demonstrate that there is no simple answer to the question of the role of morality in politics. The selections do, however, offer some important lessons for consideration. First, there appear to be no a priori grounds for choosing realism over an approach that imparts a greater role to morality. Realism is no less value-laden than moral approaches are. Both offer prescriptions as to what *should* be done and what is the best foreign policy. It is more accurate to describe realism as a counterethic than as a set of solely factual statements and explanations, as is sometimes implied.

How does one choose one ethic over another? There are two ways of trying to answer this question. One way is to ask: What is, intrinsically, the best way to live? One then does what is right. The other way is to ask: What are the consequences of a particular action? One then takes the action that produces the most good. It is possible to assess different ethical systems, including the just war tradition, idealism, realism, and the radical critique, by examining, in terms of these two questions, the global quality of life to which they give rise. Is the global quality of life that is established by following these prescriptions intrinsically the best way to live, or at least a good way to live, given historical possibilities? Are the consequences of following the prescriptions beneficial or disastrous?

As the selections are examined in light of these questions, the lessons the writer is trying to derive become clearer. To the realists, it is evident that history has shown that following just the dictates of reason or morality is not beneficial because, all too frequently, there are powerful states who will not obey these dictates and will simply take what they want through force of arms. In this situation, which according to the realists is typical in international politics, only power can ensure survival. To be without power is to court disaster, as the Melians did in the Peloponnesian War.

While it is difficult to argue, except on religious grounds, in favor of following a morality that no one obeys, it is equally true that realism tends to reduce the number of individuals and groups who will be restrained by moral considerations. It does this by increasing the number of individuals who have no motivation to obey moral rules, and by making it difficult for individuals who want to follow the rules to do so. Today, for example, we all accept the rule that in the classroom, intellectual disagreements should not be settled by dueling. If a group of students began to bring pistols to class and challenged and killed students with whom they disagreed, and, for some hypothetical reason, law enforcement agencies did nothing about it, then it would be difficult for the rest of us to refrain from bringing pistols to class, even if we accepted the general rule against dueling. Once the ideology of dueling has been accepted, it is hard to resist the practice of dueling; in the absence of the practice of dueling, however, the ideology makes little sense. (These words, written in the first edition in 1986, no longer reflect a hypothetical example for some inner-city high schools in the U.S. Instead, they reflect the reality of everyday violence, and the difficulty of escaping it, once it has become a way of life.)

As an ideology supporting violence, realism can act as a self-fulfilling prophecy, by helping to bring about the very world it deplores but accepts out of necessity. While it may be true that the worlds of the Peloponnesian War, Renaissance Italy, and World War II were realpolitik worlds, things do not always have to be that way, nor have they always been that way (just as not all high schools are plagued by violence); that is the basic insight of the idealists. There are some ways of acting at the global level that establish a higher quality of life than other ways of acting. To the extent that these more beneficial actions can be institutionalized into a set of rules, realpolitik worlds can be superseded. This is precisely what the just war tradition has attempted to do, and was successful in doing for much of the medieval period.

It should be clear that, to the extent that it provides insights to the naive, realism will have beneficial consequences in that it will alert the naive to danger. To the extent that realism provides a rationalization for the strong, it will be pernicious. One of the points made by American radicals during the Vietnam War was that American interests in Vietnam were not morally acceptable, and to respond, as realists do, that morality has no place in international politics was simply self-serving. Both radicals and those who take a just war approach place the burden of proof on those who wish to use the common people to fight wars, making them establish their case upon something other than the interests of the decision maker. Since decision makers are often advised to lie and to deceive, it behooves the rest of us to have some sort of independent basis for assessing their actions. The just war tradition and the radical critique provide such a basis.

Finally, the realists appear to be correct in arguing that idealist foreign policies that promulgate moral, religious, or ideological goals are more apt to produce total wars than are policies based only on protecting the territorial integrity and political independence of the state. Realists like Niebuhr, Morgenthau, and Kennan prescribe avoidance of messianic missions and limiting international politics to issues of survival. The problem, of course, is that most decision makers are not willing to restrict their policies in this manner. The idea that tolerance is better than fighting is, nevertheless, a particularly important lesson to remember in the nuclear age.

It must be kept in mind that the four approaches discussed in this section—realism, just war, idealism, and the radical critique—are intellectual positions that are only occasionally applied in a consistent fashion by political leaders. In recent times, just war and radical approaches have been influential primarily with religious institutions and mass movements, respectively, and not with the leaders of the most powerful states. Leaders of these states have been torn between the contradictory tendencies of idealism and realism in trying to spread their own ideologies and yet needing to confront the realities of world politics. In the United States, for example, the attempts to make the world safe for democracy, to protect small states from aggression, to aid economic development, and to promote human rights all reflect idealist goals in foreign policy that go beyond the narrow interests of territorial integrity and political independence. At the same time, there has been a recognition that moralistic condemnations, such as the nonrecognition of the People's Republic of China, during the Cold War, can be impotent, and that more messianic crusades, such as spreading democracy and human rights, can be self-defeating or at times even dangerous. There has been a constant tension in American foreign policy between idealism and realism, with presidents using idealism to justify their actions and realism to calculate their interests. On the whole, realism has held the upper hand when the United States has taken action against strong states, like the former Soviet Union. At other times, the ideology of anticommunism was so pervasive that it led to involvements, as in Vietnam, where, from the realist perspective, there was no clear threat.

These examples serve to emphasize the point that the realm of practice rarely has the clarity, consistency, or purpose that is present in the realm of ideas. This is partly because governments are eclectic in the ideas they employ; more importantly, though, it is because putting ideas into practice is very difficult, given domestic and global constraints.

FOR FURTHER READING

Realism

E. H. CARR. 1939. *The Twenty Years' Crisis.* London: Macmillan.

MARTIN WIGHT. 1946. *Power Politics.* London: Royal Institute of International Affairs.

JOHN HERZ. 1951. *Political Realism and Political Idealism.* Chicago: University of Chicago Press.

HERBERT BUTTERFIELD. 1953. *Christianity, Diplomacy and War.* London: Epworth Press.

FRIEDRICH MEINECKE. 1957. *Machiavellianism: The Doctrine of Raison d'Etat and Its Place in Modern History.* New Haven: Yale University Press.

Just War

AUGUSTINE, AURELIUS, BISHOP OF HIPPO. Freedom of the Will (*De Libero Arbitrio*) 1.5 (AD 395), Letter to Publicola (No. 47) (AD 398), Letter to Boniface (No. 189) (AD 418).

FRANCISCUS DE VICTORIA. (ca. 1487–1546). *De Indis; De Jure Belli Relectiones* (1532). Reprinted in *Classics of International Law,* edited by Ernest Nys. Washington, DC: The Carnegie Institution, 1917.

BARTOLOMÉ DE LAS CASAS. (1474–1566). *In Defense of the Indians* (ca. 1550). Northern Illinois University Press, 1992.

The Challenge of Peace: God's Promise and Our Response. 1983. (Pastoral letter on nuclear war by the U.S. Catholic bishops.) Washington, DC: U.S. Catholic Conference.

MICHAEL WALZER. 1977. *Just and Unjust Wars: A Moral Argument with Historical Illustrations.* New York: Basic Books.

Idealism

NORMAN ANGELL. 1911. *The Great Illusion.* New York: G.P. Putnam's Sons.

RICHARD A. FALK. 1975. *A Study of Future Worlds.* New York: The Free Press.

Radical Critique

HENRY DAVID THOREAU. (1817–1862). Civil Disobedience (1849). In *Walden* and *Civil Disobedience*. New York: Signet, 1960.

C. WRIGHT MILLS. 1956. *The Power Elite*. New York: Oxford University Press.

WILLIAM A. WILLIAMS. 1959. *The Tragedy of American Diplomacy*. New York: Delta Books.

NOAM CHOMSKY. 1969. "The Responsibility of Intellectuals," pp. 323–366 in Noam Chomsky, *American Power and the New Mandarins*. New York: Pantheon.

HOWARD ZINN. 1971. *The Politics of History*. Boston: Beacon Press.

Chapter 1

Realism

1. The Melian Dialogue

THUCYDIDES

84 Next summer Alcibiades sailed to Argos with twenty ships and seized 300 Argive citizens who were still suspected of being pro-Spartan. These were put by the Athenians into the nearby islands under Athenian control.

The Athenians also made an expedition against the island of Melos. They had thirty of their own ships, six from Chios, and two from Lesbos; 1,200 hoplites, 300 archers, and twenty mounted archers, all from Athens; and about 1,500 hoplites from the allies and the islanders.

The Melians are a colony from Sparta. They had refused to join the Athenian empire like the other islanders, and at first had remained neutral without helping either side; but afterwards, when the Athenians had brought force to bear on them by laying waste their land, they had become open enemies of Athens.

Now the generals Cleomedes, the son of Lycomedes, and Tisias, the son of Tisimachus, encamped with the above force in Melian territory and, before doing any harm to the land, first of all sent representatives to negotiate. The Melians did not invite these representatives to speak before the people, but asked them to make the statement for which they had come in front of the governing body and the few. The Athenian representatives then spoke as follows:

85 'So we are not to speak before the people, no doubt in case the mass of the people should hear once and for all and without interruption an argument from us which is both persuasive and incontrovertible, and should so be led astray. This, we realize, is your motive in bringing us here to speak before the few. Now suppose that you who sit here should make assurance doubly sure. Suppose that you, too, should refrain from dealing with every point in detail in a set speech, and should instead interrupt us whenever we say something controversial and deal with that before going on to the next point? Tell us first whether you approve of this suggestion of ours.'

86 The Council of the Melians replied as follows:

'No one can object to each of us putting forward our own views in a calm atmosphere. That is perfectly reasonable. What is scarcely consistent with such a proposal is the present threat, indeed the certainty, of your making war on us. We see that you have come prepared to judge the argument yourselves, and that the likely end of it all will be either war, if we prove that we are in the right, and so refuse to surrender, or else slavery.'

87 ATHENIANS: If you are going to spend the time in enumerating your suspicions about the

From *The History of the Peloponnesian War*. Translated by Rex Warner, Harmondsworth: Penguin Classics, 1954, pp. 400–408. Copyright © Rex Warner, 1954. Reprinted by permission of the publisher.

future, or if you have met here for any other reason except to look the facts in the face and on the basis of these facts to consider how you can save your city from destruction, there is no point in our going on with this discussion. If, however, you will do as we suggest, then we will speak on.

88 MELIANS: It is natural and understandable that people who are placed as we are should have recourse to all kinds of arguments and different points of view. However, you are right in saying that we are met together here to discuss the safety of our country and, if you will have it so, the discussion shall proceed on the lines that you have laid down.

89 ATHENIANS: Then we on our side will use no fine phrases saying, for example, that we have a right to our empire because we defeated the Persians, or that we have come against you now because of the injuries you have done us—a great mass of words that nobody would believe. And we ask you on your side not to imagine that you will influence us by saying that you, though a colony of Sparta, have not joined Sparta in the war, or that you have never done us any harm. Instead we recommend that you should try to get what it is possible for you to get, taking into consideration what we both really do think; since you know as well as we do that, when these matters are discussed by practical people, the standard of justice depends on the equality of power to compel and that in fact the strong do what they have the power to do and the weak accept what they have to accept.

90 MELIANS: Then in our view (since you force us to leave justice out of account and to confine ourselves to self-interest)—in our view it is at any rate useful that you should not destroy a principle that is to the general good of all men—namely, that in the case of all who fall into danger there should be such a thing as fair play and just dealing, and that such people should be allowed to use and to profit by arguments that fall short

of a mathematical accuracy. And this is a principle which affects you as much as anybody, since your own fall would be visited by the most terrible vengeance and would be an example to the world.

91 ATHENIANS: As for us, even assuming that our empire does come to an end, we are not despondent about what would happen next. One is not so much frightened of being conquered by a power which rules over others, as Sparta does (not that we are concerned with Sparta now), as of what would happen if a ruling power is attacked and defeated by its own subjects. So far as this point is concerned, you can leave it to us to face the risks involved. What we shall do now is to show you that it is for the good of our own empire that we are here and that it is for the preservation of your city that we shall say what we are going to say. We do not want any trouble in bringing you into our empire, and we want you to be spared for the good both of yourselves and of ourselves.

92 MELIANS: And how could it be just as good for us to be the slaves as for you to be the masters?

93 ATHENIANS: You, by giving in, would save yourselves from disaster; we, by not destroying you, would be able to profit from you.

94 MELIANS: So you would not agree to our being neutral, friends instead of enemies, but allies of neither side?

95 ATHENIANS: No, because it is not so much your hostility that injures us; it is rather the case that, if we were on friendly terms with you, our subjects would regard that as a sign of weakness in us, whereas your hatred is evidence of our power.

96 MELIANS: Is that your subjects' idea of fair play—that no distinction should be made between people who are quite unconnected with you and people who are mostly your

own colonists or else rebels whom you have conquered?

⁹⁷ ATHENIANS: So far as right and wrong are concerned they think that there is no difference between the two, that those who still preserve their independence do so because they are strong, and that if we fail to attack them it is because we are afraid. So that by conquering you we shall increase not only the size but the security of our empire. We rule the sea and you are islanders, and weaker islanders too than the others; it is therefore particularly important that you should not escape.

⁹⁸ MELIANS: But do you think there is no security for you in what we suggest? For here again, since you will not let us mention justice, but tell us to give in to your interests, we, too, must tell you what our interests are and, if yours and ours happen to coincide, we must try to persuade you of the fact. Is it not certain that you will make enemies of all states who are at present neutral, when they see what is happening here and naturally conclude that in course of time you will attack them too? Does not this mean that you are strengthening the enemies you have already and are forcing others to become your enemies even against their intentions and their inclinations?

⁹⁹ ATHENIANS: As a matter of fact we are not so much frightened of states on the continent. They have their liberty, and this means that it will be a long time before they begin to take precautions against us. We are more concerned about islanders like yourselves, who are still unsubdued, or subjects who have already become embittered by the constraint which our empire imposes on them. These are the people who are most likely to act in a reckless manner and to bring themselves and us, too, into the most obvious danger.

¹⁰⁰ MELIANS: Then surely, if such hazards are taken by you to keep your empire and by

your subjects to escape from it, we who are still free would show ourselves great cowards and weaklings if we failed to face everything that comes rather than submit to slavery.

¹⁰¹ ATHENIANS: No, not if you are sensible. This is no fair fight, with honour on one side and shame on the other. It is rather a question of saving your lives and not resisting those who are far too strong for you.

¹⁰² MELIANS: Yet we know that in war fortune sometimes makes the odds more level than could be expected from the difference in numbers of the two sides. And if we surrender, then all our hope is lost at once, whereas, so long as we remain in action, there is still a hope that we may yet stand upright.

¹⁰³ ATHENIANS: Hope, that comforter in danger! If one already has solid advantages to fall back upon, one can indulge in hope. It may do harm, but will not destroy one. But hope is by nature an expensive commodity, and those who are risking their all on one cast find out what it means only when they are already ruined; it never fails them in the period when such a knowledge would enable them to take precautions. Do not let this happen to you, you who are weak and whose fate depends on a single movement of the scale. And do not be like those people who, as so commonly happens, miss the chance of saving themselves in a human and practical way, and, when every clear and distinct hope has left them in their adversity, turn to what is blind and vague, to prophecies and oracles and such things which by encouraging hope lead men to ruin.

¹⁰⁴ MELIANS: It is difficult, and you may be sure that we know it, for us to oppose your power and fortune, unless the terms be equal. Nevertheless we trust that the gods will give us fortune as good as yours, because we are standing for what is right against what is wrong; and as for what we lack in power, we trust that it will be made up for by our al-

liance with the Spartans, who are bound, if for no other reason, then for honour's sake, and because we are their kinsmen, to come to our help. Our confidence, therefore, is not so entirely irrational as you think.

105 ATHENIANS: So far as the favour of the gods is concerned, we think we have as much right to that as you have. Our aims and our actions are perfectly consistent with the beliefs men hold about the gods and with the principles which govern their own conduct. Our opinion of the gods and our knowledge of men lead us to conclude that it is a general and necessary law of nature to rule whatever one can. This is not a law that we made ourselves, nor were we the first to act upon it when it was made. We found it already in existence, and we shall leave it to exist for ever among those who come after us. We are merely acting in accordance with it, and we know that you or anybody else with the same power as ours would be acting in precisely the same way. And therefore, so far as the gods are concerned, we see no good reason why we should fear to be at a disadvantage. But with regard to your views about Sparta and your confidence that she, out of a sense of honour, will come to your aid, we must say that we congratulate you on your simplicity but do not envy you your folly. In matters that concern themselves or their own constitution the Spartans are quite remarkably good; as for their relations with others, that is a long story, but it can be expressed shortly and clearly by saying that of all people we know the Spartans are most conspicuous for believing that what they like doing is honourable and what suits their interests is just. And this kind of attitude is not going to be of much help to you in your absurd quest for safety at the moment.

106 MELIANS: But this is the very point where we can feel most sure. Their own self-interest will make them refuse to betray their own colonists, the Melians, for that would mean losing the confidence of their friends among the Hellenes and doing good to their enemies.

107 ATHENIANS: You seem to forget that if one follows one's self-interest one wants to be safe, whereas the path of justice and honour involves one in danger. And, where danger is concerned, the Spartans are not, as a rule, very venturesome.

108 MELIANS: But we think that they would even endanger themselves for our sake and count the risk more worth taking than in the case of others, because we are so close to the Peloponnese that they could operate more easily, and because they can depend on us more than on others, since we are of the same race and share the same feelings.

109 ATHENIANS: Goodwill shown by the party that is asking for help does not mean security for the prospective ally. What is looked for is a positive preponderance of power in action. And the Spartans pay attention to this point even more than others do. Certainly they distrust their own native resources so much that when they attack a neighbour they bring a great army of allies with them. It is hardly likely therefore that, while we are in control of the sea, they will cross over to an island.

110 MELIANS: But they still might send others. The Cretan sea is a wide one, and it is harder for those who control it to intercept others than for those who want to slip through to do so safely. And even if they were to fail in this, they would turn against your own land and against those of your allies left unvisited by Brasidas. So, instead of troubling about a country which has nothing to do with you, you will find trouble nearer home, among your allies, and in your own country.

111 ATHENIANS: It is a possibility, something that has in fact happened before. It may happen in your case, but you are well aware that the Athenians have never yet relinquished a single siege operation through fear of others. But we are somewhat shocked to find that,

though you announced your intention of discussing how you could preserve yourselves, in all this talk you have said absolutely nothing which could justify a man in thinking that he could be preserved. Your chief points are concerned with what you hope may happen in the future, while your actual resources are too scanty to give you a chance of survival against the forces that are opposed to you at this moment. You will therefore be showing an extraordinary lack of common sense if, after you have asked us to retire from this meeting, you still fail to reach a conclusion wiser than anything you have mentioned so far. Do not be led astray by a false sense of honour—a thing which often brings men to ruin when they are faced with an obvious danger that somehow affects their pride. For in many cases men have still been able to see the dangers ahead of them, but this thing called dishonour, this word, by its own force of seduction, has drawn them into a state where they have surrendered to an idea, while in fact they have fallen voluntarily into irrevocable disaster, in dishonour that is all the more dishonourable because it has come to them from their own folly rather than their misfortune. You, if you take the right view, will be careful to avoid this. You will see that there is nothing disgraceful in giving way to the greatest city in Hellas when she is offering you such reasonable terms—alliance on a tribute-paying basis and liberty to enjoy your own property. And, when you are allowed to choose between war and safety, you will not be so insensitively arrogant as to make the wrong choice. This is the safe rule—to stand up to one's equals, to behave with deference towards one's superiors, and to treat one's inferiors with moderation. Think it over again, then, when we have withdrawn from the meeting, and let this be a point that constantly recurs to your minds—that you are discussing the fate of your country, that you have only one country, and that its future for good or ill depends on this one single decision which you are going to make.

112 The Athenians then withdrew from the discussion. The Melians, left to themselves, reached a conclusion which was much the same as they had indicated in their previous replies. Their answer was as follows:

'Our decision, Athenians, is just the same as it was at first. We are not prepared to give up in a short moment the liberty which our city has enjoyed from its foundation for 700 years. We put our trust in the fortune that the gods will send and which has saved us up to now, and in the help of men—that is, of the Spartans; and so we shall try to save ourselves. But we invite you to allow us to be friends of yours and enemies to neither side, to make a treaty which shall be agreeable to both you and us, and so to leave our country.'

113 The Melians made this reply, and the Athenians, just as they were breaking off the discussion, said:

'Well, at any rate, judging from this decision of yours, you seem to us quite unique in your ability to consider the future as something more certain than what is before your eyes, and to see uncertainties as realities, simply because you would like them to be so. As you have staked most on and trusted most in Spartans, luck, and hopes, so in all these you will find yourselves most completely deluded.'

114 The Athenian representatives then went back to the army, and the Athenian generals, finding that the Melians would not submit, immediately commenced hostilities and built a wall completely round the city of Melos, dividing the work out among the various states. Later they left behind a garrison of some of their own and some allied troops to blockade the place by land and sea, and with the greater part of their army returned home. The force left behind stayed on and continued with the siege.

115 About the same time the Argives invaded Phliasia and were ambushed by the Phliasians and the exiles from Argos, losing about eighty men.

Then, too, the Athenians at Pylos captured a great quantity of plunder from Spartan territory. Not even after this did the Spartans renounce the treaty and make war, but they issued a proclamation saying that any of their people who wished to do so were free to make raids on the Athenians. The Corinthians also made some attacks on the Athenians because of private quarrels of their own, but the rest of the Peloponnesians stayed quiet.

Meanwhile the Melians made a night attack and captured the part of the Athenian lines opposite the market-place. They killed some of the troops, and then, after bringing in corn and everything else useful that they could lay their hands on, retired again and made no further move, while the Athenians took measures to make their blockade more efficient in future. So the summer came to an end.

116 In the following winter the Spartans planned to invade the territory of Argos, but when the sacrifices for crossing the frontier turned out unfavourably, they gave up the expedition. The fact that they had intended to invade made the Argives suspect certain people in their city, some of whom they arrested, though others succeeded in escaping.

About this same time the Melians again captured another part of the Athenian lines where there were only a few of the garrison on guard. As a result of this, another force came out afterwards from Athens under the command of Philocrates, the son of Demeas. Siege operations were now carried on vigorously and, as there was also some treachery from inside, the Melians surrendered unconditionally to the Athenians, who put to death all the men of military age whom they took, and sold the women and children as slaves. Melos itself they took over for themselves, sending out later a colony of 500 men.*

---

*That there were Melian survivors, who were restored by Lysander at the end of the war, is stated by Xenophon (*Hellenica*, II, 2, 9).

2. From *The Prince*

NICCOLÒ MACHIAVELLI

CHAPTER 5: HOW CITIES OR PRINCIPALITIES ARE TO BE GOVERNED THAT PREVIOUS TO BEING CONQUERED HAD LIVED UNDER THEIR OWN LAWS

Conquered states that have been accustomed to liberty and the government of their own laws can be held by the conqueror in three different ways. The first is to ruin them; the second, for the conqueror to go and reside there in person; and the third is to allow them to continue to live under their own laws, subject to a regular tribute, and to create in them a government of a few, who will keep the country friendly to the conqueror. Such a government, having been established by the new prince, knows that it cannot maintain itself without the support of his power and friendship, and it becomes its interest therefore to sustain him. A city that has been accustomed to free institutions is much easier held by its own citizens than in any other way, if the conqueror desires to preserve it. The Spartans and the Romans will serve as examples of these different ways of holding a conquered state.

The Spartans held Athens and Thebes, creating there a government of a few; and yet they lost both these states again. The Romans, for the purpose of retaining Capua, Carthage, and Numantia, destroyed them, but did not lose them. They wished to preserve Greece in somewhat the same way that the Spartans had held it, by making her free and leaving her in the enjoyment of her own laws, but did not succeed; so that they were obliged to destroy many cities in that country for the purpose of holding it. In truth there was no other safe way of keeping possession of that country but to ruin it. And whoever becomes master of a city that has been accustomed to liberty, and does not destroy it, must himself expect to be ruined by it. For they will always resort to rebellion in the name of liberty and their ancient institutions, which will never be effaced from their memory, either by the lapse of time, or by benefits bestowed by the new master. No matter what he may do, or what precautions he may take, if he does not separate and disperse the inhabitants, they will on the first occasion invoke the name of liberty and the memory of their ancient institutions, as was done by Pisa after having been held over a hundred years in subjection by the Florentines.

But it is very different with states that have been accustomed to live under a prince. When the line of the prince is once extinguished, the inhabitants, being on the one hand accustomed to obey, and on the other having lost their ancient sovereign, can neither agree to create a new one from amongst themselves,

From *The Prince*. Translated by Christian E. Detmold; first published in the United States in 1882.

nor do they know how to live in liberty; and thus they will be less prompt to take up arms, and the new prince will readily be able to gain their good will and to assure himself of them. But republics have more vitality, a greater spirit of resentment and desire of revenge, for the memory of their ancient liberty neither can nor will permit them to remain quiet, and therefore the surest way of holding them is either to destroy them, or for the conqueror to go and live there. . . .

CHAPTER 15: OF THE MEANS BY WHICH MEN, AND ESPECIALLY PRINCES, WIN APPLAUSE, OR INCUR CENSURE

It remains now to be seen in what manner a prince should conduct himself towards his subjects and his allies; and knowing that this matter has already been treated by many others, I apprehend that my writing upon it also may be deemed presumptuous, especially as in the discussion of the same I shall differ from the rules laid down by others. But as my aim is to write something that may be useful to him for whom it is intended, it seems to me proper to pursue the real truth of the matter, rather than to indulge in mere speculation on the same; for many have imagined republics and principalities such as have never been known to exist in reality. For the manner in which men live is so different from the way in which they ought to live, that he who leaves the common course for that which he ought to follow will find that it leads him to ruin rather than to safety. For a man who, in all respects, will carry out only his professions of good, will be apt to be ruined amongst so many who are evil. A prince therefore who desires to maintain himself must learn to be not always good, but to be so or not as necessity may require. Leaving aside then the imaginary things concerning princes, and confining ourselves only to the realities, I say that all men when they are spoken of, and more especially princes, from being in a more conspicuous position, are noted for some quality that brings them either praise or censure. Thus

one is deemed liberal, another miserly (*misero*) to use a Tuscan expression (for avaricious is he who by rapine desires to gain, and miserly we call him who abstains too much from the enjoyment of his own). One man is esteemed generous, another rapacious; one cruel, another merciful; one faithless, and another faithful; one effeminate and pusillanimous, another ferocious and brave; one affable, another haughty; one lascivious, another chaste; one sincere, the other cunning; one facile, another inflexible; one grave, another frivolous; one religious, another sceptical; and so on.

I am well aware that it would be most praiseworthy for a prince to possess all of the above-named qualities that are esteemed good; but as he cannot have them all, nor entirely observe them, because of his human nature which does not permit it, he should at least be prudent enough to know how to avoid the infamy of those vices that would rob him of his state; and if possible also to guard against such as are likely to endanger it. But if that be not possible, then he may with less hesitation follow his natural inclinations. Nor need he care about incurring censure for such vices, without which the preservation of his state may be difficult. For, all things considered, it will be found that some things that seem like virtue will lead you to ruin if you follow them; whilst others, that apparently are vices, will, if followed, result in your safety and well-being. . . .

CHAPTER 17: OF CRUELTY AND CLEMENCY, AND WHETHER IT IS BETTER TO BE LOVED THAN FEARED

Coming down now to the other aforementioned qualities, I say that every prince ought to desire the reputation of being merciful, and not cruel; at the same time, he should be careful not to misuse that mercy. Cesar Borgia was reputed cruel, yet by his cruelty he reunited the Romagna to his states, and restored that province to order, peace, and loyalty; and if we carefully examine his course, we shall find it to have been really much more merciful than the course of the people of Florence, who to escape the reputation of cruelty, allowed Pistoja to be destroyed. A prince, therefore, should not mind the ill repute of cruelty, when he can thereby keep his subjects united and loyal; for a few displays of severity will really be more merciful than to allow, by an excess of clemency, disorders to occur, which are apt to result in rapine and murder; for these injure a whole community, whilst the executions ordered by the prince fall only upon a few individuals. And, above all others, the new prince will find it almost impossible to avoid the reputation of cruelty, because new states are generally exposed to many dangers. . . .

A prince, however, should be slow to believe and to act; nor should he be too easily alarmed by his own fears, and should proceed moderately and with prudence and humanity, so that an excess of confidence may not make him incautious, nor too much mistrust make him intolerant. This, then, gives rise to the question "whether it be better to be beloved than feared" or "to be feared than beloved." It will naturally be answered that it would be desirable to be both the one and the other; but as it is difficult to be both at the same time, it is much more safe to be feared than to be loved, when you have to choose between the two. For it may be said of men in general that they are ungrateful and fickle, dissemblers, avoiders of danger, and greedy of gain. So long as you shower benefits upon them, they are all yours; they offer you their blood, their substance, their lives, and their children, provided the necessity for it is far off; but when it is near at hand, then they revolt. And the prince who relies upon their words, without having otherwise provided for his security, is ruined; for friendships that are won by rewards, and not by greatness and nobility of soul, although deserved, yet are not real, and cannot be depended upon in time of adversity.

Besides, men have less hesitation in offending one who makes himself beloved than one who makes himself feared; for love holds by a bond of obligation which, as mankind is bad, is broken on every occasion whenever it is for the interest of the obliged party to break it. But fear holds by the apprehension of pun-ishment, which never leaves men. A prince, however, should make himself feared in such a manner that, if he has not won the affections of his people, he shall at least not incur their hatred; for the being feared, and not hated, can go very well together, if the prince abstains from taking the substance of his subjects, and leaves them their women. And if you should be obliged to inflict capital punishment upon any one, then be sure to do so only when there is manifest cause and proper justification for it; and, above all things, abstain from taking people's property, for men will sooner forget the death of their fathers than the loss of their patrimony. Besides, there will never be any lack of reasons for taking people's property; and a prince who once begins to live by rapine will ever find excuses for seizing other people's property. On the other hand, reasons for taking life are not so easily found, and are more readily exhausted. But when a prince is at the head of his army, with a multitude of soldiers under his command, then it is above all things necessary for him to disregard the reputation of cruelty; for without such severity an army cannot be kept together, nor disposed for any successful feat of arms. . . .

To come back now to the question whether it be better to be beloved than feared, I conclude that, as men love of their own free will, but are inspired with fear by the will of the prince, a wise prince should always rely upon himself, and not upon the will of others; but, above all, should he always strive to avoid being hated, as I have already said above.

CHAPTER 18: IN WHAT MANNER PRINCES SHOULD KEEP THEIR FAITH

It must be evident to every one that it is more praiseworthy for a prince always to maintain good faith, and practise integrity rather than craft and deceit. And yet the experience of our own times has shown that those princes have achieved great things who made small account of good faith, and who understood by cunning to circumvent the intelligence of others; and that in the end they got the better of those whose actions were dictated by loyalty and good faith. . . .

A sagacious prince then cannot and should not fulfil his pledges when their observance is contrary to his interest, and when the causes that induced him to pledge his faith no longer exist. If men were all good, then indeed this precept would be bad; but as men are naturally bad, and will not observe their faith towards you, you must, in the same way, not observe yours to them; and no prince ever yet lacked legitimate reasons with which to color his want of good faith. Innumerable modern examples could be given of this; and it could easily be shown how many treaties of peace, and how many engagements, have been made null and void by the faithlessness of princes; and he who has best known how to play the fox has ever been the most successful.

But it is necessary that the prince should know how to color this nature well, and how to be a great hypocrite and dissembler. For men are so simple, and yield so much to immediate necessity, that the deceiver will never lack dupes. . . .

It is not necessary, however, for a prince to possess all the above-mentioned qualities; but it is essential that he should at least seem to have them. I will even venture to say, that to have and to practise them constantly is pernicious, but to seem to have them is useful. For instance, a prince should seem to be merciful, faithful, humane, religious, and upright, and should even be so in reality; but he should have his mind so trained that, when occasion requires it, he may know how to change to the opposite. And it must be understood that a prince, and especially one who has but recently acquired his state, cannot perform all those things which cause men to be esteemed as good; he being often obliged, for the sake of maintaining his state, to act contrary to humanity, charity, and religion. And therefore is it necessary that he should have a versatile mind, capable of changing readily, according as the winds and changes of fortune bid him; and, as has been said above, not to swerve from the good if possible, but to know how to resort to evil if necessity demands it.

A prince then should be very careful never to allow anything to escape his lips that does not abound in the above-named five qualities, so that to see and to hear him he may seem all charity, integrity, and humanity, all uprightness, and all piety. And more than all else it is necessary for a prince to seem to possess the last quality; for mankind in general judge more by what they see and hear than by what they feel, every one being capable of the former, and but few of the latter. Everybody sees what you seem to be, but few really feel what you are; and these few dare not oppose the opinion of the many, who are protected by the majesty of the state; for the actions of all men, and especially those of princes, are judged by the result, where there is no other judge to whom to appeal.

A prince then should look mainly to the successful maintenance of his state. The means which he employs for this will always be accounted honorable, and will be praised by everybody; for the common people are always taken by appearances and by results, and it is the vulgar mass that constitutes the world. But a very few have rank and station, whilst the many have nothing to sustain them. A certain prince of our time, whom it is well not to name, never preached anything but peace and good faith; but if he had always observed either the one or the other, it would in most instances have cost him his reputation or his state. . . .

CHAPTER 21: HOW PRINCES SHOULD CONDUCT THEMSELVES TO ACQUIRE A REPUTATION

. . . It is also important for a prince to give striking examples of his interior administration (similar to those that are related of Messer Bernabo di Milano) when an occasion presents itself to reward or punish any one who has in civil affairs either rendered great service to the state, or committed some crime, so that it may be much talked about. But, above all, a prince should endeavor to invest all his actions with a character of grandeur and excellence. A prince, furthermore, becomes esteemed when he shows himself either a true friend or a real enemy; that is, when, regardless of consequences, he declares himself openly for or against another, which will always be more creditable to him than to remain neutral. For if two of your neighboring potentates should come to war amongst themselves, they are either of such character that, when either of them has been defeated, you will have cause to fear the conqueror, or not. In either case, it will always be better for you to declare yourself openly and make fair war; for if you fail to do so, you will be very apt to fall a prey to the victor, to the delight and satisfaction of the defeated party, and you will have no claim for protection or assistance from either the one or the other. For the conqueror will want no doubtful friends, who did not stand by him in time of trial; and the defeated party will not forgive you for having refused, with arms in hand, to take the chance of his fortunes. . . .

And it will always be the case that he who is not your friend will claim neutrality at your hands, whilst your friend will ask your armed intervention in his favor. Irresolute princes, for the sake of avoiding immediate danger, adopt most frequently the course of neutrality, and are generally ruined in consequence. But when a prince declares himself boldly in favor of one party, and that party proves victorious, even though the victor be powerful, and you are at his discretion, yet is he bound to you in love and obligation; and men are never so base as to repay these by such flagrant ingratitude as the oppressing you under these circumstances would be.

Moreover, victories are never so complete as to dispense the victor from all regard for justice. But when the party whom you have supported loses, then he will ever after receive you as a friend, and, when able, will assist you in turn; and thus you will have become the sharer of a fortune which in time may be retrieved.

In the second case, when the contending parties are such that you need not fear the victor, then it is the more prudent to give him your support; for you thereby aid one to ruin the other, whom he should save if he were wise; for although he has defeated his adversary, yet he remains at your discretion, inasmuch as without your assistance victory would have been impossible for him. And here it should be noted, that a prince ought carefully to avoid making common cause with any one more powerful than himself, for the purpose of attacking another power, unless he should be compelled to do so by necessity. For if the former is victorious, then you are at his mercy; and princes should, if possible, avoid placing themselves in such a position.

The Venetians allied themselves with France against the Duke of Milan, an alliance which they could easily have avoided, and which proved their ruin. But when it is unavoidable, as was the case with the Florentines when Spain and the Pope united their forces to attack Lombardy, then a prince ought to join the stronger party, for the reasons above given. Nor is it to be supposed that a state can ever adopt a course that is entirely safe; on the contrary, a prince must make up his mind to take the chance of all the doubts and uncertainties; for such is the order of things that one inconvenience cannot be avoided except at the risk of being exposed to another. And it is the province of prudence to discriminate amongst these inconveniences, and to accept the least evil for good.

A prince should also show himself a lover of virtue, and should honor all who excel in any one of the arts, and should encourage his citizens quietly to pursue their vocations, whether of commerce, agriculture, or any other human industry; so that the one may not abstain from embellishing his possessions for fear of their being taken from him, nor the other from opening new sources of commerce for fear of taxes. But the prince should provide rewards for those who are willing to do these things, and for all who strive to enlarge his city or state. And besides this, he should at suitable periods amuse his people with festivities and spectacles. And as cities are generally divided into guilds and classes, he should keep account of these bodies, and occasionally be present at their assemblies, and should set an example of his affability and magnificence; preserving, however, always the majesty of his dignity, which should never be wanting on any occasion or under any circumstances.

3. The War and American Churches

REINHOLD NIEBUHR

The Christian Church of America has never been upon a lower level of spiritual insight and moral sensitivity than in this tragic age of world conflict. Living in a suffering world, with its ears assailed by the cries of the miserable victims of tyranny and conflict, it has chosen to identify the slogan "Keep America out of the War" with the Christian gospel. . . .

. . . It is important of course that religion should not involve itself again in a holy war. It is important that Christianity should recognize that all historic struggles are struggles between sinful men and not between the righteous and the sinners; but it is just as important to save what relative decency and justice the western world still has, against the most demonic tyranny of history. Obviously the Nazis could never have gained a position in Europe from which they can place the whole of a continent under their ban if western society were really healthy. Obviously there is decay in the democratic world and there is no certainty that the capitalistic democracies will be able to rescue what is decent and just in their societies, either from internal corruption or external peril. History, however, does not present us with ideals and clear-cut choices.

Excerpted from *Christianity and Power Politics* by Reinhold Niebuhr (New York: Charles Scribner's Sons, 1940), pp. 33, 35–38, 39, 40–41, 42–47. Reprinted by permission of the author's estate.

There was a time when the socialists of Austria rightly declared that the difference between Hitler's and Schuschnigg's fascism was not very great. But when actually confronted with the peril of having Hitler's worse tyranny fastened upon Austria they wisely (though too tardily) decided that the difference might be all-important in that particular moment of history. That situation was symbolic of all historic decisions. The idea that it is possible to find a vantage point of guiltlessness from which to operate against the world is not a Christian idea but a modern rationalistic one. Ever since the eighteenth century modern secularists have been trying to find the specific causes of social sin and to eliminate them. Injustice was supposed to be caused solely by unjust governments or by faulty economic organization of society, or by human ignorance. Democracy was supposed to be the force of righteousness against monarchy. Socialism was assumed to be free of all imperialistic passions while capitalism was supposed to be the sole source of the imperial will.

"If we can't find the real cause of social injustice," said a typical modern recently, "we could be forced to go back to the absurd doctrine of original sin." That remark is a revelation of the scientific "objectivity" of modernity. The Christian idea of original sin is ruled out *a priori*. This is understandable enough in a non-Christian world. What is absurd is that modern Christianity should have accepted this modern rejection of the doctrine of original sin with such pathetic eagerness and should have spent so much energy in seeking to prove that a Christian can be just as respectable and modern as a secularist. Does he not hold to the same absurd dogma of the goodness of human nature and does he not have the same pathetic hope that if only this or that fault in the educational, social, political or economic system is corrected man will cease to be a peril to himself and to his fellowmen?

The difficulty with such optimism in regard to human nature is that it confuses every political issue in the modern world. Modern Christianity, far from offering corrective insights to this optimism, makes confusion worse confounded by exaggerating it. The secularist believes in the gradual emergence of a universal mind. The Christian believes that every man is potentially a Christ. He has forgotten that in the profoundest versions of Christianity, every man sees in Christ not only what he is and ought to be but also the true reality to which his own life stands in contradiction. Christianity does not believe, as the pessimists do, that men are by nature egotists. Nor does in hold with the optimists that egotism can be easily transcended. It believes rather that men are egotists in contradiction to their essential nature. That is the doctrine of original sin, stripped of literalistic illusions. . . .

International peace, political and economic justice and every form of social achievement represent precarious constructs in which the egoism of man is checked and yet taken for granted; and in which human sympathy and love must be exploited to the full and yet discounted. Universal peace can wait upon neither universal culture nor universal love. There can be in fact no such thing as universal peace, if we mean by it a frictionless harmony between nations and a perfect justice between men. It ought to be possible for western society to achieve a higher degree of social and political cohesion and to avoid complete anarchy. But such a possibility depends upon a degree of political realism which is lacking today in both our religious and our secular culture. It depends upon a realism which understands how tenuous and tentative every form of social peace and justice is. . . .

In one sense the logic of this isolationism is of course perfectly correct. It is not possible to make discriminate choices in politics without running the risk of ultimate involvement in conflict, because all social tensions may result in overt conflict and all forms supporting one side or the other may have the consequence of requiring a more direct support. The logic of isolationism is plausible enough but the moral implications are intolerable. If it were followed through consistently in the whole of social life each family would seek to build itself a haven of isolation lest it become involved in the horrid realities of political struggle, which are a part of every national existence. American peace as a symbol of the goodness of man can be maintained only at the price of accentuating every vice in American character, particularly the vices of Pharisaism and self-righteousness which have developed in a nation saved by two oceans from a too obvious involvement in international strife and saved by its wealth from a too obvious display of an internal social struggle. . . .

The moral and political confusion, created by religious and secular perfectionists who do not understand the involvement of all mankind in the sinful realities of history, is aggravated by perfectionists' illusions about peace. It has become almost a universal dogma of American Christianity that any kind of peace is better than war. This always means in the end that tyranny is preferred to war; for submission to the foe is the only certain alternative to resistance against the foe.

That the dogmatic assumption that nothing can be worse than war leads inevitably to an implied or explicit acceptance of tyranny is revealed by many current pronouncements in the religious world. A study conference of the Churches on the international situation held under the auspices of the Federal Council of Churches at the beginning of 1940 declared: "We are convinced that there is ground for hope that a just peace is now possible by negotiation. It is important for the welfare of mankind that the conflict end, not in a dictated but in a negotiated peace based upon the interests of all the people concerned."

This statement, which was commended by the leading Christian journal in America as containing the very essence of Christian counsel in the war situation was completely divorced from all political realities. The fact is that Hitler wanted a negotiated peace from the time he invaded Poland to the time the great offensive began. Being in possession of the continent, with the exception of France, it was obvious that a negotiated peace would have been possible only upon the basis of leaving him in possession of all the loot he had taken. If such a peace had been made the smaller nations, not yet under the Nazi heel, would have been gradually conquered by economic and political pressure. They would have had no power to resist and no incentive to resist, since they could not have looked forward to any aid in stemming the tide of Nazism. A negotiated peace, when the Churches desired it, would have been merely an easy Nazi victory.

The alternative effort to dislodge the Nazis may wreck Europe even if it succeeds, and it may fail and thus come to the same result as premature capitulation through a negotiated peace. This fact is supposed to justify the hysterical demand for peace on any terms. But our American moralists fail to understand that peoples and nations which face an imminent threat of enslavement do not make nice calculations of alternative consequences. There are critical moments in history when such calculations become irrelevant. Every instinct of survival and every decent impulse of humanity becomes engaged and prompts resistance, no matter what the consequences. The result may be tragic; but only a very vapid moralism fails to appreciate the beauty and nobility in such tragedy and continues to speculate on how much better it would have been to accept slavery without resistance than to accept it after resistance.

Just as the dogmatic insistence that nothing can possibly be worse than war leads to the explicit or implicit acceptance of tyranny, so the uncritical identification of neutrality with the Christian ethic leads to a perverse obfuscation of important moral distinctions between contending forces. *The Christian Century* has consistently criticized President Roosevelt for not being absolutely neutral. It seems not to realize that this means to condone a tyranny which has destroyed freedom, is seeking to extinguish the Christian religion, debases its subjects to robots who have no opinion and judgment of their own, threatens the Jews of Europe with complete annihilation and all the nations of Europe with subordination under the imperial dominion of a "master race."

The Christian Century answers the arguments of those who believe that civilization is imperilled by the victory of Germany with the simple assertion that this cannot be true since it is war which imperils civilization. Recognizing a certain uneasiness of conscience among Americans it counsels them to hold firm to their resolution not to have anything to do with the conflict and seeks to ease their conscience by advising them that the "Protestant conscience" of Holland and Switzerland arrived at the same conclusions. Most of the neutrals of Europe to whose conscience *The Christian Century* pointed were destroyed while it was holding them up as glorious examples.

In its simple moralism *The Christian Century* had failed to illumine the basic problem of international relations. This problem is the necessity of an obvious coincidence between national and ideal interests before nations embark upon the hazards of war. There was no question in the minds of any of the small neutral nations about the decisive character of the present conflict. Most of them hoped that Europe would be saved without their aid. Their vital interests were in every case involved ultimately but not immediately. When they became involved immediately, namely by invasion of the foe, it was too late to serve either national interest or the values of civilization which transcend national interest.

The fact that there must be some coincidence between national and ideal interests to prompt national action in a crisis is an inevitable political fact, but it is morally dubious and politically ambiguous in its import. It is morally dubious because it leaves other nations to carry the brunt of defending a civilization which transcends the mere existence of those nations. Politically it is ambiguous because the vital interests of a nation may be ultimately imperilled without being immediately imperilled. To wait until ultimate perils become immediate means to wait too long.

The Scandinavian nations would have been well advised to offer united resistance to aggression rather than wait for the extinction of the liberties of each. Holland and Belgium sought to ward off disaster by constructing a neutrality program which pretended to find equal peril in the designs of contending imperial powers. The peril was not equal. There was in fact no peril from the one side at all. The consequence of a policy which obscured the real facts was the invasion of these nations and the break-through of the German army into France. America is of course in the same position. It pretended that its vital interests would be no more endangered by a German victory than by an Allied one. The real situation is that both the ultimate cause of civilization and our own vital interests are much more seriously imperilled by Germany than the Allies. Since the victory of the German armies in Holland, Belgium and France we have gradually awakened to this fact, but probably too late.

In other words the neutrality policy which *The Christian Century* and its kind have praised as representing some kind of Christian ultimate is not only bad morals but bad politics. It represents the cardinal weakness of democracy in facing the perils of tyranny. Democracy, which must take account of the fears and apprehensions of the common people as dictatorships need not, cannot act in time. It can act in time only if it has leaders who are willing and able to anticipate perils which the common man cannot see. By the time the man in the street sees how great the peril is, the danger is so imminent as to make adequate defense preparations impossible.

This natural weakness of democracy as a form of government when dealing with foreign policy is aggravated by liberalism as the culture which has informed the life of the democratic nations. In this liberalism there is little understanding of the depth to which human malevolence may sink and the heights to which malignant power may rise. Some easy and vapid escape is sought from the terrors and woes of a tragic era.

The fact is that moralistic illusions of our liberal culture have been so great and its will-to-live has been so seriously enervated by a confused pacifism, in which Christian perfectionism and bourgeois love of ease have been curiously compounded, that our democratic world does not really deserve to survive. It may not survive. If it does it will be only because it came to its senses in the final hour and because the weaknesses of tyranny may finally outweigh its momentary advantages.

4. Political Power
A Realist Theory of International Politics

HANS J. MORGENTHAU

POLITICAL POWER

WHAT IS POLITICAL POWER?

Its Relation to the Nation as a Whole

International politics, like all politics, is a struggle for power. Whatever the ultimate aims of international politics, power is always the immediate aim. Statesmen and peoples may ultimately seek freedom, security, prosperity, or power itself. They may define their goals in terms of a religious, philosophic, economic, or social ideal. They may hope that this ideal will materialize through its own inner force, through divine intervention, or through the natural development of human affairs. They may also try to further its realization through nonpolitical means, such as technical co-operation with other nations or international organizations. But whenever they strive to realize their goal by means of international politics, they do so by striving for power. The Crusaders wanted to free the holy places from domination by the Infidels; Woodrow Wilson wanted

From *Politics among Nations: The Struggle for Power and Peace*, Third Edition, by Hans J. Morgenthau (New York: Knopf, 1960), pp. 3–4, 10–12, 14, 27–29, 31–35. Copyright 1948, 1954, © 1960 by Alfred A. Knopf, Inc. Reprinted by permission of Alfred A. Knopf. Footnotes deleted.

to make the world safe for democracy; the Nazis wanted to open Eastern Europe to German colonization, to dominate Europe, and to conquer the world. Since they all chose power to achieve these ends, they were actors on the scene of international politics.

Two conclusions follow from this concept of international politics. First, not every action that a nation performs with respect to another nation is of a political nature. . . .

Second, not all nations are at all times to the same extent involved in international politics. . . .

Its Nature

. . . When we speak of power, we mean man's control over the minds and actions of other men. By political power we refer to the mutual relations of control among the holders of public authority and between the latter and the people at large. . . .

Political power is a psychological relation between those who exercise it and those over whom it is exercised. It gives the former control over certain actions of the latter through the influence which the former exert over the latter's minds. That influence derives from three sources: the expectation of benefits, the fear of disadvantages, the respect or love for men or institutions. It may be exerted through orders, threats, persuasion, the authority or charisma of a man or of an office, or a combination of any of these. . . .

THE DEPRECIATION OF POLITICAL POWER

The aspiration for power being the distinguishing element of international politics, as of all politics, international politics is of necessity power politics. While this fact is generally recognized in the practice of international affairs, it is frequently denied in the pronouncements of scholars, publicists, and even statesmen. . . .

In recent times, the conviction that the struggle for power can be eliminated from the international scene has been connected with the great attempts at organizing the world, such as the League of Nations and the United Nations. . . .

. . . It is sufficient to state that the struggle for power is universal in time and space and is an undeniable fact of experience. It cannot be denied that throughout historic time, regardless of social, economic, and political conditions, states have met each other in contests for power. Even though anthropologists have shown that certain primitive peoples seem to be free from the desire for power, nobody has yet shown how their state of mind and the conditions under which they live can be recreated on a world-wide scale so as to eliminate the struggle for power from the international scene. It would be useless and even self-destructive to free one or the other of the peoples of the earth from the desire for power while leaving it extant in others. If the desire for power cannot be abolished everywhere in the world, those who might be cured would simply fall victims to the power of others. . . .

Regardless of particular social conditions, the decisive argument against the opinion that the struggle for power on the international scene is a mere historic accident must be derived from the nature of domestic politics. The essence of international politics is identical with its domestic counterpart. Both domestic and international politics are a struggle for power, modified only by the different conditions under which this struggle takes place in the domestic and in the international spheres.

The tendency to dominate, in particular, is an element of all human associations, from the family through fraternal and professional associations and local political organizations, to the state. On the family level, the typical conflict between the mother-in-law and her child's spouse is in its essence a struggle for power, the defense of an established power position against the attempt to establish a new one. As such it foreshadows the conflict on the international scene between the policies of the status quo and the policies of imperialism. . . .

In view of this ubiquity of the struggle for power in all social relations and on all levels of social organization, is it surprising that international politics is of necessity power politics? And would it not be rather surprising if the struggle for power were but an accidental and ephemeral attribute of international politics when it is a permanent and necessary element of all branches of domestic politics?

A REALIST THEORY OF INTERNATIONAL POLITICS

This book purports to present a theory of international politics. The test by which such a theory must be judged is not *a priori* and abstract but empirical and pragmatic. The theory, in other words, must be judged not by some preconceived abstract principle or concept unrelated to reality, but by its purpose: to bring order and meaning to a mass of phenomena which without it would remain disconnected and unintelligible. It must meet a dual test, an empirical and a logical one: Do the facts as they actually are lend themselves to the interpretation the theory has put upon them, and do the conclusions at which the theory arrives follow with logical necessity from its premises? In short, is the theory consistent with the facts and within itself?

The issue this theory raises concerns the nature of all politics. The history of modern political thought is the story of a contest between two schools that differ fundamentally in their conceptions of the nature of man, society, and politics. One believes that a rational and moral political order, derived from universally valid abstract principles, can be achieved here and now. It assumes the essential goodness and infinite malleability of human nature, and blames the failure of the social order to measure up to the rational standards on lack of knowledge and understanding, obsolescent social institutions, or the depravity of certain isolated individuals or groups. It trusts in education, reform, and the sporadic use of force to remedy these defects.

The other school believes that the world, imperfect as it is from the rational point of view, is the result of forces inherent in human nature. To improve the world one must work with those forces, not against them. This being inherently a world of opposing interests and of conflict among them, moral principles can never be fully realized, but must at best be approximated through the ever temporary balancing of interests and the ever precarious settlement of conflicts. This school, then, sees in a system of checks and balances a universal principle for all pluralist societies. It appeals to historic precedent rather than to abstract principles, and aims at the realization of the lesser evil rather than of the absolute good. . . .

Political realism believes that politics, like society in general, is governed by objective laws that have their roots in human nature. In order to improve society it is first necessary to understand the laws by which society lives. The operation of these laws being impervious to our preferences, men will challenge them only at the risk of failure.

Realism, believing as it does in the objectivity of the laws of politics, must also believe in the possibility of developing a rational theory that reflects, however imperfectly and one-sidedly, these objective laws. It believes also, then, in the possibility of distinguishing in politics between truth and opinion—between what is true objectively and rationally, supported by evidence and illuminated by reason, and what is only a subjective judgment, divorced from the facts as they are and informed by prejudice and wishful thinking. . . .

Political realism is aware of the moral significance of political action. It is also aware of the ineluctable tension between the moral command and the requirements of successful political action. And it is unwilling to gloss over and obliterate that tension and thus to obfuscate both the moral and the political issue by making it appear as though the stark facts of politics were morally more satisfying than they actually are, and the moral law less exacting than it actually is.

Realism maintains that universal moral principles cannot be applied to the actions of states in their abstract universal formulation, but that they must be filtered through the concrete circumstances of time and place. The individual may say for himself: "*Fiat justitia, pereat mundus* (Let justice be done, even if the world perish)," but the state has no right to say so in the name of those who are in its care. Both individual and state must judge political action by universal moral principles, such as that of liberty. Yet while the individual has a moral right to sacrifice himself in defense of such a moral principle, the state has no right to let its moral disapprobation of the infringement of liberty get in the way of successful political action, itself inspired by the moral principle of national survival. There can be no political morality without prudence; that is, without consideration of the political consequences of seemingly moral action. Realism, then, considers prudence—the weighing of the consequences of alternative political actions—to be the supreme virtue in politics. Ethics in the abstract judges action by its conformity with the moral law; political ethics judges action by its political consequences. . . .

Political realism refuses to identify the moral aspirations of a particular nation with the moral laws that govern the universe. As it distinguishes between truth and idolatry. All nations are tempted—and few have been able to resist the temptation for long—to clothe their own particular aspirations and actions in the moral purposes of the universe. To know that nations are subject to the moral law is one thing, while to pretend to know with certainty what is good and evil in the relations among nations is quite another. There is a world of difference between the belief that all nations stand under the judgment of God, inscrutable to the human mind, and the blasphemous conviction that God is always on one's side and that what one wills oneself cannot fail to be willed by God also.

The lighthearted equation between a particular nationalism and the counsels of Providence is morally indefensible, for it is that very sin of pride against which the Greek tragedians and the Biblical prophets have warned rulers and ruled. That equation is also politically pernicious, for it is liable to engender the distortion in judgment which, in the blindness of crusading frenzy, destroys nations and civilizations—in the name of moral principle, ideal, or God himself.

On the other hand, it is exactly the concept of interest defined in terms of power that saves us from both that moral excess and that political folly. For if we look at all nations, our own included, as political entities pursuing their respective interests defined in terms of power, we are able to do justice to all of them. And we are able to do justice to all of them in a dual sense: We are able to judge other nations as we judge our own and, having judged them in this fashion, we are then capable of pursuing policies that respect the interests of other nations, while protecting and promoting those of our own. Moderation in policy cannot fail to reflect the moderation of moral judgment. . . .

The political realist is not unaware of the existence and relevance of standards of thought other than political ones. As political realist, he cannot but subordinate these other standards to those of politics. And he parts company with other schools when they impose standards of thought appropriate to other spheres upon the political sphere. It is here that political realism takes issue with the "legalistic-moralistic approach" to international politics. That this issue is not, as has been contended, a mere figment of the imagination, but goes to the very core of the controversy, can be shown from many historical examples. . . .

This realist defense of the autonomy of the political sphere against its subversion by other modes of thought does not imply disregard for the existence and importance of these other modes of thought. It rather implies that each should be assigned its proper sphere and function. Political realism is based upon a pluralistic conception of human nature. Real man is a composite of "economic man," "political man," "moral man," "religious man," etc. A man who was nothing but "political man" would be a beast, for he would be completely lacking in moral restraints. A man who was nothing but "moral man" would be a fool, for he would be completely lacking in prudence. A man who was nothing but "religious man" would be a saint, for he would be completely lacking in worldly desires.

Recognizing that these different facets of human nature exist, political realism also recognizes that in order to understand one of them one has to deal with it on its own terms. That is to say, if I want to understand "religious man," I must for the time being abstract from the other aspects of human nature and deal with its religious aspect as if it were the only one. . . . What is true of this facet of human nature is true of all the others. No modern economist, for instance, would conceive of his science and its relations to other sciences of man in any other way. It is exactly through such a process of emancipation from other standards of thought, and the development of one appropriate to its subject matter, that economics has developed as an autonomous theory of the economic activities of man. To contribute to a similar development in the field of politics is indeed the purpose of political realism. . . .

5. Diplomacy in the Modern World

GEORGE F. KENNAN

. . . As you have no doubt surmised, I see the most serious fault of our past policy formulation to lie in something that I might call the legalistic-moralistic approach to international problems. This approach runs like a red skein through our foreign policy of the last fifty years. It has in it something of the old emphasis on arbitration treaties, something of the Hague Conferences and schemes for universal disarmament, something of the more ambitious American concepts of the role of international law, something of the League of Nations and the United Nations, something of the Kellogg Pact, something of the idea of a universal "Article 51" pact, something of the belief in World Law and World Government. But it is none of these, entirely. Let me try to describe it.

It is the belief that it should be possible to suppress the chaotic and dangerous aspirations of governments in the international field by the acceptance of some system of legal rules and restraints. This belief undoubtedly represents in part an attempt to transpose the Anglo-Saxon concept of individual law into the international field and to make it applicable to governments as it is applicable here at home

to individuals. It must also stem in part from the memory of the origin of our own political system—from the recollection that we were able, through acceptance of a common institutional and juridical framework, to reduce to harmless dimensions the conflicts of interest and aspiration among the original thirteen colonies and to bring them all into an ordered and peaceful relationship with one another. Remembering this, people are unable to understand that what might have been possible for the thirteen colonies in a given set of circumstances might not be possible in the wider international field.

It is the essence of this belief that, instead of taking the awkward conflicts of national interest and dealing with them on their merits with a view to finding the solutions least unsettling to the stability of international life, it would be better to find some formal criteria of a juridical nature by which the permissible behavior of states could be defined. There would then be judicial entities competent to measure the actions of governments against these criteria and to decide when their behavior was acceptable and when unacceptable. Behind all this, of course, lies the American assumption that the things for which other peoples in this world are apt to contend are for the most part neither creditable nor important and might justly be expected to take second place behind the desirability of an orderly world, untrou-

Reprinted from *American Diplomacy, 1900–1950* by George F. Kennan (Chicago: University of Chicago Press, 1951), pp. 95–103, by permission of The University of Chicago Press. Copyright © 1951 The University of Chicago Press.

bled by international violence. To the American mind, it is implausible that people should have positive aspirations, and ones that they regard as legitimate, more important to them than the peacefulness and orderliness of international life. From this standpoint, it is not apparent why other peoples should not join us in accepting the rules of the game in international politics, just as we accept such rules in the competition of sport in order that the game may not become too cruel and too destructive and may not assume an importance we did not mean it to have.

If they were to do this, the reasoning runs, then the troublesome and chaotic manifestations of the national ego could be contained and rendered either unsubstantial or subject to easy disposal by some method familiar and comprehensible to our American usage. Departing from this background, the mind of American statesmanship, stemming as it does in so large a part from the legal profession in our country, gropes with unfailing persistence for some institutional framework which would be capable of fulfilling this function. . . .

In the first place, the idea of the subordination of a large number of states to an international juridical regime, limiting their possibilities for aggression and injury to other states, implies that these are all states like our own, reasonably content with their international borders and status, at least to the extent that they would be willing to refrain from pressing for change without international agreement. . . .

Second, while this concept is often associated with a revolt against nationalism, it is a curious thing that it actually tends to confer upon the concept of nationality and national sovereignty an absolute value it did not have before. The very principle of "one government, one vote," regardless of physical or political differences between states, glorifies the concept of national sovereignty and makes it the exclusive form of participation in international life. It envisages a world composed exclusively of sovereign national states with a full equality of status. In doing this, it ignores the tremendous variations in the firmness and soundness of na-

tional divisions: the fact that the origins of state borders and national personalities were in many instances fortuitous or at least poorly related to realities. It also ignores the law of change. The national state pattern is not, should not be, and cannot be a fixed and static thing. By nature, it is an unstable phenomenon in a constant state of change and flux. History has shown that the will and the capacity of individual peoples to contribute to their world environment is constantly changing. It is only logical that the organizational forms (and what else are such things as borders and governments?) should change with them. The function of a system of international relationships is not to inhibit this process of change by imposing a legal strait jacket upon it but rather to facilitate it: to ease its transitions, to temper the asperities to which it often leads, to isolate and moderate the conflicts to which it gives rise, and to see that these conflicts do not assume forms too unsettling for international life in general. But this is a task for diplomacy, in the most old-fashioned sense of the term. For this, law is too abstract, too inflexible, too hard to adjust to the demands of the unpredictable and the unexpected.

By the same token, the American concept of world law ignores those means of international offense—those means of the projection of power and coercion over other peoples—which by-pass institutional forms entirely or even exploit them against themselves: such things as ideological attack, intimidation, penetration, and disguised seizure of the institutional paraphernalia of national sovereignty. It ignores, in other words, the device of the puppet state and the set of techniques by which states can be converted into puppets with no formal violation of, or challenge to, the outward attributes of their sovereignty and their independence.

This is one of the things that has caused the peoples of the satellite countries of eastern Europe to look with a certain tinge of bitterness on the United Nations. The organization failed so completely to save them from domination by a great neighboring country, a domination no less invidious by virtue of the fact that it came into being by processes we could not call "aggression." And there is indeed some justification for their feeling, because the legalistic approach to international affairs ignores in general the international significance of political problems and the deeper sources of international instability. It assumes that civil wars will remain civil and not grow into international wars. . . . It assumes, in other words, that domestic issues will not become international issues and that the world community will not be put in the position of having to make choices between rival claimants for power within the confines of the individual state.

Finally, this legalistic approach to international relations is faulty in its assumptions concerning the possibility of sanctions against offenses and violations. In general, it looks to collective action to provide such sanction against the bad behavior of states. In doing so, it forgets the limitations on the effectiveness of military coalition. It forgets that, as a circle of military associates widens in any conceivable political-military venture, the theoretical total of available military strength may increase, but only at the cost of compactness and ease of control. And the wider a coalition becomes, the more difficult it becomes to retain political unity and general agreement on the purposes and effects of what is being done. As we are seeing in the case of Korea, joint military operations against an aggressor have a different meaning for each participant and raise specific political issues for each one which are extraneous to the action in question and affect many other facets of international life. The wider the circle of military associates, the more cumbersome the problem of political control over their actions, and the more circumscribed the least common denominator of agreement. This law of diminishing returns lies so heavily on the possibilities for multilateral military action that it makes it doubtful whether the participation of smaller states can really add very much to the ability of the great powers to assure stability of international life. And this is tremendously important, for it brings us back to the realization that even under a system of world law the sanction against destructive international behavior might continue to rest basically, as it has in the past, on the alliances and relationships among the great powers themselves. There might be a state, or perhaps more than one state, which all the rest of the world community together could not successfully coerce into following a line of action to which it was violently averse. And if this is true, where are we? It seems to me that we are right back in the realm of the forgotten art of diplomacy from which we have spent fifty years trying to escape.

These, then, are some of the theoretical deficiencies that appear to me to be inherent in the legalistic approach to international affairs. But there is a greater deficiency still that I should like to mention before I close. That is the inevitable association of legalistic ideas with moralistic ones: the carrying-over into the affairs of states of the concepts of right and wrong, the assumption that state behavior is a fit subject for moral judgment. Whoever says there is a law must of course be indignant against the lawbreaker and feel a moral superiority to him. And when such indignation spills over into military contest, it knows no bounds short of the reduction of the lawbreaker to the point of complete submissiveness—namely, unconditional surrender. It is a curious thing, but it is true, that the legalistic approach to world affairs, rooted as it unquestionably is in a desire to do away with war and violence, makes violence more enduring, more terrible, and more destructive to political stability than did the older motives of national interest. A war fought in the name of high moral principle finds no early end short of some form of total domination.

In this way, we see that the legalistic approach to international problems is closely identified with the concept of total war and total victory, and the manifestations of the one spill over only too easily into the manifestations of the other. And the concept of total war is something we would all do well to think about a little in these troubled times. This is a relatively new concept, in Western civilization at any rate. It did not really appear on the scene until World War I. It characterized both of these great world wars, and both of them—as I have pointed out—were followed by great instability and disillusionment. But it is not only a question now of the desirability of this concept; it is a question of its feasibility. Actually, I wonder whether even in the past total victory was not really an illusion from the standpoint of the victors. In a sense, there is not total victory short of genocide, unless it be a victory over the minds of men. But the total military victories are rarely victories over the minds of men. And we now face the fact that it is very questionable whether in a new global conflict there could ever be any such thing as total *military* victory. I personally do not believe that there could. There might be a great weakening of the armed forces of one side or another, but I think it out of the question that there should be such a thing as a general and formal submission of the national will on either side. The attempt to achieve this unattainable goal, however, could wreak upon civilization another set of injuries fully as serious as those caused by World War I or World War II, and I leave it to you to answer the question as to how civilization could survive them.

It was asserted not long ago by a prominent American that "war's very object is victory" and that "in war there can be no substitute for victory." Perhaps the confusion here lies in what is meant by the term "victory." Perhaps the term is actually misplaced. Perhaps there can be such a thing as "victory" in a battle, whereas in war there can be only the achievement or nonachievement of your objectives. In the old days, wartime objectives were generally limited to practical ones, and it was common to measure the success of your military operations by the extent to which they brought you closer to your objectives. But where your objectives are moral and ideological ones and run to changing the attitudes and traditions of an entire people or the personality of a regime, then victory is probably something not to be achieved entirely by military means or indeed in any short space of time at all; and perhaps that is the source of our confusion.

In any case, I am frank to say that I think there is no more dangerous delusion, none that has done us a greater disservice in the past or that threatens to do us a greater disservice in the future, than the concept of total victory. And I fear that it springs in large measure from the basic faults in the approach to international affairs which I have been discussing here. If we are to get away from it, this will not mean that we shall have to abandon our respect for international law, or our hopes for its future usefulness as the gentle civilizer of events. . . . But it will mean the emergence of a new attitude among us toward many things outside our borders that are irritating and unpleasant today, . . . an attitude of detachment and soberness and readiness to reserve judgment. It will mean that we will have the modesty to admit that our own national interest is all that we are really capable of knowing and understanding—and the courage to recognize that if our own purposes and undertakings here at home are decent ones, unsullied by arrogance or hostility toward other people or delusions of superiority, then the pursuit of our national interest can never fail to be conducive to a better world. This concept is less ambitious and less inviting in its immediate prospects than those to which we have so often inclined, and less pleasing to our image of ourselves. To many it may seem to smack of cynicism and reaction. I cannot share these doubts. Whatever is realistic in concept, and founded in an endeavor to see both ourselves and others as we really are, cannot be illiberal.

Chapter 2

Just War and Idealism

---

6. Of War

THOMAS AQUINAS

QUESTION XL

ARTICLE I. Whether It Is Always Sinful to Wage War?

We proceed thus to the First Article: It seems that it is always sinful to wage war.

Objection 1. Because punishment is not inflicted except for sin. Now those who wage war are threatened by Our Lord with punishment, according to Matt. 26. 52: *All that take the sword shall perish with the sword.* Therefore all wars are unlawful.

Obj. 2. Further, Whatever is contrary to a Divine precept is a sin. But war is contrary to a Divine precept, for it is written (Matt. 5.39): *But I say to you not to resist evil;* and (Rom. 12.19): *Not revenging yourselves, my dearly beloved, but give place unto wrath.* Therefore war is always sinful.

Obj. 3. Further, Nothing, except sin, is contrary to an act of virtue. But war is contrary to peace. Therefore war is always a sin.

Obj. 4. Further, The exercise of a lawful thing is itself lawful, as is evident in exercises of the sciences. But warlike exercises which

From *Summa Theologica,* Part II of Second Part. Translated by the Fathers of the English Dominican Province. First published in the United States in 1917 by Benziger Brothers. Footnotes deleted.

take place in tournaments are forbidden by the Church, since those who are slain in these trials are deprived of ecclesiastical burial. Therefore it seems that war is a sin absolutely.

On the contrary, Augustine says in a sermon on the son of the centurion: "If the Christian Religion forbade war altogether, those who sought salutary advice in the Gospel would rather have been counselled to cast aside their arms, and to give up soldiering altogether. On the contrary, they were told: 'Do violence to no man; . . . and be content with your pay' (Luke 3.14). If he commanded them to be content with their pay, he did not forbid soldiering."

I answer that, In order for a war to be just, three things are necessary. First, the authority of the sovereign by whose command the war is to be waged. For it is not the business of a private person to declare war, because he can seek for redress of his rights from the tribunal of his superior. Moreover it is not the business of a private person to summon together the people, which has to be done in wartime. And as the care of the common weal is committed to those who are in authority, it is their business to watch over the common weal of the city, kingdom or province subject to them. And just as it is lawful for them to have recourse to the material sword in defending that common weal against internal disturbances, when they punish evildoers, according to the words of the Apostle (Rom. 13.4): *He beareth not the sword in vain: for he is God's minister, an avenger to execute wrath upon him that doth evil;* so too, it is their business to have recourse to the sword of war in defending the common weal against external enemies. Hence it is said to those who are in authority (Ps. 81. 4): *Rescue the poor: and deliver the needy out of the hand of the sinner;* and for this reason Augustine says (*Contra Faust.* xxii, 75): "The natural order conducive to peace among mortals demands that the power to declare and counsel war should be in the hands of those who hold the supreme authority."

Secondly, a just cause is required, namely that those who are attacked should be attacked because they deserve it on account of some fault. Therefore Augustine says (Q. x, *super Jos.*): "A just war is usually described as one that avenges wrongs, when a nation or state has to be punished, for refusing to make amends for the wrongs inflicted by its subjects, or to restore what it has seized unjustly."

Thirdly, it is necessary that the belligerents should have a right intention, so that they intend the advancement of good, or the avoidance of evil. Hence Augustine says (*De Verb. Dom.*): "True religion does not look upon as sinful those wars that are waged not for motives of aggrandisement, or cruelty, but with the object of securing peace, of punishing evildoers, and of uplifting the good." For it may happen that the war is declared by the legitimate authority, and for a just cause, and yet be rendered unlawful through a wicked intention. Hence Augustine says (*Contra Faust.* xxii): "The passion for inflicting harm, the cruel thirst for vengeance, an unpacific and relentless spirit, the fever of revolt, the lust of power, and such things, all these are rightly condemned in war."

Reply Obj. 1. As Augustine says (*Contra Faust.* xxii): "To take the sword is to arm oneself in order to take the life of anyone, without the command or permission of superior or lawful authority." On the other hand, to have recourse to the sword (as a private person) by the authority of the sovereign or judge, or (as a public person) through zeal for jus-

tice, and by the authority, so to speak, of God, is not to *take the sword*, but to use it as commissioned by another, and so it does not deserve punishment. And yet even those who make sinful use of the sword are not always slain with the sword, but they always perish with their own sword, because, unless they repent, they are punished eternally for their sinful use of the sword.

Reply Obj. 2. Precepts of this kind, as Augustine observes (*De Serm. Dom. in Monte,* i), should always be borne in readiness of mind, so that we be ready to obey them, and, if necessary, to refrain from resistance or self-defence. Nevertheless it is necessary sometimes for a man to act otherwise for the common good, or for the good of those with whom he is fighting. Hence Augustine says (*Ep. ad Marcellin.*): "Those whom we have to punish with a kindly severity, it is necessary to handle in many ways against their will. For when we are stripping a man of the lawlessness of sin, it is good for him to be vanquished, since nothing is more hopeless than the happiness of sinners, whence arises a guilty impunity, and an evil will, like an internal enemy."

Reply Obj. 3. Those who wage war justly aim at peace, and so they are not opposed to peace, except to the evil peace, which Our Lord came not to send upon earth (Matt. 10.34). Hence Augustine says (*Ep. ad Bonif.* clxxxix): "We do not seek peace in order to be at war, but we go to war that we may have peace. Be peaceful, therefore, in warring, so that you may vanquish those whom you war against, and bring them to the prosperity of peace."

Reply Obj. 4. Manly exercises in warlike feats of arms are not all forbidden, but those which are inordinate and perilous, and end in slaying or plundering. . . .

ARTICLE 2. Whether It Is Lawful for Clerics and Bishops to Fight?

We proceed thus to the Second Article: It seems lawful for clerics and bishops to fight.

Objection 1. For, as stated above (A. I), wars are lawful and just in so far as they protect the poor and the entire common weal from suffering at the hands of the foe. . . .

Obj. 3. Further, It seems to be the same whether a man does a thing himself, or consents to its being done by another, according to Rom. I. 32: *They who do such things, are worthy of death, and not only they that do them, but they also that consent to them that do them.* Now those, above all, seem to consent to a thing, who induce others to do it. . . .

Obj. 4. Further, Whatever is right and meritorious in itself is lawful for prelates and clerics. Now it is sometimes right and meritorious to make war, for it is written (xxiii, qu. 8, can. *Omni timore*) that "if a man die for the true faith, or to save his country, or in defence of Christians, God will give him a heavenly reward." Therefore it is lawful for bishops and clerics to fight.

On the contrary, It was said to Peter as representing bishops and clerics (Matt. 26. 53): *Put up again thy sword into the scabbard* (Vulg.,—*its place*). Therefore it is not lawful for them to fight.

I answer that, Several things are requisite for the good of a human society, and a number of things are done better and quicker by a number of persons than by one, as the Philosopher observes, while certain occupations are so inconsistent with one another, that they cannot be fittingly exercised at the same time; hence those who are assigned to important duties are forbidden to occupy themselves with things of small importance. Thus according to human laws, soldiers who are assigned to warlike pursuits are forbidden to engage in commerce.

Now warlike pursuits are altogether incompatible with the duties of a bishop and a cleric for two reasons. . . . warlike pursuits are full of unrest, so that they hinder the mind very much from the contemplation of Divine things, the praise of God, and prayers for the people, which belong to the duties of a cleric.

Therefore just as commercial enterprises are forbidden to clerics, because they entangle the mind too much, so too are warlike pursuits, according to II Tim. 2. 4: *No man being a soldier to God, entangleth himself with secular business.* . . . Therefore it is unbecoming for them to slay or shed blood, and it is more fitting that they should be ready to shed their own blood for Christ, so as to imitate in deed what they portray in their ministry. For this reason it has been decreed that those who shed blood, even without sin, become irregular. Now no man who has a certain duty to perform can lawfully do that which renders him unfit for that duty. Therefore it is altogether unlawful for clerics to fight, because war is directed to the shedding of blood.

Reply Obj. 1. Prelates ought to withstand not only the wolf who brings spiritual death upon the flock, but also the pillager and the oppressor who work bodily harm; not, however, by having recourse themselves to material arms, but by means of spiritual weapons, according to the saying of the Apostle (II Cor. 10. 4): *The weapons of our warfare are not carnal, but mighty through God.* . . .

Reply Obj. 3. As stated above (Q. XXIII, A. 4, Reply 2) every power, art or virtue that pertains to the end, has to dispose that which is directed to the end. Now, among the faithful, carnal wars should be considered as having for their end the Divine spiritual good to which clerics are deputed. Therefore it is the duty of clerics to dispose and counsel other men to engage in just wars. For they are forbidden to take up arms, not as though it were a sin, but because such an occupation is unbecoming their persons.

Reply Obj. 4. Although it is meritorious to wage a just war, nevertheless it is rendered unlawful for clerics, by reason of their being assigned to works more meritorious still. Thus the marriage act may be meritorious; and yet it becomes reprehensible in those who have vowed virginity, because they are bound to a yet greater good.

7. The World Must Be Made Safe for Democracy
The Fourteen Points

WOODROW WILSON

THE WORLD MUST BE MADE SAFE FOR DEMOCRACY

I have called the Congress into extraordinary session because there are serious, very serious, choices of policy to be made, and made immediately, which it was neither right nor constitutionally permissible that I should assume the responsibility of making.

On the third of February last I officially laid before you the extraordinary announcement of the Imperial German Government that on and after the first day of February it was its purpose to put aside all restraints of law or of humanity and use its submarines to sink every vessel that sought to approach either the ports of Great Britain and Ireland or the western coasts of Europe or any of the ports controlled by the enemies of Germany within the Mediterranean. That had seemed to be the object of the German submarine warfare earlier in the war, but since April of last year the Imperial Government had somewhat restrained the commanders of its undersea craft in conformity with its promise then given to us that passenger boats should not be sunk and that due warning would be given to all other vessels which its submarines might seek to de-

From Address to Congress Asking for Declaration of War, April 2, 1917; Address to Congress, January 8, 1918.

stroy, when no resistance was offered or escape attempted, and care taken that their crews were given at least a fair chance to save their lives in their open boats. The precautions taken were meager and haphazard enough, as was proved in distressing instance after instance in the progress of the cruel and unmanly business, but a certain degree of restraint was observed. The new policy has swept every restriction aside. Vessels of every kind, whatever their flag, their character, their cargo, their destination, their errand, have been ruthlessly sent to the bottom without warning and without thought of help or mercy for those on board, the vessels of friendly neutrals along with those of belligerents. Even hospital ships and ships carrying relief to the sorely bereaved and stricken people of Belgium, though the latter were provided with safe conduct through the proscribed areas by the German Government itself and were distinguished by unmistakable marks of identity, have been sunk with the same reckless lack of compassion or of principle.

I was for a little while unable to believe that such things would in fact be done by any government that had hitherto subscribed to the humane practices of civilized nations.

International law had its origin in the attempt to set up some law which would be respected and observed upon the seas, where no nation had right of dominion and where lay the free highways of the world. By painful stage after stage has that law been built up, with meager enough results, indeed, after all was accomplished that could be accomplished, but always with a clear view, at least, of what the heart and conscience of mankind demanded. This minimum of right the German Government has swept aside under the plea of retaliation and necessity and because it had no weapons which it could use at sea except these which it is impossible to employ as it is employing them without throwing to the winds all scruples of humanity or of respect for the understandings that were supposed to underlie the intercourse of the world. I am not now thinking of the loss of property involved, immense and serious as that is, but only of the wanton and wholesale destruction of the lives of noncombatants, men, women, and children, engaged in pursuits which have always, even in the darkest periods of modern history, been deemed innocent and legitimate. Property can be paid for; the lives of peaceful and innocent people cannot be. The present German submarine warfare against commerce is a warfare against mankind.

It is a war against all nations. American ships have been sunk, American lives taken, in ways which it has stirred us very deeply to learn of, but the ships and people of other neutral and friendly nations have been sunk and overwhelmed in the waters in the same way. There has been no discrimination. The challenge is to all mankind. Each nation must decide for itself how it will meet it. The choice we make for ourselves must be made with a moderation of counsel and a temperateness of judgment befitting our character and our motives as a nation. We must put excited feeling away. Our motive will not be revenge or the victorious assertion of the physical might of the nation, but only the vindication of right, of human right, of which we are only a single champion.

When I addressed the Congress on the twenty-sixth of February last I thought that it would suffice to assert our neutral rights with arms, our right to use the seas against unlawful interference, our right to keep our people safe against unlawful violence. But armed neutrality, it now appears, is impracticable. . . . There is one choice we cannot make, we are incapable of making: we will not choose the path of submission and suffer the most sacred rights of our Nation and our people to be ignored or violated. The wrongs against which we now array ourselves are no common wrongs; they cut to the very roots of human life.

With a profound sense of the solemn and even tragical character of the step I am taking and of the grave responsibilities which it involves, but in unhesitating obedience to what I deem my constitutional duty, I advise that the Congress declare the recent course of the Imperial German Government to be in fact nothing less than war against the Government and people of the United States; that it formally accept the status of belligerent which has thus been thrust upon it; and that it take immediate steps not only to put the country in a more thorough state of defense but also to exert all its power and employ all its resources to bring the Government of the German Empire to terms and end the war. . . .

While we do these things, these deeply momentous things, let us be very clear, and make very clear to all the world what our motives and our objects are. My own thought has not been driven from its habitual and normal course by the unhappy events of the last two months, and I do not believe that the thought of the Nation has been altered or clouded by them. I have exactly the same things in mind now that I had in mind when I addressed the Senate on the twenty-second of January last; the same that I had in mind when I addressed the Congress on the third of February and on the twenty-sixth of February. Our object now, as then, is to vindicate the principles of peace and justice in the life of the world as against selfish and autocratic power and to set up amongst the really free and self-governed peoples of the world such a concert of purpose and of action as will henceforth insure the observance of those principles. Neutrality is no longer feasible or desirable where the peace of the world is involved and the freedom of its peoples, and the menace to that peace and freedom lies in the existence of autocratic governments backed by organized force which is controlled wholly by their will, not by the will of their people. We have seen the last of neutrality in such circumstances. We are at the beginning of an age in which it will be insisted that the same standards of conduct and of responsibility for wrong done shall be observed among nations and their governments that are observed among the individual citizens of civilized states.

We have no quarrel with the German people. We have no feeling towards them but one of sympathy and friendship. It was not upon their impulse that their government acted in entering the war. It was not with their previous knowledge or approval. It was a war determined upon as wars used to be determined upon in the old, unhappy days when people were nowhere consulted by their rulers and wars were provoked and waged in the interest of dynasties or of little groups of ambitious men who were accustomed to use their fellow men as pawns and tools. Self-governed nations do not fill their neighbor states with spies or set the course of intrigue to bring about some critical posture of affairs which will give them an opportunity to strike and make conquest. Such designs can be successfully worked out only under cover and where no one has the right to ask questions. Cunningly contrived plans of deception or aggression, carried, it may be, from generation to generation, can be worked out and kept from the light only within the privacy of courts or behind the carefully guarded confidences of a narrow and privileged class. They are happily impossible where public opinion commands and insists upon full information concerning all the nation's affairs.

A steadfast concert for peace can never be maintained except by a partnership of democratic nations. No autocratic government could be trusted to keep faith within it or observe its covenants. It must be a league of honor, a partnership of opinion. Intrigue would eat its vitals away; the plottings of inner circles who could plan what they would and render account to no one would be a corruption seated at its very heart. Only free peoples can hold their purpose and their honor steady to a common end and prefer the interests of mankind to any narrow interest of their own. . . .

One of the things that has served to convince us that the Prussian autocracy was not and could never be our friend is that from the very outset of the present war it has filled our unsuspecting communities and even our offices of government with spies and set criminal intrigues everywhere afoot against our national unity of counsel, our peace within and without, our industries and our commerce. Indeed, it is now evident that its spies were here even before the war began; and it is unhappily not a matter of conjecture but a fact proved in our courts of justice that the intrigues which have more than once come perilously near to disturbing the peace and dislocating the industries of the country have been carried on at the instigation, with the support, and even under the personal direction of official agents of the Imperial Government accredited to the Government of the United States. Even in checking these things and trying to extirpate them we have sought to put the most generous interpretation possible upon them because we knew that their source lay not in any hostile feeling or purpose of the German people towards us (who were no doubt as ignorant of them as we ourselves were), but only in the selfish designs of a Government that did what it pleased and told its people nothing. But they have played their part in serving to convince us at last that that Government entertains no real friendship for us and means to act against our peace and security at its convenience. That it means to stir up enemies against us at our very doors the intercepted note to the German Minister at Mexico City is eloquent evidence.

We are accepting this challenge of hostile purpose because we know that in such a Government, following such methods, we can never have a friend; and that in the presence of its organized power, always lying in wait to accomplish we know not what purpose, there can be no assured security for the democratic Governments of the world. We are now about to accept gage of battle with this natural foe to liberty and shall, if necessary, spend the whole force of the Nation to check and nullify its pretensions and its power. We are glad now that we see the facts with no veil of false pretense about them, to fight thus for the ultimate peace of the world and for the liberation of its peoples, the German peoples included: for the rights of nations great and small and the privilege of men everywhere to choose their way of life and of obedience. The world must be made safe for democracy. Its peace must be planted upon the tested foundations of political liberty. We have no selfish ends to serve. We desire no conquest, no dominion. We seek no indemnities for ourselves, no material compensation for the sacrifices we shall freely make. We are but one of the champions of the right of mankind. We shall be satisfied when those rights have been made as secure as the faith and the freedom of nations can make them.

Just because we fight without rancor and without selfish object, seeking nothing for ourselves but what we shall wish to share with all free people, we shall, I feel confident, conduct our operations as belligerents without passion and ourselves observe with proud punctilio the principles of right and of fair play we profess to be fighting for. . . .

It is a distressing and oppressive duty, Gentlemen of the Congress, which I have performed in thus addressing you. There are, it may be, many months of fiery trial and sacrifice ahead of us. It is a fearful thing to lead this great peaceful people into war, into the most terrible and disastrous of all wars, civilization itself seeming to be in the balance. But the right is more precious than peace, and we shall fight for the things which we have always carried nearest our hearts—for democracy, for the right of those who submit to authority to have a voice in their own Governments, for the rights and liberties of small nations, for a universal dominion of right by such a concert of free peoples as shall bring peace and safety to all nations and make the world itself at last free. To such a task we can dedicate our lives and our fortunes, everything that we are and everything that we have, with the pride of those who know that the day has come when America is privileged to spend her blood and her might for the principles that gave her birth and happiness and the peace which she has treasured. God helping her, she can do no other.

THE FOURTEEN POINTS

. . . It will be our wish and purpose that the processes of peace, when they are begun, shall be absolutely open and that they shall involve and permit henceforth no secret understandings of any kind. The day of conquest and aggrandizement is gone by; so is also the day of secret covenants entered into in the interest of particular governments and likely at some unlooked-for moment to upset the peace of the world. It is this happy fact, now clear to the view of every public man whose thoughts do not still linger in an age that is dead and gone, which makes it possible for every nation whose purposes are consistent with justice and the peace of the world to avow now or at any other time the objects it has in view.

We entered this war because violations of right had occurred which touched us to the quick and made the life of our own people impossible unless they were corrected and the world secured once and for all against their recurrence. What we demand in this war, therefore, is nothing peculiar to ourselves. It is that the world be made fit and safe to live in; and particularly that it be made safe for every peace-loving nation which, like our own, wishes to live its own life, determine its own institutions, be assured of justice and fair dealing by the other people of the world as against force and selfish aggression. All the peoples of the world are in effect partners in this interest, and for our own part we see very clearly that unless justice be done to others it will not be done to us. The program of the world's peace, therefore, is our program; and that program, the only possible program, as we see it, is this:

I. Open covenants of peace, openly arrived at, after which there shall be no private international understandings of any kind but diplomacy shall proceed always frankly and in the public view.

II. Absolute freedom of navigation upon the seas, outside territorial waters, alike in peace and in war, except as the seas may be closed in whole or in part by international action for the enforcement of international covenants.

III. The removal, so far as possible, of all economic barriers and the establishment of an equality of trade conditions among all the nations consenting to the peace and associating themselves for its maintenance.

IV. Adequate guarantees given and taken that national armaments will be reduced to the lowest point consistent with domestic safety.

V. A free, open-minded, and absolutely impartial adjustment of all colonial claims, based upon a strict observance of the principle that in determining all such questions of sovereignty the interests of the populations concerned must have equal weight with the equitable claims of the government whose title is to be determined.

VI. The evacuation of all Russian territory and such a settlement of all questions affecting Russia as will secure the best and freest cooperation of the other nations of the world in obtaining for her an unhampered and unembarrassed opportunity for the independent determination of her own political development and national policy and assure her of a sincere welcome into the society of free nations under institutions of her own choosing; and, more than a welcome, assistance also of every kind that she may need and may herself desire. The treatment accorded Russia by her sister nations in the months to come will be the acid test of their good will, of their comprehension of her needs as distinguished from their own interests, and of their intelligent and unselfish sympathy.

VII. Belgium, the whole world will agree, must be evacuated and restored, without any attempt to limit the sovereignty which she enjoys in common with all other free nations. No other single act will serve as this will serve to restore confidence among the nations in the laws which they have themselves set and determined for the government of their relations with one another. Without this healing act the whole structure and validity of international law is forever impaired.

VIII. All French territory should be freed and the invaded portions restored, and the wrong done to France by Prussia in 1871 in the matter of Alsace-Lorraine, which has unsettled the peace of the world for nearly fifty years, should be righted, in order that peace may once more be made secure in the interest of all.

IX. A readjustment of the frontiers of Italy should be effected along clearly recognizable lines of nationality.

X. The peoples of Austria-Hungary, whose place among the nations we wish to see safeguarded and assured, should be accorded the freest opportunity of autonomous development.

XI. Rumania, Serbia, and Montenegro should be evacuated; occupied territories restored; Serbia accorded free and secure access to the sea; and the relations of the several Balkan states to one another determined by friendly counsel along historically established lines of allegiance and nationality; and international guarantees of the political and economic independence and territorial integrity of the several Balkan states should be entered into.

XII. The Turkish portions of the present Ottoman Empire should be assured a secure sovereignty, but the other nationalities which are now under Turkish rule should be assured an undoubted security of life and an absolutely unmolested opportunity of autonomous development, and the Dardanelles should be permanently opened as a free passage to the ships and commerce of all nations under international guarantees.

XIII. An independent Polish state should be erected which should include the territories inhabited by indisputably Polish populations, which should be assured a free and secure access to the sea, and whose political and economic independence and territorial integrity should be guaranteed by international covenant.

XIV. A general association of nations must be formed under specific covenants for the purpose of affording mutual guarantees of political independence and territorial integrity to great and small states alike.

In regard to these essential rectifications of wrong and assertions of right we feel ourselves to be intimate partners of all the governments and peoples associated together against the imperialists. We cannot be separated in interest or divided in purpose. We stand together until the end.

For such arrangements and covenants we are willing to fight and to continue to fight until they are achieved; but only because we wish the right to prevail and desire a just and stable peace such as can be secured only by removing the chief provocations to war, which this program does remove. We have no jealousy of German greatness, and there is nothing in this program that impairs it. We grudge her no achievement or distinction of learning or of pacific enterprise such as have made her record very bright and very enviable. We do not wish to injure her or to block in any way her legitimate influence or power. We do not wish to fight her either with arms or with hostile arrangements of trade if she is willing to associate herself with us and the other peace-loving nations of the world in covenants of justice and law and fair dealing. We wish her only to accept a place of equality among the peoples of the world—the new world in which we now live—instead of a place of mastery.

Neither do we presume to suggest to her any alteration or modification of her institutions. But it is necessary, we must frankly say, and necessary as a preliminary to any intelligent dealings with her on our part, that we should know whom her spokesmen speak for when they speak to us, whether for the Reichstag majority or for the military party and the men whose creed is imperial domination.

We have spoken now, surely, in terms too concrete to admit of any further doubt or question. An evident principle runs through the whole program I have outlined. It is the principle of justice to all peoples and nationalities, and their right to live on equal terms of liberty and safety with one another, whether they be strong or weak. Unless this principle be made its foundation no part of the structure of international justice can stand. The people of the United States could act upon no other principle; and to the vindication of this principle they are ready to devote their lives, their honor, and everything that they possess. The moral climax of this the culminating and final war for human liberty has come, and they are ready to put their own strength, their own highest purpose, their own integrity and devotion to the test.

Chapter 3
The Radical Critique

8. Patriotism and Government
Patriotism and Christianity

LEO TOLSTOY

PATRIOTISM AND GOVERNMENT

I have several times had occasion to express the idea that patriotism is in our time an unnatural, irrational, harmful sentiment, which causes the greater part of those calamities from which humanity suffers, and that, therefore, this sentiment ought not to be cultivated, as it now is, but, on the contrary, ought to be repressed and destroyed with all means that sensible people can command. But, strange to say, in spite of the evident and incontestable relation of the universal armaments and destructive wars, which ruin the nations, to this exclusive sentiment, all my arguments as to the obsoleteness, untimeliness, and harm of patriotism have been met either with silence or with intentional misunderstanding, or, again, with the same strange retort: "What is said is that there is harm in the bad patriotism, jingoism, chauvinism, but the real, good patriotism is a very elevated, moral sentiment, which it is not only senseless, but even criminal to condemn." But as to what this real, good patriotism consists in, . . . nothing is said. . . .

The army, the money, the school, the religion, the press, is in the hands of the ruling classes. In the schools they fan patriotism in the children by means of history, by describing their nation as the best of all the nations and always in the right; in the adults the same sentiment is roused by means of spectacles, celebrations, monuments, and a patriotic, lying press; but patriotism is chiefly roused in them by this, that, committing all kinds of unjust acts and cruelties against other nations, they provoke in these nations a hatred for their own nation, and then use this hatred for provoking such a hatred in their own nation.

The fanning of this terrible sentiment of patriotism has proceeded in the European nations in a rapidly increasing progression, and in our time has reached a stage beyond which it cannot go.

. . . Within the memory of all, not merely old men of our time, there took place an event which in the most obvious manner showed the striking stupefaction to which the men of the Christian world were brought by means of patriotism.

The German ruling classes fanned the patriotism of their popular masses to such an extent that in the second half of the century a law was proposed to the people, according to which all men without exception were to be-

---

These essays are translated respectively by Leo Wiener (1905) and Aylmer Maude, et al. (1899 version).

come soldiers; all sons, husbands, fathers, were to study murder and to become submissive slaves of the first highest rank, and to be prepared for the murder of those whom they would be ordered to kill,—the men of the oppressed nationalities and their own labourers who should defend their rights,—their fathers and brothers, as the most impudent of all rulers, William II, publicly announced.

This terrible measure, which in the rudest way offends all the best sentiments of men, has, under the influence of patriotism, been accepted without a murmur by the nation of Germany.

The consequence of this was the victory over the French. This victory still more fanned the patriotism of Germany, and later of France, Russia, and other powers, and all the people of the Continental powers without a murmur submitted to the introduction of a universal military service, that is, to slavery, which for the degree of degradation and loss of will cannot be compared with any of the ancient conditions of slavery. . . .

But more than that. Every increase of the army of one state (and every state, being on account of patriotism in danger, wishes to increase it) compels the neighbouring state to increase its army also for the sake of patriotism, which again calls forth a new increase of the first. . . .

To free people from those terrible calamities of armaments and wars, which they suffer now, and which keep growing greater and greater, we do not need congresses, nor conferences, nor treaties and tribunals, but the abolition of that implement of violence which is called the governments, and from which originate all the greatest calamities of men.

To abolish the governments only one thing is needed: it is necessary that men should understand that the sentiment of patriotism, which alone maintains this implement of violence, is a coarse, harmful, disgraceful, and bad, and above all, immoral sentiment. It is coarse, because it is characteristic of only such men as stand on the lowest stage of morality and who expect from other nations the same acts of violence that they want to practise themselves; it is harmful, because it violates the advantageous and joyous peaceful relations with other nations, and, above all, produces that organization of the governments, in which the worst man can acquire and always acquires the power; it is disgraceful, because it transforms the man not only into a slave, but also into a fighting cock, bull, gladiator, who ruins his forces and his life, not for his own purposes, but for those of his government; it is immoral, because, instead of recognizing himself as the son of God, as Christianity teaches us, or at least as a free man, who is guided by his reason,—every man, under the influence of patriotism, the slave of his government, and commits acts which are contrary to his reason and to his conscience. . . .

. . . Whoever you may be,—a Frenchman, Russian, Pole, Englishman, Irishman, German, Bohemian,—you must understand that all our real human interests, whatever they be,—agricultural, industrial, commercial, artistic, or scientific,—all these interests, like all the pleasures and joys, in no way oppose the interests of the other nations and states, and that you are, by means of a mutual interaction, exchange of services, the joy of a broad brotherly communion, of an exchange not only of wares, but also of sentiments, united with the men of the other nations.

You must understand that the questions as to who succeeds in seizing Wei-hai-wei, Port Arthur, or Cuba—whether it is your government or another—are by no means a matter of indifference to you, but that every seizure made by your government is detrimental to you, because it inevitably brings with it all kinds of influences, which your government will exert against you, in order to compel you to take part in robberies and acts of violence, which are necessary for the seizures and for the retention of what has been seized. You must understand that your life can in no way be improved by this, that Alsace will be German or French, and that Ireland and Poland are free or enslaved: no matter whose they may be, you can live wherever you please; even if you were an Alsatian, an Irishman, or a Pole,—you must understand that every fanning of patriotism will only make your position worse, because the enslavement of your nation has resulted only from the struggle of patriotisms, and that every manifestation of patriotism in one nation increases the reaction against it in another. You must understand that you can save yourselves from all your calamities only when you free yourselves from the obsolete idea of patriotism and from the obedience to the governments which is based upon it, and when you shall boldly enter into the sphere of that higher idea of the brotherly union of the nations, which

has long ago entered into life and is calling you to itself from all sides.

Let men understand that they are not the sons of any countries or governments, but the sons of God, and that, therefore, they cannot be slaves, nor enemies of other men, and all those senseless, now quite useless, pernicious institutions, bequeathed by antiquity, which are called governments, and all those sufferings, acts of violence, degradations, crimes, which they bring with them, will disappear of their own accord.

PATRIOTISM AND CHRISTIANITY

It would seem that, owing to the spread of education, of speedier locomotion, of greater intercourse between different nations, to the widening of literature, and chiefly to the decrease of danger from other nations, the fraud of patriotism ought daily to become more difficult and at length impossible to practise.

But the truth is that these very means of general external education, facilitated locomotion and intercourse, and especially the spread of literature, being captured and constantly more and more controlled by government, confer on the latter such possibilities of exciting a feeling of mutual animosity between nations, that in degree as the uselessness and harmfulness of patriotism have become manifest, so also has increased the power of the government and ruling class to excite patriotism among the people. . . .

And so, thanks to the development of literature, reading, and the facilities of travel, governments which have their agents everywhere, by means of statutes, sermons, schools, and the press, inculcate everywhere upon the people the most barbarous and erroneous ideas as to their advantages, the relationship of nations, their qualities and intentions; and the people, so crushed by labor that they have neither the time nor the power to understand the significance or test the truth of the ideas which are forced upon them or of the demands made upon them in the name of their

welfare, put themselves unmurmuringly under the yoke.

Whereas working-men who have freed themselves from unremitting labor and become educated, and who have, therefore, it might be supposed, the power of seeing through the fraud which is practised upon them, are subjected to such a coercion of threats, bribes, and all the hypnotic influence of governments, that, almost without exception, they desert to the side of the government, and by entering some well-paid and profitable employment, as priest, schoolmaster, officer, or functionary, become participators in spreading the deceit, which is destroying their comrades.

It is as if the nets were laid at the entrances to education, in which those who by some means or other escape from the masses bowed down by labor, are inevitably caught.

At first, when one understands the cruelty of all this deceit, one feels indignant in spite of oneself against those who from personal ambition or greedy advantage propagate this cruel fraud which destroys the souls as well as the bodies of men, and one feels inclined to accuse them of a sly craftiness; but the fact is that they are deceitful with no wish to deceive, but because they cannot be otherwise. And they deceive, not like Machiavellians, but with no consciousness of their deceit, and usually with the naïve assurance that they are doing something excellent and elevated, a view in which they are persistently encouraged by the sympathy and approval of all who surround them.

It is true that, being dimly aware that on this fraud is founded their power and advantageous position, they are unconsciously drawn toward it; but their action is not based on any desire to delude the people, but because they believe it to be of service to the people.

Thus emperors, kings, and their ministers, with all their coronations, manoeuvers, reviews, visiting one another, dressing up in various uniforms, going from place to place, and deliberating with serious faces as to how they may keep peace between nations supposed to be inimical to each other,—nations who would never dream of quarreling,—feel quite sure that what they are doing is very reasonable and useful.

In the same way the various ministers, diplomatists, and functionaries—dressed up in uniforms, with all sorts of ribbons and crosses, writing and docketing with great care, upon the best paper, their hazy, involved, altogether needless communications, advices, projects— are quite assured that, without their activity, the entire existence of nations would halt or become deranged.

In the same manner military men, got up in ridiculous costumes, arguing seriously with what rifle or cannon men can be most expeditiously destroyed, are quite certain that their field-days and reviews are most important and essential to the people.

So likewise the priests, journalists, writers of patriotic songs and class-books, who preach patriotism and receive liberal remuneration, are equally satisfied.

And no doubt the organizers of festivities— like the Franco-Russian fêtes—are sincerely affected while pronouncing their patriotic speeches and toasts.

All these people do what they are doing unconsciously, because they must, all their life being founded upon deceit, and because they know not how to do anything else. . . .

. . . Not long ago, Wilhelm II ordered a new throne for himself, with some special kind of ornamentation, and having dressed up in a white uniform, with a cuirass, tight breeches, and a helmet with a bird on the top, and enveloped himself in a red mantle, came out to his subjects, and sat down on this new throne, perfectly assured that his act was most necessary and important; and his subjects not only saw nothing ridiculous in it, but thought the sight most imposing.

For some time the power of the government over the people has not been maintained by force, as was the case when one nation conquered another and ruled it by force of arms, or when the rulers of an unarmed people had separate legions of janizaries or guards.

The power of the government has for some time been maintained by what is termed public opinion.

A public opinion exists that patriotism is a fine moral sentiment, and that it is right and our duty to regard one's own nation, one's own state, as the best in the world; and flowing naturally from this public opinion is another, namely, that it is right and our duty to acquiesce in the control of a government over ourselves, to subordinate ourselves to it, to serve in the army and submit ourselves to discipline, to give our earnings to the government in the form of taxes, to submit to the decisions of the law-courts, and to consider the edicts of the government as divinely right. And when such public opinion exists, a strong governmental power is formed possessing milliards of money, an organized mechanism of administration, the postal service, telegraphs, telephones, disciplined armies, law-courts, police, submissive clergy, schools, even the press; and this power maintains in the people the public opinion which it finds necessary. . . .

And indeed, one has only to remember what we profess, both as Christians and merely as men of our day, those fundamental moralities by which we are directed in our social, family, and personal existence, and the position in which we place ourselves in the name of patriotism, in order to see what a degree of contradiction we have placed between our conscience and what, thanks to an energetic government influence in this direction, we regard as our public opinion.

One has only thoughtfully to examine the most ordinary demands of patriotism, which are expected of us as the most simple and natural affair, in order to understand to what extent these requirements are at variance with that real public opinion which we already share. We all regard ourselves as free, educated, humane men, or even as Christians, and yet we are all in such a position that were Wilhelm tomorrow to take offense against Alexander, or Mr. N. to write a lively article on the Eastern Question, or Prince So-and-so to plunder some Bulgarians or Serbians, or some queen or empress to be put out by something or other, all we educated humane Christians must go and kill people of whom we have no knowledge. . . .

No feats of heroism are needed to achieve the greatest and most important changes in the existence of humanity; neither the armament of millions of soldiers, nor the construction of new roads and machines, nor the arrangement of exhibitions, nor the organization of workmen's unions, nor revolutions, nor barricades, nor explosions, nor the perfection of aërial navigation; but a change in public opinion.

And to accomplish this change no exertions of the mind are needed, nor the refutation of anything in existence, nor the invention of any extraordinary novelty; it is only needful that we should not succumb to the erroneous, already defunct, public opinion of the past, which governments have induced artificially; it is only needful that each individual should say what he really feels or thinks, or at least that he should not say what he does not think.

And if only a small body of the people were to do so at once, of their own accord, outworn public opinion would fall off us of itself, and a new, living, real opinion would assert itself. And when public opinion should thus have changed without the slightest effort, the internal condition of men's lives which so torments them would change likewise of its own accord.

One is ashamed to say how little is needed for all men to be delivered from those calamities which now oppress them; it is only needful not to lie.

Let people only be superior to the falsehood which is instilled into them, let them decline to say what they neither feel nor think, and at once such a revolution of all the organization of our life will take place as could not be attained by all the efforts of revolutionists during centuries, even were complete power within their hands.

If people would only believe that strength is not in force but in truth, would only not shrink from it either in word or deed, not say what they do not think, not do what they regard as foolish and as wrong! . . .

The governments know this, and tremble before this force, and strive in every way they can to counteract or become possessed of it.

They know that strength is not in force, but in thought and in clear expression of it, and, therefore, they are more afraid of the expression of independent thought than of armies; hence they institute censorships, bribe the press, and monopolize the control of religion and of the schools. . . .

We all complain of the senseless order of life, which is at variance with our being, and yet we refuse to use the unique and powerful weapon within our hands—the consciousness of truth and its expression; but on the contrary, under the pretext of struggling with evil, we destroy the weapon, and sacrifice it to the exigencies of an imaginary conflict.

One man does not assert the truth which he knows, because he feels himself bound to the people with whom he is engaged; another, because the truth might deprive him of the profitable position by which he maintains his family; a third, because he desires to attain reputation and authority, and then use them in the service of mankind; a fourth, because he does not wish to destroy old sacred traditions; a fifth, because he has no desire to offend people; a sixth, because the expression of the truth would arouse persecution, and disturb the excellent social activity to which he has devoted himself.

One serves as emperor, king, minister, government functionary, or soldier, and assures himself and others that the deviation from truth indispensable to his condition is redeemed by the good he does. Another, who fulfils the duties of a spiritual pastor, does not in the depths of his soul believe all he teaches, but permits the deviation from truth in view of the good he does. A third instructs men by means of literature, and notwithstanding the silence he must observe with regard to the whole truth, in order not to stir up the government and society against himself, has no doubt as to the good he does. A fourth struggles resolutely with the existing order as revolutionist or anarchist, and is quite assured that the aims he pursues are so beneficial that the neglect of the truth, or even of the falsehood, by silence, indispensable to the success of his activity, does not destroy the utility of his work. . . .

If only men were boldly and clearly to express the truth already manifest to them of the brotherhood of all nations, and the crime of exclusive devotion to one's own people, that defunct, false public opinion would slough off of itself like a dried skin,—and upon it depends the power of governments, and all the evil produced by them; and the new public opinion would stand forth, which is even now but awaiting that dropping off of the old to put forth manifestly and powerfully its demand, and establish new forms of existence in conformity with the consciousness of mankind. . . .

9. Means and Ends
Passive Resistance
The Atom Bomb, America and Japan

MOHANDAS K. GANDHI

MEANS AND ENDS

READER: Why should we not obtain our goal, which is good, by any means whatsoever, even by using violence? Shall I think of the means when I have to deal with a thief in the house? My duty is to drive him out anyhow. You seem to admit that we have received nothing, and that we shall receive nothing by petitioning. Why, then, may we not do so by using brute force? And, to retain what we may receive we shall keep up the fear by using the same force to the extent that it may be necessary. You will not find fault with a continuance of force to prevent a child from thrusting its foot into fire? Somehow or other we have to gain our end.

EDITOR: Your reasoning is plausible. It has deluded many. I have used similar arguments before now. But I think I know better now, and I shall endeavour to undeceive you. Let us first take the argument that we are justified in gaining our end by using brute force because the English gained theirs by using similar means. It is perfectly true that they used brute force and that it is possible for us to do likewise, but by using similar means we can get only the same thing that they got. You will admit that we do not want that. Your belief that there is no connection between the means and the end is a great mistake. Through that mistake even men who have been considered religious have committed grievous crimes. Your reasoning is the same as saying that we can get a rose through planting a noxious weed. If I want to cross the ocean, I can do so only by means of a vessel; if I were to use a cart for that purpose, both the cart and I would soon find the bottom. "As is the God, so is the votary" is a maxim worth considering. Its meaning has been distorted and men have gone astray. The means may be likened to a seed, the end to a tree; and there is just the same inviolable connection between the means and the end as there is between the seed and the tree. I am not likely to obtain the result flowing from the worship of God by laying my-

The first two selections are from *Hind Swaraj* or *Indian Home Rule* (1909), Chapters 16 and 17. The third is from *Harijan* (July 7, 1946). All are reprinted by permission of the Navajivan Trust (Ahmedabad, India).

self prostrate before Satan. If, therefore, any one were to say: "I want to worship God; it does not matter that I do so by means of Satan," it would be set down as ignorant folly. We reap exactly as we sow. The English in 1833 obtained greater voting power by violence. Did they by using brute force better appreciate their duty? They wanted the right of voting, which they obtained by using physical force. But real rights are a result of performance of duty; these rights they have not obtained. We, therefore, have before us in England the force of everybody wanting and insisting on his rights, nobody thinking of his duty. And, where everybody wants rights, who shall give them to whom? I do not wish to imply that they do no duties. They don't perform the duties corresponding to those rights; and as they do not perform that particular duty, namely, acquire fitness, their rights have proved a burden to them. In other words, what they have obtained is an exact result of the means they adopted. They used the means corresponding to the end. If I want to deprive you of your watch, I shall certainly have to fight for it; if I want to buy your watch, I shall have to pay for it; and if I want a gift, I shall have to plead for it; and, according to the means I employ, the watch is stolen property, my own property, or a donation. Thus we see three different results from three different means. Will you still say that means do not matter?

Now we shall take the example given by you of the thief to be driven out. I do not agree with you that the thief may be driven out by any means. If it is my father who has come to steal I shall use one kind of means. If it is an acquaintance I shall use another; and in the case of a perfect stranger I shall use a third. If it is a white man, you will perhaps say you will use means different from those you will adopt with an Indian thief. If it is a weakling, the means will be different from those to be adopted for dealing with an equal in physical strength; and if the thief is armed from top to toe, I shall simply remain quiet. Thus we have a variety of means between the father and the armed man.

Again, I fancy that I should pretend to be sleeping whether the thief was my father or that strong armed man. The reason for this is that my father would also be armed and I should succumb to the strength possessed by either and allow my things to be stolen. The strength of my father would make me weep with pity; the strength of the armed man would rouse in me anger and we should become enemies. Such is the curious situation. From these examples we may not be able to agree as to the means to be adopted in each case. I myself seem clearly to see what should be done in all these cases, but the remedy may frighten you. I therefore hesitate to place it before you. For the time being I will leave you to guess it, and if you cannot, it is clear you will have to adopt different means in each case. You will also have seen that any means will not avail to drive away the thief. You will have to adopt means to fit each case. Hence it follows that your duty is not to drive away the thief by any means you like.

Let us proceed a little further. That well-armed man has stolen your property; you have harboured the thought of his act; you are filled with anger; you argue that you want to punish that rogue, not for your own sake, but for the good of your neighbours; you have collected a number of armed men, you want to take his house by assault; he is duly informed of it, he runs away; he too is incensed. He collects his brother robbers, and sends you a defiant message that he will commit robbery in broad daylight. You are strong, you do not fear him, you are prepared to receive him. Meanwhile, the robber pesters your neighbours. They complain before you. You reply that you are doing all for their sake, you do not mind that your own goods have been stolen. Your neighbours reply that the robber never pestered them before, and that he commenced his depredations only after you declared hostilities against him. You are between Scylla and Charybdis. You are full of pity for the poor men. What they say is true. What are you to do? You will be disgraced if you now leave the robber alone. You, therefore, tell the poor men: "Never mind. Come, my wealth is yours, I will give you arms, I will teach you how to use them; you should belabour the rogue; don't you leave him alone." And so the battle grows; the robbers increase in numbers; your neighbours have deliberately put themselves to inconvenience. Thus the result of wanting to take revenge upon the robber is that you have disturbed your own peace; you are in perpetual fear of being robbed and assaulted; your courage has given place to cowardice. If you will patiently examine the argument, you will see that I have not overdrawn the picture. This is one of the means. Now let us examine the other. You set this armed robber down as an ignorant brother; you intend to reason with him at a suitable opportunity; you argue that he is, after all, a fellow man; you do not know what prompted him to steal. You, therefore, decide that, when you can, you will destroy the man's motive for stealing. Whilst you are thus reasoning with yourself, the man comes again to steal. Instead of being angry with him you take pity on him. You think that this stealing habit must be a disease with him. Henceforth, you, therefore, keep your doors and windows open, you change your sleeping-place, and you keep your things in a manner most accessible to him. The robber comes again and is confused as all this is new to him; nevertheless, he takes away your things. But his mind is agitated. He inquires about you in the village, he comes to learn about your broad and loving heart, he repents, he begs your pardon, returns you your things, and leaves off the stealing habit. He becomes your servant, and you will find for him honourable employment. This is the second method. Thus, you see, different means have brought about totally different results. I do not wish to deduce from this that robbers will act in the above manner or that all will have the same pity and love like you, but I only wish to show that fair means alone can produce fair results, and that, at least in the majority of cases, if not indeed in all, the force of love and pity is infinitely greater

than the force of arms. There is harm in the exercise of brute force, never in that of pity.

Now we will take the question of petitioning. It is a fact beyond dispute that a petition, without the backing of force, is useless. However, the late Justice Ranade used to say that petitions served a useful purpose because they were a means of educating people. They give the latter an idea of their condition and warn the rulers. From this point of view, they are not altogether useless. A petition of an equal is a sign of courtesy; a petition from a slave is a symbol of his slavery. A petition backed by force is a petition from an equal and, when he transmits his demand in the form of a petition, it testifies to his nobility. Two kinds of force can back petitions. "We shall hurt you if you do not give this," is one kind of force; it is the force of arms, whose evil results we have already examined. The second kind of force can thus be stated: "If you do not concede our demand, we shall be no longer your petitioners. You can govern us only so long as we remain the governed; we shall no longer have any dealings with you." The force implied in this may be described as love-force, soul-force, or, more popularly but less accurately, passive resistance.[1] This force is indestructible. He who uses it perfectly understands his position. We have an ancient proverb which literally means: "One negative cures thirty-six diseases." The force of arms is powerless when matched against the force of love or the soul.

Now we shall take your last illustration, that of the child thrusting its foot into fire. It will not avail you. What do you really do to the child? Supposing that it can exert so much physical force that it renders you powerless and rushes into fire, then you cannot prevent it. There are only two remedies open to you—either you must kill it in order to prevent it from perishing in the flames, or you must give your own life because you

---

[1]*Satyagraha*, what Gandhi in later years preferred to label "nonviolent resistance," to emphasize that it was an activist and not a passive strategy—ED.

do not wish to see it perish before your very eyes. You will not kill it. If your heart is not quite full of pity, it is possible that you will not surrender yourself by preceding the child and going into the fire yourself. You, therefore, helplessly allow it to go to the flames. Thus, at any rate, you are not using physical force. I hope you will not consider that it is still physical force, though of a low order, when you would forcibly prevent the child from rushing towards the fire if you could. That force is of a different order and we have to understand what it is.

Remember that, in thus preventing the child, you are minding entirely its own interest, you are exercising authority for its sole benefit. Your example does not apply to the English. In using brute force against the English you consult entirely your own, that is the national, interest. There is no question here either of pity or of love. If you say that the actions of the English, being evil, represent fire, and that they proceed to their actions through ignorance, and that therefore they occupy the position of a child and that you want to protect such a child, then you will have to overtake every evil action of that kind by whomsoever committed and, as in the case of the evil child, you will have to sacrifice yourself. If you are capable of such immeasurable pity, I wish you well in its exercise.

PASSIVE RESISTANCE

READER: Is there any historical evidence as to the success of what you have called soul-force or truth-force? No instance seems to have happened of any nation having risen through soul-force. I still think that the evil-doers will not cease doing evil without physical punishment.

EDITOR: The poet Tulsidas has said: "Of religion, pity, or love, is the root, as egotism of the body. Therefore, we should not abandon pity so long as we are alive." This appears to me to be a scientific truth. I believe in it as much as I believe in two and two being four. The force of love is the same as the force of the soul or truth. We have evidence of its working at every step. The universe would disappear without the existence of that force. But you ask for historical evidence. It is, therefore, necessary to know what history means. The Gujarati equivalent means: "It so happened." If that is the meaning of history, it is possible to give copious evidence. But, if it means the doings of kings and emperors, there can be no evidence of soul-force or passive resistance in such history. You cannot expect silver ore in a tin mine. History, as we know it, is a record of the wars of the world, and so there is a proverb among Englishmen that a nation which has no history, that is, no wars, is a happy nation. How kings played, how they became enemies of one another, how they murdered one another, is found accurately recorded in history, and if this were all that had happened in the world, it would have been ended long ago. If the story of the universe had commenced with wars, not a man would have been found alive today. Those people who have been warred against have disappeared as, for instance, the natives of Australia of whom hardly a man was left alive by the intruders. Mark, please, that these natives did not use soul-force in self-defence, and it does not require much foresight to know that the Australians will share the same fate as their victims. "Those that take the sword shall perish by the sword." With us the proverb is that professional swimmers will find a watery grave.

The fact that there are so many men still alive in the world shows that it is based not on the force of arms but on the force of truth or love. Therefore, the greatest and most unimpeachable evidence of the success of this force is to be found in the fact that, in spite of the wars of the world, it still lives on.

Thousands, indeed tens of thousands, depend for their existence on a very active working of this force. Little quarrels of millions of families in their daily lives disappear before the exercise of this force. Hundreds of nations live in peace. History does not and cannot take note of this fact. History is really a record of every interruption of the even working of the force of love or of the soul. Two brothers quarrel; one of them repents and re-awakens the love that was lying dormant in him; the two again begin to live in peace; nobody takes note of this. But if the two brothers, through the intervention of solicitors or some other reason, take up arms or go to law—which is another form of the exhibition of brute force—their doing would be immediately noticed in the press, they would be the talk of their neighbours and would probably go down to history. And what is true of families and communities is true of nations. There is no reason to believe that there is one law for families and another for nations. History, then, is a record of an interruption of the course of nature. Soul-force, being natural, is not noted in history. . . .

THE ATOM BOMB, AMERICA AND JAPAN

It has been suggested by American friends that the atom bomb will bring in Ahimsa (non-violence) as nothing else can. It will, if it is meant that its destructive power will so disgust the world that it will turn it away from violence for the time being. This is very like a man glutting himself with dainties to the point of nausea and turning away from them only to return with redoubled zeal after the effect of nausea is well over. Precisely in the same manner will the world return to violence with renewed zeal after the effect of disgust is worn out.

So far as I can see, the atomic bomb has deadened the finest feeling that has sustained mankind for ages. There used to be the so-called laws of war which made it tolerable. Now we know the naked truth. War knows no law except that of might. The atom bomb brought an empty victory to the allied arms but it resulted for the time being in destroying the soul of Japan. What has happened to the soul of the destroying nation is yet too early to see. Forces of nature act in a mysterious manner. We can but solve the mystery by deducing the unknown result from the known results of similar events. A slaveholder cannot hold a slave without putting himself or his deputy in the cage holding the slave. Let no one run away with the idea that I wish to put in a defense of Japanese misdeeds in pursuance of Japan's unworthy ambition. The difference was only one of degree. I assume that Japan's greed was more unworthy. But the greater unworthiness conferred no right on the less unworthy of destroying without mercy men, women and children of Japan in a particular area.

The moral to be legitimately drawn from the supreme tragedy of the bomb is that it will not be destroyed by counter-bombs even as violence cannot be by counter-violence. Mankind has to get out of violence only through non-violence. Hatred can be overcome only by love. Counter-hatred only increases the surface as well as the depth of hatred. I am aware that I am repeating what I have many times stated before and practiced to the best of my ability and capacity. What I first stated was itself nothing new. It was as old as the hills. Only I recited no copy-book maxim but definitely announced what I believed in every fibre of my being. Sixty years of practice in various walks of life has only enriched the belief which experience of friends has fortified. It is however the central truth by which one can stand alone without flinching. I believe in what Max Müller said years ago, namely that truth needed to be repeated as long as there were men who disbelieved it.

10. Vietnam: Setting the Moral Equation

HOWARD ZINN

. . . I would start such a discussion from the supposition that it is logically indefensible to hold to an absolutely nonviolent position, because it is at least theoretically conceivable that a small violence might be required to prevent a larger one. Those who are immediately offended by this statement should consider: World War II; the assassination attempt on Hitler; the American, French, Russian, Chinese, Cuban revolutions; possible armed revolt in South Africa; the case of Rhodesia; the Deacons in Louisiana. Keep in mind that many who support the war in Vietnam may do so on grounds which they believe similar to those used in the above cases.

The terrible thing is that once you stray from absolute nonviolence you open the door for the most shocking abuses. It is like distributing scalpels to an eager group, half of whom are surgeons and half butchers. But that is man's constant problem—how to release the truth without being devoured by it.

How can we tell butchers from surgeons, distinguish between a healing and a destructive act of violence? The first requirement is that our starting point must always be non-vi-

olence, and that the burden of proof, therefore, is on the advocate of violence to show, with a high degree of probability, that he is justified. In modern American civilization, we demand unanimity among twelve citizens before we will condemn a single person to death, but we will destroy thousands of people on the most flimsy of political assumptions (like the domino theory of revolutionary contagion).

What proof should be required? I suggest four tests:

1. Self-defense, against outside attackers or a counterrevolutionary force within, using no more violence than is needed to repel the attack, is justified. This covers that Negro housewife who several years ago in a little Georgia town, at home alone with her children, fired through the door at a gang of white men carrying guns and chains, killing one, after which the rest fled. It would sacrifice the Rhineland to Hitler in 1936, and even Austria (for the Austrians apparently preferred not to fight), but demands supporting the Loyalist government in Spain and defending Czechoslovakia in 1938. And it applies to Vietnamese fighting against American attackers who hold the strings of a puppet government.

2. Revolution is justified, for the purpose of overthrowing a deeply entrenched oppressive regime, unshakable by other means. Outside aid is permissible (because rebels, as in the American Revolution, are almost always at a

Excerpted from "Vietnam: Setting the Moral Equation," by Howard Zinn, in *The Nation* (January 17, 1966), pp. 64–69. Copyright 1966 *The Nation* magazine, The Nation Associates, Inc. Reprinted with the permission of the publisher and author.

disadvantage against the holders of power), but with the requirement that the manpower for the revolution be indigenous, for this in itself is a test of how popular the revolution is. This could cover the French, American, Mexican, Russian, Chinese, Cuban, Algerian cases. It would also cover the Vietcong rebellion. And a South African revolt, should it break out.

3. Even if one of the above conditions is met, there is no moral justification for visiting violence on the innocent. Therefore, violence in self-defense or in revolution must be focused on the evildoers, and limited to that required to achieve the goal, resisting all arguments that extra violence might speed victory. This rules out the strategic bombing of German cities in World War II, the atom bombing of Hiroshima and Nagasaki; it rules out terrorism against civilians even in a just revolution. Violence even against the guilty, when undertaken for sheer revenge, is unwarranted, which rules out capital punishment for any crime. The requirement of focused violence makes nonsensical the equating of the killing of village chiefs in South Vietnam by the Vietcong and the bombing of hospitals by American fliers; yet the former is also unjustified if it is merely an act of terror or revenge and not specifically required for a change in the social conditions of the village.

4. There is an additional factor which the conditions of modern warfare make urgent. Even if all three of the foregoing principles are met, there is a fourth which must be considered if violence is to be undertaken: the costs of self-defense or social change must not be so high, because of the intensity or the prolongation of violence, or because of the risk of proliferation, that the victory is not worth the cost. For the Soviets to defend Cuba from attack—though self-defense was called for—would not have been worth a general war; for the United States to defend Hungary from attack—though self-defense was called for—would not have been worth a general war. For China or Soviet Russia to aid the Vietcong with troops though the Vietcong cause is just, would be wrong if it seriously risked a general war.

Under certain conditions, nations should be captive rather than be destroyed, or revolutionaries should bide their time. Indeed, because of the omnipresence of the great military powers—the United States and the USSR (perhaps this is not so true for the countries battling England, France, Holland, Belgium, Portugal)—revolutionary movements may have to devise tactics short of armed revolt to overturn an oppressive regime.

The basic principle I want to get close to is that violence is most clearly justified when those whose own lives are at stake make the decision on whether the prize is worth dying for. Self-defense and guerrilla warfare, by their nature, embody this decision. Conscript armies and unfocused warfare violate it. And no one has a right to decide that someone else is better off dead than Red, or that someone else should die to defend his way of life, or that an individual (like Norman Morrison) should choose to live rather than die.

It would be foolish to pretend that this summary can be either precise or complete. Those involved in self-defense or in a revolution need no intellectual justification; their emotions reflect some inner rationality. It is those outside the direct struggle, deciding whether to support one side or stay out, who need to think clearly about principles. Americans, therefore, possessing the greatest power and being furthest removed from the problems of self-defense or revolution, need thoughtful deliberation most. All we can do in social analysis is to offer rough guides to replace nonthinking, to give the beginnings of some kind of moral calculus.

However, it takes no close measurement to conclude that the American bombings in Vietnam, directed as they are to farming areas, villages, hamlets, fit none of the criteria listed, and so are deeply immoral, whatever else is true about the situation in Southeast Asia or the world. The silence of the government's supporters on this—from Hubert Humphrey to the academic signers of advertisements—is particularly shameful, because it requires no surrender of their other arguments to concede that this is unnecessary bestiality.

Bombings aside, none of the American military activity against the Vietcong could be justified unless it were helping a determined people to defend itself against an outside attacker. That is why the Administration, hoping to confirm by verbal repetition what cannot be verified in fact, continually uses the term "aggression" to describe the Vietnamese guerrilla activities. The expert evidence, however, is overwhelming on this question:

1. Philippe Devillers, the French historian, says "the insurrection existed before the Communists decided to take part. . . . And even among the Communists, the initiative did not originate in Hanoi, but from the grass roots, where the people were literally driven by Diem to take up arms in self-defense."

2. Bernard Fall says "anti-Diem guerrillas were active long before infiltrated North Vietnamese elements joined the fray."

3. The correspondent for *Le Monde*, Jean Lacouture (in *Le Viet Nam entre deux paix*) confirms that local pressure, local conditions led to guerrilla activity.

4. Donald S. Zagoria, a specialist on Asian communism at Columbia University, wrote recently that "it is reasonably clear that we are dealing with an indigenous insurrection in the South, and that this, not Northern assistance, is the main trouble."

One test of "defense against aggression" is the behavior of the official South Vietnamese army—the "defenders" themselves. We find: a high rate of desertions; a need to herd villagers into concentration-camp "strategic hamlets" in order to control them; the use of torture to get information from other South Vietnamese, whom you might expect to be enthusiastic about "defending" their country; and all of this forcing the United States to take over virtually the entire military operation in Vietnam.

The ordinary people of Vietnam show none of the signs of a nation defending itself against "aggression," except in their noncooperation with the government and the Americans. A hundred thousand Vietnamese farmers were conducting a rebellion with mostly captured weapons (both David Halberstam and Hanson Baldwin affirmed this in *The New York Times*,

contradicting quietly what I. F. Stone demolished statistically—the State Department's White Paper on "infiltration"). Then they matched the intrusion of 150,000 American troops with 7,500 North Vietnamese soldiers (in November, 1965, American military officials estimated that five regiments of North Vietnamese, with 1,500 in each regiment, were in South Vietnam). Weapons were acquired from Communist countries, but not a single plane to match the horde of American bombers filling the skies over Vietnam. This adds up not to North Vietnamese aggression (if indeed North Vietnamese can be considered outsiders at all) but to American aggression, with a puppet government fronting for American power.

Thus, there is no valid principle on which the United States can defend either its bombing, or its military presence, in Vietnam. It is the factual emptiness of its moral claim which then leads it to seek a one-piece substitute, that comes prefabricated with its own rationale, surrounded by an emotional aura sufficient to ward off inspectors. This transplanted fossil is the Munich analogy, which, speaking with all the passion of Churchill in the Battle of Britain, declares: to surrender in Vietnam is to do what Chamberlain did at Munich; that is why the villagers must die.

The great value of the Munich analogy to the Strangeloves is that it captures so many American liberals, among many others. It backs the Vietnamese expedition with a coalition broad enough to include Barry Goldwater, Lyndon Johnson, George Meany and John Roche (thus reversing World War II's coalition, which excluded the far Right and included the radical Left). This bloc justifies the carnage in Vietnam with a huge image of invading armies, making only one small change in the subtitle: replacing the word "Fascist" with the word "Communist." Then, the whole savage arsenal of World War II—the means both justified and unjustifiable—supported by that great fund of indignation built against the Nazis, can be turned to the uses of the American Century.

To leave the Munich analogy intact, to fail to discuss communism and fascism, is to leave untouched the major premise which supports the present policy of near genocide in Vietnam. I propose here at least to initiate such a discussion.

Let's refresh our memories on what happened at Munich. Chamberlain of England and Daladier of France met Hitler and Mussolini (this was September 30, 1938) and agreed to surrender the Sudeten part of Czechoslovakia, inhabited by German-speaking people, hoping thus to prevent a general war in Europe. Chamberlain returned to England, claiming he had brought "peace in our time." Six months later, Hitler had gobbled up the rest of Czechoslovakia; then he began presenting ultimatums to Poland, and by September 3, 1939, general war had broken out in Europe.

There is strong evidence that if the Sudetenland had not been surrendered at Munich—with it went Czechoslovakia's powerful fortifications, seventy percent of its iron, steel and electric power, eighty-six percent of its chemicals, sixty-six percent of its coal—and had Hitler then gone to war, he would have been defeated quickly, with the aid of Czechoslovakia's thirty-five well-trained divisions. And if he chose, at the sign of resistance, not to go to war, then at least he would have been stopped in his expansion.

And so, the analogy continues, to let the Communist-dominated National Liberation Front win in South Vietnam (for the real obstacle in the sparring over negotiations is the role of the NLF in a new government) is to encourage more Communist expansion in Southeast Asia and beyond, and perhaps lead to a war more disastrous than the present one; to stop communism in South Vietnam is to discourage its expansion elsewhere.

We should note, first, some of the important differences between the Munich situation in 1938 and Vietnam today:

1. In 1938, the main force operating against the Czech *status quo* was an outside force, Hitler's Germany: the supporting force was the Sudeten group inside led by Konrad Henlein. Since 1958 (and traceable back to 1942), the major force operating against the *status quo* in South

Vietnam has been an inside force, formed in 1960 into the NLF: the chief supporter is not an outside nation but another part of the same nation, North Vietnam. The largest outside force in Vietnam consists of the American troops (who, interestingly, are referred to in West Germany as *Bandenkampfverbande*, Bandit Fighting Units, the name used in World War II by the Waffen S.S. units to designate the guerrillas whom they specialized in killing). To put it another way, in 1938, the Germans were trying to take over part of another country. Today, the Vietcong are trying to take over part of their own country. In 1938, the outsider was Germany. Today it is the United States.

2. The Czech government, whose interests the West surrendered to Hitler in 1938, was a strong, effective, prosperous, democratic government—the government of Benes and Masaryk. The South Vietnamese government which we support is a hollow shell of a government, unstable, unpopular, corrupt, a dictatorship of bullies and torturers, disdainful of free elections and representative government (recently they opposed establishing a National Assembly on the ground that it might lead to communism), headed by a long line of tyrants from Bao Dai to Diem to Ky, who no more deserve to be ranked with Benes and Masaryk than Governor Wallace of Alabama deserves to be compared with Robert E. Lee. It is a government whose perpetuation is not worth the loss of a single human life.

3. Standing firm in 1938 meant engaging, in order to defeat once and for all, the central threat of that time, Hitler's Germany. Fighting in Vietnam today, even if it brings total victory, does not at all engage what the United States considers the central foes—the Soviet Union and Communist China. Even if international communism *were* a single organism, to annihilate the Vietcong would be merely to remove a toenail from an elephant. To engage what we think is the source of our difficulties (Red China one day, Soviet Russia the next) would require nuclear war, and even Robert Strange McNamara doesn't seem up to that.

4. There is an important difference between the historical context of Munich, 1938, and

that of Vietnam, 1966. Munich was the culmination of a long line of surrenders and refusals
to act: when Japan invaded China in 1931,
when Mussolini invaded Ethiopia in 1935,
when Hitler remilitarized the Rhineland in
1936, when Hitler and Mussolini supported
the Franco attack on Republican Spain
1936–39, when Japan attacked China in 1937,
when Hitler took Austria in the spring of 1938.
The Vietnam crisis, on the other hand, is the
culmination of a long series of events in which
the West has on occasion held back (as in
Czechoslovakia in 1948, or Hungary in 1956),
but more often taken firm action, from the
Truman Doctrine to the Berlin blockade, to
the Korean conflict, to the Cuban blockade of
1962. So, withdrawing from Vietnam would
not reinforce a pattern in the way that the
Munich pact did. It would be another kind of
line in that jagged graph which represents recent foreign policy.

5. We have twenty years of cold-war history
to test the proposition derived from the
Munich analogy—that a firm stand in Vietnam
is worth the huge loss of life, because it will persuade the Communists there must be no more
uprisings elsewhere. But what effect did our refusal to allow the defeat of South Korea
(1950–53), or our aid in suppressing the Huk
rebellion in the Philippines (1947–55), or the
suppression of guerillas in Malaya (1948–60),
have on the guerilla warfare in South Vietnam
which started around 1958 and became consolidated under the National Liberation Front
in 1960? If our use of subversion and arms to
overthrow Guatemala in 1954 showed the
Communists in Latin America that we meant
business, then how did it happen that Castro
rebelled and won in 1959? Did our invasion of
Cuba in 1961, our blockade in 1962, show
other revolutionaries in Latin America that
they must desist? Then how explain the
Dominican uprising in 1965? And did our dispatch of Marines to Santo Domingo end the
fighting of guerillas in the mountains of Peru?

One touches the Munich analogy and it falls
apart. This suggests something more fundamental: that American policy makers and their
supporters simply do not understand either

the nature of communism or the nature of the
various uprisings that have taken place in the
postwar world. They are not able to believe that
hunger, homelessness, oppression are sufficient spurs to revolution, without outside instigation, just as Dixie governors could not
believe that Negroes marching in the streets
were not led by outside agitators.

So, communism and revolution require discussion. They are sensitive questions, which
some in the protest movement hesitate to
broach for fear of alienating allies. But they are
basic to that inversion of morality which enables the United States to surround the dirty
war in Vietnam with the righteous glow of the
war against Hitler.

A key assumption in this inversion is that
communism and Nazism are sufficiently identical to be treated alike. However, communism
as a set of ideals has attracted good people—
not racists or bullies or militarists—all over the
world. One may argue that in Communist
countries citizens had better affirm their allegiance to it, but that doesn't account for the
fact that millions in France, Italy and Indonesia
are Communist party members, that countless
others all over the world have been inspired by
Marxian ideals. And why should they not?
These ideals include peace, brotherhood,
racial equality, the classless society, the wither-
ing away of the state.

If Communists behave much better out of
power than in it, that is a commentary not on
their ideals but on weaknesses which they share
with non-Communist wielders of power. If, presumably in pursuit of their ideals, they have re-
sorted to brutal tactics, maintained suffocating
bureaucracies and rigid dogmas, that makes
them about as reprehensible as other nations,
other social systems which, while boasting of
the Judeo-Christian heritage, have fostered
war, exploitation, colonialism and race hatred.
We judge ourselves by our ideals; others by
their actions. It is a great convenience.

The ultimate values of the Nazis, let us recall, included racism, elitism, militarism and
war as ends in themselves. Unlike either the
Communist nations or the capitalist democracies, there is here no ground for appeal to

higher purposes. The ideological basis for co-existence between Communist and capitalist nations is the rough consensus of ultimate goals which they share. While war is held off, the citizens on both sides—it is to be hoped and indeed it is beginning to occur—will increasingly insist that their leaders live up to these values.

One of these professed values—which the United States is trying with difficulty to conceal by fragile arguments and feeble analogies—is the self-determination of peoples. Self-determination justifies the overthrow of entrenched oligarchies—whether foreign or domestic—in ways that will not lead to general war. China, Egypt, Indonesia, Algeria and Cuba are examples. Such revolutions tend to set up dictatorships, but they do so in the name of values which can be used to erode that same dictatorship. They therefore deserve as much general support and specific criticism as did the American revolutionaries, who set up a slave-holding government, but with a commitment to freedom which later led it, *against its wishes*, to abolitionism.

The easy use of the term "totalitarian" to cover both Nazis and Communists, or to equate the South Vietnamese regime with that of Ho Chi Minh, fails to make important distinctions, just as dogmatists of the Left sometimes fail to distinguish between Fascist states and capitalist democracies.

This view is ahistorical on two counts. First, it ignores the fact that, for the swift economic progress needed by new nations today, a Communist-led regime does an effective job (though it is not the only type of new government that can). In doing so, it raises educational and living standards and thus paves the way (as the USSR and Eastern Europe already show) for attacks from within on its own thought-control system. Second, this view forgets that the United States and Western Europe, now haughty in prosperity, with a fair degree of free expression, built their present status on the backs of either slaves or colonial people, and subjected their own laboring populations to several generations of misery before beginning to look like welfare states.

The perspective of history suggests that a united Vietnam under Ho Chi Minh is preferable to the elitist dictatorship of the South, just as Maoist China with all its faults is preferable to the rule of Chiang, and Castro's Cuba to Batista's. We do not have pure choices in the present, although we should never surrender those values which can shape the future. Right now, for Vietnam, a Communist government is probably the best avenue to that whole packet of human values which make up the common morality of mankind today: the preservation of human life, self-determination, economic security, the end of race and class oppression, that freedom of speech which an educated population begins to demand.

This is a conclusion which critics of government policy have hesitated to make. With some, it is because they simply don't believe it, but with others, it is because they don't want to rock the boat of "coalition." Yet the main obstacle to United States withdrawal is a fear that is real—that South Vietnam will then go Communist. If we fail to discuss this honestly, we leave untouched a major plank in the structure that supports U.S. action.

When the jump is made from real fears to false ones, we get something approaching lunacy in American international behavior. Richard Hofstadter, in *The Paranoid Style in American Politics*, writes of "the central preconception of the paranoid style—the existence of a vast, insidious, preternaturally effective international conspiratorial network designed to perpetrate acts of the most fiendish character."

Once, the center of the conspiracy was Russia. A political scientist doing strategic research for the government told me recently with complete calm that his institute decided not too long ago that they had been completely wrong about the premise which underlay much of American policy in the post-war period—the premise that Russia hoped to take over Western Europe by force. Yet now, with not a tremor of doubt, the whole kit and caboodle of the invading-hordes theory is transferred to China.

Paranoia starts from a base of facts, but then leaps wildly to an absurd conclusion. It is a fact that China is totalitarian in its limitation of free expression, is fierce in its expressions of hatred for the United States, that it crushed opposition in Tibet, and fought for a strip of territory on the Indian border. But let's consider India briefly: it crushed an uprising in Hyderabad, took over the state of Kerala, initiated attacks on the China border, took Goa by force, and is fierce in its insistence on Kashmir. Yet we do not accuse it of wanting to take over the world.

Of course, there is a difference. China is emotionally tied to and sometimes aids obstreperous rebellions all over the world. However, China is not the source of these rebellions. The problem is not that China wants to take over the world, but that various peoples want to take over their parts of the world, and without the courtesies that attend normal business transactions. What if the Negroes in Watts really rose up and tried to take over Los Angeles? Would we blame that on Castro?

Not only does paranoia lead the United States to see international conspiracy where there is a diversity of Communist nations based on indigenous Communist movements. It also confuses communism with a much broader movement of this century—the rising of hungry and harassed people in Asia, Africa, Latin America (and the American South). Hence we try to crush radicalism in one place (Greece, Iran, Guatemala, the Philippines, etc.) and apparently succeed, only to find a revolution—whether Communist or Socialist or nationalist or of indescribable character—springing up somewhere else. We surround the world with our navy, cover the sky with our planes, fling our money to the winds, and then a revolution takes place in Cuba, 90 miles from home. We see every rebellion everywhere as the result of some devilish plot concocted in Moscow or Peking, when what is really happening is that people everywhere want to eat and to be free, and will use desperate means and any one of a number of social systems to achieve their ends.

The other side makes the same mistake. The Russians face a revolt in Hungary or Poznan, and attribute it to bourgeois influence, or to American scheming. Stalin's paranoia led him to send scores of old Bolsheviks before the firing squad. The Chinese seem to be developing obsessions about the United States; but in their case we are doing our best to match their wildest accusations with reality. It would be paranoid for Peking to claim that the United States is surrounding China with military bases, occupying countries on its border, keeping hundreds of thousands of troops within striking distance, contemplating the bombing of its population—if it were not largely true.

A world-wide revolution is taking place, aiming to achieve the very values that all major countries, East and West, claim to uphold: self-determination, economic security, racial equality, freedom. It takes many forms—Castro's Mao's, Nasser's, Sukarno's, Senghor's, Kenyatta's. That it does not realize all its aims from the start makes it hardly more imperfect than we were in 1776. The road to freedom is stony, but people are going to march along it. What we need to do is improve the road, not blow it up.

The United States Government has tried hard to cover its moral nakedness in Vietnam. But the signs of its failure grow by the day. Facts have a way of coming to light. Also, we have recently had certain experiences which make us less naive about governments while we become more hopeful about people: the civil rights movement, the student revolt, the rise of dissent inside the Communist countries, the emergence of fresh, brave spirits in Africa, Asia, Latin America, and in our own country.

It is not our job, as citizens, to point out the difficulties of our military position (this, when true, is quite evident), or to work out clever bases for negotiating (the negotiators, when they *must*, will find a way), or to dissemble what we know is true in order to build a coalition (coalitions grow naturally from what is common to a heterogeneous group, and require each element to represent its colors as honestly as possible to make the mosaic accurate and strong). As a sign of the strange "progress" the world has made, from now on all moral transgressions take the form of irony, because they are committed against officially proclaimed values. The job of citizens, in any society, any time, is simply to point this out.

II
DEBATES OVER METHODS AND THEORY

THE TOPIC

Perhaps because international relations as a field of inquiry dates back to the times of Thucydides, it has, in the twentieth century, been very conscious of the lack of progress in accumulating knowledge. This consciousness has produced two kinds of debates within the field. The first is methodological; the second, theoretical. From time to time the field has tried to improve its knowledge by asking if the ways in which it is pursuing knowledge are flawed or could be improved by borrowing the methods of disciplines that appear to be making more progress in understanding their subject matter. In the twentieth century the following questions have always been at or near the surface: How do we know that we know? What constitutes knowledge? How do we study international relations in order to gain knowledge? These concerns can be seen mainly as disagreements over how inquiry within international relations should be defined. Some of the key disagreements center around what the purpose of the discipline is, how it can best be studied to gain knowledge, and whether it can be studied scientifically.

Such efforts to improve or change methods have been one response to the lack of cumulative knowledge. The second has been to argue that the explanations put forth by scholars are simply wrong. From this perspective, the problem is not that international relations needs a special method but that the concepts and theories used to construct explanations are leading scholars in the wrong direction. To correct this situation will require new and more accurate ways of looking at the world. If one imagines the radical changes in concepts and theories that were required to go from the traditional practices of the medicine man to the creation of modern medicine based on the sciences of biology and chemistry, one can sense the long road that it may be necessary to travel before a level of understanding equivalent to the physical sciences is attained.

THE SELECTIONS

Since the founding of the discipline in the wake of World War I, there have been three major debates over inquiry. The first, discussed in Part I, was the debate between the realists and the idealists. The realists were the first to insist that the lack of progress in the field was due to the failure to study world politics in a sufficiently scientific manner. In *The Twenty Years' Crisis*, E. H. Carr attacked idealism for confusing aspiration with reality, and maintained that a true science must first endeavor to understand how things actually are before trying to change things. Carr's work helped to make international relations primarily empirical instead of merely normative. Later realists, like Morgenthau, went on to insist that a science of international politics must be general and theoretical, and not narrowly historical; they contended, in other words, that it must delineate the fundamental laws that govern human behavior (see selection 4).

While the realists were responsible for the adoption of the general goals of science, they were more resistant to the scientific method itself. **Harold Guetzkow's** (1950) essay became an early rallying point for an emerging group of behavioralists who wanted to follow a systematic scientific strategy for acquiring cumulative knowledge about world politics. By the early 1960s, the behavioralists were having a major impact, and the field divided, sometimes bitterly, on the use of quantitative methods. This led to a second debate, one between the behavioralists and the traditionalists. The essay by **Hedley Bull** (1966) crystallizes most of the concerns of traditional scholars in the field. The defense of quantitative analysis by **J. David Singer** (1969) centers on the notion that, regardless of how elegant, insightful, or apparently relevant traditional work might be, it cannot be accepted as knowledge unless it is true, and it cannot be accepted as true unless there is systematic evidence to support it. For Singer, quantitative analysis involves following scientific rules to test hypotheses so that evidence can be used to assess the truth-claims of scholars.

As international relations enters the last decade of the twentieth century, the discipline has found itself in a third debate spurred by the post-positivist and post-modernist movements sweeping through the humanities and social sciences. Post-positivism challenges, often successfully, the standard philosophy of science that undergirds so much of conventional social science. In international relations, this debate was brought to the fore by **Yosef Lapid** (1989), who defined the most important issues post-positivism raised for the discipline and delineated both the opportunities post-positivism provides for broadening inquiry and the danger it poses in encouraging the ascendency of relativism. Of the various threads making up post-positivism, one of the most influential is post-modernism, which looks at modernity not as the progressive fulfillment of the uncovering of the truth but simply as a cultural form, one among many possible and arbitrary forms of life. This suggests that how we live in the world is not predetermined by a single law, whether it be divine law, natural law, or scientific law, but is the result of the burden of history—the numerous decisions and actions that produced today's structures and culture. From this perspective, history is seen as a series of social constructions in which beliefs and practices (like chivalry and knight errantry) create a "reality" that brings about an entire way of life that people come to see as natural, rather than as the outcome of struggle.

The selection by **Richard Ashley** and **R. B. J. Walker (1990)**, which is an introductory essay to a special issue of the *International Studies Quarterly* highlighting some of the more significant analyses of this approach, provides an overview of the issues and a sense of the tone of this form of inquiry by two of the most prominent theorists of this school of thought. Post-modernists are important because they are redefining the very terms by which we understand international relations theory, making us see discourse as a key element in the social construction of reality by deconstructing prevailing thought (see also selection 43), as well as the dominant thought of the past. In doing so, they hope to liberate people from the conceptual jails that have imprisoned thinking. It should come as no surprise, therefore, that those interested in fundamental change—critical theorists, like Ashley—or feminist scholars, like Carol Cohn (see selection 43), should be attracted to this approach.

Overlapping, but slightly predating, the third debate has been what Michael Banks calls "the inter-paradigm debate." This is a debate over whether the fundamental view scholars hold of the world is correct. Beginning in the middle 1970s, a number of scholars began questioning the dominant view of international politics as consisting of states struggling for power. These scholars questioned the focus on a single political actor and the assumption that the state itself should be regarded as a unitary rational actor. They saw the emphasis on the struggle for power as a myopic, if not obsessive, concern with only one of the many issue areas that shape the global agenda and as an oversimplification of the varieties of behavior that characterize world politics. A new emphasis on economic questions and on how non-security issues are managed in international regimes made the dominant view appear inadequate. Finally, a number of scholars were concerned that, as more and more realist hypotheses began to be tested, little systematic evidence could be marshalled to support them, and their underlying logic was often revealed to be ambiguous and imprecise.

One of the first to challenge the dominant view in a fundamental way was **John Burton** (1974). In the selection presented here, he begins by asking whether the picture of the world most scholars give us really reflects the complexity of the world we live in. In contradistinction to a dominant "billiard ball" model of "international relations" that looks primarily at relations among states, he develops a "cobweb" model of "world society" that does not assume that states control the actions of their members or that states are necessarily the center of the most important transactions that occur. Whereas the billiard ball model looks at the needs of states and their interests, Burton looks at the needs of individuals and how the frustrating of those needs can lead to crime, terrorism, and war. The dominant view places power at the center of the world and sees force and coercion as the ultimate means, but Burton sees power as only one of a number of different relationships that can exist and suggests that techniques of interpersonal conflict resolution can be used to produce integrative solutions to society's most pressing problems. In the end, the dominant view is not seen as an accurate model of the world, because the policies it produces do not seem to work very well. Burton draws upon behavioral social science to challenge the prescientific view of human nature upon which "international relations" is based and suggests the outlines of a new conception of world politics.

John Vasquez (1979) supplements Burton's challenge to the dominant approach by systematically assessing the relevant scientific evidence and finding that it gives little support to the realist paradigm. Defining *paradigm* as a set of fundamental assumptions that form a picture of the world the scholar is studying, he sketches an intellectual history of the discipline that sees realism as providing the dominant paradigm that has guided both traditional and behavioral inquiry. Next, Vasquez constructs a framework for determining whether any given paradigm is scientifically adequate. He then seeks to demonstrate that realism does not provide an accurate view of the world by showing that most of the hypotheses that have been developed in light of realist assumptions have failed to pass scientific tests. The selection concludes with a call for a new paradigm within the field.

Robert W. Cox (1981) attempts, like Burton, to develop an alternative view of world politics, but his perspective is different. He draws upon a political economy approach that has its roots in Vico, Marx, and Gramsci. In addition to providing an alternative to realism, Cox also challenges the positivistic view of theory and science that has influenced both traditionalists and behavioralists. He maintains that the view that theory is objective and value-free is too simplistic. Theory always serves a purpose and is grounded in the problems of particular groups, usually the elite groups. Although Cox does not question that good scientific theory should be objective in the sense that scholars should not fabricate evidence or distort the historical record, he shows that theory is not objective in that it comes out of, shapes, and often repairs the culture of the status quo. In contrast to this *problem-solving theory*, Cox calls for a *critical theory* of world politics that does not take existing practices and "reality" for granted, but looks at what alternative orders might be possible and how change might be brought about.

Dean Pruitt and **Jeffrey Rubin** (1986) reflect a challenge to the realist paradigm that has existed for some time, but has not had a great deal of influence within international relations because the Cold War made it seem irrelevant. The conflict resolution approach rejects the idea that international politics is fundamentally a struggle for power. In its stead, it views all politics and conflict—whether it be interpersonal, domestic, or international—as susceptible to some kind of peaceful solution based on negotiation and the use of reason. Although it emphasizes the importance of peaceful solutions, this should not be taken as necessarily denying that power is important or violence frequently efficacious. Rather, those who take a conflict resolution approach argue that there are often alternative solutions to conflict that are, less costly and mutually satisfactory. In this selection, Pruitt and Rubin discuss the use of "problem-solving" techniques for resolving conflict in a mutually acceptable fashion. The selection is particularly important for its discussion of "integrative solutions," an approach pioneered by Mary Parker Follett (1924). Integrative solutions are often referred to as "win-win" solutions, where both sides gain from the resolution of a conflict—as opposed to "win-lose" solutions, where one side wins at the expense of the other. The ending of the Cold War and the emergence of more of a consensus among the strongest states in the system (see Rosecrance, selection 44) has resulted in conflict resolution being given new attention both by scholars and diplomats, particularly as a way of dealing with ethnic disputes and conflicts in the Third World.

AN ANALYSIS OF THE TOPIC

The debate over scientific principles raises fundamental questions concerning intellectual inquiry, and some important lessons have been derived as a result.

Realism produced two lasting effects on the way in which inquiry has been conducted in the field. First, it rejected the very descriptive and narrowly factual analysis of diplomatic history and current events; in its place, it established a mode of inquiry that attempts to delineate general patterns—or what some realists called laws—from history. Thereafter, inquiry focused on explaining *why* events happened, rather than on describing *how* they occurred. Second, realism pushed normative and legalistic analysis to the periphery of the field. Realists like E. H. Carr argued that the field had to first understand and explain the fundamental laws of international politics before policy recommendations could usefully be made. Unfortunately, this advice was followed neither by the realists themselves nor by others. Consequently, the field has been plagued by attempts to apply untested theories or preliminary research findings to policy questions. Sometimes these suggestions have even been adopted by governments, as they were in the development of Western nuclear strategy (see Chapter 11).

Here the behavioralists' insistence that scholars explain how they know that they know becomes crucial. Unless explanations can be formulated so that they can be tested and researched systematically, rather than illustrated with a few anecdotes, the so-called knowledge of the field remains little more than informed and well-argued opinion. Indeed, some traditionalists, like Hedley Bull, came close to asserting that, for very important questions, informed opinion is all that is possible. The behavioralists felt that studying international relations scientifically would produce the kind of systematic body of knowledge that exists in the physical sciences. This is ultimately an empirical question, and we will just have to wait to see if behavioralists will produce this level of knowledge. It has been, after all, only a few centuries since some of the wisest philosophers argued that a science of nature was impossible!

For the present, scientific testing does serve some critical functions: Unless we at least attempt to collect and assess evidence in a nonbiased fashion, we are in danger of engaging in mythmaking. In social inquiry, there is often the risk that statements will assume the aura of truth because of the way in which they are phrased, because they are widely repeated, or because they serve the interests of certain groups. When this happens, social inquiry can easily become the captive of prevailing dogma or ideology, a concern of critical theorists. The scientific method is one of the few means by which humanity can protect itself from these kinds of self-delusion. Science, however, should not be defined so narrowly, as some behavioralists have done, that it is confined to quantitative analysis. Science consists not so much of using numbers as it does of formulating testable claims, following procedures that are open and replicable, collecting evidence in a systematic and unbiased fashion, and making valid inferences. There is no a priori reason why nonquantitative comparative historical case studies cannot fall under this rubric (see selection 42). The main point of scientific inquiry is not quantitative analysis, but to reject unsupported speculation in favor of a method that produces systematic and replicable findings.

Post-positivism has shown, however, that the epistemological foundation of the scientific method is not so well grounded that any reasonable person would be *logically* compelled to accept it. Instead, it appears that science is based on a set of consensual decisions about how to define what constitutes knowledge and what procedures will be accepted (and not accepted) as establishing that knowledge. From this viewpoint, the scientific method can be regarded simply as a set of professional norms governing a professional practice. Accepting the word of "Science" as to what is knowledge or "truth" is, as post-modernists point out, to privilege one professional practice over another (such as religion or political ideology). According to many post-modernists, science ascended to its privileged position as arbiter of empirical truth through an act of power. For some post-modernists this was an act of power that arbitrarily chose one form of truth and way of life over others.

The implication, of course, is that there is no one truth or way of knowing or even that it is illegitimate to evaluate as superior one truth or epistemology over another. The latter argument becomes particularly value-laden when certain truths and "ways of knowing" are associated with specific cultures, historical traditions, or genders. Then some post-modernists argue for the need to include different "voices" and for "diversity." Since "truth" is always an act of power, all we are really left with are the different experiences of people and the knowledge *that* experience produces. All ways of knowing become equally authentic—a position at odds not only with science, but the Western Enlightenment, which is why so much of post-modernism is an attack on the Enlightenment.

While post-positivists are correct that science is based on consensual decisions and norms, and that it ascended in the West through a process of political struggle, it does not follow that the philosophical reasons for accepting a scientific approach are arbitrary or solely political. There are, in fact, "good" reasons—logical, instrumental, and practical—for privileging science over other "ways of knowing," and Singer (1969) has outlined a number of these in his debate with Hedley Bull. More importantly, as Lapid warns, to accept all ways of knowing as equal is to embrace a relativism that says that humans are unable to evaluate and choose in any non-arbitrary fashion among competing ethical, policy, truth, or even factual claims. It is one thing to let a hundred flowers bloom; it is another to let your garden get overgrown with weeds because you are unwilling to (arbitrarily) distinguish "flowers" from "weeds."

Relativists come close to saying that humans cannot really learn new things, but only provide new interpretations or "understandings." The entire history of science and technology belies this assertion. Some theories and ways of knowing are better than others, because they are more consistent with evidence, can explain more complicated events in the past (and sometimes the future), and allow us to work in and change the world because of the "knowledge" they produce. The case for science or any kind of systematic inquiry ultimately rests on this kind of argument.

The need for theory appraisal and criteria that can distinguish "good" from "bad" theories is particularly important in the inter-paradigm debate and for the future of critical theory or any policy approach. For challengers to the dominant realist paradigm, the problem of the lack of cumulation in international relations is not due to questions of epistemology or methodology, but to the fact that the realist view of the world is inaccurate and wrong. For many of these scholars what is needed is not more tolerance of theories, but more rigorous application of existing criteria to determine which theories are flawed.

While a convincing case can be made for using existing philosophy of science for building a consensus on criteria for appraising empirical theories, the same cannot be said for normative theories, which go beyond explaining how and why international relations are conducted the way they are and discuss how politics *should* be conducted. Critical theorists, like Cox, argue that much of empirical theory is value-laden and ideological because it allows the elite (government, foundations) to define the values (like national security) that theory should serve. If critical theory were to gain more adherents in North America, as it has in some European countries, international relations theory would be free to take the problems and needs of oppressed groups or common people as the focus of its attention. Critical theory, unlike realism, would seek to explain how structures emerge and shape behavior, not in order to uncover laws that humans cannot change but to emancipate and liberate those who suffer under those structures—soldiers who die in wars that are not their business, taxpayers whose dollars go to bureaucracies that care little about their needs, a humanity that still sits on a nuclear arsenal capable of destroying the entire planet several times over.

The call for a critical theory is a criticism of existing international relations theory that echoes Marx's earlier criticism of philosophy: "The philosophers have only *interpreted* the world, in various ways; the point, however, is to *change* it" (*Theses on Feuerbach*). Post-positivism has made room for this broader range of discourse; yet, if critical theory, or any policy approach, is to do more than just become a discourse reflecting competing interests, it must develop a set of explicit criteria for evaluating and appraising policy arguments. What these criteria might be and whether a consensus on them could be established is still far from obvious. This problem constitutes one of the main tasks for those scholars pursuing these lines of inquiry.

FOR FURTHER READING

Methods

MORTON KAPLAN. 1966. The New Great Debate: Traditionalism vs. Science in International Relations. *World Politics* 19:1–20.

MICHEL FOUCAULT. 1972. *The Archaeology of Knowledge.* New York: Pantheon.

DINA A. ZINNES. 1976. *Contemporary Research in International Relations: A Perspective and a Critical Appraisal.* New York: The Free Press.

ALEXANDER L. GEORGE. 1979. "Case Studies and Theory Development: The Method of Structured, Focused Comparison," in Paul Gordon Lauren, ed., *Diplomacy: New Approaches in History, Theory, and Policy.* New York: Free Press.

Theory

MARY PARKER FOLLETT. 1924. *Creative Experience.* New York: Longmans, Green & Co.

STANLEY HOFFMANN. 1959. International Relations: The Long Road to Theory. *World Politics* 11:346–377.

MARTIN WIGHT. 1966. "Why Is There No International Relations Theory?" In Herbert Butterfield and Martin Wight, eds. *Diplomatic Investigations: Essays in the Theory of International Politics.* London: George Allen & Unwin. pp. 17–34.

ROBERT O. KEOHANE AND JOSEPH S. NYE, JR. 1977. *Power and Interdependence.* Boston: Little, Brown.

RICHARD W. MANSBACH AND JOHN A. VASQUEZ. 1981. *In Search of Theory: A New Paradigm for Global Politics.* New York: Columbia University Press.

RICHARD K. ASHLEY. 1984. The Poverty of Neorealism, *International Organization* 38 (Spring): 255–86.

MICHAEL BANKS. 1985. "The Inter-paradigm Debate," in Margot Light and A.J.R. Groom, eds., *International Relations: A Handbook of Current Theory.* Boulder, CO: Lynne Rienner.

JAMES DER DERIAN AND MICHAEL J. SHAPIRO, eds. 1989. *International/Intertextual Relations: Postmodern Readings of World Politics.* Lexington, MA: Lexington Books.

R. B. J. WALKER. 1993. *Inside/Outside: International Relations as Political Theory.* Cambridge: Cambridge University Press.

CHRISTINE SYLVESTER. 1994. *Feminist Theory and International Relations in a Postmodern Era.* Cambridge: Cambridge University Press.

CHARLES W. KEGLEY, JR., ed. 1995. *Controversies in International Relations Theory: Realism and the Neoliberal Challenge.* New York: St Martin's Press.

KEN BOOTH AND STEVE SMITH, eds. 1995. *International Relations Theory Today.* Oxford: Polity Press.

Chapter 4

Defining International Relations Inquiry

11. Long Range Research in International Relations

HAROLD GUETZKOW

This article has no practical suggestions for the conduct of either the cold or hot war with Russia. Instead it asserts that man's search for relief from wars needs to be directed by an adequate, basic theory of international relations. In lieu of offering as theory only another opinion the writer will attempt to outline some of the characteristics which an adequate theory may have eventually.

Top foreign policy makers probably feel they live in too urgent a world to concern themselves with the theories of modern social science. They devote little, if any, of their organizations' resources to theoretical studies which have no immediate bearing on day-to-day decisions. Yet, in making decisions, statesmen use assumptions about social behavior which they learned early in life and which may be valid only with reference to one ethnic group or not at all. As a result, their actions and policies are often self-defeating and their solutions to problems are severely circumscribed. In most cases the policy-maker is no doubt unaware of his assumptions about group behavior. It may be this unawareness which makes him content with inadequate and unworkable theories of international relations.

Reprinted from *The American Perspective* 4 (Fall 1950), pp. 421–440, by permission of the author.

This article contends that the surest and quickest way to world peace is an indirect one—the patient construction over the years of a basic theory of international relations. From this theory may come new and un-thought-of solutions to end wars and to guide international relations on a peaceful course.

The value of the scientific approach was emphatically underlined in World War II. The superiority of the United States' operations stemmed in large measure from successful exploitation of the world's scientific resources as they existed in 1940. Many authorities were impressed with the way in which basic natural science theory made military developments possible. Unfortunately, the reservoir of social theory is small and poor in quality, and little effort is being made to build it into a scientific resource.

This article will first consider areas in which the methodological tools used by the present-day worker in international relations must be broadened and sharpened. Then, it will suggest a few ingredients of a basic theory in international relations.

1. CONSIDERATIONS ON METHODS

Political scientists, in whose domain research on international relations has been concentrated, are in a ferment over methods. This was vividly demonstrated in the 1948 panel reports on research of the American Political Science Association. More recently the International Relations Committee of the Social Science Research Council has reviewed the impact of this development on contemporary international relations research. The following remarks come in part from these sources and in part from personal convictions regarding the direction of social science research. It is the author's belief that the following changes in our methodologies are necessary to the sound construction of basic theories in international relations.

A. The present-day trend toward analytic rather than descriptive theories of international relations needs to be reinforced.

B. The move toward theories that synthesize many causes should be emphasized.

C. Dynamic mechanisms which are assumed to explain international behavior need to be made concrete and free from vague generalities.

D. States should no longer be personified as though they behaved like individual human beings.

E. Gradually the exclusive devotion to *post-facto* explanations must give way to posing theoretical propositions which may be used for prediction and then subjected to the test of experience.

A.   In the early phases of the development of a science, there must be systematic classification and description of phenomena. At first this description tends to be verbal, and only gradually do the characteristics become measurable in dimensions which are distinct from each other. In international relations, current theory tends to be descriptive. Most contemporary works are anchored to particulars—for instance, chapters on the international relations of specific states. This approach permits detailed narration with much attention to the substance of foreign relations; but it then is very difficult to construct propositions useful in analyzing more than the single concrete situation under discussion.

The later phases of the development of a science are marked by the construction of analytic theories. The science is no longer content with descriptive generalizations but attempts to analyze relations and to develop general dynamic theories of how underlying forces bring about the phenomena observed in the earlier phases of the science. In international relations there are few signs today of such analytic theory developments. Even the more advanced power theories, which analyze international relations as the influence of one nation upon another because of the operation of national power (resources, population, and technology), are usually offered by political scientists as descriptive accounts, not as dynamic analyses. Moreover, the most advanced exponent of power theory today limits his concepts to the Western European countries.

The development of an analytical theory gives the scientist a powerful tool for discovering the mainsprings of action within a system of international relations. For instance, understanding is needed of the way in which communication, cultural uniformity, and social solidarity interact and affect the relations between nations. An analytic theory including such factors would be a valuable addition to a more fully formulated power theory. Such theory often provides unexpected derivations and quite new approaches to international affairs. One modern theorist has constructed a mathematical model of relations between states from which he deduces that military preparedness *decreases* security within the internation system—a quite unconventional conclusion! His theoretical constructions also indicated the way in which an armaments race might be slackened.

B.   Many of the older theories of international relations are unrealistic because they consider only one or a few causes. The century old balance-of-power theories, involving such concepts as "sphere of influence" and "land-vs.-sea power," tend toward one-cause explanations. Within recent years, however, there has been much progress in broadening the number of variables and the types of forces which are included in international relations theory.

The impetus for this broadening seems to have stemmed from two sources: the eminently successful German geopoliticians, and the recent rapid advances of the social sciences in the United States. When the German Academy established and the Nazis bounteously subsidized a *Laboratorium für Weltpolitik*, Haushofer and Ranse gradually incorporated the findings of more and more academic disciplines into their imperialistic geo-strategies. American social scientists are now demonstrating the fruitfulness of that "cluster of closely related disciplines called social psychology—cultural analysis—sociology." It becomes clearer that such disciplines will need to be used in the construction of basic theories of international relations.

The problems of working with a theory become more difficult as it expands to include more variables. Because "other things are not equal," it is difficult to evaluate the relative importance of one variable as contrasted with another. However, in economics, where this state of affairs grows increasingly acute, the recent methodological inventions of the Cowles Commission make it possible to handle theoretical systems involving many variables which act simultaneously. One economist has recently constructed a model of some 31 variables all included in a system of 16 simultaneous equations. He then proceeded to solve the system and to check the adequacy of his postulates against existing data. Other social sciences, on a more modest scale, are making rapid strides in handling problems which twenty years ago were thought to be impossibly complex. It will be feasible to adapt these techniques to problems in international relations.

C.   Explanations in theories of international relations are often vague. But recently there has been a tendency toward closer observation of political processes. For instance, detailed analysis of the "psychological potential" from which U.S. foreign policy springs has been made on the basis of attitude and public opinion surveys. Another development in some detail is the "self-fulfilling prophecy." The expectations (which may often be inaccurate) about the behavior of another nation are seen inducing this nation to fulfill these expectations because of acts which such a prediction leads the predictor-nation to perform. One political scientist has explored the operation of this mechanism in detail, applying the analysis to U.S. relations with Russia. His documentation suggests that the avoidance of reactions to particular expectations may eliminate self-fulfillment of the prophecy.

Such miniature systems, of course, do not cope directly with such monumental tasks as the construction of a basic theory of international relations. But the most useful theories will have to be, at first, small conceptual systems dealing with a restricted range of phenomena.

D.   The social scientist often treats the nation as though it were an individual in theorizing about international relations. This tendency has roots in the period when the acts of monarchs were identical with the acts of nations, and no distinction was necessary. Later, during neo-Darwinian times, the concept of the state as an organism became common. The lack of knowledge of the fundamental characteristics of functioning organizations allows our thinking about nations as nations to be loose and unstructured—and this vacuum in our knowledge forces us to use only those concepts available within common-sense culture.

Psychiatrists and psychologists, whose work is gradually becoming valuable to the political scientists, readily treat the nation in this personalist way. The social scientist must be alert to this bias. Despite the incautious generalizations and free extrapolations of many persuasive writers, there is not sufficient evidence to warrant such a statement as "Thus we know that the 'personality' of a nation is largely determined by the fact that parents regularly channel the behavior of their children toward the local culture patterns." By treating organizations as though they were persons, we unconsciously attribute characteristics to organizations which may be quite contrary to fact. Perhaps the results of such confusion between personality and nation have been most ridiculously demonstrated in the recent treatment of the German nation as paranoid.

E.   Few theorists venture to make predictions about future international events. Instead, they prudently limit themselves to *post facto* explanations of events. This is a realistic recognition of the limitations of our present state of social science. Lack of prediction, however, makes it difficult to test the validity of theories. In the long run, the usefulness of a theory depends upon its reliability in prediction.

Lack of interest in prediction partially stems from the background and training of students of international relations in the fields of philosophy, history and law. Distaste of predictions undoubtedly also comes from the bitter, unsuccessful attempts which lie scattered alongside the development of international relations theory. Because of the urgent demand for practical application, interest and effort have been centered on predictions of the grand strategies—just as now attention of the social scientist is focused on the American-Russian struggle.

It would be fruitful to limit at first the predictions to minor international occurrences, rather than risking an attempt to forecast important global events. Confirmation and denials of parts of theories might gradually lead to a more firmly bulwarked system, eventually enabling the social scientist to predict more and more imposing events in international relations. An aide to the policy-maker, the worker in international relations must make predictions. Yet he has never consolidated his propositions into a predictive system, so that he might test the validity of his theorizing. Until this is done, how can substantial progress be made in the construction of a testable theory of international relations?

In conclusion, what is advocated is a more thorough application of scientific methods to research in international relations. Emphasis should be given to the construction of analytic theories which specify concretely the dynamic mechanisms underlying various types of international relations. The mere building of analogies as exemplified in the personification of nations should be avoided. New theories should be capable of yielding predictions so that their validity may eventually be tested.

2. ELEMENTS NEEDED FOR THEORY CONSTRUCTION

But is it possible to construct a theory of international relations with the extension of methods proposed? What form would such theorizing take? How would it be possible to construct small islands of theory, which eventually might be tied together into a more definitive theory-system? This article can not answer these questions but presents only some explorations.

The process of theory construction requires three stages. First, using the nation as the primary unit, propositions would be developed to explain how national behaviors in the international scene originate within the state. Then, a general theory of the relations between any two states might be erected. Later, as one becomes more sure of his footing, this artificially restricted, binary theory might be elaborated into a multi-nation theory. This latter development would undoubtedly be accompanied by research on the functioning of international agencies as dynamic, supra-nation organizations.

Even the simplest theory will probably need to include propositions about four types of factors which operate to determine the foreign policy and behavior of a state:

(1) Domestic forces which are the wellspring of the state's inter-nation behaviors.
(2) The nature of the nation's decision-apparatus which translate the basic forces into foreign policies.
(3) The personal dynamics of the nation's leaders which mold the operation of the decision-making apparatus.
(4) The state of the nation's technology.

Of course, these groupings overlap. And undoubtedly much predictive potential of a theory constructed with them will come eventually from the interrelations which exist among variables.

Domestic Forces.   The distinction between "domestic" and "international" affairs, sharply drawn in the 18th and 19th century, is being gradually replaced by more realistic approaches. There are many domestic forces which pressure a nation's foreign policies into particular channels . . .

National Decision-Apparatus. How are these domestic factors, which constitute the mainspring of the nation's foreign relations, translated into national behaviors? In large measure, these forces affect foreign policies and behaviors through the decision-making and decision-executing apparatuses within the state. Hence, a basic theory of international relations needs to conceptualize these processes. . . .

Leadership Dynamics. The "great man" theory of history has long emphasized that international relations would have been quite different had different actors played the lead parts. Contemporary social scientists adopt a more moderate viewpoint. They recognize that the personal characteristics of the leader interact with social events to produce history. It will be valuable to develop a theory on how the manner in which the leader plays his role modifies the functioning of the decision-apparatus. In nations with highly centralized, monolithic administrative structures, empirical tests of this type of theory will be difficult but possible. In democratic-type organizations with multiple leadership, would it ever be possible to trace through the permutating interactions which must occur when a major foreign policy decision is reached and executed? . . .

Technology. Because the social scientist—especially the social theorist—is seldom an engineer or anthropologist, it is easy for him to forget the powerful impact the technological achievements of a nation have upon its human and social behavior systems. Although we are all impressed with the importance of atomic energy, no definitive report has yet been prepared by the social scientists on the implications of this technological advance. . . .

This outline indicates the types of forces which determine the foreign behaviors of a nation. Implicit in this formulation, of course, is the fact that the behaviors of other nations are received and interpreted through the same mechanisms. The leader characteristics, the decision-apparatus, the technological state, and the underlying needs and desires of the people all function to determine how the foreign behaviors of other nations impinge upon the state. The processes involved in interpreting the behavior of other nations are not simple. Perhaps many of the same forces which initiate foreign behaviors will also determine the way in which the foreign behaviors of other states are received. However, these forces do not operate in completely identical ways in the two situations.

After theories of the factors influencing foreign behaviors have been elaborated within particular areas, it may be found that the effects of "interaction" are important. An example is found in demographic theories of "felt" population pressure where "absolute" population pressure becomes a factor influencing foreign behavior only under certain social and economic conditions. It is the interaction of the absolute pressure and the economic conditions which makes the population pressure "felt." The enumeration of the four areas above implies a set of interrelationships among them: within a given technology the domestic forces initiate foreign behaviors through the national decision-apparatuses, all molded by the personal characteristics of the nation's leadership.

3. COMPONENTS OF AN INTER-NATION THEORY

In theorizing about the intra-nation formulation of foreign policy, one necessarily illuminates certain aspects of an inter-nation theory. At the least it seems necessary to differentiate two types of inter-nation behaviors: the more formal behavior of the state's decision-apparatus, and the informal relationships which exist between peoples of different nationalities.

Some of the same factors involved in an intra-nation theory will also determine inter-nation relations. For instance, interpersonal relations (as determined by the personality characteristics of the statesmen) will influence the outcome of international conferences. The state of technology will make changes in the traditional methods of handling international relations, as exemplified by the transformation of the ambassador from plenipotentiary to mouthpiece as a result of rapid communication between home government and delegates abroad. Finally, economic factors are known to determine power interrelations among nations, as has been so dramatically illustrated in the operation of the Marshall plan.

While these parallelisms can be extended, it is more helpful to turn now to the new types of problems which arise in considering inter-nation theory. Our intention is to indicate the applicability of social science research techniques even to these difficult problems.

Binary Theories of Inter-Nation Relations. In order to simplify the theory construction in its early phases, miniature systems might be established using pairs of nations, which would make it easier to form a concept of the problems. The pairs might be selected in such a way that empirical checks of the theory could be made with minimum cost and maximum information. As a series of binary systems was developed, the bridge to simple three-nation constructions might be made. The multi-nation theory would be very difficult to construct, but after the development of binary theories, a means would eventually suggest itself. . . .

International Organization Processes. As international contacts multiply, relationships tend to be institutionalized. Exchange of notes gradually gives way to international conferences, and conferences often acquire permanent character through the adoption of standing committees. Finally, unifying organizations arise, such as the International Labor Organization, the World Health Organization, the League of Nations or the United Nations.

It is very likely that the theory of international organization will borrow heavily from the theory of public administration. However, a separate theory will be required because of such special factors in international organization as sovereignty. Nor is there any question that these international processes are suitable for theoretical and empirical research. . . .

Problems of International Cohesion. The necessity of examining the informal relations between the populations of different states has already been noted. Public opinion not only affects the foreign policy of one state but sometimes also operates across national boundaries. A case in point is the 1948 Italian elections, which were unquestionably influenced by American public opinion as expressed in a vigorous letter-writing campaign.

These informal relations or interactions are especially relevant to the problem of developing solidarity and cohesion among nations. Although nationalist loyalty has been studied intensively, little serious work has been done on the problem of creating wider loyalties. Current work by social psychologists on the processes by which people maintain membership in multiple groups may prove to be applicable to problems of the compatibility or incompatibility of national and international loyalties.

Both the loyalty and public opinion factors indicate the way in which the direct relationship of the individual to other nations or international organizations need be considered in constructing a theory of international relations. Both would be factors in making predictions of the extent to which there is international solidarity, but it would also be necessary to give weight to the many nonpersonal forces that produce varying degrees of international cohesion. As nations become more interdependent and their international institutions develop effectiveness, another important theoretical problem emerges. To what extent does the interdependence create solidarity? Sociologists long have been concerned with this problem among groups within a nation and have come to regard interdependence as one of the main sources of group consolidation. The international version of the problem awaits sociological appraisal.

4. THE ORGANIZATION OF RESEARCH ACTIVITIES TO CONSTRUCT BASIC THEORIES OF INTERNATIONAL RELATIONS

It has been contended that with an extended methodology, it should be quite possible to construct an integrated set of theories about international relations. The formulation and testing of such theories would not, however, be easy. The sponsors of the research would need the patience of a Job and the determination of a Horatio Alger. The basic considerations implicit in the first two sections of this article would determine some characteristics of the organization which would carry out the proposed research. What follows is an attempt to focus these implications and to indicate in a tentative way how actual research might be organized.

Integrative Nature of Research Activity. The first two sections of this article stress how dependent the development of basic theories of international relations is upon the state of theoretical work on human and social behavior. The research activity will consequently need to be broad and eclectic in its orientation.

It will avoid recruiting the scientist who feels his own substantive viewpoint is a panacea. Because of difficulties always experienced in doing team research between disciplines, it may be well to devote some years to the training of mature scholars in one or two areas besides their own, so that aspects of the cross-discipline endeavour can be integrated within a single person. This may relieve some of the strains usually arising within inter-disciplinary research units.

Because of the size of the task, safeguards must be taken to avoid the growth of a research organization so large and difficult to co-ordinate that its right hand doesn't know what its left hand is doing. Full advantage should be taken of the islandic features pointed out in the second section. For instance, each time the central, integrating team of researchers uncovers a theoretical pocket, this project might be isolated for a time and become administratively divorced from the central program. The integrating team would have its hands full bringing together the developed islands of theory.

There already exist important centers devoted to fundamental research related to international relations. An example is found in the Hoover Institute and Library research on the mechanism of revolution, an essential ingredient of both the intra-national and international formulations suggested in the second section. By building careful liaison relationships, the results of such specialized centers could be profitably incorporated into the integrating team's formulations. As the central team made progress on its own, certain ramifications might appear which could be discussed with the more specialized centers. At times, these independent units might make changes in their own programs, so that their results would more readily fit into the developing global theory.

Reality-Orientation of the Research Endeavor. The mere spinning of theoretical webs is a fascinating occupation. Hence, precaution must be taken to check the extent to which the concepts conform to reality. As pointed out in section 1, the scientific method is the vehicle *par excellence* for the accomplishment of this purpose. It will be necessary to maintain a close relationship between the theoretical work and the empirical, hypothesis-checking endeavours of the research program. Only in this way can the erroneous theories be corrected, and the compounding of mistaken ideas prevented. . . .

Skeptics often claim that the social sciences will never make fundamental tests of their hypotheses because they can not experiment. Undoubtedly such limitations will make it difficult to test theories of international relations—but not impossible. Although the social scientist cannot conduct experiments at the time and place he desires them and with all scientific controls, often the events of the world can yield tests of his theories. For instance, would it not have been possible to test the validity of theoretical work on the interplay of economic and power factors in international relations at the 1950 trade agreements meetings? One might make preliminary, orientational checks of his theory on the results of the Annecy trade conferences in 1948. Then, with a revised theory, the scientist might make predictions of the outcomes of the 1950 meetings. The adequacy of one's theories would be "experimentally" checked by the deviation of the predictions from the actual outcomes. . . .

Influence of the Sponsors on the Research Work. In the end the keeper of the purse plays the tune. It is vital to the well-being of basic research in international relations that the sponsor of the activity be relatively free of biasing pressures. These pressures will probably be of two kinds: pressures to be practical and to be nationalistic. There will be forces constantly seducing the research endeavour into more practical, policy-oriented direction. Because this area is of such vital concern to governments and citizens, there will be incessant demands for devotion of the program's resources to premature application of its findings. The history of the social sciences is replete with submissions to such pressure. Yet, the basic reason we have made little world progress toward peace is that we never allow our social scientists to work with sufficient energy on the basic theoretical problems.

There will be constant pressure toward disturbance of the basic theories with nationalistic bias. The internal struggles in UNESCO arising from this source—and Russia does not even belong to UNESCO—has dissipated much of the energies of that organization. Hence, it would seem advisable to establish the research organization on a private basis, staffed with men from a number of nations whose objectivity as scientists might help them override their national biases.

Undoubtedly the German Academy's theoretical efforts in geopolitics were never allowed to reach their full potential because of the fearful operation of these two types of pressures. Yet despite these forces, in 1941 Haushofer was bold enough to stand by his quasi-scientific prediction of Nazi disaster should a Russian campaign be undertaken, even though he lost his sponsorship in so doing.

I am as fearful as my readers of the utilization of the results of basic research in international relations for immoral purposes. Derivations from the basic postulates might give rise to astoundingly successful psychological warfare programs. Perhaps some safeguard will be obtained, if the results are available simultaneously to all nations and all peoples. But even such openness in the scientist's proceedings will hardly guarantee the prevention of Machiavellian acts. The basic assumptions and many of the derivations of Nazi policy were forthrightly explained to the world in *Mein Kampf,* and particular campaigns were spelled out in some detail in books published some ten years before the operations were undertaken. Yet, statesmen remained blind and persisted in their stereotyped thinking about inter-nation relations until World War II was upon them.

The Organization Outlined. The Research Organization might consist of an inter-disciplinary Executive Integrating Team, headed by the Organization's Director, whose main task would be construction of an over-all, integrated basic theory of international relations. One member of the Executive Team would be Director of the Theory-Islands Division. Another member would be Director of an Empirical-Tests Division. The Executive Team would be assisted by an internal secretariat, which would aid the team in keeping itself appraised of both divisions' work. It would be helped in its liaison work by consultation conferences of outside experts organized for particular purposes, as well as a Liaison Staff, who would constantly search throughout the world for new theoretic and empirical developments made by other investigators, both private and in government. So that the Executive Team could devote its full energies to the creative task of constructing an integrated basic theory, the administrative functions of the Research Organization would be in the hands of an Administrative Officer and staff. In one sense, the Executive Team would be somewhat analogous to the Atomic Warfare Exploration Staff which Eisenhower set up to consider the implications of atomic weapons for military operations, without prejudice from old-line preconceptions. However, the international relations team would be much more theoretic in its interests.

In order to keep the size of the Research Organization manageable, it would be wise to allow both divisions to contract work with independent research units. By judicious selection of projects, over-lapping in research could be held to a minimum, and work stimulated in areas in which results most desperately are needed. The present operations of the Office of Naval Research might be profitably studied to gain insights on how this type of contract-stimulation of basic research could be carried out.

Although both divisions of the Research Organization would eventually function simultaneously, at first there would be emphasis upon the Theory-Islands work. Then as theories were made ready for testing by the Executive Team, the Empirical-Tests Division would undertake their validation. This Division's results would be fed back to the Executive Integrating Team to guide theory revision. Often unexpected leads obtained by the Empirical-Tests Division would need to be assigned to the Theory-Island Division for development.

Techniques for Increasing Applicability of Research Findings. After five to seven years of operation the Executive Team may decide it is time to establish a third division—the Engineering and Invention Division. It would put the basic theoretical formulations into practical applications which would aid the nations in developing better relations.

The Engineering committee within this Division would serve as consultants, perhaps on a fee basis, to governments, international organizations, and private agencies. It would help them utilize the results of the research in handling their day-to-day international relations problems. It would help such local units establish their own research operations to aid in applying the general theory to their own special needs.

Most solid scientific theories prove fruitful in providing ideas which probably would never have been conceived had there been no special frame-of-reference provided by theory. The Invention committee would have few definite responsibilities except to exploit creatively the basic theory. Their task would be to invent new devices and techniques for the conduct of international relations in ways that would eliminate the need for violent, world-devastating operations as instruments of foreign policy. Although the Executive Team will on occasion produce ideas allowing entirely new approaches to certain problems in international relations, the Invention group would be charged with the responsibility not only of developing the ideas proposed by the Executive Team but of suggesting original notions on their own.

5. CONCLUSION

In summary, a basic theory of international relations will need to be supplemented with a theory on the operation of international organizations. Because international relations are not confined to relations among nations, the final formulations will include the operation of forces deriving directly from individuals as persons. It will even be necessary to construct propositions about the effects of the operations of private economic and educational agencies on the international scene.

Out of the process of developing, integrating, and testing these bodies of theory, it is to be expected that ideas will spring which probably would never be conceived without the frame of reference provided by the theory. These ideas may concern practical applications of the theory which will aid nations in the day-to-day handling of international problems; or they may lead to new devices and techniques for the conduct of international relations. There appears to be no other approach which holds any promise of enabling men of good will to understand and control the present system of international relations, whose breakdown now threatens the world with utter devastation.

12. International Theory:
The Case for a Classical Approach

HEDLEY BULL

Two approaches to the theory of international relations at present compete for our attention. The first of these I shall call the classical approach. By this I do not mean the study and criticism of the "classics" of international relations, the writings of Hobbes, Grotius, Kant, and other great thinkers of the past who have turned their attention to international affairs. Such study does indeed exemplify the classical approach, and it provides a method that is particularly fruitful and important. What I have in mind, however, is something much wider than this: the approach to theorizing that derives from philosophy, history, and law, and that is characterized above all by explicit reliance upon the exercise of judgment and by the assumptions that if we confine ourselves to strict standards of verification and proof there is very little of significance that can be said about international relations, that general propositions about this subject must therefore derive from a scientifically imperfect process of perception or intuition, and that these general propositions cannot be accorded anything more than the tentative and

inconclusive status appropriate to their doubtful origin.

Until very recently virtually all attempts at theorizing about international relations have been founded upon the approach I have just described. We can certainly recognize it in the various twentieth-century systematizations of international theory—in works like those of Alfred Zimmern, E. H. Carr, Hans Morgenthau, Georg Schwarzenberger, Raymond Aron, and Martin Wight. And it is clearly also the method of their various precursors, whose scattered thoughts and partial treatments they have sought to draw together: political philosophers like Machiavelli and Burke, international lawyers like Vattel and Oppenheim, pamphleteers like Gentz and Cobden, historians like Heeren and Ranke. It is because this approach has so long been the standard one that we may call it classical.

The second approach I shall call the scientific one. I have chosen to call it scientific rather than scientistic so as not to prejudge the issue I wish to discuss by resort to a term of opprobrium. In using this name for the second approach, however, it is the aspirations of those who adopt it that I have in mind rather than their performance. They aspire to a theory of international relations whose propositions are based either upon logical or mathematical proof, or upon strict, empirical procedures of

Excerpted from Bull, Hedley, "International Theory: The Case for a Classical Approach," in *World Politics* 18/3 (April 1966), pp. 361–377. Copyright © 1966 by Princeton University Press. Excerpts reprinted by permission of Princeton University Press. Footnotes deleted.

verification. Some of them dismiss the classical theories of international relations as worthless, and clearly conceive themselves to be the founders of a wholly new science. Others concede that the products of the classical approach were better than nothing and perhaps even regard them with a certain affection. . . . But in either case they hope and believe that their own sort of theory will come wholly to supersede the older type; . . . they see themselves as tough-minded and expert new men, taking over an effete and woolly discipline, or pseudo-discipline, which has so far managed by some strange quirk to evade the scientific method but has always been bound to succumb to it in the end. . . .

. . . the scientific approach has contributed and is likely to contribute very little to the theory of international relations, and in so far as it is intended to encroach upon and ultimately displace the classical approach, it is positively harmful. In support of this conclusion I wish to put forward seven propositions.

The first proposition is that by confining themselves to what can be logically or mathematically proved or verified according to strict procedures, the practitioners of the scientific approach are denying themselves the only instruments that are at present available for coming to grips with the substance of the subject. In abstaining from what Morton Kaplan calls "intuitive guesses" or what William Riker calls "wisdom literature" they are committing themselves to a course of intellectual puritanism that keeps them (or would keep them if they really adhered to it) as remote from the substance of international politics as the inmates of a Victorian nunnery were from the study of sex.

To appreciate our reliance upon the capacity for judgment in the theory of international relations we have only to rehearse some of the central questions to which that theory is addressed. Some of these are at least in part moral questions, which cannot by their very nature be given any sort of objective answer, and which can only be probed, clarified, reformulated, and tentatively answered from some arbitrary standpoint, according to the

method of philosophy. Others of them are empirical questions, but of so elusive a nature that any answer we provide to them will leave some things unsaid, will be no more than an item in a conversation that has yet to be concluded. It is not merely that in *framing* hypotheses in answer to these empirical questions we are dependent on intuition or judgment (as has often been pointed out, this is as true in the natural as in the social sciences); it is that in the *testing* of them we are utterly dependent upon judgment also, upon a rough and ready observation, of a sort for which there is no room in logic or strict science, that things are this way and not that.

For example, does the collectivity of sovereign states constitute a political society or system, or does it not? If we can speak of a society of sovereign states, does it presuppose a common culture or civilization? And if it does, does such a common culture underlie the worldwide diplomatic framework in which we are attempting to operate now? What is the place of war in international society? . . . Are there just wars which it may tolerate and even require? . . . To what extent is the course of diplomatic events at any one time determined or circumscribed by the general shape or structure of the international system; by the number, relative weight, and conservative or radical disposition of its constituent states, and by the instruments for getting their way that military technology or the distribution of wealth has put into their hands; by the particular set of rules of the game underlying diplomatic practice at that time? And so on.

These are typical of the questions of which the theory of international relations essentially consists. But the scientific theorists have forsworn the means of coming directly to grips with them. When confronted with them they do one of two things. Either they shy away and devote themselves to peripheral subjects—methodologies for dealing with the subject, logical extrapolations of conceptual frameworks for thinking about it, marginalia of the subject that are susceptible of measurement or direct observation—or they break free of their own code and resort suddenly and without acknowledging that this is what they are doing to the methods of the classical approach—methods that in some cases they employ very badly, their preoccupations and training having left them still strangers to the substance of the subject.

This congenital inability of the scientific approach to deal with the crux of the subject while yet remaining true to its own terms leads me to an observation about the teaching of the subject in universities. Whatever virtues one might discern in the scientific approach, it is a wholly retrograde development that it should now form the basis of undergraduate courses of instruction in international politics, as in some universities in the United States it now does. The student whose study of international politics consists solely of an introduction to the techniques of systems theory, game theory, simulation, or content analysis is simply shut off from contact with the subject, and is unable to develop any feeling either for the play of international politics or for the moral dilemmas to which it gives rise.

The second proposition I wish to put forward arises out of the first: It is that where practitioners of the scientific approach have succeeded in casting light upon the substance of the subject it has been by stepping beyond the bounds of that approach and employing the classical method. What there is of value in their work consists essentially of judgments that are not established by the mathematical or scientific methods they employ, and which may be arrived at quite independently of them. . . .

My third proposition is that the practitioners of the scientific approach are unlikely to make progress of the sort to which they aspire. Some of the writers I have been discussing would be ready enough to admit that so far only peripheral topics have been dealt with in a rigidly scientific way. But their claim would be that it is not by its performance so far that their approach should be judged, but by the promise it contains of ultimate advance. They may even say that the modesty of their beginnings shows how faithful they are to the example of natural science: Modern physics too,

Morton Kaplan tells us, "has reared its present lofty edifice by setting itself problems that it has the tools or techniques to solve."

The hope is essentially that our knowledge of international relations will reach the point at which it becomes genuinely cumulative: that from the present welter of competing terminologies and conceptual frameworks there will eventually emerge a common language, that the various insignificant subjects that have now been scientifically charted will eventually join together and become significant, and that there will then exist a foundation of firm theory on which newcomers to the enterprise will build.

No one can say with certainty that this will not happen, but the prospects are very bleak indeed. The difficulties that the scientific theory has encountered do not appear to arise from the quality that international relations is supposed to have of a "backward" or neglected science, but from characteristics inherent in the subject matter which have been catalogued often enough: the unmanageable number of variables of which any generalization about state behavior must take account; the resistance of the material to controlled experiment; the quality it has of changing before our eyes and slipping between our fingers even as we try to categorize it; the fact that the theories we produce and the affairs that are theorized about are related not only as subject and object but also as cause and effect, thus ensuring that even our most innocent ideas contribute to their own verification or falsification.

A more likely future for the theory of international politics is that it will remain indefinitely in the philosophical stage of constant debate about fundamentals; that the works of the new scientific theorists will not prove to be solid substructure on which the next generation will build, but rather that those of them that survive at all will take their place alongside earlier works as partial and uncertain guides to an essentially intractable subject; and that successive thinkers, while learning what they can from what has gone before, will continue to feel impelled to build their own houses of theory from the foundations up.

A fourth proposition that may be advanced against many who belong to the scientific school is that they have done a great disservice to theory in this field by conceiving of it as the construction and manipulation of so-called "models." Theoretical inquiry into an empirical subject normally proceeds by way of the assertion of general connections and distinctions between events in the real world. But it is the practice of many of these writers to cast their theories in the form of a deliberately simplified abstraction from reality, which they then turn over and examine this way and that before considering what modifications must be effected if it is to be applied to the real world. A model in the strict sense is a deductive system of axioms and theorems; so fashionable has the term become, however, that it is commonly used also to refer to what is simply a metaphor or an analogy. It is only the technique of constructing models in the strict sense that is at issue here. However valuable this technique may have proved in economics and other subjects, its use in international politics is to be deplored.

The virtue that is supposed to lie in models is that by liberating us from the restraint of constant reference to reality, they leave us free to set up simple axioms based on a few variables and thenceforward to confine ourselves to rigorous deductive logic, thereby generating wide theoretical insights that will provide broad signposts to guide us in the real world even if they do not fill in the details.

I know of no model that has assisted our understanding of international relations that could not just as well have been expressed as an empirical generalization. This, however, is not the reason why we should abstain from them. The freedom of the model-builder from the discipline of looking at the world is what makes him dangerous; he slips easily into a dogmatism that empirical generalization does not allow, attributing to the model a connection with reality it does not have, and as often as not distorting the model itself by importing additional assumptions about the world in the guise of logical axioms. The very intellectual completeness and logical tidiness of the model-building operation lends it an air of authority which is often quite misleading as to its standing as a statement about the real world. . . .

The fashion for constructing models exemplifies a much wider and more long-standing trend in the study of social affairs: the substitution of methodological tools and the question "Are they useful or not?" for the assertion of propositions about the world and the question "Are they true or not?" Endemic though it has become in recent thinking, I believe this change to have been for the worse. The "usefulness" of a tool has in the end to be translated as the truth of a proposition, or a series of propositions, advanced about the world, and the effect of the substitution is simply to obscure the issue of an empirical test and to pave the way for shoddy thinking and the subordination of inquiry to practical utility. However, this is a theme that requires more amplification than it can be given here, and in introducing it I am perhaps taking on more antagonists than I need do for my present purpose.

A fifth proposition is that the work of the scientific school is in some cases distorted and impoverished by a fetish for measurement. For anyone dedicated to scientific precision, quantification of the subject must appear as the supreme ideal, whether it takes the form of the expression of theories themselves in the form of mathematical equations or simply that of the presentation of evidence amassed in quantitative form. Like the Anglican bishop a year or so ago who began his sermon on morals by saying that he did not think all sexual intercourse is necessarily wrong, I wish to take a liberal view of this matter. There is nothing inherently objectionable, just as there is nothing logically peculiar, in a theoretical statement about international politics cast in mathematical form. Nor is there any objection to the counting of phenomena. . . . The difficulty arises where the pursuit of the measurable leads us to ignore relevant differences between the phenomena that are being counted, to impute to what has been counted a significance it does not have, or to be so distracted by the possibilities that do abound in our subject for counting as to be diverted from the qualitative inquiries that are in most cases more fruitful. . . .

My sixth proposition is that there is a need for rigor and precision in the theory of international politics, but that the sort of rigor and precision of which the subject admits can be accommodated readily enough within the classical approach. Some of the targets at which the scientific theorists aim their barbs are quite legitimate ones. The classical theory of international relations has often been marked by failure to define terms, to observe logical canons of procedure, or to make assumptions explicit. It has sometimes also, especially when associated with the philosophy of history, sought to pursue into international politics implications of a fundamentally unscientific view of the world. The theory of international relations should undoubtedly attempt to be scientific in the sense of being a coherent, precise, and orderly body of knowledge, and in the sense of being consistent with the philosophical foundations of modern science. Insofar as the scientific approach is a protest against slipshod thinking and dogmatism, or against a residual providentialism, there is everything to be said for it. But much theorizing in the classical mold is not open to this sort of objection. The writings of the great international lawyers from Vitoria or Oppenheim (which, it may be argued, form the basis of the traditional literature of the subject) are rigorous and critical. There are plenty of contemporary writers who are logical and rigorous in their approach and yet do not belong to the school I have called the scientific one: Raymond Aron, Stanley Hoffmann, and Kenneth Waltz are examples. Moreover, it is not difficult to find cases where writers in the scientific vein have failed to be rigorous and critical in this sense.

My seventh and final proposition is that the practitioners of the scientific approach, by cutting themselves off from history and philosophy, have deprived themselves of the means of self-criticism, and in consequence have a view of their subject and its possibilities that is callow and brash. I hasten to add that this is not true, or not equally true, of them all. But their thinking is certainly characterized by a lack of any sense of inquiry into international politics as a continuing tradition to which they are the latest recruits; by an insensitivity to the conditions of recent history that have produced them, provided them with the preoccupations and perspectives they have, and colored these in ways of which they might not be aware; by an absence of any disposition to wonder why, if the fruits their researches promise are so great and the prospects of translating them into action so favorable, this has not been accomplished by anyone before; by an uncritical attitude toward their own assumptions, and especially toward the moral and political attitudes that have a central but unacknowledged position in much of what they say.

The scientific approach to international relations would provide a very suitable subject for the sort of criticism that Bernard Crick has applied to a wider target in his admirable book *The American Science of Politics*—criticism that would, by describing its history and social conditions, isolate the slender and parochial substructure of moral and political assumption that underlies the enterprise. There is little doubt that the conception of a science of international politics, like that of a science of politics generally, has taken root and flourished in the United States because of attitudes towards the practice of international affairs that are especially American—assumptions, in particular about the moral simplicity of problems of foreign policy, the existence of "solutions" to these problems, the receptivity of policymakers to the fruits of research, and the degree of control and manipulation that can be exerted over the whole diplomatic field by any one country. . . .

Having stated the case against the scientific approach I must return to the qualifications I introduced at the outset. I am conscious of having made a shotgun attack upon a whole flock of assorted approaches, where single rifle shots might have brought down the main targets more efficiently and at the same time spared others that may have been damaged unnecessarily.

Certainly, there are many more approaches to the theory of international relations than two, and the dichotomy that has served my present purpose obscures many other distinctions that it is important to bear in mind.

Students of international relations are divided by what are in some cases simply barriers of misunderstanding or academic prejudice. . . . But in the present controversy, eclecticism, masquerading as tolerance, is the greatest danger of all; if we are to be hospitable to every approach (because "something may come of it someday") and extend equal rights to every cliché (because "there is, after all, a grain of truth in what he says"), there will be no end to the absurdities thrust upon us. . . .

I hope I have made it clear that I see a good deal of merit in a number of the contributions that have been made by theorists who adopt a scientific approach. The argument is not that these contributions are worthless, but that what is of value in them can be accommodated readily enough within the classical approach. Moreover, the distinctive methods and aspirations these theorists have brought to the subject are leading them down a false path, and to all appeals to follow them down it we should remain absolutely deaf.

13. The Incompleat Theorist: Insight Without Evidence

J. DAVID SINGER

1. SOME DELICATE DECISIONS

. . . In Professor Bull's inventory of the scientific school's deadly sins, seven allegedly discrete propositions emerge, but despite claims to rigor and precision we quickly discover that at least one traditionalist is quite indifferent to the requirement that categories be conceptually comparable, logically exhaustive, and mutually exclusive. Rather than try to impose a degree of order on the scattershot arraignment, let me show how uncompulsive we behavioral science types can be, and skip about just as casually as the most discursive intuitionist.

After responding to these arguments with epistemological counterarguments and some anecdotal illustrations, I will try to formulate a position which may hopefully command not only the assent of the reader but of the prosecutor himself. In the process, I hope to demonstrate that the war between rigor and imagination in international politics is not only over, but that it was to some extent a

Excerpted from Singer, J. David, "The Incompleat Theorist: Insight Without Evidence," in James N. Rosenau and Klaus Knorr, eds., *Contending Approaches to International Politics* (Princeton: Princeton University Press, 1969), pp. 63–86. Copyright © 1969 by Princeton University Press. Excerpts reprinted by permission of Princeton University Press and the author. Footnotes deleted.

"phony war" all along—a war which, despite its similarity to that which most other disciplines have been through, need not have been fought but for the recalcitrance of some and the exuberance of others.

2. ALLEGATIONS AND REJOINDERS

The Puritan Intellect

The first fantasy one encounters in this morose recitation is the assertion that the scientific approach is so intellectually puritanical that it eschews the use of wisdom, insight, intuition, and judgment. Nonsense! If this were true, we would not only never write a word, but we would never address a class, consult for a government agency, cast a ballot, or even get up in the morning. The scientific view is that, while we can never be satisfied until the proposition in doubt (for example) has indeed been verified, we need hardly decline into cerebral immobility while waiting for the final word. The important difference is that the prescientific chap equates "Eureka!" with divine revelation, while the more rigorous type permits himself that moment of pleasure for basking in the warmth of private discovery, and then gets on with the job of publicly visible, explicit, reproducible authentication.

Our classicist also urges that most of the important moral, as well as theoretical, questions "cannot by their very nature be given any sort of objective answer." While I concur with his aside that the conversations of science and of ethics are always inconclusive (a somewhat milder charge), that is no reason to stop where we are, barely beyond the edge of superstition. On matters moral, scholar and layman alike have been emasculated by the folklore which sees the world of values and the world of facts as deeply and forever separate and distinct. At a certain level of generality, almost all men can find ethical consensus, but as we move toward the specific, we inevitably begin to part company. However, much of the division turns out to be not so much a matter of preference as it is one of prediction.

Very few western diplomats in 1939, for instance, *preferred* Nazi expansion in Central Europe, but most of them *predicted* that the Munich agreement would avoid it. And while few American leaders *preferred* a continuation of the war in Vietnam, many *predicted* in 1965 that rapid military escalation would terminate it. These were errors in prediction—which a more solid research base might have helped us avoid—more than disagreements over ends. To be more general, very few of those court astrologers who have urged the doctrine of "*Si vis pacem, para bellum*" on their leaders have actually preferred war; they merely predicted poorly in almost every case. In other words, even though there will inevitably be differences among men as to their preferred ultimate outcomes, or ends, the bulk of our disagreements turn on the different consequences which we expect (or predict) from the means we advocate and select. My view here is that, as our knowledge base expands and is increasingly integrated in the theoretical sense, the better our predictions will be, and therefore, the fewer policy disagreements we will have. That is, more and more value conflicts will be translatable into the more tractable form of predictive conflicts, thus bridging the gap between fact and value, and liberating our predictions from our preferences.

I certainly do not mean to argue that whenever men, individually or collectively, find themselves pursuing incompatible ends, it is always due to a failure in their knowledge. All too often we do actually want the same object (one type of scarcity) or a different set of environmental conditions (another type of scarcity). But even in those cases, greater knowledge might lead to the calculation that compromise in the short run is less costly than victory in the middle or long run. . . .

To sum up this first point, then, I defer to no one in my condemnation of a curriculum which embraces "systems theory, game theory, simulation, or content analysis" at the expense of any "contact with the subject" or "any feeling either for the play of international politics or for the moral dilemmas to which it gives rise," but utterly reject the notion that a scientific approach requires us to choose between the two. Our mission in both teaching and research is nothing more than an effective amalgamation of insight with evidence, and of substance with technique. When one of the most eminent of our traditionalists describes his method as the art of "mustering all the evidence that history, personal experience, introspection, common sense and . . . logical reasoning" make available, it is difficult to quarrel. But, it must be added that history, experience, introspection, common sense, and logic do not in themselves generate *evidence*, but ideas which must then be examined in the light of evidence.

If This Be Plagiarism

The second and closely related allegation is that the scientific approach only succeeds in casting any light upon substantive matters when it steps "beyond the bounds of that approach" and employs the classical method. As suggested above, classical concepts and historical insights are very much *within* (and not beyond) the bounds of the scientific spirit. We cannot confirm or disconfirm a proposition until it has been formulated, and the first draft of any such formulation almost invariably finds its expression in the classical mode. A great deal of careful empiricism, and a considerable amount of conceptual integration of such facts have been done by observant, experienced, sophisticated scholars from Thucydides through Carr, Wolfers, Claude, and Morgenthau. While these scholars have actually "pinned down" very little in the way of verified generalizations, they have brought shreds of partial evidence together, have developed conceptual schemes of some elegance and clarity, and have raised an impressive array of important questions. No responsible scientist would throw away that fund of wisdom and insist on beginning all over again, *tabula rasa*.

Let me try to illustrate the continuity of the prescientific and the scientific approaches by brief reference to a study of my own. In close collaboration with a diplomatic historian, I have begun a systematic inquiry into those events and conditions which most frequently coincided with the outbreak of interstate war during the period 1815–1945. Beginning with a survey of the traditional literature, we gradually assembled a number of propositions which seem to be: (a) widely accepted by historians and political scientists; (b) quite plausible on their face; and (c) generally borne out by the illustrations which their proponents have selected. By converting the traditional insights into operational language and gathering data on all relevant cases, we have already begun to find evidence which supports certain propositions, casts serious doubt on others, and leads to the revision of still others. . . . [Here Singer discusses findings from the Correlates of War project. See selections 32–33.]

I think that even this small sample of only one project's results should suffice for the nonce to illustrate the value of combining the traditional and the scientific approaches. There are, of course, a few people who will look at the results of this and similar research and tell us that they "knew it all along." My retort is of two kinds. First, and rhetorically, if the traditionalists knew this, that, or the other thing all along, how come so many of them "knew" exactly the opposite at the same time? More seriously, such a response to data-based findings reveals an alarming insensitivity to the crucial distinction between subjective belief and verifiable knowledge. Again, we are not likely to do much interesting research unless we have, and act upon, our hunches and insights, but we will never build much of a theory, no matter how high and wide we stack our *beliefs*. Conversely, a few strategically selected empirical studies can produce the evidence necessary to complete an existing theoretical edifice. It is also essential to remember that we made as many important discoveries by the incremental accumulation of modest, limited studies, many of which may seem trivial by themselves, as we do by attacking the big questions directly and all at once. Unfortunately, very few scholars make even a single great discovery in their lifetimes, regardless of discipline, but all competent research *contributes*, directly or indirectly, to those great discoveries.

The Triumph of Trivia

The third deadly sin is that our work has been, and will continue to be, restricted to peripheral and to insignificant subjects. This weakness is due, we are given to understand, not to the traditional neglect of scientific method, but to the "characteristics inherent in the subject matter." Among those factors which make our prospects "very bleak indeed" are: the unmanageable number of variables of which any generalization must take account; the difficulty of controlled experiment; the transitory and elusive nature of our material; and the extent to which our research affects the empirical world, such that "even our most innocent ideas contribute to their own verification and falsification."

As to the large number of variables, three points are worth noting. First, modern analytical tools permit us to work with as many independent and intervening variables as we care to when seeking to account for the frequency of any particular type of outcome. Second, we can always reduce this number by combining those variables which *seem* to be conceptually similar, and more to the point, we can then ascertain—via such techniques as factor analysis—the extent to which they actually are highly similar; if a dozen variables all show an extremely high covariation, we can either drop eleven of them for the moment or use them all to create a single combined variable. Third, and most important, we often start out with a large number of variables because our theory is relatively weak, but once the data are in on a sufficiently large number of cases, we can proceed to analyze them in a search for correlational patterns or causal linkages. Beginning with fairly standard bivariate techniques, we can ascertain: whether there is any statistical relationship between the observed outcome and each alleged predictor, such that it could not have occurred by sheer chance; whether that relationship is linear or more complicated; and most important, which predictor (independent variable) accounts for most of the variance, and is therefore most potent in influencing the observed result. Somewhat more complex are those techniques which permit us to combine a number of independent and intervening variables in a wide variety of ways in order to determine which ones in which pattern or sequence covary most strongly with the observed outcome, and therefore constitute the most powerful determinants. . . .

Regarding the difficulty of catching and categorizing our material, the evidence is beginning to mount that it may not be all that elusive. Many of us in comparative, as well as international, politics have begun to enjoy some fair success in observing, measuring, and recording much of the phenomena which, according to the traditionalists, would always be beyond the scientific reach, available only to the practised eye and sophisticated antennae of scholarly wisdom. If they could stop persuading themselves how "impossible" certain things are and how "intangible" the important variables are, and merely look at the literature, they would discover that the pessimism was probably unwarranted; of course, it is one thing to think that one has developed a measure of certain national or global attributes, or relationships, or behavioral events, but quite another to demonstrate that the measure is not only reliable, but valid. A measure is described as *reliable* if it is used by different observers at the same time, or the same observer at different times, and it always produces essentially the same score when applied to the same state of affairs; among familiar measures whose reliability is well demonstrated are the Dow-Jones stock market index, the United States Department of Commerce cost-of-living index, the gross national product of many industrial societies, and the periodic Gallup survey on how well the United States' President is "doing his job." To achieve that sort of acceptance and the opportunity to demonstrate its continuing reliability, a measure must embody a theoretical concept which seems important and do it in a fashion which is not only operational but persuasive. In the next several years, we may well find a few measures around which such a consensus has developed.

But reliability is far and away the simpler of the two demands one must make of a quantitative index; more difficult to satisfy and to evaluate is the demand of validity. An indicator is *valid* to the extent that it actually does measure the phenomena it is alleged to measure. There is, for example, the recent controversy over whether certain "intelligence tests" used in the United States really measure intelligence as it is generally defined and conceptualized in psychology or whether it measures achievement, or social class, or parents' educational level. The same challenges can be addressed to Galtung's measure of social position, Hart's measure of technological advancement, the Rummel and Tanter measures of foreign conflict, or the Singer and Small measures of lateral mobility, alliance aggregation, bipolarity, diplomatic status, or magnitude of war. The trouble with validity is that we never really pin it down in any final fashion. A measure may seem intuitively reasonable (and we therefore say it has "face validity"), or it may predict consistently to another variable in accord with our theory, or it may covary consistently with an "independent" measure of the same concept. None of these is really conclusive evidence of a measure's validity, but all help to make it a useful and widely accepted indicator; whereas reliability is strictly a methodological attribute, validity falls precisely at the juncture of theory and method.

The Model Is Not for Marrying

Turning to the fourth of our intellectual vices, I find some possible grounds for convergence, as well as collision, with our critic. Here we are reminded of all the things that can be—and in our field, often are—wrong with models. On the convergence side, let me readily admit that many of those we find are indeed lacking in internal rigor and consistency, often constitute little more than an intellectual exercise, and do occasionally bootleg some invisible assumptions. . . .

Models, paradigms, and conceptual schemes are merely intellectual tools by which we order and codify that which would otherwise remain a buzzing welter. Some bring us clarity and others only add to our confusion, but no matter what we call them, each of us uses abstractions to give meaning—or the illusion of meaning—to that which our senses detect. . . . Even though we must (and do) strive for the truest representation, we can never be certain that we have found it. Thus, it is as legitimate to ask whether our models are useful as it is to ask if they are true; the physical and biological sciences, for example, advanced rather nicely with tentative models that were more useful than true. In sum, I concur that our models leave much to be desired, and that they would probably be more useful were they designed to be more representational, but insist that the promising path here is to build them around concepts that are more operational, rather than more familiar, and to discard them when more accurate or more useful ones come along.

By Gauge or by Guess

Our fifth alleged flaw is the "fetish for measurement". . . . We are arraigned here on three subsidiary counts. First, we tend to "ignore relevant differences between the phenomena that are being counted." This is partly an empirical question and partly an epistemological one; in due course the various measurement efforts will show us where we have erred in lumping the unlumpable. But it seems to me that this undue preoccupation, yea obsession, with the unique, the discrete, the non-comparable, is what has largely kept history from developing into a cumulative discipline, and has led to so much frivolous debate between the quantifiers and the antiquantifiers in sociology, psychology, economics, and political science. The fact is that no two events, conditions, or relationships are ever exactly alike; they must always differ in *some* regard, even if it is only in time-space location. The question is whether they are sufficiently similar to permit comparison and combination for the theoretical purposes at hand. To borrow a metaphor of which the antiquantifiers are quite fond, there is absolutely nothing wrong with adding apples and oranges if fruit is the subject at hand! And if we want to generalize at a more restricted level, we had better distinguish not only between apples and oranges, but between McIntosh and Golden Delicious as well. If we cannot combine and aggregate, with due attention to the matter of relevant differences, we cannot make empirical generalizations; and in the absence of such generalizations, we may generate a great deal of speculation, but blessed little theory.

The second allegation here is that we attach more significance to a quantitative indicator or a statistical regularity than it deserves. This, too, is primarily an empirical question, and if we can discover that a common enemy unifies a nation only under certain limited conditions, that the percentage of national product going to foreign trade decreases rather than increases as productivity rises, that domestic conditions correlate with a nation's foreign policy only under special conditions, that estimates of relative military power become distorted as diplomatic tension rises, or that nations are more war-prone when their status is falling rather than rising, we must conclude that the quantifying exercises were useful. Once more, there is something to the charge, and, as suggested above, we must be careful not to equate reliability and plausibility with validity in our measures. . . .

A final point here is Bull's willingness to take seriously only those quantitative results which "confirm some intuitive impression." Here again is the old faith in the folklore and conventional wisdom of a particular time and place. When rigorous methods produce results which are intuitively reasonable, we should not only find this reassuring, but should be careful to avoid pointing out that we "knew it all along." As I suggested above, it would be most instructive to go through our scholarly literature and see how often we have known one thing all along in one section or chapter and something quite different in the following section or chapter. The fact is, we seldom even know what we know, because our assertions are usually made in regard to a small and highly selective sample of cases and in an extremely limited context.

No Monopoly on Precision

The sixth item in Bull's "propositional inventory" is his allegation that the practitioners of the classical approach are as likely to be precise, coherent, and orderly as are members of the scientific school. He reminds us that in the past many classicists (especially the international lawyers) have indeed shown real conceptual rigor, and that the self-styled scientists have often failed in this regard. The claim is all too true, but beside the point. First, the ratio of high-to-low verbal and conceptual precision in the literature of the two schools would certainly not be flattering to those on the classicist side. When social scientists do historical work, we set up our coding rules and then examine *all* the cases which qualify; there is much less of a tendency to ransack history in search of those isolated cases which satisfy one's theoretical or rhetorical requirements of the moment. We need only glance through both sets of literature for tentative but striking evidence of this difference. Closely related, and perhaps an inevitable corollary of this difference, is the fact that when most traditionalists do a serious historical analysis, it takes the form of a case study, whereas the scientist knows that: (a) one can never describe all the variables relevant to a given case, and (b) that what happened only once before is not much of a guide to what will happen in the future. Thus, we tend to select a *few* variables on (please note) intuitive grounds or on the basis of prior research findings, and then examine their interrelationship over *many* historical cases.

Second, and in addition to specific procedures, the scientific researcher usually has an intellectual style that substantially increases the probability of better performance in this regard. Even when we deal with a variable that need not be operationalized in the study at hand, we tend to ask how it *could* be so refined and clarified. Once in the habit of thinking operationally, it is difficult to settle for constructs and propositions that are not—or could not be translated into—"machine readable" form. As the traditionally trained scholar moves further in this direction, and looks at propositions as interesting problems to be investigated or hypotheses to be tested—rather than as the revealed truth—the gap will begin to close. But vague and fuzzy notions cannot be put to the test, and whatever respect for precision there is in the classical tradition will have to be resurrected and mobilized.

The Rootless Wanderers

Our seventh deadly sin is that we have often cut ourselves off from history and philosophy, with certain dire consequences, among which is the loss of some basis for stringent self-criticism. I take the charge to mean that it is from those two intellectual *disciplines*—rather than the phenomena they study—that the severance has occurred. . . . The fact is, unhappily, that the charge of our being ahistorical is far from unfounded, and an appreciable fraction of the modernists do indeed restrict themselves to the study of only the most recent past or the more trivial problems, and largely for the reason implied in Bull's earlier point: because the data are more available or the cases are more amenable to our methods. But this criticism applies equally to the more traditional scholars. . . .

As to our philosophical rootlessness, the picture seems to be more mixed, with the modernists quite alert to the epistemological concerns of philosophy but often indifferent to its normative concerns. For example, the traditionalists seem much more willing than the modernists to speak out on matters of public policy, with the latter often hiding behind the argument that our knowledge is still much too inadequate, or that we should not use our status as "experts" to exercise more political influence than other citizens. . . .

The more ethical position, it seems to me, is to recognize that individual responsibility cannot be put on the shelf until we are absolutely certain of our political perceptions and predictions. First, most social events will always retain an element of the probabilistic, . . . Second, if we withhold expression of our judgments until our science is more fully developed, we run a fairly high risk that so many errors in judgment will have been made that the situations we face then will be even less tractable than those of the present, . . .

. . . As retarded as our discipline may be, we have as great a right and responsibility to take public stands in our area of special competence as the engineer, medical researcher, lobbyist, sales manager, planner, or land speculator have in theirs. In my view, knowledge is meant to energize, not paralyze. . . .

Returning to the original charge, my other reason for hoping that he refers not to the substance, but the style, of history and philosophy is that we probably have little more to learn from them in terms of method or concept. At the risk of alienating some of my favorite colleagues, I would say that these disciplines have gone almost as far as they can go in adding to social science knowledge in any appreciable way. True, the historian can continue to pile up facts and do his case studies, but only as he borrows from the social sciences can he produce hard evidence or compelling interpretations of the past; one reason that we must heed Bull's implied advice and move into historical research is that otherwise our understanding of the past will remain in the hands of the literati, responding to one revisionist or counter-revisionist interpretation after another, as the consensus ebbs and flows. Of course, some historians are beginning to shift to the scientific mode now, but while encouraging that trend, it is up to the social scientists to meet them halfway, chronologically as well as methodologically. As to the philosophers, their discipline is too broad and diverse to permit any sweeping statements, ranging as it does from theology to philosophy of science, but logic, deduction, speculation and introspection can only carry us so far. Thus, while new formulations in philosophy (and mathematics) can be expected, the odds are that the scientist himself will continue to be his own best philosopher and theorist, as long as he looks up from his data matrix and statistical significance tables periodically, and asks "what does it all mean?" . . .

3. CONCLUSION

My thesis should now be quite clear, but in the unlikely event that my touch has been too light or my rhetoric too subtle, let me reiterate it here in the baldest terms. All kinds of men contemplate and think about all kinds of problems. Some are intrigued with physical problems, ranging from biology to celestial mechanics; some are more preoccupied with social phenomena, from child development to world politics; and some are intrigued with that elusive interface at which the physical and the social domains appear to meet, whether in psychophysiology or human ecology. When men first began to think about any of these problems, they had little to go on. There was not much in the way of recorded experiences, philosophical schemes, tools of observation, or techniques of measurement. Over the centuries, however, some knowledge began to accumulate; witch doctors, court astrologers, and theologians all contributed—even in their errors—to the growth in understanding of the world around us. Philosophical schemes and cosmologies, inclined planes and brass instruments, psychoanalysis and mathematical statistics all tended to further the increase in knowledge. In some fields of inquiry, progress was quite rapid. In others, due to social taboos as well as the inherent complexity of the phenomena, things did not move quite as well. Thus, long after Lavoisier had demonstrated the fallaciousness of the phlogiston theory, and the systematic observations of Galileo and Brahe had discredited the Ptolemaic conception of astronomy, students of social phenomena—relying on authority rather than evidence—continued to accept notions that were equally inaccurate.

Where do we stand now? In some of the social sciences, progress has been steady and impressive; in others, it has been more halting. It would seem that those disciplines which are most advanced are precisely those in which imagination and insight have been combined with—not divorced from—rigor and precision. In each of these, one finds that the early work, no matter how creative, remained largely speculative, with several theoretical schemes—often equally plausible—contending for position. Until systematic observation, operationally derived evidence, and replicable analytical procedures were introduced, skillful rhetoric and academic gamesmanship often carried the day. Thus, in sociology, Comte and Spencer played a key role in the transition from speculation to measurement; Hume and Smith come to mind as those who represent the convergence of theoretical insight and systematic quantification in economics; and in psychology, one might select Wundt and Titchener as the scholars who bridged the gap between the preoperational and the operational. At the other pole, such social science disciplines as anthropology and psychiatry remain largely impressionistic—but far from nonempirical—in their evidence, and thus unimpressive in their theory.

We in political science stand very much at the threshold. In certain subfields, operational measurement and the quantitative evidence which result are more or less taken for granted now; opinion surveys, voting studies, and roll-call analyses are, except in the intellectual backwaters, seen as necessary—but not sufficient—ingredients in the growth of political theory. But in international politics, there are still those few who raise the same old spectres, rattle the same old skeletons, and flog the same old horses. They sometimes tell us that Thucydides or Machiavelli or Mahan knew all there was to know and at other times they tell us that the subject matter is intrinsically unknowable. Perhaps the best answer to both assertions is to "look at the record"; a decade ago there was little published scientific research beyond the pioneering work of Quincy Wright's *Study of War* and Lewis Richardson's scattered articles. Five years ago, a handful of us were getting underway and perhaps a dozen or so data-based papers had appeared. In mid-1967, I find . . . in the English language journals almost 100 articles that bring hard evidence to bear on theoretically significant questions, and more than a dozen books. Whether the traditionalists will find these persuasive—or as Bull recognizes, whether they will even read them—is uncertain. The quality is clearly uneven, the theoretical relevance is mixed, the methodological sophistication ranges from naïve to fantastic, the policy payoffs seem to differ enormously, and the craftsmanship runs from slovenly to compulsive, but the work is already beginning to add up. . . .

My point, then, is that there is no longer much doubt that we can make the study of international politics (or better still, world politics) into a scientific discipline worthy of the name. But it requires the devotees of both warring camps to come together in collaboration if not in sublime unity. We on the scientific side have little ground for exultation. Whatever progress we have already made is due in large measure to the wisdom, insight, and creativity of those from whom we have learned. What is more, the war would not be over if the traditionalists had waited for us to meet them half way. It is a tribute to the classical tradition, in which many of us were of course reared, that its heritage is rich and strong enough to permit the sort of growth and development which now is well along. All that remains is for those in the scientific camp to shift from the digital to the analog computer and recognize that every serious scholar's work is on the same continuum. If we modernists can master the substantive, normative, and judgmental end of it as well as the traditionalists are mastering the concepts and methods at our end, convergence will be complete, and the "war" will not have been in vain.

14. The Third Debate: On the Prospects of International Theory in a Post-Positivist Era

YOSEF LAPID

"The search for a better theory forms the third debate . . . [It] is potentially the richest, most promising and exciting that we have ever had in international relations."

MICHAEL BANKS (1986:17)

Excursions into metatheory are notoriously controversial in the social sciences. One finds, on the one hand, the conviction that such concerns "are too important to be taken for granted and too much a part of our ongoing research enterprises to be left to philosophers to think about." Furthermore, "Those who try to ignore philosophy only succeed in reinventing it." One finds, on the other hand, a prescription for a rigorous philosophy-avoidance strategy for the practicing social scientist. Especially in the early stages of theorizing, so this argument goes, misplaced pursuits of epistemology and philosophy of science are bound to be inconclusive and are likely to come at the expense of actual research.

Be that as it may, it is hardly disputable that the demise of the empiricist-positivist promise for a cumulative behavioral science recently has forced scholars from nearly all the social

From *International Studies Quarterly* (1989) 33, 235–251. © 1989 International Studies Association. Reprinted by permission of ISA and the author. Most footnotes and citations, including those for direct quotations, have been suppressed.

disciplines to reexamine the ontological, epistemological, and axiological foundations of their scientific endeavors. As a result, the human sciences are currently undergoing an acute bout of self-doubt and heightened metatheoretical ferment. Indeed, some of the most highly prized premises of Western academic discourse concerning the nature of our social knowledge, its acquisition, and its utility—including shibboleths such as "truth," "rationality," "objectivity," "reality," and "consensus"—have come under renewed critical reflection. . . .

As we shall see shortly, this far-reaching and still evolving intellectual transition in the philosophical and social disciplines has left its mark on international relations scholarship. Following the "idealism versus realism" schism of the 1920s and 1930s, and transcending the more recent "history versus science" exchange of the 1950s and 1960s, in the late 1980s the discipline stands in the midst of a third discipline-defining debate. It is noteworthy that in terms of methodological and theoretical innovations the field of international relations was and still is "an absorber and importer, not a producer in its own right." Hence, *prima facie*, there are reasons to suspect that just as the "second debate"—the "history versus science" controversy—was wedded to the ascendance of positivism in Western social science, so is the "third debate" linked, historically and intellectually, to the confluence of diverse anti-positivistic philosophical and sociological trends.

Submitting that the third debate in international relations theory parallels the intellectual ferment that other social sciences are presently undergoing and that this debate constitutes a diffuse and still maturing disciplinary effort to reassess theoretical options in a "post-positivist" era, this essay explores the debate's etiology and assesses its implications for current and future prospects for theoretical growth. . . .

THE THIRD DEBATE: DISARRAY OR THEORETICAL RESTRUCTURING?

Few observers would seriously contest the suggestion that the field of international studies has experienced in recent years sustained theoretical effervescence. But beyond a vague uneasiness over the fact that no reduction seems to be obtaining in the diversity of conceptualizations and higher-order theories, one looks in vain for a more specific consensus on the current state and future direction of the discipline. . . . we find at the pessimistic end of the spectrum scholars who are either reluctant or unable to detect a coherent pattern in the rampant theoretical speculation. Such observers deplore the dazing pace with which new ideas are superficially introduced into international relations theory, only to be discarded subsequently with inexplicable urgency. They seem thoroughly confused by the "amount of debris on the battlefield of international relations theory" and feel understandably frustrated at facing this vast intellectual disarray "with few guides on making choices." Hence, they conclude that "in both theory and practice international politics can bring on despair. This is an occupational hazard in the field for which there is no remedy."

Others, to be sure, would strongly disagree with such a gloomy reading. They would counter that the lively chorus of contending theoretical voices in the field of international

relations constitutes a "dialogue" or a "debate" with the power to transform the international relations discipline. Yet even among this group there is conspicuously little agreement about who is debating whom, along what lines of contention, and with what prospects of success. . . . But . . . it is imperative to highlight some notable commonalities among those who do acknowledge a coherent and consequential pattern in the current intellectual cacophony in the international relations field. For at a minimum one finds, for example, a shared recognition that the third debate marks a clear end to the positivist epistemological consensus that was hardly shaken in the course of the "history versus science" controversy. Whereas the second debate was preoccupied with quarrels over methodology narrowly defined, the third debate is typically expected to facilitate trailblazing ideas about the nature and progression of knowledge in the international relations field. One also finds a shared appreciation that theory in this field is "in the process of being restructured," a restructuring which is recognized moreover as being "linked directly to a similar set of debates occurring in contemporary social and political theory."

THE THIRD DEBATE: A POST-POSITIVIST PROFILE

Especially when compared with the simplistic coherence of the positivist philosophical movement, post-positivism is not a unitary philosophical platform. It presents itself as a rather loosely patched-up umbrella for a confusing array of only remotely related philosophical articulations. Hence, if one wishes to refer meaningfully to post-positivism as an alternative philosophical position—perhaps ushering in a new era in international relations theory—one first must identify some areas of convergence in the general ideas presented by this "new philosophy of science."

A detailed analysis of such convergent post-positivist views is, however, well beyond the scope of this paper. I will deliberately restrict my attention to three themes which seem to have been particularly influential in determining the tone, agenda, and mood of the current debate in international relaposttions theory. These themes—the preoccupation with meta-scientific units (paradigmatism), the concern with underlying premises and assumptions (perspectivism), and the drift towards methodological pluralism (relativism)—are, of course, interrelated. They will, however, be treated separately here to elucidate more clearly their distinct impact on the current theoretical debate.

The Concern with Meta-Scientific Units (Paradigmatism)

Post-positivism has wrought a notable change in the understanding and choice of proper units of analysis in the study of scientific development. In sharp contrast to the positivist choice of the empirically corroborated law or generalization as the fundamental unit of scientific achievement, the new philosophy of science insists that only relatively long-lived, large-scale, and multi-tiered constructs—such as "paradigms," "research-programmes," "research traditions," "super-theories," "global theories," and "weltanschauungen"—should qualify as basic knowledge-producing, knowiedge-accumulating, and knowledge-conserving units. For theories do not come to us separately; hence they should not be handled as self-contained entities.

Above all, the new philosophical posture portrays scientific knowledge as a triadic complex consisting of 1) a "phenomenic" axis covering the empirical content of scientific theories; 2) an "analytic" axis covering hypotheses, explanations, and theoretical models; and 3) a "thematic" axis covering reality-defining assumptions, epistemological premises, and other types of distinctly "ideological" or "metaphysical" ingredients. The novelty of this underlying post-positivist project—postulating an irreducibly three-dimensional space for scientific knowledge—is the explicit negation of the cardinal positivist premise which affirms the "eliminability of the human" and places (or replaces) the scientist

"at the center of the social-intellectual-ethical complex known as science."

Paradigmatism thus asserts that meta-scientific constructs come and go in complete packages. It follows that only broader conjunctures of interrelated theories, including their unstated premises and underlying assumptions, can qualify as proper units of development and appraisal in science. It follows, furthermore, that empirical evidence in the usual sense of registering "objectively" what one sees is of only limited utility in scientific evaluative appraisal. For in sharp contrast with the phenomenic axis, the thematic axis—although challengeable perhaps in some other way—is not refutable by direct empirical observation. This partially explains why science is not "one great totalitarian engine taking everyone relentlessly to the same inevitable goal." At the same time it also raises the challenge of formulating alternative, "rational" criteria of evaluative appraisal which acknowledge and confront rather than deny or ignore the non-empirical nature of at least one integral component of all scientific knowledge.

Returning to our principal concern with international relations theory, I submit that "paradigmatism"—in the specific sense of an enhanced post-positivist concern with meta-scientific constructs which incorporate integral thematic components as a precondition of scientific intelligibility—presents itself as one of the most notable characteristics of the third debate. For even a cursory glance at the literature reveals that studies involving bivariate and multivariate relations, which flourished throughout the 1960s and early 1970s, now are held in general disrepute. The intellectual exchange is no longer between individual scholars or isolated theories, but between "models," "paradigms," "research programs" and "research traditions," or "discourses." The chosen unit differs in accordance with respective preferences for Kuhnian (1962), Lakatosian (1970), Laudanian (1984), or other more fashionably "post-modernist" constructs. But we find in each case a remarkable concurrence with the underlying tenet which postulates that significant theoretical modifications and choices must always take into account the supportive meta-scientific domains in which they are holistically embedded.

It is in this general context, I suggest, that one can best understand the marked popularity of countless efforts to recast the fragmented theoretical turnout of the international relations field in terms of contending meta-theoretical constructs. There is also the related propensity to go beyond simple shopping lists of would-be paradigms or perspectives by launching more ambitious projects of paradigm demolition, paradigm synthesis or paradigm proliferation. And, arguably, such is the logic that also informs, for instance, Kratochwil and Ruggie's (1986) choice of the historically evolving "research program" (international organization) over the isolated theory (regimes) as their prime unit of evaluative appraisal.

The common denominator of these endeavors is the implicit belief that the substitution of new meta-theoretical constructs for more traditional units of scientific appraisal is somehow essential to locating and stimulating genuine theoretical growth. Fortunately—as indicated by the tendency to up-grade theoretical revisions to would-be "paradigm clashes" or putative "progressive" or "degenerative problem-shifts"—the impact of paradigmatism on current theoretical preoccupations in the international relations field has started penetrating well beyond a technical recasting of its fragmented theoretical corpus into revamped and more fashionably holistic blueprints. New questions are being raised about the dynamics of emergence, persistence, and the decline of meta-theoretical constructs in the field. The extent to which contending paradigms are truly "incommensurable"—incompatible and even incommunicable with one another—is more seriously examined. And the potential for fruitful dialogue between or syntheses of contending paradigmatic approaches is more systematically explored.

Most important, in this process of expanding paradigmatism the third debate has progressively taken the format of "a discourse about the choice of analytic frameworks." In this more sophisticated sense paradigmatism focuses on the difficult task of formulating and applying valid—as opposed to invalid—evaluative procedures at the paradigmatic level. Needless to say, for the time being these promising developments have expressed themselves mainly in a far greater sensitivity to, rather than the actual resolution of, new and hereto ignored sets of meta-theoretical problems. But given this, it is still possible to summarize by reiterating the remarkable role played by the post-positivist reformulation of the unit of scientific appraisal in determining the specifically "inter-paradigmatic" profile of the current debate in international relations theory. This I submit differentiates in a fundamental rather than a faddish way the current controversy from its two predecessors in the field.

The Focus on Premises and Assumptions: Perspectivism

In addition to the reformulation of the unit of scientific achievement, post-positivism also invokes a deliberate shift to the thematic level of underlying ontological, epistemological, and axiological premises and assumptions. Such a refocusing is considered necessary in view of the remarkable willingness of both natural and social scientists to disregard empirical data that appear to contradict theories that (for them) have reached thematic status. Sometimes, therefore, impasses in the growth of knowledge may be created and reproduced less by observational mistakes (in the phenomenic axis) or by narrowly defined theoretical flaws (in the analytic axis) than by generalized crises of basic presuppositions (the thematic axis).

Once a set of guiding assumptions is elevated to thematic status, the perspectivist argument suggests, it becomes highly resistant to both evidence and logical criticism. And occasionally, under the fiat of premises that endure in the face of all negative tests, the entire process of theorizing may be forced to proceed along unacceptably restrictive or misleading lines. . . .

Highlighting assumptions as an important source of our scientific ignorance is different, however, from submitting that they always serve to distort theoretical inquiry. To the contrary, *similar* sets of assumptions invariably serve as enabling sources of valid scientific knowledge. Perspectivism submits, in short, that we are encapsulated in sets of presuppositions which may hinder *or* facilitate theoretical growth. And if guiding assumptions are the source of both our ignorance and our knowledge, it follows that "the focal point of challenge in science should become our weltanschauungen."

It should not be difficult to establish that the current debate in international relations theory also is characterized by a shift of attention toward the domain of thematic premises and assumptions. This refocusing expresses itself in a manifest eagerness of international relations scholars, from even radically opposed theoretical camps, to leave the phenomenic and analytic planes in order to devote more energetic attention to the "hidden" domain of key underlying assumptions. Perspectivism is implicit, for instance, in insights concerning the "inescapability of theory" and in ensuing concerns with becoming "the prisoner of unstated assumptions." It is manifest also in a more explicit sensitivity to the need "to become clearly aware of the perspective which gives rise to theorizing."

To be sure, the perspectivist accent is most audible among a small but vocal group of "post-positivist," "post-structuralist," and "post-modernist" critics of mainstream international relations theory. As indicated by Richard Ashley's recent work, these "rebels" utilize "deconstructive" and "genealogical" tools deliberately designed to automatically "target" assumptive theoretical headquarters. These intellectual technologies postulate that meaning and understanding are not intrinsic to the world but, on the contrary, are continuously constructed, defended, and challenged. Their main purpose is to "problemize" answers, make "strange" what has become familiar, and reverse the process of construction in order to reveal how problematic are the taken-for-granted structures ("anarchy" for instance) of our social and political world.

The growing fascination with the thematic component of our current knowledge of world politics is by no means restricted to an elite vanguard of post-modernist rebels. Robert Jervis (1988) has recently demonstrated that modernists can be quite effective—and, of course, far more accessible than their post-modernist colleagues—in exposing major assumptive traps in current theory. . . .

Although it is possible to argue that the preoccupation with underlying assumptions is anything but new to international relations theory, my point is that this preoccupation has acquired new significance in the context of the third debate. Perspectivism, as defined in this study, denotes something more fundamental than a ritualistic insistence that "we must examine our assumptions about the behavior of the actors in international arenas more carefully." It refers to more than "a rejection of empiricism in favor of a theoretical approach that accepts the place of data in a subordinate position." On the basis of these brief illustrations, it seems reasonable to conclude that perspectivism in the sense of a strong post-positivist focus on thematic premises and assumptions has been internalized as a foremost characteristic of the third debate in international relations theory.

The Drift Toward Methodological Pluralism: Relativism

"The current fierce attack on science, objectivity, truth, and even rationality and logic," says J.O. Wisdom, "may well be the fiercest ever mounted in history (1987:159;). The new epistemology associated with Fleck, Polanyi, Kuhn, Feyerabend and others is, indeed, often attacked as having extremely relativistic implications. This new relativism is far more radical than previous versions because it is "second order," that is, "it questions not individual assertions for their lack of evidence but the implied and embedded standards, criteria, norms and principles that *make judgments possible and give them privileged status*" (D'Amico,

1986:139; my emphasis). By undermining objectivity and truth, this relativization of philosophical thinking has greatly complicated the task of providing effective legitimation of knowledge and has rendered problematic the demarcation of science from non-science.

The massive move toward relativism has had at least three noteworthy ramifications. First, all versions of *methodological monism* seeking to institutionalize standardized, explicit, and unchanging criteria for regulating scientific domains—including the positivist conception of the scientific method—have been rendered suspect by this new intellectual climate. Far from consenting that epistemic criteria are destined to remain essentially unchanged over time and place, the new epistemology unapologetically suggests that it is itself socially mutable and historically contingent. And, following methodologically from such epistemological relativism, "a vigorous pluralism is called for. When it comes to theoretical ideas 'let the hundred flowers bloom'."

Second, the growing recognition of a multitude of potentially fruitful research strategies also has facilitated a better understanding of science as a polymorphic as opposed to monolithic entity. As the end product of scientific activity, social knowledge is now more typically seen as a complex of equally privileged but only loosely integratable forms. . . .

Finally, the post-positivist endorsement of epistemological and methodological diversity has undermined the classic fascination with scientific consensus, resulting in "a new-wave preoccupation with scientific dissensus." This intriguing eclipse of consensus as a prime desideratum in social science is of primary importance, for it signals a collapse of the highly influential Kuhnian equation of an inability to achieve paradigmatic consensus with an inability to achieve significant theoretical growth.

Returning to our main focus of interest, we note that the post-positivist bent toward relativism and its ensuing methodological ramifications have clearly influenced the tone and substance of the third debate in international relations theory. It is hardly accidental, for instance, that despite high emotional and intellectual stakes, the current controversy has not been characterized by the focused intransigence that marked the two previous debates. In tune with the post-positivist "plea for tolerance in matters theoretical," scholars have resisted the temptation to seize upon the current intellectual transition as an opportunity to impose a new set of exclusive epistemological principles and prescriptions.

Reflecting a deepening suspicion of methodological monism, even scholars who are otherwise sympathetic to positivist orthodoxy now feel obliged to concede the dangers of "monolithic dogmatism." The discipline as a whole now seems favorably disposed to consider alternative epistemologies "rather than replacement of one kind of science by another." . . .

Finally, it was perhaps inevitable that the expanding acceptance of a polymorphic image of science and the growing popularity of methodological pluralism also would lead to a reexamination of scientific dissensus and its relationship to scientific progress. As a result, the search for "un-Kuhnian" versions of progress is already well underway in international relations theory. Irrespective of other disagreements concerning the theoretical prospects of the field, one now finds considerable consensus that "the way forward for [international relations theory] that finds itself in difficulties is not to pursue 'normalcy' of the Kuhnian kind but to work towards a diversity of strong paradigms."

THE GROUNDS FOR POST-POSITIVIST OPTIMISM

Granted that some post-positivist messages have been trickling down from the new philosophy of science, why should these tenets translate into greater optimism about the prospects of international relations theory? On what basis and in what sense can one posit that the third debate "provides stimulus, hope, and even excitement in the demanding business of analyzing international relations"? (Banks, 1985:20). What are the new promises of international relations theory from a post-positivist standpoint, and what is the post-positivist substitute for the embattled and rapidly fading El Dorado of positivist science?

In seeking an answer to this question it will be useful to take a second look at the three post-positivist themes that surfaced in our previous discussion. Closer scrutiny suggests that, under certain conditions, each of them can provide fertile ground for rejuvenated theoretical optimism. To begin, the preoccupation with meta-scientific constructs provides an attractive substitute for the positivist choice of the empirically corroborated law or generalization as the fundamental unit of scientific achievement. For despite many valiant efforts, scholars were ultimately forced to concede the manifest absence of cumulative progress defined in the rigorous terms of the empiricist-positivist scientific blueprint.

Provided that one is willing to live with charitable definitions of "paradigms" or "research programs," it is possible to document a rather impressive record of actual and forthcoming theoretical growth in international relations theory. . . . And if the popularity of Lakatos's methodology continues to rise among theorists, one may safely anticipate that we will soon have as many, if not more, correspondingly reconstructed "research programs." . . .

The belief that social scientists are invariably better equipped to cut through assumptive as opposed to empirical impasses is perhaps overly optimistic. By pointing, nonetheless, to the nonempirical sphere of thematic premises and pre-suppositions, perspectivism has facilitated a relative "liberation of theory from observation." And this liberation was destined to be interpreted by at least some scholars as a good reason for renewed hopefulness. "Having passed through a phase in which facts have dominated theory," one of them notes approvingly, "the logic of our scholarship is carrying us into a phase in which theory dominates facts" (Banks, 1986:9).

This takes us directly to perhaps the richest mine of optimism embedded in the post-positivist credos of the third debate. Like other social scientists, international relations theorists

can derive renewed confidence in their scientific credentials from the post-positivist move toward relativism and methodological pluralism. For the positivist scientific promise was arrogant and brutal in its simplicity: "This is the model of a scientific enterprise, take it or leave it."

For too long the tragedy of international relations scholars was, of course, that they proved incapable of either fruitfully adopting or decisively rejecting the grail of positivist science. Via positivism the discipline became locked in a sterile and frustrating worshipful relationship to the natural sciences. Presently emerging from this self-imposed positivist trap, many scholars are favorably impressed by the new latitude of maneuver offered by a multitude of post-positivist idioms of enquiry. And although notably lacking the exclusive luster of the positivist "mantle of science," the post-positivist counterpart—or counterparts—are far more accommodating in their acknowledged posture of tolerance and humility.

The endorsement of methodological pluralism, the emergence of a polymorphic image of science, and the reassuring notion that in the social sciences even permanent dissensus is not a scientific disaster have neutralized the once intimidating bite of the positivist "anti-scientific" label. Small wonder that currently issued verdicts of condemnation to "a life of intellectual pluralism" no longer carry their traditional message of scientific despair. Following a necessary period of digestion of post-positivist ideas, it is now more fashionable to posit that "much of the strength of the discipline comes from the plurality of its theoretical orientations."

Arguably it is this feeling of an exceptional "opening up" of international theory which above all sustains the hope that, by presenting unprecedented theoretical potentialities, the impact of the third debate may exceed by far the significance of the two previous ones. For some the main opportunity is to overcome U.S.-inspired nationalistic parochialism and create a "genuinely international theory applicable to all." Others seem more concerned with related problems of paradigmatic sectarianism, identifying opportunities for new and more energetic syntheses of realism and Liberalism or realism and Marxism.

Still others have identified opportunities for revamping the empiricist-positivist orthodoxy with "holistic" or "interpretive" correctives; grounding political realism and international theory in the supposedly superior principles of a "realist philosophy of science"; endorsing the epistemological foundations of critical theory as "the next stage in the development of International Relations theory"; and adopting a "post-structuralist discourse" which, we are told, "expands the agenda of social theory, posing questions that other discourses must *refuse* to ask."

Other interpretations of the precise nature of the post-positivist promise are readily available. What seems common to many of these theoretical projects is their striking ambition. In their combined effect the themes of paradigmatism, perspectivism, and relativism—in conjunction with the post-positivist plea for tolerance in matters theoretical—apparently have generated a reservoir of energy which seems to be best released by theorizing on a grandiose scale. Indeed, as Rosenau remarks, "this is not a time for nit-picking, for finding fault with rogue definitions, imprecise formulations and skewed data" (1986:850).

THE LIMITS OF POST-POSITIVIST OPTIMISM

How durable and consequential will the current season of hope be in the international relations discipline? Are we truly on the verge of a new era in international theory or is it more likely that the adrenaline rush of the third debate, like others, will have only negligible long-term implications? A definitive answer to this question would be risky and premature at this point, for we must keep in mind that the current surge of optimism is admittedly heuristic. It is, in other words, an enthusiasm of newly initiated departures rather than a sober celebration of safe arrivals. Hence prudence and fairness and the post-positivist spirit of tolerance itself demand a patient awaiting of further, more substantive, research findings.

Having acknowledged this it is nonetheless appropriate to add some observations on the hazards of excessive post-positivist optimism. In referring to possible problems and difficulties, my purpose is not to deprecate the revitalizing theoretical energy released by the third debate. It is rather to further delimit its scope in the spirit of constructive criticism. For clarity and consistency we will return, for the last time, to the three post-positivist trademarks of the third debate. Starting with "paradigmatism," one should notice in particular the danger of misappropriating this valuable post-positivist corrective for propaganda and polemical uses. Philosophers of science have long suspected, in fact, that one major reason social scientists turn to philosophy is to fabricate a more "respectable" anchor for the claim of being a "progressive science." There are reasons to suspect that such a line of reasoning may stand behind some current attempts to reconstruct the corpus of international theory in terms of "paradigms," "research programs," and other meta-scientific units of analysis.

Consider the fact that, as typically applied to the international relations field, Lakatos's methodology of scientific appraisal has consistently resulted in rather optimistic readings of both its past theoretical growth and its future prospects. . . .

But the problem goes far beyond cavalier invocations of would-be philosophical authorities. With the consolidation of international relations as a "dividing discipline," contending sets of criteria for judging scientific acceptability proliferate. Ironically, this opens up tempting opportunities for instant scientific redemption of vast bodies of theoretical literature by simple shifts of epistemic standards of appraisal. Would-be scientific contributions such as Allison's "models" of foreign policy decision-making, which might be considered unacceptable if judged by strict positivist criteria, may appear more promising if "interpretive" or "hermeneutical" standards are invoked. Without questioning the considerable merits of multiple criteria for evaluating claims, scholars in the field should beware lest they come to resemble the proverbial archer who shoots his arrow and then draws a bull's eye around it. . . . Especially if seen as a miracle drug, enthusiastic paradigmatism which makes light of the critical distinction between promising and misleading lines of inquiry at the meta-scientific level might lead us straight into new but equally damaging traps at the paradigmatic level.

A more sober look at the true merits of post-positivist perspectivism reveals at least three noteworthy risks. First, the preprogramming capacity of assumptive frameworks is often vastly exaggerated or reified. Perspectivism can play a constructive role only in so far as it acknowledges the historic and dynamic character of cognitive schemes and assumptive frameworks. Otherwise, "we lock the subject into himself unable ever to see more than he knows." This reminder seems particularly pertinent in view of the still popular rehearsals of rigid matrixes of underlying assumptions which mechanistically incapacitate realist thinking about contemporary world affairs. Seen in this simplistic manner—but *not* otherwise—perspectivism as revealed in the debate over realism may justifiably be dismissed as a source of confusion."

This takes us to a second set of hazards, namely that of embedding the fixation on guiding assumptions in a superficial understanding of the ramifications of what has been popularized by Kuhn and by Feyerabend as the "incommensurability" thesis. This in turn can result in equally damaging denials *or* exaggerations of the problem of comparison and communication between sets of thematic assumptions. Rather than defining the problem away by assuming automatic commensuration (portraying "models" as merely different "facets" of the same complex "reality"), and instead of building up the problem to "suicidal" proportions (by insisting that "genuine" paradigms "are defined by their fundamental incommensurabilities with other interpretations"), scholars interested in understanding the implications of post-positivist perspectivism for international theory must pay considerably more attention to philosophical efforts to devise new roads to commensurability.

A third danger which merits brief mention in this context lurks in the often-voiced concern that the shift of focus toward the lofty domain of guiding assumptions will come at the expense of empirical or lower level theoretical studies. Should it drift into such parasitic directions, the post-positivist "liberation of theory from data" could indeed lead us "into the dead end of metatheory" (Skocpol, 1987:12).

Finally, we will briefly examine the notorious pitfalls of post-positivist relativism. To be sure, methodological pluralism richly benefits from all the virtues of relativism. Unfortunately, it also suffers from some of its worse vices. If adopted uncritically or taken to its logical conclusion, methodological pluralism may deteriorate into a condition of epistemological anarchy under which almost any position can legitimately claim equal hearing. And to the extent that such an equality between different types of knowledge prevails, mere theoretical proliferation becomes practically indistinguishable from genuine theoretical growth.

It is hardly a secret, of course, that the international relations field is already seriously afflicted by some of the hazards of unreflective methodological pluralism. . . . The "Newton syndrome" and the seemingly universal desire to engage in grandiose theorizing have already resulted in an excessive fragmentation of the field. To borrow an apt metaphor, the field of international relations indeed "resembles nothing as much as the Learnean Hydra; each time one conceptual head is lopped off, another two appear in its place." If the relativistic excesses of methodological pluralism and fickle allegiances lead to hopeless theoretical incoherence, the optimistic message of post-positivist pluralism ironically may result in a backlash of some new dogmatic version of methodological monism.

IN LIEU OF CONCLUSION: A "PIANISSIMO" BRAVO?

Much more could be said on the promises and hazards of post-positivism in international relations theory. It is certainly useful to note that the third debate offers as many dead ends as it opens promising paths for future research. But acknowledging such hazards is not to deny that theoretical creativity may be greater today than at any time since the emergence of international relations as a distinct discipline. For we must keep in mind Isaiah Berlin's brilliant insight concerning the propensity of all great liberating ideas to turn into "suffocating straitjackets." When all angles are carefully considered, the hazards are not sufficient to seriously challenge the conclusion that the third debate has indeed generated some unparalleled theoretical potentialities. . . .

Whether these theoretical potentialities will bear fruit in the foreseeable future remains to be seen, but one thing seems reasonably clear. For many years the international relations discipline has had the dubious honor of being among the least self-reflexive of the Western social science. . . . The third debate is the beginning of a slow but progressive loss of patience with this posture of intellectual hibernation. The debate has stimulated theoretical and epistemological ferment in international relations theory, forging links with other disciplines undergoing a similar process. It has called attention to new notions of scientific objectivity, forcing a reconsideration of the role of the international relations theorist in the scientific process. It has called into question received criteria for evaluating theoretical constructs (such as empirical validity, prediction, and explanation), allowing theories to be reexamined in terms of their historical context, their ideological underpinnings, the forms of society which they foster or sustain, and the metaphors and literary tropes that inform their construction.

Although the controversy fueled by postpositivist ideas in some ways has aggravated the dangers of epistemological anarchism, it also has alerted scholars to the problem of understanding "the notion of criticism where known methods of refutation are inapplicable." Although we may be unable to disprove a "themata" or a "weltanschauung" with traditional empirical or logical methods, we may find them to be overly restrictive or impossible to

work with, as shown by Jervis's (1988) critique of the "anarchy/game theory" framework or by Kratochwill and Ruggie's rebuff of positivism in the context of regime analysis (1986:766).* . . .

In the space cleared by the weakening of deeply rooted urges for firm foundations, invariant truths, and unities of knowledge, an optimistic hope is now being planted—as hinted by the demand to make room for new "problematiques" and "to open up the field to critical approaches which have hitherto been marginalised, neglected, or dismissed by the discipline"—that, as in other social disciplines, knowledge in the field of international relations may be cumulative "not in possessing ever-more-refined answers about fixed questions but in possessing an ever-rich repertoire of questions." In this process, the discipline's level of reflexivity and its means for sustaining critical and self-conscious direction have been vitally enriched. . . .

"The task," as highlighted by the third debate, is neither the discovery of some ahistorical and universal scientific method nor the attainment of some objectively validated truth about world politics. It is rather a matter of promoting a more reflexive intellectual environment in which debate, criticism, and novelty can freely circulate. The international relations scholarly community—like all communities of inquiry—is communicatively constituted, and its success is partially conditioned by its ability to sustain and enhance the quality of argument in the context of deeply entrenched paradigmatic diversity. . . . we can agree, I hope, that the "exclusive and chloroforming world of the 1950s . . . is one to which few friends of International Relations or social science more generally would want to return" (Halliday, 1987:216). And on this minimal basis I for one am prepared to add a pianissimo "bravo" to the cheers of those already celebrating the

---

*Wisdom calls this "the enabling criterion." It asks whether a weltanschauung "can do its job or gets in the way of its own goal" (Wisdom, 1987:161).

would-be splendors of post-positivism in international relations theory.

REFERENCES

BANKS, M. (1985) Where We Are Now. *Review of International Studies* 11:215–33.

BANKS, M. (1986) The International Relations Discipline: Asset or Liability for Conflict Resolution. In *International Conflict Resolution*, edited by E. E. Azar and J. M. Burton, pp. 5–27. Boulder: Lynne Rienner Publishers.

D'AMICO, R. (1986) Going Relativist. *Telos* 67:135–45.

HALLIDAY, F. (1987) State and Society in International Relations: A Second Agenda. *Millennium* 16(2):216–29.

JERVIS, R. (1988) Realism, Game Theory, and Cooperation. *World Politics* **XL**(3):317–49.

KRATOCHWIL, F. AND J. G. RUGGIE. (1986) International Organization: A State of the Art on the Art of the State. *International Organization* 40(4):753–75.

KUHN, T. S. (1962) *The Structure of Scientific Revolution.* Chicago: University of Chicago Press.

LAKATOS I. (1970) Falsification and the Methodology of Scientific Research Programmes. In *Criticism and the Growth of Knowledge*, edited by I. Lakatos and A. Musgrave. Cambridge: Cambridge University Press.

LAUDAN, L. (1984) *Science and Values.* Berkeley: University of California Press.

ROSENAU, J. N. (1986) Before Cooperation: Hegemons, Regimes, and Habit-Driven Actors in World Politics. *International Organization* 40(4):849–94.

SKOCPOL T. (1987) The Dead End of Metatheory. *Contemporary Sociology* 16(1):10–12.

WISDOM, J. O. (1987) *Challengeability in Modern Science.* Dorset: Blackmore Press.

15. Speaking the Language of Exile: Dissident Thought in International Studies

RICHARD K. ASHLEY AND R. B. J. WALKER

You will have understood that I am speaking the language of exile. This language of the exile muffles a cry, it doesn't ever shout. . . . Our present age is one of exile. How can we avoid sinking into the mire of common sense, if not by becoming a stranger to one's own country, language, sex and identity? Writing is impossible without some kind of exile.

Exile is already in itself a form of dissidence, since it involves uprooting oneself from a family, a country or a language. More importantly, it is an irreligious act that cuts all ties, . . . including those that bind him to the belief that the thing called life has A Meaning guaranteed by the dead father.

JULIA KRISTEVA
"A New Type of Intellectual: The Dissident"

Think, if you will, of all of those familiar times and places in modern life where genres blur, narratives of knowing and doing intersect in mutually destabilizing ways, contingency threatens to displace necessity, the very identity of the subject is put in doubt, and human beings live and toil as exiles, deprived of any absolute territory of being to call home. Think, in particular, of the marginal instances of:

the working mother who must daily pass back and forth across the mutually intruding, never stable frontiers of career-life and home-life—each with its own distinctive, historically elaborated narratives of truth and meaning and each with its own gender-marked implications for what the normal subject will naturally do and therefore effortlessly be;

the draft-age youth whose identity is simultaneously claimed in national narratives of "national security" and the universalizing narratives of the "rights of man"; . . .

the alien worker, whose movement within a national territory is constrained by a national narrative of "law," but who at the same time is deprived of many of the powers and protections attending a narrative of "citizenship"; . . .

the Santiago or Los Angeles barrio-dweller who finds himself amidst the narratives of a "market" that fails to include him, the narratives of "honor" within a culture now displaced, the narratives of "education" that promise to rectify and uplift him and the narratives of "law and order" that threaten to render him a criminal object of police cudgels should education fail;

the participant in the environmental or cultural movement who subscribes to a narrative of the inescapable "interconnectedness" of dispersed locales but who, at the same time, would resist a narrative of "rationalization" that anticipates a necessary progress toward a universal and uniform order; . . .

From *International Studies Quarterly* (1990) 34, 259–266. © 1990 International Studies Association. Reprinted by permission of ISA Footnotes and most citations suppressed.

These marginal sites are no doubt very different, but beyond noticing that they are proliferating in modern global life today, we can say that they have at least four things in common. First, these sites are intrinsically ambiguous. In none of these instances can one refer to a time and place sharply bounded, a homogeneous territory in which categories are fixed, values are stable, and common sense meanings are sure. In none of these sites is there a unique and ultimate sovereign identity—be it the identity of the individual or the institutional structures of a social whole or community—to which one can appeal in fixing meanings and interpreting conduct. Here the words "I" and "we" have no certain referent. Here, exiled from the certain truths of every modern narrative of life, one can never confidently invoke an "everybody who knows" because one can never be sure just who this "everybody" is. As a result, one cannot speak as an economist might of rational individuals whose identities are given and who, in order to find their way and give meaning to their lives, need only deploy their available means to serve their self-generated interests under external constraints. One cannot speak as a moral philosopher might of the responsible human being who has a duty to ground his conduct in the transcendent principles of an ethical community. And one cannot speak as a sociologist might of social actors who habitually replicate an eternal yesterday, measure their practices by reference to a recognized norm, or project social values already inscribed in a coherent order.

Second, it follows that these marginal times and places are sites of struggle, where power is conspicuously at work. They are deterritorialized sites where people confront and must know how to resist a diversity of representational practices that would traverse them, claim their time, control their space and their bodies, impose limitations on what can be said and done, and decide their being. This is not to say that people here oppose some personified actor who, as external "enemy number one," administers power over them. Since the differences between inside and outside are here uncertain, none can be clearly defined. This is also not to say that people here resist power in the name of the life and freedom of some sovereign identity, some community of truth, some absolute and identical source of meaning that is victimized and repressed by power. In these sites, again, identity is never sure, community is always uncertain, meaning is always in doubt. Instead, people here confront arbitrary cultural practices that work to discipline ambiguity and impose effects of identity and meaning by erecting exclusionary boundaries that separate the natural and necessary domicile of certain being from the contingencies and chance events that the self must know as problems, difficulties, and dangers to be exteriorized and brought under control. Here, in other words, power is not negative and repressive but positive and productive. Practices of power do not deny the autonomy of subjects already present so much as they work to impose and fix ways of knowing and doing that shall be recognized as natural and necessary to autonomous being. They work to produce effects of presence, of identity, of a territorial ground and origin of meaning. And they work by discriminantly reading and representing ambiguous circumstances to impose differences between that which may be counted as the certainty of presence and that which must be regarded as the absence beyond its bounds.

Third, these marginal sites thus resist knowing in the sense celebrated in modern culture, where to "know" is to construct a coherent representation that excludes contesting interpretations and controls meaning from the standpoint of a sovereign subject whose word is the origin of truth beyond doubt. In modern culture, it is the male-marked figure of "man"—reasoning man who is at home and at one with the public discourse of "reasonable humanity"—who is understood to be the sovereign subject of knowledge. It is the figure of "man" who is understood to be the origin of language, the condition of all knowledge, the maker of history, and the source of truth and meaning in the world. And although in modern discourse this figure of sovereign "man" is understood to exist in opposition to an ambiguous and indeterminate history that here and now limits him, escapes his mastery, and eludes the penetration of his thought, modern discourse nonetheless invests in this figure of "man" the promise of transcendence: through reason, man may subdue history, quiet all uncertainty, clarify all ambiguity, and achieve total knowledge, total autonomy, and total power. This is the promise implicit in every claim of modern "knowledge"—a claim always uttered as if by "man" and in the name of "man." This, too, is the promise that the disciplines of modern social science make—a promise of knowledge and power on behalf of a universal sovereign figure of "man" whose voice a discipline would speak. And this, as it happens, is the same promise that legitimates the violence of the modern state—the promise, inscribed in a compact with "man," to secure and defend the "domesticated" time and space of reasoning "man" in opposition to the recalcitrant and dangerous forces of history that resist the sway of "man's" reason.

Yet it is characteristic of the marginal sites just considered that they resist knowing in this sense and, in doing so, put just this promise in doubt. They resist this modern form of knowing because here, in these local times and places, the figure of "man" is anything but an indubitable presence whose voice can be simply spoken in the representation of people's circumstances, intentions, and conduct. Any figure of "man" whose sovereign right to speak truth might here be asserted is immediately recognized as one among many arbitrary interpretations; it is seen as a knowledgeable practice of power, itself arbitrarily constructed, that is put to work to tame ambiguities, control meaning, and impose limitations on what people can do and say.

Accordingly, from the various "central" standpoints of modern culture that would speak the sovereign voice of "man," the various marginal zones of life can be cast only negatively, as a fearsome moment of abjection. To the extent that they resist the imposition of some coherent "man-centered" narrative, these sites can be understood only to signal an entropic moment, a moment that escapes "man's" rational control, a moment that spells the death of "man." They can be regarded only as moments that the modern person must endlessly defer or promise to master in the name of a life, a truth, an identity in itself. Uncertainty, indeterminancy, darkness, disorder, turbulance, irrationality, ungovernability, terror, and anarchy—these are words that modern discourse uses to mark off these marginal places and times. These words demarcate marginal places and times as voids of truth and meaning that must be feared, exiled, and, if they persist, disciplined by the violent imposition of the certain voices of truth they lack.

Fourth, while these various marginal times and places defy the control of modern forms of knowledge—while they defy stable representation from the standpoint of one or another unique figuration of sovereign "man"—it must not be thought that they can be known only thus, as "voids" yet to be brought under control of "man's" reason. When one allows that these deterritorialized zones are multiplying so that it can be said that "our present age is one of exile," it makes sense to listen to the exiles who live and move in these contested marginal zones, respecting the dissident practices they undertake. And when one listens in this way, it becomes plain that these are proliferating times and places where exciting things of uncertain consequence are happening in global political life. To be sure, the exiles might speak in wavering timbre. After all, these are sites where the disciplining metaphysical faiths of modern culture are put in doubt, constructs of sovereign "man" cannot be made practically effective, and putatively objective boundaries of conduct authorized from sovereign perspectives are seen not only to be arbitrary but also to produce a scarcity of resources by which people might struggle to make life possible. People here are disposed to question identity as much as they are inclined to be dubious of all universal narratives and transcendental ends. If voices are here heard to flutter, hesitate, and show doubt, however, the wavering cannot be equated with an anxious quavering. It cannot be equated with a fear of death that must be calmed by the imposition of a certain identity and a universal narrative in which an identity might secure an exclusionary territory to call home. For the questioning of "self" does not here signal a "deficiency," a "lacuna that must be filled." Ambiguity and uncertainty are not here regarded as sources of fear in themselves.

Ambiguity, uncertainty, and the ceaseless questioning of identity—these are resources of the exiles. They are the resources of those who would live and move in these paradoxical marginal spaces and times and who, in order to do so, must struggle to resist knowledgeable practices of power that would impose upon them a certain identity, a set of limitations on what can be done, an order of "truth." They are resources that make possible what Julia Kristeva would call the work of "dissidence," the politicizing work of thought. In Michel Foucault's phrasing (1973:386), they are indicative of the opening of "a space in which it is once more possible to think." Here, where identity is always in process and territorial boundaries of modern life are seen to be arbitrarily imposed, the limits authored from one or another sovereign standpoint can be questioned and transgressed, hitherto closed-off cultural connections can be explored, and new cultural resources can be cultivated thereby. Here it becomes possible to explore, generate, and circulate new, often distinctly joyful, but always dissident ways of thinking, doing, and being political.

We do not call attention to these proliferating marginal sites of modern politics in order to highlight lapses in contemporary global political theory, some specific domains of conduct that theorists have yet to take seriously enough. We do so in order to suggest that these deterritorialized and decentered sites of political life already have their counterparts at the margins of modern international studies. Kristeva has suggested that "A spectre haunts Europe: the dissident." We want to suggest that for some years now, a "spectre" has haunted the "European continent" of international studies. It is the spectre of a widely proliferating and distinctly dissident theoretical attitude

spoken in uncertain voice by women and men who, for various reasons, know themselves as exiles from the territories of theory and theorizing solemnly affirmed at the supposedly sovereign centers of a discipline. It is the spectre of a work of global political theory, a dissident work of *thought*, that happily finds its extraterritorial place—its politicized "nonplace"—at the uncertain interstices of international theory and practice.

These proliferating works of thought are not difficult to find. In the published literature, more so in the informal xero-circuits of the field, and still more so in the seminar papers of graduate students, one can detect an increasing volume and variety of work whose principal business is to interrogate limits, to explore how they are imposed, to demonstrate their arbitrariness, and to think *other*-wise, that is, in a way that makes possible the testing of limitations and the exploration of excluded possibilities. Some know their activity as reflection on ontology, on epistemology, on methodology—on what many call the unspoken presuppositions of a discipline. Some know their activity as exploration into the possibility of a post-positivist international relations discourse, a post-empiricist science of international relations, or a critical theory of global politics. Others know their activity as a kind of history, albeit one that does not aspire to remember an originary past but to expose and undo the arbitrary practices by which "counter-memories" are forgotten in the construction of a "necessary" present. Still others know their activity as attempts to set up a series of relays between international relations theory, on the one hand, and European social theory, feminist theory, and/or contemporary literary theory, on the other. And many more simply do their works of thought, not pausing to give their works a name but simply proceeding straightaway to a "ruthless and irreverent dismantling of the workings of discourse, thought, and existence" (Kristeva) in modern global life. However they are known and presented, moreover, these works of thought are to be heard insistently questioning the time-honored dualisms upon which modern theory and practice have long pivoted. Identity/difference, man/history, present/past, present/future, inside/outside, domestic/international, sovereignty/anarchy, community/war, male/female, realism/idealism, speech/language, agent/structure, particular/universal, cultural/material, theory/practice, center/periphery, state/society, politics/economics, revolution/reform—these and countless other dichotomies have been examined in their practical workings, turned, rethought, and exposed as arbitrary cultural constructs by which, in modern culture, modes of subjectivity, objectivity, and conduct are imposed.

As seen from the standpoints that would claim to occupy the center of a discipline, it is true, these marginal works of thought are known primarily as indications of a negativity: a crisis of confidence, a loss of faith, a degeneration of reigning paradigms, an organic crisis in which, as Gramscians would say, "the old is dying and the new cannot yet be born." So cast, they are known to mark an interregnum, a time of delay between paradigms. So cast, also, they are subject to the discipline implicit in questions that modern theorists who long for a center, a secure source of meaning guaranteed by a "dead father," so readily ask. Can they not prove their merits by configuring themselves as a new paradigm whose knowledge claims would bear a promise of control in the name of "man?" If they aspire to be taken seriously, can they not configure themselves as a theoretical counter-hegemony that could speak a sovereign voice, assume a name, take a position, command a space, secure a home, set down a law, and lay claim to the center of a discipline? The discipline is ready to hear affirmative answers to these questions—answers that would affirm that the study of international politics is indeed a business of making heroic promises on behalf of a universal sovereign figure. To those works of thought that answer no, the discipline turns a deaf ear when it can.

It is characteristic of these exile works of thought, though, that they will answer no. For these dissident works are like the marginal sites discussed earlier in that they resist assimilation to modern modes of knowing in the interest of the power of the modern figures of sovereign man and sovereign state. They share the three other features of these marginal sites as well. These dissident works of global political theory move in intrinsically ambiguous sites, where respect for the play of difference and the undecidability of history displace the assertion of identity, including the assertion of one or another interpretation of a universal identity of sovereign "man". They move in politicized sites where power is conspicuously at work and subject to meticulous examination. And they constitute exciting works of experimentation and exploration that would transgress arbitrary limits, open up hitherto closed off connections, and enable the construction and circulation of new ways of knowing and doing politics. Requiring "ceaseless analysis, vigilance and will to subversion," these marginal works of thought "necessarily enter into complicity with other dissident practices in the modern Western world."

The purpose of this special issue, then, is not to announce a new and powerful perspective on global politics for which a discipline must make way. The contributions to this issue do not speak a sovereign voice or proclaim a credo. They do not fabricate and ritualize a story of origins that would supply unity to these dissident works of thought. They stake out no territory to be defended, no boundaries that might separate citizens of a new discipline from those who are alien to it. They neither write nor exemplify a manual of war by which soldiers of a new mode of global political theory might be taught to seize, defend, and extend a domain. They issue no promises. They bear no flag.

Our intention in these pages, on the contrary, is to provide an opportunity for a public celebration of what these dissident works of thought already celebrate in countless scattered locales of research labor: difference, not identity; the questioning and transgression of limits, not the assertion of boundaries and frameworks; a readiness to question how meaning and order are imposed, not the search for a source of meaning and order already in place; the unrelenting and meticulous analysis of the workings of power in modern global life, not the longing for a sovereign figure (be it man, God, nation, state, paradigm, or research program) that promises a deliverance from power; the struggle for freedom, not a religious desire to produce some territorial domicile of self-evident being that men of innocent faith can call home. Our intention, too, is to enable the further circulation of the new strategies of questioning, analysis, and resistance that these works of thought have found to be effective in one or another site and that might prove provocative and workable in other sites as well. In short, we do not want to "shout," as if a voice raised in *International Studies Quarterly* might bespeak the arrival of a new movement that would storm and take the capitals of international studies. We want instead to make it possible to listen attentively to the "muffled cries" of dissidence that are already everywhere to be heard.

. . . These papers range across a variety of topics that are no doubt familiar to readers of the *Quarterly*: surveillance, simulation and computer-assisted war gaming, the acceleration of weapons delivery, alliance politics, arms transfers, the local politics of ecological and anti-nuclear movements, the politics of international debt, and the production and transformation of political institutions, to name a few. Yet any attempt to introduce these papers and say what they must mean would be to do violence to them. For while these papers range across topics with familiar names, they do not approach them from the standpoint of some sovereign subject, some center of interpretation with which authors and readers are one. They do not pretend to project an originary word of truth and power beyond doubt, a voice of "man" that promises to settle the ambiguities of life once and for all. . . . [T]hese papers show that the refusal to embrace one or another sovereign standpoint and its pretenses of territorial being does not entail either a flight to a kind of idealism or a retreat to political passivity. It instead enables a disciplined, critical labor of thought that takes seriously those unfinalized power political struggles in which the question is no longer which sovereign shall win and which shall lose but how, if at all, a sovereign-centered territorialization of political life can be made to prevail. . . .

. . . Thus, while the contributors to this issue . . . refuse to be seduced by a strategy of reading that would draw them into abstractly theoretical discussions or self-enclosing simulations of idealized realities that function only to redeem some notion of sovereign scholarly being. Instead, these scholars do what, we suspect, scholars of international studies in general are inclined to do. They get on with their work. They engage the intrinsically problematical realities of a world that affords few people today anything resembling a domestic haven of self-evident being exempt from the play of power. Like all exiles from the supposed sovereign territories of modern culture, these scholars undertake a critical task, a task of dissidence to which Foucault (1984:50) has gestured. It is a task of working "on our limits, that is, a patient labor giving form to our impatience for liberty."

REFERENCES

FOUCAULT, M. (1973) *The Order of Things: An Archaeology of the Human Sciences*. New York: Random House.

———. (1984) What is Enlightenment? In *The Foucault Reader*, edited by P. Rabinow. New York: Pantheon.

Chapter 5

Challenging the Realist Paradigm

16. International Relations or World Society?

JOHN BURTON

INTRODUCTION

The title is intended to raise the question, what is the nature of that thing out there that is the subject matter of international relations? What is the reality we try to describe and understand? As will be seen, this question has both intellectual and policy implications.

At the intellectual level, there are two issues. The first is whether the legal entities we call states are the main and the significant actors, that is, whether a description and explanation of the behavior of the inter-state system would hold the answers to the policy problems we all seek to solve, or whether we can find these only by studying the whole of world society, of which the inter-state system is only one part. The second is whether our descriptions and theories of behavior, be it of states or other units, are based on reliable observations, or merely reflect vague impressions about aggression, power, authority, national interests, law and order, deviance and other political-sociological phenomena.

The two issues are related. If states were the dominant actors, then some reliable predictions could be made about the inter-state sys-

From *The Study of World Society: A London Perspective* by John Burton, et al., Occasional Paper no. 1, International Studies Association, pp. 3–10, 19–20, 22–27. © 1974 by ISA Reprinted by permission of the author.

tem merely by adequate descriptive studies of diplomatic history, trading relations, international institutions, strategies, alliances and other aspects of the interactions of states. If, on the other hand, transactions across national boundaries, that are not wholly initiated and controlled by state authorities, were found to be influential on the behavior of states and on other units in the wider world society, then reliable studies would need to be made of behavior at all social levels, of the nature of authority and responses to authority, of human values, of ethnic and other sympathy relationships that cross national boundaries, and of the spillover into the wider political environment of social and political unrest within states. How we perceive that thing out there determines, therefore, how we define our field: is reality effectively the system of states, or is it the wider world society? And the way we define our field determines the scope of behavioral knowledge that is relevant.

What is out there, whether relations between nations or a more complex world society, is not merely a matter of interest to philosophers and theorists. The relations between perception and reality are of special interest to practitioners because policy flows from perceptions of reality. . . .

It is to be noted that there has been a continuing process of change in thought and, correspondingly, in remedies, as experience, especially failure, has forced new approaches. The inter-state system and thinking about it have moved from national defenses, to power balances and alliance structures, to collective security, to attempts at disarmament. But these changes in thought and policies have been, over the centuries, no more than superficial variations on the one continuing theme of threat and defense within the international and the inter-state systems. Traditional hypotheses that designate states as the main if not sole actors also imply that the preservation of states and their institutions, and the inter-state system and its institutions, are the prime concern of policy. They accept law and order imposed by state and inter-state authorities as the necessary condition of social stability and peaceful relations within and between states. These hypotheses have persisted over time despite the fact that they have failed to produce policies that achieve these objectives. Deviance at the social and the inter-state level have not been contained, as is shown by rising crime figures and a persistent condition of war at both inter-state and intra-state levels.

Failure of policies does not, of course, disprove the hypotheses on which they are based. It may well be that they are valid, that the inter-state system is the only significant one, that human behavior at other levels is not significant, and that there are no possible outcomes of state policies of law and order except frequent failure reflected in a condition of war or conflict at one level or another. Alternatively, it may be that these hypotheses were realistic at one point of time, but are no longer because of altered conditions—once again raising the question of what is reality. Certainly, the contemporary political-sociological environment of states, and contemporary thinking about authority, decision-making, role behavior, conflict, values, and related topics at many different levels of social behavior, have given rise to doubts and questioning about the reality of the hypothesized power-oriented inter-state system where before there was seemingly certainty and acceptance. If empirical evidence and theoretical analysis invalidate traditional hypotheses, and if other hypotheses

emerge that allow a different perception of reality and also more reliably explain behavior, then new policy opportunities will be created.

Through the ages political scientists and practitioners have been working at the ground-floor or earthy level of observation of the practices of states and statesmen. Contemporary thinking in international relations is relatively analytical, as is to be expected in an age of research and scientific inquiry. It is at a basement level, resting on empirical evidence and theories derived from other studies of behavior—individual, group, industrial, communal.

In fact, there now appears to be an even lower or even more fundamental level of knowledge to explore. To what extent have our own creations, our own pre-theories and notions of human and institutional behavior, our own expectations of behavior, resulted in that behavior? To what degree have our images of reality, which could be false, made a reality of our imagination? By adopting policies that reflect our pre-theories about the dominance of the state-system, of its inherent instability, have we established inter-state relations that are based on aggressiveness and power? Have we, in short, been self-creating over the years and in so being have we been self-defeating—bringing about a conflictual international system which it was our desire to avoid? However, I do not intend, on this occasion, to dig below the basement and to explore these interesting sub-basement possibilities. We are concerned now with the basement level only: is our image of inter-state relations that we believe to be the dominant relations in world society an accurate reflection of reality, or merely a reflection of some untested and probably false theories of behavior?

The ground floor level, then, is narrowly concerned with inter-state relations, essentially power relations, and the image of world society is one in which the relative power of states determines international relations. The basement level is concerned with world society as a whole, making no arbitrary boundaries between that which is national and that which is international, and consequently no arbitrary boundaries among the general body of knowledge about man and his environment—psychological, sociological, economic or political. . . . The boundaries of the field of interest are thus extended to include all behavior, even the behavior of non-human systems such as electronic ones.

In the interests of exposition, let us remind ourselves of the two different models that are employed at the ground floor and basement levels. The image or model of international relations based on the power relations of states has been called the "billiard ball" model [Wolfers 1962:19]. It represents the notion of different sized balls coming into contact one with the other, the subsequent direction taken by each being the outcome of the relative momentum and velocity of those in collision. The contact is on the hard surfaces of the outside; what goes on within each state is of no concern to any other. This is "domestic jurisdiction." These billiard balls have physical boundaries, and in this image one of the main roles of the state is to defend these boundaries and to control transactions across them.

It could be said that any interactions between points inside and outside states are under the control of a central authority located within the geographical boundary, and that, therefore, ultimately, all interactions are between authorities. But this is the formal, and not the practical, description of affairs. In reality, not all interactions across state boundaries are through and under the control of state authorities, as many modern states are finding. A concept of systems interacting is more realistic than a concept of states interacting. A system has no geographical boundaries. The system comprises points between which there is interaction. Inside each system there are sub-systems of interaction. One can draw the geographical area around a factory, but the factory itself comprises a set of systems and sub-systems by which management is put into office, by which certain production and distribution activities are carried out, and so on. The total activity can be broken down and analyzed in this way. Most systems at some level or other cut across state boundaries, just as factory transactions do when its members participate in external systems such as unions.

The interaction of states is only one of many systems of interaction in world society. If we were to analyze systems separately—communications, tourism, trade, science—and superimpose one on another, we would get a build-up of interactions. The map of world society would be one cobweb of transactions imposed on another, and the image of world society would be one of concentrations of interactions at some points, and linkages across national boundaries, sometimes clustered, sometimes infrequent [Burton 1968:8].

Which of these two models or images depicts better that thing out there which we are studying is an empirical question. The second one appears to be nearer contemporary reality. The evidence is before us in terms of communications, movements of people, the epidemic spread of ideas and ideologies, transnational corporations, functional institutions that are universal, tourism, migration, sympathies and support across boundaries and other increased transactions associated with the post-1945 era. This apparent evidence is supported by studies of politics. There has been an erosion of authority of central governments because they cannot contain revisionist minority movements which win support in the wider world society. Central authorities have failed to deal effectively with the complex problems of inflation, unemployment, housing and education. Major industrial societies are moving toward forms of government that are sub-system dominant, many of the sub-systems being international. The life of the ordinary person—whether or not he has adequate education for his children, what is the real value of his savings, whether his particular job is secure and whether he has the prospect of a job—is largely determined by decisions taken outside his national environment, and frequently at a non-governmental level. The role and nature of government is altering, away from defensive postures toward assisting adjustment to change, and this is itself supporting evidence that already we have effectively moved away from the billiard ball relationship that may have existed in the past, to an interaction process within a world society.

It is not to be denied that when authorities are deciding policies, the basis of thinking is probably determined, not by the empirical evidence, and not even by their own perceptions of reality, but by the logical consequences of the approach adopted. The two perceptions lead to radically different analyses of behavior at all levels, to radically different policies, sometimes challenging philosophies, attitudes, values and interests to an unacceptable degree. The ground floor model is the one that is comfortable for ruling elites, for the powerful, for the privileged, for those in authoritative role positions, for those, in short, who wish no radical change in the social, economic and political institutions that exist within their own segments of world society. The basement model is perceived by them as a subversive one. It represents the inexorable incursions of alien behavior, of anarchy and permissiveness, expressed in terms of political participation and self-fulfillment, which themselves are seen from an elitist posture to be the cause of the erosion of authority and the breakdown of law and order.

It is my intention to deal with the theoretical and then with some practical consequences of the two different approaches, the traditional and the more analytical, the aim throughout being to answer the question, what is the nature of that thing out there, and the related question, has the failure of traditional methods of social engineering and control been despite the validity of traditional assumptions made about "reality," or because of their invalidity?

THEORY

At the ground level, the questions asked relate to the stability of society, the preservation of states, the observance of law and the national and international deterrents that are required to preserve the inter-state system. The study fields are national interests, defense, strategy, institutions and law.

At the basement level a different set of questions is asked, and there are different fields of study. Is the prime goal of social organization at the national and international levels the preservation of societies and their institutions or, alternatively, is it the closing of the Galtung gap between the actual and potential development of the person and the groups with which he is affiliated [Galtung 1969:168]? Are the prime causes of war and conflict the violence of the individual and nation against established norms, or the violence imposed on the individual by the structures of national and world society? The fields of study are authority relationships, human values, system ability to respond to change, role behavior, ethnic identity, conflict and integration, and social mobilization.

The traditional study of international relations is the study of behavior at one level, to a marked degree divorced from studies of behavior at other social levels. Despite attempts to be analytical in some aspects, such as decision-making and strategic interactions, it remains essentially descriptive and rests on crude hypotheses concerning behavior, such as human aggressiveness, and the effectiveness of coercive power. International relations is not unique in this respect. . . .

The study of world society seeks to focus on some high levels of interaction, but in the perspective of the whole behavior. It is seeking to define and to explain the field and problems of special interest to international relations scholars, by reference to behavior at all social levels. It is, therefore, initially concerned with human behavior. Inevitably it is less concerned than traditional studies are with institutional behavior, strategy, power relationships and even the complexities of decision-making within a particular structure. Each of these are the excretions of behavior, but not explanations of it. The starting point is man, and his social behavior, and the special study is this behavior at an inter-communal, international, or inter-state level. The nature and effectiveness of the institutions that accompany this behavior are also of interest. The value orientation is explicit: it is those of man, not those of institutions; the development of man, not the preservation of institutions for their own sake.

The model adopted is one of interactions, the cobweb model. This, like the billiard ball model, is a descriptive model—it reflects the empirical evidence. But it is also the model that reflects the axiomatic element in all human behavior, that is, relationships. The starting point is, therefore, not behavior but a more operational definition of behavior—relationships. No progress can be made in the study of any level of behavior unless there is description and an explanation of relationships, how they evolve, how they are learned, what patterns emerge, and why there is observance of and deviance from them. Yet it is the immediate reaction of some that such a behavioral study of relationships is outside the field of interest of international relations, despite the use of "relations" in this traditional title of our subject matter. The world society approach postulates that the study of relationships is the common field of all behavioral studies, whatever the level. It is the inadequacy of the implied and unstated assumptions about relationships that has limited the explanatory and predictive value of past studies. Our literature is literally studded with references to aggressiveness, acquisition, fear, racial differences, religious and ideological commitments and a host of other notions. But there is no evidence that relationships are studied or understood. We fall back, in both theory and policy, on law and order, natural and supernatural coercion and power as the means of controlling behavior. Human behavioral relations seem to be treated as though they are the creation of social institutions, and in policy human values are subordinated to institutional needs, thus creating conflictual social relationships. What is now needed at every level of behavioral sciences in every culture is a reexamination of basic hypotheses: what is the nature of relationships. In the field of international relations the traditional hypotheses about relationships that rest so much on coercion have led to policies of defense, balances, alliances, collective security and deterrents, and perhaps created a society that is hooked on these supports. The study of relationships is not merely well within our area of interests, but an essential part of it.

The two different approaches and sets of questions rest on significantly different conceptions of the human condition. There are those at the ground floor level who claim to be "political realists." They have a Calvinistic conception of behavior related very closely to traditional normative notions reflected in legal thinking. Their assumption appears to be that, generally speaking, persons and states conform to agreed norms of behavior because of coercion and threat, together with some sense of moral obligation. The questions they ask are why does the minority not conform and how can it be made to conform? At the basement level, . . . it is appreciated that non-social behavior is predominant. . . . Only twenty percent of crime is recorded in most developed industrial states. In addition to unrecorded crime there are the lawful practices of those who take advantage of the economic and financial systems to profit by means which cause more human suffering than many acts of crime. The situation at the international level is no different. The question to be asked from the basement is, why does the minority of socially motivated citizens or units not commit violence against others? While at the ground floor level aggressive behavior, personal and national, is the main focus of attention, at the basement level more attention is given to cooperative behavior because it is this which is the exceptional and interesting phenomenon. The operative question is not how to coerce or to deter, but what conditions produce integrative behavior.

Behind these different conceptions of the condition of man are quite fundamentally different theories of behavior. These typically remain unstated, yet they are at the heart of differences between these two approaches. At the ground floor level man is inherently evil, anti-social and aggressive, or has lived so long in frustrating circumstances that he tends to have these behavioral characteristics. The role of the state is to control his behavior, and the role of the inter-state system is to deter aggressive responses. The state is given a legitimate monopoly on violence, and the endeavor has been to endow the inter-state system with a similar monopoly in this wider field. The state thus comes to be perceived as the most powerful and therefore the main, if not the only, significant actor in the national and international arena. The preservation of its institutions, which are assumed to have consensual support, in the face of disruptive elements is its main task. Coercion, deterrence, punishment are the means of preserving social organizations and curbing deviant behavior both nationally and internationally. But the empirical evidence at all levels is that these processes do not deter.

At the basement level, on the other hand, a deeper analysis of behavior leads to quite different conclusions about the integrative processes in any society, the means of avoiding deviant behavior, and the purposes of social organization. The role of the state appears not to be a determining or effective one, especially its coercive role in the maintenance of law and order. . . .

POLICY

So far we have been concerned with the way in which conceptual thinking is influenced by the model or image of the world that we adopt. Now let us consider how policy propositions are affected by the approach adopted. By way of example let us take theories about the origins of conflict.

At the ground floor level, conflict is an aberration, a breakdown in social or authority relationships. Furthermore, it is inevitable either because of the nature of man or because of the environment of scarce resources in which he survives. The enforcement of law and order is not merely or mainly to preserve social institutions and the state; it is also to protect citizens from each other.

If human relations are assumed to be zero-sum, and, moreover, on a material plane—that is, if the gain of one equals the loss of another in acquiring some resource—and if in this environment of zero-sum relationship the unit response is aggressive, as it would surely be, then social relations must be determined by open warfare, by threat of violence, or by the imposition and enforcement by third parties of a set of norms. This is the essential connection between power politics and law and order, and perhaps why so many leading power politicians are or were lawyers.

However, there is a false assumption inherent in the ground floor notion of a coercive authority. Let us leave aside the question whether the employment of coercion, threat or violence raises any moral issues. Let us leave aside, also, questions as to whether greater sympathy should be felt for deviants, small states or individual delinquents, because they may have had an unfavorable environment. The assumption is that policies of coercion deter. The average prison sentence in Britain was 28 percent longer in 1971 than it was in 1961, but there was no apparent positive effect. In education, in industrial relations and in communal relations, threat and coercion are found not to be effective deterrents. This is the empirical position. At the inter-state level coercion by victory in war, by judicial settlement, by the pressure of expectations associated with mediation and conciliation, is not effective. At all levels, the tendency is to respond to failure by applying more of the same medicine and not to acknowledge that the initial analysis was probably faulty. When "law and order" fails, the level of coercion is increased.

Let us dwell a little on this problem of deterrence, let us examine the theoretical reasons why deterrence does not deter, and the conditions which generate social behavior. This is the heart of the problem of integrative behavior, the solution to which the study of international relations has been devoted. At the ground floor level, behavior that confronts "law and order" is variously labeled anarchy, permissiveness, subversion or moral degeneration. When legal authorities are challenged, conflict and latent conflict can, on the basis of these labels, justifiably be dealt with by the imposition of law and order by coercive means. Where the authority is in a majority, the justification of coercion is on grounds of democratic principles and the maintenance of law and order. But the appeal to democracy and to law and order is clearly a rationalization, for when "law and order" is maintained by a minority, there is not even the semblance of democracy to justify coercion. In South Africa and Rhodesia, minorities impose their authority. What is clear now in world society is that when important values are believed to be threatened, no coercive power, nor even majority power, can contain even relatively small minorities. Authority, in our times, is required to win a legitimized support, and not merely to rely upon a legal status maintained by power. This applies at all social levels. . . .

Modern industrial society tends to destroy and not to build relationships. Technological developments require shifts in occupation and changes in living environments. There is no identity, or relationship on a personal basis, with a monopolized industry, a large company, or the society as a whole represented by the tax gatherer. Even an employee does not identify with a large business whose managers are merely names in the press. In exchange terms there is no motivation for observing the rules. In the absence of internalized norms you do not pay your fare or for your shopping unless clearly required to do so. This is a situation that will get worse as industrial society gets larger and even more anonymous. The "outsider," the "alienated," the "dropout," now comprise a growing sub-culture. . . .

Having thus deviated, having not observed the norms of society, the subject is required to experience a form of punishment or negative satisfaction. Punishment, even physical punishment, by a parent is usually in the context of a relationship. It is not the physical hurt that has any effect. Within a system of relationships, physical or any other punishment is a means of communicating disapproval. What is at stake is the relationship, and to preserve this the child is prepared to conform if necessary. . . . But punishment by a parent, teacher or authority with whom there is no valued relationship rests entirely on the physical pain or the deprivation inflicted, with which the human organism has a physical and mental capacity

to cope. It is this form of punishment, unassociated with valued relationships, that the court, authorities and society inflict. Behavior is not altered by it in the direction intended: on the contrary, the behavioral response is to damage the person or property of that parent, teacher, authority or society as soon as opportunity offers. . . .

If this analysis is valid, traditional means of allegiance to authority and observation of its norms—that is, the traditional deterrents— must be self-defeating. . . .

Can such an analysis be applied at a much higher systems level? Rhodesia, South Africa, Northern Ireland, tribal states, Japan in its imperialist circumstances? Maybe behavior that accords with the norms of the rest of world society cannot easily be promoted merely by encouraging valued relationships; but it is clear that unacceptable behavior is not likely to be deterred by sanctions and other means of coercion. A Security Council with arms at its disposal would have been an ineffective and dangerous instrument; world government with a monopoly of power would be as a colonial force facing an independence movement.

Hence, at the ground floor level there is this intellectual and practical dilemma: on the assumption that relationships are zero-sum, that there are scarce values to be shared among aggressive people, third party determination, supported by coercion, is necessary if conflict or warfare is to be avoided. But coercion, even the implied coercion of mediation, is not effective, and usually not acceptable. Therefore, either the assumption that relationships are zero-sum is false, or there is nothing that can be done to avoid conflictual relationships. There are no answers to the problems of conflict except violence or its suppression by the violence of third parties.

This, indeed, is the contemporary view of social organization, national and international: when law and order fails there is despair because there appears to be no alternative to increased coercion and escalated conflict. It is not satisfying to argue only that relationships must be rebuilt by education, urban planning, social measures and altered legal norms and processes. This takes too long for practical purposes, and in any event the nature of industrial society and international relations is such that whatever these measures achieve is likely to be more than offset by further destruction of relationships. What, then, can be the controlling or organizing influence in any society if coercion is ineffective and if valued relationships do not suffice as inducements for the observation of otherwise unacceptable legal and social norms? On what basis can the Cold War be settled, communities in Cyprus and Northern Ireland come to terms, and contending parties in the Middle East live in peace together?

There are two aspects in the answer to this question, one analytical and one procedural.

At the basement level, theoretical and empirical evidence suggests that human relationships at all levels are not the simple fixed sums one associated with a struggle for scarce resources and the aggressiveness that accompanies such a struggle. Scarcity in itself is not a source of conflict. On the contrary, it is the reason for integrative behavior. It is the scarcity of resources, and the need to make the optimum use of scarce resources, that leads to specialization and exchange relationships based on comparative costs. Scarcity creates communities. At the international level, a richly endowed country that can produce everything more cheaply in terms of labor and capital than another, still gains by exchanging some products with that other. Scarcity is an integrative influence. But the distribution of scarce resources can be a source of conflict. Galtung, by implication, adopts this view when he provides that violence against the person or group is measured by the gap between actual and potential development within the limits of what is possible: the inevitable gap created by the inadequacy of resources is not violence. Our problem area is allocation, not scarcity, relative deprivation, not deprivation. It follows that processes by which the allocation of resources is determined are also a source of conflict, which is why participation and legit-

imization are important behavioral considerations. When attention is directed toward the allocation of resources, and not their scarcity, the area of interest is that of non-material values, security, participation, freedom of choice and others. Conflict involves many values, including such non-material ones. Probably values are commonly held, that is, they reflect universal needs—physiological, social and political. Value priorities, however, differ in different cultures and in different circumstances. Furthermore, they become confused with tactics. A value attached to security can easily be confused with a value attached to occupation of a strategic height, which in practice can create conditions of insecurity. Conflict, therefore, also involves definition of values. In addition, there are costs of attainment that have to be taken into account, in particular, the loss of other values. Costing relates to perceptions of the behavior and values of others. Conflictual relationships are, therefore, typically potentially and actually altering and alterable as priorities, re-definitions, costs and perceptions interact over time. Conflict is in this sense essentially a subjective relationship to which the ground floor level, zero-sum notion of an objective struggle over a scarce resource is not meaningful.

The procedural aspect of the answer to the question, how can integrative behavior be achieved in the absence of enforced norms, follows from this analytical aspect. We are seeking relationships that need no coercive support. Relationships that require no support are exchange ones from which there is mutual benefit—that is, essentially functional relationships that have their source in the organization of a scarcity of resources in the satisfaction of infinite demands. Such functional relationships are by definition associated with participatory decision-making processes: functional exchange relationships are reciprocal and involve the free decision-making of relevant parties.

Let us draw a vertical axis on which we can plot points between positive-sum outcomes of relationships and zero-sum, and a horizontal axis on which we can plot points between war and lesser forms of coercion such as judicial settlement and arbitration and cooperative processes. [See Figure 5.1—ED.]

The ground floor level of traditional studies has been concerned with the lower left segment: the assumption of a cake to be divided gives rise to the need for coercive settlements. The basement level is concerned with the top right segment, exchange behavior that requires no coercive support. This diagram serves to bring to attention the way in which war, arbitration and third party coercive settlements follow logically and necessarily from the assumption that relationships are zero-sum—win-lose. But coercion is not effective. Hence, conflictual relations are continuing and inevitable. But once this fundamental assumption is challenged, once relationships are perceived as mutually profitable, coercion is not required.

The differences can be featured in many ways: at the ground level the processes of controlling relationships rely upon bargaining, relative power positions, alliance resources, legal norms based on the past practices of powerful states and historical claims to territories and rights. At the basement level the processes are those applicable to problem-solving: how can the best use of scarce resources be organized? Where there are conflictual relations arising out of the allocation of scarce resources, as in Rhodesia and in most communities, the relevant questions are, what are the costs of maintaining this disparity, what are the other values at stake, what options are possible, is there clarity in defining values, interests, goals, tactics, and are perceptions of the motivations and values of the opposing party accurate?

Once, therefore, this basic assumption that relationships are zero-sum is overcome, the ground level dilemma is also overcome. In place of coercive controls of relationships, there are possible alternatives in social engineering. In particular, the role of third parties is not judicial on the basis of legal norms, but to assist the parties concerned in redefining their values, in reassessing their costing, in reperceiving their relationships and in exploring alternative functional means of achieving their ends.

This is no new observation to those engaged in social case work and to some management consultants. If we conceive of interstate relations as bound by the same behavioral rules as are all other social interactions, if we do not make some arbitrary distinction between different system levels of behavior, then it should not be regarded as a novel observation to make in the field of international relations. There is at least some empirical work that would support the validity of this approach at the communal and interstate levels [Burton 1969].

CONCLUDING REMARKS

The billiard ball image, and policies based on it that promote the status of state authorities and inhibit processes of political and social change, confront basic trends. An examination of systemic needs and of fundamental human values leads to quite different policies. Restrictive state intervention that inhibits change, from tariff policies to assistance to non-legitimized authorities, creates structures that can exist only within a threat or power system. Constructive intervention, from retraining labor to promoting political and social change of a character that establishes continuing legitimization of authority, creates structures that are self-supporting. The processes by which this is achieved and, in particular, processes whereby conflict is

FIGURE 5.1

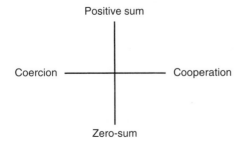

transformed from a perceived zero-sum or win-lose relationship into a positive and problem-solving one, are probably the key which we seek. The prescriptive message is let us help world society to evolve in the direction of flow dictated by human needs and environmental conditions, by assisting change and adjustment to it, and not by confronting it with preservation orders, and intervention and aggressions in the name of legal norms and law and order.

REFERENCES

BURTON, J. W. 1968. *Systems, States, Diplomacy and Rules.* Cambridge: Cambridge University Press.

———. 1969. *Conflict and Communication.* New York: Macmillan and Free Press.

GALTUNG, JOHAN. 1969. Violence, Peace and Peace Research. *Journal of Peace Research*, Vol. 7 no. 3.: 167–191.

WOLFERS, A. 1962. *Discord and Collaboration.* Baltimore: Johns Hopkins University Press.

17. Coloring It Morgenthau: New Evidence for an Old Thesis on Quantitative International Politics*

JOHN A. VASQUEZ

In the last decade a number of scholars have criticized the dominant paradigm in international relations inquiry. Two major criticisms have been levelled at some of the advocates of paradigm change: they do not clearly demonstrate the dominance of a specific paradigm, and they have produced no data-based studies to demonstrate the obsolescence of the fundamental assumptions of the field. This paper attempts to meet these criticisms by systematically testing what has become known as the "Color It Morgenthau" thesis, namely the claim that the realist paradigm has dominated quantitative international relations and has up to this time failed to explain behavior adequately.

Reprinted from *British Journal of International Studies*, 5 (1979), pp. 210–228, with the permission of Butterworth Scientific Ltd. Footnotes deleted.

*This article grew out of my collaboration with John Handelman, Michael O'Leary, and William Coplin on 'Color It Morgenthau: A Data-Based Assessment of Quantitative International Relations Research' (International Studies Association, March 1973).

KUHN AND THE "COLOR IT MORGENTHAU" THESIS

In the second edition of *The Structure of Scientific Revolutions* Kuhn defines *paradigm* as an exemplar that makes a set of fundamental assumptions to form a picture of the world the scholar is studying. A dominant paradigm is usually provided by a single work that is seen as so unprecedented in its achievement that it becomes an exemplar of scientific analysis in a particular field. Scholarly behavior in this period, which Kuhn calls *normal science*, is characterized by extensive articulation of the paradigm in order to construct theories, collection of facts that the paradigm has declared as important for understanding "reality," and use of those facts to test hypotheses. Paradigms are displaced when an anomaly(ies) emerges that the paradigm cannot explain away. This anomaly leads to a crisis in the field and the breakdown of normal research activity. A number of rival paradigms emerge; eventually one that explains the anomaly(ies) gains dominance, and the process repeats itself.

The "Color It Morgenthau" thesis employs Kuhn to make two claims. The first is that international relations inquiry, as practiced in the U.S., has developed as a science along the lines suggested by Kuhn and is currently in a normal science stage with all the major activities of the field (theory construction, data collection and research) being directed by the realist paradigm. The second is that the failure of the behavioral research of the sixties to produce many strong findings constitutes an anomaly that challenges the belief that the realist paradigm can adequately explain behavior.

THE RESEARCH DESIGN

Operationalizing the Realist Paradigm

The realist paradigm can be operationalized by looking at the fundamental assumptions it makes about the world:

1. Nation-states or their decision-makers are the most important actors for understanding international relations.
2. There is a sharp distinction between domestic politics and international relations.
3. International relations is the struggle for power and peace. Understanding how and why that struggle occurs and suggesting ways for regulating it is the purpose of the discipline. All research that is not at least indirectly related to this purpose is trivial.

To determine if quantitative scholars accept these assumptions, a content analysis of the variables in their data collections and research hypotheses will be performed. A coding scheme . . . was developed by selecting indicators for each of the three assumptions.

The first part of the coding scheme lists all the possible actors an international relations scholar could study. If a variable refers only to nations and not to any other actor, then it is . . . taken as evidence that the first two realist assumptions have been accepted. This is valid since it is reasonable to expect that a variable based on these assumptions would tend to focus primarily on nations and neglect other actors. Consequently, if a variable focuses on any other actor or the nation in conjunction with non-national actors, then the work is

taken as evidence that the first two assumptions of the realist paradigm have been rejected.

In order to determine if the critical third assumption is accepted, it is necessary to examine whether the variable emphasizes studying the struggle for power and peace. If the variable employed one of the following topics of inquiry: conflict-cooperation, alliances, power (including geographical-political-economic- and socio-cultural characteristics), isolationism-involvement in world affairs, integration, propaganda, and supranationalism—it was viewed as accepting the third assumption of the realist paradigm.

These foci were taken as indicators because a textual and content analysis of Morgenthau's *Politics among Nations* revealed that they were all important topics of inquiry. . . .

To determine if a hypothesis was guided by realist assumptions, all its variables had to have actor *and* topic codes that were declared realist in the coding scheme. In other words, every variable in the hypothesis had to employ all three assumptions of the realist paradigm before the hypothesis could be declared as realist.

. . . the coding scheme has been found to be quite reliable. It has been applied to different documents (books, abstracts, data files, and hypotheses) in a series of tests employing various coders with reliability scores ranging from .86 to .93.

Testing Paradigm Dominance

If the "Color It Morgenthau" thesis is correct in asserting that the realist paradigm has dominated international relations inquiry, then it logically follows that the two major activities of quantitative scholars—data making and hypothesis testing—would be directed by the realist paradigm. Hence the following two propositions provide a valid test of the claim on paradigm dominance:

1. The realist paradigm guided data making in the field of international relations in the 1950s and 1960s.
2. The realist paradigm guided research in the field of international relations in the same period.

The sample employed to test the first proposition consists of 1650 variables on file with the International Relations Archive of the Inter-University Consortium for Political Research (ICPR) by May 1971. This sample consists of all data that was readily and routinely available to scholars. The sample employed to test proposition two consists of 7,827 hypotheses. The sample was derived by recording every hypothesis tested by inductive or "correlational" statistics in articles classified in Susan Jones and J. David Singer, *Beyond Conjecture in International Politics*, as correlational-explanatory. . . . Jones and Singer purport to have abstracted every data-based article on international politics published prior to 1970.

. . . If the "Color It Morgenthau" thesis is correct, then it will be expected that variables in data sets and in the 7,827 hypotheses will be characterized by (*a*) an acceptance of the three fundamental assumptions of the realist paradigm, (*b*) the use of national power as the primary independent variable, and (*c*) the use of inter-nation conflict-cooperation as the primary dependent variable. In addition, it would be expected that the most frequently tested proposition would be the one that links the primary independent and dependent variables.

Testing Paradigm Adequacy

. . . Any evaluation is only as good as the criteria it employs. The major criterion that will be employed in this design is the ability of a paradigm to produce knowledge. This criterion is a necessary condition for an adequate paradigm; other criteria such as policy relevance and parsimony are secondary criteria that determine the value of the produced knowledge.

Whether a paradigm has produced any knowledge can be determined by the empirical content of its theories, i.e., by the extent to which the theories give rise to hypotheses that fail to be falsified. This requirement maintains that a scientifically useful paradigm will be one that provides scholars with a view of the world

permitting them to formulate hypotheses that fail to be falsified. This criterion will be called the *criterion of accuracy* since it reflects the ability of the paradigm to accurately predict behavior. It is a valid criterion because, if a paradigm's hypotheses were falsified consistently, it would make little sense to say that the paradigm was producing knowledge.

However, it might be argued that the criterion of accuracy by itself is an invalid test because the falsified hypotheses could consist of mostly non-essential hypotheses that did not really embody the "core" or "heart" of the paradigm's perspective. To control for this possibility, a second criterion, the *criterion of centrality*, has been introduced. It requires that only the central hypotheses of a paradigm have to fail to be falsified. This is a valid criterion in combination with the first because, if neither the essential nor non-essential propositions of a paradigm fail to be falsified, then in what sense is the paradigm fulfilling its promise to be an adequate guide to inquiry?

Nevertheless, some scholars may argue that, even if a paradigm failed to satisfy both the criteria of accuracy and centrality, it might be an adequate guide to inquiry if it produced a few "pearls of wisdom." To control for this possibility the *criterion of scientific importance* has been introduced. It maintains that hypotheses that have succeeded in passing empirical tests should be non-obvious and theoretically significant for building the science of the discipline. Clearly, if a paradigm failed to satisfy this criterion as well as the previous two it could hardly be said to be producing knowledge and fulfilling its major purpose.

To determine the extent to which the realist paradigm satisfies the three criteria of paradigm adequacy, the following propositions will be tested:

3. The realist paradigm should tend to produce hypotheses that fail to be falsified.
4. The central propositions of the realist paradigm should tend to produce hypotheses that fail to be falsified.
5. Realist hypotheses that fail to be falsified should be of scientific importance.

... Although the three propositions are fairly explicit, they still leave unresolved the standard of success that will be employed in the tests. How many hypotheses, for example, must fail to be falsified? This is an important question because the success rate of a paradigm would probably be a function not only of the validity of a paradigm, but of the general methodological sophistication of the field. To set a fixed standard, therefore, might be invalid. To deal with this problem, the success rate of hypotheses that accept all three realist assumptions will be compared with those that reject one or more of the assumptions. By employing this procedure it is possible to make the inference that hypothesis tests validly reflect paradigm adequacy, and not the methodological skill of the field or a specific scholar.

The rationale for this conclusion is quite simple and uncontroversial. One can assume that the extent to which realist hypotheses included in the sample adequately test the theoretical premises of the paradigm will vary; i.e., that some are properly derived, measured, tested, etc. and that others are not. Likewise one would assume that the quality of hypotheses that rejected one or more of the realist assumptions would also vary. All that is necessary to make the inference on paradigm adequacy is that the quality of hypothesis tests for realist and non-realist findings be relatively equal; i.e., that the proportion of poor non-realist tests equal the proportion of poor realist

tests. . . . Thus if the test results should reveal a consistent difference between the performance of hypotheses that accept realist assumptions and those that do not, it would be acceptable to infer that the accuracy of the hypotheses played an important role in the test finding.

It should be clear from the above that all this test design can ascertain is the relative success of accepting or rejecting realist assumptions. It cannot assess the performance of specific alternative paradigms such as Marxism or Idealism; nor can it evaluate the performance of specific realist substantive theories. But it does not need to accomplish these tasks to test the adequacy claim of the "Color It Morgenthau" thesis.

Before these propositions can be tested, it is necessary to operationalize and measure the phrase "fail to be falsified." A hypothesis can be said to have failed to be falsified to *the extent to which when tested by inductive and descriptive statistics it is found to be statistically significant and to have a strong measure of association.* Two indices, Predictive Power Index (A) and (B), were constructed to measure this criterion and are reported in Tables 5.1 and 5.2. Both indices establish their categories on the basis of squaring "correlations" (as in explained variance), and are used only for measures of association that range from 0.00 to |1.00|. PI(A) includes all statistically non-significant findings no matter how high their measures of association in

TABLE 5.1   Predictive Power Index A

	PI(A)		
	Category	*Significance*	*Range of measures*
Very Weak (Inadequate Hypothesis)	10	n.s. or not reported	0.00 to |.32|
	20	.05 or not reported	|.33| to |.45|
	30	.05 or not reported	|.46| to |.55|
	40	.05 or not reported	|.56| to |.63|
	50	.05 or not reported	|.64| to |.71|
	60	.05 or not reported	|.72| to |.77|
	70	.05 or not reported	|.78| to |.84|
Very Strong (Adequate Hypothesis)	71+	.05 or not reported	|.85| to |1.00|

TABLE 5.2   Predictive Power Index B

	PI(B)		
	Category	*Significance*	*Range of measures*
Very Weak (Inadequate Hypothesis)	25	n.s. or not reported	0.00 to I.50I
	50	.05 or not reported	I.51I to I.71I
	75	.05 or not reported	I.72I to I.87I
Very Strong (Adequate Hypothesis)	100	.05 or not reported	I.88I to I1.00I

category 10 (i.e., very weak). The other categories in PI(A) include only those "correlations" that were (i) greater than I.33I and significant at the .05 level or (ii) were greater than I.33I and were reported without a significance test. PI(B) differs from PI(A) only in that there are four categories in the scale. In this case non-significant findings are placed in category 25.

Whether or not Predictive Power Indices A and B provide a good or valid measure depends on the purpose for which they were created. In this analysis the indices are being employed as a means of interpreting how accurate a prediction the hypothesis provides. To say simply that a hypothesis has been "supported" or "not supported," as has been done in other analyses that review a large number of findings, loses a tremendous amount of information and often does not even provide a reliable measure since the rules employed for determining "supported" are not specified. On the other hand, to repeat the actual finding would not provide much interpretation and would be an exhausting process. Predictive Power Indices A and B try to strike a balance between providing too much or too little information, while at the same time providing a reliable measure.

The research design established for testing the claim on paradigm adequacy is quite strict. If the "Color It Morgenthau" thesis is correct it would be expected that hypotheses that reject one or more of the three fundamental realist assumptions would tend to do better on the criteria of accuracy and scientific importance than hypotheses that accept realist assumptions. In addition, if the "Color It

Morgenthau" thesis is correct, it would be expected that non-central hypotheses would do better in passing empirical tests than the central realist hypotheses. Although the "Color It Morgenthau" thesis makes these predictions, the opposite are the common expectations of the field. The findings should therefore provide some hard evidence to decide a controversial claim.

THE FINDINGS

The first test of the proposition that the realist paradigm guided the data making activities of quantitative international relations scholars found that about three-quarters of the data on file in the International Relations Archive of the ICPR consist of data that can be employed as realist indicators (Realist = 1236 (74.9%), Non-Realist = 414 (25.1%)). Furthermore, the rank ordering of specific variables in the sample . . . shows that about two-thirds of the data on file are indicators of the two central concepts of the realist paradigm: national power and inter-nation conflict-cooperation. Clearly both findings fail to falsify proposition (1); therefore it can be concluded that the realist paradigm guided data making in the field during the 1950s and 1960s. Although the findings demonstrate that a large amount of data can be used to test realist hypotheses, it remains to be seen if scholars have actually employed the data in that manner.

The tests of the proposition that the realist paradigm has guided the research activities of quantitative international relations scholars found that the attention of quantitative scholars has been devoted overwhelmingly to testing realist hypotheses. Of the 7,827 hypotheses, 92.9 percent (7,275) are realist and only 7.1 percent (552) are non-realist. This finding demonstrates that data on realist indicators are much more frequently analyzed than other data.

Tables 6–8 demonstrate that of all the possible realist indicators and hypotheses that could be studied, the central ones receive the predominant attention.* These tests show: (1) that national power is the most frequently employed independent variable, constituting almost sixty percent of all the employed independent variables, (2) that inter-nation conflict-cooperation is the most frequently employed dependent variable, constituting about sixty percent of all the employed dependent variables, and finally, . . . the most frequently tested hypothesis in the field is the one that employs national power to explain inter-nation conflict-cooperation (41.7% of the hypotheses). Clearly all the findings confirm that proposition (2) has failed to be falsified, and that the realist paradigm guided research in the field in the 1950s and 1960s.

The above evidence supports the domination claim of the "Color It Morgenthau" thesis. The evidence shows that data collection is not a random process, but is devoted primarily to gathering realist indicators with special attention to the central concepts in the realist paradigm. In addition, the evidence shows that hypothesis testing within the field has not been a haphazard process but highly focused on testing realist hypotheses.

The "Color It Morgenthau" thesis also claims that the realist paradigm has failed to adequately explain international behavior. . . . Proposition 3 applies the criterion of accuracy, which states that hypotheses that accept the three fundamental assumptions of the realist paradigm should tend to fail to be falsified more frequently than hypotheses that reject one or more of the realist assumptions. Using PI(B) the test of proposi-

tion 3 shows that although neither realist nor non-realist hypotheses were very successful in explaining behavior, the non-realist hypotheses do consistently better. Of the 7,158 realist hypotheses 93.1 percent (6,661) fall into category 25 (i.e., they are statistically insignificant and/or have measures of association less than |.50|) compared with 83.1 percent (432) of the non-realist hypotheses. Turning to the stronger categories 75 and 100 only 2.2 percent of the realist hypotheses fall into these categories (i.e., they are not statistically insignificant and have measures of association of at least |.72|) compared to 4.6 percent of the non-realist. These findings indicate that the realist paradigm has not been very successful in passing empirical tests. Although early success would not be expected, neither would one expect that over ninety percent of over 7,000 realist hypotheses would be falsified. Finally, the fact that hypotheses rejecting one or more of the realist assumptions could more successfully pass empirical tests raises serious questions about the accuracy of the realist paradigm. It can be concluded that . . . the realist paradigm has failed to satisfy the criterion of accuracy.

Proposition 4 applies the criterion of centrality, which states that only the central propositions of the realist paradigm need to fail to be falsified in order for the paradigm to be declared adequate. The content and textual analysis of *Politics among Nations* revealed that the central proposition in that work was the attempt to explain inter-nation conflict-cooperation by the use of national power. The test of this proposition separates this hypothesis and its reverse from all the other hypotheses in the sample. . . . the two central hypotheses constitute 41.1 percent of the sample. Employing the more precise PI(A) measure, it can be seen that HY 1 (national power correlated with inter-nation conflict-cooperation) does very poorly with 91.7 percent of its findings falling in category 10 (i.e., they are either statistically insignificant or have a measure of association of less than |.33|). If categories 10 and 20 are combined then 98.2

---

*Tables 6–11, which report the data analysis, have been deleted.

percent of the tests of HY 1 are falsified. Relating the concepts in the reverse manner (HY 2) does not help much since 95.1 percent of these hypotheses fall into categories 10 and 20. Examining the strong categories of 70 and 71+ confirms the above finding. HY 1 produces only four out of 2,994 tests in these categories and HY 2 produces only one out of 162 tests.

These results are hardly encouraging for the realist paradigm. A comparison with the "other" hypotheses tested in the field shows that the central hypotheses of the realist paradigm do less well than the non-central or non-realist hypotheses. . . . It can be concluded that . . . the realist paradigm has failed to satisfy the criterion of centrality.

Proposition 5 applies the criterion of scientific importance, which states that realist hypotheses that failed to be falsified should produce findings that are non-obvious and theoretically significant for building a science of international relations. In order to test the proposition the 181 realist and nonrealist hypotheses that fell into categories 75 and 100 of PI(B) were separated from the total sample and classified as either trivial or non-trivial. Given the rather small number of cases and problems of measuring "triviality," the results of this test must be interpreted with caution. Nevertheless, the test shows that non-realist hypotheses are relatively more successful than realist hypotheses in producing scientifically important findings. About two-thirds (69.5 percent) of the realist findings were declared trivial compared to about one half (54.2 percent) of the non-realist hypotheses. This finding suggests that accepting rather than rejecting realist assumptions does not result in comparatively more scientifically important findings. In other words, it cannot be claimed that, despite the poor performance of the realist paradigm on the first two criteria, its assumptions might be able to produce more important findings than a paradigm that rejected them. It can be concluded that . . . the realist paradigm has failed to satisfy the criterion of scientific importance.

CONCLUSION: WHERE DO WE GO FROM HERE?

The failure of the realist paradigm to satisfy the three criteria of adequacy poses an anomaly that the field must explain. The use of quantitative analysis to test aspects of the realist paradigm, which began in 1956 and was well underway by the mid-sixties, has not produced much knowledge, although it has commanded a great deal of effort. The field has not, as was expected, moved "beyond conjecture." The question that must be answered is, why? The "Color It Morgenthau" thesis has answered that question by suggesting that the view of the world provided by the realist paradigm is incorrect. However there are a number of competing *ad hoc* explanations that can be offered and must be evaluated before a definite conclusion can be reached.

There are six *ad hoc* explanations that could be offered to account for the findings of the previous tests: (*a*) the findings are to be expected because of the youthfulness of the field; (*b*) the findings are due to the bivariate character of many of the hypotheses being tested, and as more complex relationships are tested the success rate of the realist paradigm will go up; (*c*) the findings might be due to the inaccuracy of one large article included in the sample; (*d*) the findings are due to the particular statistics that are employed; (*e*) the findings show that quantitative analysis is inadequate and not that the realist paradigm is inadequate; (*f*) the findings are due to measurement error in articles providing the sample.

Three of the *ad hoc* explanations were tested and falsified: those that attribute the findings to the effects of the bivariate character of hypotheses (Kendall's Tau$_c$ = 0.04), article size (Kendall's Tau$_c$ = –0.05), and statistics employed (Kendall's Tau$_c$ = 0.03). The remaining three *ad hoc* explanations all have conceptual problems that make them difficult to test. The *ad hoc* explanation that attributed the findings to the youthfulness of the field was falsified (Kendall's Tau$_c$ = 0.019), but because it could be argued that the entire pre-1970 period was youthful, the test was declared inconclusive. While this explanation is plausible, at some point in time adherents to this explanation must specify that the youthful period is over; otherwise the explanation will never be able to be falsified. The *ad hoc* explanation that quantitative analysis is inadequate is primarily a philosophical claim that cannot be tested precisely, because it is what constitutes testing that is the subject of the debate. Finally the *ad hoc* explanation of measurement error poses a logical problem. Every research finding is either a product of the research design or "reality." There is no conclusive test that can determine which source is responsible for a finding. While this explanation has some credence, unless adherents are willing to specify when they will accept null findings as legitimate evidence, this explanation cannot be falsified.

While the last three *ad hoc* explanations cannot be directly tested they all imply future research strategies that can be evaluated and compared with the research strategy offered by the "Color It Morgenthau" thesis. The research strategy implied by the *ad hoc* explanation on the inadequacy of quantitative methods suggests that there is nothing fundamentally wrong with the realist paradigm and that the field should return to traditional methods of analysis prevalent prior to the behavioral revolt. The problems with this recommendation are that: (*a*) it fails to explain why the "defective" method was more successful with non-realist than realist hypotheses and (*b*) it sidesteps all the epistemological arguments made against the traditional method during the last decade. It is therefore rejected.

The research strategy implied by both the youthfulness of the field and measurement error *ad hoc* explanations is that the anomaly is only temporary, and that as the methodological sophistication of the field grows the number of findings will improve. The advantage of this strategy is that it allows scholars to build on the work already done. . . .

The research strategy implied by the "Color It Morgenthau" thesis is that more paradigm diversity should be introduced into the field. More attention should be devoted to: (*a*) developing new paradigms, (*b*) articulating and elaborating already existing paradigms, such as Marxism and Transnational Relations, and (*c*) collecting data and conducting research on hypotheses derived from these new paradigms. Until such work is conducted, the adequacy of rival paradigms cannot be evaluated. Unless such work is encouraged, adherents of the realist paradigm can always claim that, despite its poor performance, there is no available rival to replace it.

It should be clear that the research strategies suggested by the two *ad hoc* explanations and by the "Color It Morgenthau" thesis are not mutually exlusive. . . .

Because of the various *ad hoc* explanations, the present analysis cannot reach a definitive assessment of the adequacy of the realist paradigm. However, it has raised the following questions about its adequacy: if the view of the world presented by the realist paradigm is correct or useful as a guide to understanding, then why have so many hypotheses that have been guided by this view been consistently falsified? If the view of the realist paradigm is correct, then why have hypotheses that have rejected the view been falsified proportionally less often? If the view of the realist paradigm is correct, then why have the central realist propositions, which have been extensively elaborated and tested, been consistently falsified? If the view of the realist paradigm is correct, then why has the realist paradigm produced only 48 scientifically important findings out of 7,158 realist hypotheses that have been tested since 1956? . . .

18. Social Forces, States and World Orders: Beyond International Relations Theory

ROBERT W. COX

. . . ON PERSPECTIVES AND PURPOSES

Theory is always *for* someone and *for* some purpose. All theories have a perspective. Perspectives derive from a position in time and space, specifically social and political time and space. The world is seen from a standpoint definable in terms of nation or social class, of dominance or subordination, of rising or declining power, of a sense of immobility or of present crisis, of past experience, and of hopes and expectations for the future. Of course, sophisticated theory is never just the expression of a perspective. The more sophisticated a theory is, the more it reflects upon and transcends its own perspective; but the initial perspective is always contained within a theory and is relevant to its explication. There is, accordingly, no such thing as theory in itself, divorced from a standpoint in time and space. When any theory so represents itself, it is the more important to examine it as ideology, and to lay bare its concealed perspective.

To each such perspective the enveloping world raises a number of issues; the pressures

of social reality present themselves to consciousness as problems. A primary task of theory is to become clearly aware of these problems, to enable the mind to come to grips with the reality it confronts. Thus, as reality changes, old concepts have to be adjusted or rejected and new concepts forged in an initial dialogue between the theorist and the particular world he tries to comprehend. This initial dialogue concerns the *problematic* proper with a particular perspective. Social and political theory is history-bound at its origin, since it is always traceable to an historically-conditioned awareness of certain problems and issues, a problematic, while at the same time it attempts to transcend the particularity of its historical origins in order to place them within the framework of some general propositions or laws.

Beginning with its problematic, theory can serve two distinct purposes. One is a simple, direct response: to be a guide to help solve the problems posed within the terms of the particular perspective which was the point of departure. The other is more reflective upon the process of theorising itself: to become clearly aware of the perspective which gives rise to theorising, and its relation to other perspectives (to achieve a perspective on perspectives); and to open up the possibility of choosing a different valid perspective from which the prob-

Reprinted from *Millennium: Journal of International Studies* 10, no. 2 (1981), pp. 128–137, with the permission of the publisher and author. Footnotes deleted.

lematic becomes one of creating an alternative world. Each of these purposes gives rise to a different kind of theory.

The first purpose gives rise to *problem-solving theory*. It takes the world as it finds it, with the prevailing social and power relationships and the institutions into which they are organised, as the given framework for action. The general aim of problem-solving is to make these relationships and institutions work smoothly by dealing effectively with particular sources of trouble. Since the general pattern of institutions and relationships is not called into question, particular problems can be considered in relation to the specialised areas of activity in which they arise. Problem-solving theories are thus fragmented among a multiplicity of spheres or aspects of action, each of which assumes a certain stability in the other spheres (which enables them in practice to be ignored) when confronting a problem arising within its own. The strength of the problem-solving approach lies in its ability to fix limits or parameters to a problem area and to reduce the statement of a particular problem to a limited number of variables which are amenable to relatively close and precise examination. The *ceteris paribus* assumption, upon which such theorising is based, makes it possible to arrive at statements of laws or regularities which appear to have general validity but which imply, of course, the institutional and relational parameters assumed in the problem-solving approach.

The second purpose leads to *critical theory*. It is critical in the sense that it stands apart from the prevailing order of the world and asks how that order came about. Critical theory, unlike problem-solving theory, does not take institutions and social and power relations for granted but calls them into question by concerning itself with their origins and how and whether they might be in the process of changing. It is directed towards an appraisal of the very framework for action, or problematic, which problem-solving theory accepts as its parameters. Critical theory is directed to the social and political complex as a whole rather than to the separate parts. As a matter of prac-

tice, critical theory, like problem-solving theory, takes as its starting point some aspect or particular sphere of human activity. But whereas the problem-solving approach leads to further analytical sub-division and limitation of the issue to be dealt with, the critical approach leads toward the construction of a larger picture of the whole of which the initially contemplated part is just one component, and seeks to understand the processes of change in which both parts and whole are involved.

Critical theory is theory of history in the sense of being concerned not just with the past but with a continuing process of historical change. Problem-solving theory is non-historical or ahistorical, since it, in effect, posits a continuing present (the permanence of the institutions and power relations which constitute its parameters). The strength of the one is the weakness of the other. Because it deals with a changing reality, critical theory must continually adjust its concepts to the changing object it seeks to understand and explain. These concepts and the accompanying methods of enquiry seem to lack the precision that can be achieved by problem-solving theory, which posits a fixed order as its point of reference. This relative strength of problem-solving theory, however, rests upon a false premise, since the social and political order is not fixed but (at least in a long-range perspective) is changing. Moreover, the assumption of fixity is not merely a convenience of method, but also an ideological bias. Problem-solving theories can be represented, in the broader perspective of critical theory, as serving particular national, sectional, or class interests, which are comfortable within the given order. Indeed, the purpose served by problem-solving theory is conservative, since it aims to solve the problems arising in various parts of a complex whole in order to smooth the functioning of the whole. This aim rather belies the frequent claim of problem-solving theory to be value-free. It is methodologically value-free insofar as it treats the variables it considers as objects (as the chemist treats molecules or the physicist forces and motion); but it is value-bound by virtue of the fact that it implicitly accepts the prevailing order as its own framework. Critical theory contains problem-solving theories within itself, but contains them in the form of identifiable ideologies, thereby pointing to their conservative consequences, not to their usefulness as guides to action. Problem-solving theory tends to ignore this kind of critique as being irrelevant to its purposes and in any case, as not detracting from its practical applicability. Problem-solving theory stakes its claims on its greater precision and, to the extent that it recognises critical theory at all, challenges the possibility of achieving any scientific knowledge of historical processes.

Critical theory is, of course, not unconcerned with the problems of the real world. Its aims are just as practical as those of problem-solving theory, but it approaches practice from a perspective which transcends that of the existing order, which problem-solving theory takes as its starting point. Critical theory allows for a normative choice in favour of a social and political order different from the prevailing order, but it limits the range of choice to alternative orders which are feasible transformations of the existing world. A principal objective of critical theory, therefore, is to clarify this range of possible alternatives. Critical theory thus contains an element of utopianism in the sense that it can represent a coherent picture of an alternative order, but its utopianism is constrained by its comprehension of historical processes. It must reject improbable alternatives just as it rejects the permanency of the existing order. In this way critical theory can be a guide to strategic action for bringing about an alternative order, whereas problem-solving theory is a guide to tactical actions which, intended or unintended, sustain the existing order.

The perspectives of different historical periods favour one or the other kind of theory. Periods of apparent stability or fixity in power relations favour the problem-solving approach. The Cold War was one such period. In international relations, it fostered a concentration upon the problems of how to manage an apparently enduring relationship between two superpowers. However, a condition of uncertainty in power relations beckons to critical theory as people seek to understand the opportunities and risks of change. Thus the events of the 1970s generated a sense of greater fluidity in power relationships, of a many-faceted crisis, crossing the threshold of uncertainty and opening the opportunity for a new development of critical theory directed to the problems of world order. To reason about possible future world orders now, however, requires a broadening of our enquiry beyond conventional international relations, so as to encompass basic processes at work in the development of social forces and forms of state, and in the structure of global political economy. Such, at least, is the central argument of this essay.

REALISM, MARXISM AND AN APPROACH TO A CRITICAL THEORY OF WORLD ORDER

Currents of theory which include works of sophistication usually share some of the features of both problem-solving theory and critical theory but tend to emphasise one approach over the other. Two currents which have had something important to say about inter-state relations and world orders—realism and Marxism—are considered here as a preliminary to an attempted development of the critical approach.

The realist theory of international relations had its origin in an historical mode of thought. Friedrich Meinecke, in his study on *raison d'état*, traced it to the political theory of Machiavelli and the diplomacy of Renaissance Italian city-states, which marked the emergence of a sense of the specific interests of particular states quite distinct from the general norms propagated by the ideologically dominant institution of medieval society, the Christian church. In perceiving the doctrines and principles underlying the conduct of states as a reaction to specific historical circumstances, Meinecke's interpretation of *raison d'état* is a contribution to critical theory.

Other scholars associated with the realist tradition, such as E. H. Carr and Luwig Dehio, have continued this historical mode of thought, delineating the particular configurations of forces which fixed the framework for international behaviour in different periods and trying to understand institutions, theories and events within their historical contexts.

Since the Second World War, some American scholars, notably Hans Morgenthau and Kenneth Waltz, have transformed realism into a form of problem-solving theory. Though individuals of considerable historical learning, they have tended to adopt the fixed ahistorical view of the framework for action characteristic of problem-solving theory, rather than standing back from this framework, in the manner of E. H. Carr, and treating it as historically conditioned and thus susceptible to change. It is no accident that this tendency in theory coincided with the Cold War, which imposed the category of bi-polarity upon international relations, and an overriding concern for the defense of American power as a bulwark of the maintenance of order.

The generalised form of the framework for action postulated by this new American realism (which we shall henceforth call neo-realism, which is the ideological form abstracted from the real historical framework imposed by the Cold War) is characterised by three levels, each of which can be understood in terms of what classical philosophers would call substances or essences, i.e., fundamental and unchanging substrata of changing and accidental manifestations or phenomena. These basic realities were conceived as: (1) the nature of man, understood in terms of Augustinian original sin or the Hobbesian "perpetual and restless desire for power after power that ceaseth only in death"; (2) the nature of states, which differ in their domestic constitutions and in their capabilities for mobilising strength, but are similar in their fixation with a particular concept of national interest (a Leibnizian *monad*) as a guide to their actions; and (3) the nature of the state system, which places rational constraints upon the unbridled pursuit of rival national interests through the mechanism of the balance of power.

Having arrived at this view of underlying substances, history becomes for neo-realists a quarry providing materials with which to illustrate variations on always recurrent themes. The mode of thought ceases to be historical even though the materials used are derived from history. Moreover, this mode of reasoning dictates that, with respect to essentials, the future will always be like the past.

In addition, this core of neo-realist theory has extended itself into such areas as game theory, in which the notion of substance at the level of human nature is presented as a rationality assumed to be common to the competing actors who appraise the stakes at issue, the alternative strategies, and the respective payoffs in a similar manner. This idea of a common rationality reinforces the non-historical mode of thinking. Other modes of thought are to be castigated as inapt, and incomprehensible in their own terms (which makes it difficult to account for the irruption into international affairs of a phenomenon like Islamic integralism, for instance).

The "common rationality" of neo-realism arises from its polemic with liberal internationalism. For neo-realism, this rationality is the one appropriate response to a postulated anarchic state system. Morality is effective only to the extent that it is enforced by physical power. This has given neo-realism the appearance of being a non-normative theory. It is "value-free" in its exclusion of moral goals (wherein it sees the weakness of liberal internationalism) and in its reduction of problems to their physical power relations. This non-normative quality is, however, only superficial. There is a latent normative element which derives from the assumptions of neo-realist theory: security within the postulated inter-state system depends upon each of the major actors understanding this system in the same way, that is to say, upon each of them adopting neo-realist rationality as a guide to action. Neo-realist theory derives from its foundations the prediction that the actors, from their experiences within the system, will tend to think in this way; but the theory also performs a proselytising function as the advocate of this form of rationality. To the neo-realist theorist, this proselytising function (wherein lies the normative role of neo-realism) is particularly urgent in states which have attained power in excess of that required to balance rivals, since such states may be tempted to discard the rationality of neo-realism and try to impose their own moral sense of order, particularly if, as in the case of the United States, cultural tradition has encouraged more optimistic and moralistic alternative views of the nature of man, the state and world order.

The debate between neo-realists and liberal internationalists reproduces, with up-to-date materials, the seventeenth century challenge presented by the civil philosophy of Hobbes to the natural law theory of Grotius. Each of the arguments is grounded in different views of the essences of man, the state and the inter-state system. An alternative which offered the possibility of getting beyond this opposition of mutually exclusive concepts was pointed out by the eighteenth century Neapolitan Giambattista Vico, for whom the nature of man and of human institutions (amongst which must be included the state and the inter-state system) should not be thought of in terms of unchanging substances but rather as a continuing creation of new forms. In the duality of continuity and change, where neo-realism stresses continuity, the Vichian perspective stresses change; as Vico wrote, ". . . this world of nations has certainly been made by men, and its guise must therefore be found within the modifications of our own human mind."

This should not be taken as a statement of radical idealism, (i.e., that the world is a creation of mind). For Vico, ever-changing forms of mind were shaped by the complex of social relations in the genesis of which class struggle played the principal rôle, as it later did for Marx. Mind is, however, the thread connecting the present with the past, a means of access to a knowledge of these changing modes of social reality. Human nature (the modifications of mind) and human institutions are identical with human history; they are to be understood in genetic and not in essentialist terms (as in neo-realism) or in teleological terms (as in functionalism). One cannot, in this Vichian perspective, properly abstract man and the state from history so as to define their substances or essences as *prior to* history, history being but the record of interactions of manifestations of these substances. A proper study of human affairs should be able to reveal both the coherence of minds and institutions characteristic of different ages, and the process whereby one such coherent pattern—which we can call an historical structure—succeeds another. Vico's project, which we would now call social science, was to arrive at a "mental dictionary," or set of common concepts, with which one is able to comprehend the process of "ideal eternal history," or what is most general and common in the sequence of changes undergone by human nature and institutions. The error which Vico criticised as the "conceit of scholars," who will have it that "what they know is as old as the world," consists in taking a form of thought derived from a particular phase of history (and thus from a particular structure of social relations) and assuming it to be universally valid. This is an error of neo-realism and, more generally, the flawed foundation of all problem-solving theory. It does not, of course, negate the practical utility of neo-realism and problem-solving theories within their ideological limits. The Vichian approach, by contrast, is that of critical theory.

How does Marxism relate to this method or approach to a theory of world order? In the first place, it is impossible, without grave risk of confusion, to consider Marxism as a single current of thought. For our purposes, it is necessary to distinguish two divergent Marxist currents, analogous to the bifurcation between the old realism and the new. There is a Marxism which reasons historically and seeks to explain, as well as to promote, changes in social relations; there is also a Marxism, designed as a framework for the analysis of the capitalist state and society, which turns its back on historical knowledge in favour of a more static and abstract conceptualisation of the mode of production. The first we may call by the name under which it recognises itself: historical materialism. It is evident in the historical works of Marx, in those of present-day Marxist historians such as Eric Hobsbawm, and in the thought of Gramsci. It has also influenced some who would not be considered (or consider themselves) Marxist in any strict sense, such as many of the French historians associated with the *Annales*. The second is represented by the so-called structural Marxism of Althusser and Poulantzas ("so-called" in order to distinguish their use of "structure" from the concept of historical structure in this essay) and most commonly takes the form of an exegesis of *Capital* and other sacred tests. Structural Marxism shares some of the features of the neo-realist problem-solving approach such as its ahistorical, essentialist epistemology, though not its precision in handling data nor, since it has remained very largely a study in abstractions, its practical applicability to concrete problems. To this extent it does not concern us here. Historical materialism is, however, a foremost source of critical theory and it corrects neo-realism in four important respects.

The first concerns dialectic, a term which, like Marxism, has been appropriated to express a variety of not always compatible meanings, so its usage requires some definition. It is used here at two levels: the level of logic and the level of real history. At the level of logic, it means a dialogue seeking truth through the exploration of contradictions. One aspect of this is the continual confrontation of concepts with the reality they are supposed to represent and their adjustment to this reality as it continually changes. Another aspect, which is part of the method of adjusting concepts, is the knowledge that each assertion concerning reality contains implicitly its opposite and that both assertion and opposite are not mutually exclusive but share some measure of the truth sought, a truth, moreover, that is always in motion, never to be encapsulated in some definitive form. At the level of real history, dialectic is the potential for alternative forms of development arising from the confrontation of opposed social forces in any concrete historical situation.

Both realism and historical materialism direct attention to conflict. Neo-realism sees conflict as inherent in the human condition, a constant factor flowing directly from the power-seeking essence of human nature and taking the political form of a continual reshuffling of power among the players in a zero-sum game, which is always played according to its own innate rules. Historical materialism sees in conflict the process of a continual remaking of human nature and the creation of new patterns of social relations which change the rules of the game and out of which—if historical materialism remains true to its own logic and method—new forms of conflict may be expected ultimately to arise. In other words, neo-realism sees conflict as a recurrent consequence of a continuing structure, whereas historical materialism sees conflict as a possible cause of structural change.

Second, by its focus on imperialism, historical materialism adds a vertical dimension of power to the horizontal dimension of rivalry among the most powerful states, which draws the almost exclusive attention of neo-realism. This dimension is the dominance and subordination of metropole over hinterland, centre over periphery, in a world political economy.

Third, historical materialism enlarges the realist perspective through its concern with the relationship between the state and civil society. Marxists, like non-Marxists, are divided between those who see the state as the mere expression of the particular interests in civil society and those who see the state as an autonomous force expressing some kind of general interest. This, for Marxists, would be the general interest of capitalism as distinct from the particular interests of capitalists. Gramsci contrasted historical materialism, which recognises the efficacy of ethical and cultural sources of political action (though always relating them with the economic sphere), with what he called historical economism or the reduction of everything to technological and material interests. Neo-realist theory in the United States has returned to the state/civil society relationship, though it has treated civil society as a constraint upon the state and a limitation imposed by particular interests upon *raison d'état*, which is conceived of, and defined as, independent of civil society. The sense of a reciprocal relationship between structure (economic relations) and superstructure (the ethico-political sphere) in Gramsci's thinking contains the potential for considering state/society complexes as the constituent entities of a world order and for exploring the particular historical forms taken by these complexes.

Fourth, historical materialism focuses upon the production process as a critical element in the explanation of the particular historical form taken by a state/society complex. The production of goods and services, which creates both the wealth of a society and the basis for a state's ability to mobilise power behind its foreign policy, takes place through a power relationship between those who control and those who execute the tasks of production. Political conflict and the action of the state either maintain, or bring about changes in, these power relations of production. Historical materialism examines the connections between power in production, power in the state, and power in international relations. Neo-realism has, by contrast, virtually ignored the production process. This is the point on which the problem-solving bias of neo-realism is most clearly to be distinguished from the critical approach of historical materialism. Neo-realism implicitly takes the production process and the power relations inherent in it as a given element of the national interest, and therefore as part of its parameters. Historical materialism is sensitive to the dialectical possibilities of change in the sphere of production which could affect the other spheres, such as those of the state and world order.

This discussion has distinguished two kinds of theorising as preliminary to proposing a critical approach to a theory of world order. Some of the basic premises for such a critical theory can now be restated:

1. an awareness that action is never absolutely free but takes place within a framework for action which constitutes its problematic. Critical theory would start with this framework, which means starting with historical enquiry or an appreciation of the human experience that gives rise to the need for theory;

2. a realisation that not only action but also theory is shaped by the problematic. Critical theory is conscious of its own reality but through this consciousness can achieve a broader time-perspective and become less relative than problem-solving theory. It knows that the task of theorising can never be finished in an enclosed system but must continually be begun anew;

3. the framework for action changes over time and a principal goal of critical theory is to understand these changes;

4. this framework has the form of an historical structure, a particular combination of thought patterns, material conditions and human institutions which has a certain coherence among its elements. These structures do not determine people's actions in any mechanical sense but constitute the context of habits, pressures, expectations and constraints within which action takes place;

5. the framework or structure within which action takes place is to be viewed, not from the top in terms of the requisites for its equilibrium or reproduction (which would quickly lead back to problem-solving), but rather from the bottom or from outside in terms of the conflicts which arise within it and open the possibility of its transformation.

FRAMEWORKS FOR ACTION: HISTORICAL STRUCTURES

At its most abstract, the notion of a framework for action or historical structure is a picture of a particular configuration of forces. This configuration does not determine actions in any direct, mechanical way but imposes pressures and constraints. Individuals and groups may move with the pressures or resist and oppose them, but they cannot ignore them. To the extent that they do successfully resist a prevailing historical structure, they buttress their actions with an alternative, emerging configuration of forces, a rival structure.

Three categories of forces (expressed as potentials) interact in a structure: material capabilities, ideas and institutions. No one-way determinism need be assumed among these three; the relationships can be assumed to be reciprocal. The question of which way the lines of force run is always an historical question to be answered by a study of the particular case.

Material capabilities are productive and destructive potentials. In their dynamic form these exist as technological and organisational capabilities, and in their accumulated forms as natural resources which technology can transform, stocks of equipment (e.g., industries and armaments), and the wealth which can command these.

Ideas are broadly of two kinds. One kind consists of intersubjective meanings, or those shared notions of the nature of social relations which tend to perpetuate habits and expectations of behaviour. Examples of intersubjective meanings in contemporary world politics are the notions that people are organised and commanded by states which have authority over defined territories; that states relate to one another through diplomatic agents as being in the common interest of all states; and that certain kinds of behaviour are to be expected when conflict arises between states, such as negotiation, confrontation, or war. These notions, though durable over long periods of time, are historically conditioned. The realities of world politics have not always been represented in precisely this way and may not be in the future. It is possible to trace the origins of such ideas and also to detect signs of a weakening of some of them.

The other kind of ideas relevant to an historical structure are collective images of social order held by different groups of people. These are differing views as to both the nature and the legitimacy of prevailing power relations, the meanings of justice and public good, and so forth. Whereas intersubjective meanings are broadly common throughout a particular historical structure and constitute the common ground of social discourse (including conflict), collective images may be several and opposed. The clash of rival collective images provides evidence of the potential for alternative paths of development and raises questions as to the possible material and institutional basis for the emergence of an alternative structure.

Institutionalisation is a means of stablising and perpetuating a particular order. Institutions reflect the power relations prevailing at their point of origin and tend, at least initially, to encourage collective images consistent with these power relations. Eventually, institutions take on their own life; they can become either a battleground of opposing tendencies, or stimulate the creation of rival institutions reflecting different tendencies. Institutions are particular amalgams of ideas and material power which in turn influence the development of ideas and material capabilities.

There is a close connection between institutionalisation and what Gramsci called hegemony. Institutions provide ways of dealing with internal conflicts so as to minimise the use of force. (They may, of course, also maximise the capacity for using force in external conflicts, but we are considering here only the internal conflicts covered by an institution.) There is an enforcement potential in the material power relations underlying any structure, in that the strong can clobber the weak if they think it necessary. But force will not have to be used in order to ensure the dominance of the strong to the extent that the weak accept the prevailing power relations as legitimate. This the weak may do if the strong see their mission as hegemonic and not merely dominant or dictatorial, that is, if they are willing to make concessions that will secure the weak's acquiescence in their leadership and if they can express this leadership in terms of universal or general interests, rather than just as serving their own particular interests. Institutions may become the anchor for such a hegemonic strategy since they lend themselves both to the representations of diverse interests and to the universalisation of policy.

It is convenient to be able to distinguish between hegemonic and non-hegemonic structures, that is to say between those in which the power basis of the structure tends to recede into the background of consciousness and those in which the management of power relations is always in the forefront. Hegemony cannot, however, be reduced to an institutional dimension. One must beware of allowing a focus upon institutions to obscure either changes in the relationship of material forces, or the emergence of ideological challenge to an erstwhile prevailing order. Institutions may be out of phase with these other aspects of reality and their efficacy as a means of regulating conflict (and thus their hegemonic function) thereby undermined. They may be an expression of hegemony but cannot be taken as identical to hegemony. . . .

19. Conflict Resolution: Problem Solving

DEAN G. PRUITT AND JEFFREY Z. RUBIN

[E]scalating conflict often reaches the point where both parties find the further use of contentious tactics either unworkable or unwise. If yielding, withdrawing, and inaction are also ruled out, as they frequently are, the solution to such a stalemate must eventually be found in problem solving. . . . Problem solving can be defined as any effort to locate a mutually acceptable solution to the controversy.

Problem solving is by no means always the last step in a controversy. Indeed, it is often the approach taken first, especially when relations with Other are valued and there is perceived common ground. (This is because it does not run the risk of antagonizing Other in the way that heavy pressure tactics do.) Many controversies are resolved through initial problem solving and never escalate. Still other controversies display a picture-frame progression of events: Problem solving is tried first but it fails. The parties then turn to contentious behavior, and the controversy escalates for a while, until a stalemate is reached and problem solving is reasserted.

At its best, problem solving involves a joint effort to find a mutually acceptable solution. The parties or their representatives talk freely to one another. They exchange information about their interests and priorities, work together to identify the true issues dividing them, brainstorm in search of alternatives that bridge their opposing interests, and collectively evaluate these alternatives from the viewpoint of their mutual welfare.

However, a full problem-solving discussion of this kind is not always practical because of the realities of divergent interests. One or both parties may fear that such openness will deny them an opportunity for competitive gain or give the other party such an opportunity. When these fears exist, individual problem solving is a practical alternative. A single person or small partisan group can perform all the functions just described: seeking insight into the other party's interests, identifying the true issues, devising mutually beneficial alternatives, and evaluating these alternatives from a joint perspective. Another approach is for a third party to do the problem solving.

There are many arguments for engaging in problem solving. One is that this strategy reduces the likelihood of runaway escalation. This is because it does not pose a threat to Other and is psychologically incompatible with the use of heavy contentious tactics. As the saying goes, "It is better to jaw-jaw than to war-war." Problem solving also encourages the discovery of compromises and integrative options that serve both parties' interests.

From Dean G. Pruitt and Jeffrey Z. Rubin, *Social Conflict: Escalation, Stalemate, and Settlement.* (New York: Random House, 1986), pp. 139–148. Reprinted by permission of McGraw-Hill, Inc. and the authors. Citations suppressed.

Problem solving is not without its risks, however. Individual efforts to find a mutually acceptable solution tend to weaken Party's own resolve and may also (if there is ambiguity about Party's strength) telegraph weakness to Other. Also, problem-solving discussions can be more advantageous to one party than the other. For instance, they are likely to provide greater benefit to the more verbal of the two parties, who is often better armed with statistics and other persuasive devices. An example is a discussion between labor and management in which union leaders are poorly educated. If the less verbal party has greater threat capacity, as is sometimes true of the labor representative, that party may be able to achieve a larger outcome from contentious behavior than from problem solving. . . .

The next section deals with the impact of problem solving on the outcome of conflict. One possible outcome, the development of an integrative solution, receives special emphasis. Following that, we examine the techniques people use to fashion integrative solutions. Five types of integrative solutions are described, along with the refocusing questions that make it possible to devise these solutions. . . .

OUTCOMES OF PROBLEM SOLVING

Successful problem solving can lead to three broad classes of outcomes: compromise, agreement on a procedure for deciding who will win, or integrative solution.

Compromise

A *compromise* is an agreement reached when both parties concede to some middle ground along an obvious dimension. A good example is a decision to settle a wage dispute by splitting the difference between the two parties' proposals. . . . The popular use of the term "compromise" is somewhat broader; it often means any agreement in which the parties abandon their initial demands. But we have adopted a narrower definition in order to distinguish compromises from integrative solutions.

Compromises can sometimes be very good for both parties and sometimes very bad. But most commonly they provide both parties a middling outcome—by no means as good as what they had hoped for or as bad as what they might have got. Where it can be achieved, an integrative solution is usually much better for both parties than a compromise. Yet many controversies end in compromise. Among the reasons for this are aspirations that are not sufficiently high, time pressure that makes it hard to embark on a search for new options, fear of prolonged conflict, and a societally endorsed fetish for "fairness" that often attracts unwarranted attention to the 50–50 division. In addition, compromises sometimes grow out of an unduly escalated episode. So much energy has been devoted to trying to beat the other party, and so much attention is focused on partisan options, that the parties cannot engage in creative efforts to devise new alternatives. Hence, when they finally see that they are in a hurting stalemate, they reach out in desperation for an obvious compromise.

Agreement on a Procedure for Deciding Who Will Win

Compromise is not the only kind of solution that seems fair. Sometimes the outcome of problem solving is a procedure for deciding who will win—that is, a rule for awarding one party all it is asking while the other gets little or nothing. Examples of such a procedure include:

- Tossing a coin, with victory for the winner.
- Comparing needs, with victory for the party who feels most strongly about the issue under consideration.
- Submitting to a third-party decision, with victory for the disputant whose position seems most cogent to a judge or arbitrator.
- Voting, with victory to the party who can command a majority of some deliberative body.

It is sometimes essential to use one of these procedures—for example, when there are only two possible outcomes (such as I go first or you go first). But in most cases, more integrative solutions are available if the parties will only seek them out. This means that norms of fairness and legitimate procedures like voting can sometimes be snakes in the grass, undermining the parties' will to look for more integrative solutions and the benefits that come with such solutions.

Integrative Solutions

An integrative solution is one that reconciles (that is, integrates) the two parties' interests. Integrative solutions produce the highest joint outcomes of the three types of agreement. Consider, for example, the story of two sisters who are quarreling over an orange. A compromise agreement is reached to split the fruit in half—whereupon the first sister squeezes her half for juice while the other uses the peel from her half in a cake. Both would clearly have profited more from the integrative solution of giving the first sister all the juice and the second all the peel. But, intent on compromise, they never found it.

In this story, it is possible for a *fully* integrative solution to be reached, one that totally satisfies both parties' aspirations. However, most integrative solutions are not quite so successful. They *partially* reconcile the parties' interests, leaving them fairly content but not quite so happy as if they had achieved all they had hoped for.

Integrative solutions sometimes entail known alternatives, but more often they involve the development of novel alternatives and hence require some creativity and imagination. For this reason, it is proper to say that they usually emerge from a process of creative thinking. Integrative solutions can be devised by either of the parties acting separately, by the two of them in joint session, or by a third party such as a mediator.

Situations that allow for the development of integrative solutions are said to be high in "integrative potential." . . . There is more integrative potential in most situations than is usually assumed. Hence a skilled and sustained problem-solving effort is often richly rewarded.

Although it is true that problem solving can lead to any of the three possible outcomes—compromise, agreement on a procedure for deciding who will win, or integrative solution—parties to conflict are strongly advised to pursue integrative solutions if at all possible. This advice is given for four main reasons.

1. If aspirations are high and there is resistance to yielding on both sides, it may be impossible to resolve the conflict unless a way can be found to join the two parties' interests.
2. Agreements involving higher joint benefit are likely to be more stable. Compromises, coin tosses, and other mechanical agreements are often unsatisfying to one or both parties, causing the issue to come up again at a later time.
3. Because they are mutually rewarding, integrative solutions tend to strengthen the relationship between the parties. Strengthened relationships usually have inherent value and also facilitate the development of integrative solutions in subsequent situations.
4. Integrative solutions ordinarily contribute to the welfare of the broader community of which the two parties are members. For example, a firm usually benefits as a whole when its departments are able to reconcile their differences creatively.

. . . Problem solving is especially likely to lead to integrative solutions when aspirations are high, time pressure is low, fear of conflict is low, and the parties are not overly impressed by the importance of fairness.

TYPES OF INTEGRATIVE SOLUTIONS

If integrative solutions are so important to achieve, how do they emerge? What are the routes for moving from opposing demands to an alternative that reconciles the two parties' interests? We have identified five such routes, leading to five types of integrative solutions: expanding the pie, nonspecific compensation, logrolling, cost cutting, and bridging. In addition to its theoretical value, this typology should be useful as a check list for any bargainer or mediator seeking a way to settle a controversy.

In order to increase the theoretical and practical value of our presentation, we shall mention in connection with each type of solution the kind of information that is needed in order to formulate such a solution and several refocusing questions that can aid in the search for such a solution. The types of solutions will be listed in order of the difficulty of getting the necessary information—with the least difficult listed first. . . .

Expanding the Pie

Some conflicts hinge on a resource shortage. Time, money, space, automobiles, handsome men, or what have you—all are in long demand but short supply. In such circumstances, integrative solutions can be devised by expanding the pie, which means increasing the available resources. For example, . . . [when] two milk companies were vying to be first to unload cans on a platform, the controversy was resolved when somebody thought of widening the platform.

Expanding the pie is a useful formula when the parties find one another's proposals inherently acceptable but reject them because they pose opportunity costs. . . . However, expanding the pie is by no means a universal remedy. If there are inherent costs, as opposed to opportunity costs, in the other party's proposal, broadening the pie may yield strikingly poor results. Other types of integrative solutions are better in such cases.

The information requirements for expanding the pie are very slim. All that is required is knowledge of the parties' demands. No analysis of the interests underlying these demands is needed. However, this does not mean that such a solution is always easy to find. There may be no resource shortage, or it may be expensive to enlarge the pool of resources. Furthermore, it may not be apparent that the problem hinges on a resource shortage. In an argument over who goes first on the loading platform, it may not be clear that the real issue is the size of the platform.

Several refocusing questions can be useful in seeking a solution by expanding the pie.

How can both parties get what they want? Does the conflict hinge on a resource shortage? How can the critical resource be expanded?

Nonspecific Compensation

In nonspecific compensation, Party gets what he or she wants, and Other is repaid in some unrelated coin. Compensation is "nonspecific" when it does not deal with the precise costs incurred by the other party. An . . . example is a supervisor giving an employee a bonus for going without dinner in order to meet a deadline.

Compensation usually comes from the party whose demands are granted, because that party is "buying" concessions from the other. But it can also originate with a third party or even with the party who is compensated. An example of the latter is an employee who pampers himself or herself by finding a nice office to work in while going without dinner.

Two kinds of information are useful for devising a solution via nonspecific compensation: (1) information about one or more realms of value to the other party, for example, knowledge that he or she values love or attention or is money-mad; (2) information about how badly that party is hurt by making the concessions; such information is useful for devising adequate compensation. If only one of these kinds of information (or neither) is available, it may be possible to conduct an "auction" for the other party's acquiescence, changing the sort of benefit offered or raising one's offer in trial-and-error fashion, until a formula is found to which he or she can agree.

Refocusing questions that can help locate a means of compensation include: What does the other party value that I can supply? How valuable is this to the other party? How much is the other party hurting in conceding to me?

Though it is often useful, nonspecific compensation has its limitations. These are mainly due to normative constraints. For example, it is not proper to pay a government employee for food. . . .

When there are normative constraints against a compensatory scheme that is nevertheless desired by the parties, three strategies are available for avoiding community awareness of the transaction: making a secret agreement, secretly transferring one or both benefits, and delayed sequential enactment of the benefits (such that the two parties' actions are so separated in time that outsiders do not see the connection). A traveler who places a $20 bill in his or her passport at a foreign airport is making a secret transfer. An example of a secret agreement that was also sequentially enacted can be seen in the American pledge to withdraw missiles from Turkey during the Cuban missile crisis. This withdrawal was delayed for four months after the Russians took their missiles out of Cuba, presumably so that the connection would not be obvious. One can only assume that the American president feared that, if this agreement became known, he would be criticized by opposition politicians or nervous allies.

Compensatory schemes often take the form of promises—guarantees of later benefit in exchange for present compliance. . . .

Logrolling

In a solution by logrolling, each party concedes on issues that are of low priority to itself and high priority to the other party. In this way, each gets that part of its demands that it deems most important. Like the other types of solutions, logrolling is not a universal route to integrative solutions. It is possible only when several issues are under consideration and the parties have different priorities among these issues. Suppose . . . a hypothetical case of bargaining between labor and management in which labor initially demands a 20 percent increase in overtime rate and 20 more minutes of rest breaks and management indicates unwillingness to provide either concession. If the overtime rate is especially important for labor and if long rest breaks are particularly abhorrent to management, a reasonably integrative solution can be achieved by labor dropping its demands for more rest breaks in exchange for management giving in on the overtime rate. This sort of solution is typically better for both parties than a compromise on the two issues, such as a 10 percent increase in overtime rate and 10 more minutes of rest time.

Logrolling can be viewed as a variant of nonspecific compensation in which each party is compensated for making concessions desired by the other.

To develop solutions by logrolling, it is useful to have information about the two parties priorities among the issues so that concessions can be matched up, but it is not necessary to have information about the nature of the interests (goals and values) underlying these priorities. Information about priorities is not always easy to get. One reason for this is that people often try to conceal their priorities for fear that they will be forced to concede on issues of lesser importance to themselves without receiving compensation. Another reason is that people often erroneously project their own priorities onto others, assuming that what they want is what the other wants also.

Solutions by logrolling can also be developed by a process of trial and error in which one systematically offers a series of possible packages, keeping one's own aspirations as high as possible, until an alternative is found that is acceptable to the other party.

Refocusing questions that can be useful for developing solutions by logrolling include: Which issues are of higher priority and which of lower priority to myself? Which issues are of higher priority and which of lower priority to the other party? Are some of my high-priority issues of lower priority to the other party and vice versa?

Cost Cutting

In solutions by cost cutting, Party gets what he or she wants, and Other's costs are reduced or eliminated. The result is high joint benefit, not because Party has changed his or her position but because Other suffers less. . . .

Information about the nature of the other party's costs is, of course, helpful for developing solutions by cost cutting. This is a deeper kind of information than knowledge of that party's priorities. It involves knowing something about the interests—the values and needs—underlying that party's overt position.

Refocusing questions for developing solutions by cost cutting include: What costs are posed for the other party by my proposal? How can these costs be mitigated or eliminated?

Bridging

In bridging, neither party achieves its initial demands, but a new option is devised that satisfies the most important interests underlying those demands. For example, suppose [there are] . . . two women reading in a library room. One wants to open the window for ventilation, the other to keep it closed in order not to catch cold. The ultimate solution involves opening a window in the next room, thereby letting in the fresh air while avoiding a draft.

Bridging typically stems from a reformulation of the issue(s) on the basis of an analysis of the underlying interests. . . . The reformulation process can be carried out by either or both parties or by a third party who is trying to help.

It is rare that a solution can be found that bridges all of the two parties' interests, as the window in the next room of the library does.

More often higher-priority interests are served while lower-priority interests are discarded. . . .

It follows that people who seek to develop bridging solutions must usually have information about the nature of the two parties' interests and about their priorities among these interests. Information about priorities among interests is different from information about priorities among issues (which is useful for developing solutions by logrolling). Issues are the concrete matters under discussion now; interests are the hidden concerns that underlie preferences with respect to issues.

To achieve an optimal solution by bridging, the information just described should be used as follows: In an initial phase, one's search model should include all of the interests on both sides. But if this does not generate a mutually acceptable alternative, some of the lower-priority interests should be discarded from the model and the search begun anew. The result will not be an ideal solution, but it is likely to be one that is mutually acceptable. . . .

Refocusing questions that can be raised in seaching for a solution by bridging include: What are the two parties' basic interests? What are the priorities among these interests? How can both sets of high-priority interests be achieved?

III
FOREIGN POLICY
AND GLOBAL CONFLICT

THE TOPIC

Understanding foreign policy and explaining global conflict have been the two main empirical endeavors of the field of international relations. As the following selections show, these are interrelated questions. Chapter 6 begins with general explanations of foreign policy. Some of the path-breaking work that has been done on the subject of crisis is presented in Chapter 7. Chapter 8 presents selections from a variety of disciplines and historical periods to address the field's central problem: war. Chapter 9 covers the subject of imperialism. While other empirical research has been conducted, these areas embody the best and most influential work.

THE SELECTIONS

The selections in Chapter 6 can be grouped into three categories. Morgenthau (1952) and Wolfers (1952) deal with the concept of national interest both as an explanation of foreign policy and as a basis for the conduct of foreign affairs. Guetzkow and Valadez (1968, 1981), Jervis (1976), and Allison and Halperin (1972) analyze processes by which foreign policy decisions are made. Finally, Rosenau (1966) presents a general explanation of foreign policy behavior.

The end of World War II, the creation of the United Nations, the emergence of the Cold War, and the onset of the Korean War provided severe tests for the application of idealist and realist ideas about foreign policy. The shattered hopes for a postwar era of peace and the circumlocution that the Korean War was a police action did much to ensure the intellectual triumph of realism. Both **Morgenthau's** (1952) essay and his book *In Defense of the National Interest* cogently present the case for basing foreign policy on the national interest (cf. Wilson, selection 7), although, with his typical acumen, he recognizes the potential problems posed by the ambiguity of the concept. In a series of articles later collected in *Discord and Collaboration*, **Arnold Wolfers** elucidates and reformulates some of the fundamental assumptions and concepts of realism. In the selection reprinted here, he details the empirical obfuscations and policy risks inherent in the concept of national interest. Many of the problems he outlines were to materialize later during the Vietnam and Watergate era to haunt the American polity. Ironically, Wolfers's analysis eventually led most political scientists to abandon the concept just at the time when Morgenthau's analysis provided the intellectual rationale for policymakers to embrace it. While scholars have developed other concepts to explain foreign policy, no other concept that can be used to make and evaluate foreign policy has gained wide acceptance. The most closely related concept has been that of class interest, which shares many of the same conceptual problems. Clearly, the need for new concepts to evaluate policy stands as one of the major challenges to the field.

During the 1950s and 1960s, the behavioralists focused attention on empirical questions rather than on questions related purely to policy. Snyder, Bruck, and Sapin introduced the decision-making approach to the field in 1954. Instead of attempting to deduce a country's foreign policy on the basis of its national interest, they emphasized the need to try to explain foreign policy by examining the factors that influence officials to make a particular decision.

Studying foreign policy decision making is difficult, however, because the process is usually inaccessible to scholarly observation, and often secret. One of the more innovative attempts to resolve this problem was through the use of simulation. Early simulation involved individuals' playing roles in a "game" in which the rules and procedures were intended to represent the "reality" of world politics. Scholars often use role-playing simulations in much the same way that social psychologists use experiments, testing specific hypotheses by observing how players with different characteristics play the game. This technique was introduced into the field in the late 1950s by **Harold Guetzkow**, who with others developed the Inter-Nation Simulation.

A simulation, however, involves more than just a procedure for testing hypotheses. The rules that make up the game and the "programs" used to determine the consequences of decisions form a theory of how world politics work. In the article excerpted here, Guetzkow and Valadez examine the extent to which the underlying theory of the simulation is a valid representation of "reality" and review some of the findings on the effect personal characteristics have on making foreign policy decisions. Even though the selection deals with only one aspect of the research, the reader can gain a sense of the scope and rigor of one of the major projects in the field. Early role-playing simulations have given rise to all-computer simulations, which in turn have served as a foundation for the use of artificial intelligence to replicate foreign policy decisions.

Since decision making involves cognitive and social psychology, it is clear that political science has much to learn from research in that area. **Robert Jervis's** (1976) work has been in the forefront of integrating and applying the findings of this research to the diplomatic record in order to improve our understanding of the dynamics of foreign policy. In the selection reprinted here, he argues that individuals' images and beliefs about foreign policy are determined by the lessons they derive from history. Since these lessons are often overdrawn and difficult to change, Jervis's work raises questions about the soundness of foreign policy making and provides insights about its dynamics.

The work on bureaucratic politics also deals with foreign policy making but from the perspective of the organization, rather than that of the individual. In their important essay, **Allison** and **Halperin** (1972) attack the realist idea that the nation is a unitary rational actor that produces foreign policy in the national interest. Instead, they see foreign policy as a product of the pulling and hauling of bureaucratic actors, each with its own organizational interests. Because this indicates that foreign policy is often formulated primarily for domestic or organizational reasons, it is erroneous to assume that foreign policy is basically a set of intentional communications and interactions between states guided by a rational decision-making framework. While the insight associated with this approach has not given rise to a general explanation of foreign policy, it has undercut confidence in deductive attempts to explain decisions on the basis of national interest.

As the focus on decision making evolved from the 1950s through the 1970s, others attempted to develop more general explanations of foreign policy. The most influential of these attempts was **Rosenau's** (1966) "pre-theory." His work makes two advances over that of Snyder et al. First, he reduces the long checklist of factors that might affect a decision to five variable clusters; second, he rank-orders the potency of these factors on the basis of the nation's attributes and the issue under contention. Rosenau's contribution is important because it moved the field toward the creation of testable hypotheses that could explain the behavior of states. In doing so, Rosenau gave rise to a school of comparative foreign policy that has researched and reformulated many of his propositions.

Because the United States was involved in a number of dramatic crises during the Cold War, and because many wars are preceded by crises, it is not an accident that crisis research became a focus of the behavioralists. Chapter 7 includes representative selections from some of the best work on this topic. The article by **Charles Hermann** (1969) has continued to receive wide attention; in it, he defines *crisis* as a situation that, as a decision maker perceives it, involves a high threat to the state, a short time in which to decide, and the element of surprise. Using these three dimensions, he develops a typology of situations that a decision maker could face, and then offers propositions to explain and predict how these situations would affect foreign policy decision making. In his other work, Hermann used the Inter-Nation Simulation to test his propositions; later in the 1970s, he was instrumental in collecting event data (quantitative analysis of news reports) in the CREON project, which linked his focus on decision making with Rosenau's pre-theory of foreign policy behavior.

The selection by **Holsti**, **North**, and **Brody** (1968) attempts to delineate the role of perception in the escalation of crisis to war. This selection was one of the most important articles to come out of the Stanford Studies on Conflict and Integration, directed by Robert North. The project was significant because it was the first to use the technique of content analysis to gather data from previously secret government documents. It not only serves as an exemplar of scientific research, but also elucidates the dynamics of hostile spirals that lead to war. Later, Robert North and Nazli Choucri (see selection 36), supplemented this research with an investigation of the long-term factors that, from 1870 to 1914, led to World War I.

Such studies demonstrate that important pieces of knowledge can be created by the application of scientific and statistical techniques. Equally important in the study of crisis has been the application of game theory. Originally a branch of mathematics, game-theoretic models of "chicken," "prisoner's dilemma," and "zero-sum games" have been applied to questions related to nuclear war and arms control. The selection by **Glenn Snyder** and **Paul Diesing** (1977) applies game theory to a set of historical crises to see if the structure of the crisis conforms to certain games. They then examine the extent to which the "game structure" shapes crisis bargaining.

War has been a focus of inquiry for a long time, and it has received the attention of several disciplines. The works in Chapter 8 were selected to reflect this richness: their authors are practitioners of political philosophy, anthropology, physics, and political science.

The selection by **Hobbes** (1651) provides an insight that has been central in analyses of world politics; namely, that in a state of anarchy, war is constant and insecurity prevalent. Although Hobbes was reacting to the English Civil War, his notion that the state of nature is anarchic, and that without government there is nothing to prevent war, has long been seen by many as an accurate image of the international system. For Hobbes, war is a natural condition, given human nature, which he sees as "a perpetual and restless desire of power after power, that ceases only in death."[1] The solution to war is for all individuals to disarm and to give complete obedience to an all-powerful sovereign. At the global level, this solution would entail a world government. Hobbes's contribution is that he not only provided the basis for much of the work on global anarchy, but also developed one of the main explanations of the need for government.

Unlike Hobbes, **Margaret Mead** (1940) does not believe that war is inherent in human nature. If this were the case, she cogently points out in her essay, then it should be found in all societies; but it is not. She and other anthropologists have located peaceful societies. To Mead, war is a learned custom that does not have a biological basis. Her focus on peaceful societies is representative of an area of inquiry in the field that explains war by looking at what has enabled peaceful societies to avoid it.

The work of **Lewis Richardson** was the first major attempt to investigate war through the application of the scientific method and statistical procedures. As with others who were writing at the time, Richardson reacted to World War I with horror. He resolved to find the causes of war. A Quaker, he retired from a very successful career in physics and meteorology to investigate the subject of war. His two major works, *Statistics of Deadly Quarrels* and *Arms and Insecurity*, were published posthumously in 1960. In the former, he collected data on deadly quarrels and then examined their common attributes. His analysis was particularly important for the *way* in which he studied war and for his use of statistical models and reasoning. In *Arms and Insecurity*, a portion of which is reprinted here, he attempts to use mathematics to explain arms races as an action-reaction process that often results in war. His specific model as well as his use of mathematical deduction provided the foundation for much of the work on arms races.

---

[1]Thomas Hobbes, *Leviathan*, Part I, Chapter 11, second paragraph.

Although the contemporary scientific study of war can be traced back to the work of Lewis Richardson, his research had little influence until the 1960s. Prior to that time, the analysis of war that received the most attention was Quincy Wright's monumental tome, *A Study of War*, begun in 1926 and completed in 1942. Building on the efforts of Richardson and Wright, J. David Singer in the middle 1960s initiated the Correlates of War project, which involved several scholars and a host of graduate students. This project has been the main source of scientific data on war, militarized disputes, alliances, and national capability. Analysis of these data form the bulk of the scientific findings on war. The selection by **Stuart Bremer** (1992) looks at factors associated with the onset of war, while the selection by **Frank Wayman**, **J. David Singer**, and **Gary Goertz** (1983) examines factors associated with winning wars. Bremer finds that war is more probable between neighbors than between non-neighbors, especially if at least one is less economically advanced or non-democratic, there is no overwhelming preponderance of capability between the states, and one side is a major state (see also Maoz and Russett, selection 51). Wayman, Singer, and Goertz find that winning wars and success in militarized disputes is generally a function of a state's economic capability, rather than its military capability. This implies that the outcome of many wars (but not all) can be predicted beforehand, especially if both sides are equally motivated.

Closely related to the study of war has been the analysis of imperialism, the subject of Chapter 9. Imperialism, which has been perceived as a cause of war, is also a subject of inquiry in its own right. Although imperialism was a concern in ancient times, the seminal modern study is that of Hobson (1902). His work greatly influenced **Lenin**, (1916) who made it the basis of his own analysis, *Imperialism: The Highest Stage of Capitalism*, which remains the best-known work on the subject and the starting point for most Marxist analyses of imperialism.

Primarily because of the political climate within the United States and because of the influence of the Cold War, most studies on imperialism were not conducted by international relations scholars. **Johan Galtung's** "A Structural Theory of Imperialism," published in 1971, renewed interest in the study of the subject. In it he employs sociological concepts to analyze the imperialistic relationship between the center and the periphery in today's world. In so doing, he shows that the ending of colonialism has not ended imperialism, which has continued in more subtle ways.

In the mid-1970s, behavioralists within the United States became more interested in testing and reformulating propositions on imperialism. One of the most significant efforts was that of **Choucri** and **North**, (1975) who examined the relationship among domestic factors, expansion, imperial rivalries, and the onset of World War I. Their work is particularly important in linking the earlier work on the 1914 crisis with the more structural approach of the contemporary Marxists.

Meanwhile, the relationship between center and periphery continued as a focus of inquiry. Latin American researchers, including Cardoso and Faletto, saw this relationship as one of dependency, and used it to explain why Third World countries are not industrializing more rapidly. This work set the stage for a much broader area of inquiry, led by Immanuel Wallerstein (selection 47), that looks at how a single world political economy emerged.

FOR FURTHER READING

Foreign Policy

CHARLES A. BEARD. 1934. *The Idea of the National Interest.* New York: Macmillan.

RICHARD C. SNYDER, H. W. BRUCK, and BURTON SAPIN, eds. 1962. *Foreign Policy Decision-Making: An Approach.* New York: Free Press.

RUDOLPH J. RUMMEL. 1972. *The Dimensions of Nations.* Beverly Hills: Sage.

JACK SNYDER. 1991. *Myths of Empire: Domestic Politics and International Ambition.* Ithaca: Cornell University Press.

Crisis

CHARLES A. MCCLELLAND. 1972. "The Beginning, Duration, and Abatement of International Crises: Comparison in Two Conflict Arenas." In Charles F. Hermann, ed. *International Crises: Insights from Behavioral Research.* New York: Free Press.

RICHARD NED LEBOW. 1981. *Between Peace and War: The Nature of International Crises.* Baltimore: Johns Hopkins University Press.

MICHAEL BRECHER. 1993. *Crisis in World Politics.* Oxford: Pergamon.

RUSSELL J. LENG. 1993. *Interstate Crisis Behavior, 1816–1980: Realism versus Reciprocity.* Cambridge: Cambridge University Press.

War

SIGMUND FREUD. 1930. *Civilization and Its Discontents.* London: Hogarth Press.

QUINCY WRIGHT. 1942. *A Study of War.* Chicago: University of Chicago Press.

J. DAVID SINGER. 1979, 1980. *The Correlates of War,* Vols. I & II. New York: Free Press.

R. J. RUMMEL. 1979. *War, Power, Peace,* Vol. 4: *Understanding Conflict and War.* Beverly Hills, Calif.: Sage Publications.

BRUCE BUENO DE MESQUITA. 1981. *The War Trap.* New Haven: Yale University Press.

JACK S. LEVY. 1989. "The Causes of War: A Review of Theories and Evidence," in P. Tetlock et al. (eds.) *Behavior, Society, and Nuclear War,* Vol I. New York: Oxford University Press.

RANDOLPH M. SIVERSON AND HARVEY STARR. 1991. *The Diffusion of War.* Ann Arbor: University of Michigan Press.

JOHN A. VASQUEZ. 1993. *The War Puzzle.* Cambridge: Cambridge University Press.

Imperialism

J. A. HOBSON. 1902. *Imperialism: A Study.* London: George Allen and Unwin, 1938.

JOSEPH SCHUMPETER. 1919. "The Sociology of Imperialism," in *Imperialism and Social Classes.* New York: Meridian Books, 1958.

RONALD ROBINSON AND JOHN GALLAGHER. 1961. *Africa and the Victorians.* London: Macmillan.

FERNANDO HENRIQUE CARDOSO AND ENZO FALETTO. 1979. *Dependency and Development in Latin America.* Berkeley: University of California Press.

Chapter 6
Explanations of Foreign Policy

20. Another "Great Debate": The National Interest of the United States

HANS J. MORGENTHAU

. . . The issue which the present debate raises concerns the nature of all politics and, more particularly, of the American tradition in foreign policy. The history of modern political thought is the story of a contest between two schools which differ fundamentally in their conception of the nature of man, society, and politics. One believes that a rational and moral political order, derived from universally valid abstract principles, can be achieved here and now. . . .

The other school believes that the world, imperfect as it is from the rational point of view, is the result of forces which are inherent in human nature. . . . This being inherently a world of opposing interests and of conflict among them, moral principles can never be fully realized, but at best approximated through the ever temporary balancing of interests and the ever precarious settlement of conflicts. . . .

Yet what is the national interest? How can we define it and give it the content which will make it a guide for action? This is one of the relevant questions to which the current debate has given rise.

Excerpted from "Another 'Great Debate': The National Interest of the United States," by Hans J. Morgenthau, *American Political Science Review*, 46 (1952), pp. 961–978. Reprinted by permission of the publisher. Footnotes deleted.

It has been frequently argued against the realist conception of foreign policy that its key concept, the national interest, does not provide an acceptable standard for political action. This argument is in the main based upon two grounds: the elusiveness of the concept and its susceptibility to interpretations, such as limitless imperialism and narrow nationalism, which are not in keeping with the American tradition in foreign policy. The argument has substance as far as it goes, but it does not invalidate the usefulness of the concept.

The concept of the national interest is similar in two respects to the "great generalities" of the Constitution, such as the general welfare and due process. It contains a residual meaning which is inherent in the concept itself, but beyond these minimum requirements its content can run the whole gamut of meanings which are logically compatible with it. That content is determined by the political traditions and the total cultural context within which a nation formulates its foreign policy. The concept of the national interest, then, contains two elements, one that is logically required and in that sense necessary, and one that is variable and determined by circumstances.

Any foreign policy which operates under the standard of the national interest must obviously have some reference to the physical, political, and cultural entity which we call a nation. In a world where a number of sovereign nations compete with and oppose each other for power, the foreign policies of all nations must necessarily refer to their survival as their minimum requirements. Thus all nations do what they cannot help but do: protect their physical, political, and cultural identity against encroachments by other nations. . . .

The survival of a political unit, such as a nation, in its identity is the irreducible minimum, the necessary element of its interests vis-à-vis other units. Taken in isolation, the determination of its content in a concrete situation is relatively simple; for it encompasses the integrity of the nation's territory, of its political institutions, and of its culture. Thus bipartisanship in foreign policy, especially in times of war, has been most easily achieved in the promotion of these minimum requirements of the national interest. The situation is different with respect to the variable elements of the national interests. All the cross currents of personalities, public opinion, sectional interests, partisan politics, and political and moral folkways are brought to bear upon their determination. In consequence, the contribution which science can make to this field, as to all fields of policy formation, is limited. It can identify the different agencies of the government which contribute to the determination of the variable elements of the national interest and assess their relative weight. It can separate the long-range objectives of foreign policy from the short-term ones which are the means for the achievement of the former and can tentatively establish their rational relations. Finally, it can analyze the variable elements of the national interest in terms of their legitimacy and their compatibility with other national values and with the national interest of other nations. . . .

The legitimacy of the national interest must be determined in the face of possible usurpation by subnational, other-national, and supranational interests. On the subnational level we find group interests, represented particularly by ethnic and economic groups, who tend to identify themselves with the national interest. Charles A. Beard has emphasized, however

one-sidedly, the extent to which the economic interests of certain groups have been presented as those of the United States. Group interests exert, of course, constant pressure upon the conduct of our foreign policy, claiming their identity with the national interest. It is, however, doubtful that, with the exception of a few spectacular cases, they have been successful in determining the course of American foreign policy. It is much more likely, given the nature of American domestic politics, that American foreign policy, insofar as it is the object of pressures by sectional interests, will normally be a compromise between divergent sectional interests. The concept of the national interest, as it emerges from this contest as the actual guide for foreign policy, may well fall short of what would be rationally required by the overall interests of the United States. Yet the concept of the national interest which emerges from this contest of conflicting sectional interests is also more than any particular sectional interest or their sum total. It is, as it were, the lowest common denominator where sectional interests and the national interest meet in an uneasy compromise which may leave much to be desired in view of all the interests concerned. . . .

The more acute problem arises at the present time from the importance which the public and government officials, at least in their public utterances, attribute to the values represented and the policies pursued by international organizations either as alternatives or supplements to the values and policies for which the national government stands. It is frequently asserted that the foreign policy of the United States pursues no objectives apart from those of the United Nations, that, in other words, the foreign policy of the United States is actually identical with the policy of the United Nations. This assertion cannot refer to anything real in actual politics to support it. For the constitutional structure of international organizations, such as the United Nations, and their procedural practices make it impossible for them to pursue interests apart from those of the member-states which dominate their policy-forming bodies. . . .

The real issue in view of the problem that concerns us here is not whether the so-called interests of the United Nations, which do not exist apart from the interests of its most influential members, have superseded the national interests of the United States, but for what kind of interests the United States has secured United Nations support. While these interests cannot be United Nations interests, they do not need to be national interests either. Here we are in the presence of that modern phenomenon which has been variously described as "utopianism," "sentimentalism," "moralism," the "legalistic-moralistic approach." The common denominator of all these tendencies in modern political thought is the substitution for the national interest of a supranational standard of action which is generally identified with an international organization, such as the United Nations. The national interest is here not being usurped by sub- or supranational interests. . . . What challenges the national interest here is a mere figment of the imagination, a product of wishful thinking, which is postulated as a valid norm for international conduct, without being valid either there or anywhere else. At this point we touch the core of the present controversy between utopianism and realism in international affairs. . . .

The national interest as such must be defended against usurpation by non-national interests. Yet once that task is accomplished, a rational order must be established among the values which make up the national interest and among the resources to be committed to them. While the interests which a nation may pursue in its relation with other nations are of infinite variety and magnitude, the resources which are available for the pursuit of such interests are necessarily limited in quantity and kind. No nation has the resources to promote all desirable objectives with equal vigor; all nations must therefore allocate their scarce resources as rationally as possible. The indispensable precondition of such rational allocation is a clear understanding of the distinction between the necessary and variable elements of the national interest. Given the contentious manner in which in democracies the variable elements of the national interest are generally determined, the advocates of an extensive conception of the national interest will inevitably present certain variable elements of the national interest as though their attainment were necessary for the nation's survival. In other words, the necessary elements of the national interest have a tendency to swallow up the variable elements so that in the end all kinds of objectives, actual or potential, are justified in terms of national survival. . . .

The concept of the national interest presupposes neither a naturally harmonious, peaceful world nor the inevitability of war as a consequence of the pursuit by all nations of their national interest. Quite to the contrary, it assumes continuous conflict and threat of war, to be minimized through the continuous adjustment of conflicting interests by diplomatic action. No such assumption would be warranted if all nations at all times conceived of their national interest only in terms of their survival and, in turn, defined their interest in survival in restrictive and rational terms. As it is, their conception of the national interest is subject to all the hazards of misinterpretation, usurpation, and misjudgment to which reference has been made above. To minimize these hazards is the first task of a foreign policy which seeks the defense of the national interest by peaceful means. Its second task is the defense of the national interest, restrictively and rationally defined, against the national interests of other nations which may or may not be thus defined. If they are not, it becomes the task of armed diplomacy to convince the nations concerned that their legitimate interests have nothing to fear from a restrictive and rational foreign policy and that their illegitimate interests have nothing to gain in the face of armed might rationally employed. . . .

21. "National Security" as an Ambiguous Symbol

ARNOLD WOLFERS

Statesmen, publicists and scholars who wish to be considered realists, as many do today, are inclined to insist that the foreign policy they advocate is dictated by the national interest, more specifically by the national security interest. It is not surprising that this should be so. Today any reference to the pursuit of security is likely to ring a sympathetic chord.

However, when political formulas such as "national interest" or "national security" gain popularity they need to be scrutinized with particular care. They may not mean the same thing to different people. They may not have any precise meaning at all. Thus, while appearing to offer guidance and a basis for broad consensus they may be permitting everyone to label whatever policy he favors with an attractive and possibly deceptive name.

In a very vague and general way "national interest" does suggest a direction of policy which can be distinguished from several others which may present themselves as alternatives. It indicates that the policy is designed to promote demands which are ascribed to the nation rather than to individuals, sub-national groups or mankind as a whole. It emphasizes that the policy subordinates other interests to those of the nation. But beyond this, it has very little meaning. . . .

. . .The question is raised, therefore, whether this seemingly more precise formula of national security offers statesmen a meaningful guide for action. Can they be expected to know what it means? Can policies be distinguished and judged on the ground that they do or do not serve this interest?

The term national security, like national interest, is well enough established in the political discourse of international relations to designate an objective of policy distinguishable from others. We know roughly what people have in mind if they complain that their government is neglecting national security or demanding excessive sacrifices for the sake of enhancing it. Usually those who raise the cry for a policy oriented exclusively toward this interest are afraid their country underestimates the external dangers facing it or is being diverted into idealistic channels unmindful of these dangers. Moreover, the symbol suggests protection through power and therefore figures more frequently in the speech of those who believe in reliance on national power than of those who place their confidence in model behavior, international cooperation, or the United Nations to carry their country safely through the tempests of international conflict. For these reasons it would be an exaggeration

Reprinted from *Political Science Quarterly* 67 (December 1952), pp. 481–502, by permission of the publisher. Footnotes deleted.

150

to claim that the symbol of national security is nothing but a stimulus to semantic confusion, though closer analysis will show that if used without specifications it leaves room for more confusion than sound political counsel or scientific usage can afford.

The demand for a policy of national security is primarily normative in character. It is supposed to indicate what the policy of a nation should be in order to be either expedient—a rational means toward an accepted end—or moral, the best or least evil course of action. The value judgments implicit in these normative exhortations will be discussed.

Before doing so, attention should be drawn to an assertion of fact which is implicit if not explicit in most appeals for a policy guided by national security. Such appeals usually assume that nations in fact have made security their goal except when idealism or utopianism of their leaders has led them to stray from the traditional path. If such conformity of behavior actually existed, it would be proper to infer that a country deviating from the established pattern of conduct would risk being penalized. This would greatly strengthen the normative arguments. The trouble with the contention of fact, however, is that the term "security" covers a range of goals so wide that highly divergent policies can be interpreted as policies of security.

Security points to some degree of protection of values previously acquired. In Walter Lippmann's words, a nation is secure to the extent to which it is not in danger of having to sacrifice core values, if it wishes to avoid war, and is able, if challenged, to maintain them by victory in such a war. What this definition implies is that security rises and falls with the ability of a nation to deter an attack, or to defeat it. This is in accord with common usage of the term.

Security is a value, then, of which a nation can have more or less and which it can aspire to have in greater or lesser measure. It has much in common, in this respect, with power or wealth, two other values of great importance in international affairs. But while wealth measures the amount of a nation's material pos-

sessions, and power its ability to control the actions of others, security, in an objective sense, measures the absence of threats to acquired values, in a subjective sense, the absence of fear that such values will be attacked. In both respects a nation's security can run a wide gamut from almost complete insecurity or sense of insecurity at one pole, to almost complete security or absence of fear at the other. . . .

This point, however, should not be overstressed. There can be no quarrel with the generalization that most nations, most of the time—the great Powers particularly—have shown, and had reason to show, an active concern about some lack of security and have been prepared to make sacrifices for its enhancement. Danger and the awareness of it have been, and continue to be, sufficiently widespread to guarantee some uniformity in this respect. But a generalization which leaves room both for the frantic kind of struggle for more security which characterized French policy at times and for the neglect of security apparent in American foreign policy after the close of both World Wars throws little light on the behavior of nations. The demand for conformity would have meaning only if it could be said—as it could under the conditions postulated in the working hypothesis of pure power politics—that nations normally subordinate all other values to the maximization of their security, which, however, is obviously not the case.

There have been many instances of struggles for more security taking the form of an unrestrained race for armaments, alliances, strategic boundaries and the like; but one need only recall the many heated parliamentary debates on arms appropriations to realize how uncertain has been the extent to which people will consent to sacrifice for additional increments of security. Even when there has been no question that armaments would mean more security, the cost in taxes, the reduction in social benefits or the sheer discomfort involved has militated effectively against further effort. . . .

It might be objected that in the long run nations are not so free to choose the amount of effort they will put into security. Are they not under a kind of compulsion to spare no effort provided they wish to survive? This objection again would make sense only if the hypothesis of pure power politics were a realistic image of actual world affairs. In fact, however, a glance at history will suffice to show that survival has only exceptionally been at stake, particularly for the major Powers. If nations were not concerned with the protection of values other than their survival as independent states, most of them, most of the time, would not have had to be seriously worried about their security, despite what manipulators of public opinion engaged in mustering greater security efforts may have said to the contrary. What "compulsion" there is, then, is a function not merely of the will of others, real or imagined, to destroy the nation's independence but of national desires and ambitions to retain a wealth of other values such as rank, respect, material possessions and special privileges. It would seem to be a fair guess that the efforts for security by a particular nation will tend to vary, other things being equal, with the range of values for which protection is being sought.

In respect to this range there may seem to exist a considerable degree of uniformity. . . . But there is deviation in two directions. Some nations seek protection for more marginal values as well. There was a time when United States policy could afford to be concerned mainly with the protection of the foreign investments or markets of its nationals, its "core values" being out of danger, or when Britain was extending its national self to include large and only vaguely circumscribed "regions of special interest." It is a well-known and portentous phenomenon that bases, security zones and the like may be demanded and acquired for the purpose of protecting values acquired earlier; and they then become new national values requiring protection themselves. Pushed to its logical conclusion, such spatial extension of the range of values does not stop short of world domination. . . .

The lack of uniformity does not end here. A policy is not characterized by its goal, in this case security, alone. In order to become im-

itable, the means by which the goal is pursued must be taken into account as well. Thus, if two nations were both endeavoring to maximize their security but one were placing all its reliance on armaments and alliances, the other on meticulous neutrality, a policy maker seeking to emulate their behavior would be at a loss where to turn. . . .

After all that has been said little is left of the sweeping generalization that in actual practice nations, guided by their national security interest, tend to pursue a uniform and therefore imitable policy of security. . . .

The actual behavior of nations, past and present, does not affect the normative proposition, to which we shall now turn our attention. According to this proposition nations are called upon to give priority to national security and thus to consent to any sacrifice of value which will provide an additional increment of security. It may be expedient, moral or both for nations to do so even if they should have failed to heed such advice in the past and for the most part are not living up to it today.

The first question, then, is whether some definable security policy can be said to be generally expedient. Because the choice of goals is not a matter of expediency, it would seem to make no sense to ask whether it is expedient for nations to be concerned with the goal of security itself; only the means used to this end, so it would seem, can be judged as to their fitness—their instrumental rationality—to promote security. Yet, this is not so. Security, like other aims, may be an intermediate rather than an ultimate goal, in which case it can be judged as a means to these more ultimate ends.

Traditionally, the protection and preservation of national core values have been considered ends in themselves, at least by those who followed in the footsteps of Machiavelli. . . .

When one sets out to define in terms of expediency the level of security to which a nation should aspire, one might be tempted to assume that the sky is the limit. Is not insecurity of any kind an evil from which any rational policy maker would want to rescue his country? Yet, there are obvious reasons why this is not so.

In the first place, every increment of security must be paid by additional sacrifices of other values usually of a kind more exacting than the mere expenditure of precious time on the part of policy makers. At a certain point, then, by something like the economic law of diminishing returns, the gain in security no longer compensates for the added costs of attaining it. As in the case of economic value comparisons and preferences, there is frequently disagreement among different layers of policy makers as to where the line should be drawn. This is true particularly because absolute security is out of the question unless a country is capable of world domination, in which case, however, the insecurities and fears would be "internalized" and probably magnified. Because nations must "live dangerously," then, to some extent, whatever they consent to do about it, a modicum of additional but only relative security may easily become unattractive to those who have to bear the chief burden. Nothing renders the task of statesmen in a democracy more difficult than the reluctance of the people to follow them very far along the road to high and costly security levels.

In the second place, national security policies when based on the accumulation of power have a way of defeating themselves if the target level is set too high. This is due to the fact that "power of resistance" cannot be unmistakably distinguished from "power of aggression." What a country does to bolster its own security through power can be interpreted by others, therefore, as a threat to their security. If this occurs, the vicious circle of what John Herz has described as the "security dilemma" sets in: the efforts of one side provoke countermeasures by the other which in turn tend to wipe out the gains of the first. Theoretically there seems to be no escape from this frustrating consequence; in practice, however, there are ways to convince those who might feel threatened that the accumulation of power is not intended and will never be used for attack. The chief way is that of keeping the target level within moderate bounds and of avoiding placing oneself in a position where it

has to be raised suddenly and drastically. The desire to escape from this vicious circle presupposes a security policy of much self-restraint and moderation, especially in the choice of the target level. It can never be expedient to pursue a security policy which by the fact of provocation or incentive to others fails to increase the nation's relative power position and capability of resistance. . . .

The reason why "power of resistance" is not the general panacea which some believe it to be lies in the nature of security itself. If security, in the objective sense of the term at least, rises and falls with the presence or absence of aggressive intentions on the part of others, the attitude and behavior of those from whom the threat emanates are of prime importance. Such attitude and behavior need not be beyond the realm of influence by the country seeking to bolster its security. Whenever they do not lie beyond this realm the most effective and least costly security policy consists in inducing the opponent to give up his aggressive intentions.

While there is no easy way to determine when means can and should be used which are directed not at resistance but at the prevention of the desire of others to attack, it will clarify the issue to sketch the type of hypotheses which would link specific security policies, as expedient, to some of the most typical political constellations.

One can think of nations lined up between the two poles of maximum and minimum "attack propensity," with those unalterably committed to attack, provided it promises success, at one pole and those whom no amount of opportunity for successful attack could induce to undertake it at the other. While security in respect to the first group can come exclusively as a result of "positions of strength" sufficient to deter or defeat attack, nothing could do more to undermine security in respect to the second group than to start accumulating power of a kind which would provoke fear and countermoves.

Unfortunately it can never be known with certainty, in practice, what position within the continuum one's opponent actually occupies.

Statesmen cannot be blamed, moreover, if caution and suspicion lead them to assume a closer proximity to the first pole than hindsight proves to have been justified. We believe we have ample proof that the Soviet Union today is at or very close to the first pole, while Canadian policy makers probably place the United States in its intentions toward Canada at the second pole.

It is fair to assume that, wherever the issue of security becomes a matter of serious concern, statesmen will usually be dealing with potential opponents who occupy a position somewhere between but much closer to the first of the two poles. This means, then, that an attack must be feared as a possibility, even though the intention to launch it cannot be considered to have crystallized to the point where nothing could change it. If this be true, a security policy in order to be expedient cannot avoid accumulating power of resistance and yet cannot let it go at that. Efforts have to be made simultaneously toward the goal of removing the incentives to attack. This is only another way of saying that security policy must seek to bring opponents to occupy a position as close to the second pole as conditions and capabilities permit.

Such a twofold policy presents the greatest dilemmas because efforts to change the intentions of an opponent may run counter to the efforts to build up strength against him. The dangers of any policy of concessions, symbolized by "Munich," cannot be underestimated. The paradox of this situation must be faced, however, if security policy is to be expedient. It implies that national security policy, except when directed against a country unalterably committed to attack, is the more rational the more it succeeds in taking the interests, including the security interests, of the other side into consideration. Only in doing so can it hope to minimize the willingness of the other to resort to violence. Rather than to insist, then, that under all conditions security be sought by reliance on nothing but defensive power and be pushed in a spirit of national selfishness toward the highest targets, it should be stressed that in most instances efforts to satisfy

legitimate demands of others are likely to promise better results in terms of security. . . .

We can now focus our attention on the moral issue, if such there be. Those who advocate a policy devoted to national security are not always aware of the fact—if they do not explicitly deny it—that they are passing moral judgment when they advise a nation to pursue the goal of national security or when they insist that such means as the accumulation of coercive power—or its use—should be employed for this purpose.

Nations like individuals or other groups may value things not because they consider them good or less evil than their alternative; they may value them because they satisfy their pride, heighten their sense of self-esteem or reduce their fears. However, no policy, or human act in general, can escape becoming a subject for moral judgment—whether by the conscience of the actor himself or by others— which calls for the sacrifice of other values, as any security policy is bound to do. Here it becomes a matter of comparing and weighing values in order to decide which of them are deemed sufficiently good to justify the evil of sacrificing others. If someone insists that his country should do more to build up its strength, he is implying, knowingly or not, that more security is sufficiently desirable to warrant such evils as the cut in much-needed social welfare benefits or as the extension of the period of military service. . . .

The moral issue will be resolved in one of several ways depending on the ethical code upon which the decision is based. From one extreme point of view it is argued that every sacrifice, especially if imposed on other nations, is justified provided it contributes in any way to national security. Clearly this implies a position that places national security at the apex of the value pyramid and assumes it to constitute an absolute good to which all other values must be subordinated. Few will be found to take this position because if they subscribed to a nationalistic ethics of this extreme type they would probably go beyond security—the mere preservation of values—and insist that the nation is justified in conquering whatever it can use as *Lebensraum* or otherwise. At the opposite extreme are the absolute pacifists, who consider the use of coercive power an absolute evil and condemn any security policy, therefore, which places reliance on such power.

For anyone who does not share these extreme views the moral issue raised by the quest for national security is anything but clear-cut and simple. He should have no doubts about the right of a nation to protect and preserve values to which it has a legitimate title or even about its moral duty to pursue a policy meant to serve such preservation. But he cannot consider security the supreme law as Machiavelli would have the statesmen regard the *ragione di stato*. Somewhere a line is drawn, which in every instance he must seek to discover, that divides the realm of neglect, the "too-little," from the realm of excess, the "too-much." Even Hans Morgenthau, who extols the moral duty of self-preservation, seems to take it for granted that naked force shall be used for security in reaction only to violent attack, not for preventive war.

Decision makers are faced with the moral problem, then, of choosing first the values which deserve protection, with national independence ranking high not merely for its own sake but for the guarantee it may offer to values like liberty, justice and peace. He must further decide which level of security to make his target. This will frequently be his most difficult moral task though terms such as adequacy or fair share indicate the kind of standards that may guide him. Finally, he must choose the means and thus by scrupulous computation of values compare the sacrifices, which his choice of means implies, with the security they promise to provide.

It follows that policies of national security, far from being all good or all evil, may be morally praiseworthy or condemnable depending on their specific character and the particular circumstances of the case. They may be praised for their self-restraint and the consideration which this implies for values other than security; they may instead be condemned for being inadequate to protect national values. Again, they may be praised in one instance for the consideration given to the interests of others, particularly of weaker nations, or condemned in another because of the recklessness with which national values are risked on the altar of some chimera. The target level falls under moral judgment for being too ambitious, egotistical and provocative or for being inadequate; the means employed for being unnecessarily costly in other values or for being ineffective. This wide range of variety which arises out of the multitude of variables affecting the value computation would make it impossible, and in fact meaningless, to pass moral judgment, positive or negative, on "national security policy in general."

It is this lack of moral homogeneity which in matters of security policy justifies attacks on so-called moralism, though not on moral evaluation. The "moralistic approach" is taken to mean a wholesale condemnation either of any concern with national security—as being an expression of national egotism—or of a security policy relying on coercive and therefore evil power. The exponent of such "moralism" is assumed to believe that security for all peoples can be had today by the exclusive use of such "good" and altruistic means as model behavior and persuasion, a spirit of conciliation, international organization or world government. If there are any utopians who cling to this notion, and have influence on policy, it makes sense to continue to disabuse them of what can surely be proved to be dangerous illusions.

It is worth emphasizing, however, that the opposite line of argument, which without regard for the special circumstances would praise everything done for national security or more particularly everything done for the enhancement of national power of resistance, is no less guilty of applying simple and abstract moral principles and of failing to judge each case realistically on its merits.

In conclusion, it can be said, then, that normative admonitions to conduct a foreign policy guided by the national security interest are no less ambiguous and misleading than the statement of fact concerning past behavior which was discussed earlier. In order to be meaningful such admonitions would have to specify the degree of security which a nation shall aspire to attain and the means by which it is to be attained in a given situation. It may be good advice in one instance to appeal for greater effort and more armaments; it may be no less expedient and morally advisable in another instance to call for moderation and for greater reliance on means other than coercive power. Because the pendulum of public opinion swings so easily from extreme complacency to extreme apprehension, from utopian reliance on "good will" to disillusioned faith in naked force only, it is particularly important to be wary of any simple panacea, even of one that parades in the realist garb of a policy guided solely by the national security interest.

22. Simulation and "Reality": Validity Research

HAROLD GUETZKOW AND JOSEPH J. VALADEZ

. . . A simulated construction is but theory. It provides no shortcut or magical route to the "proof" of the validity of the verbal and mathematical components it contains. Thus, there is a need for a systematic examination of the extent of the congruences between empirical analyses of world processes and simulations of international relations. This essay attempts such an examination.

It is still convenient to employ the definition of simulation of behavioral processes written some years ago: "an operating representation, in reduced and/or simplified form, of relations among social units (or entities) by means of symbolic and/or replicate component parts" (Guetzkow, 1959: 184).

Within the perspective that simulation is operating theory, let us proceed with our central task: To what extent are simulations of international processes being verified? . . .

Excerpted from Harold Guetzkow and Joseph J. Valadez, eds. *Simulated International Processes: Theories and Research in Global Modeling* (Beverly Hills, Calif.: Sage Publications, 1981), pp. 253–327. Copyright © 1981 Sage Publications, Inc. Reprinted by permission of the publisher and the authors. This essay is an updated and revised version of Harold Guetzkow's "Some Correspondences between Simulations and 'Realities' in International Relations," in Morton A. Kaplan, ed., *New Approaches in International Relations* (New York: St. Martin's Press, 1968), pp. 202–269. This excerpt contains only some of the findings from INS and none of the more recent findings reported from IPS and SIPER. Footnotes and selected references deleted.

INTER-NATION SIMULATION

"Decision-Makers and Their Nations"

In considering "Decision-Makers and Their Nations," it is convenient first to discuss individuals serving in the INS as surrogates for the decision-makers of the world. Attention will be given next to these humans assembled in groups, along with the political, economic, and military programs which function together as representations of the nation-state.

Humans as Surrogates. Because of the difficulties involved in programming the decision-making within a nation, given the present development of work in "artificial intelligence" . . . humans are used in the Inter-Nation Simulation to handle these activities. . . .

Personal Characteristics. Perhaps the most focused evidence available on the impact of personal style on outputs from the humans who constitute the decision-making units within the Inter-Nation Simulation is presented by Michael J. Driver (1965, 1977). . . . Richard A. Brody (1963) and Driver selected 336 participants for their sixteen runs of the simulation on the basis of each individual's cognitive simplicity/complexity. Driver found that outputs of the high school seniors and graduates who served as his decision-makers conformed to the findings obtained in many other situations (Harvey et al., 1961; Schroder et al., 1967).

Driver (1977: Table 13.1; 342) noted how those surrogates with simpler conceptual structures, as determined on a pretest, tended to involve their nations in more aggressive behavior than did those with more complex, abstract conceptual structures ($\chi^2 = 7.1^{**}$ $p < .005$; correspondence rating: much).

This same characteristic was investigated by Hermann et al. (1974) in a study of decision-making in response to an unidentified attack. The simulators hypothesized that cognitive complexity of the participating 325 U.S. Naval petty officers would be inversely related to the decision to counterattack a suspected foe. This prediction was found to be consistent with Driver's conclusion that individuals with less complex cognitive structures tend to exhibit more aggressive behavior than the more complex thinkers. The correlation, though in the predicted direction ($\beta = -.13$, $b = -.12$, $s = .15$, $t = .84$, df = 11/27) was weak (correspondence rating: little).

The success of Suedfeld and his associates in adapting the complexity concepts and techniques to historical, archival materials (Suedfeld and Tetlock, 1977; Suedfeld and Rank, 1976) gives one further confidence in the homomorphy of the simulation and the reference materials offered by Driver and the Hermanns. "Complexity of the messages produced by governmental leaders was significantly lower in crises that ended in war" (Suedfeld and Tetlock, 1977; 169).

The operation of personal characteristics of surrogates within simulations may be pinpointed, too, both in terms of a particular set of personality traits, namely "self-esteem" and "defensiveness," and in terms of a particular situation, namely "crisis." Personal characteristics are related intimately to the way in which individuals handle crises. . . . Margaret G. Hermann (1965) has replicated aspects of these phenomena (Lazarus and Baker, 1956) concerned with self-esteem and defensiveness in her observations of 163 U.S. Naval petty officers (average age, 32.5 years) who conducted decision-making in eleven replications of a crisis-permeated simulation of policy-making (C. F. Hermann, 1969: Ch. 3). Along with many

other outcomes she found that as the simulated crisis produced more negative affect, the decision-makers high in self-esteem and high in defensiveness ("avoiders") decreased their attempts to seek aid from other nations and they decreased their search for information about the threat. Conversely, those low in self-esteem but high in defensiveness ("affiliators") increased their attempts to affiliate and increased their search for information (M. G. Hermann, 1965: 73). . . . The results are statistically significant ($F = 4.37^{**}$; correspondence rating: much).

Self-esteem, independent of defensiveness, has been found to be associated with avoidance behavior (Hermann and Hermann, 1967; Block and Thomas, 1955; Cohen, 1959; Leventhal and Perloe, 1962; Silverman, 1964). Hermann et al. (1974) examined this personality characteristic in U.S. Naval petty officers as it related to the decision to launch nuclear weapons in response to a simulated unidentified attack. Predicting self-esteem to be inversely related to this decision, the simulators monitored some ten INS runs conducted at the Great Lakes Naval Training Center. Statistical results strongly supported this hypothesis ($\beta = -.35$, $b = -.33$, $s = .13$, $t = 2.56$, df = 6/32, $p < .05$; correspondence rating: much; Hermann et al., 1974: 88).

Hermann-like findings corresponding to field and laboratory work reported by Harold M. Schroder et al. (1967) have been obtained in a "tactical game situation" less rich than the Inter-Nation Simulation, in which crisis was created by increasing information loads. Using three measures of information-handling (delegated information searches; self-initiated information searches . . . and integrated utilization of sought-for information in subsequent decision-making), Streufert et al. (1965) obtained statistically significant impact of levels of information load upon information-handling by 185 college students, assembled into fourteen teams serving as decision-makers. And using the same personality measures employed by Driver in his operation with Brody of the Inter-Nation Simulation, the researchers obtained dramatic as well as statistically significant differences in the effects of crisis upon information-handling for those surrogates with structurally complex styles, as contrasted with those with structurally simple styles (. . . correspondence rating: much).

Thus, both in ordinary and in crisis situations within two simulations, the surrogate decision-makers behaved in ways similar to ways other individuals act in field and laboratory studies. In the end, however, it may be expeditious to use surrogates who match particular international actors for work within the Inter-Nation Simulation. An attempt to encompass the entire personality of the participants was made by M. G. Hermann (Hermann and Hermann, 1967) in her use of a semantic differential instrument and the California Psychological Inventory (CPI), which yielded a profile of some thirteen traits in a disguised simulation of the activities within and among the countries that became involved in World War I during the summer of 1914. Working as a clinical psychologist, Hermann prepared personality profiles for each of ten actors who played significant roles in the 1914 crisis, on the basis of personal letters, autobiographical materials, and biographies. Then she matched these profiles to those of potential participants, choosing ten from an available population of 101 high school graduates for use as surrogates. The findings from this pilot study are suggestive: One realization with matched participants (M-Run) came closer to producing an output similar to the unfolding of historical events, as they are described by the historian Luigi Albertini (1953), than did a second realization (A-Run), in which another ten surrogates were less well matched than in the M-Run (correspondence rating: some). More definitive validation study covering key personal characteristics of relevance to policy-makers acting in the international scene awaits the production of comparable research in reference materials. . . .

To this point our review of the operation of personal characteristics in the Inter-Nation Simulation has focused on their impact upon the outputs of the surrogates. It is also of interest to know to what extent the very processes producing the consequences are themselves homomorphic to those which create outcomes in the reference system. Are the "right" outputs being produced for the "wrong" reasons? There are three researches of relevance which examine how processes of perception mediate the impact of personal characteristics upon outcomes in the simulation.

1. Studies of President Woodrow Wilson and Secretary of State John Foster Dulles made by other researchers suggested to Michael J. Shapiro that their personal styles exemplified the frequently verified relations between cognitive rigidity and a tendency to perceive conflicts in moral rather than instrumental terms, and also to be relatively unreceptive to change. Using Driver's measures of cognitive style, as derived from the Adorno/California F-Scale and the Schroder/Streufert Situational Interpretation Test (SIT) (1966: Table 1; 10), Shapiro checked whether the same processes held within these Brody-Driver simulations. He found that cognitive rigidity correlated significantly ($r = .51**$ for the F-Scale; $r = .69**$ for SIT) with the extent to which 336 high school students, serving as participants, evaluated environmental stimuli in moral categories, as revealed in coding the messages generated in the course of the simulation. But he found that neither rigidity measure was correlated with fixity of beliefs and attitudes about decision-makers in other nations (the r's being $-.01$ and $.12$, respectively; correspondence rating: some, 1966: Table 2; 12).

2. . . . Driver (1977) was able to measure changes in the dimensionality of the perceptions of the nations' decision-makers as they moved from ordinary to tense to dangerous situations within the 112 simulated nations in his research with Brody (1963). Corresponding to the findings in laboratory and field situations, including those analyzed in studies of natural disasters (such as panics during fires and floods), Driver noted that the dimensionality of the perceptions of the 336 high school students used as surrogates changed curvilinearly, from simple to more complex to less complex, as the inter-nation situation moved from run-of-the-day interaction through con-

flict and into war (Schroder et al., 1967: 66–81; Driver, 1977: 353). Driver found that even the content of the framework, in terms of which of the other nations were perceived as similar or different from one another, varied as the distinctions among the nations were made in terms of two to three, and then three to five, and then reduced to two or three dimensions again. For example, Driver (1962: 243) noted that "economic power dimensions are first transformed into military power and finally replaced altogether by alliance concerns as the clouds of war gather" (correspondence rating: much).

3. In quite a different way, C. F. Hermann obtained findings which converge with those of Driver, and noted that in crisis as compared with noncrisis there was a tendency—slight, but statistically significant—for his petty officers to perceive "events as involving a number of different alternatives or only one or two alternatives" . . . even though content coding revealed no such differences in frequency in alternatives found in messages and conference statements exchanged in the course of the simulation (Hermann, 1969: 171). In his illustrations from the literature on international crisis behavior of political decision-makers, Hermann listed observations (1969: 161–165) that also are congruent with Driver's findings (correspondence rating: some).

In all three of these sets of findings there is somewhat convergent evidence as to how processes of perception operate within the surrogate decision-makers in realizations of the Inter-Nation Simulation. Two processes are displayed: the correlation of cognitive rigidity with the extent to which participants evaluate environmental stimuli in moral categories, and the tendency toward reduction in the perceived richness of the situation in crisis. The reference data used in making the comparisons with the simulations consisted of case materials, along with anecdotal observations. The evidence samples but limited aspects of perceptual phenomena, even though both ordinary and political decision-makers were compared with the surrogates. A codification of perceptions and misperceptions in interna-

tional politics was completed by Jervis (1976) after the studies reviewed immediately above were undertaken. Its use of both laboratory experiments and international cases summarizes rich evidence of the common ways in which the "processes of perception" operate in the human, whether the individual is in the (simulation) laboratory or the foreign office. Within these confines, it seems the outputs deriving from the personal characteristics are being produced for at least some of the "right" reasons. . . .

Surrogate Groups and Programs as "Nations." In making an assessment of "decision-makers and their nations," it is useful not only to consider the decision-makers per se, but also to explore how the surrogates function when assembled as decision-making groups, as well as how the consequences of their decisions are programmed as the outputs of their nations. "Individual and group components of the Inter-Nation Simulation are meshed into an operating model through both structured and free, self-developing interactive processes. In general, programmed assumptions are used for setting the foundations of the simulation, serving to provide operating rules for the decision-makers whereby they may handle the political, economic, and military aspects of their nations" (Guetzkow, 1981b: 64). Let us now examine aspects of the validity of the processes within these "nations" in the simulation. . . .

Organizational Characteristics: Decision-making Groups and Roles Therein. In their East Algonian Exercise, Crow and Noel (1977: 400–401) demonstrated the effects of an organizational context upon their decision-makers, at least in one experiment with respect to one output—the level of military response used to control a simulated military insurrection. Those with high-risk preferences tended to respond throughout at a higher level than those with low-risk preferences ($F = 9.27**$, df $= 1/24$). But in both instances, as the individual moved from private decision-making to a situation in which there was a high probability of winning the war and in which he needed to come to consensus with three other "top-level leaders of Algo, all equal in authority and responsibility" (1977: 387), there was a reduction in the level of response ($F = 4.29*$, df = 1/24). Some writers about politics (e.g., Acheson, 1960; Neustadt, 1960) believe that a committee system tends "to inhibit innovation, boldness, and creativity with the result that any decision is a consensus or compromise based on the lowest common denominator of agreement" (Crow and Noel, 1977: 396). As Henry Kissinger (1962: 356) speculates, "the system stresses avoidance of risk rather than boldness of conception."

In two of Crow and Noel's other experiments in the East Algonian Exercise, in which military response levels made in the course of rendering individual "pregroup" judgments were compared with the outcomes of group consensus, there were no clear effects of organizational context shown, despite the similarity of these experiments to the one mentioned earlier. In one, there was an interaction effect between the simulated situation and the organizational context, but in a contrary direction. When the opponent was presented as highly aggressive the decision-makers shifted to a significantly ($F = 11.1*$, df = 1/20) higher level of military response as a result of group decision—in this experiment, from a level of 7.4 to 9.2 (1977: Table 15.4; 401)—a result contrary to current verbal speculation among students of politics. Yet, such findings are in keeping with results from social psychological experiments by M. A. Wallach and N. Kogan (1965), in which group discussions permit shifts to accept greater risks because "each individual can feel less than proportionally to blame for the possible failure of a risky decision" (Crow and Noel, 1977: 396; correspondence rating: incongruent). Both results may be valued, although there is dissatisfaction with the limitations of both criteria: the unsystematic nature of field observation and the lack of "richness" of the laboratory.

More in line with the results from these social psychological experiments were simulation outputs reported by Hermann et al. (1974:

89). In accordance with Kogan and Wallach's (1967) findings, the simulators expected that group decision-makers were less likely to respond aggressively to an unidentified attack and accept the risk of delay. Statistical analysis of simulation outputs did not contradict this hypothesis that groups mitigate aggressive decision-making ($\beta = -.32$, $b = -.31$, $s = .12$, $t = 2.61$, $p < .05$; correspondence rating: much . . .).

In his simulation study of crises in foreign policy-making, C. F. Hermann (1969) probed the development of consensus within sixty-six decision-making groups comprising eleven runs of an Inter-Nation Simulation with U.S. Naval petty officers as participants (see pp. 261–266). In an "event and decision form," Hermann (1969: 206–207) queried his participants a number of times as to whether a crisis they "recently or are now experiencing" had made the nation's goals "easier/harder to attain," covering such goals as "office-holding," "alliance development," and an ability to "preserve nation as separate unit." Although this experimenter demanded no actual group decision after focused discussion on the matter, as was the case in the East Algonian Exercise conducted by Crow and Noel (1977), crisis induced considerably more consensus, as measured by the agreement among three or four office-holders within each nation that "one or more goals had been made more difficult to attain" (1969: 159). In a set of forty-eight paired samples of crisis versus noncrisis events, consensus existed for two-thirds of the non-crisis situations; the consensus increased significantly ($\chi^2 = 7.2$, $p = .004$) to 100 percent in the crisis situations (1969: Table 18; 159). In discussing his hypothesis that "In crisis as compared to non-crisis, the frequency of consensus among decision-makers as to the national goals affected by the situation is increased," Hermann (1969: 155–157) indicated that such a tendency toward increased consensus is documented by the general literature on conflict (Mack and Snyder, 1957: 234) and on disaster (Thompson and Hawkes, 1962: 278), and by the specific case studies of U.S. decision-making within the Korean (Snyder and Paige,

1958: 375) and the Cuban (Larson, 1963: 225) crises (correspondence rating: some).

This relationship between crisis conditions and intra-group communication processes was further investigated in the Robinson et al. (1969) study of intervening variables influencing group consensus in two sets of INS simulations—at the Great Lakes Naval Training Station and the Western Behavioral Sciences Institute—and the all-person MIT political game. The acts of searching for information and alternatives are typically characteristic of decision-making . . . ; the simulators expected that the time pressures of crisis situations may inhibit these, thus accelerating group decision. It was suggested that this decision-making may thus be based on a deficient intelligence system. Previous research has reported that one reason the search for alternative courses of action becomes limited in crisis is that decision-makers tend to be satisfied earlier than during times of stability (Simon, 1957; March, 1962). Though the MIT game produced nonsignificant results ($\chi^2 = .10$, n.s.), both INS studies produced findings corresponding to empirical research suggesting that there is less search for alternative courses of action in crisis (Great Lakes: $\chi^2 = 4.22$, $p < .05$; WBSI: $\chi^2 = 13.60$, $p < .01$; correspondence rating: much). The number of alternatives open to national leaders is perceived by them to be significantly less in crisis (Snyder and Paige, 1958; Holsti, 1965). This same reduction occurred in the simulation studies (Great Lakes: $\chi^2 = 5.62$, $p < .01$; WBSI: $\chi^2 = 9.77$, $p < .01$). As before, the MIT game exhibited non-significant findings ($\chi^2 = .10$, n.s.; correspondence rating: much).

As part of the starting conditions within the Inter-Nation Simulation, roles are designated within each group responsible for the nation's decision-making—a procedure which contrasts with the usual RAND/MIT practice of having each "team" work without assigned activities for any participant in their political-military exercises. In this way, an attempt is made within INS to induce a "division of labor" among the participants so that each position gains its perspective, as commonly occurs in

roles found in bureaucracies (Katz and Kahn, 1966: Ch. 7, 171–198). Thus, the group as a surrogate tends to function less as a small, "face-to-face" group, instead taking on some characteristics of an organization (Guetzkow and Bowes, 1957).

Druckman's (1965, 1986) study of ethnocentrism indicated that tendencies toward "bias" as found in laboratory and field studies (Rosenblatt, 1964) occur among the roles within the simulation. For example, those in low status roles within the simulated executive decision-making groups in WINSAFE II (Raser and Crow, 1964), especially the marginal decision-maker who was aspiring to office, were found to be "most favorably disposed toward the in-group and least favorably disposed toward all out-groups, allies and enemies" (Druckman, 1968: 62). Likewise, following observations made by Gordon Allport, Leonard Berkowitz, Robert Hamblin, and George Homans, Druckman (1968: 61) theorized that "the role with the most international contacts with opposite members of equal status . . . should be least ethnocentric." Druckman found that "the foreign minister or external decision-maker was the least ethnocentric role" (1965: 124–125; cf. Druckman, 1968: 62). The external decision-maker rated his own group least favorably and the out-group's allies and enemies most favorably (correspondence rating: much). Thus, role differentiations in the Inter-Nation Simulation may be homomorphic to those which occur in government offices handling decision-making for countries within the international system, although there is no direct evidence on this matter from a study (Argyris, 1967) made within the U.S. Department of State. . . .

EPILOG

Given the barefoot quality of our assessments of correspondences between outcomes of the simulations and the reference materials, it is easy to realize that our listing of congruences is but a first step in the task of making adequate estimates of the validities involved. In the perspective of a sophisticated philosophical analysis, . . . it is reassuring to note that ". . . These are hypotheses based upon crude inductive generalization, but they constitute the logical starting point. Each of them is rather shaky, owing to the childish quality of the induction by enumeration which supports it, but the more sophisticated inferences that follow can be well founded. As evidence accumulates and further inductions are made, the results become more and more securely established" (Salmon, 1967: 131–132). It is to be hoped that others will join in meeting the exciting challenges posed by our validity problems, moving beyond mere enumeration.

Now that we have apparently entered an era in which the construction and application of simulations is blooming, might this not also be the time to refine methods with which our as yet coarse models might increase in validity? Following completion of the project on Simulated International Processes (see Guetzkow, 1981a), a second project, Computer Simulations for Decision-Making in International Affairs (CSDMIA), commenced at Northwestern University to move in this direction. Through construction of modular simulations, various components of international relations processes can be individually formulated and refined. "Once analyzed, these 'mini-modules' are specified as computer simulation modules operable both independently and within the context of a more comprehensive simulation framework, i.e., Bremer's SIPER" (Guetzkow et al., 1977: 6). Each mini-simulation constitutes a mini-theory; through experimentation each may be individually refined. Will such an effort increase the overall validity of the entire simulation, despite Bremer's difficulty in his utilization of a somewhat comparable strategy in the economic realm of SIPER?

Improvements and extensions of extant simulations, however, depend upon how well our colleagues assume the burdens of validating their work. To date, emphasis among simulation builders has been more upon the venture of model construction, with the scholar working as an artist, rather than upon

involvement in checking correspondences between the simulations and their respective reference systems, as is incumbent upon the scholar who works as a social scientist or policy-influencer. This obligation, however, does not belong solely to the simulator. As Morton Gorden (1967) pointed out, the verbal theorist shares in the same obligations. When simulator and verbal theorist ground their work in empirical materials, then they may fruitfully join hands with mathematical and simulation theorists in constructing homomorphic models of the international system which will have fidelity. Then their constructions will represent the world more adequately, as it is now and as it may evolve with simulated alternative futures, unfolding the "realities" of the decades ahead.

REFERENCES

ACHESON, D. G. 1960. The President and the Secretary of State. In D. K. Price, ed. *The Secretary of State.* Englewood Cliffs, N.J.: Prentice-Hall, Inc.

ALBERTINI, L. 1953. *The Origins of the War of 1914.* Ed. and trans. by I. M. Massy. London: Oxford University Press.

ARGYRIS, C. 1967. *Some Causes of Organizational Ineffectiveness Within the Department of State.* Washington, D.C.: Government Printing Office (for the Center for International Systems Research; DS Publication 8180).

BLOCK, J., AND H. THOMAS. 1955. Is satisfaction with self a measure of adjustment? *Journal of Abnormal and Social Psychology* 51: 254–259.

*BRODY, R. A. 1963. Some systemic effects of the spread of nuclear-weapons technology: A study through simulation of a multinuclear future. *Journal of Conflict Resolution* 7(4): 663–753.

COHEN, A. R. 1959. Situation structure, self-esteem, and threat-oriented reactions to power. In D. Cartwright, ed. *Studies in Social Power.* Ann Arbor: University of Michigan Press.

CROW, W. J., AND R. NOEL. 1977. An experiment in simulated historical decision-making. In M. G. Hermann with T. Milburn, eds. *A Psychological Examination of Political Leaders*, pp. 385–405. New York: Macmillan.

*DRIVER, M. J. 1962. Conceptual structure and group processes in an Inter-Nation Simulation, Part 1: The perception of simulated nations: A multidimensional analysis of social perceptions as affected by situational stress and characteristic levels of complexity in perceivers, Ph.D. dissertation, Princeton University.

*———. 1965. A structure analysis of aggression, stress, and personality in an Inter-Nation Simulation. Paper 97, Krannert Graduate School, Purdue University.

*———. 1977. Individual differences as determinants of aggression in the Inter-Nation Simulation. In M. G. Hermann with T. Milburn, eds. *A Psychological Examination of Political Leaders*, pp. 337–353. New York: Macmillan.

*DRUCKMAN, D. 1965. Ethnocentric bias in the Inter-Nation Simulation. M.A. thesis, Northwestern University.

*———. 1968. Ethnocentrism in the Inter-Nation Simulation. *Journal of Conflict Resolution* 12 (March): 45–68.

*GORDEN, M. 1967. International relations theory in the TEMPER simulation. Evanston, Ill.: Simulated International Processes project, Northwestern University.

*GUETZKOW, H. 1959. A use of simulation in the study of inter-nation relations. *Behavioral Science* 4(3): 183–191.

———. 1981a. Simulated International Processes: An incomplete history, pp. 13–21 in H. Guetzkow and J. J. Valadez, eds. *Simulated International Processes: Theories and Research in Global Modeling*. Beverly Hills, Calif.: Sage.

———. 1981b. The Inter-Nation Simulation, pp. 23–64 in H. Guetzkow and J. J. Valadez, eds. *Simulated International Processes: Theories and Research in Global Modeling*. Beverly Hills, Calif.: Sage.

——— AND A. E. BOWES. 1957. The development of organizations in a laboratory. *Management Science* 3: 380–402.

———, W. L. HOLLIST, AND M. D. WARD. 1977. Computer simulations for decision-making in international affairs: Moving toward consolidation of research in international relations through empirical analysis and computer simulation. *International Peace Research Newsletter* 25/3: 5–13.

HARVEY, O. J., D. E. HUNT, AND H. M. SCHRODER. 1961. *Conceptual Systems and Personality Organization*. New York: John Wiley.

*HERMANN, C. F. 1969. *Crises in Foreign Policy: An Analysis*. Indianapolis: Bobbs-Merrill.

——— AND M. G. HERMANN. 1967. An attempt to simulate the outbreak of World War I. *American Political Science Review* 61/2: 400–416.

———, ———, AND R. CANTOR. 1974. Counterattack or delay: Characteristics influencing decision-makers' responses to the simulation of an unidentified attack. *Journal of Conflict Resolution* 18: 75–106.

*HERMANN, M. G. 1965. Stress, self-esteem and defensiveness in an Inter-Nation Simulation. Ph.D. dissertation, Northwestern University.

HOLSTI, O. R. 1965. The 1914 case. *American Political Science Review* 59/2: 365–378.

JERVIS, R. 1976. *Perception and Misperceptions in International Politics*. Princeton, N.J.: Princeton University Press.

KATZ, D. AND R. L. KAHN. 1966. *The Social Psychology of Organizations*. New York: John Wiley.

KISSINGER, H. A. 1961. *The Necessity for Choice: Prospects of American Foreign Policy*. New York: Harper & Row.

KOGAN, N. AND M. A. WALLACH. 1967. Risk taking as a function of the situation, the person, and the group. In *New Directions in Psychology*. New York: Holt, Rinehart & Winston.

LARSON, D. L. 1963. *The "Cuban Crisis" of 1962*. Boston: Houghton Mifflin.

LAZARUS, R. S. AND R. W. BAKER. 1956. Personality and psychological stress: A theoretical and methodological framework. *Psychology Newsletter* 8: 21–32.

LEVENTHAL, H. AND S. I. PERLOE. 1962. A relationship between self-esteem and persuasibility. *Journal of Abnormal and Social Psychology* 64: 385–388.

MACK, R. W. AND R. C. SNYDER. 1957. The analysis of social conflict: Toward an overview and synthesis. *Journal of Conflict Resolution* 1: 212–248.

MARCH, J. G. 1962. Some recent substantive and methodological developments in theory of organizational decision-making. In A. Ranney, ed. *Essays on the Behavioral Study of Politics*. Urbana: University of Illinois Press.

NEUSTADT, R. 1960. *Presidential Power*. New York: John Wiley.

*RASER, J. R. AND W. J. CROW. WINSAFE II: An Inter-Nation Simulation study of deterrence postures embodying capacity to delay response. La Jolla, Calif.: Western Behavioral Sciences Institute.

*ROBINSON, J. A., C. F. HERMANN, AND M. G. HERMANN. 1969. Search under crisis in political gaming and simulation in D. G. Pruitt and R. C. Snyder, eds. *Theory and Research on the Causes of War*, pp. 80–94. Englewood Cliffs, N.J.: Prentice-Hall, Inc.

ROSENBLATT, P. C. 1964. Origins and effects of group ethnocentrism and nationalism. *Journal of Conflict Resolution* 8/2: 131–146.

SALMON, W. C. 1967. *The Foundations of Scientific Inference*. Pittsburgh: University of Pittsburgh Press.

SCHRODER, H. M., M. J. DRIVER, AND S. STREUFERT. 1967. *Human Information Processing*. New York: Holt, Rinehart & Winston.

*SHAPIRO, M. J. 1966. Cognitive rigidity and moral judgments in an inter-nation simulation. Evanston, Ill.: Northwestern University.

SILVERMAN, I. 1964. Differential effects of ego threat upon persuasibility for high and low self-esteem subjects. *Journal of Abnormal and Social Psychology* 69: 567–572.

SIMON, H. A. 1957. *Models of Man*. New York: John Wiley.

———

*Asterisked entries are studies involving the Northwestern project on Simulated International Processes.

SNYDER, R. C. AND G. D. PAIGE. 1958. The United States decision to resist aggression in Korea: The application of an analytical scheme. *Administrative Science Quarterly* 3: 341–378.

STREUFERT, S., M. A. CLARDY, M. J. DRIVER, M. KARLINS, H. M. SCHRODER, AND P. SUEDFELD. 1965. A tactical game for the analysis of complex decision-making in individuals and groups. *Psychological Reports* 17: 723–727.

SUEDFELD, P. AND A. D. RANK. 1976. Revolutionary leaders: Long-term success as a function of changes in conceptual complexity. *Journal of Personality and Social Psychology* 34/2: 169–178.

——— AND P. TETLOCK. 1977. Integrative complexity of communications in international crises. *Journal of Conflict Resolution* 21/1: 169–184.

THOMPSON, J. D. AND R. W. HAWKES. 1962. Disaster, community organization, and administrative process. In G. W. Baker and D. W. Chapman, eds. *Man and Society in Disaster*. New York: Basic Books.

TUCKER, L. R. AND S. L. MESSICK. 1963. An individual differences model for multi-dimensional scaling. *Psychometrika* 28/4: 333–367.

WALLACH, M. A. AND N. KOGAN. 1965. The roles of information, discussion, and consensus in group risk taking. *Journal of Experimental Social Psychology* 65: 75–86.

23. How Decision-Makers Learn from History

ROBERT JERVIS

How do past events influence current perceptions? Some have argued that they do not. A. J. P. Taylor says that "men use the past to prop up their own prejudices." Stanley Hoffmann agrees with John Fairbank that Americans tend to use history as a "grabbag from which each advocate pulls out a 'lesson' to prove his point." Herbert Butterfield argues that "Those who [in 1919] talked of 'avoiding the mistakes of 1815' were using history to ratify the prejudices they had already." In this view, international experiences do not affect statesmen's perceptions. Instead, analogies are seized upon only to bolster pre-existing beliefs and preferences. This chapter will contend that this argument is wrong. What one learns from key events in international history is an important factor in determining the images that shape the interpretation of incoming information. If history merely reinforced established beliefs, people with different outlooks would not draw the same lessons from events, people would not disproportionately use as analogies events they experienced firsthand, and historical experiences would not alter decision-makers' views.

Excerpted from *Perception and Misperception in International Politics* by Robert Jervis, pp. 217, 228, 230–233, 238–239, 253, 261, 266–269, 281–282. Copyright © 1976 by Princeton University Press. Reprinted by permission of Princeton University Press and the author. Footnotes deleted.

Where can the statesman find the concepts he needs to interpret others' behavior and guide his own actions?. . . Decision-makers learn broad, general lessons from history, but this kind of learning hinders rather than aids productive thinking. Decision-makers apply an analogy in its broad outlines to many disparate cases. There is generality—indeed too much generality—both in the kinds of situations that are seen as similar to the earlier one and in the range of aspects of the case that are seen as similar. But because the learning has not involved an understanding of many of the important causal relations, it is not general in the sense of grasping the crucial characteristics of the situation and the patterns that are likely to recur in the future. Decision-makers usually fail to strip away from the past event those facets that depend on the ephemeral context. They often mistake things that are highly specific and situation-bound for more general characteristics because they assume that the most salient aspects of the results were caused by the most salient aspects of the preceding situation. People pay more attention to *what* has happened than to *why* it has happened. Thus learning is superficial, overgeneralized, and based on *post hoc, ergo propter hoc* reasoning. As a result, the lessons learned will be applied to a wide variety of situations without a careful effort to determine whether the cases are similar on crucial dimensions. . . .

Derived from the sloppy search for causes and their location in large events is the tendency to slight the importance of the conditions and circumstances under which the outcome occurred. When a person constructs an account of events that stresses the overriding importance of a few variables and simple connections between them, he will learn a set of rigid rules that will not be a good guide to a changing world. If he has correctly identified a major cause, and if other factors are either unimportant or can be neglected because they are constant in all the cases he will confront, he can indeed use one event as an analogy to many others. But if the previous outcome depended on the interaction of several factors, the application of the lessons without a careful analysis of the two situations will be misleading. The person will see the world as more unchanging than it is and will learn overgeneralized lessons. . . .

A similar overgeneralization caused by learning a noncontingent rule was responsible for Admiral Halsey's mistake in the battle for Leyte Gulf in sending all his forces in pursuit of a Japanese decoy fleet, thereby leaving the American invasion forces open to attack from another Japanese fleet. The decoy fleet looked powerful to Halsey because it contained aircraft carriers; yet all but one of these were small, converted ships of "trivial military value." The other Japanese fleet, although without carriers, was built around modern battleships that constituted the greater menace. The problem was that Halsey was guided by "two axioms . . . (a) 'the enemy's main force is where his carriers are'. . . , and (b) 'don't divide the fleet in the presence of the enemy.'" Both axioms had been useful earlier in the war, but were no longer valid once the Japanese carriers were unimportant and the American fleet large enough to deal with two forces simultaneously. Halsey and his staff had not learned why the axioms should be followed; they did not understand the detailed causal linkages; and so, not noticing the importance of changed circumstances, they applied the axioms when they were no longer appropriate. . . .

Further problems arise as outcomes are often categorized as "success" or "failure." This determination is usually made by applying a simple standard, such as whether the actor was better off at the end of the encounter than it was before. With a successful outcome, relatively little attention is paid to the costs of the policy, the possibility that others might have worked even better, or the possibility that success was largely attributable to luck and that the policy might just as easily have failed. It is especially rare for decision-makers to ask themselves whether the favorable outcome might have been produced in spite of, not because of, their choices. The result is that, as we will discuss later in this chapter, policies that were followed by success will be too quickly repeated in the future. The other side of this coin is that in cases of failure it is usually assumed that the rejected alternatives would have produced better results. The possibility that the outcome, although undesired, was better than that which would have been secured by most alternatives is infrequently considered. Furthermore, a more extreme assumption is often made: not only would most alternatives have fared better but the decision-makers should have known this. In other words, the information available at the time should have led statesmen to recognize the situation and take appropriate steps. The lessons drawn thus rarely leave room for the possibility that, although the policy was not as good as alternative ones, it may still have been the best one to choose given the information available. It can be argued, for example, that although appeasing Hitler was a bad policy there was no way to have known this at the time. Not only was German behavior compatible with that of a normal revisionist state, but Hitler was a rare exception—very few decision-makers were willing to try to expand recklessly as he was. If this is true, it might not be wise for later statesmen to adjust their perceptual predispositions so as to be quicker to see aggressors and slower to see others as controllable revisionists. . . .

Although a full-scale treatment of this subject cannot be given here, we should note that when an event affects the perceptual predispositions of many members of an organization we can speak of organizational learning. The lessons can become institutionalized in textbooks, rules, and even language itself—e.g. the development of the pejorative meaning of "appeasement" after 1939. Lessons become working assumptions and form the basis for future planning. In the military they involve not only strategic and tactical thinking but the conduct of maneuvers, formal instruction, and standing orders. . . .

Past successes and failures are reflected in changes in organizational routines and guidelines. . . . Success is apt to consolidate the power of those who advocated the policy, defeat to undermine it and strengthen the hand of those who had different views. Thus Japan's initial success in World War II reinforced the position of the dominant group in that country, which believed it could win a limited victory, and made it even more difficult for dissenters to ask what Japan would do if the Allies refused to accept the verdict of a short struggle. An event will exercise an especially powerful influence over an organization's memory if the organization's structure is altered so that part of it (perhaps a newly created part) has a special interest in seeing that the previous event is taken as the model for the future.

EVENTS FROM WHICH PEOPLE LEARN MOST

The four variables that influence the degree to which an event affects later perceptual predispositions are whether or not the person experienced the event firsthand, whether it occurred early in his adult life or career, whether it had important consequences for him or his nation, and whether he is familiar with a range of international events that facilitate alternative perceptions. We can make only two observations about the relative importance of these variables and the way they interact. First, when several of the variables are positive (e.g. firsthand participation in dealing with an important national problem) the event

will have especially great salience. But it would be attempting too much precision to say whether the impact of the variables is additive or multiplicative. Second, events that are terribly important for the nation (e.g. wars) can have so great an impact that the perceptual predispositions of those who did not participate in the making of the policy will be affected almost as much as those who did. . . .

GENERATIONAL EFFECTS

. . . Since the concerns and events that are most important in any period of time pervade the society, all those who come of age at the time are affected similarly. Because, as we discussed above, the orientation that is first formed is not easily replaced but instead structures the interpretation of later events, the result is a generational or cohort effect. As Karl Mannheim pointed out, individuals "who share the same year of birth are endowed, to that extent, with a common location in the historical dimension of the social process" which predisposes them to a "certain characteristic mode of thought and experience, and [creates] a characteristic type of historically relevant faction." . . .

To find the source of the basic political ideas that a person holds one must often go back to the events that demanded attention in his early life. Sometimes he will explicitly use these events as analogies for specific current events. More often they will support a general outlook. Thus two contending generations of French diplomats offered conflicting policies toward Britain in the late 1870s based on the different climates that had dominated their early adulthood: the older ones who learned about international politics in the period when France was recovering from the defeat of Napoleon favored a policy of conciliation "based upon an acceptance of French weakness," while the younger ones who were "bred in the tradition of Republican opposition to Napoleon III" called for a more assertive and independent course.

. . . Although a pure generation model would imply that events would have no immediate effect on the images held by those in power, this is obviously not true. The Munich analogy was applied in the late 1940s as well as in the late 1950s. Three factors explain this. First, important events often change a state's political leadership, bringing to power those whose views were appropriate to the earlier event. Thus those who wanted to stand firm against the Soviets were elected and appointed to office after World War II. Second, these upheavals often bring younger people into the government, people for whom the recent event constituted a formative experience. Third, as we will discuss below, events that are very important, like major wars, can change the cognitive predispositions of those who had other formative experiences.

The combination of both immediate and delayed effects can produce generational cycles in policies. A new policy or general orientation forms in reaction to a traumatic event, usually a war or a dramatic failure of the old views. The new policy and underlying beliefs receive support not only from those in power but also from those younger people who will govern 20 years later. Indeed the latter group has learned the lessons especially well, but because of the flawed nature of the way they will have learned, the lessons will be oversimplified and overgeneralized and therefore will be likely to be applied to inappropriate situations. And because their perceptual predispositions will have been so strongly affected, these people will be very slow to abandon their views. This will insure that, when the lessons are misapplied, the failure of the policy will be important and dramatic and so will set a new generation on its course.

THE LAST WAR

. . . Because of the dramatic and pervasive nature of a war and its consequences, the experiences associated with it—the diplomacy that preceded it, the methods of fighting it, the alliances that were formed, and the way the war was terminated—will deeply influence the perceptual predispositions of most citizens. Major

wars so dominate the life of the country that in a real sense all those old enough to remember it will have experienced it firsthand. Thus, members of the British cabinet who were not active in politics before World War II, as well as those who had served during that period, applied the appeasement model to relations with Nasser. And the diplomacy of this period had important enough consequences for the United States, which was not an active participant, to make the Munich analogy at least as salient for this country as for Britain and France.

What was believed to have caused the last war will be considered likely to cause the next one. The impact of the two world wars on later perceptions shows that as generals are prepared to fight the last war, diplomats are prepared to avoid it. The League of Nations was constructed to deal with the kinds of events that were believed to have been responsible for the preceding conflict. Thus because the First World War had seemed to erupt so suddenly, much attention was paid to mechanisms for enforcing a "cooling off" period. But this did not help keep the peace in the 1930s. "The Italo-Abbyssinian dispute, which ended in war in October 1935, began in December 1934. The cooling-off procedures which occupied the intervening months played into Italy's hands because it had no intention of being 'cooled off' and used those months to hot up its preparations for war. Only when the war itself began was the League's machinery galvanized into real action against the aggressor." More generally, appeasement in the 1930s grew out of the belief that World War I could have been avoided by intelligent and conciliatory diplomacy. Thus statesmen were especially alert to the danger of spirals of hostility and were highly sensitive to the possibility that incompatibility might be illusory. Similarly, beliefs about the origins of the Second World War made the West more apt to see Russia and China as aggressors to whom few concessions could safely be made. Western leaders would have been even quicker to see Russia as aggressive had the period following the end of the First World War been marked by fierce conflict between the former allies instead of a resurgence of the threat from the defeated enemy. The Congress of Vienna had occurred too long before to shape decision-makers' perceptions.

The American perception of the nature of the communist threat has similarly shifted with the most recent armed conflict. The Second World War contributed to a perceptual sensitivity to all-out attack. Perceptual thresholds were altered by the Korean War, which led to the expectation that limited wars would probably recur and would resemble Korea in their causes and their military manifestations. So Dulles and others concluded that the American alliance system had to be expanded to reduce the risk that the communists would misjudge American commitments. And many military officers not only felt that the armies of our Asian allies should be trained to repel conventional attacks but held to this view in the face of mounting guerrilla warfare in South Vietnam. After the nature of the latest war became unmistakable, it became the model for the future. And ambiguous cases—e.g. the conflict in Cambodia—were seen as guerrilla warfare and subversion when, if they had occurred in the 1950s, they would have been considered a conventional invasion, resembling Korea.

Specific lessons are also drawn from the most recent war. For example, the 1939 Soviet demand for a naval base on the northern shore of the Gulf of Finland was rooted in the memory of the battles of the Russian Civil War. Stalin told the Finns that the winner of World War II "will sail into the Gulf of Finland. Yudenitch attacked along the Gulf, and later the British did the same." The tsars, he pointed out, had had a base at Porkkala to close the gulf to enemy warships. The Soviet Union had the same need. But Stalin did not examine the reasons why it had been advantageous to have guns on both sides of the gulf to see if changes in circumstances and technology had altered the tactics of attack and defense. Even though the Finns pointed out that the gulf was too narrow to permit a naval assault under modern conditions as long as either shore was defended, the Soviets would not budge. Because

the French expected World War I to be short, they sent as many men as possible to the front and left few behind for industrial production. Because they believed in the supremacy of the offensive, they launched ill-prepared attacks. In the interwar years they altered their military doctrine and army structure to correct the earlier deficiencies, and so produced a force that was ill-equipped for the changed circumstances. Similarly, because the American army was all in one place in the First World War, the interwar plans for the relations between Washington and the field "assumed a major effort in a main theatre—a single front—overseas. Significantly, there was no thought of huge forces deployed in a global war waged in many theatres." And because France had not fallen in World War I, until June 1940 "army planners continued to think in terms of such dock facilities as those of Cherbourg and Le Havre for the easy transfer of America's land power onto the European continent." Finally, because Nazi Germany was seen not only as an unprovoked aggressor but as initially weak and easy to have stopped had the Allies acted quickly, soldiers and diplomats learned not only that they must stand firm but that it is possible and advantageous to respond before the offender reaches full strength. Thus the United States air force's postwar plans stressed the need for military force "capable of immediate action to forestall any armed threat to this country before it gains momentum."

Only if the next confrontation is likely to resemble the last will this effect aid decision-making. It is reasonable for states to adopt many of the military tactics and forms of organization displayed by the winner in the most recent war, but for many basic questions—e.g. the intentions of other actors, the costs and benefits of alliances, the possibilities of staying neutral—there usually is no reason why the recent past will be a better guide than the remote past or why what happened to one's state will be more informative than what happened to others. Before 1914 statesmen realized that overestimating others' hostility could lead to an unnecessary war. Before 1939 statesmen knew that it was not wise to make concessions to a leader who sought to overthrow the system. And unless one believes that the recent event represents a trend (e.g. that Hitler's behavior not only shows the danger of appeasement but also demonstrates that modern conditions breed aggressive states), the occurrence of another instance of a well-known phenomenon should not call for a large change in the decision-maker's estimate of the probability of such a situation recurring. But it does produce drastic changes, and thereby often decreases the accuracy of later perceptions.

It is usually the last major war, rather than the earlier ones, that has most impact because major wars rarely come more than once a generation and most people have firsthand memories of only the most recent one. Earlier wars have only been read about and so will not create such powerful predispositions. When wars occur more frequently and the person remembers not only the lessons of the last one but the contradicting lessons of the conflict that occurred early in his adulthood, the impact of both will be diluted. . . .

SUMMARY

Recent international history is a powerful source of beliefs about international relations and images of other countries. Events that are seen firsthand, that happen early in the person's adult life, and that affect him and his country have great impact on his later perceptual predispositions. While these events do in fact contain valuable information, the learning process is beset with three linked flaws that seriously affect the quality of decision-making. First, there is often little reason why those events that provide analogies should in fact be the best guides to the future. Why should the last war, rather than earlier ones, most closely resemble the contemporary situation? Why should what has happened to the decision-maker and his state be so much more relevant than the fates of others? Second, because outcomes are learned without careful attention to details of causation, lessons are superficial and over-generalized. Analogies are applied to a wide range of events with little sensitivity to variations in the situation. Furthermore, people employ lessons taken from a major event to explain a general situation rather than trying to see what smaller and often less dramatic aspects of the past case can be used to help understand contemporary events. Third, decision-makers do not examine a variety of analogies before selecting the one that they believe sheds the most light on their situation. Instead, because of their predispositions, they see the present as like recent and dramatic events without carefully considering alternative models or the implications of this way of perceiving. They thereby fail to apply fully their intelligence to some of the most important questions they face.

24. Bureaucratic Politics: A Paradigm and Some Policy Implications

GRAHAM T. ALLISON AND MORTON H. HALPERIN*

During the Tet holiday of 1968, North Vietnamese troops launched massive attacks on a large number of South Vietnamese cities. *Why?*

In December 1950, the Chinese Communists intervened in the Korean War. Today some Senators raise the specter of Chinese Communist intervention in the Vietnamese War. Will Communist China intervene in Vietnam? . . .

In the mid-1960's, the U.S. put a lid on American strategic weapons: 1000 Minutemen, 54 Titans, and 640 Polaris, and a limited number of bombers. Administration officials an-

nounced these limits, recognizing that the Soviets would build up to a position of parity but hoping that Moscow would not go for superiority. If in the mid-1960's a Secretary of Defense had wanted to persuade the Soviet Union not to deploy an ICBM fleet that would seriously threaten U.S. forces, how might he have proceeded?

The first question asks for an explanation; the second for a prediction; the third for a plan. These are three central activities in which both analysts of international politics and makers of foreign policy engage. In response to the first question, most analysts begin by considering various objectives that the North Vietnamese might have had in mind: for example, to shock the American public and thereby affect the presidential election; to collapse the government of South Vietnam; to cause a massive uprising of military and civilians in South Vietnam, thus bringing total victory; or to take the cities and keep them. By examining the problems that Hanoi faced and the character of the action they chose, analysts eliminate some of these aims as implausible. Explanation then consists in constructing a calculation that permits us to understand why, in the particular situation, with certain objections, one would have chosen to launch the Tet offensive. In attempting to predict whether the Communist Chinese

Excerpted from "Bureaucratic Politics: A Paradigm and Some Policy Implications," by Graham T. Allison and Morton H. Halperin, *World Politics* 24 (Spring 1972), Supplement. Excerpts reprinted by permission of Princeton University Press.

*This presentation of a bureaucratic politics approach to foreign policy builds upon previous works of both authors. Specifically, it takes as a point of departure Allison's "Conceptual Models and the Cuban Missile Crisis," *American Political Science Review*, LXIII (September 1970) and *Essence of Decision: Explaining the Cuban Missile Crisis* (Boston 1971); and Halperin's *Bureaucratic Politics and Foreign Policy* (1974). Here we focus on the further development of "Model III," recognizing that organizations can be included as players in the game of bureaucratic politics, treating the factors emphasized by an organizational process approach as constraints, developing the notion of shared attitudes, and introducing a distinction between "decision games" and "action games."

will intervene in the Vietnamese War, and if so, in what fashion, most analysts would consider (1) Chinese national security interests in Vietnam, (2) the likelihood of the collapse of the North Vietnamese in the absence of Chinese Communist intervention, (3) the contribution of Chinese Communist troops to the North Vietnamese efforts, and (4) indications of Chinese Communist intentions, for example, warnings to the U.S., pledges to the North Vietnamese, statements about Chinese interests, etc. These considerations would then be combined in some intuitive fashion to yield a prediction. In recommending U.S. actions to persuade the Soviets to stop with rough parity, and not to push for "superiority," many analysts would have focused on Soviet national security interests. They would then consider American actions that would affect those interests in such a way that deploying larger strategic forces would be counterproductive.

Characteristic of each of these three answers is a basic approach: a fundamental set of assumptions and categories for thinking about foreign affairs. This approach depends primarily on the assumption that events in international politics consist of the more or less purposive acts of unified national governments and that governmental behavior can be understood by analogy with the intelligent, coordinated acts of individual human beings. Following this approach, analysts focus on the interests and goals of a nation, the alternative courses of actions available, and the costs and benefits of each alternative. An event has been explained when the analyst has shown, for example, how the Tet offensive was a reasonable choice, given Hanoi's strategic objectives. Predictions are generated by calculating the rational thing to do in a certain situation, given specified objectives. Recommended plans concentrate on analyzing other nations' strategic interests and ways of affecting their calculations about the consequences of actions.

Let the reader consider, for example, how he would explain the Soviet invasion of Czechoslovakia in 1968, or North Vietnamese activity in Laos or Cambodia. One typically puts himself in the place of the nation or the national government confronted with a problem of foreign affairs and tries to figure out how he might have chosen the action in question. If I had been the Soviet Union faced with the threat of Czech liberalization, or the Czech threat to the economy of the Bloc, what would I have done? Moreover, this is not simply the way we react to current events. It is the way most analysts, most of the time, structure their most careful explanations and predictions of important occurrences in foreign affairs.

Few readers will find the simple assertion of this point persuasive. Obviously there are several variants of this basic approach. Obviously the approach does not capture the entire analysis of those who employ it. Obviously not all analysts rely on this approach all of the time. But as one of us has argued at much greater length elsewhere, this framework, which has been labelled Model I, has been the dominant approach to the study of foreign policy and international politics. (Even analysts primarily concerned with discovering causal relations between variables—for example, between environmental or intra-national factors—and specific outcomes, when called upon to explain or predict, display a tendency to rely on the assumption of purposive unitary nations coping within the constraints established by these causal relations.)

This traditional approach to international politics has much to recommend it. As a "lens" it reduces the organizational and political complications of government to the simplification of a single actor. The array of details about a happening can be seen to cluster around the major features of an action. Through this lens, the confused and even contradictory factors that influence an occurrence become a single dynamic: the *choice* of the alternative that achieved a certain goal. This approach permits a quick, imaginative sorting out of the problem of explanation or prediction. It serves as a productive shorthand, requiring a minimum of information. It can yield an informative summary of tendencies, for example, by identifying the weight of strategic costs and benefits.

But this simplification—like all simplifications—obscures as well as reveals. In particular, it obscures the persistently neglected fact of bureaucracy: the "maker" of government policy is not one calculating decision-maker, but rather a conglomerate of large organizations and political actors who differ substantially about what their government should do on any particular issue and who compete in attempting to affect both governmental decisions and the actions of their government.

The purpose of this paper is to present an alternative approach that focuses on intra-national factors, in particular Bureaucratic Politics, in explaining national behavior in international relations. The argument is that these factors are very important, underemphasized in the current literature, yet critical when one is concerned with planning policy. Section 1 of this paper presents the alternative approach: a Bureaucratic Politics Model. Our hope is that the framework is sufficiently general to apply to the behavior of most modern governments in industrialized nations, though it will be obvious that our primary base is the U.S. government. Section 2 suggests how this approach can be applied to understand how one nation influences the behavior of another. . . .

A BUREAUCRATIC POLITICS MODEL

Our purpose here is to outline a rough-cut framework for focusing primarily on the individuals within a government, and the interaction among them, as determinants of the actions of a government in international politics. What a government does in any particular instance can be understood largely as a result of bargaining among players positioned hierarchically in the government. The bargaining follows regularized circuits. Both the bargaining and the results are importantly affected by a number of constraints, in particular, organizational processes and shared values.

In contrast with Model I, this Bureaucratic Politics Model sees no unitary actor but rather many actors as players—players who focus not on a single strategic issue but on many diverse intra-national problems as well. Players choose in terms of no consistent set of strategic objectives, but rather according to various conceptions of national security, organizational, domestic, and personal interests. Players make governmental decisions not by a single rational choice, but by pulling and hauling. (This by no means implies that individual players are not acting rationally, given their interests.) . . .

Suggestive Propositions About Decisions

1. Decisions of a government seldom reflect a single coherent, consistent set of calculations about national security interests.

2. Decisions by definition assign specific actions to specific players, but they typically leave considerable leeway both about which subordinates should be involved and what specific actions should be taken.

3. Decisions typically reflect considerable compromise. Compromise results from a need to gain adherence, a need to avoid harming strongly felt interests (including organizational interests), and the need to hedge against the dire predictions of other participants.

4. Decisions are rarely tailored to facilitate monitoring. As a result, senior players have great difficulty in checking on the faithful implementation of a decision.

5. Decisions that direct substantial changes in action typically reflect a coincidence of (a) a deadline for a President or senior players that focuses them on a problem and fuels the search for a solution and (b) the interests of junior players committed to a specific solution and in search of a problem.

About Actions

1. Presidential decisions will be faithfully implemented when: a President's involvement is unambiguous, his words are unambiguous, his order is widely publicized, the men who receive it have control of everything needed to carry it out, and those men have no apparent doubt of his authority to issue the decision.

2. Major new departures in foreign policy typically stem from some decision by central players. But the specific details of the action taken are determined in large part by standard operating procedure and programs existing in the organizations at the time.

3. Ambassadors and field commanders feel less obliged to faithfully implement decisions because they typically have not been involved in the decision game. They feel they know better what actions one should want from another government and how to get those actions.

4. The larger the number of players who can act independently on an issue, the less the government's action will reflect decisions of the government on that issue.

5. Where a decision leaves leeway for the organization that is implementing it, that organization will act so as to maximize its organizational interest within constraints. . . .

INTERACTION BETWEEN NATIONS

How does the behavior of one nation affect that of another?

Most analysts of international politics approach this question by applying a version of Model I to the behavior of each nation. This approach leads them to treat the interaction between nations as if it resulted from a competition between two purposive individuals. Each nation's actions are seen to be an attempt to influence the actions of the other by affecting its strategic calculus. The behavior of each nation is explained as a reaction to the behavior of the other.

Consider how analysts who take this approach explain arms races. Nation *A* builds military forces for the purpose of influencing nation *B*. If it fears that nation *B* is stronger and hence may be tempted to attack or to exploit its military superiority, nation *A* will increase the size of its own forces. Nation *B*, observing this buildup, and fearful of the increased strength of nation *A*, in turn increases its own forces.

The Bureaucratic Politics Model suggests an alternative answer to the question of how one nation's behavior affects the behavior of

another. Explanation focuses primarily on processes internal to each nation. The actions of a nation result not from an agreed upon calculus of strategic interests, but rather from pulling and hauling among individuals with differing perceptions and stakes. These arise not only from differing conceptions of national security interest but also from differing domestic, organizational and personal interests. The influence of one nation's actions on another result from the actions' impact on the stands, or on the power of players in decision or action games in the other nation.

From this alternative perspective, the explanation of an "arms race" is to be found primarily within each nation—in particular in the process by which each one procures and deploys military forces. At any given time some players in nation *A* will take stands in favor of increasing defense expenditures and procuring particular weapons systems. The interests that lead them to these stands will be diverse. Career officers in the armed services, for example, will seek additional funds for forces controlled by their services. Other players' stands will be affected by their perceptions of how particular decisions will affect the influence of particular players. Actions by another nation will be interpreted by those seeking additional weapons to enhance their arguments and influence. These actions will affect decisions to increase defense spending if they affect senior players' perceptions of what is necessary for national security or of what is necessary to promote their other interests.

Model I analysis can be relied on to predict the fact that a large increase in nation *A*'s defense budget will produce an increase in nation *B*'s defense spending. But the size of that increase and, even more importantly, the specific characteristics of weapons purchased with the increase are better explained or predicted by the Bureaucratic Politics Model. In general, Model I is more useful for explaining actions where national security interests dominate, where shared values lead to a consensus on what the national security requires, and where actions flow rather directly from decisions. The bureaucratic politics model is more useful where there is data on the interests of players and the rules of the game, where organizational and domestic interests predominate, or where one wishes to treat the details of action.

The Bureaucratic Politics Model suggests a number of propositions about the way actions of one nation affect the actions of another. We shall attempt to formulate these propositions explicitly. But before presenting propositions, it should be useful to consider in a more general manner the process of national interaction as it looks through the lens of bureaucratic politics.

The Bureaucratic Politics Model's emphasis on intra-national processes stems not only from the fact that individuals within nations do the acting, but also from the observation that the satisfaction of players' interests are to be found overwhelmingly at home. Political leaders of a nation rise and fall depending on whether they satisfy domestic needs. Individuals advance in the bureaucracy when they meet the standards set by political leaders or by career ladders. Organizations prosper or decline depending on domestic support in that bureaucracy and beyond it—but within the nation. These struggles are what preoccupy players in foreign-policy bureaucracies. Threats to interests from rival organizations, or competing political groups, are far more real than threats from abroad.

This is not to say that players do not have national security interests. No leader wants to see his nation attacked, and few desire to send their soldiers off to fight in distant wars. Some leaders are committed to a conception of world order. Some players have a wide range of interests beyond the borders of the nation. Even when players are concerned about national security interests, however, they are likely to see the battles as being won or lost mainly at home. This has become a truism of the Vietnam war, but it is true for other policies as well. For President Harry S. Truman the problem of the Marshall Plan was how to get Congress to establish the program and vote the funds, not how to get European governments to take the money or use it wisely. For President Dwight D. Eisenhower the problem of arms control was how to get imaginative proposals from his associates. For planners in the Pentagon, the drive to get the forces necessary to defend the nation is stymied, not by foreign governments, but by rival services, the Secretary of Defense, and the President.

It is not that actions of other nations do not matter, but rather they matter if and when they influence domestic struggles. A player's efforts to accomplish his objectives—whether to advance domestic political interests, organizational interests, personal interests, or national security interests—are sometimes affected by what he and other players come to believe about the actions of other nations. A German chancellor whose domestic position depends upon his reputation for being able to get what the Federal Republic needs from the United States will be concerned about American actions that lead his colleagues and opponents to conclude Washington no longer listens to him. An American Secretary of Defense or President who wishes to cut defense spending will see that his position requires Soviet actions that permit him to argue that the nation's security can be protected with reduced forces. . . . Since actions by other nations can affect the stands players take, and thereby affect decisions and actions, we must consider how actions of other nations enter into the process of decision bargaining and how they affect actions.

Many nations are doing many things at any given time. Not all of these foreign activities become relevant to decision or action games within a nation. Those that do are the actions reported by the nation's foreign office or intelligence organizations, or by senior players directly. Intelligence organizations are not perfect and neutral transmission belts. They notice what their images of the world lead them to think will be important to senior players. They report events and opinions according to established procedures and in ways designed to protect their own organizational interests. Senior players notice what may help them or their opponents and relate mainly to the former. If a new interpretation of another nation's actions comes to be accepted among senior players, some players will see new opportunities to seek decisions or actions. Others will see threats to ongoing actions or desired new ones; still others will be unconcerned.

Reports of the actions of other nations will never be more than one of many influences on decisions and actions. However, when players are evenly divided, or new action suggests to many a substantial change in anticipated future actions, these reports of another nation's actions can be decisive. The Japanese attack on Pearl Harbor, to take an extreme example, affected the perceptions of many Americans about whether the national security required American forces to engage in war against Japan. The Soviet ABM deployment may well have tipped the balance in the hard-fought American controversy over whether to deploy an ABM. President Lyndon Johnson's estimate of the effect of not deploying an American ABM system on his reelection prospects may have been substantially changed by the possibility that he could be charged with permitting an "ABM gap."

When the actions of one nation are effective in changing the behavior of a second, the new action is rarely what was intended by any player in the first nation. Changes in stands will lead to desired changes in action, which in turn will produce desired changes in the action of another nation only: when a clear signal is sent, when someone in the other nation already wants to take the desired action and the action increases that player's influence. More often, the effects are marginal or unintended.

Propositions About National Interaction

1. The actions of nation *A* that appear to an outside observer to be designed to influence the actions of nation *B* will in fact be a combination of: (a) routine patterns of behavior; (b) maneuvers in decision games that are incidentally visible to other nations or deliberately visible, since to be effective they must appear to be a "signal"; (c) actions by players in the absence of decisions; (d) actions fol-

lowing a decision game not related to influencing nation *B*; as well as (e) actions following a decision game related to influencing nation *B*.

2. Reports and interpretations of these actions provided to senior players by participants in nation *B* (in the Foreign Office and Intelligence) charged with observing, reporting, explaining and predicting actions of other nations will be affected by (a) the perceptual tendencies of all individuals; (b) the use of Model I analysis or (c) even if not, the lack of required data and understanding; and (d) the standard operating procedures and interests of these organizations.

A. These players share the perceptual tendencies of all individuals. This means, for example, that

(1) New information will be fitted into their existing attitudes and images;

(2) Reports that should lead to a change in plans will be distorted so as to "save their theory";

(3) Clues that signal a significant change in the probabilities of events will be lost in the surrounding noise.

Examples: Evidence of a Japanese attack on Pearl Harbor was explained away. One senior military officer urged that the United States proceed to invade Cuba even after the Soviets agreed to remove their missiles.

B. Because these players use Model I they tend to assume that the actions were: (1) designed and executed, in effect, by a single individual; (2) designed carefully to influence their nation; (3) designed with a world view like their own; and (4) designed without regard to the domestic and bureaucratic politics of nation *A*.

Examples: Khrushchev warned Kennedy of the difficulty he had during the Cuban missile crisis of convincing his associates that an American U-2 which crossed into Soviet territory was not an indication that the United States was about to attack. The American intelligence community persists in predicting Soviet force structure on the basis of Model I analysis. . . .

6. Changes in actions of one nation will succeed in changing the actions of a second nation in a desired direction only to the extent that (a) the actions of the first nation send a clear, consistent, simple signal and (b) some participants in the other nation want, in pursuit of their own interests, to change behavior in the desired way, and (c) this signal serves to increase the influence of these participants.

25. Pre-Theories and Theories of Foreign Policy

JAMES N. ROSENAU

3

. . . Two basic shortcomings, one philosophical and the other conceptual, would appear to be holding back the development of foreign policy theory. Let us look first at the philosophical shortcoming. If theoretical development in a field is to flourish, empirical materials which have been similarly processed must be available. It is no more possible to construct models of human behavior out of raw data than it is to erect a building out of fallen trees and unbaked clay. . . . So it is with the construction and use of social theories. There must be, as it were, pre-theory which renders the raw materials comparable and ready for theorizing. The materials may serve as the basis for all kinds of theories—abstract or empirical, single- or multi-country, pure or applied—but until they have been similarly processed, theorizing is not likely to occur or, if it does, the results are not likely to be very useful.

Unlike economics, sociology, and other areas of political science, the field of foreign policy research has not subjected its materials

Excerpted from R. Barry Farrell, ed., *Approaches to Comparative and International Politics* (Evanston, Illinois: Northwestern University Press, 1966), pp. 27–93. Copyright © 1966 Northwestern University Press. Reprinted by permission of the publisher and author. Most footnotes deleted.

to this preliminary processing. Instead, as noted above, each country and each international situation in which it participates is normally treated as unique and nonrecurrent, with the result that most available studies do not treat foreign policy phenomena in a comparable way. Thus it is that the same data pertaining to the external behavior of the Soviet Union are interpreted by one observer as illustrative of Khrushchev's flexibility, by another as reflective of pent-up consumer demands, and by still another as indicative of the Sino-Soviet conflict. . . .

It must be emphasized that the preliminary processing of foreign policy materials involves considerably more than methodological tidiness. We are not referring here to techniques of gathering and handling data, albeit there is much that could be said about the need for standardization in this respect. Nor do we have in mind the desirability of orienting foreign policy research toward the use of quantified materials and operationalized concepts, albeit again good arguments could be advanced on behalf of such procedures. Rather, the preliminary processing to which foreign policy materials must be subjected is of a much more basic order. It involves the need to develop an explicit conception of where causation is located in international affairs. Should foreign policy researchers proceed on the assumption that identifiable human beings are the causative agents? Or should they treat political roles, governmental structures, societal processes, or international systems as the source of external behavior? And if they presume that causation is located in all these sources, to what extent and under what circumstances is each source more or less causal than the others? Few researchers in the field process their materials in terms of some kind of explicit answer to these questions. Most of them, in other words, are not aware of the philosophy of foreign policy analysis they employ, or, more broadly, they are unaware of their pre-theories of foreign policy.

To be sure, foreign policy researchers are not so unsophisticated as to fail to recognize that causation can be attributed to a variety of actors and entities. For years now it has been commonplace to avoid single-cause deterministic explanations and to assert the legitimacy of explaining the same event in a variety of ways. Rather than serving to discipline research, however, this greater sophistication has in some ways supplied a license for undisciplined inquiry. Now it is equally commonplace to assume that one's obligations as a researcher are discharged by articulating the premise that external behavior results from a combination of many factors, both external and internal, *without* indicating how the various factors combine under different circumstances. Having rejected single-cause explanations, in other words, most foreign policy researchers seem to feel they are therefore free *not* to be consistent in their manner of ascribing causation. Deterministic theories have philosophical roots, much foreign policy research seems to say, so that in abandoning the theories it is also necessary to give up the practice of locating one's work in a pre-theoretical context. . . .

Nothing could be further from the truth. . . .

Perhaps the best way to indicate exactly what a pre-theory of foreign policy involves is by outlining the main ingredients of any pre-theory and then indicating how the author has integrated these ingredients into his own particular pre-theory. Although the statement is subject to modification and elaboration, it does not seem unreasonable to assert that all pre-theories of foreign policy are either five-dimensional or translatable into five dimensions. That is, all foreign policy analysts either explain the external behavior of societies in terms of five sets of variables or they proceed in such a way that their explanations can be recast in terms of the five sets. Listed in order of increasing temporal and spatial distance from the external behaviors for which they serve as sources, the five sets are what we shall call the idiosyncratic, role, governmental, societal, and systemic variables.

The first set encompasses the idiosyncracies of the decision-makers who determine and implement the foreign policies of a nation. Idiosyncratic variables include all those aspects of a decision-maker—his values, talents, and prior experiences—that distinguish his foreign policy choices or behavior from those of every other decision-maker. John Foster Dulles' religious values, De Gaulle's vision of a glorious France, and Khrushchev's political skills are frequently mentioned examples of idiosyncratic variables. The second set of variables pertains to the external behavior of officials that is generated by the roles they occupy and that would be likely to occur irrespective of the idiosyncracies of the role occupants. Regardless of who he is, for example, the U.S. ambassador to the United Nations is likely to defend American and Western positions in the Security Council and General Assembly. Governmental variables refer to those aspects of a government's structure that limit or enhance the foreign policy choices made by decision-makers. The impact of executive-legislative relations on American foreign policy exemplifies the operation of governmental values. The fourth cluster of variables consists of those non-governmental aspects of a society which influence its external behavior. The major value orientations of a society, its degree of national unity, and the extent of its industrialization are but a few of the societal variables which can contribute to the contents of a nation's external aspirations and policies. As for systemic variables, these include any non-human aspects of a society's external environment or any actions occurring abroad that condition or otherwise influence the choices made by its officials. Geographical "realities" and ideological challenges from potential aggressors are obvious examples of systemic variables which can shape the decisions and actions of foreign policy officials.

But these are only the ingredients of a pretheory of foreign policy. To formulate the pretheory itself one has to assess their *relative potencies.* That is, one has to decide which set of variables contributes most to external behavior, which ranks next in influence, and so on through all the sets. There is no need to specify exactly how large a slice of the pie is accounted for by each set of variables. Such precise specifications are characteristics of theories and not of the general framework within which data are organized. At this pre-theoretical level it is sufficient merely to have an idea of the relative potencies of the main sources of external behavior. . . .

Attaching causal priorities to the various sets of variables is extremely difficult. Most of us would rather treat causation as idiographic than work out a consistent pre-theory to account for the relative strength of each variable under different types of conditions. One way to overcome this tendency and compel oneself to differentiate the variables is that of engaging in the exercise of mentally manipulating the variables in actual situations. Consider, for example, the U.S.-sponsored invasion of Cuba's Bay of Pigs in April 1961. To what extent was that external behavior a function of the idiosyncratic characteristics of John F. Kennedy (to cite, for purposes of simplicity, only one of the actors who made the invasion decision)? Were his youth, his commitments to action, his affiliations with the Democratic party, his self-confidence, his close election victory—and so on through an endless list—relevant to the launching of the invasion and, if so, to what extent? Would any President have undertaken to oust the Castro regime upon assuming office in 1961? If so, how much potency should be attributed to such role-derived variables? Suppose everything else about the circumstances of April 1961 were unchanged except that Warren Harding or Richard Nixon

occupied the White House; would the invasion have occurred? Or hold everything constant but the form of government. Stretch the imagination and conceive of the U.S. as having a cabinet system of government with Kennedy as prime minister; would the action toward Cuba have been any different? Did legislative pressure derived from a decentralized policy-making system generate an impulse to "do something" about Castro, and, if so, to what extent did these governmental variables contribute to the external behavior? Similarly, in order to pre-theorize about the potency of the societal variables, assume once more a presidential form of government. Place Kennedy in office a few months after a narrow election victory, and imagine the Cuban situation as arising in 1921, 1931, or 1951; would the America of the roaring twenties, the depression, or the McCarthy era have "permitted," "encouraged," or otherwise become involved in a refugee-mounted invasion? If the United States were a closed, authoritarian society rather than an open, democratic one, to what extent would the action toward Cuba have been different? Lastly, hold the idiosyncratic, role, governmental, and societal variables constant in the imagination, and posit Cuba as 9000 rather than 90 miles off the Florida coast; would the invasion have nevertheless been launched? If it is estimated that no effort would have been made to span such a distance, does this mean that systemic variables should always be treated as overriding, or is their potency diminished under certain conditions?

The formulation of a pre-theory of foreign policy can be further stimulated by expanding this mental exercise to include other countries and other situations. Instead of Kennedy, the presidency, and the U.S. of 1961 undertaking action toward Cuba, engage in a similar process of holding variables constant with respect to the actions taken by Khrushchev, the monolithic Russian decision-making structure, and the U.S.S.R. of 1956 toward the uprising in Hungary. Or apply the exercise to the actions directed at the Suez Canal by Eden, the cabinet system, and the England of 1956. Or take still another situation, that of the attack on Goa carried out by the charismatic Nehru and the modernizing India of 1961. In all four cases a more powerful nation initiated military action against a less powerful neighbor that had come to represent values antagonistic to the interests of the attacker. Are we therefore to conclude that the external behavior of the U.S., Russia, England, and India stemmed from the same combination of external and internal sources? Should the fact that the attacked society was geographically near the attacking society in all four instances be interpreted as indicating that systemic variables are always relatively more potent than any other type? Or is it reasonable to attribute greater causation to idiosyncratic factors in one instance and to societal factors in another? If so, what is the rationale for subjecting these seemingly similar situations to different kinds of analysis?

Reflection about questions similar to those raised in the two previous paragraphs has led this observer to a crude pre-theory of foreign policy in which the relative potencies of the five sets of variables are assessed in terms of distinctions between large and small countries, between developed and underdeveloped economies, and between open and closed political systems. As can be seen in Table 6.1, these three continua give rise to eight types of countries and eight different rankings of relative potency. There is no need here to elaborate at length on the reasoning underlying each ranking.[1] The point is not to demonstrate the va-

lidity of the rankings but rather to indicate what the construction of a pre-theory of foreign policy involves and why it is a necessary prerequisite to the development of theory. Indeed, given the present undeveloped state of the field, the rankings can be neither proved nor disproved. They reflect the author's way of organizing materials for close inspection and not the inspections themselves. To be theoretical in nature, the rankings would have to specify *how much* more potent each set of variables is than those below it on each scale, and the variables themselves would have to be causally linked to specific forms of external behavior.

To be sure, as in all things, it is possible to have poor and unsound pre-theories of foreign policy as well as wise and insightful ones. The author's pre-theory may well exaggerate the potency of some variables and underrate others, in which case the theories which his pre-theory generates or supports will in the long run be less productive and enlightening than those based on pre-theories which more closely approximate empirical reality. Yet, to repeat, this pre-theory is not much more than an orientation and is not at present subject to verification.

One suspects that many foreign policy analysts would reject this pre-theory, not because they conceive of different rankings or even different sets of variables but rather because the very idea of explicating a pre-theory strikes them as premature or even impossible. . . .

The fact is, however, that one cannot avoid having a pre-theory of foreign policy whenever one takes on the task of tracing causation. Even the most historical-minded analyst makes the initial assumption that events derive from an underlying order, that every external behavior of every society stems from some source and is therefore, at least theoretically, explicable. To assume otherwise—to view the external behaviors of societies as random and impulsive, as occurring for no reason, and as therefore unknowable—is to render analysis useless and to condemn the analyst to perpetual failure. Since we cannot avoid the presumption of an

---

[1]Suffice it to note that the potency of a systemic variable is considered to vary inversely with the size of a country (there being greater resources available to larger countries and thus lesser dependence on the international system than is the case with smaller countries), that the potency of an idiosyncratic factor is assumed to be greater in less developed economies (there being fewer of the restraints which bureaucracy and large-scale organization impose in more developed economies), that for the same reason a role variable is accorded greater potency in more developed economies, that a societal variable is considered to be more potent in open polities than in closed ones (there being a lesser need for officials in the latter to heed nongovernmental demands in the former), and that for the same reason governmental variables are more potent than societal variables in closed polities than in open ones.

TABLE 6.1 An Abbreviated Presentation of the Author's Pre-Theory of Foreign Policy, in Which Five Sets of Variables Underlying the External Behavior of Societies are Ranked According to Their Relative Potencies in Eight Types of Societies

Geography and physical resources	LARGE COUNTRY				SMALL COUNTRY			
State of the economy	Developed		Underdeveloped		Developed		Underdeveloped	
State of the polity	Open	Closed	Open	Closed	Open	Closed	Open	Closed
Rankings of the variables	Role Societal Governmental Systemic Idiosyncratic	Role Idiosyncratic Governmental Systemic Societal	Idiosyncratic Role Societal Systemic Governmental	Idiosyncratic Role Governmental Systemic Societal	Role Systemic Societal Governmental Idiosyncratic	Role Systemic Idiosyncratic Governmental Societal	Idiosyncratic Systemic Role Societal Governmental	Idiosyncratic Systemic Role Governmental Societal
Illustrative examples	U.S.	U.S.S.R.	India	Red China	Holland	Czechoslovakia	Kenya	Ghana

underlying order, neither can we avoid having some conception of its nature. Yet causation is not self-revealing. The underlying order does not simply manifest itself for the diligent analyst who gathers every scrap of evidence and then takes a long, hard look at what he has accumulated. . . .

While it is thus impossible to avoid possession of a pre-theory of foreign policy, it is quite easy to avoid awareness of one's pre-theory and to proceed as if one started over with each situation. Explicating one's conception of the order that underlies the external behavior of societies can be an excruciating process. . . .

But, it may be asked, if the purpose of all this soul searching and anguish is that of facilitating the development of general theory, how will the self-conscious employment of pre-theories of foreign policy allow the field to move beyond its present position? As previously implied, the answer lies in the assumption that the widespread use of explicit pre-theories will result in the accumulation of materials that are sufficiently processed to provide a basis for comparing the external behavior of societies. If most researchers were to gather and present their data in the context of their views about the extent to which individuals, roles, governments, societies, and international systems serve as causal agents in foreign affairs, then even though these views might represent a variety of pre-theories, it should be possible to discern patterns and draw contrasts among diverse types of policies and situations. Theoretical development is not in any way dependent on the emergence of a consensus with respect to the most desirable pre-theory of foreign policy. Comparison and theorizing can ensue as long as each researcher makes clear what variables he considers central to causation and the relative potencies he ascribes to them. For even if one analyst ascribes the greatest potency to idiosyncratic variables, while another views them as having relatively little potency and still another regards them as impotent, they will have all provided data justifying their respective assumptions,

and in so doing they will have given the theoretician the materials he needs to fashion if-then propositions and to move to ever higher levels of generalization.

4

But all will not be solved simply by the explication of pre-theories. This is a necessary condition of progress toward general theory, but it is not a sufficient one. Research in the foreign policy field would appear to be hindered by conceptual as well as philosophical shortcomings, and we will not be able to move forward until these more specific obstacles are also surmounted. Not only must similarly processed materials be available if general theory is to flourish, but researchers must also possess appropriate concepts for compiling them into meaningful patterns. Although rendered similar through the explication of pre-theories, the materials do not fall in place by themselves. Concepts are necessary to give them structure and thereby facilitate the formulation of if-then propositions. . . .

Two interrelated conceptual problems seem to be holding back the development of general theories of external behavior. One concerns the tendency of researchers to maintain a rigid distinction between national and international political systems in the face of mounting evidence that the distinction is breaking down. The second difficulty involves an inclination to ignore the implications of equally clear-cut indications that the functioning of political systems can vary significantly from one type of issue to another. Let us anticipate much of the ensuing discussion by noting that the interrelationship of the two problems is such that a new kind of political system, the *penetrated system*, is needed to comprehend the fusion of national and international systems in certain kinds of *issue-areas*.

. . . The national society is now so penetrated by the external world that it is no longer the only source of legitimacy or even of the employment of coercive techniques.

The probability that most social processes will culminate at the national level has diminished, and instead the "most inclusive" structures through which groups strive to attain goals are increasingly becoming a composite of subnational, national, and supranational elements.

It must be emphasized that these changes involve considerably more than a significant increase in the influence wielded by nonmembers of national societies. We are not simply asserting the proposition that the external world impinges ever more pervasively on the life of national societies, albeit such a proposition can hardly be denied. Nor are we talking merely about the growing interdependence of national political systems. Our contention is rather that in certain respects national political systems now permeate, as well as depend on, each other and that their functioning now embraces actors who are not formally members of the system. These nonmembers not only exert influence upon national systems but actually participate in the processes through which such systems allocate values, coordinate goal-directed efforts, and legitimately employ coercion. They not only engage in bargaining with the system, but they actually bargain within the system, taking positions on behalf of one or another of its components. Most important, the participation of nonmembers of the society in value-allocative and goal-attainment processes is accepted by both its officialdom and its citizenry, so that the decisions to which nonmembers contribute are no less authoritative and legitimate than are those in which they do not participate. Such external penetration may not always be gladly accepted by the officials and citizens of a society, but what renders decisions legitimate and authoritative is that they are felt to be binding, irrespective of whether they are accepted regretfully or willingly. . . .

The foregoing considerations not only lead to the conclusion that cogent political analysis requires a readiness to treat the functioning of national systems as increasingly dependent on external events and trends, but they also suggest the need to identify a new type of political system that will account for phenomena which not even a less rigid use of the national-international distinction renders comprehensible. Such a system might be called the *penetrated political system,* and its essential characteristics might be defined in the following way: A penetrated political system is one in which *nonmembers of a national society participate directly and authoritatively, through actions taken jointly with the society's members, in either the allocation of its values or the mobilization of support on behalf of its goals.* The political processes of a penetrated system are conceived to be structurally different from both those of an international political system and those of a national political system. In the former, nonmembers indirectly and nonauthoritatively influence the allocation of a society's values and the mobilization of support for its goals through autonomous rather than through joint action. In the latter, nonmembers of a society do not direct action toward it and thus do not contribute in any way to the allocation of its values or the attainment of its goals.

Obviously operationalization of these distinctions will prove difficult. When does an interaction between two actors consist of autonomous acts, and when does it amount to joint action? When are nonmembers of a society participants in its politics, and when are they just influential nonparticipants? Furthermore, how extensive must the participation by nonmembers be in order that a penetrated political system may come into existence? . . .

. . . One final point with respect to penetrated systems needs to be made. As it stands at present, our formulation suffers from a lack of differentiation. While the analysis points to the conclusion that all national societies in the modern world are susceptible of swift transformation into penetrated systems, it treats all such systems as if they were similarly transformed and structured. Yet obviously there is a vast difference between the penetrated systems that have developed in Vietnam and the Congo and those that have evolved with respect to British or Indian defenses. In the former cases penetration is thorough-going, whereas in the latter it is limited to the allocation of a highly restricted set of values. . . . Accordingly, so as to differentiate degrees of penetration as well as the structural differences to which they give rise, it seems appropriate to distinguish between multi-issue and single-issue penetrated systems, the distinction being based on whether nonmembers participate in the allocation of a variety of values or of only a selected set of values.

5

The conclusion that national societies can be organized as penetrated political systems with respect to some types of issues—or issue-areas—and as national political systems with respect to others is consistent with mounting evidence that the functioning of any type of political system can vary significantly from one issue-area to another. Data descriptive of local, party, legislative, national, and international systems are converging around the finding that different types of issue-areas elicit different sets of motives on the part of different actors in a political system, that different system members are thus activated in different issue-areas, and that the different interaction patterns which result from these variations produce different degrees of stability and coherence for each of the issue-areas in which systemic processes are operative. . . .

. . . In the foreign policy field, too, there are numerous indications that the nature of the issue constitutes a crucial variable in the processes whereby the external behavior of national societies is generated. In the United States, for example, the complex of internal influences brought to bear in the ratification of treaties would seem to be entirely different from that which underlies the allocation of economic and military assistance to other countries. One has the impression that much the same could be said about other societies that maintain foreign aid programs.

Whether they are impressionistic or systematic, in short, the data on issue-areas are too impressive to ignore. Conceptual allowance must be made for them if theorizing in the foreign policy field is to flourish. Indeed, the emergence of issue-areas is as pronounced and significant as is the breakdown of the national-international distinction. Taken together, the two trends point to the radical conclusion that the boundaries of political systems ought to be drawn vertically in terms of issue-areas as well as horizontally in terms of geographic areas. . . . Let us turn, therefore, to the task of specifying more precisely the nature of issue-areas and the location of vertical systems within them.

Stated formally, an issue-area is conceived to consist of *(1) a cluster of values, the allocation or potential allocation of which (2) leads the affected or potentially affected actors to differ so greatly over (a) the way in which the values should be allocated or (b) the horizontal levels at which the allocations should be authorized that (3) they engage in distinctive behavior designed to mobilize support for the attainment of their particular values.* If a cluster of values does not lead to differences among those affected by it, then the issue-area is not considered to exist for that group of actors, and their relationships with respect to the values are not considered to form a vertical system. . . .

It will be noted that the boundaries of vertical systems are delineated not by the common membership of the actors who sustain them (as horizontal systems are), but rather by the distinctiveness of the values and the behavior they encompass. The actors determine the state of a vertical system—whether it is active, dormant, or nonexistent—but the boundaries of the system are independent of the identity of the actors who are active within it. . . .

This is not to imply, of course, that either the actors, the values, or the behavior that form the parameters of a vertical system are simple to identify. A number of operational problems will have to be resolved before empirical research on vertical phenomena yield worthwhile results. In particular, answers to three questions must be developed: How are the values over which men differ to be clustered together into issue-areas? At what level of abstraction should they be clustered? What characteristics render the behavior evoked by one cluster of values distinctive from that stimulated by other clusters?

The general line of response to the first two questions seems reasonably clear. A typology of issue-areas ought to be something more than a mere cataloguing of the matters over which men are divided at any moment in time. For vertical systems to be of analytic utility, they must persist beyond the life of particular actors. As has already been implied, not much would be accomplished if "issue-area" meant nothing more than the conventional usage, in which an "issue" is equated with any and every concrete historical conflict that ensues between identifiable individuals or groups. In brief, a typology of issue-areas must be cast in sufficiently abstract terms to encompass past and future clusters of values as well as present ones. Obviously, too, the level of abstraction must be high enough to allow for clusters of values that evoke behavior within all types of horizontal systems, from local communities to the global community. At the same time the typology cannot be so generalized as to erase the distinctiveness of the behavior which characterizes the vertical systems in each of its areas.

For the present, of course, any typology must be largely arbitrary. Until systematic and extensive data on the distinctive nature of certain issue-areas are accumulated, the lines dividing them cannot be drawn with much certainty. In order to suggest further dimensions of the concept, however, let us adopt a simple typology which seems to meet the above criteria. Let us conceive of all behavior designed to bring about the authoritative allocation of values as occurring in any one of four issue-areas: the *territorial, status, human resources,* and *nonhuman resources* areas, each of which encompasses the distinctive motives, actions, and interactions evoked by the clusters of values that are linked to, respectively, the allocation of territorial jurisdiction, the allocation of status within horizontal political

systems or within nonpolitical systems, the development and allocation of human resources, and the development and allocation of nonhuman resources. . . .

In other words, each of the four issue-areas is conceived to embrace a number of vertical political systems, and the boundaries of each vertical system are in turn conceived to be determined by the scope of the interaction that occurs within it. Thus, as implied above, some vertical systems may function exclusively at local horizontal levels; others may be national in scope; still others may be confined to interaction at the international level. . . .

. . . But how, it may well be asked, does this particular typology meet the criterion that the value clusters in each area must evoke distinctive motives, actions, and interactions on the part of the affected actors? Granted that the values themselves differ, why should it be presumed that these differences are sufficient to produce differentiation in the functioning of the systems that allocate the values in each issue-area? . . . In the case of the foregoing typology the four issue-areas were derived from an impression that the motives, actions, and interactions of political actors are crucially related to the degree of tangibility of both the values which have to be allocated and the means which have to be employed to effect allocation. With respect to motives and actions, it was reasoned that the affected actors would be more strongly motivated and more persistently active the *greater* the tangibility of the *means* (since the rewards and costs to the actor of allocating a particular cluster of values are likely to be clearer the more easily comprehensible are the means necessary to realize the values); and that the more actors affected and active, the *lesser* the tangibility of the *ends* (since tangibility involves specificity, and thus the aspirations of a greater number of actors are likely to be encompassed by issues in which intangible goals are at stake). With respect to interaction, the presumption was made that the *greater* the tangibility of both the *ends* and *means* involved in an allocative process, the more the tendency to bargain among the affected actors would increase. In short, among the distinctive characteristics of an issue-area are the number of affected actors, the intensity of their motivations to act, the frequency with which they act, and the extent of their readiness to bargain with each other.

That four main issue-areas derive from the foregoing is readily apparent. The processes of allocating tangible values through the use of tangible means will differ significantly from those in which intangible ends and means are involved; both of these will in turn be distinguished from the processes whereby tangible values are allocated through the utilization of intangible means; and still a fourth pattern of distinctive motives, actions, and interactions will occur whenever tangible means are employed to achieve intangible ends. In short, we have fashioned a 2 × 2 matrix, each cell of which corresponds more or less closely to one of the four kinds of values that are presumed to sustain political behavior [see Figure 6.1].

Although crude and impressionistic, this

FIGURE 6.1

derivation of the distinctiveness of the issue-area does seem to hold up when one engages in the exercise of locating empirical findings in the matrix. Let us take Dahl's data as an example, and assume for purposes of illustration that the tangible-intangible scale of ends is op-

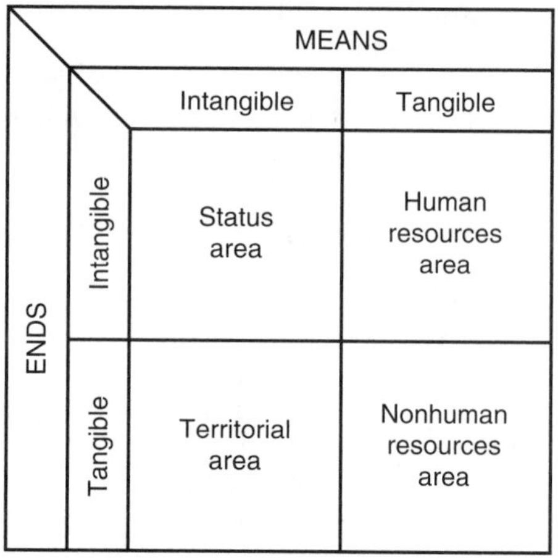

TABLE 6.2 A Further Elaboration of the Author's Pre-Theory of Foreign Policy, in Which Five Sets of Variables Underlying the External Behavior of Societies Are Ranked According to Their Relative Potencies in Sixteen Types of Societies and Three Types of Issue-Areas

LARGE COUNTRY

Developed Economy												Underdeveloped Economy											
Open Polity						*Closed Polity*						*Open Polity*						*Closed Polity*					
Penetrated			*Non-penetrated*			*Penetrated*			*Non-penetrated*			*Penetrated*			*Non-penetrated*			*Penetrated*			*Non-penetrated*		
status area	*nonhuman resource area*	*other area*	*status area*	*nonhuman resource area*	*other area*	*status area*	*nonhuman resource area*	*other area*	*status area*	*nonhuman resource area*	*other area*	*status area*	*nonhuman resource area*	*other area*	*status area*	*nonhuman resource area*	*other area*	*status area*	*nonhuman resource area*	*other area*	*status area*	*nonhuman resource area*	*other area*
so	r	r	so	r	r	r	r	r	r	r	r	i	i	i	i	i	i	i	i	i	i	i	i
r	sy	so	r	g	so	i	i	i	i	i	i	r	r	r	so	r	r	r	r	r	r	r	r
sy	so	sy	g	so	g	g	g	g	so	g	g	so	sy	sy	r	sy	so	sy	sy	sy	g	g	g
g	g	g	sy	sy	sy	so	sy	sy	g	sy	so	sy	g	so	sy	so	sy	so	g	g	so	sy	sy
i	i	i	i	i	i	sy	so	so	sy	so	sy	g	so	g	g	g	g	g	so	so	sy	so	so

i = idiosyncratic variables   r = role variables   g = governmental variables erationalized in terms of whether the values involved can be photographed with a camera and that the tangibility of means is measured by the extent to which money must be expended in order to acquire the values. The values represented by education cannot be photographed, albeit money is necessary to build the schools and pay the teachers—prerequisites to the realization of education values. Hence vertical systems designed to process educational issues fall in the human resources areas of the matrix. Similarly, nominations in New Haven are not photographable, and, unlike the building and maintenance of a school system, money is not needed to have them allocated in a desired fashion. Thus they would be classified in the status area. Likewise, urban redevelopment in New Haven—or the need for it—is readily photographable, and great quantities of money must be committed to its realization, thereby locating it in the nonhuman resources area. Since Dahl offers no data for the territorial area, let us conclude this exercise with the example of Berlin as a vertical political system. In this case recent history—especially since the erection of the wall in August 1961—testifies poignantly to the photographability of the values involved. Yet diplomatic persuasion, rather than money and the military capabilities it buys, must obviously serve as the means through which a Berlin settlement will ultimately be accomplished.

The impression that the fit between this formulation and empirical phenomena is sufficient to warrant further development of the typology is reinforced by one other consideration. The assumption that the tangibility of ends and means determines the number of affected actors and the extent of their readiness to bargain with each other permits specific conclusions about distinctive characteristics of at least two of the issue-areas. On the one hand, the status area, being composed of both intangible ends and means, is likely to evoke more uncompromising political behavior on the part of more actors than any of the other three; on the other hand, the nonhuman resources area, being composed of both tangible ends and means, is likely to evoke more

Table 6.2 Continued

SMALL COUNTRY																							
Developed Economy												Underdeveloped Economy											
Open Polity						Closed Polity						Open Polity						Closed Polity					
Penetrated			Non-penetrated			Penetrated			Non-penetrated			Penetrated			Non-penetrated			Penetrated			Non-penetrated		
status area	nonhuman resource area	other area	status area	nonhuman resource area	other area	status area	nonhuman resource area	other area	status area	nonhuman resource area	other area	status area	nonhuman resource area	other area	status area	nonhuman resource area	other area	status area	nonhuman resource area	other area	status area	nonhuman resource area	other area
sy	sy	sy	r	r	r	sy	sy	sy	r	r	r	sy	sy	sy	i	i	i	sy	sy	sy	i	i	i
so	r	r	so	sy	sy	r	r	r	sy	sy	sy	i	i	i	sy	sy	sy	i	i	i	sy	sy	sy
r	g	so	sy	g	so	i	i	i	i	i	i	so	r	r	so	r	r	r	r	r	r	r	r
g	so	g	g	so	g	so	g	g	so	g	g	r	g	so	r	g	so	so	g	g	so	g	g
i	i	i	i	i	i	g	so	so	g	so	so	g	so	g	g	so	g	g	so	so	g	so	so

so = societal variables   sy = systemic variables

bargaining on the part of fewer actors than any of the other areas. That these two conclusions correspond to the differences between concrete vertical systems in each area can be readily demonstrated. Compare, for instance, the processes whereby values pertaining to civil rights are allocated with those that mark the allocation of values in the field of transportation (e.g., the development of rivers, harbors, and roads). Clearly more persons are aroused by the former cluster than by the latter, and plainly, too, uncompromising positions are as characteristic of civil rights issues as horse-trading is of rivers and harbors allocations.

Indeed, it is noteworthy that these characteristics of the status area would seem to be so powerful as to create still another distinctive characteristic of that area: The boundaries of vertical systems in the status area would appear to be more capable of expansion than are systems in any other area. Because they arouse a greater number of actors and a more uncompromising set of orientations, status issues can quickly move upward, downward, and sideward, once they are activated. The demand for civil rights in Angola, the attempt of James Meredith to enter the University of Mississippi, and the recognition of Communist China are illustrative of the vertical dynamism of status issues. Their horizontal dynamism—their capacity for intruding upon other issue-areas—is exemplified by the current civil rights debate in the United States. . . .

6

The implications of the foregoing conceptual adjustments for the construction of foreign policy theory are clear. If the above formulation has any validity, the external behavior of horizontal systems at the national level is likely to vary so greatly in scope, intensity, and flexibility in each of the four issue-areas that any theory of foreign policy will have to include if-then propositions which reflect these variations. Similarly theoretical account will have to be taken of the external behavior of penetrated systems. Their relations with the rest of

the world will obviously be partly a function of differences in the degree and nature of the penetration they experience. Moreover, since the extent and manner of penetration are likely to vary from one issue-area to the next, any theory will have to encompass these additional differences.

Indeed the penetrated and vertical systems concepts would seem to be sufficiently important to warrant revision at the pre-theoretical level. It seems reasonable to presume, for instance, that the relative potency of systemic variables would be greater in penetrated systems than in those which are strictly of a national kind. Thus the pre-theory summarized in Table 6.1 could fruitfully be doubled in scope by subdividing each of the eight columns into "penetrated" and "nonpenetrated" categories and introducing eight new rankings which elevate the systemic variables, say, one notch in each of the eight penetrated systems. Likewise, if the distinctive characteristics of the status and nonhuman resources areas have been correctly estimated, it is easy to envision still another expansion of the pre-theory—a twofold expansion in which societal variables are elevated one position in the rankings for status areas (because more members of the system are likely to be aroused to make more uncompromising demands) and lowered one rank in those for nonhuman resources areas (because fewer system members are likely to make less stringent demands). Table 6.2 presents these possible expansions of the pre-theory which the penetrated and vertical systems concepts facilitate.

While these concepts greatly complicate the task of theory building, they do not dictate or limit the kind of theory that can be constructed. As emphasized throughout, all we have done in this paper is to identify and amplify the materials out of which any theory of foreign policy must be fashioned. A wide range of theories can be built out of these materials, and nothing inherent in the latter determines the design, elegance, and utility of the former. These qualities must be supplied by the analyst, which is what makes the task of theory building awesome and challenging.

Chapter 7
Crisis

26. International Crisis as a Situational Variable

CHARLES F. HERMANN

1

Interpreters of international politics have discussed numerous variables in their efforts to understand the variety of actions taken in the name of nation-states and other international actors. Single acts of foreign policy as well as patterns of interaction have been explained in terms of goals and national interests, the available national capabilities, the type of government, the personalities of national leaders, the influential nongovernmental agents within a country, or the human and nonhuman environment outside the country. One cluster of variables of potential value in explaining the behavior of international actors characterizes the situation that provides the occasion for action. Situational analysis, as it has been applied in other areas, assumes that the action of an agent (in this case an international actor) is a function of the immediate situation it confronts.

With appreciation for the multiplicity of variables operating in international politics and with the availability of multivariate techniques of analysis, students of world affairs have increasingly avoided reliance on simplistic, single-factor explanations of their subject. No reversal of this trend is intended in this discussion of situational analysis. Rather this essay suggests that for the explication of some foreign policy actions, specific situational variables should be examined together with other factors. Situational variables are among a number of independent variables that can be expected to contribute significantly in accounting for variation in international actions.

Assuming that a researcher plans to include reference to the immediate situation, what specific variables can he use to characterize the event? Some time ago Snyder and his associates observed: "We ought to recognize that a systematic frame of reference for the study of international politics will require several typologies, one of which will be concerned with situations." As a step in the development of a typology of situations, individual categories of situations can be isolated and defined. Crisis constitutes one possible category if only because it has been analyzed so frequently by observers of international politics. . . .

Reprinted with the permission of the author and The Free Press, a Division of Simon & Schuster Inc. from *International Politics and Foreign Policy*, revised edition, James N. Rosenau, ed., pp. 409–421. Copyright © 1969 by The Free Press. Footnotes deleted.

2

Definitions of crisis which identify a specific class of situations can be constructed with reference to either of two approaches which are among those prevalent in the contemporary study of international politics. These two are the systemic and decision-making approaches. . . .

We shall stipulate that a system is a set of actors (for example, nations, international organizations, and so on) interacting with one another in established patterns and through designated structures. In any given international political system, critical variables must be maintained within certain limits or the instability of the system will be greatly increased—perhaps to the point where a new system will be formed. A crisis is a situation which disrupts the system or some part of the system (that is, a subsystem such as an alliance or an individual actor). More specifically, a crisis is a situation that creates an abrupt or sudden change in one or more of the basic systemic variables. . . .

3

As the name suggests, central to the decision-making approach is the process by which decisions are made on questions of policy. Also basic to this organizing framework are the persons who, as individuals or in some collective form, constitute the authoritative decision-makers. The decision-makers behave according to their interpretation of the situation, not according to its "objective" character as viewed by some theoretical omnipotent observer. Therefore, in attempting to explain how different kinds of situations influence the type of choice that is made, the analyst must interpret the situation as it is perceived by the decision-makers.

The use of crisis as a situational variable which partially explains the policy-makers' decision is not unlike the stimulus-response model familiar to psychologists. Crisis acts as a stimulus; the decision represents a response. . . .

Those analysts who have studied crisis using the decision-making framework display no more agreement regarding the definition of crisis than do their counterparts who have applied the systemic approach. As before, we stipulate a definition which delimits a class of situations and contains some of the properties frequently associated with crisis. Specifically, a crisis is a situation that (1) threatens high-priority goals of the decision-making unit, (2) restricts the amount of time available for response before the decision is transformed, and (3) surprises the members of the decision-making unit by its occurrence. Threat, time, and surprise all have been cited as traits of crisis, although seldom have all three properties been combined. Underlying the proposed definition is the hypothesis that if all three traits are present then the decision process will be substantially different than if only one or two of the characteristics appear. Contained in the set of events specified by this definition are many that observers commonly refer to as crises for American policy-makers, for example, the 1950 decision to defend South Korea, the 1962 Cuban missile episode, and the 1965 decision to send marines to the Dominican Republic. But other situations would not be considered crises for policy-makers in the Unites States; the 1958 ultimatum on Berlin, the extended Greek-Turkish-Cypriot dispute, and the mission in 1964 to rescue Europeans in Stanleyville (Congo) are illustrative in this regard. The exclusion of these and other situations that do not contain at least one of the three traits does not deny the importance of these situations or the significant consequences of the resulting decisions. The classification of them as noncrises simply indicates that these situations may be different with respect to the decision process in some systematic ways from those included in the crisis set.

Before hypothesizing how the decision process in crisis differs from noncrisis, we must return to the perceptual problem. The proposed definition clearly refers to the decision-makers' perceptions of crisis situations, but how can this definition be implemented? The ideal answer is as obvious as it is difficult to achieve. Through interviews the researcher would get decision-makers to assess the amount of threat, time, and surprise they thought a given situation involved. Even if interviews should not be feasible, however, perceptual data on each crisis trait can be developed through the use of the public statements of policy-makers, their memoirs, and reports of their perceptions by other political leaders and by journalists.

Once we assume that the decision-makers' perceptions of a situation can be measured, a phenomenological question arises: Do the elements of the definition represent actual properties of situations as well as images in the minds of policy-makers? That is, do these qualities represent measurable stimuli independent of perceptions? Experimental data have been assembled elsewhere that offer an affirmative reply to this inquiry. Without reviewing that evidence we may note that situations do vary in the extent to which they obstruct goals sought by policy-makers, and hence, situations differ in measurable threat. Moreover, most situations contain dynamic elements which lead to their evolution after a measurable period of time regardless of whether these aspects of the situations are recognized by the affected decision-makers. Finally, the frequency with which similar events have occurred in the past and the existence of contingency planning are indicators of the amount of potential surprise contained in a situation. In short, the three crisis traits can be measured directly as properties of the situation or indirectly as perceptions of the decision-makers.

Because situations differ in their degree of threat, in their duration through time, and in their amount of surprise, each of the three traits that define a crisis can be conceived as one extreme on a dimension with scale positions for every possible quantity of each property. When taken together at right angles, these three scales form a three-dimensional space in which all situations can be located according to their degree of threat, time, and awareness (surprise). In Figure 7.1, this space has been closed to form a cube, the eight corners of

which represent all possible combinations of the extreme values of the three dimensions. Thus, the corners of the cube represent ideal types of situations with respect to threat, time, and awareness. Few, if any, actual situations can be considered to correspond to these ideal types, but as the location in the cube of a specific situation approaches one of the corners, that situation can be treated as influencing decision-making in a manner similar to the ideal type.

To illustrate the location of a situation along a dimension, consider the element of decision time in both the Korean crisis of 1950 and the Cuban crisis of 1962. As the South Korean army crumbled before the North Korean advance, the initial optimism of American decision-makers changed to a realization that unless the United States intervened quickly the invaders would control the entire peninsula. The first meeting with the President to discuss the Korean situation occurred on Sunday evening, June 25. After a series of steps taken in the next several days to support the faltering South Korean army, President Truman decided early Friday morning, June 30, to commit American ground forces. Although Truman and his advisers considered the time to be extremely short, other situations such as the detection of a launched ballistic missile attack could offer even less time for decision. Thus, on the time dimension the Korean decision would be located near the short time end of the scale, but would not be at the most extreme point. The Cuban missile crisis also presented short decision time because, as the American policy-makers observed, once the missiles were operational they would be extremely difficult to remove without the possibility that some of them would be launched in retaliation. With missiles prepared for firing, the situation facing the leaders of the United States would be drastically altered. The first presidential session on that crisis occurred on the morning of Tuesday, October 26; the following Tuesday President Kennedy issued the "Proclamation of the Interdiction of Offensive Weapons" that ordered the blockade to begin the next morning. In actual time the decision in the missile

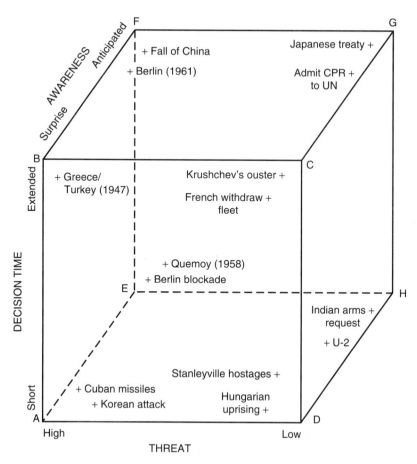

FIGURE 7.1   A situational cube representing the three dimensions of threat, decision time, and awareness, with illustrative situations from the perspective of American decision-makers. (*Note*: The representation of a three-dimensional space in a two-dimensional diagram makes it difficult to interpret the locations of the situations; their positions should not be considered exact in any case.)

A. Crisis Situation
   High Threat/Short Time/Surprise
B. Innovative Situation
   High Threat/Extended Time/Surprise
C. Inertia Situation
   Low Threat/Extended Time/Surprise
D. Circumstantial Situation
   Low Threat/Short Time/Surprise

E. Reflexive Situation
   High Threat/Short Time/Anticipated
F. Deliberative Situation
   High Threat/Extended Time/Anticipated
G. Routinized Situation
   Low Threat/Extended Time/Anticipated
H. Administrative Situation
   Low Threat/Short Time/Anticipated

crisis was more extended than that in the Korean crisis. If the decision-maker's perceptions of available time are used, some evidence indicates that the Korean crisis as compared to the Cuban crisis involved even less time than estimates based on clock or calendar. Despite these differences, the perceived time for both decisions puts them near the extreme of short time and both decision processes could be expected to bear resemblance to ideal type situations involving short decision time.

Hypothesized differences in decision-making introduced by crisis can be indicated by comparing crises with the other types of situations represented by the corners of the cube in Figure 7.1. The more decision-makers perceive a situation to approximate the specified characteristics of crisis, the more applicable the following comments should be.

CRISIS SITUATIONS

In a crisis, with its extreme danger to national goals, the highest level of governmental officials makes the decision. The time limitations together with the ability of these high-ranking decision-makers to commit the government allow them to ignore usual bureaucratic procedures. Information about the situation is at a premium because of the short time for collecting new intelligence and the absence of the serious data-gathering that precedes expected situations of importance. To a greater degree than in other situations the inputs that provide the basis for choice must be other than information about the immediate situation. For example, decision-makers may have a tendency to rely on incomplete analogies with previous situations or on their prior judgments about the friendliness or hostility of the source of the crisis. Although some substantive disagreements may occur among the policy-makers, personal antagonisms remain subdued because of a felt need for ultimate consensus. Compared to the policies made in response to other situations, crisis decisions tend more toward under- or over-reaction. An extreme response is encouraged by certain constraints imposed by the decision process (e.g., minimal information, increased importance of the decision-makers' personalities). The high stakes of a crisis decision and the uncertainty surrounding the outcome lead the decision-makers to remain quite anxious after the decision. Consequently, they expend considerable energy in the post-decision phase seeking support for their policy from allies and others.

INNOVATIVE SITUATIONS

A situation perceived to contain high threat and surprise but an extended amount of time can be described as encouraging an innovative decision. The threat to high-priority objectives increases the likelihood that the situation will receive the attention of the most able men available and, similarly, that considerable energy will be devoted to investigating the problem. Unlike a crisis decision, the greater time allows the government to undertake considerable search—a process motivated by the threat. Occasionally individuals in an agency charged with conducting foreign policy have programs or ideas that they have been unable to gain support for under normal conditions. A situation of the innovative type, for which there is no planned response and an openness to new ideas, will be sought by such individuals as an opportunity to obtain acceptance for their proposals. As in crises, *ad hoc* groups may be organized for the consideration of the situation, but they are not as free as crisis decision-makers to ignore normal administrative procedures.

Consider the following illustrations of innovative decisions. The deteriorating economic and political situation in Western Europe became increasingly visible to policy-makers in Washington during the last months of 1946. Against this background on February 21, 1947, the British surprised American officials by notifying them that beginning the first of April, Britain would be forced to discontinue financial assistance to embattled Greece. The same note also indicated that the British government would be unable to supply all the military assis-

tance required by Turkey. That incident resulted in what Jones has called "the fifteen
weeks" that culminated in the Marshall Plan. . . .

INERTIA SITUATIONS

Situations perceived as involving low threat,
extended time, and surprise often lead to inertia decisions, that is, to decisions not to act
or to discussions that never result in a decision.
The surprise quality of the situation makes less
likely the existence of preparations appropriate for coping with it. Being unexpected, no
agency or bureau may see the situation as
salient to its own plans. As a result the situation may be discussed by the various offices to
which it is referred without the commitment
of any agency. A decision is further inhibited
by the absence of any sense of urgency. Given
the number of policy situations at any given
time that pose considerable danger to the objectives of policy-makers, this type of situation
has difficulty being assigned a place on the
crowded agenda of men with the authority to
commit the state. . . .

CIRCUMSTANTIAL SITUATIONS

Circumstantial decisions are increasingly
likely in situations that policy-makers recognize as involving low threat, short time, and
surprise. Like crises these are situational conditions that require a quick decision if a choice
is to be made before the situation is transformed in some manner that makes action
more difficult. But unlike crises, and more like
inertia decisions, the stakes in the present type
of situation are not high. A failure to make the
"right" decision in time is not seen as leaving
important national goals in jeopardy. Under
these conditions whether or not the nation's
policy-makers reach a decision depends on
other circumstances that exist at the time the
situation is recognized. In other words, the
three situational variables are not likely to be
critical determinants in the low threat, short
time, and surprise configuration. . . .

REFLEXIVE SITUATIONS

The first four classes of situations involved surprise; the remaining four (located at the back
of the cube in Figure 7.1) mark the opposite
end of the awareness dimension. The lower
left-hand corner of the cube represents situations that are recognized by policy-makers as
containing high threat, short time, and anticipation. This situational configuration increases the probability of reflexive decisions.
With decision time at a premium, no elaborate
search routines or consultations are possible
to disclose methods for coping with the situation. In this sense the decision process is similar to that for crises, the difference being that
for reflexive decisions the policy-makers have
expected the situation to occur. Because they
will experience a serious threat to their goals
if it does develop, the policy-makers probably
produce a contingency plan in the period before the situation emerges. Once the situation
appears, minor alterations may be made in the
proposed plan, but time pressures deny decision-makers the chance to consider major alternatives. In fact, the knowledge that they
have already considered the problem may lead
policy-makers to an almost reflexive response.
Under these circumstances the decision
process will be more rapid than in a crisis.

The blockade of Berlin in 1948 provides an
example. American decision-makers perceived
the threat to their objectives to be severe. They
also recognized decision time to be restricted
both by the dwindling supply of essential commodities in Berlin and by the need for a rapid
response to assure Europeans of the commitment of the United States. As early as January
1948, the Soviets introduced various restrictions on transportation moving through East
Germany to Berlin. By early April, General Clay
had proposed to Washington an airlift to
Berlin—at least for American dependents—if
access on the ground were denied. When the
Soviets began to stop traffic on June 24, Clay
called for an airlift to begin the following day
as an interim measure. After a month, the
President and his advisers agreed to continue
this temporary measure on an increased scale

for the duration of the blockade. The confrontation over the Taiwan Straits in 1958 may be another illustration of a situation containing the characteristics that lead to a reflexive decision. Policy-makers in the United States considered the shelling of Quemoy and Matsu islands—which began on August 23—as a serious threat requiring a quick decision if the islands were to be defended. American intelligence detected clues of the forthcoming assault during the first days of August, which added to the sense of anticipation already created by previous encounters. When the shelling of the islands began, the United States quickly responded by reinforcing the Seventh Fleet, which was operating in the area. Although engaging in overstatement, Stewart Alsop revealed the reflexive nature of the American reaction with his observation: "There is little real significance in the inner history of the 1958 crisis, simply because the basic decisions had already been made in 1954 and 1955."

DELIBERATIVE SITUATIONS

The combination of high threat, extended time, and anticipation often results in a decision process that can be described as deliberative. The reaction of decision-makers parallels that for the innovative decision in many respects. High threat increases the probability that the situation receives careful attention, but unlike a crisis, the deliberations are not limited to a small group of the highest-ranking officials. Consideration of the problem occurs at different levels and in different agencies. The time available for discussion both prior to the actual appearance of the situation (as a result of anticipation) and after it emerges (as a result of extended decision time) can lead to organizational difficulties. Many groups in and out of government may become committed to a particular method of handling the problem. As the following examples indicate, deliberative situations increase the likelihood of hard bargaining between groups with alternative proposals.

. . . The Soviet ultimatum on June 4, 1961, created [this] type of situation. The Soviet government warned that it would sign a separate peace treaty with East Germany within six months unless the Western powers withdrew their military forces from Berlin which was to become a demilitarized city. The U.S.S.R. had made a similar demand in November 1958. Moreover, Khrushchev for months before the formal note was dispatched had boasted that he would sign such a treaty. Despite the anticipated quality of the situation and the relatively extended period of time for decision, the American decision-makers perceived it as quite threatening. The decision process in response to this situation involved considerable internal dissent among United States policy-makers as well as sharp divisions between the Western allies.

ROUTINIZED SITUATIONS

A diagonal running through the center of the cube in Figure 7.1 which has crisis decisions at one end has routinized decisions located at the other extreme. Routinized decisions frequently occur in low threat, extended time, and anticipated situations. Many, but not all, situations of this type are anticipated because they reappear with considerable regularity. Agencies charged with the conduct of foreign policy develop programmed routines for meeting recurrent low threat situations. Because established procedures are available, these situations tend to be dealt with by policy-makers at the lower and middle levels of the organization. The decision process follows one of two general patterns. In the first pattern decision-makers treat the problem in the same manner as they have treated previous situations of the same genus. Execution of the recommended course of action follows prompt agreement, unless temporary delays develop because policy-makers, whose approval is required, are engaged in more urgent business. If the situation lacks precedent or becomes the pawn in an interagency dispute, it follows the second pattern. Under these circumstances it may never come to a decision or may lie fallow until personnel change. Fear of bureaucratic obstruction provides one reason why policy-makers offer strong resistance to proposals for altering the response to an issue for which there are established procedures. . . .

ADMINISTRATIVE SITUATIONS

The final corner of the situational cube represents low threat, short time, and anticipation—a combination that usually results in a decision process described in this essay as administrative. Administrative decisions engage middle-level officials of foreign policy organizations, men who have the authority to energize selected parts of the decision machinery for quick responses to situations that contain limited threat. Efforts to seek out new information about the situation are limited by the short decision time and by the relatively low priority of low threat situations in gaining access to the government's facilities for search. In a fashion similar to reflexive decisions, the treatment of an administrative decision depends on the extent to which policy-makers have taken advantage of their expectation that the situation is likely to occur. If they anticipate that the situation will involve minimal threat, policy-makers may be reluctant to invest much time in the preparation of a possible response. On the other hand, when a low threat situation materializes they have less of a felt need for some kind of action than do the participants in a reflexive decision. Hence, those engaged in an administrative decision are unlikely to act at all unless they are confident that the proposed response is appropriate to the situation. In brief, a low threat, short time, anticipated situation will mobilize existing work groups who will not engage in any significant amount of bargaining or search and who will reach a decision only if they are confident in their choice at the time it is made. . . .

A[n] . . . illustration of the administrative type of situation is the Indian request for arms during the October 1962 border conflict with China. The issue of military aid to India had been extensively explored during the previous months, especially since May when it appeared that India might turn to the Soviet Union for military support. When Prime Minister Nehru made an urgent appeal to the United States on October 29, the United States decision followed with such speed that the first shipments arrived within the week. This American decision was made while the highest levels of the government remained involved in the Cuban missile crisis.

We should reiterate that the statements about the decision processes that develop in response to various types of situations are hypotheses which may or may not be confirmed by further research. Thus, the statement about confidence in administrative decisions could be recast in the customary form for hypotheses as follows: The less threat and decision time and the more anticipation that decision-makers perceive in a given situation, the greater will be their initial confidence in any decision made about that situation. We hypothesize that situational variables increase the tendency for the occurrence of a certain kind of process or decision, but these variables alone may not determine the outcome. Other variables reinforce or alter the influence of the specified situational variables. It is possible, of course, that the effect of some situational configurations—perhaps crisis—is so strong that the impact of other variables seldom changes the situational effect on the decision. The question of how much variance in decisions is accounted for by particular situational variables is a matter for empirical research.

The situational cube offers one technique for increasing the cumulative knowledge about crises using the decision-making approach. The use of any classification scheme encourages the analyst to compare a particular situation with others he believes to be similar in specified qualities and to distinguish it from those assumed to be different. . . .

The examples used for the situational cube illustrate that previously written case studies can provide material for evaluating hypotheses about the effect of crises on decisions once these propositions have been advanced. As in the systemic approach, however, certain problems arise in reinterpreting a series of prepared studies, each describing an individual situation. The original authors may have excluded important information necessary for inspection of the hypotheses or they may have attached different meanings to important variables. If the same analyst examines a number of cases with the hypothesis in mind, some of these problems are overcome. Nevertheless, as we move from the statement of hypotheses about crisis as a situational variable to the rigorous testing of these hypotheses, the case study necessarily must be augmented by other methods of analysis. This requirement, together with more exact definitions of the situational variable, seems necessary for further crisis analysis using either the systemic or decision-making approach.

27. Perception and Action in the 1914 Crisis

OLE R. HOLSTI, ROBERT C. NORTH, AND RICHARD A. BRODY

RELATING PERCEPTIONS
TO BEHAVIOR:
THE INTERACTION MODEL

We are interested not only in what national decision makers *perceive*—or say they perceive—
about themselves and others. We are also
interested in what they actually *do*. How are
these perceptual and action elements to be
brought together systematically and correlated for meaningful analysis? Basically, we are
interested in internation "communication" in
the sense that this concept can be used to characterize all transactions between nations. This
indicates that both the verbal *and* and physical
acts have information potential. The acts of
one nation can be considered as inputs to
other nations. The basic problem is this: given
some input to a nation, what additional information do we need to account for the nation's
foreign policy response?

The conceptual framework we have selected for such analysis is a two-step mediated
stimulus-response ($S–r : s–R$) model. These elements are as follows: A stimulus (S) is an event
in the environment which may or may not be
perceived by a given actor, and which two or
more actors may perceive and evaluate differently. A stimulus may be a physical event or a
verbal act. The stimuli relevant to international politics tend to originate with the acts of
other nations (or are perceived as) directed toward a nation in question. This is not to say
that domestic problems (for example, pressure for tariffs) have no relevance. Rather, it is
to assert that the impetus for most decisions,
especially in crisis, is extra-national. Input behavior (S) can be described in terms of the clarity and salience of the stimulus. Clarity is a
function of both the nature of the acts and its
intensity. Is the act physical or verbal? Is it at a
high or low level of intensity? These characteristics may play a considerable part in determining the manner in which the nation-state
responds (R). On the other hand, physical acts
of moderate to high intensity may have a low
level of salience; even a very clear stimulus may
find the actors focused elsewhere. For example, during the early weeks of the 1914 crisis,
British decision makers were primarily concerned with the Ulster situation rather than
the events on the Continent.

A response (R) is an action of an actor, without respect to his intent or how either he or
other actors may perceive it. Both S's and R's
are non-evaluative and non-affective. For example, on July 29, 1914, Russia, in response to
the declaration of war, ordered a partial mo-

Reprinted with the permission of The Free Press, a
Division of Simon & Schuster Inc. from *Quantitative
International Politics*, J. David Singer, ed., pp. 132–139, 141,
145–147, 152–158. Copyright © 1968 by The Free Press.
Most footnotes and selected references deleted.

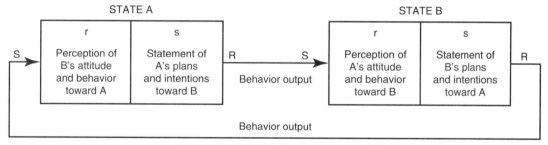

FIGURE 7.2 The Interaction Model

bilization of the southern district (*R*). Although the intention behind it was only to deter Austria-Hungary from invading Serbia, this action served as a stimulus (*S*) to Germany, which, within hours, responded by threatening a mobilization of its own (*R*).

In the model, the perception (*r*) of the stimulus (*S*) within the national decision system corresponds to the "definition of the situation" in the decision-making literature (Snyder et al., 1962; March and Simon, 1958). For example, during the crisis leading up to World War I, Germany perceived that Russia was threatening German borders. Finally, (*s*) represents the actor's expressions of his own intentions, plans, actions, or attitude toward another actor; for example, Germany asserted an intention of supporting Austria-Hungary. Both (*r*) and (*s*) carry evaluative and affective loadings. In the case of the Russian partial mobilization (*R*), although the intent behind it (*s*) was aimed solely at Austria-Hungary, it was perceived (*r*) as a serious threat by German decision-makers, who expressed their own intent (*s*) to take similar action. Three days later Germany ordered a general mobilization (*R*).

Operationally, it would be much simpler, of course, to confine oneself only to *S* and *R*, as do many traditional theories of international politics. In many situations and for many decision-makers the best predictor of state A's action response toward state B will be the nature of state B's actions. If the latter were unambiguously dangerous, one would expect them to be negatively valued by almost any individual or group in a decision-making role.

Predicting President Roosevelt's response to the attack on Pearl Harbor would not be difficult. However, not all—or even most—internation actions are so unambiguous. Consider, for example, Chamberlain's and Churchill's perceptions of Hitler's invitation to confer at Munich on the fate of Czechoslovakia.

There have been serious doubts about the feasibility of quantifying perceptual and affective data, and the inclination, until recently, has been to emphasize "hard" variables and aggregate data: to measure gross national products and populations, or to count troops or planes or ships or megatons, and assume that decision-makers respond to the "objective" value assigned to these capabilities by the investigator. As important as these "objective" data are, they may fail to take into sufficient account how human beings react to the factors discussed above. Many of the crucial problems of international politics concern such questions as decision-making, communication, and negotiation under varying conditions of stress. For this purpose, valuable indicators of tension are subjective ones, that is, those revealed by the decision-makers themselves. "Objective" indicators of tensions, such as rising defense budget, while useful as supplementary information, may not indicate that a particular decision-maker felt himself to be under the pressure of high stress. Moreover, objective data are usually compiled on an annual, quarterly, or monthly basis. These indices may well be used to reveal the trend toward an environment conducive to crisis (Wright, 1957 . . .)—such as Europe in

1914 or the cold war since 1945—but are less useful for the intensive study of a *short* time period. Thus it is particularly important for the investigator who seeks to analyze short-term changes in the international system— such as the crisis situation—to incorporate subjective data into his model.

COLLECTING THE PERCEPTUAL DATA

The selection of the 1914 crisis as the initial case in which to attempt rigorous quantitative analyses of conflict at the international level was based on several considerations. The available documentation relating to the outbreak of World War I surpasses that of any crisis of similar magnitude. Among the major nations involved, only the Serbian archives have remained relatively inaccessible to the investigator. Moreover, a generation of careful scholarship has produced published and readily accessible document collections of unquestioned authenticity, including those of Austria-Hungary (1930), France (1936), Great Britain (1926), Germany (Montgelas and Schücking, 1924), and Russia (1934). The forged, altered, or incomplete collections—produced by the various governments while passions and charges of "war guilt" still ran high—have been superseded. Finally, the crisis is a classic example of war through escalation. The minor war between Austria-Hungary and Serbia—which crisis-hardened European diplomats expected to remain localized—engulfed nearly the entire continent within ten days. The existing international system—still referred to by many as the classic example of a functioning "balance of power" system—was unable to cope with the situation as it had previously done in the recurring Balkan crises. While extensive war plans had been drawn up by the various general staffs, there is little evidence that any European decision-maker wanted or expected a general war—at least in 1914.

The perceptual data were derived in whole from documents authored by selected British, French, Russian, German, and Austro-Hungarian decision-makers. Those persons filling key roles such as head of state, head of government, or foreign minister were selected, unless there was a clear indication—from such standard sources as Fay (1928) or Albertini (1953)—that the person had no part whatsoever in the formulation of decisions. In addition, certain other persons who played a prominent part in the events were added. The complete list of decision-makers whose messages were subjected to content analysis is found in Table 7.1

One issue that must be resolved in a satisfactory manner in research which is so heavily dependent upon diplomatic documents is that of *sampling*. Three potential sources of error are present. First, do the published documents represent a faithful sample of the communication between decision-makers? One difficulty is represented by that portion of communication which is not recorded— for example, face-to-face conversations, telephone messages, or conferences in which no official minutes are recorded. While the basic "sense" of such communication can often be cross-checked against diaries, memoirs, or other such sources, this type of communication represents a source of sampling error of generally unknown proportions.

A second potential source of sampling error is found in the adequacy of document collections themselves. Possible sources of loss are those attributable to misfiling or destruction of documents—either intentionally or inadvertently—and bias or carelessness by those commissioned to collect and publish them. Even in the case of intentionally destroyed documents, however, the historian or social scientist is not helpless. For example, if A destroys his copy of a message sent to B, it should still be found among B's documents.

The documents published in various collections used in this study of the 1914 crisis appear to be complete. . . .

A third source of potential sampling error is in the selection of documents for content analysis by the investigator. The data in the present paper are derived from the *complete* uni-

TABLE 7.1   1914 Decision-Makers Selected for Documentary Content Analysis

Position[a]	*Austria Hungary*	*Germany*	*England*	*France*	*Russia*
Head of State	Franz Joseph	Wilhelm II	George V	Poincaré	Nicholas II
Head of Government	Stügkh[b] Tisza	Bethmann-Hollweg	Asquith	Viviani	
Secretary for Foreign Affairs	Berchtold	Jagow	Grey	Viviani	Sazonov
Undersecretary for Foreign Affairs	Forgach Macchio Hoyos	Zimmermann Stumm	Nicolson	Bienvenu-Martin Berthelot Ferry	
Minister of War/Chief of General Staff	Conrad	Moltke		Messimy	Sukomlinov
Others			Haldane[c]		

[a]Position refers to functionally equivalent roles, not to formal titles, which vary from nation to nation.
[b]Stügkh was Austro-Hungarian Minister-President; Tisza was Hungarian Prime Minister.
[c]Lord Chancellor.

verse, rather than a sample thereof: the *verbatim text* of published documents meeting the criteria of authorship and time (June 27–August 4).

The initial step in the exploitation of these documents was to devise perceptual units that could be defined, recognized by separate investigators, counted, and ranked along scales of more-to-less intensity. The units used in these analyses of international crisis—the *perceptions*—have been abstracted from the documents in terms of the following elements: *the perceiving party or actor; the perceived party or actors; the action or attitude; and the target party or actor.* For example, the assertion by a Russian decision-maker that "The Austrian, as well as German, hope is for the ultimate annihilation of Serbia," was coded as follows:

Perceiver	Perceived	Action or Attitude	Target
Russia	Austrian	hope is for the ultimate annihilation of	Serbia
Russia	German	hope is for the ultimate annihilation of	Serbia

The 1914 documents yielded over 5,000 such cognitive and affective perceptions.

The analysis of these data has gone through three fairly distinctive states: (1) the use of only *frequency* of perceptions; (2) the recoding of the documents, and scaling of the perceptions for the *intensity* of various attributes; and (3) correlational analyses between perceptions and the various types of "*hard*" and *action* data.

Using frequency of themes as a technique of analysis, an initial paper tested two basic hypotheses about the relationships between perceptions of threat and perceptions of capability in international crisis (Zinnes, North, Koch, 1961). Theodore Abel, in his survey of decisions to go to war—including the case of 1914—had concluded that, "in no case is the decision precipitated by emotional tensions, sentimentality, crowd behavior, or other irrational motivations" (1941, p. 855). The evidence presented in that initial study strongly supported a contrary hypothesis: *If perceptions of anxiety, fear, threat, or injury are great enough, even the perception of one's own inferior capability will fail to deter a nation from going to war.*

Using perceptual data—but no action data—from the 1914 crisis, Dina A. Zinnes tested four hypotheses about the relationships between perceptions of hostility and expressions of hostility by key decision-makers (Zinnes, 1963). In the 1914 case it was found that a nation-state tends to express hostility to the degree that it sees itself to be the target of another state's hostility; and such a nation-state, on identifying the source of perceived injury, tends then to express hostility toward the perceived offending state.

Although these studies reinforced the belief that content analysis of documentary material provides a rich source of data, they also revealed the importance of measuring *intensity* as well as *frequency* of perceptions. Thus the entire set of documents was recoded for perceptions of: hostility, friendship, frustration, satisfaction, and desire to change the *status quo*. Each item was next typed on a separate card and masked to conceal the identity of the various actors. Thus the example cited above would appear as:

> *X*'s hope is for the ultimate annihilation of Z
> *Y*'s hope is for the ultimate annihilation of Z

The entire set of cards for each category (for example, hostility) was then scaled for intensity by a series of three judges on a forced-distribution scale of 1 to 9 by the Q-Sort technique. The quantitative results were then aggregated into twelve time periods, each containing approximately one twelfth of the documentation.

After the complete recoding and scaling of the 1914 documents, the hypotheses relating perceptions of capability and injury were re-examined. It was found that decision-makers of each nation most strongly felt themselves to be the victims of injury precisely at that time when its leaders were making policy decisions of the most crucial nature (Holsti and North, 1965). As mentioned, perceptions of its inferior capability did not deter a nation such as Germany from going to war. The Kaiser's desperate reaction to the events which were engulfing him—perhaps best characterized by his assertion, "If we are to bleed to death, England shall at least lose India" (Montgelas and Schücking, 1924, p. 350)—is the reaction of a decision-maker under such severe stress that any action is preferable to the burden of the sustained tension.

This reaction in the face of an adversary's greater capabilities—a reaction strikingly familiar to instances in the Peloponnesian Wars, the wars between Spain and England during the sixteenth century, and the Japanese decision to strike at Pearl Harbor (Holsti, 1963)—are not unrelated to the dilemmas of our own age of missiles and nuclear war-heads. These findings underscore the need for re-examining that "common sense" and almost irresistible "conventional wisdom" which argues that deterrence is merely a matter of piling up more and/or better weapons that the opponent can amass.

COLLECTING THE BEHAVIORAL DATA

These initial studies were based solely on perceptual data, without a systematic attempt to correlate them against other data. Critics of content analysis have frequently pointed to the lack of studies in which inferences based on content data are tested against independent material (Berelson, 1952, pp. 74–75). For example, is there any significant relationship between what policy-makers say and write and the actual decisions they make? If there is not, then the value of content analysis as a research technique is placed in serious doubt. The next reasonable step, therefore, was to examine the relationship between perceptions and a series of "hard" indices. Financial data such as stock and bond prices, gold movements, commodity futures, interest rates, and other items lend themselves to this purpose. Reliable data on these indicators, measured and reported on a daily basis, are readily accessible.

The relationship between the level of tension, revealed through the content analysis of documents, and political decision-making may be investigated directly or indirectly. The direct approach involves a search for correlation between the results of the content analysis and such actions as troop movements, mobilization, breaking of diplomatic relations and the like. The indirect approach involves a correlation of the "soft" variables with a set of indices which are presumed to be sensitive to international tension levels.

The financial indicators discussed here are of the latter type. Although they respond to events other than international political crises, the history of 1914 rules out other causes of fluctuation. Given fluctuations of financial indicators, correlated with increases and decreases in international tension, these indicators can be used to check the validity of content analysis data. If the latter covary both with the political/military actions of nations participating in the crisis and with the fluctuations of financial indicators that respond to the tensions born of these actions, confidence in the content analysis techniques is substantially enhanced. . . .

The Flow of Gold

. . . When the movement of gold is compared to the daily fluctuations in the intensity of perceived hostility there is a significant correlation ($r_s = .85$). It is interesting to note, for example, that the drop in perceiver hostility on Monday, July 27, is matched by a sharp rise in the influx of gold. During the preceding weekend many observers and participants, including the Kaiser and Winston Churchill, had felt that the Serbian reply to the ultimatum marked the end of the crisis. Similarly the steady rise in hostility starting on July 28 corresponds to the withdrawal of gold in panic proportions. . . .

The Prices of Securities

The data analyzed here consist of twenty of the most important stocks and bonds for Serbia, Russia, France, Germany, Austria-Hungary, England, and Belgium, traded on the London, St. Petersburg, Paris, Berlin, Vienna and Brussels exchanges. To facilitate interpretation, the price of each security is given as a percentage of its value during the pre-crisis week (June 20–26). The index is the average value for the twenty securities. When the composite index is compared to the fluctuations in the intensity of perceived hostility,

there is again an evident similarity. The decrease in perceived hostility on July 27 is matched by a slight rise in the value of securities. Some individual shares of those nations most intimately involved in the Austro-Serbian dispute rose quite markedly—Serbian Bonds (2.5%), Russian Bonds (2.5%), and Austrian Credit Shares (1.7%). Subsequently there was a virtual collapse in prices, corresponding to the rise in perceived hostility. The figures on the extent of the collapse in the last few days of the crisis are actually stated conservatively. In the first place, many of the quoted prices were, according to observers, nominal and thus higher than the actual price for which one could sell his securities (*Economist*, August 1, 1914, p. 231). Secondly, for the purpose of the index, the price of a security that was no longer traded—usually due to the closing of various exchanges—is carried through July 30 at the last quoted price. . . .

In contrast, the paper losses in values of the stocks and bonds of the major participants in the crisis were staggering. In the ten-day period ending July 30, the value of 387 representative British stocks fell by £188,000,000. By July 25, the value of the securities of twenty-three German industrial firms had dropped from £79,000,000 to £65,900,000—and the worst was yet to come! In one sense the "cost" of the war reached catastrophic proportions even before the first shot was fired (*Economist*, August 1, 1914, p. 229; August 29, 1914, p. 383). Thus the comparison with the securities of belligerents and neutrals during the crisis strongly suggests that the virtual collapse of prices during July 1914 was directly related to rising international tensions. . . .

RELATING PERCEPTION AND MILITARY ACTION

The next step was to test the basic interaction ($S–r:s–R$) model with the data. Students of conflict have frequently asserted that parties acting in crisis situations reveal more or less consistent patterns of rising tensions and escalation leading to violence. Within the context of international politics, the line of reasoning can be summarized as follows: If state A—correctly or incorrectly—perceives itself threatened by state B, there is a high probability that A will respond with threats of hostile action. As state B begins to perceive this hostility directed toward itself, it is probable that B, too, will behave in a hostile (and defensive) fashion. This threatening behavior by B will confirm for A that its initial perceptions were correct, and A will be inclined to increase its hostile (and defensive) activity. Thereafter, the exchanges between the two parties will become increasingly negative, threatening, and injurious (North, 1962).

An initial and partial test of this sequence of interaction was carried out by correlating perceptual, or affective, data from 1914 with the spiral of military mobilizations just prior to the outbreak of World War I (North et al., 1964). The findings suggest that mobilizations accounted for a considerable part—but by no means all—of the variance in hostility. There was a steady rise in hostility *prior to* any acts of mobilization, and thus, to some degree, the decision-makers were responding to verbal threats and diplomatic moves, rather than to troop movements, in earlier phases of the crisis. This study thus revealed the necessity of correlating perceptual data with other types of action data. It also underscored the importance of testing hypotheses in other crisis situations, since there was little in the 1914 data to suggest under what conditions the exchange of threats leads to "deescalation," as appears to have happened in the October, 1962, Cuban crisis, rather than to a conflict spiral.

The action data (*S* and *R* in the model) were expanded to include all events of a military character involving nations in the 1914 crisis either as agents or targets of actions. These were gathered from standard military histories of the period (Edmunds, 1937; McEntee, 1937; Frothingham, 1924) and such usually reliable newspapers as the *New York Times*, *Times* (London), and *Le Temps* (Paris). Wherever possible the reports were verified in an authoritative history of the crisis (Albertini, 1953). If

serious doubt existed about the accuracy of an item—in the closing days of the crisis newspapers were filled with many unsubstantiated charges and countercharges—the item was discarded. As with the documentary data, the action data were coded in a uniform format; that is, according to the *agent* of action, the *action*, and the *target* of action. Unless the target of action was *explicit*, it was coded as general. The coding yielded three hundred and fifty-four military actions, of which the following are examples:

Agent	Action	Target
French Chamber	approves a 3-year military law	(general)
German fleet	leaves Norway for home ports	(general)
Austrian army	bombarded	Belgrade
Churchill (Britain)	orders shadowing in the Mediterranean of	two German battle-cruisers
Germany	declares war on	France

. . . For purposes of combining action and perceptual data in the *S–r:s–R* model, both the *s* and *r* stages in the model are operationalized solely in terms of the hostility variable. Previous studies involving multivariant analysis, which have revealed hostility to be the best predictor of action, are supported in the present study. With violence of action as the dependent variable, only the rank-order correlation coefficient for hostility ($r_s = .66$) is statistically significant. A convenient starting point is to assume congruence across the *S–r:s–R* model. In these terms it is postulated—however tentatively—that a given amount of violence (or any other quality which the investigator wishes to measure) in an environmental stimulus (*S*) will yield an appropriate level of expressed affective response (*r*) which, in turn, will stimulate an expressed "intent" (*s*) of like affective loading and a response (*R*) at about the same level of violence as the original stimulus (*S*). Where data from historical crisis situations provide incongruent patterns across the model, other sources of variance must be sought to account for the discrepancy between the expected and obtained relationship. . . .

Previous studies have suggested that in situations where two or more actor-nations are minimally engaged or involved in an interaction, the environmental stimulus (S) may yield an accurate prediction of an actor-nation's response (R). Stated somewhat differently, S may be the best predictor of R in circumstances where the actor-nations perceive that neither the penalties nor the rewards are likely to be of any great significance (Zaninovich, 1964).

The first hypothesis specifies the conditions under which the degree of congruence between S and R is high or low.

The correlation between input action (S) and policy response (R) will be better in a situation of low involvement than in one of high involvement.

This suggests that in the *low* involvement situation, the analysis of perceptions (s and r) may be less crucial and that "objective" criteria may give the analyst adequate information. Rummel's (1964) findings that domestic data predict state behavior fairly well—except under conditions of high conflict—can be interpreted as lending support to this hypothesis.

Of the two coalitions engaged in the crisis, the Triple Entente was engaged for a much shorter period. During the month between June 27 and July 27, that coalition revealed a total of only 40 perceptions of hostility compared to 171 for the Dual Alliance; in the late period (July 28 to August 4) the figures were 229 and 270 respectively.[1] This certainly coincides with the historians' consensus.

. . . The degree of congruence between S and R for the less-engaged coalition, the Triple Entente, is considerably lower ($r_s = .463$) than that for the Dual Alliance ($r_s = .678$). Several explanations are possible. First, at least two

members of the Triple Entente—England and France—acted (R) with a high level of violence only relatively late in the crisis period, withholding action until the threat (S) from the Dual Alliance was quite clearly defined.

On the other hand, the actions of the Dual Alliance—and particularly Austria-Hungary's actions in the early and middle part of the crisis period leading to a hoped-for local war—were not commensurate with the level of violence displayed by either Serbia or other members of the Triple Entente. There were two overlapping crises which became one at midnight August 4. The first was the result of a rather deliberately planned local war that had little to do with the actions of the other major powers and in which the members of the Triple Entente were only minimally engaged; the second resulted in an unplanned escalation into general war, engulfing all the nations.

A second hypothesis including the S and R (action) stages of the model is concerned not only with congruence or lack of congruence, but with the direction of differences.

In a situation of low involvement, policy response (R) will tend to be at a lower level of violence than the input action (S), whereas in a high-involvement situation, the policy response (R) will tend to be at a higher level of violence than the input action (S).

In terms of the events of 1914, the hypothesis suggests that the nations of the Triple Entente would under-respond to actions from the other side, whereas those of the Dual Alliance would be over-reacting to the threat from the Triple Entente. A Mann-Whitney U Test to compare the magnitude of the difference between input (S) and output (R) action reveals that the values for the Dual Alliance are indeed consistently negative (indicating over-reaction), whereas those of the Triple Entente are positive (under-reaction) on balance.

The inability to predict reactions (R) solely on the basis of action (S) suggests an examination of the relationship between action, perceptual, and situational variables.

Where such lack of congruence between input and output action exists, the interven-

[1] $\chi^2 = 45.8$, and with df = 1, $P = < .001$. [This is statistically significant.—ED.].

ing perceptions may perform either an accelerating or decelerating function. This suggests the hypothesis that

In the low-involvement situation, r will tend to be at a lower level than S, whereas in the high-involvement situation r will tend to be higher than S.

Intuitively the hypothesis makes sense. In a period of relative calm and low involvement, perceptual distortion will probably tend in the direction of under-perception; one may even be lulled into a false sense of security by failing to perceive a real threat. The British and French reaction to Nazi Germany—until the aggressive actions of Hitler became so unambiguous that even Chamberlain and Daladier perceived the danger—is a case in point. During a period of intense stress, on the other hand, when all fingers are near or on the trigger, even the most innocent action may be perceived as a threat of great magnitude. This pattern is much like that exhibited by Kaiser Wilhelm during the intense crisis leading up to World War I. Although possessor of the world's second ranking navy, at one point he perceived the presence of a few Russian torpedo boats in the Baltic as adequate cause for alerting the entire German fleet (Montgelas and Schücking, 1924, p. 223).

The hypothesis is supported by the 1914 data. Table 12[2] reveals the difference between the level of input action (S) and perceptions of those actions (r). The leaders of the Dual Alliance consistently overperceived the level of violence in the actions of the other coalition.

The same hypothesis can also be tested in a somewhat different way. The first six periods (June 27–July 27) have been described as those in which the members of the Dual Alliance were highly involved in the events in the Balkans, whereas those of the Triple Entente were not. On the other hand, during the culminating periods of the crisis (July 28–August 4), nations in both alliances were

being drawn into war. Thus, if the hypothesis is correct, differences in the way in which actions (S) are perceived (r) by nations of the two coalitions should be greatest during the early stages of the crisis. When the data in Table 7.12 are reanalyzed in this manner, the hypothesis is again supported. The difference between the two coalitions in regard to the S–r link during the early period is statistically significant ($U = 4$, $p = .013$), whereas in the later period it is not ($U = 11$, p = n.s.).

A further hypothesis within the model relates perceptions of one's own intent, with perceptions of the intent of others. Boulding (1959), Osgood (1962), and many others have pointed to the propensity of nations to perceive their own intentions in the best light possible, while attributing more hostile motives to those of others.

To the extent that there is a difference between perceptions of the other's policy (r) and statements of own intent (s), perceptions of hostility in r will tend to be higher than in s in *both* the low-involvement and the high-involvement situations.

The figures in Table 13 support the hypothesis both in that the level of perceived hostility for (r) is consistently higher than for (s) and in that there is no significant difference between the two coalitions.[3] The final intervening perceptual link in the model is that between the perception of one's own behavior (s) and the level of violence in the actual response (R). The hypothesis is that

In the situation of low involvement, statements of intent (s) will tend to be higher than action responses (R), whereas in the high-involvement situation, s will tend to be lower than R.

Again there is at least intuitive support for the hypothesis. In a situation of high involvement, whether the action is essentially cooperative or conflictual, the effort one makes often far surpasses stated intent. . . . In the case

---

[2]Table 12, which has been deleted, shows a statistically significant relationship: $U = 32$, $p = < .025$—ED.

[3]Table 13, which has been deleted, shows no statistically significant relationship: $U = 67$, p = n.s.—ED.

where one feels little stress, on the other hand, the propensity of promises to run ahead of performance appears enhanced. . . .

Table 14,[4] however, reveals that there is, in fact, no difference between the two coalitions in regard to the *s–R* linkage. In both cases, *R* is consistently higher than *s*; that is, the states in both coalitions tended to react at a higher level of violence than suggested by the statements of intent by their various leaders.

SUMMARY OF FINDINGS

The analysis of the 1914 crisis began with an assumption basic to most traditional theories of international politics—that is, the assumption of congruence between input (*S*) and output (*R*) action. The data revealed, however, a significant difference between the two coalitions corresponding to the different levels of involvement in the situation. . . .

Having failed to account for the escalation from a local incident to a general war with only the action variables, the perceptual variables (*r*) and (*s*) were analyzed. The various links across the model were examined and no significant difference between the two coalitions in regard to the *s–R* step was found: (*R*) was higher than (*s*) in both cases. As predicted, there was little difference between the Triple Entente and Dual Alliance in the *r–s* link, both perceiving themselves as less hostile than the other coalition. A significant difference did appear at the *S–r* step, however. The leaders of the Dual Alliance consistently over-perceived the actions of the Triple Entente. Thus the *S–r* link served a "magnifying" function. The decision-makers of the Triple Entente, on the other hand, tended to under-perceive the actions of the Dual Alliance. This difference in perceiving the environment (the *S–r* link) is consistent with the pronounced tendency of the Dual Alliance to respond at a higher level of violence than the Triple Entente. . . .

---

[4]Table 7.14, which has been deleted, shows that *U* = 50, *p* = n.s.—Ed.

REFERENCES

ABEL, THEODORE. 1941. The Element of Decision in the Pattern of War. *American Sociological Review.* (Dec): 853–859.

ALBERTINI, LUIGI. 1953. *The Origins of the War of 1914.* 3 vols. New York: Oxford University Press.

BERELSON, BERNARD. 1952. *Content Analysis in Communication Research* New York: Free Press.

BOULDING, KENNETH E. 1959. National Images and International Systems. *Journal of Conflict Resolution* 3: 120–131.

EDMUNDS, SIR JAMES E. 1937. *Official History of the War, Military Operations: France and Belgium 1914.* 3d ed. London: Macmillan.

FAY, SIDNEY B. 1928. *The Origins of the World War.* New York: Macmillan.

FROTHINGHAM, THOMAS C. 1924. *The Naval History of the World War: Offensive Operations, 1914–1915.* Cambridge: Harvard University Press.

HOLSTI, OLE R. 1963. The Value of International Tension Measurement. *Journal of Conflict Resolution* 7: 608–617.

———— AND ROBERT C. NORTH. 1965. Perceptions of Hostility and Economic Variables. *Comparing Nations,* ed. Richard L. Merritt. New Haven: Yale University Press.

McENTEE, GIRARD L. 1937. *Military History of the World War.* New York: Scribner's.

MARCH, JAMES G., AND HERBERT A. SIMON. 1958. *Organizations.* New York: John Wiley.

MONTGELAS, MAX., AND WALTER SCHÜCKING, eds. 1924. *Outbreak of the World War: German Documents Collected by Karl Kautsky.* New York: Oxford University Press.

NORTH, ROBERT C. 1962. Decision-making in Crises: An Introduction. *Journal of Conflict Resolution* 6:197–200.

————, RICHARD A. BRODY AND OLE R. HOLSTI. 1964. Some Empirical Data on the Conflict Spiral. *Peace Research Society Papers.* I: 1–14.

OSGOOD, CHARLES E. 1962. *An Alternative to War or Surrender.* Urbana, Ill.: University of Illinois Press.

RUMMEL, RUDOLPH J. 1964. Testing Some Possible Predictors of Conflict Behavior within and between Nations. *Peace Research Society Papers I:* 79–111.

SNYDER, RICHARD C., H. W. BRUCK, AND BURTON SAPIN, eds. 1962. *Foreign Policy Decision-Making.* New York: Free Press.

WRIGHT, QUINCY. 1957. Design for a Research Proposal on International Conflict and the Factors Causing Their Aggravation or Amelioration. *Western Political Quarterly* 10: 263–275.

ZANINOVICH, GEORGE. 1964. An Empirical Theory of State Response: The Sino-Soviet Case. Ph.D. dissertation, Stanford University.

ZINNES, DINA A. 1963. Expression and Perception of Hostility in Interstate Relations. Ph.D. dissertation, Stanford University.

ZINNES, DINA A., ROBERT C. NORTH, AND HOWARD E. KOCH, Jr. 1961. Capability, Threat and the Outbreak of War. In James N. Rosenau, ed., *International Politics and Foreign Policy: A Reader in Research and Theory.* New York: Free Press.

28. From *Conflict Among Nations*

GLENN H. SNYDER AND PAUL DIESING

FORMAL MODELS OF BARGAINING

. . . We now survey the various types of strategic models that we have attempted to apply to crises, some of which proved more useful than others. Some of them, such as Prisoner's Dilemma or Chicken, were available and quite thoroughly analyzed in the existing literature before we did the case studies; others we invented to fit situations that emerged from our empirical research.

Normal Form, 2 × 2

In this type of model one focuses on the basic strategic situation and leaves out all details. The whole temporal development of a crisis is ignored and with it all particular tactics, communications, and changes of tactics. The obvious disadvantage is that the model leaves out the whole of the bargaining process, and all strategies that may be available to the players except the very simplest ones—"make concessions" or "stand firm." Moreover, these two labels are so simple that they obscure the vari-

Excerpted from *Conflict Among Nations: Bargaining, Decision Making, and System Structure in International Crises* (Princeton: Princeton University Press, 1977), pp. 39–48, 480–484, 488–497. Copyright © 1977 by Princeton University Press. Reprinted by permission of Princeton University Press. Footnotes deleted.

ety of actual behavior that might be employed in following them.

The advantage of this drastic simplification is that it brings out the basic structure of crises. Also on the positive side, these models may be used, as we shall see later, as frameworks to classify tactics, and they allow us to describe a greater variety of bargaining situations than do the utility models. We can also make use of the conclusions reached in experimental gaming, most of which uses 2 × 2 models.

The basic structure of a generalized crisis is given in Figure 7.3. The two essential strategic possibilities are to hold pretty much to one's original demands, D, and to make some concessions or accommodations to the opponent's demands, C. Holding to one's original demands usually requires the use of various coercive tactics to induce the opponent to accommodate. We shall therefore refer to C as the accommodative strategy and to D as the coercive or stand-firm strategy.

Since there are four possible outcomes, each player has four possible payoffs, one for each outcome. We use the standard labels originated by Rapoport for these payoffs. The payoff for deadlock, DD, we label P; the payoff for compromise, CC, we label R; the payoff for making unilateral concessions, yielding, we label S; and the payoff for getting one's way is T. The four payoffs are always arranged as given in Figure 7.4, with the first letter of a pair

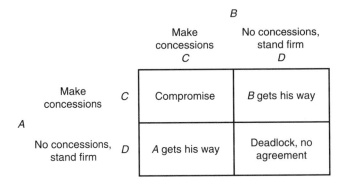

FIGURE 7.3   A Generalized Bargaining Game

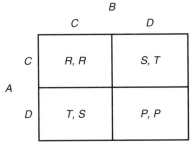

FIGURE 7.4   Payoffs from a Generalized Game

representing *A*'s payoff and the second representing *B*'s payoff.

These letters all originally had a heuristic meaning in the Prisoner's Dilemma game, but since the meanings are more or less misleading when applied to other games, we omit them. . . .

Symmetric Games: The Four Mixed Motive Games. Anatol Rapoport and Melvin Guyer have shown that if the numbers in a 2 × 2 game matrix are considered to represent the ordinal preference rankings of the players over the four possible outcomes, rather than cardinal utilities, then there are exactly 78 2 × 2 games. Out of these, 12 are *symmetric* games in the sense that the ordinal rankings are the same for each player. All the rest are *asymmetric*—the preference orderings are different. Of the 12 symmetric games, eight are of little or no theoretical interest, either because there is no conflict (both players give highest preference

to the same outcome) or because the outcome is completely determined. The remaining four are "interesting"; Rapoport calls them the "archetypes" of the 2 × 2 game. We chose to start with these four in attempting to apply game models to crises; they are shown in Figure 7.5. A few of the other games, both symmetric and asymmetric, turned out to be useful when we explored the empirical cases; they will be shown subsequently. Since the payoffs represent ordinal rankings rather than cardinal magnitudes, we show them by the positive numbers 1 through 4, i.e., from "least preferred" to "most preferred," even though in real play some of the outcomes may be losses and thus have negative utility. Each game is strictly defined by the ordinal ranking of the four payoffs, and the four games together represent all possible rankings of mixed-motive games. *T* is always the most preferred payoff, *T* = 4th, since we defined *T* as "win" or "get one's way." This requires a rearrangement of Hero, which at one time was defined as S > T > R > P.

In all four games the 1st payoff is more or less disastrous; 2[d] is the minimax payoff, the minimum a player can insure for himself no matter what the other does; 3[d] is the best accommodative payoff; and *T* = 4th is the best coercive payoff. The games are mixed motive not just in the sense that both common and conflicting interests are present; this is true of all bargaining. Rather, the common and conflicting interests are so intermingled that neither kind of interest can be pursued without inducing a reversal of attention to the other. In

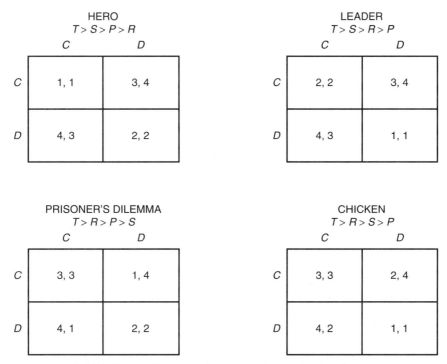

FIGURE 7.5 The Four Symmetric Mixed-Motive Games

other words, the players are caught between opposite inducements and must vacillate between them. $T = 4^{th}$ induces them to play against each other, to struggle and coerce, since T can be achieved only at the cost of a lesser payoff to the other. However, the payoff for both yielding to this inducement is $P = 1^{st}$ or 2^d, and both could do better than 2^d by coordinating their strategies. In other words, a strategy of struggle induces a reversal of strategy to accommodation. But the attempt to coordinate strategies inevitably leads back to conflict. In Prisoner's Dilemma and Chicken there is the danger of a double cross, a switch to D, which induces suspicion and a temptation to preempt D; in Hero and Leader there are two opposed ways to coordinate, and the players must struggle over the question of how to coordinate. But if both struggle, they are back at DD; there is no guaranteed way out.

Prisoner's Dilemma and Chicken are adversary games in that the interests of the parties are more completely opposed than in the other two. If one player plays D or commits himself to it, the other can do no better than minimax, which usually in actual cases has negative utility. In Prisoner's Dilemma, he gets this by playing D to avoid the disastrous 1 payoff. In Chicken, he gets it by accommodating to the other's coercive pressure. The chief difference between the two games is that in Chicken the worst outcome is mutual coercion, and yielding to the other's coercive pressure is only the second worst, whereas in Prisoner's Dilemma the reverse is true. In both of these adversary games compromise is quite possible, in Prisoner's Dilemma because of the knowledge or fear that a D strategy will be reciprocated, and in Chicken because of the inability of the parties to commit themselves credibly.

We should mention at this point that we are *not* assuming simultaneous play, which takes us another step away from game theory orthodoxy and toward real world conditions. Our players move in sequence; thus the second player's choice is taken in full knowledge of what the first has already chosen. The difference is particularly important with respect to the way we shall be using the Prisoner's Dilemma model. Most discussions of the Prisoner's Dilemma assume simultaneous play. With this assumption, either or both players are either tempted to play *D* to exploit an opponent who is expected to cooperate or they are driven to play *D* in fear that the other will succumb to such temptation. From either or both of these motivations both players must logically choose *D* strategies, and the outcome is mutual "punishment"—worse than what they might have achieved had each cooperated. However, in a sequential-move game, the "dilemma" in the Prisoner's Dilemma disappears. That is, there is no problem about guessing whether or not the opponent is trustworthy and whether to double-cross him if he is or to preempt if he isn't. This is because even if the opponent proves to be non-cooperative— plays his *D* strategy—there is time to counter with one's own *D* strategy, thus avoiding the disastrous *CD* or *DC* outcomes. Since both parties know that such countering is inevitable, neither has any incentive to play *D* and the logical outcome of the Prisoner's Dilemma with sequential moves is *CC*, mutual cooperation. One would expect, therefore, that there would be no crises with a Prisoner's Dilemma structure. As we shall see, however, this is not the case, since one or both parties may initially misperceive the other's preference ordering, believing he is playing a Chicken game, for example. Moreover, there are Prisoner's Dilemma situations in some crises where the simultaneous move version of the game is approached in the sense that, although it is possible to counter the opponent's *D* strategy in time to avoid the *worst* outcome, it is still *costly* to let him play it first and thus there is some incentive to preempt.

Hero and Leader would appear to be alliance games since even though one party plays coercively, the other can still achieve the fairly high payoff of 3 by accommodating. In contrast to the two adversary games, both 3 and 4 payoffs for both parties lie in NE or SW cells. Accommodating the other in his attempt to gain his best payoff is better than resisting it by attempting to get one's own best payoff. As a working hypothesis, it seemed to us that this was roughly analogous to the position of allies during a crisis, wherein the partners might each favor different strategies for dealing with the opponent, but value the preservation of the alliance over the adoption of their preferred strategy *vis à vis* the opponent. Hence they might argue or bargain about the optimum crisis strategy to adopt, but each would, in the end, prefer to go along with the other's preference rather than disrupt the alliance. Compromise (CC) is not a logical outcome in Hero and Leader because its payoff is less than going along with the partner's preferred strategy.

There may also be alliance games that take a Prisoner's Dilemma or Chicken form, that is, games in which compromise is possible.

A fifth symmetric game that showed up in our cases is Deadlock (Fig. 7.6). This is not a mixed-motive game, since both players prefer firmness (*D*) to either appeasing the opponent or compromising with him. Mathematically the outcome of Deadlock is *DD*, since *D* dominates *C* for both players, and empirically the outcome is war. However, there can be complications in actual play that do not appear in the mathematics of the game. The essential difference between Deadlock and Prisoner's Dilemma is that in the latter there is some compromise (*R,R*) available, which both parties would prefer to no agreement (*P,P*).

FIGURE 7.6 Deadlock

Asymmetric Games. Called Bluff (Fig. 7.7) is Prisoner's Dilemma for player *A* and Chicken for player *B*. Player *A* can play a *D* strategy confidently, knowing that player *B*, who is playing Chicken, must ultimately play *C*. Although this game seems to combine Chicken and Prisoner's Dilemma, its dynamics are different from either of them and therefore it deserves its own heuristic name. We name it "Called Bluff," because from *A*'s standpoint, if *B* threatens to play *D* he is a bluffer whom *A* can and must call, although *A* must do it carefully to avoid an accidental *DD* outcome. In our cases, this game also appears frequently as a misperception game; that is, the "caller" thinks the game is Called Bluff when actually it is Prisoner's Dilemma or Deadlock.

In the game shown in Figure 7.8, *A*'s preference ordering is the same as in Deadlock; he prefers no agreement (possibly war) to any conceivable compromise, though his highest preference is *T* (4), resulting from *B* playing *C* to his *D*. However, the game itself is not Deadlock, since *B* is in Chicken and prefers

compromise or even capitulation to no agreement. We call this game "Bully" because *A*, who is assured of a 3 payoff regardless of *B*'s strategy, can bully and threaten *B* with impunity. He can in fact force *B* to yield, play *C* to his *D* threats, and thus obtain his maximum payoff of 4.

In Big Bully (Fig. 7.9), *B* is again in Chicken, but *A* prefers no agreement and probably war not only over any conceivable compromise but also over *B*'s total capitulation. This distinguishes the game from Bully, where *A*, though unwilling to compromise, would accept *B*'s yielding to his (*A*'s) demands rather than no agreement or war. *A* is a "big bully" because his demands on *B* are intended only as a pretext for the use of force. Big Bully is exemplified by Austria vs. Serbia, 1914, and Germany vs. Czechoslovakia, 1938, abstracting out the complicating alliance relationships in both cases. *B*'s game may become transformed into Prisoner's Dilemma as a consequence of *A*'s humiliating threats and insults, which prompt him to prefer fighting a losing war, thereby salvaging some dignity, to knuckling under to *A*'s demands.

Protector (Fig. 7.10) is an alliance game between two unequal partners. *A*, the great power "protector," has preferences ordered as in Bully, while *B*'s (the client's) are ranked as in Leader. Assume that *B* is in conflict with some other state; *A* plays the role of supporter (in varying possible degrees). *B*'s *D* strategy is to stand firm against the other state's demands and make demands himself; his *C* strategy is to make concessions desired by *A*. *A*'s *C* strategy

FIGURE 7.7   Called Bluff

FIGURE 7.8   Bully

FIGURE 7.9   Big Bully

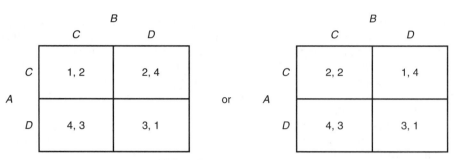

FIGURE 7.10 Protector

is to support *B*'s position fully; his *D* strategy is to provide limited defensive support. *A* can enforce concessions by threatening to withhold support because *B*'s alternative of standing firm alone against the opponent is disastrous. In short, since *A*'s *D* strategy is dominating, *B* must follow his "protector" and make the concessions demanded by *A* as the condition for the latter's support. . . .

CRISIS BARGAINING: GENERAL SUMMARY

Game Models and Crisis Structures

The best formal model for our purposes turned out to be the simple 2 × 2 game matrix, which we used to portray the "structure" of a crisis. Here the word *structure* obviously means something different than the structure of the entire international system in terms of the distribution of military power. It means the ordinal ranking, by the crisis participants, of their values for each of the four gross outcomes: win, lose, compromise, or breakdown. (Breakdown in most cases translates to expected cost (probability × estimated cost) of war or initiation of violence.) Thus, "structure" mainly shows the interests engaged in the conflict for each party, although their relative military strength enters into the *P* (breakdown) values in the matrices. Since interests and military strength are the principal components of crisis bargaining power, the game structure gives a crude ap-

proximation of the relative bargaining power of the parties.

Using the 2 × 2 model, we found nine different types of bargaining structures in our cases. Four were symmetrical, both parties having the same preference orderings across the four outcomes. The rest were asymmetrical, with a different ranking for each actor. Each type reflected a different combination of interests and power between the parties and each had its own dynamic of resolution and probable outcome.

Table 7.2 summarizes the crisis structures, the empirical cases of each one and their typical outcomes. (We remind the reader that Leader and Protector are alliance or détente bargaining structures that may either precede or occur simultaneously with an adversary crisis. Some of the other structures may also characterize alliance bargaining situations, not all of which are listed.)

We used ordinal rather than cardinal numbers in the game models, first because ordinal rankings were sufficient to show the general structure of the conflict situation and, second, because it was impossible, even roughly, to estimate the *amount* of value that the parties attached to various outcomes.

In some cases, even the assignment of ordinal rankings involved a certain amount of guesswork. All actors were of course clear from the start about their own rankings of *T*, *S*, and *R*—the gross outcomes win, lose, or compromise—even though the exact empirical content of these outcomes might not be clear for a while. But for only a little more

TABLE 7.2   Crisis Structures and Outcomes

	Structures	*Cases*	*Typical Outcomes*
Symmetrical			
	1. Prisoner's Dilemma	Agadir, 1911 Berlin, 1958–1962 Yom Kippur, 1973	Compromise

	2. Chicken	Munich, 1938
		  (late phase)
		Berlin, 1948
		Lebanon, 1958
		Iran, 1946
		  (early phase)
			One side capitulates

	3. Leader	Bosnia, 1908
		  (early phase)
		Germany-Austria, 1914
		Ruhr, 1923
		Iran, 1946 (early phase)
			One partner leads, the
			  other follows; or
			  alliance or détente
			  breaks up

	4. Deadlock	U.S.-Japan, 1940–41	War
Asymmetrical			

	5. Called Bluff (one
	party in Prisoner's
	Dilemma; other in
	Chicken)
		Morocco, 1905
		Quemoy, 1958
		Cuba, 1962
			Capitulation by Chicken
			  party or unequal
			  compromise

	6. Bully (Bully-
	Chicken)
		Fashoda, 1898
		Bosnia, 1909
		  (later phase)
			Capitulation by Chicken
			  party

	7. Bully-Prisoner's Dilemma	Germany–Austria vs. Russia–France, 1914	War

	8. Big Bully (Big Bully-
	Chicken)
		Munich, 1938
		  (early phase)
			War (avoided in this case
			  by shift of German
			  Structure to Chicken
			  or Bully)

	9. Protector (Bully-
	Leader)
		Suez, 1956 (U.S.–Great
		  Britain)
		Quemoy, 1958
		  (U.S.–Taiwan)
			Dominant ally protects
			  and restrains client

than half of them could we say with confidence that they were aware from the beginning of how they ranked P—the expected cost (value) of bargaining breakdown or war—in relation to the other three outcomes. In these cases we had to guess what their ranking would have been had they been forced to make one. For example, there is no evidence that Hitler in 1938 actually compared the costs of war with England and France against the value of his objectives in Czechoslovakia until the peak of the crisis in late September.

When he did compare them, he found he was playing Chicken, but our judgment that he was playing Chicken from the beginning is only hypothetical. The example clearly suggests one reason why the P-function is not always clearly established at first: the player does not think he needs to worry about it because he is sure the opponent will *not* fight. In other cases the extent or likelihood of allied support—a vital component of expected war costs—does not become clear until later in the crisis.

In still other cases the *P*-value is not fully faced up to as long as diplomacy and other non-violent options are still available, and may never be evaluated if such options succeed. The critical value comparison in a crisis is between *S* and *P*—the cost of yielding vs. the expected costs of war—and people will tend not to make this comparison realistically until they absolutely have to. . . .

Our crisis structures were constructed from the actual or presumed rankings of outcomes by each party separately. But neither party could be sure of the other's rankings. This was an additional source of uncertainty about the "name of the game" for the parties, in addition to the initial uncertainty about their own rankings. Sometimes they, in effect, made an estimate of the other party's prefer-ences fairly early on, but quite often these estimates proved to be wrong. In other words, often a party's subjective picture of the crisis structure was at variance with the actual structure. This was quite typical, in fact, for at least one party in most crises; if it were not for its mistaken guess about the opponent's value rankings, the crisis would not have occurred at all. Germany in 1905 comes to mind: France was estimated to be Chicken because England would not provide support; when the British did join the fray, France turned out to be in Prisoner's Dilemma. If they had not mispredicted British behavior, the Germans would not have challenged. Of course, it is a party's subjective estimate of the crisis structure, not the actual structure, that governs its behavior. . . .

Chapter 8
War

29. Of the Natural Condition of Mankind as Concerning Their Felicity and Misery

THOMAS HOBBES

Nature has made men so equal in the faculties of the body and mind as that, though there be found one man sometimes manifestly stronger in body or of quicker mind than another, yet, when all is reckoned together, the difference between man and man is not so considerable as that one man can thereupon claim to himself any benefit to which another may not pretend as well as he. For as to the strength of body, the weakest has strength enough to kill the strongest, either by secret machination or by confederacy with others that are in the same danger with himself.

And as to the faculties of the mind, setting aside the arts grounded upon words, and especially that skill of proceeding upon general and infallible rules called science—which very few have and but in few things, as being not a native faculty born with us, nor attained, as prudence, while we look after somewhat else— I find yet a greater equality among men than that of strength. For prudence is but experience, which equal time equally bestows on all men in those things they equally apply themselves unto. That which may perhaps make such equality incredible is but a vain conceit of one's own wisdom, which almost all men think they have in a greater degree than the vulgar—that is, than all men but themselves

and a few others whom, by fame or for concurring with themselves, they approve. For such is the nature of men that howsoever they may acknowledge many others to be more witty or more eloquent or more learned, yet they will hardly believe there be many so wise as themselves; for they see their own wit at hand and other men's at a distance. But this proves rather that men are in that point equal than unequal. For there is not ordinarily a greater sign of the equal distribution of anything than that every man is contented with his share.

From this equality of ability arises equality of hope in the attaining of our ends. And therefore if any two men desire the same thing, which nevertheless they cannot both enjoy, they become enemies; and in the way to their end, which is principally their own conservation, and sometimes their delectation only, endeavor to destroy or subdue one another. And from hence it comes to pass that where an invader has no more to fear than another man's single power, if one plant, sow, build, or possess a convenient seat, others may probably be expected to come prepared with forces united to dispossess and deprive him, not only of the fruit of his labor, but also of his life or liberty. And the invader again is in the like danger of another.

And from this diffidence of one another there is no way for any man to secure himself

From *Leviathan*, Part I, Ch. 13.

so reasonable as anticipation—that is, by force or wiles to master the persons of all men he can, so long till he see no other power great enough to endanger him; and this is no more than his own conservation requires, and is generally allowed. Also, because there be some that take pleasure in contemplating their own power in the acts of conquest, which they pursue farther than their security requires, if others that otherwise would be glad to be at ease within modest bounds should not by invasion increase their power, they would not be able, long time, by standing only on their defense, to subsist. And by consequence, such augmentation of dominion over men being necessary to a man's conservation, it ought to be allowed him.

Again, men have no pleasure, but on the contrary a great deal of grief, in keeping company where there is no power able to overawe them all. For every man looks that his companion should value him at the same rate he sets upon himself; and upon all signs of contempt or undervaluing naturally endeavors, as far as he dares (which among them that have no common power to keep them in quiet is far enough to make them destroy each other), to extort a greater value from his contemners by damage and from others by the example.

So that in the nature of man we find three principal causes of quarrel: first, competition; secondly, diffidence; thirdly, glory.

The first makes men invade for gain, the second for safety, and the third for reputation. The first use violence to make themselves masters of other men's persons, wives, children, and cattle; the second, to defend them; the third, for trifles, as a word, a smile, a different opinion, and any other sign of undervalue, either direct in their persons or by reflection in their kindred, their friends, their nation, their profession, or their name.

Hereby it is manifest that, during the time men live without a common power to keep them all in awe, they are in that condition which is called war, and such a war as is of every man against every man. For WAR consists not in battle only, or the act of fighting, but in a tract of time wherein the will to contend by bat-

tle is sufficiently known; and therefore the notion of *time* is to be considered in the nature of war as it is in the nature of weather. For as the nature of foul weather lies not in a shower or two of rain but in an inclination thereto of many days together, so the nature of war consists not in actual fighting but in the known disposition thereto during all the time there is no assurance to the contrary. All other time is PEACE.

Whatsoever, therefore, is consequent to a time of war where every man is enemy to every man, the same is consequent to the time wherein men live without other security than what their own strength and their own invention shall furnish them withal. In such condition there is no place for industry, because the fruit thereof is uncertain: and consequently no culture of the earth; no navigation nor use of the commodities that may be imported by sea; no commodious building; no instruments of moving and removing such things as require much force; no knowledge of the face of the earth; no account of time; no arts; no letters; no society; and, which is worst of all, continual fear and danger of violent death; and the life of man solitary, poor, nasty, brutish, and short.

It may seem strange to some man that has not well weighed these things that nature should thus dissociate and render men apt to invade and destroy one another; and he may therefore, not trusting to this inference made from the passions, desire perhaps to have the same confirmed by experience. Let him therefore consider with himself—when taking a journey he arms himself and seeks to go well accompanied, when going to sleep he locks his doors, when even in his house he locks his chests, and this when he knows there be laws and public officers, armed, to revenge all injuries shall be done him—what opinion he has of his fellow subjects when he rides armed, of his fellow citizens when he locks his doors, and of his children and servants when he locks his chests. Does he not there as much accuse mankind by his actions as I do by my words? But neither of us accuse man's nature in it. The desires and other passions of man are in themselves no sin. No more are the actions that proceed from those passions till they know a law that forbids them, which, till laws be made, they cannot know, nor can any law be made till they have agreed upon the person that shall make it.

It may peradventure be thought there was never such a time nor condition of war as this, and I believe it was never generally so over all the world; but there are many places where they live so now. For the savage people in many places of America, except the government of small families, the concord whereof depends on natural lust, have no government at all and live at this day in that brutish manner as I said before. Howsoever, it may be perceived what manner of life there would be where there were no common power to fear by the manner of life which men that have formerly lived under a peaceful government use to degenerate into in a civil war.

But though there had never been any time wherein particular men were in a condition of war one against another, yet in all times kings and persons of sovereign authority, because of their independency, are in continual jealousies and in the state and posture of gladiators, having their weapons pointing and their eyes fixed on one another—that is, their forts, garrisons, and guns upon the frontiers of their kingdoms, and continual spies upon their neighbors—which is a posture of war. But because they uphold thereby the industry of their subjects, there does not follow from it that misery which accompanies the liberty of particular men.

To this war of every man against every man, this also is consequent: that nothing can be unjust. The notions of right and wrong, justice and injustice, have there no place. Where there is no common power, there is no law; where no law, no injustice. Force and fraud are in war the two cardinal virtues. Justice and injustice are none of the faculties neither of the body nor mind. If they were, they might be in a man that were alone in the world, as well as his senses and passions. They are qualities that relate to men in society, not in solitude. It is consequent also to the same condition that there be no propriety, no dominion, no *mine* and *thine* distinct; but only that to be every man's that he can get, and for so long as he can keep it. And thus much for the ill condition which man by mere nature is actually placed in, though with a possibility to come out of it consisting partly in the passions, partly in his reason.

The passions that incline men to peace are fear of death, desire of such things as are necessary to commodious living, and a hope by their industry to obtain them. And reason suggests convenient articles of peace, upon which men may be drawn to agreement. These articles are they which otherwise are called the Laws of Nature, whereof I shall speak more particularly in the two following chapters.

30. Warfare Is Only an Invention— Not a Biological Necessity

MARGARET MEAD

Is war a biological necessity, a sociological inevitability or just a bad invention? Those who argue for the first view endow man with such pugnacious instincts that some outlet in aggressive behavior is necessary if man is to reach full human stature. It was this point of view which lay back of William James's famous essay, "The Moral Equivalent of War," in which he tried to retain the warlike virtues and channel them in new directions. A similar point of view has lain back of the Soviet Union's attempt to make competition between groups rather than between individuals. A basic, competitive, aggressive, warring human nature is assumed, and those who wish to outlaw war or outlaw competitiveness merely try to find new and less socially destructive ways in which these biologically given aspects of man's nature can find expression. Then there are those who take the second view: warfare is the inevitable concomitant of the development of the state, the struggle for land and natural resources of class societies springing, not from the nature of man, but from the nature of history. War is nevertheless inevitable unless we change our social system and outlaw classes, the struggle for power, and possessions; and in the event of our success warfare would disappear, as a symptom vanishes when the disease is cured.

One may hold a sort of compromise position between these two extremes; one may claim that all aggression springs from the frustration of man's biologically determined drives and that, since all forms of culture are frustrating, it is certain each new generation will be aggressive and the aggression will find its natural and inevitable expression in race war, class war, nationalistic war and so on. All three of these positions are very popular today among those who think seriously about the problems of war and its possible prevention, but I wish to urge another point of view, less defeatist perhaps than the first and third, and more accurate than the second: that is, that warfare, by which I mean recognized conflict between two groups *as groups*, in which each group puts an army (even if the army is only fifteen pygmies) into the field to fight and kill, if possible, some of the members of the army of the other group—that warfare of this sort is an invention like any other of the inventions in terms of which we order our lives, such as writing, marriage, cooking our food instead of eating it raw, trial by jury or burial of the dead, and so on. Some of this list any one will grant are inventions: trial by jury is confined to very limited portions of the globe; we know that

Reprinted from *Asia* 40/8 (August 1940) pp. 402–405 by permission of the author's estate. Also reprinted in *Anthropology, A Human Science* (Princeton: D. Van Nostrand Co., 1964), pp. 126–133.

there are tribes that do not bury their dead but instead expose or cremate them; and we know that only part of the human race has had the knowledge of writing as its cultural inheritance. But, whenever a way of doing things is found universally, such as the use of fire or the practice of some form of marriage, we tend to think at once that it is not an invention at all but an attribute of humanity itself. And yet even such universals as marriage and the use of fire are inventions like the rest, very basic ones, inventions which were perhaps necessary if human history was to take the turn that it has taken, but nevertheless inventions. At some point in his social development man was undoubtedly without the institution of marriage or the knowledge of the use of fire.

The case for warfare is much clearer because there are peoples even today who have no warfare. Of these the Eskimo are perhaps the most conspicuous examples, but the Lepchas of Sikkim described by Geoffrey Gorer in *Himalayan Village* are as good. Neither of these peoples understands war, not even defensive warfare. The idea of warfare is lacking, and this idea is as essential to really carrying on war as an alphabet or syllabary is to writing. But whereas the Lepchas are a gentle, unquarrelsome people, and the advocates of other points of view might argue that they are not full human beings or that they had never been frustrated and so had no aggression to expand in warfare, the Eskimo case gives no such possibility of interpretation. The Eskimo are not a mild and meek people; many of them are turbulent and troublesome. Fights, theft of wives, murder, cannibalism, occur among them—all outbursts of passionate men goaded by desire or intolerable circumstance. Here are men faced with hunger, men faced with loss of their wives, men faced with the threat of extermination by other men, and here are orphan children, growing up miserably with no one to care for them, mocked and neglected by those about them. The personality necessary for war, the circumstances necessary to goad men to desperation are present, but there is no war. When a traveling Eskimo entered a settlement he might have to fight the strongest man in the settlement to establish his position among them, but this was a test of strength and bravery, not war. The idea of warfare, of one *group* organizing against another *group* to maim and wound and kill them was absent. And without that idea passions might rage but there was no war.

But, it may be argued, isn't this because the Eskimo have such a low and undeveloped form of social organization? They own no land, they move from place to place, camping, it is true, season after season on the same site, but this is not something to fight for as the modern nations of the world fight for land and raw materials. They have no permanent possessions that can be looted, no towns that can be burned. They have no social classes to produce stress and strains within the society which might force it to go to war outside. Doesn't the absence of war among the Eskimo, while disproving the biological necessity of war, just go to confirm the point that it is the state of development of the society which accounts for war, and nothing else?

We find the answer among the pygmy peoples of the Andaman Islands in the Bay of Bengal. The Andamans also represent an exceedingly low level of society; they are a hunting and food-gathering people; they live in tiny hordes without any class stratification; their houses are simpler than the snow houses of the Eskimo. But they knew about warfare. The army might contain only fifteen determined pygmies marching in a straight line, but it was the real thing none the less. Tiny army met tiny army in open battle, blows were exchanged, casualties suffered, and the state of warfare could only be concluded by a peace-making ceremony.

Similarly, among the Australian aborigines, who built no permanent dwellings but wandered from water hole to water hole over their almost desert country, warfare—and rules of "international law"—were highly developed. The student of social evolution will seek in vain for his obvious causes of war, struggle for lands, struggle for power of one group over another, expansion of population, need to divert the minds of a populace restive under tyranny, or even the ambition of a successful leader to enhance his own prestige. All are absent, but warfare as a practice remained, and men engaged in it and killed one another in the course of a war because killing is what is done in wars.

From instances like these it becomes apparent that an inquiry into the causes of war misses the fundamental point as completely as does an insistence upon the biological necessity of war. If a people have an idea of going to war and the idea that war is the way in which certain situations, defined within their society, are to be handled, they will sometimes go to war. If they are a mild and unaggressive people, like the Pueblo Indians, they may limit themselves to defensive warfare; but they will be forced to think in terms of war because there are peoples near them who have warfare as a pattern, and offensive, raiding, pillaging warfare at that. When the pattern of warfare is known, people like the Pueblo Indians will defend themselves, taking advantage of their natural defenses, the *mesa* village site, and people like the Lepchas, having no natural defenses and no idea of warfare, will merely submit to the invader. But the essential point remains the same. There is a way of behaving which is known to a given people and labeled as an appropriate form of behavior; a bold and warlike people like the Sioux or the Maori may label warfare as desirable as well as possible; a mild people like the Pueblo Indians may label warfare as undesirable; but to the minds of both people the possibility of warfare is present. Their thoughts, their hopes, their plans are oriented about this idea, that warfare may be selected as the way to meet some situation.

So simple peoples and civilized peoples, mild peoples and violent, assertive peoples, will all go to war if they have the invention, just as those peoples who have the custom of dueling will have duels and peoples who have the pattern of vendetta will indulge in vendetta. And, conversely, peoples who do not know of dueling will not fight duels, even though their wives are seduced and their daughters ravished; they may on occasion commit murder but they will not fight duels. Cultures which lack the idea of vendetta will not meet every

quarrel in this way. A people can use only the forms it has. So the Balinese have their special way of dealing with a quarrel between two individuals: if the two feel that the causes of quarrel are heavy they may go and register their quarrel in the temple before the gods, and, making offerings, they may swear never to have anything to do with each other again. Today they register such mutual "not-speaking" with the Dutch government officials. But in other societies, although individuals might feel as full of animosity and as unwilling to have any further contact as do the Balinese, they cannot register their quarrel with the gods and go on quietly about their business because registering quarrels with the gods is not an invention of which they know.

Yet, if it be granted that warfare is after all an invention, it may nevertheless be an invention that lends itself to certain types of personality, to the exigent needs of autocrats, to the expansionist desires of crowded peoples, to the desire for plunder and rape and loot which is engendered by a dull and frustrating life. What, then, can we say of this congruence between warfare and its uses? If it is a form which fits so well, is not this congruence the essential point? But even here the primitive material causes us to wonder, because there are tribes who go to war merely for glory, having no quarrel with the enemy, suffering from no tyrant within their boundaries, anxious neither for land nor loot nor women, but merely anxious to win prestige which within that tribe has been declared obtainable only by war and without which no young man can hope to win his sweetheart's smile of approval. But if, as was the case with the Bush Negroes of Dutch Guiana, it is artistic ability which is necessary to win a girl's approval, the same young man would have to be carving rather than going out on a war party.

In many parts of the world, war is a game in which the individual can win counters—counters which bring him prestige in the eyes of his own sex or of the opposite sex; he plays for these counters as he might, in our society, strive for a tennis championship. Warfare is a frame for such prestige-seeking merely because it calls for the display of certain skills and certain virtues; all of these skills—riding straight, shooting straight, dodging the missiles of the enemy and sending one's own straight to the mark—can be equally well exercised in some other framework and, equally, the virtues—endurance, bravery, loyalty, steadfastness—can be displayed in other contexts. The tie-up between proving oneself a man and proving this by a success in organized killing is due to a definition which many societies have made of manliness. And often, even in those societies which counted success in warfare a proof of human worth, strange turns were given to the idea, as when the plains Indians gave their highest awards to the man who touched a live enemy rather than to the man who brought in a scalp—from a dead enemy—because the latter was less risky. Warfare is just an invention known to the majority of human societies by which they permit their young men either to accumulate prestige or avenge their honor or acquire loot or wives or slaves or sago lands or cattle or appease the blood lust of their gods or the restless souls of the recently dead. It is just an invention, older and more widespread than the jury system, but none the less an invention.

But, once we have said this, have we said anything at all? Despite a few instances, dear to the hearts of controversialists, of the loss of the useful arts, once an invention is made which proves congruent with human needs or social forms, it tends to persist. Grant that war is an invention, that it is not a biological necessity nor the outcome of certain special types of social forms, still, once the invention is made, what are we to do about it? The Indian who had been subsisting on the buffalo for generations because with his primitive weapons he could slaughter only a limited number of buffalo did not return to his primitive weapons when he saw that the white man's more efficient weapons were exterminating the buffalo. A desire for the white man's cloth may mortgage the South Sea Islander to the white man's plantation, but he does not return to making bark cloth, which would have left him free. Once an invention

is known and accepted, men do not easily relinquish it. The skilled workers may smash the first steam looms which they feel are to be their undoing, but they accept them in the end, and no movement which has insisted upon the mere abandonment of usable inventions has ever had much success. Warfare is here, as part of our thought; the deeds of warriors are immortalized in the words of our poets; the toys of our children are modeled upon the weapons of the soldier; the frame of reference within which our statesmen and our diplomats work always contains war. If we know that it is not inevitable, that it is due to historical accident that warfare is one of the ways in which we think of behaving, are we given any hope by that? What hope is there of persuading nations to abandon war, nations so thoroughly imbued with the idea that resort to war is, if not actually desirable and noble, at least inevitable whenever certain defined circumstances arise?

In answer to this question I think we might turn to the history of other social inventions, and inventions which must once have seemed as firmly entrenched as warfare. Take the methods of trial which preceded the jury system: ordeal and trial by combat. Unfair, capricious, alien as they are to our feeling today, they were once the only methods open to individuals accused of some offense. The invention of trial by jury gradually replaced these methods until only witches, and finally not even witches, had to resort to the ordeal. And for a long time the jury system seemed the one best and finest method of settling legal disputes, but today new inventions, trial before judges only or before commissions, are replacing the jury system. In each case the old method was replaced by a new social invention; the ordeal did not go out because people thought it unjust or wrong, it went out because a method more congruent with the institutions and feelings of the period was invented. And, if we despair over the way in which war seems such an ingrained habit of most of the human race, we can take comfort from the fact that a poor invention will usually give place to a better invention.

For this, two conditions at least are necessary. The people must recognize the defects of the old invention, and some one must make a new one. Propaganda against warfare, documentation of its terrible cost in human suffering and social waste, these prepare the ground by teaching people to feel that warfare is a defective social institution. There is further needed a belief that social invention is possible and the invention of new methods which will render warfare as out-of-date as the tractor is making the plow, or the motor car the horse and buggy. A form of behavior becomes out-of-date only when something else takes its place, and in order to invent forms of behavior which will make war obsolete, it is a first requirement to believe that an invention is possible.

31. The Use of Mathematics
Arms Races

LEWIS F. RICHARDSON

THE USE OF MATHEMATICS

Literary people have sometimes wrongly supposed that mathematical expressions can be used to describe the actions of only such objects as follow laws of a rigid mechanical, deterministic type in all particulars. The answer to that assertion is the growth of statistical science and its applications to life-insurance, to the molecular chaos in a gas, and to many other features of social life, of biology, and of physics. The usual condition for mathematical treatment is that, if the individual phenomena are not determinate, then they must be numerous. An appreciation of the service rendered by mathematics to economics will be found in Marshall's *Principles of Economics* (1910). It therefore seems reasonable to inquire whether mathematical language can also express the behavior of people in another situation where they act together in large groups, namely in relation to war.

William James even went so far as to use mathematics in his discussion of free will

(1902). "The facts," he wrote, "may be most briefly symbolized thus, P standing for the propensity, I for the ideal impulse, and E for the effort:

$$I \text{ per se} < P.$$
$$I + E > P."$$

To have to translate one's verbal statements into mathematical formulae compels one carefully to scrutinize the ideas therein expressed. Next the possession of formulae makes it much easier to deduce the consequences. In this way absurd implications, which might have passed unnoticed in a verbal statement, are brought clearly into view and stimulate one to amend the formula. An additional advantage of a mathematical mode of expression is its brevity, which greatly diminishes the labor of memorizing the idea expressed. If the statements of an individual become the subject of a controversy, this definiteness and brevity lead to a speeding up of discussions over disputable points, so that obscurities can be cleared away, errors refuted, and truth found and expressed more quickly than could have been done had a more cumbrous method of discussion been pursued.

Arms and Insecurity (Pacific Grove, Calif.: Boxwood Press, 1960), pp. xvii–xviii, 12–17, 19. Reprinted by permission of the Boxwood Press. Citations deleted.

Mathematical expressions have, however, their special tendencies to pervert thought: the definiteness may be spurious, existing in the equations but not in the phenomena to be described; and the brevity may be due to the omission of the more important things, simply because they cannot be mathematized. Against these faults we must constantly be on our guard. It will probably be impossible to avoid them entirely, and so they ought to be realized and admitted.

A fundamental rule of scientific method is Ockham's so-called "razor," to the effect that: "Entities are not to be postulated without necessity." For shaving off the superabundant growth of mathematical uncertainties and difficulties I have made frequent appeal to an analogous rule: "Formulae are not to be complicated without good evidence." This is a diffident and groping empiricism. . . .

Mathematics has been used in this book both inductively to summarize facts, and deductively to trace the consequences of hypotheses. By mistaking the intention it is possible to complain that the inductions do not follow from the previous hypotheses, and that the deductions go beyond the known facts. Certainly that is so, but it is no cause for complaint, rather for rejoicing.

Those who say, "You can prove anything by statistics," should instead say, "Unfortunately we do not understand statistical method sufficiently well to enable us to distinguish arguments that are genuine from those that are false."

To anyone who believes that words are the proper medium of expression I commend the following exercise: Translate into words $Ax^2 + Bx + C = 0$, remembering that x, A, B, C are not words. Proceed in words, not using any algebraic symbols, to find and prove the solution of the equation. Read your words to schoolboys who are approaching, but have not yet done, quadratic equations. Set them examples in words alone.

There are people who despise theories and take a pride in their adherence to facts. Even such a person must admit that the ordinary process of recognition involves an element of theory. Has he never recognized in the street an acquaintance who showed no recognition in return? Or cut open an egg to find it uneatable? Such mistakes draw our attention to our false theories; and indicate that our correct recognitions involve correct theories. All ordinary political discussions are chock-full of theories, most of them unspoken. Pure mathematicians on the contrary strive to make their assumptions explicit. Dare we do that in matters which touch our feelings?

ARMS RACES

It is an old Proverb *Maxima bella ex levissimis causis*: the greatest Feuds have had the smallest Beginnings.
WILLIAM PENN (1693)

1. FREE WILL

CHAIRMAN: I now call on Dr. Richardson to explain his science of foreign politics.

CRITIC: Sir! I beg to move the previous question: that we do not waste our time on such an absurdity. How can anyone possibly make scientific statements about foreign politics? These are questions of right, of loyalty, of power, of the dignity of free choice. They touch a little on law but are far beyond the reach of any science.

AUTHOR: I admit that the discussion of free choice is better left to the dramatists. But nowadays science does usefully treat many phenomena that are only in part deterministic—witness the many social applications of statistics and the astounding progress of theories as to the probable position of an electron.

CRITIC: The electron? That surely is irrelevant. On glancing at your summary, I see mathematical equations with the symbol *t* in them. Does *t* stand for time?

AUTHOR: You have guessed rightly.

CRITIC: Can you predict the date at which the next war will break out?

AUTHOR: No, of course not. The equations are merely a description of what people would do if they did not stop to think. Why are so many nations reluctantly but steadily increasing their armaments as if they were mechanically compelled to do so? Because, I say, they follow their traditions, which are fixtures, and their instincts, which are mechanical and because they have not yet made a sufficiently strenuous intellectual and moral effort to control the situation. The process described by the ensuing equations is not to be thought of as inevitable. It is what *would occur if instinct and tradition were allowed to act uncontrolled.* In this respect the equations have some analogy to a dream. For a dream often warns an individual of the antisocial acts that his instincts would lead him to commit, if he were not wakeful.

CRITIC: Dreams, if you like. But why equations? History is not mechanical.

> The world's like a horse.
> We balance on a stirrup
> To manage the course
> Of Power in Europe.

AUTHOR: Wait until you see the statistics of arms races!

CRITIC: This author has the wrong background, for he appears to have been trained in physical science, which is the study of what merely exists whereas the proper training is strategy, the art of confounding our enemies. For we are sure always to have lots of enemies.

AUTHOR: Mr. Chairman, that last sentence is, in the phraseology of the lawcourts, my case. For those who neglect the objective good of the whole, in order to study strategy, are likely always to have lots of enemies.

CHAIRMAN: I think we might go on.

2. LINEAR THEORY OF TWO NATIONS

Introduction

This theory is about general tendencies common to all nations; about how they resent defiance, how they suspect defense to be concealed *aggression*, how they respond to imports by sending out exports; about how expenditure on armaments is restrained by the difficulty of paying for them; and, lastly, about grievances and their queer irrational ways, so that a halting apology may be received as though it were an added insult.

A rule of the theoretical game is that a nation is to be represented by a single variable, its outward attitude of threatening or co-operation. So the great statesmen, who collect, emphasize, and direct the national will, need not be mentioned by name. This is politics without personalities.

The various motives which lead a nation in time of peace to increase or decrease its preparations for war may be classified according to the manner of its dependence on its own existing preparations and on those of other nations. For simplicity, the nations are here regarded as forming two groups. There are motives such as revenge or dissatisfaction with the results of treaties; these motives are independent of existing armaments. Then there is the very strong motive of fear, which moves each group to increase its armaments because of the existence of those of the opposing group. Also there is rivalry, which, more than fear, attends to the difference between the armaments of the two groups rather than to the magnitude of those of the other group. Lastly, there is always a tendency for each group to reduce its armaments in order to economize expenditure and effort.

What the result of all these motives may be is not at all evident when they are stated in words. It is here that mathematics can give powerful aid. But before the mathematician can get to work on the problem, the data must be stated precisely; and precision may seem inappropriate to sociology. Would it not be more polite to remain content with a modest vagueness? No! For, unless our statements are in terms so precise that it would be possible in them to make a definite mistake, it will be impossible in them to make a definite advance in science.

Permit me to discuss a generalized public speech, fictitious but typical of the year 1937. The Defense Minister of Jedesland, when introducing his estimates, said:

The intentions of our country are entirely pacific. We have given ample evidence of this by the treaties which we have recently concluded with our neighbors. Yet, when we consider the state of unrest in the world at large and the menaces by which we are surrounded, we should be failing in our duty as a government if we did not take adequate steps to increase the defenses of our beloved land.

We have now to translate that into mathematics. At first sight there might seem to be no way of doing it, and, on second thoughts, perhaps too many ways. But we can shave the problem clean with Ockham's razor. This principle in its usual form runs "entities are not to be multiplied without necessity," Mathematical physics has progressed by trying out first the simplest formulae that described the broad features of the early experiments and by leaving complicated formulae to wait for more accurate experiments. By "entities" let us understand terms and coefficients in formulae, and let us restate Ockham's rule as "formulae are not to be complicated without good evidence" or briefly "try out the easiest formulae first."

Now the simplest representation of what that generalized defense minister said is this:

$$dx/dt = ky \qquad ...(1)$$

where t is time, x represents his own defenses, y represents the menaces by which he is surrounded, and k is a positive constant, which will be named a "defense coefficient." Let us for simplicity assume that what he euphemistically called "surroundings" is, in fact, a single nation. Its defense minister asserts similarly that

$$dy/dt = kx \qquad ...(2)$$

If x and y are ever both positive, they then, according to equations (1) and (2), are both increasing; and so they will become more positive, and go on increasing faster and faster without any end to the process.[1] The system described by equations (1) and (2) is evidently unstable. In fact, we know that the process of increasing defenses was altered by the outbreak of war. A failure of equations to describe both small and very large disturbances is familiar in many departments of applied mathematics and need not unduly dispirit us: for example, Hooke's law is important in connection with the strength of materials, although it does not describe fracture.

But can we really believe that the international system is inevitably unstable? Surely the cost of armaments exercises some restraint. Leading statesmen have expressed this opinion. Thus Mr. Winston Churchill records that on 3 November 1909, while he was President of the Board of Trade, he began a minute to the Cabinet with these words:

Believing that there are practically no checks upon German naval expansion except those imposed by the increasing difficulties of getting money, I have had the enclosed report prepared with a view to showing how far those limitations are becoming effective. It is clear that they are becoming terribly effective.

Again, the German Chancellor, Prince Bülow in 1914, wrote:

It is just possible that the effect of convulsively straining her military resources to the uttermost may, by reacting on the economic and social conditions of

---

[1]A quantitative argument, which is not necessary for the understanding of this introduction, but which some readers may prefer, goes as follows. The general solution of equations (1) and (2) is

$$x = Ae^{kt} + Be^{-kt}. \qquad ...(3)$$
$$y = Ae^{kt} - Be^{-kt} \qquad ...(4)$$

If at t_0 both x and y are positive, then so is $x + y$ and therefore also A. But $k > 0$. So, as $t \to \infty$, both $x \to \infty$ and $y \to \infty$.

France, hasten the return of pacific feelings. . . . Should the three-year military service entail an income tax, this would also probably have a sobering effect.

So let the equations be improved into

$$dx/dt = ky - \alpha x, \qquad \ldots(5)$$
$$dx/dt = lx - \beta y, \qquad \ldots(6)$$

where α and β are positive constants representing the fatigue and expense of keeping up defenses, and k and l are positive defense coefficients, which we now regard as possibly unequal.

Let us compare this statement with some opinions of statesmen. Sir Edward Grey, who was British Foreign Secretary when World War I broke out, afterward wrote:

The increase of armaments that is intended in each nation to produce consciousness of strength, and a sense of security, does not produce these effects. On the contrary, it produces a consciousness of the strength of other nations and a sense of fear. . . . The enormous growth of armaments in Europe, the sense of insecurity and fear caused by them—it was these that made war inevitable. . . . This is the real and final account of the origin of the Great War.

Sir Edward Grey's statement is symbolized by the terms in k and l. Compare also Thucydides' account of the cause of the Peloponnesian war: "The real though unavowed cause I believe to have been the growth of Athenian power, which terrified the Lacedaemonians and forced them into war . . ." (Jowett, 1881). When this opinion of Sir Edward Grey was quoted by Mr. Noel Baker, M.P., in the House of Commons on 20 July 1936, Mr. L. S. Amery, M.P., said in reply:

With all respect to the memory of an eminent statesman, I believe that statement to be entirely mistaken. The armaments were only the symptoms of the conflict of ambitions and ideals, of those nationalist forces, which created the war. The War was brought about because Serbia, Italy, Rumania passionately desired the incorporation in their States of territories which at that time belonged to the Austrian Empire and which the Austrian

Government were not prepared to abandon without a struggle. France was prepared if the opportunity ever came to make an effort to recover Alsace-Lorraine. It was in those facts, in those insoluble conflicts of ambitions and not in the armaments themselves that the cause of the War lay.

Mr. Amery's objections should, I think, be met, not by leaving out Sir Edward Grey's terms, but by inserting additional terms, namely, g and h, to represent grievances and ambitions, provisionally regarded as constants, so that the equations become:

$$dx/dt = ky - \alpha x + g, \qquad \ldots(7)$$
$$dx/dt = lx - \beta x + h. \qquad \ldots(8)$$

These equations were published in 1935, as a simplification of an earlier theory.

In *Generalized Foreign Politics*, written in the years 1937–1939, the g and h were called the "grievances." Many people think that this was too sympathetic a name for what they call "aggressive intentions." From the mathematical point of view, g and h represent any motives which, while affecting warlike preparations, remain constant independently of the amount of such preparations at home or abroad. From the psychological point of view such motives could include deeply rooted prejudices, standing grievances, old unsatisfied ambitions, wicked and persistent dreams of world conquest, or, on the contrary, a permanent feeling of contentment. This list is too long to be recited on every occasion; so, for short, g and h are still usually called the "grievances"—a name which indicates that g is a positive number when its side is dissatisfied and a negative number when the prevailing mood of that side is contentment.

A well-known literary man objected that grievances and ambitions are imponderables; so what sense could there be in regarding them as measurable? The answer is that x and y can be counted, in men or money, and that x and y are partly the numerical effects of those "imponderables."

The preparations for war of the two groups may be regarded as the rectangular co-ordinates or a particle in an "international plane," so that every point in this plane represents one conceivable instantaneous international situation. The differential equations are then the equations of motion of the particle.

A hint will now be taken from Plato's advice concerning astronomy (*Republic*). We shall pursue foreign politics with the help of problems, just as we pursue geometry, but tentatively.

If *g, h, x, y* are all made zero simultaneously, the equations show that *x* and *y* remain zero. That ideal condition is *permanent peace by disarmament and satisfaction*. It has existed since 1817 on the frontier between the United States and Canada; also since 1905 on the frontier between Norway and Sweden (for the treaties see *League of Nations Armaments Year-Book* [1937]).

The equations further imply that *mutual disarmament without satisfaction* is not permanent, for, if *x* and *y* instantaneously vanish, $dx/dt = g$ and $dy/dt = h$.

Unilateral disarmament corresponds to putting $y = 0$ at a certain instant. We have at that time

$$dx/dt = -\alpha x + g, \quad dy/dt = lx + h.$$

The second of these equations implies that *y* will not remain zero if the grievance *h* is positive; later, when *y* has grown, the term *ky* will cause *x* to grow also. So, according to the equations, unilateral disarmament is not permanent. This accords with the historical fact that Germany, whose army was reduced by the Treaty of Versailles in 1919 to 100,000 men, a level far below that of several of her neighbors, insisted on rearming during the years 1933–36.

A *race in armaments*, such as was in progress in 1912, occurs when the defense terms predominate in the second members of the equations. If those were the only terms, we should have

$$dx/dt = ky, \quad dy/dt = lx,$$

and both *x* and *y* would tend to the same infinity, which, if positive, we may interpret as war. But, for large *x* and *y*, linearity may fail. . . .

Development of the Theory

The Opposite to War. The generalizing spirit of mathematics is very suggestive. It draws our attention to the possibility of "negative preparedness for war" and invites us to assign a name to it and to inquire whether the above general statements still hold true when the signs of the variables are changed. As a preliminary, let us consider, not nations, but only two people, and let us compare quarreling with falling in love. If hatred may be regarded as negative love, these two activities are opposite. Yet there are important resemblances between them. The chief stimulus to falling deeply in love is any sign of love from the other person, just as the chief stimulus to becoming more annoyed is any insult or injury from the other person. When quarreling is represented by $dx/dt = ky$, and $dy/dt = lx$, these same two equations with *k* and *l* still positive can also represent falling in love. For if *x* and *y* are ever both negative, they then, according to the equations, are both becoming more negative and will continue to do so, faster and faster, without any end to the process, as far as it is described by the equations.

Now, returning to the study of nations, we notice that the classical antithesis of "war and peace" is not appropriate here. For war is an intense activity, whereas peace, in the sense of a mere tranquil inattention to the doings of foreigners, resembles zero rather than a negative quantity. Negative preparedness for war must mean that the group directs toward foreigners an activity designed to please rather than to annoy them. Thus a suitable name for negative preparedness for wars seems to be "co-operation."

Just as armaments provoke counter-armaments, so assistance evokes reciprocal assistance; for example, imports and exports tend to equality. Also there is a tendency to reduce co-operation on account of the fatigue and expense which it involves. Thus it appears that the general statements remain broadly true when the preparedness changes from positive to negative. The most extensive form of international co-operation is foreign trade. There exist also more than 500 international associations, having little or no connection with one another but listed by the League of Nations (1936). The extreme form of international cooperation, corresponding to the infinity opposite to war, would appear to be a world-state, as imagined, for instance, by H. G. Wells in his book *The Shape of Things To Come* (1933).

Quarreling is here regarded as a positive activity, making friends as a negative activity. That happened because the equations were first written during World War I. It might be better to reverse the convention of signs. But the change has not been made in this book. . . .

32. Dangerous Dyads:
Conditions Affecting the Likelihood of Interstate War, 1816–1965

STUART A. BREMER

Clausewitz's assertion that war is "nothing but a duel on a large scale" reminds us that one of the core questions in the study of conflict is "who fights whom?" A good deal of theoretical speculation and some empirical evidence suggest that war is more likely to occur between states that are geographically proximate, roughly equal in power, major powers, allied, undemocratic, economically advanced, and/or militarized than between those that are not. Some of the component propensities in this summary statement are so widely assumed to be true that they have become "stylized facts" that, to some observers, need no further verification. But a closer scrutiny of the empirical evidence on which this confidence is based reveals one or more critical deficiencies in the relevant research. . . .

To discover or verify the relative importance of the seven factors listed at the outset of this

From Stuart A. Bremer, "Dangerous Dyads," *Journal of Conflict Resolution*, Vol. 36 No. 2, June 1992 309–341. © 1992 Sage Publications, Inc. Reprinted by permission of Sage Publications, Inc. and the author. Footnotes and most citations suppressed. Detailed methodological discussion, particularly of Poission regression, has been omitted. Readers seeking this information and references to the relevant literature should consult the original, especially pp. 332–333.

article, a broad spatial-temporal domain (i.e., all states, 1816–1965) is used here, and the interstate dyad is the unit of analysis. A uniform measure of war that clearly reflects the focus of this study—the onset of interstate war—is employed, and both bivariate and multivariate analyses are conducted. Given that the primary mission of this article is of a "fact finding" nature, no elaborate formal models will be presented, nor will I dwell at length on subtle theoretical issues. . . .

SEVEN PREDICTORS OF WAR

Geographical Proximity and War

The proposition that war is more likely to occur between states that are geographically proximate than between those that are not is disputed by few, and even considered trivial by some, perhaps because of the strong geopolitical component that is inherent in the very act of war. Boxers, after all, cannot fight until they are physically able to reach one another. This analogy is somewhat misleading, however, since the proposition does not state that war is more likely if the armed forces of two states are within striking distance of one another. Rather it argues that war is more likely between states that share a common border zone, regardless of whether that border zone is a heavily fortified no-man's land or an almost forgotten boundary for which little physical evidence exists save its designation on maps.

A stronger and more interesting argument for why geographical proximity promotes war builds on the notion that proximity engenders serious conflicts of interest between states, a fraction of which are bound to lead to war. Shared access to a physical area can lead directly to interstate friction, even if the states involved agree as to where the border lies between them. A common example of this is where insurgents use the territory of an adjacent state as a basing area, and the state thus being used is unable or unwilling to suppress the insurgents' activities on its territory. A large variety of other examples of how proximity can introduce an unwelcome degree of interdependence between states can be cited. Because this enforced "common fate" breeds frustrations and rivalries between states, so the argument runs, interstate tension increases and, ceteris paribus, war is more likely.

The empirical evidence linking war and proximity is scattered but generally consistent. Several studies have found an association between the number of borders states have and their foreign conflict behavior generally or war involvement specifically. These studies do not enable us to conclude that sharing a common border increases the likelihood of conflict and war between a given pair of states because they do not demonstrate that the increased conflict involvement of states with many neighbors is directed toward those neighbors. Thus, the evidence that these studies present for the proposition must be considered indirect.

More direct evidence is to be found in studies by Gleditsch and Singer (1975), Garnham (1976), and Gochman (1990a). Gleditsch and Singer found that the average intercapital distance between warring states was significantly less than the average such distance between all states over the period from 1816 to 1965. Garnham also employed an intercapital mea-

sure of distance to assess proximity, and found that the distance between warring pairs of states was significantly less than what would be expected by chance. This led him to conclude that "international war is more probable between more proximate pairs of nation-states" (p. 240). Gochman reported that about two-thirds of militarized interstate disputes occurring between 1816 and 1976 were between states that shared a common land border or were separated by 150 miles or less of water. Gochman also found that the proportion of disputes in which contiguity was present has tended to increase with the passage of time. Hence, if any trend is present in the effect of proximity on conflict, it would appear to be in the opposite direction from that commonly thought; that is, proximity may be more salient today than it was a century and a half ago.

Power Parity and War

Whether equality in power between states promotes war or peace has been hotly debated in the theoretical literature. Both sides make convincing arguments that appeal to common sense. One side argues that states that are radically different in power should not engage in war because the clearly weaker side would not be so foolish as to initiate or allow itself to be drawn into a war it cannot win. Hence, at the dyadic level, preponderance promotes peace. The other side of the debate argues that when two states are relatively equal in power, neither can be certain of victory, and they therefore deter one another from war. Ergo, power parity promotes peace between states. The first of these two views is found in more contemporary treatments of the question (e.g., Organski 1968; see selection 38), whereas the second prevails in the older balance of power tradition.

Although many empirical studies have examined the relationship between power and war, very few have looked specifically at the dyadic level. Garnham (1976) examined two-nation wars during the period from 1816 to 1965 and found that warring pairs of states were more equal with respect to several power-base measures (i.e., area, population, fuel consumption, iron and steel production) than would be expected by chance. This led him to conclude that power parity is more likely to lead to war than preponderance. Weede (1976) restricted his analysis to a smaller spatial-temporal domain (i.e., contiguous Asian dyads over the period from 1950 to 1969), but found essentially the same result, that is, that preponderance of power promotes peace. More recently, Gochman (1990b) found evidence to support the proposition that major powers are more likely to engage in war with other major powers when their capabilities are relatively equal. After reviewing the empirical literature on dyadic power and war, Sullivan concludes that "though the findings do not speak with one voice, a tendency seems to be, with some certain exceptions, that situations of preponderance are more likely associated with nonwar than the opposite" (1990, 129), an assessment with which I essentially agree.

Power Status and War

As with geographical proximity and war, there may be a tautological element in the proposition that major powers are more likely to engage in war than minor powers. It can be quite convincingly argued that major powers achieve and maintain their status as such because, in large measure, they pursue an active, interventionist, perhaps even aggressive, foreign policy that brings them more frequently into violent conflict with other states. The literature on war making and state making suggests that the two phenomena are intimately connected. To the extent that this is true, it may be impossible to determine on balance whether states become major powers because they engage frequently in war or states engage frequently in war because they are major powers. A true test of the two propositions may come when and if Germany and Japan are readmitted to the major power club.

The nondyadic empirical evidence is quite clear (Bremer 1980; Small and Singer 1982); major powers are much more likely to become involved in wars than minor powers. Ceteris paribus, dyads that contain one or more major powers should be more war prone than those that do not.

Alliance and War

In the modern era, alliances tend to be seen as defining "security communities" among their members, and, as such, it is expected that they will reduce the likelihood of war between members. In truth, this expectation may be based largely on a few durable and institutionalized alliances like NATO in the post-World War II era rather than on alliances in general. Yet the assumption that allies are more likely to resolve disputes by means other than war and, therefore, are less likely to engage in war with one another seems deeply ingrained in conventional wisdom. The older, more traditional view of alliances sees them as growing out of expediency and reflecting nothing deeper than a temporary need of two or more states to coordinate their actions against one or more other states. In this second view, alliances are not seen as contracts but rather as bargains, wherein it is understood by all parties that each has the right to withdraw quickly should a better deal come along. Under this conception of alliances as limited, transient arrangements, war between allies should be neither more nor less frequent than between nonallied states. In theory, then, alliances may or may not reduce the chances of war between allies, but they should not increase the likelihood of war between allies.

Perhaps for this reason, Bueno de Mesquita's assertion that "war is much more likely between very close allies than between enemies" (1982, 30) was a counterintuitive, if not startling, deduction from his expected utility theory. And the empirical evidence he offered (1981, 159–64) seemed to confirm this assertion. After a thoughtful review of Bueno de Mesquita's arguments and evidence, Ray concluded that "in light of the fact that it would be surprising to find that allies are even as conflict prone as unallied pairs of states, it is not unreasonable to conclude that allied dyads were disproportionately involved in international conflict with each other in the 1816–1974 time period" (Ray 1990, 86). Thus, contrary to most theoretical expectations, war appears to be more likely between allied states than between nonallied states, at least since the end of the Napoleonic era.

Democracy and War

At a time when democracy seems to be experiencing a resurgence, the argument that democracies are less war prone (at least *vis-à-vis* one another) gives some grounds for optimism about an otherwise turbulent future. The philosophical justifications for why democratic states should be less war prone than others will not be repeated here (see Doyle, 1986) [see also Maoz and Russett, selection 51]. Instead, I will focus on the empirical debate that has been underway for some years.

Until recently, the prevailing appraisal of the empirical evidence regarding the linkage between democracy and war proneness supported the conclusion that democracies were neither more nor less war prone than other states. . . . [Newer studies have] found strong evidence that democracies tend not to go to war with one another, but little evidence that democracies tend to be less war prone overall.

Most of the studies surveyed above contain one or more serious design flaws, such as using a monadic level of analysis when a dyadic one is called for, failing to control for the number of democracies, or using an inappropriate measure of war. Nevertheless, the weight of evidence they yield clearly supports the proposition that democracies have a much lower likelihood of becoming involved in wars against other democracies than would be expected by chance. Russett has even gone so far as to assert that "this is one of the strongest nontrivial and nontautological generalizations that can be made about international relations" (1990, 123). The evidence as to whether or not democracies are less war prone overall is far less conclusive, but the absence of strong evidence to the contrary leads one to conclude that democracies have been neither more nor less war prone than nondemocracies.

Development and War

The rise of international political economy as a subfield has resensitized many to the importance of economic factors and international conflict. A central focus of much of the literature in this area is the way in which economically advanced states relate to each other and, more importantly, to states that are not economically advanced. Although war appears not to be a central concern of most of those engaged in research in this area, two propositions relating to war can be deduced from their work. The first derives from the Leninist thesis that states that are more economically advanced will tend to come into sharp conflict with one another as they compete for markets and resources in a largely zero-sum world. Of course, a critical caveat for the Leninist thesis is that these states be capitalistic in nature, and this is, no doubt, an important theoretical distinction. Unfortunately it is not a distinction that can be used meaningfully in empirical analyses because, with few exceptions over the last two centuries, all more advanced states have also been capitalistic. For this reason the proposition examined here is simply that more advanced states are more likely to start wars with one another than are other states.[1]

The second proposition that is suggested by this literature is that war is more likely between more advanced and less advanced states than between pairs of more or less advanced states. This would follow from an admittedly unsophisticated dependencia theory that states that the likelihood of war increases when a more advanced economy attempts to penetrate a less advanced economy, or when a less advanced economy attempts to shake off the yoke imposed by a more advanced economy.

---

[1]This proposition is also broadly consistent with the lateral pressure theory (Choucri and North) [see selection 36] because it posits, ceteris paribus, that technologically advanced societies should exhibit high levels of conflict among themselves.

If this pattern of conflict were widespread, then one would expect to see a disproportionate amount of war between more and less advanced economies.

Efforts to uncover empirical studies that bear directly on these propositions were unsuccessful. . . .

Militarization and War

According to the old maxim, "states that seek peace should prepare for war." The questions that concern us here are whether states that devote a disproportionate share of their resources to military preparedness succeed in reducing their chances of war, as the maxim implies they should, or will such states exhibit a higher likelihood of war? I should emphasize that more militarized states are not necessarily those with the largest absolute military capability. Several countries in the Middle East, for example, maintain armed forces much larger than most other countries of comparable size and are more militarized, as I use the term here, even though their armed forces are small in a global sense.

The war-avoidance properties of militarization flow clearly from the logic of deterrence. If a state can persuade a potential attacker that the costs of war will be high relative to the expected gains, then the odds of being attacked will be lower. And this logic applies to small states as well as large since, although small states may not be able to avoid defeat in wars with large states, they can, by extensive military preparations, guarantee that victory will be costly to the large states and thereby deter attacks. According to deterrence theory, then, more militarization means less war.

As is usually the case, for each maxim there is an equally convincing counter-maxim. In this instance it would be that "those who live by the sword, die by the sword." For a variety of reasons, states that prepare for war may get exactly that for which they prepare. The construction of a "garrison state" may call forth leaders that are bellicose and unyielding rather than flexible and accommodating. The militarization of a society may cause leaders and followers alike to conclude that war is inevitable rather than merely possible. Justifying the sacrifices that high degrees of military preparedness require may strengthen enemy images and even lead to collective paranoia. And, of course, other states may not see the defensive motivation behind the heightened military posture, and perceive instead a substantial threat to their own security. On balance, I find the second argument more persuasive than the first so the exact proposition under examination is stated accordingly; that is, pairs of more militarized states are more likely to begin wars than other states.

The empirical evidence on this proposition is, at best, indirect. The most germane comes from the numerous but inconclusive studies on the relationship between arms races and war. On one side of this question we find Wallace (1982), who has presented evidence that arms races do increase the likelihood of war between racing states. On the other side, we find Diehl (1983). . . who disputes this connection. To a great extent the outcome of this debate hinges on the definition of what constitutes an arms race.

Even if it were shown conclusively that arms races increase the likelihood of war, this would not constitute direct confirming evidence for the proposition under consideration here for two reasons. First, the arms race thesis is dynamic while the militarization hypothesis is static. That is, continued increases in preparedness are central to the former, while high levels of preparedness are the concern of the latter. Second, the arms race thesis is not concerned with the relative defense effort of racing states, while the militarization hypothesis is. Two states could be involved in a low level arms race with neither reaching the stage of militarization referred to here, although continued, large increases in resources devoted to the military should eventually lead to that stage.

DEFINITIONS AND MEASUREMENTS

Given the way in which our seven key propositions are stated and the underlying theoretical arguments from which they derive, it seems obvious that the interstate dyad is the appropriate level of analysis. An interstate dyad is defined as any pair of states that are members of the interstate system, where system membership is defined by the standard Correlates of War rules. Because I wish to test the veracity of the propositions over a long historical period (i.e., from 1816 to 1965) rather than at only one point in time, the basic observational unit must be time based, and I have selected the year as the time unit. Hence, the interstate dyad-year is the observational unit employed in the analyses that follow. Aggregating over time and space yields a population of 202,778 nondirectional interstate dyad-years during the 1816 to 1965 span.[2]

Defining War Occurrence

One of the key reasons that the findings derived from empirical studies of war do not add up in a cumulative fashion is the wide variation in operational definitions of war that have been employed. Thus, for example, two studies may, as this one does, accept the Correlates of War definition of what constitutes a war, yet adopt quite different measures of war participation (e.g., nation-months of war underway versus battle deaths begun), and, by doing so, make it virtually impossible to compare their findings in any direct way. Too often, I think, the measurement of war has been guided by statistical considerations or by an eclecticism that sees the various war measures as more or less substitutable rather than by a deeper theoretical examination of the questions under review.

As stated above, the seven propositions under examination deal only with the likelihood of wars between states and say little directly about the length, severity, or ultimate size of those wars that do occur. Hence, measures of war that rest on the latter are inappropriate for this study. . . .

I share the growing view that war must be seen as a process rather than only an event,

and, according to this view, it is important to distinguish between the occurrence of a war and how it evolves thereafter. In other words, the question of why wars begin is fundamentally different from the questions of why wars grow in size, duration, or severity. Studies that fail to make this distinction are fundamentally flawed. If we turn back to the seven propositions under study, it seems clear that their focus is the likelihood that a war will begin between two states and not the likelihood that a state will join an ongoing war. Hence, I will examine only the original participants in a given war and disregard subsequent joiners in the analyses that follow.

If all wars began as one-on-one confrontations, then for each of the 56 interstate wars that began during the period under study there would be one dyad of original participants, but the historical record is not quite so simple. In 13 of the 56 qualifying wars, two or more states became involved in war with one or more other states on the very first day of the war. These may be instances of genuine collusion or very fast joining behavior (I favor the former interpretation), but unfortunately the available historical evidence does not allow us to distinguish reliably between the two. In view of this, we are left with little choice but to treat these simultaneous outbreaks of dyadic war as independent events even though we strongly suspect they are not. Employing this assumption, one finds 93 cases of war onset at the dyadic level during the period from 1816 to 1965. Because the year *prior* to the beginning of each war was used as the observation point for the seven independent variables rather than the year of the war itself, three of the 56 wars are not usable due to the fact that not all of the participants on one side were members of the interstate system in the year prior to the war. This reduces the number of war dyads by eight, leaving a total of 85.

Geographical Proximity

To ascertain whether any given pair of states are geographically proximate to one another, I turned to the Correlates of War contiguity

---

[2]A nondirectional dyad is one in which no distinction is made between the U.S.-USSR and USSR-U.S. dyads, for example. In directional dyads this differentiation is, of course, retained.

data set. In that data set, four types of direct state-to-state contiguity are distinguished: contiguous by land, or separated by 12, 24, or 150 miles or less of water. In this study I have chosen to disregard the tripartite water distance distinction and deal with only three types of contiguity. Thus, in a given year, a dyad is either land contiguous, sea contiguous (i.e., separated by 150 miles of water or less), or not contiguous. At this time, unfortunately, the contiguity data extend only from 1816 to 1965, and it is this limitation that essentially defines the temporal span of the whole study. Applying these criteria to the 202,778 interstate dyad-years yielded 10,542 cases of land contiguity, 3,019 cases of sea contiguity, and 189,217 cases of no contiguity.

Relative Power

To assess the degree to which any pair of states is equal in power, I have used the Correlates of War material capabilities data set that covers the period from 1816 to 1985 and records the military personnel, military expenditures, iron and steel production, energy consumption (after 1859), urban population, and total population for state system members. In the usual fashion, I first derived indexes of military, economic, and demographic capability by computing each state's average share of system-wide capability across the two variables within each of the three dimensions and then averaged these values to arrive at the Composite Index of National Capability (or CINC).

Based on these CINC scores, I computed the larger-to-smaller capability ratios for all dyad-years and classified them into three groups. If the capability ratio was less than or equal to three, then the dyad was considered to constitute a case of small power difference. If the ratio was larger than 10, then the power difference was coded as large, whereas a ratio between 3 and 10 was coded as a medium power difference. If either of the CINC scores was missing (or equal to zero) for a ratio calculation, then the power difference score for that dyad was coded as missing also.

The 3-to-1 threshold was chosen because of its prominence in the folklore of military strategy while 10-to-1 threshold is quite arbitrary. To my surprise, the use of these thresholds yielded roughly equal groups of dyad-years. That is, 74,620 of the 202,778 dyad-years were found to exhibit a large power difference, 56,432 were characterized by a medium power difference, and 62,055 by a small power difference. The 9,671 remaining cases (less than 5%) were missing.

Power Status

To investigate the effects of power status, each dyad-year was examined to determine whether both, one, or neither of the relevant states were or was a major power in that year. Accordingly, the dyad was coded as having a power status of major-major, major-minor, or minor-minor. The identity and qualifying years for major powers were the same as those defined by Small and Singer (1982) and used by many other analysts. Applying these criteria across the entire spatial-temporal domain yielded the following breakdown: 2,267 major-major dyad-years, 36,907 major-minor dyad-years, and 163,604 minor-minor dyad-years.

Alliance

To distinguish those dyads that are allied from those that are not, I have used the Correlates of War formal alliance data set (Small and Singer 1969) as amended and modified by Alan Sabrosky. In that data set formal alliances among nations are divided into three types: mutual defense pacts, neutrality agreements, and ententes. Using this data set, I was able to classify each dyad-year as falling into one of four groups: defense, neutrality, entente, and none. The total number of dyad-years this produced were 11,176; 647; 3,531; and 187,424, respectively.

Democracy

Defining and measuring democracy is difficult, and especially so when a dichotomous measure is desired. Therefore, in this study I will draw on two different efforts to classify political systems. The first is the dichotomous division of states done by Steve Chan (Chan 1984) in which a state is classified as democratic if its chief executive is directly or indirectly elected in a popular fashion and its legislative branch is also elected and able to constrain the executive in an effective manner (see Chan 1984, 629–31 for further details). Using this data set, which covers the period from 1816 to 1980, I was able to assign each of the dyad-years to one of three groups: both states democratic (21,644), one democratic state (78,349), and both states undemocratic (99,580). In addition, data were missing for 3,205 dyad-years, and these were assigned to the missing group.

The second data collection I use to assess whether or not states are democratic is Ted Robert Gurr's Polity II data set (Gurr, Jaggers, and Moore 1989), which contains, among other things, a variable reflecting the degree of "institutionalized democracy" found in a state in a given year. Like Chan's measure, this index is based on the competitiveness of leader selection processes and constraints on executive authority. In its raw form, this index varies from 0 to 10 (undemocratic to democratic). I dichotomized the variable by classifying states as democratic that had a value of 5 or greater on Gurr's index and otherwise as undemocratic. Using the Gurr-based index I found 22,859 dyad-years in which both states were democratic, 80,668 with one democratic state, and 80,801 with neither state democratic. This left 18,450 dyad-years coded as missing when values were missing for one or both states.

Development

Given the paucity of macroeconomic time-series data for years prior to World War II, any effort to differentiate more advanced economies from less advanced economies based on, for example, GNP or GDP per capita would suffer from serious design deficiencies. Rather than abandoning the effort to consider the relationship between development and war, I derived an index based on the Correlates

of War material capabilities data set that may capture some of the economic differentiation between states that is sought.

It will be recalled that in deriving the composite index of national capability, two component indexes assessing the economic and demographic dimensions were used. In a general sense, these component indexes reflect the share of system-wide economic and demographic capabilities that a state possesses in any given year. A more economically advanced state should be characterized by possessing a share of system-wide economic capability that is greater than its share of system-wide demographic capability. Hence, in years when this was found to be true, I classified a state as more advanced; otherwise, less advanced. The next step involved examining each pair of states in each year and assigning it to one of three groups: both more advanced (7,160 dyad-years), one more advanced (61,823 dyad-years), and both less advanced (128,939 dyad-years). The remaining 4,856 dyad-years had to be assigned to the missing group because data were not available for one or both of the relevant states.

Militarization

As with measuring development, assessing whether states are more or less militarized over the century and a half under study is difficult, given the lack of historical data. Ideally, one would wish to measure what is sometimes referred to as defense effort (i.e., the ratio of defense expenditures to GNP), but this is not a viable measure for most states in most years over the century and a half under consideration due to the insufficiency of macroeconomic data. Instead, I relied on the material capabilities data set discussed above, and classified a state as more militarized if its share of system-wide military capabilities was greater than its share of system-wide demographic capabilities. I classified it less militarized if this was not true. The classification of each dyad-year was then based on whether both, one, or neither of the two states making up the dyad were more militarized in that year. This produced 29,366; 87,720; and 76,467 dyad-years, respectively, leaving 9,225 dyad-years as missing due to the absence of data for one or both sides.

BIVARIATE RESULTS

To begin the assessment of the relative merit of the seven propositions stated in the introduction, I use a simple and straightforward method. I calculate and compare the conditional probabilities of war in a dyad-year given the presence of the conditions specified by each proposition. The degree to which the conditional probabilities relevant to a proposition vary from one another is then used as evidence for the proposition. The relevant information is found in Table 8.1. For each dyad type, the first column in this table shows the observed number of war onsets, together with the expected number of onsets (in parentheses) if the type distinctions are ignored. The latter are the products of the unconditional dyadic probability of war (85/202,778) and the number of dyad-years each dyad type was observed, which is given in the second column. The third column contains the conditional probability of war, pr (War), for each dyad type, which is the observed number of war onsets divided by the total dyad-years. These probabilities have been multiplied by 1,000 to facilitate reading. To help distinguish large and small effects, I include as well in the table standard normal (Z) values and their associated probabilities. These are derived from a difference of proportions test where each group is posited to be a random sample drawn from a known population. The Z and pr(Z) values reflect, then, the likelihood of obtaining a conditional probability of war this different from the unconditional probability of war if the distinction used to define the group was truly irrelevant to war propensity.

Proximity and War. The top of Table 8.1 reveals the probabilities of war in a dyad-year when the 202,778 dyad-years are segregated by geographical proximity. It is obvious that the presence of land or sea contiguity significantly increases the probability of war occurring in a dyad, with land contiguous dyads being slightly more war prone than sea contiguous ones. Ignoring the latter distinction yields a probability of war per dyad-year, given either land or sea contiguity, of .0045. Because this value is 35 times greater than the probability of war when contiguity is absent, there can be little doubt that the effect of state-to-state contiguity on the occurrence of war is quite strong. The large Z values and their small associated probabilities strongly reinforce this conclusion.

Power Difference and War. The conditional probabilities of war onset given large, medium, or small power differences are the next shown in Table 8.1. The first impression conveyed by these results is that, relatively speaking, the three probabilities do not differ all that much from one another. The Z values are all within the +1 to –1 range, suggesting that the power difference distinction is not much better than a random split. Together, these values lead to the conclusion that the effect of power difference is, at best, small. The effect that is present, however, is in the direction postulated; that is, war is about one-third more likely in dyads characterized by small or medium power differences than in those with large power differences.

Power Status and War. The next set of conditional probabilities in Table 8.1 are obtained when the whole set of dyad-years is divided into subsets based on the power status of the states involved. Major-major dyads have the highest probability of war, whereas minor-minor dyads have the lowest probability of war, and, because the probability of war in the former is about 10 times larger than the latter, the proposition that major-major dyads are more war prone seems to have considerable merit. In addition, because the probability of war in dyads that include one major power is about 5 times greater than those that contain no major power, it appears that the effect of power status may be additive rather than interactive. The absolute Z values are all greater than 3,

TABLE 8.1 Conditional Probabilities of War by Dyad Type, 1816–1965

Dyad Type	*War Dyads*	*Total Dyads*	*pr(War)**	*Z*	*pr(Z)*
		Proximity and war			
Land contiguous	48 (4.4)	10,542	4.55	20.74	<.0001
Sea contiguous	13 (1.3)	3,019	4.31	10.43	<.0001
Not contiguous	24 (79.3)	189,217	0.13	−6.21	<.0001
		Power difference and war			
Large difference	27 (31.3)	74,620	0.36	−0.77	.22
Medium difference	28 (23.7)	56,432	0.50	0.89	.19
Small difference	29 (26.0)	62,055	0.47	0.59	.28
Missing	1	9,671			
		Power status and war			
Major-major	5 (1.0)	2,267	2.21	4.16	<.0001
Major-minor	42 (15.5)	36,907	1.14	6.75	<.0001
Minor-minor	38 (68.6)	163,604	0.23	−3.69	.0001
		Alliance and war			
Defense pact	20 (4.7)	11,176	1.79	7.08	<.0001
Neutrality treaty	2 (0.3)	647	3.09	3.32	.0004
Entente	1 (1.5)	3,531	0.28	−0.39	.35
No alliance	62 (78.6)	187,424	0.33	−1.87	.031
		Democracy and war (Chan)			
Both democratic	1 (9.1)	21,644	0.05	−2.68	.0043
One democratic	14 (32.8)	78,349	0.18	−3.29	.0005
Both not democratic	70 (41.7)	99,580	0.70	+4.37	<.0001
Missing	0	3,205			
		Democracy and war (Gurr)			
Both democratic	2 (9.6)	22,859	0.09	−2.45	.0071
One democratic	25 (33.8)	80,668	0.31	−1.52	.0643
Both not democratic	36 (33.9)	80,801	0.45	+0.37	.3557
Missing	22	18,450			
		Development and war			
Both advanced	6 (3.0)	7,160	0.84	+1.73	.0418
One advanced	25 (25.9)	61,823	0.40	−0.18	.4286
Both not advanced	54 (54.0)	128,939	0.42	−0.01	.496
Missing	0	4,856			
		Militarization and war			
Both more militarized	38 (12.3)	29,366	1.29	+7.32	<.0001
One more militarized	30 (36.8)	87,720	0.34	−1.12	.1314
Both less militarized	16 (32.1)	76,467	0.21	−2.84	.0023
Missing	1	9,225			

*To facilitate reading all probabilities have been multiplied by 1,000.

which confirms the conclusion that the power status of a dyad has a major impact on its war propensity.

Alliance and War. The conditional probabilities of war onset when members of a dyad are linked by different types of formal alliance bonds are shown next in Table 8.1. Both the defense pact and neutrality treaty categories show significantly higher than expected war probabilities, whereas the opposite is true for ententes. However, due to the small number of war dyads in the neutrality and entente categories, a better estimate of the impact of alliance on war may be obtained by collapsing some of the categories. If the three types of alliance are merged, the conditional probability of war given any alliance is .0015 ($Z = +6.53$) versus .00033 when no alliance is present, a likelihood ratio of about 4.5 to 1. If instead, because of their low relative frequency of war, ententes are combined with the no alliance category, then the corresponding probabilities are .0019 ($Z = +9.88$) and .00033, yielding a likelihood ratio of 5.6 to 1. Hence, regardless of how ententes are coded, the likelihood of war in allied dyads is about 5 times greater than that in nonallied dyads. These results confirm the paradoxical proposition that alliances encourage war between members rather than inhibiting it.

Democracy and War. Proposition 5 stated that war between undemocratic dyads is more likely than between democratic dyads, and the results obtained using Chan's (1984) data shown in Table 8.1 support this assertion. The probability of war onset between democracies is much smaller than between states that are not democratic, or, stated in the direction specified by the proposition, war onset between pairs of undemocratic states is about 14 times as likely as between pairs of democratic states. Because war onset in undemocratic dyads is about 4 times as likely as between mixed (i.e., one democratic, one undemocratic) pairs of states, it appears that the contention of some that both states must be democratic before the war-inhibiting effect of

democracy is felt is unsupported. If the latter were true, then the probabilities of war onset when one or neither state was undemocratic should both be about .00047 rather than .00018 and .00070 respectively. The large Z and small pr(Z) values indicate that the presence of a democracy in a dyad significantly reduces its war propensity. Shifting over to the Gurr (et al., 1989) based index of democracy yields similar but not identical results. As shown in Table 8.1, the probability that two undemocratic states will begin a war is much greater than the probability that two democratic states will do so. But, unlike the Chan-based results, we do not find a significant difference in the probability of war between dyads containing one or no democratic states. In these results, then, we find evidence only for what has been called the "joint democracy" effect . . .

Development and War. The sixth proposition stated that war was more likely to occur between states that are economically advanced than between those that are not, and the results shown in Table 8.1 lend support to it. Dyads containing two advanced states are twice as likely to begin wars as those that contain one or fewer advanced states, but the Z values indicate that this effect is quite weak.

Militarization and War. The last part of Table 8.1 reveals the conditional probabilities of war when dyads are grouped according to whether both, one, or neither of the states involved are more militarized. Pairs of more militarized states are about six times as likely to begin a war in a given year than pairs of less militarized states, and, based on the small size of the probability of war in mixed dyads, one might conclude that the effect of militarization is largely interactive. Naturally, the argument that this relationship between militarization and war is spurious, due to the tendency for states preparing for war to become more militarized in preparation for the coming war, cannot be refuted. However, regardless of whether the proposition is causal or merely descriptive in nature, the assertion that militarized pairs of states are more likely to begin wars finds support here.

All seven propositions set forth at the beginning of this article have found support in the simple bivariate analyses, but some of the relationships found are stronger than others. From strongest to weakest, I would rank the various effects as follows: (1) Proximity, (2) Power status, (3) Alliance, (4) Militarization, (5) Democracy, (6) Development, (7) Power difference.

It is interesting that the factor that has received perhaps the greatest amount of theoretical attention, power difference, is found here to be the weakest predictor of war onset. If subsequent analyses bear out the weak effects of relative power, the potential implications for international relations theory may be truly profound. But such a judgment must await the results of more complex analyses such as those presented below.

MULTIVARIATE RESULTS

There are a variety of reasons for suspecting that the bivariate analyses reported above do not provide a sound basis for identifying types of dyads that are particularly war prone. Chief among these is the suspicion that the seven factors dealt with here are not uncorrelated with one another. Under this condition, apparently strong relationships with war may be spurious and weak relationships with war may become strong when the effects of other factors are removed. And, of course, not only the strengths of association may be affected, but also their direction as well. For example, the bivariate results suggest that both contiguity and alliance increase the likelihood of war onset in a dyad, but an analysis of the joint effects of both factors reveals that the existence of an alliance between a pair of contiguous states *decreases* their likelihood of war, and the conclusion that alliances make war more likely is not fully warranted.

In order to assess the joint and individual effects of the seven factors under consideration on war onset, all dyad-years were recoded to re-

flect the most war prone conditions revealed by the bivariate analyses. For example, the contiguity variable was assigned a value of one if the dyad was contiguous by land or sea (as defined above) and zero if not. . . .[3] Because each of the seven variables is now binary in nature, they jointly define 2^7 or 128 possible dyad types. . . .

The question to be addressed here is the relative contribution of each of the seven factors under consideration to the likelihood of war beginning within dyads. Because the dependent variable, number of war onsets, is bounded (i.e., may not be less than zero) and discrete (i.e., only integer values are possible) the standard regression model is not appropriate. However, the Poisson regression model is, because it assumes that the dependent variable has precisely those characteristics mentioned above. . . . [Hence,] the Poisson regression model would seem to be well suited to the problem at hand." . . .

An examination of the coefficients in Table 8.2 reveals that the majority of our expectations stemming from the bivariate analyses are confirmed, but a few are not. Because the seven variables were coded in such a way that values of one were assigned to the more war-prone condition identified in the bivariate analyses, the naive expectation is that the signs of the seven coefficients will be positive. The strongest predictor of the seven is contiguity, and, as expected, its presence significantly increases the likelihood of war in a dyad. Second in importance is the absence of democracy in a dyad, which also increases a dyad's likelihood of war. The third most important factor, both more advanced, does not have the expected positive effect, however. The next two factors, which measure the presence of a major power and overwhelming preponderance in a dyad, both have a similar, positive impact on the likelihood of war. The existence of an alliance within a dyad slightly *decreases* the likelihood of war starting within that dyad. The final condition, both militarized, has a very weak positive effect and adds virtually

---

[3]Table 2 in the original article, which summarized this information, has been omitted.

TABLE 8.2 Multivariate Poisson Regression Analysis of Dyadic War Onset, 1816–1965

Variable	Coefficient	Standard Error	t Ratio	Significance
Intercept	−5.468	1.206	−4.53	.00001
Log (dyad-years)	0.471	0.130	3.62	.0003
Contiguous	1.780	0.362	4.91	<.00001
Both not democratic	1.285	0.295	4.35	.00001
Both more advanced	−1.275	0.507	−2.52	.01184
At least one major	0.658	0.263	2.50	.01239
No large power difference	0.619	0.243	2.54	.01098
Allied	−0.397	0.287	−1.38	.16641
Both militarized	0.098	0.240	0.41	.683

nothing to the explanatory power of the equation. This lack of any significant relationship between militarization and war is surprising because readiness for war is seen by some as a dangerous condition in and of itself, and by others as an early warning indicator of war. Joint preparedness, as measured here, does not seem to constitute either of these.

The failure to find any significant effect of militarization on war led to some experimentation with the possible interaction of this factor with the six others. Only one combination proved noteworthy, and that was the condition of both militarized and allied. Substituting the product of these two variables in place of the militarization term yields the results shown in Table 8.3. The log-likelihood value increases to −92.555, suggesting a notable improvement in the model, and, more importantly, the contributions of the seven factors become clearer and stronger. In particular, the alliance coefficient now shows a strong, negative association between being allied and the likelihood of war, and the interaction term shows a strong positive association with war. Hence, by itself, the existence of an alliance reduces the chances of war in a dyad, but this effect is nullified if the parties to the dyad are both more militarized.

In order to understand better the relative importance of the seven factors, let us consider a hypothetical dyad and its expected number of war onsets over a 100-year period. To begin, I will assume that the dyad has the predicted characteristics of a least war-prone one; that is, it is composed of noncontiguous, allied minor

powers, at least one of which is democratic and one of which is less militarized, and one state has overwhelming preponderance over the other. The expected number of wars that would originate in such a dyad over 100 years is about 0.003, based on the coefficients of the revised model.

Table 8.4 summarizes how the stepwise alteration of each factor transforms the dyad from least war prone to most war prone. It is readily apparent that contiguity has the strongest impact, followed closely by economic status and alliance. The presence or absence of joint democracy is next in importance, with relative power and power status having significantly less of an impact. As expected, the interaction term makes only a small contribution to the expected number of wars because its main effect is reflected in the alliance term. The third column in Table 8.4 shows the proportionate increase in the expected number of wars that each factor makes; the reader can readily assess the relative importance of the seven factors.

IMPLICATIONS AND CONCLUSIONS

In closing I will consider some implications for theory and research, beginning with the individual factors and concluding with the overall pattern they reveal.

The importance of contiguity in accounting for the onset of interstate war argues that it should be commonly included in almost all

TABLE 8.3   Revised Multivariate Poisson Regression Analysis of Dyadic War Onset, 1816–1965

Variable	Coefficient	Standard Error	t Ratio	Significance
Intercept	−4.950	1.077	−4.60	<.0001
Log (dyad-years)	0.425	0.118	3.61	.0003
Contiguous	1.683	0.342	4.92	<.0001
Both not democratic	1.273	0.294	4.33	<.0001
Both more advanced	−1.412	0.498	−2.83	.0046
At least one major	0.545	0.257	2.12	.0342
No large power difference	0.607	0.243	2.50	.0123
Allied	−1.464	0.539	−2.72	.0066
Both militarized and allied	1.541	0.557	2.77	.0056

studies of war, if only as a control variable. Whether it is only a measure of opportunity for war, or whether it taps something deeper that reflects the willingness to engage in war as well, is unclear, but its importance is not, and the argument for its inclusion applies to all levels of analysis. These results suggest that Diehl's conclusion that "although geography may not be the most important factor in international relations, its significance justifies increased and more careful attention from scholars of international conflict" (1991, 24) is true, but understated, for in this competition between many purportedly important preconditions for war, contiguity finished first.

Alliances have been found to reduce significantly the likelihood of war between allies, except under the special condition where both are more militarized, in which case they have almost no impact. Thus our theoretical ex-

pectations are generally confirmed and the bivariate finding that alliances promote war between allies is shown to be essentially spurious. There is nothing in this finding inconsistent with the argument that alliances promote the spread of war, once it breaks out, however.

In the economic sphere, these results suggest that the likelihood of war starting between "have" states is considerably lower than between "have" and "have not" or between "have not" states. This could reflect a mutual recognition among advanced economies that war is, in Mueller's words, "abhorrent—repulsive, immoral, and uncivilized—and methodologically ineffective—futile" (1989, 217), or, less charitably, it may indicate the presence of cartel-like collusion among richer states to avoid war between themselves in order to maintain their exalted economic positions. More conclusively, the (neo)-Leninist notion that com-

TABLE 8.4   Expected War Onsets per Dyad in a Century

Action	Expected Wars	Proportionate Increase
Start with least war-prone dyad	0.003	
Add contiguity	0.015	5.4
Remove alliance	0.066	4.3
Make one or both less advanced	0.300	4.6
Make one or both not democratic	0.963	3.2
Remove overwhelming preponderance	1.767	1.8
Give one or both major power status	3.048	1.7
Add alliance and make both militarized	3.290	1.1
Result: most war-prone dyad	3.290	

petition between advanced economies is a major determinant of war has found little support. However, more research is certainly needed on this factor before any definitive conclusions can be drawn.

Democracy has once again shown itself to be a war-reducing factor, and its effect is readily apparent even after the effects of many other factors have been removed. It would not appear that the bivariate relationship between democracy and war is spurious, as some have contended; on the contrary, democracy is once again shown to be a quite powerful inhibitor of war. More studies are needed to ascertain more precisely what it is about democracy that serves to inhibit war.

The results obtained in these analyses clearly support the position that power preponderance is more conducive to peace in a dyad than the lack thereof. Although its effect is not as strong as others considered here, and certainly weaker than hard-core realists would have us believe, the existence of overwhelming preponderance is, ceteris paribus, a "pacifying condition." It should be noted that these are precisely the dyads where one side should perceive itself to have a high probability of winning any war, based on relative capabilities. According to expected utility theory (Bueno de Mesquita 1981), the decision for war is based on this probability times the utility of victory. If we can assume that the utility of victory is independent of the probability of victory across our 200,000 dyads, then, if this theory is true, we should observe that dyads with large power differences are the more war-prone ones, precisely the opposite of what has been found here. This suggests that some reexamination of a basic premise of expected utility theory may be in order. At the very least, the way in which the probability of victory is typically operationalized should be questioned.

I have long felt that the designation of some states as major powers was an overly subjective classification and somewhat *ad hoc.* With respect to war, there is also the distinct possibility that the well-established propensity for major powers to engage in war is tautological (i.e., states are considered major powers be-

cause they fight many wars). In view of this I would have preferred to find *no* significant association between power status and war after controlling for other factors like power difference. Yet, under this condition, the major power effect remains and is found to be about as influential as power preponderance. This suggests to me that there is another important characteristic, for which the major power designation serves as a proxy, that remains to be identified.

Perhaps the most important contribution of this study is that it provides, for the first time, a direct assessment of the relative importance of more than a few factors that are alleged to promote or inhibit the outbreak of war. In order of declining importance, the conditions that characterize a dangerous, war-prone dyad are:

1. presence of contiguity
2. absence of alliance
3. absence of more advanced economy
4. absence of democratic polity
5. absence of overwhelming preponderance
6. presence of major power.

The first four of these are each over twice as important as each of the last two. If the order of this list were compared to that of the implicit research priorities that have guided war and peace research, the correlation would not be positive. This leads to the rather sobering conclusion that our priorities may be seriously distorted.

Taken together these results give a stronger endorsement to the idealist prescription for peace than to the realist one. Core components of the Wilsonian recipe for a more peaceful world were: establish collective security alliances, spread democracy, promote economic progress, and reduce armament levels. All of these save the last have been found to reduce strongly the likelihood of war at the dyadic level, and even the last factor is not discredited given that nothing in these findings suggests that high levels of military preparedness reduce the likelihood of war. In contrast, some of the primary concerns of realists, that is, relative power and power status in this analysis, have been shown to be less important than the above. Moreover, realists generally dismiss domestic factors as unimportant, yet these results suggest that they have a greater impact on the likelihood of war than others which they consider far more important. Certainly the results reported here do not constitute a head-to-head test of idealism versus realism (perhaps such a test is not possible), but they do suggest that a deeper examination of the idealist position might bring us closer to understanding the conditions that foster peace. We now have neorealism; perhaps it's time to seriously entertain neoidealism.

REFERENCES

BREMER, S. A. 1980. The trials of nations. In *The Correlates of War: II. Testing Some Realpolitik Models*, edited by J. D. Singer. New York: Free Press.

BUENO DE MESQUITA, B. 1981. *The War Trap.* New Haven, CT: Yale University Press.

———. 1982. Where war is likely in the next year or two. *U.S. News and World Report*, May 3.

CHAN, S. 1984. Mirror, mirror on the wall . . . are the freer countries more pacific? *Journal of Conflict Resolution* 28:617–48.

DIEHL, P. F. 1983. Arms races and escalation: A closer look. *Journal of Peace Research* 20:205–12.

———. 1991. Geography and war: A review and assessment of the empirical literature. *International Interactions* 17:11–27.

DOYLE, M. W. 1986. Liberalism and world politics. *American Political Science Review* 80:1151–69.

GARNHAM, D. 1976. Dyadic international war, 1816–1965: The role of power parity and geographical proximity. *Western Political Quarterly* 29:231–42.

GLEDITSCH, N. P., AND J. D. SINGER. 1975. Distance and international war, 1816–1965. In *Proceedings of the International Peace Research Association Fifth General Conference*, edited by M. R. Khan. Oslo: International Peace Research Association.

GOCHMAN, C. S. 1990a. The geography of conflict: Militarized interstate disputes since 1816. Paper presented at the 31st annual meeting of the International Studies Association, Washington, DC, April 10–14.

———. 1990b. Capability-driven disputes. In *Prisoners of War: Nation-States in the Modern Era*, edited by C. S. Gochman and A. N. Sabrosky. Lexington, MA: Lexington Books.

GURR, T. R., K. JAGGERS, AND W. H. MOORE. 1989. Polity II. *DDIR Update* 3(4):1–7.

MUELLER, J. 1989. *Retreat from Doomsday.* New York: Basic Books.

ORGANSKI, A. F. K. 1968. *World Politics.* 2d ed. New York: Knopf.

RAY, J. L. 1990. Friends as foes: International conflict and wars between formal allies. In *Prisoners of War: Nation-States in the Modern Era*, edited by C. S. Gochman and A. N. Sabrosky. Lexington, MA: Lexington Books.

RUSSETT, B. 1990. *Controlling the Sword: The Democratic Governance of National Security.* Cambridge, MA: Harvard University Press.

SMALL, M., AND J. D. SINGER. 1969. Formal alliances, 1816–1965: An extension of the basic data. *Journal of Peace Research* 6:257–82.

———. 1982. *Resort to Arms: International and Civil Wars, 1816–1980.* Beverly Hills, CA: Sage.

SULLIVAN, M. P. 1990. *Power in Contemporary International Politics.* Columbia: University of South Carolina Press.

WALLACE, M. D. 1982. Armaments and escalation: Two competing hypotheses. *International Studies Quarterly* 26: 37–51.

WEEDE, E. 1976. Overwhelming preponderance as a pacifying condition among contiguous Asian dyads, 1950–1969. *Journal of Conflict Resolution* 20:395–412.

33. Capabilities, Allocations, and Success in Militarized Disputes and Wars, 1816–1976

FRANK W. WAYMAN, J. DAVID SINGER, AND GARY GOERTZ

It is often suggested that power is to the study of politics as wealth is to the study of economics, but that whereas wealth is rather easily measured, power remains a more elusive phenomenon. Nowhere is this more apparent than in the study—and practice—of international politics. We have attended to the concept of power for centuries, built our models and predicated our policies upon it, yet we still remain far from an agreed definition, not to mention a valid and reliable way of measuring it.

This suggests the need for further work in several areas. First, it seems that much conceptual clarification remains to be done, despite the work of a number of scholars. Second is the need for a set of more valid, reliable, empirically vindicated indicators of power and the related concepts of capability and influence, building on previous efforts in this direction. Third, and perhaps most important, is the need for research that examines the efficacy

From *International Studies Quarterly* (1983) 27, 497–515. © 1983 International Studies Association. Reprinted by permission of I.S.A. and the authors. Most footnotes and citations suppressed.

Authors' note: We are grateful to the National Science Foundation and the University of Michigan-Dearborn Grants Committee for research support. We would also like to dedicate this study to the memory of Alexander Mark Wayman.

of different forms of power as an instrument of political influence. Work of this latter sort is most crucial, inasmuch as careful evaluation of the role of various indicators in the crucible of political struggle can help establish the validity of alternative indicators, while at the same time contributing to greater conceptual clarity.

In this paper our primary concern is with this third focus. . . . In particular, we examine one aspect of power that all of these researchers agree is intrinsic to an understanding of its role in international politics: the material capabilities available to the state, and the extent to which these can be brought to bear in the exercise of interstate influence. More specifically, our concern here is with the historical efficacy of material capabilities—especially those that are allocated to the military establishment—in achieving success in military confrontations and in all-out war. Whatever else is subsumed under the rubric of power, the ability of a state to have its way in conflict is an element that must be considered. This point may appear commonplace; the necessity of armed forces in the pursuit of success in conflict is so readily assumed that one must look diligently to find, since the rise of the modern interstate system, that rare state that somehow manages to survive without such forces. Be that as it may, our intent here is to measure as validly as possible—though in no way conclusively—the extent to which the states' armed forces and the industrial–demographic base on which they rest do indeed lead to victory in war and to prevailing in disputes at the brink of war. . . .

These considerations lead us, in turn, to formulate what might be called the capability–security hypothesis: that there is a curvilinear relationship between a state's level of security and the level of its military capabilities. In an essentially anarchic international system, in which there are always scarcities, especially the scarcity of security, and in which force or the threat of force is the final arbiter, the *absence* of armed forces can be a dangerous temptation to even a moderately armed neighbor, making some modest level of preparedness a useful deterrent. But at the other end of the preparedness spectrum, there is also a serious danger. Excessively *high levels* of militarization can not only provoke an arms buildup and/or adventurous behavior on the part of potential enemies, but become a temptation to a state's own political elites to embark on their own military adventures. This temptation arises partly out of the domestic consequences of over-preparedness, since it usually increases the influence of the pro-military elements while decreasing that of countervailing elements in the society, and reduces the availability of economic, diplomatic, and cultural resources as alternative instruments, thereby reducing the range of options likely to be considered when the need for interstate influence is indicated. Externally, over-preparedness tends to stimulate the same within rivals and/or neighboring societies, further enhancing the escalatory process on both sides.

It is, of course, one thing to posit such a curvilinear relationship and quite another to put it to the empirical test. To be satisfactory, such a test requires: (a) a sufficiently large spatial–temporal domain and (b) the generation of an appropriate data base, including of course indicators of (c) military capabilities and (d) security. While we think we satisfy three of these requirements here, the fourth, an indicator of national security, is satisfied to

only a limited extent. The concept of national security is so broad and elusive, and the possible range of indicators so varied, that we must settle for indicators that fall short of tapping the entire range of the concept.

We conceptualize national security in the context of the Correlates of War Project's research loci as a relatively low frequency of *involvement* in wars and military disputes, and a relatively high frequency of *success* when such events occur. Here we consider only the latter. A subsequent paper will examine the relationship of capabilities to frequency of involvement in wars and disputes. While we realize that national security is a more complex and multidimensional concept, and that our definition would be too restrictive for many whose scholarly interests are different than ours, we believe that measuring success in war and in militarized disputes over 160 years is not a bad way to begin. It is to these procedural matters we first turn.

EMPIRICAL DOMAIN, DATA, AND INDICATORS

While much of the empirical work in our field suggests otherwise, one can hardly claim to generalize on the basis of a few cases, a brief historical period, or one particular region. Thus, in order to provide a strong basis for generalization we continue in this project's tradition by examining: (a) all interstate wars in the international system from the end of the Napoleonic Wars up through 1976, the last year for which the relevant data base is relatively complete and (b) all militarized disputes in which there was at least one major power on each side, for the same 160-year period. Elsewhere, we have defended the length (and the brevity!) of our temporal domain, and specified the criteria for inclusion in the interstate system and the major power subsystem, along with the fluctuating membership of both since 1816. Here, we need merely reiterate the states that have constituted the major power grouping, and the years up through 1976 during which each qualified for inclusion:

Austria-Hungary (1816–1918); Prussia/ Germany (1816–1918; 1925–1945); Russia/USSR (1816–1917; 1922–); France (1816–1940; 1945–); United Kingdom (1816–); Italy (1860–1943); Japan (1895–1945); United States (1898–); China (1949–).

The Population of Cases

For an investigation of the sort proposed here, we need not examine the data for each state and each year that it was in the larger system, or in the more restricted major power subsystem. Since we are concerned only with the states' success or failure in militarized disputes and in interstate wars, we need consider only the data for those particular states and years. This requires, of course, a specification of disputes and wars and their participants.

With respect to wars, we differentiate among three types (omitting, of course, civil wars): (a) interstate; (b) imperial; and (c) colonial. Our concern here is with the first type only. We define interstate war as sustained military combat between the official armed forces of at least two sovereign members of the interstate system which results in at least 1000 fatalities among the combat personnel. (Detailed criteria, justification, and emerging data describing these 69 interstate wars are found in *Resort to Arms* (Small and Singer, 1982), along with data for the 51 imperial or colonial wars.)

It should be noted that every war is preceded by a militarized dispute, though most such disputes (about 88%) end in stalemate, compromise, or capitulation rather than war. How do we recognize these militarized disputes, and how are they differentiated from less serious, non-militarized disputes? Identifying all qualifying interstate disputes, and the candidate cases from which they emerge, was much more difficult than identifying the qualifying wars; the latter have left many more traces, on both the battlefield and in the archives. We can bury our dead, but we cannot bury our wars. Disputes, on the other hand, often leave no corpses, and governments frequently have good reason to either conceal or distort these confrontational events. However, by systematically combing through such compilations as Langer's (1968) *Encyclopedia of World History* and the Dupuy and Dupuy (1977) *Encyclopaedia of Military History*, plus the diplomatic and military histories of every state for every year that it was a system member, we believe that our N of 967 (of which 101 had a major power on each side) is very close to complete. For an interstate dispute to qualify as 'militarized', one of the protagonists had to have committed one of the following acts: (a) an explicit threat to resort to war; (b) the mobilization of inactive forces; (c) the deployment or redeployment of active forces; or (d) the actual use of force short of war.

In this paper, we examine major-major disputes and all wars. We included only major-major disputes because they are the only ones for which dispute outcomes have been coded to date, because these disputes are usually of greater salience in our field, and because they are the ones that most frequently escalate to war.

Measuring Success in Wars and Disputes

Turning now to our two sets of variables—outcomes and predictor—how do we propose to measure them? While the concepts one thinks of as reflecting national security have seldom been approached in an operational fashion, there are some fairly obvious approaches. Here, we defer the joys of trying to measure security on an interval scale and resort to relatively unambiguous, if not always precise, *nominal* categories. That is, we will classify as successful those states or coalitions that 'won' in each dispute and each war, no matter how pyrrhic the victory. Of course, the state that systematically avoids brink-of-war confrontation as well as wars themselves, while still managing to have its way, would score very high on national security. . . .

In war—at least until World War III—one state or coalition usually emerges victorious in the sense that its forces are sufficiently superior at the close of combat that the other side seeks a cessation of hostilities. The victors may even have suffered greater casualties and loss of more material and/or territory, yet, in the eyes of the participants, contemporary observers, and later historians, one side is the victor and the other the vanquished. Of the 69 interstate wars from 1816 to 1976 studied here, there were only two in which the scholarly consensus ruled the outcome a 'draw', and both of them since World War II: the Korean War of 1950 and the Israeli-Egyptian War of Attrition in 1969–1970, leaving a population of 67 for our concerns.

Measuring success in war, while not without its problems (O'Connor, 1969), is simpler than measuring success in a militarized dispute. But despite the uneven quality of knowledge and the ambiguity of interpretation, even when the facts are accurate and fairly complete, we again find a satisfactory consensus among observers. First of all, if a militarized dispute escalates to war (and nine of our 101 major-major ones do), the outcome of the war determines the outcome of the dispute, with military victory coded as success, and defeat coded as failure. By turning to the case histories, we find sufficient evidence to code all of our dispute outcomes as win, lose, or draw for the initiator (i.e., the party making the first move in the interaction sequence). We do this by first identifying the initiator's objectives and intentions in setting the sequence in motion, as expressed in fairy explicit demands and requests. The coding problem arises, however, when we next try to estimate the extent to which the initiator's demands have been met (within six months of the final act in the dispute sequence). We rely on historians' accounts of the extent to which demands were met by opponents and, following Maoz, we code a win for the initiator if:

(1) the balance of demand-satisfaction clearly favors the initiator . . . [or] (2) the balance of victory in military operations clearly favors the initiator . . . If demands were satisfied despite the failure in military operations, but the date in which the political demands were met followed the military operations, [we] code a 'win'. Similarly, if demands were not met but the following military operations were successful, [we] code 'win' (Maoz, 1982:231).

We code a 'tie' if the balance of demand-satisfaction or balance of victory in military operations is roughly equal, or if 'there are sharp discrepancies between demand-satisfaction and the outcomes of military operations which cannot be resolved' by determining which was the more recent (Maoz, 1982:321). In these terms, nearly half of the cases are classified as a tie or draw. One final problem here is whether to treat only the losses as failure, or to include the 'draw' outcomes as well, producing a lower success score. The latter strategy seems reasonable, inasmuch as a failure to win can hardly be classed as a successful outcome for the initiator. Just to be sure, we code our outcomes both ways.

Measuring Military Capabilities and Allocations

. . . We begin with a six-dimensional indicator of each state's material capabilities for each year it was in the system. We use total population and urban population (*not* percent urban) to tap the demographic dimensions, commercial energy consumption and iron/steel production to tap the industrial dimensions, and military expenditures and active duty armed force levels to tap the military dimensions. Our concern here is with the industrial and military capability dimensions, although we also look briefly at the efficacy of the demographic indicators in a state's ability to prevail in disputes and war. In order to compare the capabilities of opposing states or coalitions, we begin with the basic score for each in the year that the dispute or war began, total that score for all of the major powers, and then calculate the percentage share held by each. . . .

Turning from the measurement of material capabilities we next face the economic policy question of the allocation of national resources to the military sector. We eschew calling these allocations a 'burden', partly to avoid the normative connotation and partly because, for some countries at some periods in their early development, the allocation of resources to military preparedness has been economically advantageous rather than burdensome. What we seek here is an indicator of the fraction of a country's industrial or demographic resources that have been allocated to military preparedness. As suggested in our introduction, many practitioners and observers contend that this, rather than the absolute levels of expenditure, personnel, infrastructure, or hardware, offers a more valid measure of capability inasmuch as it allegedly reflects national will or resolve. Whether that argument is compelling or not, it is clear that allocation ratios *do* tap an important and different aspect of a state's capacity to protect its interests and enhance its security; and as we discuss shortly, there is almost no correlation between allocation and capability scores.

With these considerations in mind, we go on to measure military allocations in three ways. To get at the share of the industrial base allocated in each country each year, we compute the ratio between military expenditures and overall industrial capabilities as reflected in both the energy consumption and iron–steel production figures. Because we have energy figures only since 1870, but need to go back to 1816, we also use the military expenditures to iron–steel ratio alone. As with the absolute estimates, we make our cross-country comparisons by converting both the numerators and denominators into each country's percentage shares. Thus, if a country accounts for 5% of the major power system's energy consumption and 5% of its military expenditures in a given year, its allocation ratio would have a value of 1; if 10% of the major power system's expenditures, the value would be 2. On the demographic side, for our third allocations ratio, we use the same procedures, dividing the active duty armed forces level by the estimated total population of the country that year. . . .

It might also be useful here if we looked at the extent of covariation of our several indicators of capability and of preparedness/allocation ratios, partly to illuminate the general patterns and partly to address the problem of multi-collinearity in our logit analyses (logit being a regression-like procedure for nominal

dependent variables). . . . The results are hardly surprising. Quite prominent is the high association between the two industrial capability indicators and the urban population levels, as well as that between military expenditures and these three factors. Equally relevant, but perhaps less expected, are the moderate to high *negative* correlations between these three indicators of industrialization and the military expenditure/steel and energy ratio. That is, one might have expected that the more economically developed a country was, the *more* it would allocate to preparedness, but what we see here is that the less-developed countries tend to put more of their resources into the military sector. Finally, we note the relative absence of any serious multi-collinearity problems between allocation and capability measures. For example, our most-used allocation indicator (expenditures/iron and steel production—because it goes back to 1816) is not significantly correlated with any of the six material capability scores.

VICTORY AND DEFEAT IN WAR

Having laid out the theoretical considerations guiding this investigation, along with the complexities of our raw and generated data base, we may now turn to our analyses. First, we examine the separate effects of material capabilities and of military allocation ratios on the outcome of interstate *wars* for the two initial protagonists, and then we do the same for all the participants on both sides. In the second half of the analysis, our focus is on the outcome of militarized *disputes*, again distinguishing between the initial disputants and all who eventually participated.

As noted in our introduction, practitioners have traditionally been attentive to the importance of being able to evaluate the capabilities of rivals and allies and thus predict with some confidence the outcome of some contemplated confrontation or war. But if it is true that states rarely go to war, or the brink of war, without a strong belief in their chances of success, as is often claimed, then leaders—by definition—have been wrong just about half the time. A more sophisticated model would recognize that political and military elites often go to, and over, the brink, even when they are dubious or pessimistic about the likelihood of success.

In any event, given the importance of this calculation, there has been no dearth of efforts to measure the war-making capacity of states; of greater interest here, however, are the efforts to ascertain which factors have actually accounted for success or failure in the past. . . .

Turning to our own effort, we selected four of the six components, leaving out urban population and energy consumption because of missing data on these variables for the minor powers. In Table 8.5 we look at the association between the four initiator-to-target capability indicators and the distribution of victory and defeat for the initial protagonists in the interstate wars for whose participants we have all the relevant capabilities data.

Worth noting at the outset is that initiators of war are superior to their targets about twice as often as they are equal or weaker. While this may seem impressive, it reminds us that in well over a third of the cases the initiator is weaker than or approximately equal to the target state. The correlation between strength and victory is measured by the ordinal correlation coefficient, tau-beta. Whenever the absolute value of tau-beta is two (or more) times its standard error, the ordinal association between strength and victory is statistically significant at approximately the 0.05 level (or better). Examining these statistics and the frequencies of victory, we see that industrial strength as reflected in iron and steel output is the most critical of those factors examined, and that armed force size and military expenditure are fairly important elements, followed by total population, which has an effect in the predicted direction but which, unlike the others, is too weak to be statistically significant.

TABLE 8.5 Initiator's Success in Interstate Wars as a Function of *Capabilities vis-à-vis* Target, 1816–1976.*

Capability dimension	Initiator is:	N	Frequency of victory (%)	Tau-beta	S.E.	Approximate significance level
Military personnel	Stronger	28	64			
	Equal	12	42	0.16	0.07	0.05
	Weaker	19	47			
Military expenditure	Stronger	28	57			
	Equal	7	57	0.16	0.07	0.05
	Weaker	14	36			
Steel Stronger		27	74			
	Equal	14	29	0.41	0.06	0.001
	Weaker	14	29			
Total population	Stronger	30	57			
	Equal	6	50	0.06	0.07	not significant
	Weaker	20	50			

*The Ns vary for reasons of missing data; these data are not available for all states involved in wars; the major problems are Latin American countries and Turkey during the 19th century.

In devising criteria for 'stronger', 'same', and 'weaker' there are two main considerations: (1) that 'weaker' or 'stronger' represent significant differences between the two parties and (2) that there should be a large enough N in each cell for the statistical techniques to be valid. The thresholds chosen were a compromise between these two criteria. . . .

The importance of the industrial factor does not mean, of course, that military expenditures and personnel are negligible. Recall that these capabilities were measured in the year the war started and, as World War II demonstrated, the economic base provides the potential for an effective development of military capabilities *during* the fighting. For this reason, the findings reported here, which are related to actual power, are consistent with Alcock and Newcombe (1970), who find that the best predictors of perceived power are economic capability in peacetime and military capability in wartime.

Shifting from basic capabilities to the military allocation indicators for the first participants, major and non-major powers, we turn to Table 8.6.

Here we find the first of our counter-intuitive results. While a heavy allocation of manpower to the armed forces tends to pay off with moderate frequency in military victory, heavy monetary allocations do not. That is, and bearing in mind the relatively small population of cases here, those initiators which allocate more of their economic and industrial resources to military expenditure on the eve of war emerge victorious in only half the cases, whereas the under-allocators win 70% of the time.

Before leaving this discussion, it might be useful to ascertain whether the 'determinants' of victory in war are any different if we com-

pare the capabilities of not only the initial combatants, but those of the entire coalition on each side in wars that expand beyond the dyadic. The patterns are remarkably similar, with superiority in military personnel and total population somewhat more critical, expenditure about the same, and iron-steel production somewhat less critical.

Moreover, the unexpected pattern again is uncovered when we compare the ratios of military spending to the industrial base of the coalitions using iron and steel production as the indicator. When the initiating coalition's expenditure allocation is greater than that of the target, it wins 60% of the time, but when it is 'under-allocating' the success score rises to 78%, with a tau-beta coefficient of –0.17 and an 0.09 standard error. To put it another way, initiators have a better win–lose record than targets, in both the dyadic and multi-party cases, but they fare quite a bit better if they are not 'over-allocating' funds to the military sector on the eve of war.

SUCCESS AND FAILURE IN MILITARIZED DISPUTES

While the difference between success and failure in interstate war may mean the survival or extinction of a state or a regime, war remains a relatively rare event: an average of only six

TABLE 8.6 Initiator's Success in Interstate Wars as a Function of Military *Allocations vis-à-vis* Target, 1816–1976.*

Allocation dimension	Initiator allocates:	N	Frequency of victory (%)	Tau-beta	S.E.	Approximate significance level
Military expenditure to steel	More	8	50			
	Same	3	0	–0.21	0.11	0.05
	Less	10	70			
Military personnel to total population	More	17	65			
	Same	24	50	0.16	0.07	0.05
	Less	14	43			

*The *N*s vary here for reasons given in the note to Table 8.5, and the fact that if a country has no steel production (e.g. 19th-century Latin America) the indicator Military expenditure to steel is undefined, hence missing.

per decade throughout the international system since the Napoleonic era. Militarized disputes, on the other hand, occur with much greater frequency. . . .

Before examining our own findings, let us briefly look at the results of those few prior empirical efforts. In an important pioneering study, Blechman and Kaplan (1978) examined those 12 cases since World War II in which the US mobilized, displayed, or used force short of war *vis-à-vis* the USSR. They found that neither regional nor global military superiority was as critical in prevailing as was demonstrating higher resolve or defending a client state where the *status quo* was threatened. Similarly, using more operational criteria, Maoz (1982) found that demonstrating resolve by initiating most of the escalatory moves was more critical than greater military or material capabilities. . . .

Looking at the results in Table 8.7, note that we not only examine the effects of all six capability dimension ratios but, given the greater frequency with which militarized disputes end up in a draw (as compared to wars), we show that frequency for each of the capability comparisons. Note also (as with the war analyses) that the ratios reflect only the first major power participant on each side if there were more than one on either.

While the associations are not dramatic, the results are quite different from those that turn up in the case of victory in war. Prevailing in these disputes is associated with superiority in the 'industrialization' dimensions only: energy, iron and steel, and urban population. When the initiator enjoyed superiority on these three dimensions, success followed more often than failure. But note the very high number of draws; if we treat these as non-success/failure, the advantage of industrial superiority is appreciably muted. More important, however, is the frequency with which superiority on the other three dimensions leads to *failure*. All else being equal, these figures suggest that superiority in military personnel and expenditure, as well as in total population, is actually a *disadvantage* for the initiating power. And, as noted above, the high

frequency of draws further weakens the case for superior military strength.

As with the war outcomes, we must attend not only to relative capabilities but the extent to which each of the protagonists is allocating personnel and money to military preparedness. As Table 8.8 indicates, we find once again that over-allocation to the military is not at all advantageous, but in the case of disputes the costs of higher allocation are even greater than in wars. The initiator prevails twice as often when it is allocating *less* money to the military than when it is allocating more than its adversary, and even in the case of military personnel per capita, such allocation is almost as disadvantageous.

Once again, recognizing that those states that join in after a war or dispute has begun might change the patterns, we compared the figures for the two sides in disputes when there were multiple protagonists. Here the results are much the same, with superiority on the industrial and demographic dimensions advantageous to the initiator, and military superiority again a net liability. Shifting from these capability ratios to the ways in which the major powers allocate their industrial and demographic resources to preparedness, we again find the now familiar pattern: the greater the military expenditures in terms of the iron–steel and the combined industrial base, the lower the frequency of prevailing, and the same holds true for armed forces per capita.

SUMMARIZING THE RESULTS

Having examined a rather diverse set of bivariate relationships, we find a highly consistent set of results, although they are not sufficiently high in statistical significance to make a conclusive case. In war, it is advantageous to have an overall superiority in industrial and demographic as well as military terms, and it is advantageous to be over-mobilized in terms of armed forces per capita. All of these indicators are associated with victory in interstate war from 1816 to 1976. But those initiators of war who were over-allocating in terms of expendi-

TABLE 8.7 Initiator's Success in Major-Major Disputes as a Function of *Capabilities vis-à-vis* Target, 1816–1976.

Capability dimension	Initiator	N	Frequency of prevailing (%)	Frequency of draws (%)	Tau-beta and S.E.	Approximate significance level
Military personnel	Stronger	34	27	53	−0.09	not
	Equal	39	26	49	(0.06)	significant
	Weaker	26	39	50		
Military expenditure	Stronger	33	21	61	−0.09	not
	Equal	34	27	53	(0.06)	significant
	Weaker	33	39	39		
Industrial energy*	Stronger	35	29	60	+0.16	
	Equal	14	29	50	(0.06)	0.05
	Weaker	36	19	53		
Steel	Stronger	39	39	49	+0.21	0.01
	Equal	25	28	56	(0.06)	
	Weaker	35	20	49		
Urban population	Stronger	35	31	49	+0.08	not
	Equal	40	28	63	(0.06)	significant
	Weaker	24	29	33		
Total population	Stronger	32	28	44	−0.08	not
	Equal	36	33	53	(0.06)	significant
	Weaker	22	32	50		

*There is a decrease of 15 in the *N* in this case because energy consumption data are available only after 1870.

tures *vis-à-vis* the industrial base were defeated in war more often than they were victorious.

In militarized disputes, we again find that industrial and urban capabilities are associated with prevailing, but that whatever value there is in military superiority in war fades away in disputes; the weaker party in terms of both personnel and expenditure is more frequently the successful protagonist. And if we look at allocation ratios, the counter-intuitive pattern is

TABLE 8.8 Initiator's Success in Major-Major Disputes as a Function of Military *Allocations vis-à-vis* Target, 1816–1976.

Allocation dimension	Initiator is:	N	Frequency of prevailing (%)	Frequency of draws (%)	Tau-beta and S.E.	Approximate significance level
Military expenditure to steel	More	40	23	48	−0.24	0.001
	Same	24	17	67	(0.06)	
	Less	35	46	43		
Military expenditure to steel and energy	More	40	18	50	−0.26	0.001
	Same	17	24	65	(0.06)	
	Less	28	36	57		
Military personnel to total population	More	27	30	59	−0.09	not
	Same	33	21	46	(0.06)	significant
	Less	27	44	48		

even more pronounced. Whether for the initial participants or entire coalitions, the side whose resources are more heavily committed to military preparedness prevails less often than the one that is under-allocating. Examining the correlations, one sees that in past wars the initial party won if it was stronger than its opponent in all four scrutinized material capabilities, especially iron and steel production (tau-beta = 0.41 [see Table 8.5]). If the war expanded beyond the two original parties, the initial party fared best by building a coalition that was stronger in military personnel (tau-beta = 0.30), steel production (tau-beta = 0.28), and total population (tau-beta = 0.25). For both the initial parties and coalitions, the winning side was more heavily allocated in military personnel but more lightly allocated in military expenditures.

As for winning disputes, the initial party fared best when stronger in the industrial capabilities (tau-beta = 0.21 and 0.16) and (to a lesser extent) urban population (tau-beta = 0.08 [see Table 8.7]). The other capabilities appear counter-productive, as do heavier military allocations of all three sorts. Whereas in war the winner's profile was different for initial parties than for coalitions, in disputes the profile is basically the same for initial parties and for coalitions.

To further consider the stability of these results, we carried out a set of multivariate logit analyses, with the following results. The factor most associated with success in wars and in disputes is the steel production ratio, and the military expenditure ratio is also associated with victory more often than not. The military personnel ratio, however, is associated with defeat most of the time, as are the allocation indicators, especially that reflecting military expenditure as a fraction of the country's industrial base. The general profile of a successful state thus suggested would be one that, when compared with its rival, has a relatively heavy industrial base, moderately high military expenditures, relatively low military personnel preparedness (both absolute and relative to population), and a relatively low military expenditure allocation. The multivariate results

are generally consistent with the bivariate results, with, however, the exception of the effect of the personnel figures in wars. Do the multivariate results mean that higher levels of military personnel *in the absence of* higher expenditures and industrial base are more likely to draw one into the vortex of a lost war than to give one a basis for victory? The inconsistencies with the bivariate results could be further examined using causal models to judge whether inferences from the bivariate association between personnel and victory in war are spurious, or whether the multivariate results are misleading because of interaction effects, reduced *N* or multi-collinearity. . . .

CONCLUSIONS

While it is recognized rather infrequently, a few scholars have observed that states arm and spend for a number of reasons beyond the obvious. In addition to the pursuit of national security as traditionally defined, we might note some of the other considerations. One of these is that of nation-building, . . . Another, in more established states, is that of economic growth . . . But the general expectation is that any economic disadvantages resulting from high levels of preparedness will be more than counterbalanced by the gains in national security. More specifically, it is usually asserted that, at the very least, the state will be secure from domination by the rival of the moment and, in addition, will be able to prevail if involved in a crisis or confrontation, and emerge victorious if drawn into the crucible of war.

As is already evident, this first systematic data-based investigation hardly confirms such expectations. To the contrary, we find that victory in war depends more upon a country's industrial base than on the extremes to which such resources are allocated to the armed forces. As we noted at the outset, this is not to suggest that total disarmament is thus the preferred strategy, but merely to emphasize that a state can be not only under-armed, but over-armed. And this conclusion is even more powerfully indicated by our analysis of militarized disputes between major powers and coalitions thereof. There we find not only that industrial capabilities are more critical than military preparedness, but that those powers that 'under-allocate' to the military have, over a span of 160 years, enjoyed a significantly higher rate of success in these brink of war confrontations than those that have 'over-allocated'. Despite the tentative nature of these findings, and the absence of a fully formulated theoretical model, we now suspect that Frederick the Great was soon to be wide of the mark when he wrote to the Countess Von Gotha in 1760 that 'God is always with the strongest battalions'.

REFERENCES

ALCOCK, N., AND A. NEWCOMBE (1970) Perception of National Power. *Journal of Conflict Resolution* 14:335–343.

BLECHMAN, B., AND S. KAPLAN (1978) *Force Without War*. Washington DC: Brookings.

MAOZ, Z. (1982) *Paths to Conflict: International Dispute Initiation, 1816–1976*. Boulder: Westview.

O'CONNOR, R. (1969) Victory in Modern War. *Journal of Peace Research* 4:367–385.

Chapter 9
Imperialism

34. The Place of Imperialism in History

V. I. LENIN

We have seen that in its economic essence imperialism is monopoly capitalism. This in itself determines its place in history, for monopoly that grows out of the soil of free competition, and precisely out of free competition, is the transition from the capitalist system to a higher socioeconomic order. We must take special note of the four principal types of monopoly, or principal manifestations of monopoly capitalism, which are characteristic of the epoch we are examining.

Firstly, monopoly arose out of the concentration of production at a very high stage. This refers to the monopolist capitalist associations, cartels, syndicates and trusts. We have seen the important part these play in present-day economic life. At the beginning of the twentieth century, monopolies had acquired complete supremacy in the advanced countries, and although the first steps towards the formation of the cartels were taken by countries enjoying the protection of high tariffs (Germany, America), Great Britain, with her system of free trade, revealed the same basic phenomenon, only a little later, namely, the birth of monopoly out of the concentration of production.

Secondly, monopolies have stimulated the seizure of the most important sources of raw materials, especially for the basic and most highly cartelised industries in capitalist society: the coal and iron industries. The monopoly of the most important sources of raw materials has enormously increased the power of big capital, and has sharpened the antagonism between cartelised and noncartelised industry.

Thirdly, monopoly has sprung from the banks. The banks have developed from modest middleman enterprises into the monopolists of finance capital. Some three to five of the biggest banks in each of the foremost capitalist countries have achieved the "personal link-up" between industrial and bank capital, and have concentrated in their hands the control of thousands upon thousands of millions which form the greater part of the capital and income of entire countries. A financial oligarchy, which throws a close network of dependence relationships over all the economic and political institutions of present-day bourgeois society without exception—such is the most striking manifestation of this monopoly.

Fourthly, monopoly has grown out of colonial policy. To the numerous "old" motives of colonial policy, finance capital has added the struggle for the sources of raw materials, for the export of capital, for spheres of influence, i.e., for spheres for profitable deals, conces-

From *Imperialism: The Highest Stage of Capitalism*, Chapter 10. Published in Volume 22 of the *Collected Works* (Moscow: Progress Publishers, 1964), pp. 298–304. Translated by Yuri Sdobnikov. Footnotes deleted.

sions, monopoly profits and so on, economic territory in general. When the colonies of the European powers, for instance, comprised only one-tenth of the territory of Africa (as was the case in 1876), colonial policy was able to develop by methods other than those of monopoly—by the "free grabbing" of territories, so to speak. But when nine-tenths of Africa had been seized (by 1900), when the whole world had been divided up, there was inevitably ushered in the era of monopoly possession of colonies and, consequently, of particularly intense struggle for the division and the redivision of the world.

The extent to which monopolist capital has intensified all the contradictions of capitalism is generally known. It is sufficient to mention the high cost of living and the tyranny of the cartels. This intensification of contradictions constitutes the most powerful driving force of the transitional period of history, which began from the time of the final victory of world finance capital.

Monopolies, oligarchy, the striving for domination and not for freedom, the exploitation of an increasing number of small or weak nations by a handful of the richest or most powerful nations—all these have given birth to those distinctive characteristics of imperialism which compel us to define it as parasitic or decaying capitalism. More and more prominently there emerges, as one of the tendencies of imperialism, the creation of the "rentier state," the usurer state, in which the bourgeoisie to an ever-increasing degree lives on the proceeds of capital exports and by "clipping coupons." It would be a mistake to believe that this tendency to decay precludes the rapid growth of capitalism. It does not. In the epoch of imperialism, certain branches of industry, certain strata of the bourgeoisie and certain countries betray, to a greater or lesser degree, now one and now another of these tendencies. On the whole, capitalism is growing far more rapidly than before; but this growth is not only becoming more and more uneven in general, its unevenness also manifests itself, in particular, in the decay of the countries which are richest in capital (Britain).

In regard to the rapidity of Germany's economic development, Riesser, the author of the book on the big German banks, states:

The progress of the preceding period (1848–70), which had not been exactly slow, compares with the rapidity with which the whole of Germany's national economy, and with it German banking, progressed during this period (1870–1905) in about the same way as the speed of the mail coach in the good old days compares with the speed of the present-day automobile . . . which is whizzing past so fast that it endangers not only innocent pedestrians in its path, but also the occupants of the car.

In its turn, this finance capital which has grown with such extraordinary rapidity is not unwilling, precisely because it has grown so quickly, to pass on to a more "tranquil" possession of colonies which have to be seized—and not only by peaceful methods—from richer nations. In the United States, economic development in the last decades has been even more rapid than in Germany, *and for this very reason*, the parasitic features of modern American capitalism have stood out with particular prominence. On the other hand, a comparison of, say, the republican American bourgeoisie with the monarchist Japanese or German bourgeoisie shows that the most pronounced political distinction diminishes to an extreme degree in the epoch of imperialism—not because it is unimportant in general, but because in all these cases we are talking about a bourgeoisie which has definite features of parasitism.

The receipt of high monopoly profits by the capitalists in one of the numerous branches of industry, in one of the numerous countries, etc., makes it economically possible for them to bribe certain sections of the workers, and for a time a fairly considerable minority of them, and win them to the side of the bourgeoisie of a given industry or given nation against all the others. The intensification of antagonisms between imperialist nations for the division of the world increases this urge. And so there is created that bond between imperialism and opportunism, which revealed itself first and most clearly in Great Britain, owing to the fact that certain features of imperialist development were observable there much earlier than in other countries. Some writers, L. Martov, for example, are prone to wave aside the connection between imperialism and opportunism in the working-class movement—a particularly glaring fact at the present time—by resorting to "official optimism" (*à la* Kautsky and Huysmans) like the following: the cause of the opponents of capitalism would be hopeless if it were progressive capitalism that led to the increase of opportunism, or if it were the best-paid workers who were inclined towards opportunism, etc. We must have no illusions about "optimism" of this kind. It is optimism in respect of opportunism; it is optimism which serves to conceal opportunism. As a matter of fact the extraordinary rapidity and the particularly revolting character of the development of opportunism is by no means a guarantee that its victory will be durable: the rapid growth of a painful abscess on a healthy body can only cause it to burst more quickly and thus relieve the body of it. The most dangerous of all in this respect are those who do wish to understand that the fight against imperialism is a sham and humbug unless it is inseparably bound up with the fight against opportunism.

From all that has been said . . . on the economic essence of imperialism, it follows that we must define it as capitalism in transition, or, more precisely, as moribund capitalism. It is very instructive in this respect to note that bourgeois economists, in describing modern capitalism, frequently employ catchwords and phrases like "interlocking," "absence of isolation," etc., "in conformity with their functions and course of development," banks are "not purely private business enterprises; they are more and more outgrowing the sphere of purely private business regulation." And this very Riesser, whose words I have just quoted, declares with all seriousness that the "prophecy" of the Marxists concerning "socialization" has "not come true"!

What then does this catchword "interlocking" express? It merely expresses the most striking feature of the process going on before our eyes. It shows that the observer counts the separate trees, but cannot see the wood. It slavishly copies the superficial, the fortuitous, the chaotic. It reveals the observer as one who is overwhelmed by the mass of raw material and is utterly incapable of appreciating its meaning and importance. Ownership of shares, the relations between owners of private property "interlock in a haphazard way." But underlying this interlocking, its very base, are the changing social relations of production. When a big enterprise assumes gigantic proportions, and, on the basis of an exact computation of mass data, organises according to plan the supply of primary raw materials to the extent of two-thirds, or three-fourths, of all that is necessary for tens of millions of people; when the raw materials are transported in a systematic and organised manner to the most suitable places of production, sometimes situated hundreds or thousands of miles from each other; when a single centre directs all the consecutive stages of processing the material right up to the manufacture of numerous varieties of finished articles; when these products are distributed according to a single plan among tens and hundreds of millions of consumers (the marketing of oil in America and Germany by the American oil trust)—then it becomes evident that we have socialisation of production, and not mere "interlocking"; that private economic and private property relations constitute a shell which no longer fits its contents, a shell which must inevitably decay if its removal is artificially delayed, a shell which may remain in a state of decay for a fairly long period (if, at the worst, the cure of the opportunist abscess is protracted), but which will inevitably be removed.

The enthusiastic admirer of German imperialism, Schulze-Gaevernitz, exclaims:

Once the supreme management of the German banks has been entrusted to the hands of a dozen persons, their activity is even today more significant for the public good than that of the majority of the Ministers of State. . . . (The "interlocking" of bankers, ministers, magnates of industry and rentiers is here conveniently forgotten.) If we imagine the development of those tendencies we have noted carried to their logical conclusion we will have: the money capital of the nation united in the banks; the banks themselves combined into cartels; the investment capital of the nation cast in the shape of securities. Then the forecast of that genius Saint-Simon will be fulfilled: "The present anarchy of production, which corresponds to the fact that economic relations are developing without uniform regulation, must make way for organisation in production. Production will no longer be directed by isolated manufacturers, independent of each other and ignorant of man's economic needs; that will be done by a certain public institution. A central committee of management, being able to survey the large field of social economy from a more elevated point of view, will regulate it for the benefit of the whole society, will put the means of production into suitable hands, and above all will take care that there be constant harmony between production and consumption. Institutions already exist which have assumed as part of their functions a certain organisation of economic labour, the banks." We are still a long way from the fulfillment of Saint-Simon's forecast, but we are on the way towards it: Marxism, different from what Marx imagined, but different only in form.

A crushing "refutation" of Marx, indeed, which retreats a step from Marx's precise, scientific analysis to Saint-Simon's guess-work, the guess-work of a genius, but guess-work all the same.

35. A Structural Theory of Imperialism

JOHAN GALTUNG

1. INTRODUCTION

This theory takes as its point of departure two of the most glaring facts about this world: the tremendous inequality, within and between nations, in almost all aspects of human living conditions, including the power to decide over those living conditions; *and* the resistance of this inequality to change. The world consists of Center and Periphery nations; and each nation, in turn, has its centers and periphery. Hence, our concern is with the mechanism underlying this discrepancy, particularly between the center in the Center and the periphery in the Periphery. In other words, how to conceive of, how to explain, and how to counteract inequality as one of the major forms of *structural violence.* Any theory of liberation from structural violence presupposes theoretically and practically adequate ideas of the dominance system against which the liberation is directed; and the special type of dominance system to be discussed here is *imperialism.*

Imperialism will be conceived of as a dominance relation between collectivities, particularly between nations. It is a sophisticated type of dominance relation which cuts across nations, basing itself on a bridgehead which the center in the Center nation establishes in the center of the Periphery nation, for the joint benefit of both. It should not be confused with other ways in which one collectivity can dominate another in the sense of exercising power over it. Thus, a military occupation of B by A may seriously curtail B's freedom of action, but is not for that reason an imperialist relationship unless it is set up in a special way. The same applies to the *threat* of conquest and possible occupation, as in a balance of power relationship. Moreover, *subversive* activities may also be brought to a stage where a nation is dominated by the pin-pricks exercised against it from below, but this is clearly different from imperialism.

Thus, imperialism is a species in a genus of dominance and power relationships. It is a subtype of something, and has itself subtypes to be explored later. Dominance relations between nations and other collectivities will not disappear with the disappearance of imperialism; nor will the end to one type of imperialism (e.g. political, or economic) guarantee the end to another type of imperialism (e.g. economic or cultural). Our view is not reductionist in the traditional sense pursued in marxist-leninist theory, which conceives of imperialism as an economic relationship under private capitalism, motivated by the need for expand-

Reprinted from "A Structural Theory of Imperialism" by Johan Galtung, *Journal of Peace Research* [8]/2 (1971), pp. 81–91, 106–109, by permission of Universitets forlaget, Oslo. Footnotes deleted.

ing markets, and which bases the theory of dominance on a theory of imperialism. According to this view, imperialism and dominance will fall like dominoes when the capitalistic conditions for economic imperialism no longer obtain. According to the view we develop here, imperialism is a more general structural relationship between two collectivities, and has to be understood at a general level in order to be understood and counteracted in its more specific manifestations—just like smallpox is better understood in a context of a theory of epidemic diseases, and these diseases better understood in a context of general pathology.

Briefly stated, imperialism is a system that splits up collectivities and relates some of the parts to each other in relations of *harmony of interest*, and other parts in relations of *disharmony of interest*, or *conflict of interest*.

2. DEFINING "CONFLICT OF INTEREST"

"Conflict of interest" is a special case of conflict in general, defined as a situation where parties are pursuing incompatible goals. In our special case, these goals are stipulated by an outsider as the "true" interests of the parties, disregarding wholly or completely what the parties themselves say explicitly are the values they pursue. One reason for this is the rejection of the dogma of unlimited rationality: actors do *not* necessarily know, or they are unable to express, what their interest is. Another, more important, reason is that rationality is unevenly distributed, that some may dominate the minds of others, and that this may lead to "false consciousness." Thus, learning to suppress one's own true interests may be a major part of socialization in general and education in particular.

Let us refer to this true interest as LC, *living condition*. It may perhaps be measured by using such indicators as income, standard of living in the usual materialistic sense—but notions of *quality of life* would certainly also enter, not to mention notions of *autonomy*. But the precise content of LC is less important for our purpose than the definition of conflict of interest:

There is *conflict*, or *disharmony of interest*, if the two parties are coupled together in such a way that the LC *gap* between them is *increasing*;

There is *no conflict*, or *harmony of interest*, if the two parties are coupled together in such a way that the LC *gap* between them is *decreasing down to zero*. . . .

. . . There is the problem of what to do with the case of a *constant gap*. The parties grow together, at the same rate, but the gap between them is constant. Is that harmony or disharmony of interest? We would refer to it as disharmony, for the parties are coupled such that they will not be brought together. Even if they *grow* parallel to each other it is impossible to put it down as a case of harmony, when the distribution of value is so unequal. On the contrary, this is the case of disharmony that has reached a state of equilibrium . . .

And then, in conclusion: it is clear that the concept of interest used here is based on an ideology, or a *value premise of equality*. An interaction relation and interaction structure set up such that inequality is the result is seen as a coupling not in the interest of the weaker party. This is a value premise like so many other value premises in social science explorations, such as "direct violence is bad," "economic growth is good," "conflict should be resolved," etc. As in all other types of social science, the goal should not be an "objective" social science freed from all such value premises, but a more honest social science where the value premises are made explicit.

3. DEFINING "IMPERIALISM"

We shall now define imperialism by using the building blocks presented in the preceding two sections. In our two-nation world, imperialism can be defined as one way in which the Center nation has power over the Periphery nation, so as to bring about a condition of disharmony of interest between them. Concretely, *Imperialism* is a relation between a Center and a Periphery nation so that

(1) there is *harmony of interest* between the *center in the Center* nation and the *center in the Periphery* nation,

(2) There is more *disharmony of interest* within the Periphery nation than within the Center nations,

(3) there is *disharmony of interest* between the *periphery in the Center* nation and the *periphery in the Periphery* nation.

. . . This complex definition, borrowing largely from Lenin, needs spelling out. The basic idea is, as mentioned, that the center in the Center nation has a bridgehead in the Periphery nation, and a well-chosen one: the center in the Periphery nation. This is established such that the Periphery center is tied to the Center center with the best possible tie: the tie of harmony of interest. They are linked so that they go up together and down, even under, together. How this is done in concrete terms will be explored in the subsequent sections. . . .

In the Periphery nation, the center grows more than the periphery, due partly to how interaction between center and periphery is organized. Without necessarily thinking of economic interaction, the center is more enriched than the periphery—in ways to be explored below. However, for part of this enrichment, the center in the Periphery only serves as a transmission belt (e.g., as commercial firms, trading companies) for value (e.g., raw materials) forwarded to the Center nation. This value enters the Center in the center, with some of it drizzling down to the periphery in the Center. Importantly, there is less disharmony of interest in the Center than in the Periphery, so that *the total arrangement is largely in the interest of the periphery in the Center*. Within the Center the two parties may be opposed to each other. But in the total game, the periphery see themselves more as the partners of the center in the Center than as the partners of the periphery in the Periphery—and this is the essential trick of that game. Alliance-formation between the two peripheries is avoided,

while the Center nation becomes more and the Periphery nation less cohesive—and hence less able to develop long-term strategies.

Actually, concerning the three criteria in the definition of imperialism as given above, it is clear that no. (3) is implied by nos. (1) and (2). The two centers are tied together and the Center periphery is tied to its center: that is the whole essence of the situation. If we now presuppose that the center in the Periphery is a smaller proportion of that nation than the center in the Center, we can also draw one more implication: *there is disharmony of interest between the Center nation as a whole and the Periphery nation as a whole*. But that type of finding, frequently referred to, is highly misleading because it blurs the harmony of interest between the two centers, and leads to the belief that imperialism is merely an international relationship, *not a combination of intra- and international relations*. . . .

4. THE MECHANISMS OF IMPERIALISM

The two basic mechanisms of imperialism both concern the *relation* between the parties concerned, particularly between the nations. The first mechanism concerns the *interaction relation* itself, the second how these relations are put together in a larger interaction structure:

(1) the principle of *vertical interaction relation*

(2) the principle of *feudal interaction structure*. . . .

To study whether the interaction is symmetric or asymmetric, on equal or unequal terms, *two* factors arising from the interaction have to be examined:

(1) *the value-exchange between the actors—inter-actor effects*

(2) *the effects inside the actors—intra-actor effects* . . .

It is certainly meaningful and important to talk in terms of unequal exchange or asymmetric interaction, but not quite unproblematic what its precise meaning should be. For that reason, it may be helpful to think in terms of three stages or types of exploitation, partly reflecting historical *processes* in chronological order, and partly reflecting types of *thinking* about exploitation.

In the first stage of exploitation, A simply engages in looting and takes away the raw materials without offering anything in return. If he steals out of pure nature there is no human interaction involved, but we assume that he forces "natives" to work for him and do the extraction work. It is like the slave-owner who lives on the work produced by slaves—which is quantatively not too different from the land-owner who has land-workers working for him five out of seven days a week.

In the second stage, A starts offering something "in return." Oil, pitch, land, etc. is "bought" for a couple of beads—it is no longer simply taken away without asking any questions about ownership. The price paid is ridiculous. However, as power relations in the international systems change, perhaps mainly by bringing the power level of the weaker party up from zero to some low positive value, A had to contribute more: for instance, pay more for the oil. The question is now whether there is a cut-off point after which the exchange becomes equal, and what the criterion for that cut-off point would be. Absence of subjective dissatisfaction—B says that he is now content? Objective market values or the number of man-hours that have gone into the production on either side?

There are difficulties with all these conceptions. But instead of elaborating on this, we shall rather direct our attention to the shared failure of all these attempts to look at *intra-actor* effects. Does the interaction have enriching or impoverishing effects *inside* the actor, or does it just lead to a stand-still? This type of question leads us to the third stage of exploitation, where there may be some balance in the flow between the actors, but great differences in the effect the interaction has within them. . . .

If the first mechanism, the *vertical interaction relation*, is the major factor behind inequality, then the second mechanism, the *feudal interaction structure*, is the factor that maintains and reinforces this inequality by protecting it. There are four rules defining this particular interaction structure:

1. interaction between Center and Periphery is *vertical*
2. interaction between Periphery and Periphery is *missing*
3. multilateral interaction involving all three is *missing*
4. interaction with the outside world is *monopolized* by the Center, with two implications:
   a. Periphery interaction with Center nations is *missing*
   b. Center as well as Periphery interaction with Periphery nations belonging to other Center nations is *missing* . . .

Some important *economic* consequences of this structure should be spelled out.

First and most obvious: the *concentration on trade partners*. A Periphery nation should, as a result of these two mechanisms, have most of its trade with "its" Center nation. In other words, empirically we would expect high levels of *import concentrations* as well as *export concentration* in the Periphery, as opposed to the Center, which is more free to extend its trade relations in almost any direction—except in the pure case, with the Periphery of other Center nations.

Second, and not so obvious, is the *commodity concentration*: the tendency for Periphery nations to have only one or very few primary products to export. This would be a trivial matter if it could be explained entirely in terms of geography, if, e.g., oil countries were systematically poor as to ore, ore countries poor as to bananas and coffee, etc. But this can hardly be assumed to be the general case: Nature does not distribute its riches that way. There is a historical rather than a geographical explanation to this. A territory may have been exploited for the raw materials most easily available and/or most needed in the Center, and this, in turn, leads to a certain social structure, to communication lines to the deposits, to trade structures, to the emergence of certain center groups, (often based on ownership of that particular raw material), and so on. To start exploiting a new kind of raw material in the same territory might upset carefully designed local balances; hence, it might be easier to have a fresh start for that new raw material in virgin territory with no bridgehead already prepared for imperialist exploits. In order to substantiate this hypothesis we would have to demonstrate that there are particularly underutilized and systematically underexplored deposits precisely in countries where one type of raw material has already been exploited.

The combined effect of these two consequences is a *dependency* of the Periphery on the Center. Since the Periphery usually has a much smaller GNP, the trade between them is a much higher percentage of the GNP for the Periphery, and with both partner and commodity concentration, the Periphery becomes particularly vulnerable to fluctuations in demands and prices. At the same time the center in the Periphery depends on the Center for its supply of consumer goods. Import substitution industries will usually lead to consumer goods that look homespun and unchic, particularly if there is planned obsolescence in the production of these goods in the Center, plus a demand for equality between the two centers maintained by demonstration effects and frequent visits to the Center.

However, the most important consequence is political and has to do with the systematic utilization of feudal interaction structures as a way of protecting the Center against the Periphery. The feudal interaction structure is in social science language nothing but an expression of the old political maxim *divide et impera*, divide and rule, as a strategy used systematically by the Center relative to the Periphery nations. How could—for example—a small foggy island in the North Sea rule over one quarter of the world? By isolating the Periphery parts from each other, by having them geographically at sufficient distance from each other to impede any real alliance formation, by having separate deals with them so as to tie them to the Center in particularistic ways, by reducing multilateralism to a minimum with all kinds of graded membership, *and* by having the Mother country assume the role of window to the world.

However, this point can be much more clearly seen if we combine the two mechanisms and extend what has been said so far for relations between Center and Periphery *nations* to relations between center and periphery *groups* within nations. Under an imperialist structure the two mechanisms are used not only between nations but also within nations, but less so in the Center nation than in the Periphery nation. In other words, there is vertical division of labor within as well as between nations. And these two levels of organization are intimately linked to each other (as A. G. Frank always has emphasized) in the sense that the center in the Periphery interaction structure is also that group with which the Center nation has its harmony of interest, the group used as a bridgehead.

Thus, the combined operation of the two mechanisms at the two levels builds into the structure a subtle grid of protection measures against the major potential source of 'trouble', the periphery in the Periphery. To summarize the major items in this grid:

1. the general impoverishment of pP brought about by vertical division of labor within the Periphery nation, and particularly by the high level of inequality (e.g., differential access to means of communication) and disharmony of interest in the Periphery nation;
2. the way in which interaction, mobilization, and organization of pP are impeded by the feudal structure *within* Periphery nations;
3. the general impoverishment of the Periphery nation brought about by vertical division of labor, particularly in terms of means of destruction and communication;
4. the way in which interaction, mobilization, and organization of the Periphery nations are impeded by the feudal interaction structure *between* nations
   a. making it difficult to interact with other Periphery nations "belonging" to the same Center nations,
   b. making it even more difficult to interact with Periphery nations "belonging" to other Center nations:

5. the way it which it is a fortiori difficult for the peripheries in Periphery nations to interact, mobilize, and organize

   a. intra-nationally because of (1) and (2),

   b. inter-nationally because of (3) and (4),

   c. in addition, because the center in the Periphery has the monopoly on international interaction in all directions and cannot be counted on to interact in the interest of its own periphery;

6. the way in which pP cannot appeal to pC or cC either because of the disharmony of interest.

Obviously, the more perfectly the mechanisms of imperialism within and between nations are put to work, the less overt machinery of oppression is needed and the smaller can the center groups be, relative to the total population involved. *Only imperfect, amateurish imperialism needs weapons; professional imperialism is based on structural rather than direct violence. . . .*

10. CONCLUSION: SOME STRATEGIC IMPLICATIONS

From a general scheme, we cannot arrive at more than general policy implications that can serve as guide-lines, as strategies. More concreteness is needed to arrive at the first tactical steps. But theory developed in peace research should lead to such guide-lines; if it merely reflects what is empirical, not what is potential, then it is not good theory.

Our point of departure is once more that the world is divided into have's and have-not's, in have and have-not nations. To decrease the gap, one aspect of the fight against structural violence, redistribution by taking from the have's and giving to the have-not's, is not enough: the structure has to be changed. The imperialist structure has inter-national as well as intra-national aspects and will consequently have to be changed at both levels.

However, let us start with the international changes needed, for a point of departure. Following closely the analysis of the mechanisms of imperialism in order to establish anti-mechanisms, we get Table 9.1.

Again, at this general level it is impossible to indicate the first steps that would lead from vertical, feudal interaction towards horizontalization and defeudalization. These are guidelines only. And their implementation should certainly not be seen as a sufficient condition for the process of genuine development to start in the Periphery, with the possible result that the gap between Center and Periphery may be decreasing again, but as a necessary condition. Very many of the findings in "liberal" development theory may become valid precisely when today's periphery nations become autonomous through structural change. Hence, the basic formulas of horizontalization and defeudalization are necessary conditions, not panaceas.

But another question that certainly has to be asked is what this presupposes in terms of intranational strategies. In one sense the answer is simple: Table 9.1 also applies to the relation between center and periphery within a nation, not only between nations. As such it gives four general guide-lines for a revolutionary process that would abolish the exploitation of the periphery by the Center.

But this is too abstract, so let us return to the question in more concrete terms. The major difficulty with the international strategies in Table 9.1 is obviously that these would not be in the interest of the center in the Periphery. Nothing in these strategies would guarantee them the living conditions they already enjoy, very often on par with (or even above) the living conditions of the center in the Center. They would have all reasons to resist such changes. In fact, from a purely human point of view this group is perhaps the most exposed group in the whole international system, on the one hand the pawn and instrument of the center in the Center and on the other hand the exploiters of the periphery in the Periphery. In such a cross-pressure it seems reasonable to expect that the group will sooner or later have to choose sides. Either it will have to relocate and join the center in the Center, or it will have to stand in solidarity with the periphery in the Periphery.

TABLE 9.1 Strategies for Structural Change of the International Dominance System

I. HORIZONTALIZATION

1. Horizontalization Center-Periphery

a. *exchange on more equal terms,* either by reducing the division of labor or by more horizontal division of labor that would equalize spin-off effects. Concretely this would mean that Center nations would have to start importing processed products from Periphery nations, and engage in intra- rather than inter-sector trade, and even intra- rather than inter-commodity trade.

b. *reduction of vertical interaction,* down to total decoupling in case exchange on more equal terms is unacceptable or does not work.

c. *self-reliance,* partly in order to develop import substitutes, and partly in order for Periphery nations to define themselves what products they need rather than adapting the preference scales developed in the Center.

II. DEFEUDALIZATION

2. Defeudalization Center-Periphery

a. *exchange on equal terms,* intra- rather than inter-sector, but obviously at a lower level where degree of processing is concerned than under 1.a. above. It may imply exchanges of raw materials, or exchanges of semi-processed goods. Obviously, which Periphery country should interact horizontally with which other Periphery countries would depend on the nature of the economic exchange and the concrete geo-political situation.

b. *development of viable organization of Periphery countries for international class conflict.* Such organizations seem to depend for their viability not only on commitment to an ideology (rejection of past and present as well as visions for the future), but also seem to function better if they are built around an exchange relation of the type indicated in 2.a. The exact purpose of the organization would be to force Center nations to change their policies in the direction of 1.a., and also to command a better redistribution of capital and technology from the Center. This would also be the organization that could organize a strike on the delivery of raw materials in case Center nations do not conform with these types of structural changes, as an analogy to the denial of human manpower typical of the intranational strikes.

3. Multilateralization Center-Periphery

a. *multinational, symmetric organization should be established wherever possible,* the system of international organizations should be taken out of phase 3 and moved towards phase 4. These organizations would serve as concrete instruments for horizontal rela-

tionships between Center and Periphery, and between Periphery and Periphery.

b. *destruction of multi-national asymmetric organization* if they do not change in the direction of 3.a. above by withdrawl of Periphery participation.

c. *self-reliance with the Periphery itself building multi-national symmetric organizations,* retaining some contact with the Center for conflict articulation. This pattern might also apply to the UN and the UN Agencies unless they pursue policies of the types indicated above.

d. *establishment of global or trans-national organizations* that could serve to globalize the world's means of communication and means of production in order to establish a universally accessible communication network and a production system that would give top priority to the needs of the periphery of the Periphery.

4. Extra-bloc activity

a. *Periphery-Center contacts extended to other Centers,* but in accordance with the program indicated in 1.a. and 1.b. above.

b. *Periphery-Periphery contacts extended to other Periphery countries,* but in accordance with points 2 and 3 above. For the latter the Algiers Group of 77 would be an important, although weak model, and the conferences of non-aligned states another. At the first conference in Beograd in 1961 there were 25 participants, at the second in 1964 in Cairo 47 participants, and at the 1970 Lusaka conference there were 54 participants (the number of observers was, 3, 10, and 12 respectively).

We can now, building on the *criteria* of imperialism, formulate a new set of strategies that would have more immediate domestic implications and support the international strategies of Table 9.1, as shown in Table 9.2.

At this point we choose to stop. These strategies . . . are only presented here in brief outline in order to indicate what to us seems to be a crucial criterion against which any theory should be tested: is it indicative of a

---

TABLE 9.2   Strategies for Structural Change of the Intra-national Dominance System

I. REDUCED HARMONY BETWEEN THE CENTERS

1. Reduction to neutral or no relationship

This type of situation arises often when there is a crisis in the center of the Center, for instance due to internal war in the Center or external war between two or more Center nations. In this situation the Periphery attains some kind of autonomy because the Center can no longer exercise minute control—as seems to be the case for many countries in Latin America during the Second World War.

2. Change to negative relationship between the centers

In the general theory it has been postulated that there is "harmony" between the two centers, but social relations being complex such a harmony is hardly ever complete. There may be some privileges that cC reserve for themselves (such as taxation *without* representation) or some privileges that cP reserve for themselves (such as the right to maintain slavery or racist society). In general tensions may arise precisely because the model of complete harmony and similarity is not realized. The result may be a *nationalist* fight for liberation. . . .

II. REDUCED DISHARMONY IN THE PERIPHERY

3. Violent revolution in the Periphery

According to this formula the internal disharmony of interest is eliminated by eliminating cP as a class, by using means of force. This can be done partly by killing them, partly by means of imprisonment, and partly by giving them the chance to relocate, for instance by using their ties with cC so as to settle where they really belong—in the Center. A new regime is then introduced which perhaps may have its center, but certainly not a center that is tied with relations of harmony to the old cC.

4. Non-violent revolutions in the Periphery

In this approach cP are not eliminated as persons, but as a part of the Periphery structure be-

cause the rest of the Periphery nation refuses to interact with them. They become non-functional socially rather than eliminated in a physical sense. To give them new tasks in a new society becomes an important part of the non-violent revolution.

5. Cooperation between the peripheries in the Periphery

Since international relations are so dominated by the centers in the Periphery, more of international relations has to be carried out by the peoples themselves in patterns of non-governmental foreign policy. The Havana-based *Tricontinental* (OSPAAAL) is an important example.

III. CHANGES IN THE CENTER

6. Increased disharmony in the Center

In this case pC may no longer side with cC as it should according to nationalist ideology in the Center, but find that the Periphery nation in general and pP in particular is the natural ally. It is difficult to see how this can have consequences that could be beneficial to the Periphery unless the two countries are contiguous, or unless this might be a factor behind the types of development outlined in I,1 and I,2 above.

7. Changes in the goals of the Center

. . . The Center might itself choose to stop imperialist policies, not because it is forced to do so from below . . . , but out of its own decision. Thus, cC might see that this is a *wrong* policy to pursue, e.g., because of the exploitation it leads to, because of the dangers for world peace, because of relations to other nations, etc. . . . But in general we would believe more in Periphery-generated strategies than in Center-generated ones, since the latter may easily lead to a new form of dependence on the Center.

practice, does it indicate who the actors behind that practice could be? A theory should not only be evaluated according to its potential as a reservoir of hypothesis implications to be tested against present reality (data), but as much—or perhaps more—as a reservoir of policy implications to be tested against potential reality (goals, values). What we have tried to do here is an effort in both directions.

36. From *Nations in Conflict*

NAZLI CHOUCRI AND ROBERT C. NORTH

The purpose of this chapter is to present the conceptual framework within which we have analyzed the policies and actions contributing to war. In general there seem to be at least three major processes that generate conflict and warfare among nations: domestic growth and the external expansion of interests; competition for resources, markets, superiority in arms, and strategic advantage; and the dynamics of crisis.

One of our problems has been to avoid essentially linear causal assumptions—we are interested in dynamic relationships, in which feedback mechanisms are continuously in play. We believe that among great powers the fundamental processes, even allowing for variations in detail, mode, and style of behavior, are universal enough not to be affected themselves by modes, styles, or most events.

By themselves, some of the propositions put forward in this chapter may seem self-evident; it is only when they are considered together that the implications for international conflict and war become fully apparent. We do not believe that war is in any sense inevitable, but our findings do suggest that the tap roots of large-scale violence reach far down into the basic structure of societies and are shaped by human population, technology, and access to resources.

Because individuals are the ultimate source of all increases in population, all advances in knowledge and skills, all social, political, and economic change, and therefore of the behavior of nations, the individual is our basic unit of analysis. All the variables in this study are aggregations of what individual humans have done. (Nevertheless, individuals and the society of which they are a part are intensely interactive. What the individual does or does not do affects the conditions and dispositions of the state, and the conditions and dispositions of the state affect the attitudes and behavior of individuals.)

Man is critically dependent on his physical environment. As biological organisms, humans have certain basic needs, namely, air, food, water, and territory. *In a growing population there will be an increasing demand for basic resources.* In addition to plants and animals required for food, human beings acquire other, harder-to-get resources; the technology of this acquisition brings about both environmental and social changes. A society that can produce electronic computers is likely to be organized quite differently than a society in which steam engines represent the highest level of technology, and even more differently

From *Nations in Conflict* by Nazli Choucri and Robert C. North (San Francisco: W. H. Freeman, 1975), pp. 14–25. Copyright © 1975 by W. H. Freeman and Company. All rights reserved. Reprinted by permission of the publisher and the authors. Footnotes deleted.

than societies with only crude hand tools. Advances in technology tend not only to increase the range and amount of resources available to a society, but to influence individual and social behavior as well.

Advances in technology often lead to a greater concentration of population. Moreover, historically, the denser the population and the higher the level of technology, the greater is the division and institutionalization of labor. Bureaucratization seems to develop with increases in both the levels and density of population and the advancement of technology.

The more advanced the level of technology in a society, the greater will be the kinds and quantity of resources needed by society to sustain that technology and advance it further. At the same time, demands are likely to increase as technology alters a society's perception of its "needs." Each new level of technology influences manufacturing, transportation, and communication, creating social change and thus new economic and political institutions. Advances in technology, when combined with increases in population, often contribute to the dilemma of rising demands and insufficient domestic resources.

A society (especially one with a growing population) with insufficient resources within its own territory will be seriously constrained in its activities unless it finds some way of acquiring the resources it demands. Whether and how a society reaches for resources beyond its sovereignty is conditioned by location, level of population, level of technology, and the resources, technology, needs, power, and friendliness of neighboring states.

Overall, the entire history of man has been characterized by growth—that is, by larger populations, more advanced technologies, the ability to employ larger amounts of energy for human purposes, and the tendency to demand larger amounts of a wider range of resources and finished products—all requiring more complex modes of governance.

One function of governments is to articulate priorities and to establish these by influencing the allocation of technology, resources, and labor and thus shape national capabilities.

Examples of capabilities are agriculture, the skills and implements of trade, the techniques and capital for sophisticated finance, light industry, heavy industry, specific enterprises such as the manufacture of chemicals or textiles, and naval and military establishments. Governments directly influence these allocations through the spending of public monies and through tax policy, and indirectly through, for example, wage and price controls, rationing of commodities, and restrictions on imports and exports.

Ordinarily, natural resources, capital labor, and technology are limited, so that choices have to be made with respect to the development of national capabilities. These choices reveal the actual or operational, in contrast to the professed, values of a society. Often, the choices become institutionalized and difficult to alter in any significant way. Moreover, they are reinforced insofar as existing capabilities determine what other capabilities can be developed to meet growing demands.

When demands are unmet and existing capabilities are insufficient to satisfy them, new capabilities may have to be developed. But a society can develop particular capabilities (including resources) *only if it has the necessary existing capabilities to do so.* Moreover, if national capabilities cannot be attained at a reasonable cost within national boundaries, they may be sought beyond. Any activity—selling wheat, buying oil, investing capital, increasing the labor force, or moving troops—takes on new meaning once it is extended into foreign territory. We use the term "lateral pressure" to refer to the process of foreign expansion of any activity.

There are three aspects of this process that must be distinguished: (1) the *disposition* to extend activities beyond national boundaries; (2) the particular *activities* that result from the disposition to act; and (3) the *impact* that these activities have on the people of another country and their environment. When we discuss lateral pressure in this study we shall be explicitly concerned with the *measurable activities* of this process—although the other two aspects should be kept in mind.

Lateral pressure can be manifested in many different types of activities, depending on the nature of the demands that are not being satisfied domestically and on the capabilities that are available. Lateral pressure is not likely to be expressed unless both demands and capabilities are above some threshold. A society may demand particular commodities that are unavailable domestically, but be wholly lacking in the capabilities—the capital, the credit, the commercial institutions, the shipping facilities, and so-forth—required to obtain those commodities. In such a case the demand for those commodities will not generate lateral pressure. On the other hand, a society may demand certain commodities (cotton and rubber, for example) that are unavailable domestically *and* have the capabilities for acquiring them. In this case the combination of demand and capabilities will create the *predisposition* to reach beyond national boundaries to satisfy demands. Now there are two major possibilities. The predisposition may be acted on—the desired resources are acquired—or the country may be prevented from doing so by another state. Thus, if a country demanding resources also lacks the naval or military capabilities necessary to overcome resistance by another country, the *predisposition* for lateral pressure will not be acted on.

Virtually any mode in which lateral pressure is expressed—commercial activities, dispatch of troops into foreign territory, establishment of naval or military bases, acquisition of colonial territory, even missionary activities—may contribute to international conflict and violence. Obviously, however, some activities are more likely than others to lead to violence. Moreover, international differences in the extent and intensity of lateral pressure contribute substantially to international conflict.

Conceivably, a country generating many demands and possessing capabilities appropriate for pursuing activities abroad may "turn inward." It may not require any great amount of resources from beyond its borders; it may use techniques to uncover hitherto inaccessible resources or find new uses for its resources; it may locate sufficient capital investment fields at home; it may not require foreign markets for its goods; or it may exchange international competition for power, prestige, and status. It would be difficult, however, to identify modern, industrialized countries that do not manifest strong, extensive lateral pressure in some form.

Lateral pressure may be expressed in many types of activities other than those associated with the search for raw materials, markets, or living space. During the great period of world exploration in the sixteenth century, some Europeans were as interested in finding Christians as spices; others wanted military or naval bases, or simply adventure. Nevertheless, Christianization was ordinarily undertaken by societies that were equally interested in spices (or some other product) and, more importantly, were able to build ships and mount large expeditions. Today, as well as during the nineteenth century, business has often "gone abroad" for cheaper labor and resources, new markets and fresh opportunities for investment. As in the sixteenth century, today's foreign commerce may also be connected with a desire for national security, status, prestige, or military advantage. Lateral pressure can therefore be the outcome of both public (or national) and private aims.

For some supporters of colonial policies in nineteenth-century Europe the "policy of colonial expansion was undoubtedly good business." For others, a strong colonial policy was a patriotic ideal, the "pride of standing in the front rank of the nations which were shaping the world of the future, the delight in ruling and the excitement of competing with foreign rivals. . . ." In either case, a policy of growth and expansion was difficult to reverse, once undertaken. National growth can generate a strong demand for greater growth and thus create ever higher demand for resources. Surpluses for such resources as labor and capital generate demands for further research and development, exploration, investment and other enterprise and growth.

The disposition toward foreign activities is not always sound economically. A nation's foreign policy may encourage foreign activities solely for national prestige. Foreign activities may be profitable only so long as the government, often at a huge cost to the taxpayer, protects trade routes and maintains a secure environment for overseas enterprises.

An industrialized country with strong military capabilities may extend its activities into (and even establish domination over) a country with a much larger population that generates comparatively higher demands, but which has a less advanced technology and lower level of industrialization. For example, although the population of India was larger than that of Britain, England enjoyed a considerable advantage over India by virtue of a difference in technological efficiency.

After the Renaissance a relatively few European countries (and, more recently, the United States and Japan) were able to extend their interests throughout the world. This expansion of interests was so widespread and long-lasting that it became institutionalized through colonies, protectorates, lease-holds, unequal alliances, client-state arrangements, and exploitative trade. Many white men thus inferred that they were innately superior, and were preordained to preside over and exploit societies with lower capability.

Although lateral pressure encompasses some of the propositions about imperialism put forward by J. A. Hobson, V. I. Lenin, and others, the two concepts are not synonymous. The demands of a capitalist economy may contribute to lateral pressure in important ways, but capitalism is not a necessary condition for lateral pressure; both pre-capitalist and socialist societies may generate lateral pressure. Similarly, although class conflict may contribute to lateral pressure, it is not a necessary condition.

As a nation or empire extends its activities, and hence its interests, the feeling may develop among the leaders of such a state or the citizenry or both, that these "national interests" ought to be protected. National interests tend to be intensely subjective among those who define and proclaim them, so that it is often extremely difficult to predict which interests are likely to be defended by arms. The critical factor in deter-

mining the importance to a nation of an interest is not the kind of interest, but the existence of the feeling that the interest must be defended (and then the intensity of this feeling, measured by the social costs that a nation is willing to incur in the defense of this interest).

The protection of national interests in far off places may lead to war between colonial powers and their subject populations, or to attempts at attracting, equipping, and financing local power elites benefiting from foreign control. During the late nineteenth and early twentieth centuries, Britain, France, and Germany engaged in such activities throughout much of Africa and Asia. For example, the Afghan Wars were to a large extent a manifestation of British and Russian expansionism in Central Asia. The history of French control in Indochina and British domination in Burma and Siam offer other examples.

Large differences in capabilities between countries mean grossly unequal political and economic relations between them. In most cases of intensive interaction between societies, the nation with vastly greater capabilities tends to dominate the other, even when domination is not a deliberate policy. Such relations invite the domination and exploitation of the weaker country by the stronger. Differences in capabilities between major powers are likely to have a different meaning. *When two or more major powers extend their respective interests outward, there is a strong probability that these interests will be opposing, and the activities of these nations may collide.* These activities may be diplomatic, commercial, military, or so forth, and thus involve quite different levels of intensity. Depending upon the intensity, such conflicts of interests and activities may contribute to the outbreak of war between strong countries, or between their client states, or both. The Fashoda Incident, the Moroccan Crisis, and the Bosnian Crisis of 1908–1909 are examples of military confrontations resulting from conflicts of interest between major powers before WWI.

Collisions can lead to the withdrawal of one (or both) of the parties, an agreement between them, or continuing conflict. In general the stronger the lateral pressure manifested by rival countries, the greater is the likelihood of the intensification of competition of conflict over territory, resources, markets, political or diplomatic influence, military or naval power, status, or prestige. Such behavior tends to be characteristic of the international relations of powerful states and empires.

The more intense the competition becomes, the greater is the likelihood that it will lead to arms competition, crisis, or possibly armed conflict. Major wars often emerge from a two-fold process: internally generated pressures, and mutual comparison, competition, rivalry, and conflict on a number of salient dimensions. Each of these processes is closely related to the other, and each can be accounted for to a remarkable degree by the interaction among three variables: population, technology, and access to resources.

Thus, international competition and conflict are closely linked to domestic growth, with the result that a country's domestic and foreign activities are likely to be intensely interdependent. Just as domestic growth may contribute to a country's foreign activities, so its foreign activities, in conflict with those of other countries, may generate further domestic demands and growth.

Although any activity by one country in or near the boundary of another country, or within the sphere of interest of another, may generate conflict and even violence, some activities are likely to have a stronger influence on international affairs than others. During the years between 1870 and 1914 we would expect that colonial expansion would be especially important for its effect on relations among the major powers. In another era, other manifestations of lateral pressure might be more important—troops overseas, military bases on foreign territory, outside investment in former colonial areas, military aid, technical assistance. In the late nineteenth and early twentieth centuries competition for colonial territory and spheres of control was the principal international concern. A major factor in Bismarck's turn to imperialism and colonial-

ism may have been the fear that "if he failed to authorize the hoisting of the German flag, the flag of another European power would quickly go up." The British, leaders of the world's largest empire, felt threatened on many occasions when it appeared that some other power might secure a territorial advantage in some part of the world.

States and empires do not stand still relative to one another in population, technology, territory, resources, military capability, or strategic advantage. Compared with each other, some are growing while others are declining, and thus the condition of the international system is perpetual change. A nation may find itself at a relative disadvantage in the world competition for resources, markets, prestige, or strategic superiority. In this eventuality, such a nation's leaders will look for means of improving the nation's relative position. This may involve increases in military or naval capabilities, or improvements in heavy industry. One method of increasing capabilities is to secure favorable alliances. Such bonds normally imply the pooling of some capabilities for the maintenance of shared interests. In defense alliances, the partners are able to complement one another's military capabilities.

Alliances are not always formed only to enhance national capabilities. Alliances, treaties and other international compacts are often concluded to end or moderate conflicts of interests. But although these arrangements may ameliorate conflict, they may also create conflict. Whenever some compact is achieved between two nations not previously allied, it is likely to damage relations between at least one of the parties and any rivals, unless comparable compacts are made with these. Under such circumstances, the alignment of one group of nations may encourage other nations to create a competing bloc. Although relationships improved between Britain and France after 1904 and between Britain and Russia after 1907 as a result of alliances, none of these three powers achieved alliance with Germany. In such a case the amelioration of conflict among only some powers may be suspected of contributing in the long run to conflict among all the powers.

Broad alliance patterns (including distribution of capabilities within and across alliance boundaries) may define the structure of the international system. From the viewpoint of a nation's leaders, a strong or strategically placed ally may be viewed as organic to their own national power. A leading power may seek an alliance to prevent a growing power from overtaking it in some area, or a growing power may seek an alliance in order to overtake a stronger power. There is usually a price for alliances, however, since international compacts impose some constraints upon a nation's activities.

Competition may give rise to "antagonizing," the term given by Arthur Gladstone to "the process by which each side forms an increasingly unfavorable picture of the other as evil, hostile, and dangerous." No matter which side initiates the process, antagonizing tends to become mutual. "When one side criticizes, distrusts, ridicules, or denounces the other, the other side is likely to reply in kind." The more intense the competition and antagonizing, the greater is the probability of interactions being transformed from insult to injury. Thereafter, "when one side takes actions which are or threaten to be harmful to the other side, the other side is even more likely to reply in kind."

With respect to the interactions between two rival countries, the difference between them on any salient dimension—territorial acquisition, trade, armaments, prestige, etc.—can be a powerful factor in motivating further competition or conflict. *An increase in the political, economic or military strength and effectiveness of one nation will tend to generate new demands in the rival nation and a disposition among its leaders to increase appropriate capabilities.* For example, if Nation A with a higher naval budget than Nation B adds further increments, Nation B is likely to increase its naval budget. Also, if Nation B with a lower budget tries to catch up with A, then the latter is likely to add increments in an effort to maintain its advantage. Nevertheless, we show in Part III that arms increases are sometimes better-explained by domestic growth factors than by international competition.

A nation may respond to an increase in the strength and effectiveness of another nation, e.g., trade, by increasing its own strength and effectiveness in a wholly different area, e.g., colonial territory, military strength, or naval power. This possibility tends to complicate the Richardson-type model of arms races in that increases in the military budgets (or shipping tonnage, etc.) of nations may be attributable to increases by a rival nation in some area *other than* military capability.

The interdependency between a country's domestic growth and military expenditures, on the one hand, and the interdependency between military budgets of rival countries are of considerable importance in the great-power system prior to WWI. Most of the major powers were growing or expanding on a number of dimensions—in colonial territory, military expenditures, trade, and so forth. The stronger these tendencies were after 1900—the more the European countries absorbed available territory for colonialization, the higher their military and naval budgets grew, and the stiffer the competition for the world's resources became—the more some leaders saw the possibilities for further growth threatened and their own policy options narrowing, rather than expanding along with the increased power of their nations. The larger the colonial commitments and spheres of interest of Britain and France, for example, the greater was the dissatisfaction of German leaders, who saw the area of unclaimed territories rapidly diminishing. The greater the armaments expenditures of one major power, the stronger the feeling of commitment was likely to be on the part of its rivals to increase their own military expenditures. Finally, as the powers began to adhere to one or another alliance, the more limited appeared to be the possibilities for negotiation and peaceful diplomacy between alliances.

National decisions are frequently thought of as being made in direct response to some perceived threat by another nation, or as steps directed toward certain widely shared and explicit goals, such as "survival of country." But the processes involved in policy formation and action are often exceedingly complex. National decision, even in an authoritarian state, are usually the outcome of communications—often indirect, subtle, and difficult to trace—among the head of state, his advisers and agents, and the citizenry. Such data as levels and rates of change in population, technology, trade, investment, and colonial expansion are in every case the accumulation and aggregation of the effects of decisions made by individual human beings acting singly, in partnership, or in small groups.

The size of a nation's population at any given time is an outcome of millions of private decisions ("conscious" or "unconscious") to have or not have children. So, too, a country's general level of technology is the outcome of large numbers of research and production enterprises undertaken by individuals working singly, in private firms, and in agencies of government. The decision of ten million Germans to have a second cup of coffee could affect their country's relations with Brazil. In a modern state problems of national security are analyzed by hundreds and perhaps thousands of different institutions. Furthermore, different approaches to national defense are taken simultaneously by dozens or hundreds of research and planning centers in and out of government, and in imperfect communication with one another. Thus, a nation's military budget can be as much the outcome of the personal ambition and interests of bureaucrats in war and navy departments as it is of interactions with rival powers. Often, the accumulation of countless individual decisions creates

TABLE 9.3 The Conceptual Model

Components of the Model	Description-Rationale	Measure[a]
Expansion	Demands resulting from the interactive effects of population and technological growth give rise to activities beyond national borders.	Colonial area.
Conflict of interest	Expanding nations are likely to collide in their activities outside national boundaries; such collisions have some potential for violence.	Metricized measure of violence in *intersections* (conflicts specifically over colonial issues) between major powers.
Military capability	States, by definition, have military establishments; these grow as a result of domestic growth and competition with military establishments of other nations.	Military budgets.
Alliance	Nations assess their power, resources, and capabilities in comparison with other nations and attempt to enhance themselves through international alliances.	Total alliances.
Violence-behavior	Nations engage in international violence as a consequence of expansion, military capability, and alliances.	Metricized measure of violence in actions directed toward all other nations.[b]

[a]Data are established for *each* nation and aggregated *annually* for the years 1870–1914. . . .
[b]Target nations include not only the six major powers in the study, but all states.

tendencies that were not planned or foreseen. Despite these complexities, since this study focuses on the interaction of certain macrolevel events—growth, expansion, and competition of nations—we shall be concerned only with the *outcomes* of decision-making processes and not with decision-making itself.

National attributes (the levels and rates of change of certain variables) can provide valuable data for studying the processes that lead to war. Chapter 2 presents profiles of the national attributes of the six major European powers during the 45 years prior to WWI. These profiles are an important consideration in the history of the interaction of these powers (presented in Part II) and are the data base for our quantitative analysis (reported in Part III).

Despite our best efforts, the propositions put forward here are crude, and greater precision is required before we can approach a true theory. Our thoughts, observations, assumptions, and propositions constitute at best a "proto-theory." The specific components (variables) of the processes we are studying are presented in Table 9.3. In Part III we introduce an operational model (a system of simultaneous equations) designed to capture some of the complexities of the interdependency and interaction of these components. Even then, we assume that our tentative theory will be only a first cut into the problem, and that the propositions will have to be subjected to much more testing than that reported in this book.

IV

THE SEARCH FOR PEACE

THE TOPIC

Throughout the ages, one of the goals of international relations inquiry has been to find a way to bring about peace. Chapters 10 through 14 present approaches to peace that have attracted attention in our own day: the balance of power, nuclear deterrence, concert of powers, the establishment of a world political economy, the rise of a democratic security community, and international law and world government. Each of these approaches entails a peace proposal or set of proposals that can be evaluated in terms of its viability and feasibility. A proposal can be said to be *viable* if, once implemented, it will actually bring about peace. In other words, a proposal is viable if, in principle, it will work. A proposal can be said to be *feasible* if it *can* be implemented—in other words, if it is sufficiently practical and not too costly. Unfortunately, the solutions that often appear to be the most viable, like world government, do not seem very feasible; and the solutions which can be implemented, like deterrence, may not be viable.

Despite many noble attempts, war has obviously not been eliminated. Therefore, many peace proposals seek not to abolish war but to mitigate its effects. They try to do this by constraining the capability of each side (balance of power and nuclear deterrence), by circumscribing the conditions under which war will be used as an instrument of policy and the methods by which it will be fought (nuclear deterrence concert of power), or by providing alternative means of conflict resolution and an atmosphere that encourages peaceful change (e.g., a concert of power, a world government, or the rules guiding a stable world political economy or a democratic peace).

THE SELECTIONS

Perhaps the oldest mechanism for preserving peace has been the maintenance of a balance of power. As long ago as the time of Thucydides, the breakdown of a balance of power was seen as a cause of war:

> What made war inevitable was the growth of Athenian power and the fear which this caused in Sparta.[1]

---

[1]Thucydides, *History of the Peloponnesian War*, translated by Rex Warner (Harmondsworth: Penguin classics, 1954), p. 25.

Throughout European history, and particularly in the last four centuries, the balance of power has been cited as a justification for policy and has been lauded by some as the only realistic proposal for maintaining peace. Nevertheless, it has been fraught with problems. At the practical level, it has not provided a very permanent solution; wars have occurred throughout the last four centuries. Those who have argued in favor of the viability of the balance of power have maintained that these wars occurred when the balance was disrupted. This contention is not very persuasive, since it concedes that a balance may be difficult to implement at the point at which it is needed most—when war threatens. Thus, this argument saves the viability of the proposal, but sacrifices its feasibility. Conversely, others have argued that the balance can be implemented, but that it will not prevent war; states will fight each other whether they are equal or unequal in capability.

At the conceptual level, the proposal has difficulties because it means different things. Some, such as Kenneth Waltz (1979), see it as an automatic and natural phenomenon, like Adam Smith's invisible hand; if one nation increases in power, one or more other nations will move in a law-like fashion to match and counter that power. Others view it as a conscious policy that decision makers must meticulously follow if it is to work. Still others see it as a popular symbol with which to marshal support and rationalize a position that has been taken for other reasons. In this guise, the balance of power is a form of propaganda.[2]

Regardless of whether, in Ernst Haas's (1953) words, it is a prescription, an empirical concept, or propaganda, it is unclear why the balance of power should work. Thucydides and other ancients commented that if one state gained too much power there would be nothing to stop it from subjecting all others. This certainly points out a potential danger, but it does not follow that peace will be produced from a balance. All a balance will prevent is an "easy" victory. War may, and often does, occur among relative equals. This has led many scholars to argue that security can be attained not through a balance of power, but only through a preponderance of power. The other side will only be prevented from attacking if it knows it will lose the war. While this argument makes sense, what is to prevent the preponderant power from attacking?

These kinds of conceptual and theoretical problems, coupled with the balance of power's limited historical success, have undermined scholarly confidence in the balance of power as a peace proposal. Indeed, it can be argued that neither a balance of power nor a preponderance of power is associated with peace, but rather each is associated with a different types of war! From this perspective, the balance of power has been associated with total wars like the Peloponnesian War, the Punic Wars, the Thirty Years War, the Napoleonic Wars, and World Wars I and II. These were wars of rivalry among relative equals. Conversely, a preponderance of power has been associated with imperial wars of conquest. A balance of power may prevent the latter wars in the short run, but in so doing often produces conditions that lead to total wars between rivals.

---

[2]These points are made by Ernst Haas, in "The Balance of Power: Prescription, Concept, or Propaganda?" *World Politics* 5 (1953), pp. 442–477. Similar criticisms were made in the eighteenth century by Johann Heinrich Gottlob von Justi; see Per Maurseth, "Balance of Power Thinking from the Renaissance to the French Revolution," *Journal of Peace Research*, No. 2, (1964) pp. 131–132.

The selections in Chapter 10 examine some of these issues in detail. In an article that provides an overview of his important (1957) book, *System and Process in International Politics*, **Morton Kaplan** employs systems language to analyze the balance of power. He describes how the basic elements of the European balance of power can be viewed as a system of behavior that is supported by a given structure, and how a change in the structure can produce different systems. Kaplan's main contribution is to provide political scientists with a set of propositions that elaborate in systematic fashion the role of power in shaping world politics. Since some of his six systems are more peaceful than others, his work is also useful for those who seek to avoid or limit war through a change in the system. Next, **A. F. K. Organski** (1958) in a cogent analysis explains why the balance of power usually does not bring peace. He then goes on to present his power-transition thesis, which asserts that war is most likely when the dominant or most powerful state is being surpassed by a rising state. If this thesis is true, then it is clear that the balance of power is often only a stopgap measure before a major war. Reacting to criticisms of the balance-of-power concept, **Kenneth Waltz** (1979) attempts to place it on a new theoretical foundation by analyzing the structure of the system. Waltz's analysis also a heralded the emergence of a neo-realist movement within international relations that sought to resurrect a number of classic realist ideas by reshaping them on the basis of an economic logic. In the Waltz selection, for example, analogies to the market play an important function. Waltz, however, does not really provide any new empirical evidence on the way the balance of power operates or on the notion that it prevents war. Also, his defense of the balance of power is not typical of such traditional realists as Morgenthau, who were very critical of the concept. Nevertheless, Waltz makes an important contribution to the debate by his emphasis on the role of *structure* in shaping behavior.

With the advent of nuclear weapons, balance-of-power thinking was supplanted by the concept of nuclear deterrence. The nuclear balance of terror, although horribly frightening, seemed to achieve the positive aspects of both the balance of power and the preponderance of power without the negative aspects. As long as each side was able to absorb an initial attack and to retaliate, power was relatively equal, as in the balance of power. Thus, wars of conquest resulting from inequality could be prevented. Conversely, the tremendous destructive capability of nuclear weapons insured that both sides would lose a nuclear war. As long as this mutual assured destruction was in place, each side had, in effect, a preponderance of power. Thus, wars of rivalry could be prevented.

Chapter 11 reprints the most influential and relevant thought on these questions. The chapter begins with a selection from **Clausewitz** (1780–1831), the Prussian military theorist, because his work has been seen as particularly relevant to the nuclear dilemma. Now that war can be so catastrophic and final, it is important to remember exactly what war is, how it is related to politics, and what functions it serves. Clausewitz addressed these questions for his century; his insistence that "war is a mere continuation of policy by other means," has been particularly relevant to nuclear theorists because it makes it clear that the purpose of force is to win a set of political decisions.

Beginning in the late 1950s, a group of American scholars examined issues concerning nuclear weapons and developed what became in effect an

American doctrine of deterrence. The work of Bernard Brodie, Herman Kahn, Thomas Schelling, and Henry Kissinger is of special importance. Brodie was among the first to perceive that nuclear weapons would change old notions of the balance of power and make strategy even more important. **Herman Kahn**, in his work at the RAND Corporation, was one of the main architects of nuclear deterrence. In the selection reprinted here, he defines three types of deterrence and the underlying logic of each. One of the problems that Kahn (1960) points out in this analysis and in his larger work, *On Thermonuclear War*, is that if deterrence against direct attack works, then it is hard to believe that the United States would risk nuclear annihilation to protect a Berlin, let alone a Taiwan.

This was known as the problem of credibility and was the focus of much of the work of Thomas Schelling, who was also associated with RAND. Schelling pointed out that it is easier to deter someone from taking an action than it is to compel them to do something. His elucidation of this distinction between deterrence and "compellence," along with his work on credibility, make Schelling as important a figure as Herman Kahn.

The deductive arguments of Brodie, Kahn, and Schelling, coupled with the public pronouncements of John Foster Dulles and later of Robert McNamara, gradually transformed nuclear deterrence from a theory and policy into a dogma and doctrine. Yet there was little empirical evidence to support it. The first major quantitative test was conducted by Bruce Russett (1963), who found certain crucial aspects of deterrence theory were incorrect. More influential were the comparative case studies conducted eleven years later by **Alexander George** and **Richard Smoke** (1974). In a changed political atmosphere, their analyses raised very serious questions about the empirical accuracy of much of deterrence doctrine. Their review of American actions shows that deterrence theory provided decision makers with insufficient guidance, and that decision makers often deviated from the guidance that was provided. If deterrence theory is unable to accurately describe and explain the actions of American decision makers, then it is doubtful that it could predict how the Russians or Chinese would react in a nuclear confrontation. Yet it is precisely this information that it purports to provide. The selection reprinted here is from their conclusion.

The implications of George and Smoke's analysis are very disturbing as we enter a multi-nuclear world. Critics of nuclear strategy, like Anatol Rapoport, have often pointed out the risks of conducting diplomacy at the brink; but if decision makers do not even make the kinds of cost-benefit calculations upon which deterrence is based, then the risks are even greater. It may very well be that the absence of a nuclear war between the U.S. and U.S.S.R. was not due simply to nuclear deterrence, but to such other irenic factors as the fact that the U.S. and U.S.S.R. were not contiguous and were not fighting over territory, that they were willing to accept a de facto division of Europe, that they did not seriously attempt to overthrow each other's governments, and that they were prepared to lose limited wars in the periphery to avoid escalation to total war. If this is the case, then nuclear proliferation is even more dangerous than we had thought, because it is not likely that these irenic factors will be present among other states.

One of the ways in which the defense establishment was able to inculcate its ideas about nuclear strategy was through inviting scholars to summer institutes where they learned about nuclear doctrine. The selection by **Carol Cohn** is a reflection on one such experience. Her analysis is important because it demonstrates the power of concepts and the language in which they are embedded to shape and control thought. To learn a discipline is to become disciplined by the dominant language of a field and to learn how to think in a certain manner. It is this disciplining effect of theoretical language that many post-modernists are rebelling against. Cohn uses a conceptual analysis called "de-construction" to show how the language of defense intellectuals shapes meaning by including some things in its reality and marginalizing or excluding other things (like moral values). Cohn's critique is also important as one of the early, if not seminal, feminist reconceptualizations of security. Here her analysis provides us with important insights, not only in terms of her uncovering of sexual imagery (with its obvious Freudian implications), but also in terms of her juxtaposition of her values with the "rational" de-personalized values of the defense intellectuals and her description of how such congenial seminars can bring about a "militarization of the mind."

The passing of the Cold War brought an end to the immediate danger of nuclear holocaust. In its wake has arisen a peace *among the strongest states* in the system not seen since the end of the Napoleonic Wars. Despite the Persian Gulf War, the Yugoslav Civil War, and a host of ethnic conflicts, like the 1994 massacres in Rwanda, the probability of war among major states—U.S., Russia, China, Germany, Japan, France, and Britain—is the lowest it has been in the twentieth century.

This peace is much deeper than the uneasy nuclear "peace" of the Cold War. Unlike the era we have just passed, the present is one where there are no fundamental issues over which the strongest states will fight each other. The selections in Chapters 12 and 13 provide different views about how this has come about, and how peace might be managed and extended. The selections in Chapter 12 examine the role that global leadership has played in shaping a world order that will insure peace. **Richard Rosecrance** delineates the historical deficiencies of either the balance of power or nuclear deterrence to provide a real peace. He argues in favor of a concert of powers, whereby a negotiated consensus among major states will form a kind of global governance and loose management of the system.

A concert of power is different from a collective security system, primarily in that the former aims at self-interested management of relations among the strongest without any expectation that "aggression" will always be fought; whereas collective security requires that all states come together to fight every "aggressor" no matter who is the target. Logically, this makes collective security (in principle) more viable because all states are committed beforehand to fight against an "aggressor." Since this is known, "aggressors" should be "deterred," because a coalition of all against one would normally have an overwhelming preponderance of power, insuring the defeat of the state that attacked. While many contemporary scholars see a concert system as feasible, the attempt to convert the UN system into a true collective security system is seen as not feasible precisely because this kind of commitment cannot usually be obtained and, if obtained, not sustained. **Inis Claude Jr.'s** trenchant 1962 critique of collective security makes many of these points and seems more relevant than ever. Indeed, some of his warnings, especially about the costs of intervention, apply equally well to the concert proposal.

Two of the main characteristics of the new world order are the decline of the two superpowers and the ascendency of global capitalism. The role that the world political economy plays in shaping world order is the focus of the selections by Robert Keohane and Immanuel Wallerstein, who provide different perspectives on the current world political economy as well as tracing its historical development from its origins in the sixteenth century to its domination by the United States.

The selection by **Robert Keohane** (1984) approaches the question of a world political economy from the question of what makes selfish power-seeking states cooperate sufficiently to create such an economy. He sees cooperation as deriving from a system of rules and institutions that are created and sustained by a hegemon. Now that American hegemony is declining, will cooperation and the system itself survive? He argues, for a variety of reasons, that it will. Keohane's analysis represents an attempt to reformulate realism by taking account of the importance of values, rules, and institutions for moderating the struggle for power and explaining the emergence of cooperation. In this sense, it can be contrasted with the more Marxist-informed discourse of Wallerstein and of Cox (see selection 18).

Immanuel Wallerstein (1974) is more responsible than any other scholar for the idea that the economy of any single nation can only be understood in terms of the world economy. He provides a broad historical explanation of the evolution of this world economy and an analysis of why the current arrangement has prevented the emergence of a world empire. Like many classics in international relations, Wallerstein's work comes from outside the field. With the decline of American economic hegemony, as indicated by the abandonment of the gold standard and then by the Arab oil embargo, his work received wide attention and helped to promote a new emphasis on political economy within the field.

Both the Keohane and Wallerstein selections suggest that the possibility for a new concert of powers is a logical (albeit not inevitable) outcome from the increasing integration of a single global economy. Although the two authors come from very different political and theoretical perspectives, they both agree that the economic foundation of the system has had a profound impact on the system's political structure and global leadership. Liberals will go on to argue that the world economy will run more smoothly if a grand consensus can be established among the strongest states and institutionalized. The incentive for such a consensus is that all states' absolute material benefits will rise, even if some gain more than others.

The selections in Chapter 13 provide a theoretical discussion of what appears to be an emerging democratic security community whose members are at peace and do not anticipate, at any level, the possibility of going to war with each other. One of the earliest to suggest the idea that democratic states might not fight each other was **Immanuel Kant** (1724–1804), the great German philosopher who provided an outline for a "perpetual peace" among republican nations (i.e., states having a separation of powers). The long essay presents a treaty that outlines rules and conditions that would shape relations between states in such a manner that war would not occur. Being republican (note Kant uses the term "democracy" in a pejorative manner to refer to a tyranny of the majority without any individual rights) is important, but in itself not sufficient to bring about peace. Kant's solution is more complicated than that; his treaty also prohibits the acquiring of another state or the use of what today we would call covert activities, calls for the gradual abolition of armies, and guarantees the right to visit other countries. In this work can be found many of the ideas of contemporary liberalism—the idea that people (as opposed to kings) are hesitant to enter war, that commerce is inherently antithetical to war and will eventually play a role in circumscribing it, and that publicity and the public's right to know will make clear whether some decision is just (cf. Wilson, selection 7). The hypothetical treaty is intended to form a moral foundation for an eventual pacific union (*foedus pacificum*) or federation of peoples who will not fight (and see no need to fight) each other because they share the principles outlined in the treaty. In writing the essay, Kant was following in the footsteps of other eighteenth-century thinkers who presented their ideas of what was necessary to create a perpetual peace in Europe, especially the Abbé de Saint-Pierre, who first used the term "perpetual peace" in 1713.

Kant's essay reminds one of **Karl Deutsch's** (1957) analysis that within Europe there might emerge after the Second World War (given sufficient economic integration) a pluralistic security-community where war was unthinkable. Clearly, within the North Atlantic region (which includes all of Western Europe) such a security-community has been in existence now for some time. In this article, Deutsch elucidates the conceptual differences between integration and amalgamation and how they relate to the economic and political foundations of peace.

The idea that democracies do not fight each other was first demonstrated statistically by **Dean Babst** in 1962. Long ignored, his article gained recognition by scientific peace researchers only in the 1980s. The relationship, although confirmed and elaborated by Rummel (1983), had been overshadowed by the statistical relationship that democratic states do not fight any fewer wars than other types of states, i.e., that they are not necessarily inherently pacific. Michael Doyle's prescient 1986 essay on liberalism helped place the hypothesis that democratic states do not fight each other at center stage. Since the late 1980s, a tremendous amount of attention has been given to this hypothesis and possible deviant cases (see James Lee Ray, 1995). **Zeev Maoz** and **Bruce Russett** have been in the vanguard of the effort to demonstrate the statistical accuracy of the relationship. In the article reprinted here, they go beyond the simple statement that democracies do not fight each other and attempt to test two competing explanations of why this might be the case. They conclude that democracies tend not to fight each other both because they have shared norms about how disagreements should be handled and because there are institutional constraints that prevent democratic states from going to war that are not present in other types of states. Both these factors are discussed by Kant and both are supported by the statistical evidence; the normative factors, however, seem, empirically, to be more important.

Maoz and Russett's analysis helps us begin to understand what might be at the root of the democratic peace. This is important because without an understanding of its causes, it is difficult to evaluate its viability as a global solution to war. Some critics are still suspicious of the idea, because they are not convinced that democratic states are any less aggressive or imperialistic than non-democratic states. There is an ideological tendency in this peace proposal to imply that wars that do occur are the fault of non-democratic states, a position enunciated by Wilson. This does not seem to conform to the historical record, especially when strong democratic states attack weaker people, as they did in the heyday of imperialism, or engage in messianic crusades, for which they seem to have a peculiar penchant (see Kennan, selection 5). It also overlooks the fact that many democratic states in the post-Napoleonic era were beneficiaries of the status quo, and therefore had no need to fight wars with democratic or non-democratic states; whereas non-democratic states, like Germany, Japan, Italy, and the Soviet Union, were revisionist and could often only pursue their agenda through threatening force. Finally, one of the reasons democratic states may not fight each other may be that they do not have territorial disputes, having, like England and France, used war to establish their boundaries in a pre-democratic era. In other words, democratic states may not fight each other simply because they have no need in the current historical era to do so.

Nevertheless, it may still be the case that even if democratic states have serious disputes, they may not go to war because they do not resort to power politics (a syndrome of behavior often associated with war between relative equals) in dealing with one another. If it is the absence of power politics behavior that is at the root of the democratic peace, then one way to get non-democratic states to become peaceful is to establish conditions where they need not resort to power politics in order to resolve disputes. If this cannot be done, then the other way to peace is for non-democratic states to become democratic. The problem with this proposal is that the alternatives are to either wait for the entire world to become democratic, an unlikely prospect in the short run, or to use coercive techniques to encourage the spreading of democracy. The latter, however, seems to contradict the rationale given for the viability of the democratic peace proposal.

Historically, the most common proposal for ending war has been to create a world government and to establish international law. Dante, Hobbes, and Rousseau all discussed this proposal in a trenchant manner. The heart of the argument lies in the assumption that, in a state of anarchy (the absence of government and law), war occurs naturally because there is nothing to prevent it (see Waltz, selection 39); it occurs whenever a side is willing to fight rather than lose. Thus, in an anarchic state, war provides the same function as government does—a way of making decisions authoritatively. According to this argument, world government and international law can become a substitute for war if nations will accept them as nonviolent and binding bases for reaching political agreement. To provide empirical support for this argument, proponents of world government often point to the relative absence of domestic violence within nations that have legitimate governments. They argue that, just as domestic government put an end to the state of nature within a given territory, so can world government end global anarchy.

The problem with this proposal seems to lie not so much in its viability—it probably would work if a world government could be created and its decisions accepted—but in its feasibility—how can a world government be created? Contemporary critics of world government and international law have regarded this proposal as utopian, because the conditions necessary for creating an effective world government or enforcing international law do not exist.

Such realist critics as Reinhold Niebuhr and Hans Morgenthau have argued that the League of Nations and the United Nations could not become a proto-world government, because government presupposes community. Since there was and is no world community, there can be no world government. Realists as well as other critics point out that the mere existence of government will not prevent violence—as revolutions and civil wars make abundantly clear. It is necessary to discover the conditions that produce *effective* government. In recent years, these criticisms have led some scholars to investigate the causes of community formation and its consequences for the prospects of creating government. Some hoped that such knowledge could be used to aid in the development of a world community, which could then serve as a foundation for the creation of a world government. At the time of its formation, UNESCO was actually charged with such a mission. By 1950, this lofty goal and similar ones in the United Nations were swept away by the Cold War.

While the feasibility of world government is an obvious problem, many have also questioned its desirability. Some do not want peace at the price of justice, or equality, or freedom, or some other value they hold dear. Likewise, they may be hesitant to join a government or support a law that benefits others more than themselves, or that institutionalizes the status quo and makes change difficult, or that reduces their autonomy and places the right to make decisions into the hands of an international body. For all these reasons, there is very little support for a world government among states in today's world.

Nonetheless, authoritative decisions at the global level—particularly economic decisions—are often made that affect the everyday lives of millions of people. What to produce—cocoa for the world market or staples for local consumption? What price to charge? Should austerity measures be instituted? The answers to all these questions are increasingly influenced, if not determined, by those outside one's nation-state—the global market, multinational corporations, the World Bank. States may be legally sovereign, but they are rarely economically sovereign. This has led many to argue that there is a single world political economy ordered around capitalist practices that makes for a greater degree of order and cooperation than is apparent in the realist notion of anarchy. The world political economy serves as evidence that it is possible to form global institutions and a global order that move the international system away from a state of nature (see Hobbes, selection 29) and toward a world society (see Burton, selection 16), even if we are far away from a world community and world government. Whether the world political economy will provide the material foundation for a more peaceful world is an open question, but it must be remembered that the current capitalist world system, itself, was established through violence and domination and that it is not necessarily the most just system possible, since it distributes benefits and costs in such a way that it is easy for the wealthy to make money and difficult for the poor to end their exploitation (see Galtung, selection 35).

Chapter 14 presents three selections on international law and world government. The first is by **Hugo Grotius** (1583–1645), who is commonly recognized as the father of international law. Grotius was a seventeenth-century Dutch jurist best known for promulgating the principle of freedom of the seas and for establishing the foundation of modern international law. The selection reprinted here is from his prolegomena to *The Law of War and Peace*, first published in 1625. In it, he makes the argument that international law, as a reflection of natural law, is in the best interest of all states. The second selection, by **Grenville Clark** and **Louis Sohn**, was first published in 1958; it presents the case for converting the United Nations into a quasi-world government. In the last selection, **Inis Claude, Jr.** delineates some of the difficulties in drawing an analogy between domestic government and world government. In particular, he points out that advocates of world government, like Clark and Sohn, often ignore the fact that government is based not so much on the "rule of law" as on the "rule of politics."

AN ANALYSIS OF THE TOPIC

The search for peace in the post-Cold War era must begin with an analysis of the viability and feasibility of peace proposals. The prospects for peace are brighter now than they have been in some time. Can international relations theory offer any guidance at this propitious moment of history? Much of the scholarship suggests that the balance of power is neither a viable nor feasible mechanism for avoiding conventional war. At the nuclear level, the balance-of-power proposal was replaced by the notion of nuclear deterrence, which was widely credited with preventing war between the United States and the U.S.S.R. The extent to which deterrence actually works is now being questioned. The fact that the two states avoided nuclear war may have nothing to do with the principles of deterrence. If that is the case, then nuclear proliferation is quite ominous, because deterrence cannot be relied upon. Even where it seems to work, as in the Cold War, the peace is an uneasy and highly risky one.

The attempt to create a concert of powers points humanity in a different direction. A concert of powers might operate in much the same manner as the Concert of Europe did in 1815. It provides the best hope for establishing a kind of global security regime that would help prevent war and/or mitigate it if prevention failed. If a concert of powers is going to be able to control nuclear proliferation, the major security problem still on the horizon, it will eventually have to include most of the regional powers in the world.

The viability of a concert, however, is tenuous, as Rosecrance points out by saying that concerts tend to last for only around ten years. So long as no fundamental issue arises over which major states would fight each other, a concert of powers provides sufficient management to prevent other issues from getting out of hand. A concert can also prevent major states from getting dragged into conflicts by minor states. More importantly, a concert can help manage potential rivalries among major states by creating understandings and "rules of the game" that regulate competition. Finally, a concert can help stabilize a system by doing what it can to either resolve or mitigate conflict that occurs among regional powers or minor states. All these effects make a concert system viable, but it is a proposal that can work and be implemented only in special conditions, for it depends very much on the willingness of major states to cooperate and make compromises. For the moment these conditions are being met, but for how long they will remain is not clear. In short, a concert of powers is limited as a peace proposal primarily because it depends on the good will, or at least tolerance, of the strongest states in the system.

The democratic peace provides some clues as to what might produce long-term good will among states, namely, create a habit of relating to each other on a basis of mutually acceptable norms, which usually means not treating each other in a power politics fashion. It also seems to entail resorting to conflict resolution techniques (see Pruitt and Rubin, selection 19) to handle outstanding disputes, rather than trying to take advantage through the use of force. The extent to which these norms can be passed along to non-democratic states and institutionalized in the system as a whole will determine if a democratic peace can be converted into a global peace. In order for that to happen, however, certain very violence-prone issues, like territorial disputes, will either have to be kept off the agenda or be handled in a considerably less realpolitik and more conflict-resolution fashion.

No contemporary world order is likely to evolve into a world government, because major states do not find it in their interests. Nevertheless, the absence of world government does not mean the absence of governance. A concert system may be able to create a sufficient consensus on rules of the game to establish a working security regime. The path to world order may not lie in simply trying to expand this regime to include all issues and actors. Too great an extension may precipitate collapse. The concert must concentrate on preserving peace among the strongest states and managing their own relations so that they do not permit wars involving weaker states to drag them into a war with each other. The concert also has a responsibility to try to prevent wars by taking an active conflict resolution role, but it will not be able to prevent all wars, particularly where territorial and ethnic questions are involved. In these cases, it should work to mitigate suffering and develop rules of engagement that will keep wars limited. Such rules were often successful during the Cold War in preventing direct U.S.-Soviet military combat.

A true world order will involve more than just a security regime, however. There must be a variety of regimes, each with different rules and participants, and each confined to an identifiable set of issues. There need to be regimes devoted to the oceans, trade, energy, development, food, telecommunications, health, and so forth, and most of these are already present in some form. The governance of the world political economy provides an important example of how a successful international regime can make important decisions, even though it may not solve all problems. The ways in which these less violence-prone issues are resolved will provide important precedents for the future and may help create sufficient cultural, social, economic, and political ties to create a sense of community. David Mitrany (1943) thought that such a process would help bring about "a working peace system" because cooperation in one issue area would "spill over" into cooperation in another area. Such a system seems to have worked in Western Europe, one of the most war-torn areas in world history.

The key point about regime creation, as Claude and philosophers like Edmund Burke would insist, is that the creation of such regimes must be worked out in practice and on the basis of experience, not by the imposition of rationalistic schemes; only then will they have any chance of being feasible. In addition, the underlying economic relations, as Marx and other economic philosophers have argued, must create sufficient abundance to meet fundamental material needs so that states and people do not feel that the only way of improving their condition is to use force. This will work to keep certain war-prone issues off the agenda and to ameliorate contention on the issues that remain. This brief discussion should indicate that international relations theory can provide insight and guidance in the search for peace. Whether those insights will be used wisely will depend upon the actions of world leaders, their followers, and mass political movements.

FOR FURTHER READING

Balance of Power

David Hume. 1752. "Of the Balance of Power," in David Hume, *Essays: Moral, Political, and Literary.*

Ernst B. Haas. 1953. The Balance of Power: Prescription, Concept, or Propaganda? *World Politics* 5: 442–477.

Edward V. Gulick. 1955. *Europe's Classical Balance of Power.* Ithaca, NY: Cornell University Press.

Nuclear Deterrence

Bernard Brodie. 1945. The Atomic Bomb and American Security. Memorandum No. 18, Yale Institute of International Studies.

Thomas C. Schelling. 1960. *The Strategy of Conflict.* New York: Oxford University Press.

Anatol Rapoport. 1960. *Fights, Games and Debates.* Ann Arbor: University of Michigan Press.

Bruce Russett. 1963. The Calculus of Deterrence. *Journal of Conflict Resolution,* Vol. 7 (June): 97–109.

Patrick Morgan. 1983. *Deterrence: A Conceptual Analysis.* Beverly Hills, Calif.: Sage.

Feminist Perspectives

Jean Bethke Elshtain. 1987. *Women and War.* New York: Basic Books.

Cynthia Enloe. 1989. *Bananas, Beaches, and Bases.* London: Pandora.

V. Spike Peterson, ed. 1992. *Gendered States: Feminist (Re)Visions of International Relations Theory.* Boulder: Lynne Rienner.

J. Ann Tickner. 1992. *Gender in International Relations: Feminist Perspectives on Achieving Security.* New York: Columbia University Press.

World Order, Democratic Peace

Charles A. Kupchan and Clifford A. Kupchan. 1991. Concerts, Collective Security, and the Future of Europe. *International Security,* Vol. 16 (Summer): 114–161.

Ernst Haas. 1961. International Integration: The European and the Universal Process. *International Organization* 15: 366–392.

Rudolph J. Rummel. 1983. Libertarianism and International Violence. *Journal of Conflict Resolution,* Vol. 27 (March): 27–71.

Michael W. Doyle. 1986. Liberalism and World Politics. *American Political Science Review,* Vol. 80 (December): 1151–1169.

WILLIAM J. DIXON. 1994. Democracy and the Peaceful Settlement of International Conflict. *American Political Science Review,* Vol. 88 (March): 14–32.

JAMES LEE RAY (1995) *Democracy and International Conflict.* Columbia, S.C.: University of South Carolina Press.

Political Economy

KARL MARX. (1818–1883). *A Contribution to the Critique of Political Economy* (1859), 2nd ed. translated by N.I. Stone, Chicago: Charles H. Kern & Co., 1904.

FERNAND BRAUDEL. 1973. *The Mediterranean and the Mediterranean World in the Age of Phillip II.* New York: Harper and Row.

STEPHEN KRASNER. 1978. *Defending the National Interest.* Princeton: Princeton University Press.

PETER A. GOUREVITCH. 1986. *Politics in Hard Times.* Ithaca, NY: Cornell University Press.

ROBERT GILPIN. 1987. *The Political Economy of International Relations.* Princeton: Princeton University Press.

PAUL KENNEDY. 1987. *The Rise and Fall of the Great Powers: Economic Change and Military Conflict from 1500 to 2000.* New York: Random House.

International Law, World Government

DANTE ALIGHIERI (1256–1321). *On World Government* (De Monarchia) (ca. 1310–1313). Indianapolis: Bobbs-Merrill, 1976.

JEAN JACQUES ROUSSEAU (1712–1778). *A Lasting Peace through the Federation of Europe* (1761).

EMMERICH DE VATTEL (1714–1767). *The Law of Nations* (1758).

DAVID MITRANY. 1943. *A Working Peace System.* Chicago: Quadrangle Books, 1966.

HANS KELSEN. 1952. *Principles of International Law.* New York: Rinehart.

HEDLEY BULL. 1966. Society and Anarchy in International Relations. In *Diplomatic Investigations,* edited by Herbert Butterfield and Martin Wight. Cambridge, Mass.: Harvard University Press.

ROBERT AXELROD. 1981. *The Evolution of Cooperation.* New York: Basic Books.

CHARLES W. KEGLEY, JR. AND GREGORY A. RAYMOND. 1990. *When Trust Breaks Down.* Columbia: University of South Carolina Press.

Chapter 10

The Balance of Power

37. Some Problems of International Systems Research

MORTON A. KAPLAN

This essay will attempt to provide a brief and non-technical account of some of the theoretical models employed in *System and Process in International Politics. . . .* A number of theoretical considerations underlie this essay. One is that some pattern of repeatable or characteristic behavior does occur within the international system. Another is that this behavior falls into a pattern because the elements of the pattern are internally consistent and because they satisfy needs that are both international and national in scope. A third is that international patterns of behavior are related, in ways that can be specified, to the characteristics of the entities participating in international politics and to the functions they perform. . . .

Just as it is possible to build alternative models of political systems, e.g., democratic or totalitarian, and of family systems, e.g., nuclear families, extended families or monogamous or polygamous families, so it is possible to build different models of international systems. . . . Six alternative models of international systems are presented in this section. These models do not exhaust the possibilities.

They are, however, intended to explore the continuum of possibilities. In their present stage of development the models are heuristic. Yet, if they have some degree of adequacy, they may permit a more meaningful organization of existing knowledge and more productive organization of future research. Only two of the models—the "balance of power" system and the loose bipolar system—have historical counterparts.

"BALANCE OF POWER" SYSTEM

. . . The "balance of power" international system is an international social system that does not have as a component a political subsystem. The actors within the system are exclusively national actors, such as France, Germany, Italy, etc. Five national actors—as a minimum—must fall within the classification "essential national actor" to enable the system to work.

The "balance of power" international system is characterized by the operation of the following essential rules, which constitute the characteristic behavior of the system: (1) increase capabilities, but negotiate rather than fight; (2) fight rather than fail to increase capabilities; (3) stop fighting rather than eliminate an essential actor; (4) oppose any coalition or single actor that tends to assume

———
Excerpted from "Some Problems of International Systems Research," by Morton A. Kaplan, first published in *International Political Communities: An Anthology* (Garden City, N. Y.: Anchor, 1966), pp. 469–486. Reprinted by permission of the author. Footnotes deleted.

a position of predominance within the system; (5) constrain actors who subscribe to supra-national organizational principles; and (6) permit defeated or constrained essential national actors to re-enter the system as acceptable role partners, or act to bring some previously inessential actor within the essential actor classification. Treat all essential actors as acceptable role partners.

The first two rules of the "balance of power" international system reflect the fact that no political sub-system exists within the international social system. Therefore, essential national actors must rely upon themselves or upon their allies for protection. However, if they are weak, their allies may desert them. Therefore, an essential national actor must ultimately be capable of protecting its own national values. The third essential rule illustrates the fact that other nations are valuable as potential allies. In addition, nationality may set limits on potential expansion.

The fourth and fifth rules give recognition to the fact that a predominant coalition or national actor would constitute a threat to the interests of other national actors. Moreover, if a coalition were to become predominant, then the largest member of that coalition might also become predominant over the lesser members of its own coalition. For this reason members of a successful coalition may be alienated; they may also be able to bargain for more from the losers than from their own allies.

The sixth rule states that membership in the system is dependent upon only behavior that corresponds with the essential rules or norms of the "balance of power" system. If the number of essential actors is reduced, the "balance of power" international system will become unstable. Therefore, maintaining the number of essential national actors above a critical lower bound is a necessary condition for the stability of the system. This is best done by returning to full membership in the system defeated actors or reformed deviant actors.

Although any particular action or alignment may be the product of "accidents," i.e., of the set of specific conditions producing the action or alignment, including such elements as chance meetings or personality factors, a high correlation between the pattern of national behavior and the essential rules of the international system would represent a confirmation of the predictions of the theory. . . .

The number of essential rules cannot be reduced. The failure of any rule to operate will result in the failure of at least one other rule. . . . The rules of the system are interdependent. For instance, the failure to restore or to replace defeated essential national actors eventually will interfere with the formation of coalitions capable of constraining deviant national actors or potentially predominant coalitions. . . .

The rules, in short, are equilibrium rules for the system. This does not, however, imply that the rules will be followed by the actors because they are equilibrium rules, unless an actor has an interest in maintaining the equilibrium of the system. The constraints on the actor must motivate it to behave consonantly with the rules; or, if one or more actors are not so motivated, the others must be motivated to act in a way which forces the deviant actors back to rule-consonant behavior. Thus the rules may be viewed normatively, that is, as describing the behavior which will maintain the equilibrium of the system or as predictive, that is, as predicting that actors will so behave if the other variables of the system and the environment are at their equilibrium settings. If the other variables of the system and the environment are not at their equilibrium settings, deviant behavior is expected.

It is relatively easy to find historical examples illustrating the operation of the "balance of power" system. The European states would have accepted Napoleon had he been willing to play according to the rules of the game. The restoration of the Bourbons permitted the application of rule three. Had this not been possible, the international system would immediately have become unstable. Readmission of France to the international system after restoration fulfilled rule six.

The European concert, so ably described by Mowat, illustrates rule one. The *entente cordiale* illustrates rule four and the history of the eighteenth and nineteenth centuries rule two. Perhaps the best example of rule three, however, can be found in the diplomacy of Bismark at Sadowa, although his motivation was more complex than the rule alone would indicate. It is not the purpose of this essay to multiply historical illustrations. The reader can make his own survey to determine whether international behavior tended to correspond to these rules during the eighteenth and nineteenth centuries.

The changes in conditions that may make the "balance of power" international system unstable are: the existence of an essential national actor who does not play according to the rules of the game, such as one who acts contrary to the essential rules of the system; in the example discussed, a player who seeks hegemony; failures of information which prevent a national actor from taking the required measures to protect its own international position; capability changes that become cumulative and thus increase an initial disparity between the capabilities of essential national actors; conflicts between the prescriptions of different rules under some conditions; difficulties arising from the logistics of the "balancing" process, the small number of essential actors, or an inflexibility of the "balancing" mechanism. . . .

Instability may result, although the various national actors have no intention of overthrowing the "balance of power" system. . . . Even the endeavor to defeat Napoleon and to restrict France to her historic limits had some effects of this kind. This effort, although conforming to rules four, five, and six, also aggrandized Prussia and hence upset the internal equilibrium among the German actors. This episode may have triggered the process which later led to Prussian hegemony within Germany and to German hegemony within Europe. Thus, a dynamic process was set off for which shifts within alignments or coalitions were not able to compensate. . . .

The "balance of power" system has the following consequences. Alliances tend to be specific, of short duration, and to shift according to advantage and not according to ideology (even within war). Wars tend to be limited in objectives. There is a wide range of international law that applies universally within the system. Among the most significant rules of applicable law are those dealing with the rules of war and the doctrine of non-intervention.

The "balance of power" system in its ideal form is a system in which any combination of actors within alliances is possible so long as no alliance gains a marked preponderance in capabilities. The system tends to be maintained by the fact that even should any nation desire to become predominant itself, it must, to protect its own interests, act to prevent any other nation from accomplishing such an objective. Like Adam Smith's "unseen hand" of competition, the international system is policed informally by self-interest, without the necessity of a political sub-system.

The rise of powerful deviant actors, inadequate counter-measures by non-deviant actors, new international ideologies, and the growth of supranational organizations like the Communist bloc with its internationally organized political parties, sounded the death knell for the "balance of power" international system.

LOOSE BIPOLAR SYSTEM

In its place, after an initial period of instability, the loose bipolar system appeared. This system differs in many important respects from the "balance of power" system. Supranational actors participate within the international system. These supranational actors may be bloc actors like NATO or the Communist bloc or universal actors like the United Nations. Nearly all national actors belong to the universal actor organization and many—including most of the major national actors—belong to one or the other of the major blocs. Some national actors, however, may be non-members of bloc organizations.

In distinction to the "balance of power" international system, in which the rules applied uniformly to all national actors, the essential rules of the loose bipolar system distinguish, for instance, between the role functions of actors who are members of blocs and those who are not.

In the "balance of power" system, the role of the "balancer" was an integrating role because it prevented any alliance from becoming predominant. In the ideal form of the system, any national actor is qualified to fill that role. In the loose bipolar system, however, the integrating role is a mediatory role. The actor filling it does not join on one side or the other but mediates between the contending sides. Therefore, only non-bloc members or universal actor organizations can fill the integrative role in the loose bipolar system. . . .

With only two major groupings in the bipolar system, any rapid change in military capabilities tends to make this system unstable. For this reason, possession of second-strike nuclear systems by both major blocs is a factor for stability within the system.

The rules of the loose bipolar system follow:

1. All blocs subscribing to hierarchical or mixed hierarchical integrating principles are to eliminate the rival bloc.
2. All blocs subscribing to hierarchical or mixed hierarchial integrating principles are to negotiate rather than to fight, to fight minor wars rather than major wars, and to fight major wars—under given risk and cost factors—rather than to fail to eliminate the rival bloc.
3. All bloc actors are to increase their capabilities relative to those of the opposing bloc.
4. All bloc actors subscribing to non-hierarchical organizational principles are to negotiate rather than to fight to increase capabilities, to fight minor wars rather than to fail to increase capabilities, but to refrain from initiating major wars for this purpose.
5. All bloc actors are to engage in major war rather than to permit the rival bloc to attain a position of preponderant strength.
6. All bloc members are to subordinate objectives of the universal actor to the objectives of their bloc in the event of gross conflict between these objectives but to subordinate the objectives of the rival bloc to those of the universal actor.
7. All non-bloc member national actors are to coordinate their national objectives with those of the universal actor and to attempt to subordi-

nate the objectives of bloc actors to those of the universal actor.
8. Bloc actors are to attempt to extend the membership of their bloc but to tolerate the non-member position of a given national actor if the alternative is to force that national actor to join the rival bloc or to support its objectives.
9. Non-bloc member national actors are to act to reduce the danger of war between the bloc actors.
10. Non-bloc members are to refuse to support the policies of one bloc actor as against the other except in their roles as members of a universal actor.
11. Universal actors are to reduce the incompatibility between the blocs.
12. Universal actors are to mobilize non-bloc member national actors against cases of gross deviation, e.g., resort to force by a bloc actor. This rule, unless counterbalanced by the other rules, would enable the universal actor to become the prototype of a universal international system.

. . . The consequences of the loose bipolar system are as follows. Alliances tend to be long-term, to be based on permanent and not on shifting interests, and to have ideological components. Wars, except for the fear of nuclears, would tend to be unlimited. However, the fears concerning nuclear escalation are so great that there is, in fact, a greater dampening of war than in the "balance of power" system. Thus, wars tend to be quite limited; and even limited wars are rare. In the field of law, there are fewer restrictions on intervention than in the "balance of power" system and the limitations which do exist stem largely from the fear of escalation. The universal organization is used primarily for mediation and to some extent for war dampening.

TIGHT BIPOLAR SYSTEM

The tight bipolar international system represents a modification of the loose bipolar system in which non-bloc member actors and universal actors either disappear entirely or cease to be significant. Unless both blocs are hierarchically organized, however, the system will tend toward instability.

There is no integrative or mediatory role in the tight bipolar system. Therefore there will tend to be a high degree of dysfunctional tension in the system. For this reason, the tight bipolar system will not be a highly stable or well-integrated system.

UNIVERSAL SYSTEM

The universal international system might develop as a consequence of the functioning of a universal actor organization in a loose bipolar system. The universal system, as distinguished from those international systems previously discussed, would have a political system as a sub-system of the international social system. However, it is possible that this political system would be of the confederated type, i.e., that it would operate on territorial governments rather than directly on human individuals.

The universal international system would be an integrated and solidary system. Although informal political groupings might take place within the system, conflicts of interest would be settled according to the political rules of the system. Moreover a body of political officials and administrators would exist whose primary loyalty would be to the international system itself rather than to any territorial sub-system of the international system.

Whether or not the universal international system is a stable system depends upon the extent to which it has direct access to resources and facilities and upon the ratio between its capabilities and the capabilities of the national actors who are members of the system.

HIERARCHICAL SYSTEM

The hierarchical international system may be democratic or authoritarian in form. If it evolves from a universal international system—perhaps because the satisfactions arising from the successful operation of such a uni-

versal international system lead to a desire for an even more integrated and solidary international system—it is likely to be a democratic system. If, on the other hand, the hierarchical system is imposed upon willing national actors by a victorious or powerful bloc, then the international system is likely to be authoritarian.

The hierarchical system contains a political system. Within it, functional lines of organization are stronger than geographical lines. This highly integrated characteristic of the hierarchical international system makes for greater stability. Functional cross-cutting makes it most difficult to organize successfully against the international system or to withdraw from it. Even if the constitution of the system were to permit such withdrawal, the integration of facilities over time would raise the costs of withdrawal too high.

UNIT VETO SYSTEM

Consider a world in which some twenty-odd nations have nuclear systems capable of a not incredible first strike. That is, each nation would have a nuclear system that would not completely reduce enemy forces in a first strike but that might nonetheless reduce the enemy forces so much, if everything went according to plan, that a war begun by a first strike might be contemplated. However, even a successful first strike would then leave a nation launching such an attack, because of its depleted arsenal, quite vulnerable to attack by a third nation—an attack that might not be unlikely either if its own attack had been without provocation or if the other nation were malevolent. In any event, the vulnerability of the attacker to subsequent attack by a third state would tend to inhibit such a first strike except in the most extremely provocative circumstances.

There would be little need for specific alliances in this world. To the extent that alliances did occur, one would expect them to be of a nonideological nature. Nations might ally themselves in pacts establishing an obligation to retaliate against any "aggressor" who launched a nuclear attack, which exceeded certain specified proportions, against an alliance member.

In this system one does not expect large counter-value or counter-force wars. If nuclear weapons are used at all, they will tend to be used in limited retaliations for purposes of warning or in other strictly limited ways. The wars that do occur will tend to be non-nuclear and limited in geographic area and means of war-fighting. Sublimited wars will occur more often than actual wars.

The system, however, might seem to have some potentiality for triggering wars or for catalytic wars. That is, if one nation engages in a counter-force attack, this in some views would likely trigger an attack on it by a third state. Or an anonymous attack or accident might catalyze a series of wars. These possibilities cannot be denied, particularly if tensions within the system become high. Nonetheless first strikes and accidental wars are unlikely because credible first-strike forces will not exist and because adequate command and control systems will be available. . . . Nations equipped with nuclear forces in the unit veto system will tend to be self-sufficient and to reject outside pressures, even if coming from universal organizations. In particular, the functions of the universal organization dealing with political change will tend to be minimized. This will be reinforced by the disappearance of the colonial question as an important issue in world politics.

The foreign policies of the great nuclear powers will tend to be isolationist. Alliances, as specified, will recede in importance. Hegemonial ambitions will be curbed—primarily by an obvious inability to achieve them. Protective functions will tend to be shifted to "other" shoulders, when aggression does occur, since no "natural" assignment of this function will be possible. (That is, almost any one of the nuclear powers could play the role; there is no particular pressure on any particular nation to assume it.) . . .

38. The Power Transition

A. F. K. ORGANSKI

. . . It is claimed that a balance of power brings peace. We have seen that there were periods when an equal distribution of power between contenders actually existed or was thought to have existed by the parties involved, but examination revealed that these periods were the exception rather than the rule. Still closer examination reveals that they were periods of war, not periods of peace.

In the 18th century, the last century of the period called the golden age of the balance of power, there were constant wars. In the 19th century, after the Napoleonic Wars, there was almost continuous peace. The balance of power is usually given a good share of the credit for this peaceful century, but as we have seen, there was no balance at all, but rather a vast preponderance of power in the hands of England and France. A local balance of power between France and Germany erupted into the Franco-Prussion War, and German miscalculations that her power balanced that of her probable enemies resulted in World War I, bringing an end to the century of peace.

In the years between the two World Wars, we again had peace and a preponderance of power on the side of the Allies. Once Germany rose again to the point where the power of the Axis nations in fact approximated that of the European allies, war broke out again, the attack predicated on the erroneous assumption that the power of the United States was not involved. Now we are again in the period of peace, where the United States holds the preponderance of power.

The relationship between peace and the balance of power appears to be exactly the opposite of what has been claimed. The periods of balance, real or imagined, are periods of warfare, while the periods of known preponderance are periods of peace. If this is true, the time to worry about the dangers of a third world war is not now, when the predominance of the West is so obvious, but in the future, when industrialization may bring the Communist world abreast of us in power.

The claim that a balance of power is conducive to peace does not stand up. Indeed, it is not even logical. It stands to reason that nations will not fight unless they believe they have a good chance of winning, but this is true for both sides only when the two are fairly evenly matched, or at least when they believe they are. Thus a balance of power increases the chances of war. A preponderance of power on one side, on the other hand, increases the chances for peace, for the greatly stronger side need not fight at all to get what it wants. . . . [One of] the conditions that make for inter-

Excerpted from *World Politics* by A.F.K. Organski (New York: Knopf, 1958), pp. 292–93, 325–33, 338. Copyright © 1958 by A.F.K. Organski. Reprinted by permission of Alfred A. Knopf, Inc. and the author.

national peace . . . is *not* an equal distribution of power.

There is one last point that must be raised about the balance of power. According to the theory, the danger of aggression is to be expected from the stronger nation. A powerful nation intent on maximizing its power is expected to press its advantage and make war upon its neighbors if it ever succeeds in achieving a clear preponderance of power. Here again, the facts do not back up the theory. Nations with preponderant power have indeed dominated their neighbors, but they have not been the ones to start the major wars that have marked recent history. This role has fallen almost without exception to the weaker side. The theory of the balance of power provides no possible explanation for Germany's action in the two World Wars or for Japan's attack upon the United States. It does not explain the two great wars of recent history. . . .

We are now in position to understand more clearly why the usual distribution of power in the world has not been a balance but rather a preponderance of power in the hands of one nation and its allies. And we can understand why world peace has coincided with periods of unchallenged supremacy of power while the periods of approximate balance have been the periods of war. As we have noted, wars occur when a great power in a secondary position challenges the top nation and its allies for control. Thus the usual major conflict is between the top nation (and its allies) and the challenger that is about to catch up with it in power.

In some respects the international order has striking similarities with that of a national society; it is legitimized by an ideology and rooted in the power differential of the groups that compose it. Peace is possible only when those possessing preponderant power are in firm control and are satisfied with the *status quo* or with the way in which it promises to develop in a peaceful context. Peace is threatened whenever a powerful nation is dissatisfied with the *status quo* and is powerful enough to attempt to change things in the face of opposition from those who control the existing international order.

Degree of power and degree of satisfaction, then, become important national characteristics to be considered when trying to locate the nations that are most likely to disturb world peace. We can classify all the nations of the world in terms of these two characteristics, achieving four categories which turn out to be of major importance in international politics.

CLASSIFICATION OF NATIONS: 1. THE POWERFUL AND SATISFIED

The international order is best visualized if one thinks of a pyramid with one nation at the top and many nations at the bottom. Those at the top of the pyramid are most powerful and those at the bottom least powerful. As we move downward in terms of power, the number of nations in each layer is greater than the number in the layer above it. . . .

Together, the dominant nation and the great powers allied with it make up our first group of nations: the powerful and the satisfied. At present, this group includes the United States, Britain, France (though France is falling fast into the position of a middle power), and, since their defeat in World War II, Western Germany, Italy, and Japan. Satisfaction is, of course, a relative term. Perhaps no nation is ever completely satisfied, but in a general way it can be said that these nations are satisfied with the present international order and its working rules, for they feel that the present order offers them the best chance of obtaining the goals they have in mind. The dominant nation is necessarily more satisfied with the existing international order than with any other since it is to a large extent *her* international order. Other nations (such as England and France today) may be satisfied because they realized their full power potential before the present order was established, and thus their power assured them a full measure of what they regarded as their rightful share of benefits. Still other great powers (such as the defeated Axis powers) may be considered satisfied because they can no longer hope to achieve the domination they once sought and are thus content to accept a place in the international order that seems likely to allow them substantial rewards.

2. THE POWERFUL AND DISSATISFIED

Some of the great powers, however, are not satisfied with the way things are run on the international scene, and they make up our second category, that of the powerful and dissatisfied. From this group come the challengers who seek to upset the existing international order and establish a new order in its place. When nations are dissatisfied and at the same time powerful enough to possess the means of doing something about their dissatisfaction, trouble can be expected.

As we have seen in our brief historical sketch, the nations that are powerful and dissatisfied are usually nations that have grown to full power after the existing international order was fully established and the benefits already allocated. These parvenus had no share in the creation of the international order, and the dominant nation and its supporters are not usually willing to grant the newcomers more than a small part of the advantages they receive. Certainly they are unwilling to share the source of all their privileges: the rule of international society. To do so would be to abandon to a newcomer the preferred position they hold. As far as the dominant nation is concerned and, even more pointedly, as far as great nations that support the dominant nation are concerned, the challengers are to be kept in their place.

The challengers, for their part, are seeking to establish a new place for themselves in international society, a place to which they feel their growing power entitles them. Often these nations have grown rapidly in power and expect to continue to grow. They have reason to believe that they can rival or surpass in power the dominant nation, and they are unwilling to accept a subordinate position in international affairs when dominance would give them much greater benefits and privileges.

A rapid rise in power thus produces dissatisfaction in itself. At the same time, a rapid rise in power is likely to be accompanied by dissatisfaction of a different sort. In the present period such rapid rises have been brought about largely through industrialization. Rapid industrialization, however, produces many internal strains and grievances, and the temptation is great for the national government of a nation undergoing such changes to channel some of the dissatisfaction into aggressive attitudes and actions toward the outside in order to divert criticism from the government or other powerful groups within the nation. Industrialization is the source of much of the international "trouble" of the present period, for it expands the aspirations of men and helps to make them dissatisfied with their lot and at the same time it increases their power to do something about their dissatisfaction, i.e., to wrest a greater share of the good things of life from those who currently control them.

The role of challenger, of course, is not a permanent role, nor is it one that all great powers go through. Some of the great powers never fill it. These are the nations that accept a supporting role in the dominant international order, nations we have classified as "powerful and satisfied." Dissatisfied, powerful nations, however, are likely to become challengers, at least for a time. Those who succeed become dominant (and so satisfied) nations eventually. Those who fail conclusively may fall back and accept a secondary supporting role in the international order they have tried to overturn, as Germany appears to have done after two defeats, thus joining the ranks of the satisfied and the powerful by a different path. However, as long as they remain outside the dominant international order and have hopes of overturning it or taking over its leadership through combat, such nations are serious threats to world peace. It is the powerful and dissatisfied nations that start world wars. . . .

Peace, then, is most likely to be maintained when the powerful and satisfied nations together with their allies enjoy a huge preponderance in power over the challenger and its allies, i.e., when the power of those who support the *status quo* is so great that no military challenge to them could hope to achieve success. War is most likely when the power of the dissatisfied challenger and its allies begins to approximate the power of those who support the *status quo.*

It must be stressed that such a peace is not necessarily a peace with justice. Protestations to the contrary notwithstanding, dominant nations are interested primarily in their own welfare, not in that of the rest of the world, and the two are not always compatible. Nor is the challenger necessarily on the side of right. Challengers often claim to speak for all of oppressed humanity, for all the underdogs who suffer under the existing international order, but they, too, are primarily interested in their own welfare, and once a new international order is successfully established, the underdogs are likely to find that they are still underdogs who have merely exchanged one set of world leaders for another.

Nor is peace exactly synonymous with the maintenance of the *status quo.* . . . [C]hange is constant. The international distribution of power is constantly shifting and with it many of the other arrangements that depend upon power. The possibilities of peaceful change should not be underestimated, but neither should the frequency with which major changes are brought about through war. As the challenger grows more powerful, it begins to demand new arrangements and changes in the international order which will give it a larger share of the benefits it desires. In theory, those who dominate the existing international order could make way for the newcomer and welcome it into the top ranks, giving up some of their privileges in the process. In practice, however, such action is rare. The challenger demands a place at the top and is rebuffed. Desiring change and unable to bring it about peacefully, the challenger all too often turns to war.

It might be expected that a wise challenger, growing in power through internal development, would hold back from threatening the existing international order until it had reached a point where it was as powerful as the dominant nation and its allies, for surely it would seem foolish to attack while weaker than the enemy. If this expectation were correct, the risk of war would be greatest when the two opposing camps were almost exactly equal in power, and if war broke out before this point, it would take the form of a preventive war launched by the dominant nation to knock off a competitor before it became strong enough to upset the existing international order.

In fact, however, this not what has happened in recent history. Germany, Italy, and Japan attacked the dominant nation and its allies long *before* they equalled them in power, and the attack was launched by the challengers, not by the dominant camp. If history repeats itself, the next world war will be started by the Soviet Union and it will be launched *before* the Soviet bloc is as powerful as the United States and its allies, thus diminishing the chances of a Communist victory. However, history may not repeat itself, for the Soviet Union is not Germany, and there are other factors involved besides the relative power of the two camps. . . .

Thus wars are most likely when there is an approaching balance of power between the dominant nation and a major challenger. However, there are other factors which also operate to make war more or less likely. Specifically, war is most apt to occur: if the challenger is of such a size that at its peak it will roughly equal the dominant nation in power; if the rise of the challenger is rapid; if the dominant nation is inflexible in its policies; if there is no tradition of friendship between the dominant nation and the challenger; and if the challenger sets out to replace the existing international order with a competitive order of its own.

39. From *Theory of International Politics*

KENNETH N. WALTZ

POLITICAL STRUCTURES

. . . I defined domestic political structures first by the principle according to which they are organized or ordered, second by the differentiation of units and the specification of their functions, and third by the distribution of capabilities across units. Let us see how the three terms of the definition apply to international politics.

Ordering Principles

Structural questions are questions about the arrangements of the parts of a system. The parts of domestic political systems stand in relations of super- and subordination. Some are entitled to command; others are required to obey. Domestic systems are centralized and hierarchic. The parts of international-political systems stand in relations of coordination. Formally, each is the equal of all the others. None is entitled to command; none is required to obey. International systems are decentralized and anarchic. The ordering principles of the two structures are distinctly different, in-

Excerpted from Kenneth N. Waltz, *Theory of International Politics* (Reading, Mass.: Addison-Wesley, 1979), pp. 88–93, 100–101, 111, 117–123. Reprinted by permission of MsGraw-Hill, Inc. and the author. Footnotes and selected citations deleted.

deed, contrary to each other. Domestic political structures have governmental institutions and offices as their concrete counterparts. International politics, in contrast, has been called "politics in the absence of government" (Fox 1959, p. 35). International organizations do exist, and in ever-growing numbers. Supranational agents able to act effectively, however, either themselves acquire some of the attributes and capabilities of states, as did the medieval papacy in the era of Innocent III, or they soon reveal their inability to act in important ways except with the support, or at least the acquiescence, of the principal states concerned with the matters at hand. Whatever elements of authority emerge internationally are barely once removed from the capability that provides the foundation for the appearance of those elements. Authority quickly reduces to a particular expression of capability. In the absence of agents with system-wide authority, formal relations of super- and subordination fail to develop.

The first term of a structural definition states the principle by which the system is ordered. Structure is an organizational concept. The prominent characteristic of international politics, however, seems to be the lack of order and of organization. How can one think of international politics as being any kind of an order at all? The anarchy of politics internationally is often referred to. If structure is an organizational concept, the terms "structure" and "anarchy" seem to be in contradiction. If international politics is "politics in the absence of government," what are we in the presence of? In looking for international structure, one is brought face to face with the invisible, an uncomfortable position to be in.

The problem is this: how to conceive of an order without an orderer and of organizational effects where formal organization is lacking. Because these are difficult questions, I shall answer them through analogy with microeconomic theory. Reasoning by analogy is helpful where one can move from a domain for which theory is well developed to one where it is not. Reasoning by analogy is permissible where different domains are structurally similar.

Classical economic theory, developed by Adam Smith and his followers, is microtheory. Political scientists tend to think that microtheory is theory about small-scale matters, a usage that ill accords with its established meaning. The term "micro" in economic theory indicates the way in which the theory is constructed rather than the scope of the matters it pertains to. Microeconomic theory describes how an order is spontaneously formed from the self-interested acts and interactions of individual units—in this case, persons and firms. The theory then turns upon the two central concepts of the economic units and of the market. Economic units and economic markets are concepts, not descriptive realities or concrete entities. This must be emphasized since from the early eighteenth century to the present, from the sociologist Auguste Comte to the psychologist George Katona, economic theory has been faulted because its assumptions fail to correspond with realities. Unrealistically, economic theorists conceive of an economy operating in isolation from its society and polity. Unrealistically, economists think of the acting unit, the famous "economic man," as a single-minded profit maximizer. They single out one aspect of man and leave aside the wondrous variety of human life. As any moderately sensible economist knows, "economic man" does not exist. Anyone who

asks businessmen how they make their decisions will find that the assumption that men are economic maximizers grossly distorts their characters. The assumption that men behave as economic men, which is known to be false as a descriptive statement, turns out to be useful in the construction of theory.

Markets are the second major concept invented by microeconomic theorists. Two general questions must be asked about markets: How are they formed? How do they work? The answer to the first question is this: The market of a decentralized economy is individualist in origin, spontaneously generated, and unintended. The market arises out of the activities of separate units—persons and firms—whose aims and efforts are directed not toward creating an order but rather toward fulfilling their own internally defined interests by whatever means they can muster. The individual unit acts for itself. From the coaction of like units emerges a structure that affects and constrains all of them. Once formed, a market becomes a force in itself, and a force that the constitutive units acting singly or in small numbers cannot control. Instead, in lesser or greater degree as market conditions vary, the creators become the creatures of the market that their activity gave rise to. Adam Smith's great achievement was to show how self-interested, greed-driven actions may produce good social outcomes if only political and social conditions permit free competition. If a laissez-faire economy is harmonious, it is so because the intentions of actors do *not* correspond with the outcomes their actions produce.... Each would like to work less hard and price his product higher. Taken together, all have to work harder and price their products lower. Each firm seeks to increase its profit; the result of many firms doing so drives the profit rate downward. Each man seeks his own end, and, in doing so, produces a result that was no part of his intention. Out of the mean ambition of its members, the greater good of society is produced.

The market is a cause interposed between the economic actors and the results they produce. It conditions their calculations, their behaviors, and their interactions. It is not an agent in the sense of A being the agent that produces outcome X. Rather it is a structural cause. A market constrains the units that comprise it from taking certain actions and disposes them toward taking others.

International-political systems, like economic markets, are formed by the coaction of self-regarding units. International structures are defined in terms of the primary political units of an era, be they city states, empires, or nations. Structures emerge from the coexistence of states. No state intends to participate in the formation of a structure by which it and others will be constrained. International-political systems, like economic markets, are individualist in origin, spontaneously generated, and unintended. In both systems, structures are formed by the coaction of their units. Whether those units live, prosper, or die depends on their own efforts. Both systems are formed and maintained on a principle of self-help that applies to the units. To say that the two realms are structurally similar is not to proclaim their identity. Economically, the self-help principle applies within governmentally contrived limits. Market economies are hedged about in ways that channel energies constructively. One may think of pure food-and-drug standards, antitrust laws, securities and exchange regulations, laws against shooting a competitor, and rules forbidding false claims in advertising. International politics is more nearly a realm in which anything goes. International politics is structurally similar to a market economy insofar as the self-help principle is allowed to operate in the latter.

In a microtheory, whether of international politics or of economics, the motivation of the actors is assumed rather than realistically described. I assume that states seek to ensure their survival. The assumption is a radical simplification made for the sake of constructing a theory. The question to ask of the assumption, as ever, is not whether it is true but whether it is the most sensible and useful one that can be made. Whether it is a useful assumption depends on whether a theory based on the assumption can be contrived, a theory from

which important consequences not otherwise obvious can be inferred. Whether it is a sensible assumption can be directly discussed.

Beyond the survival motive, the aims of states may be endlessly varied; they may range from the ambition to conquer the world to the desire merely to be left alone. Survival is a prerequisite to achieving any goals that states may have, other than the goal of promoting their own disappearance as political entities. The survival motive is taken as the ground of action in a world where the security of states is not assured, rather than as a realistic description of the impulse that lies behind every act of state. The assumption allows for the fact that no state always acts exclusively to ensure its survival. It allows for the fact that some states may persistently seek goals that they value more highly than survival; they may, for example, prefer amalgamation with other states to their own survival in form. It allows for the fact that in pursuit of its security no state will act with perfect knowledge and wisdom—if indeed we could know what those terms might mean. Some systems have high requirements for their functioning. . . . Competitive economic and international-political systems work differently. Out of the interactions of their parts they develop structures that reward or punish behavior that conforms more or less nearly to the system's requirements. Recall my description of the constraints of the British parliamentary system. Why should a would-be Prime Minister not strike out on a bold course of his own? Why not behave in ways markedly different from those of typical British political leaders? Anyone can, of course, and some who aspire to become Prime Minister do so. They rarely come to the top. Except in deepest crisis, the system selects others to hold the highest office. One may behave as one likes to. Patterns of behavior nevertheless emerge, and they derive from the structural constraints of the system.

Actors may perceive the structure that constrains them and understand how it serves to reward some kinds of behavior and to penalize others. But then again they either may not see it or, seeing it, may for any of many reasons fail to conform their actions to the patterns that are most often rewarded and least often punished. To say that "the structure selects" means simply that those who conform to accepted and successful practices more often rise to the top and are likelier to stay there. The game one has to win is defined by the structure that determines the kind of player who is likely to prosper.

Where selection according to behavior occurs, no enforced standard of behavior is required for the system to operate, although either system may work better if some standards are enforced or accepted. Internationally, the environment of states' action, or the structure of their system, is set by the fact that some states prefer survival over other ends obtainable in the short run and act with relative efficiency to achieve that end. States may alter their behavior because of the structure they form through interaction with other states. But in what ways and why? To answer these questions we must complete the definition of international structure. . . .

- Structures are defined, first, according to the principle by which a system is ordered. Systems are transformed if one ordering principle replaces another. To move from an anarchic to a hierarchic realm is to move from one system to another.

- Structures are defined, second, by the specification of functions of differentiated units. Hierarchic systems change if functions are differently defined and allotted. For anarchic systems, the criterion of systems change derived from the second part of the definition drops out since the system is composed of like units.

- Structures are defined, third, by the distribution of capabilities across units. Changes in this distribution are changes of system whether the system be an anarchic or a hierarchic one.

ANARCHIC STRUCTURES AND BALANCES OF POWER

. . . To achieve their objectives and maintain their security, units in a condition of anarchy—be they people, corporations, states, or whatever—must rely on the means they can generate and the arrangements they can make for themselves. Self-help is necessarily the principle of action in an anarchic order. A self-help situation is one of high risk—of bankruptcy in the economic realm and of war in a world of free states. . . . Wherever agents and agencies are coupled by force and competition rather than by authority and law, we expect to find . . . behaviors and outcomes . . . closely identified with the approach to politics suggested by the rubric *Realpolitik.*

Realpolitik indicates the methods by which foreign policy is conducted and provides a rationale for them. Structural constraints explain why the methods are repeatedly used despite differences in the persons and states who use them. Balance-of-power theory purports to explain the result that such methods produce. Rather, that is what the theory should do. If there is any distinctively political theory of international politics, balance-of-power theory is it. And yet one cannot find a statement of the theory that is generally accepted. Carefully surveying the copious balance-of-power literature, Ernst Haas (1953) discovered eight distinct meanings of the term, and Martin Wight found nine (1966). Hans Morgenthau, in his profound historical and analytic treatment of the subject, makes use of four different definitions (1973). Balance of power is seen by some as being akin to a law of nature; by others, as simply an outrage. Some view it as a guide to statesmen; others as a cloak that disguises their imperialist policies. Some believe that a balance of power is the best guarantee of the security of states and the peace of the world; others, that it has ruined states by causing most of the wars they have fought.

To believe that one can cut through such confusion may seem quixotic. I shall nevertheless try. It will help to hark back to several basic propositions about theory. (1) A theory contains at least one theoretical assumption. Such assumptions are not factual. One therefore cannot legitimately ask if they are true, but only if they are useful. (2) Theories must be evaluated in terms of what they claim to explain. Balance-of-power theory claims to explain the results of states' actions, under given conditions, and those results may not be fore-shadowed in any of the actors' motives or be contained as objectives in their policies. (3) Theory, as a general explanatory system, cannot account for particularities.

Most of the confusions in balance-of-power theory, and criticisms of it, derive from misunderstanding these three points. A balance-of-power theory, properly stated, begins with assumptions about states: They are unitary actors who, at a minimum, seek their own preservation and, at a maximum, drive for universal domination. States, or those who act for them, try in more or less sensible ways to use the means available in order to achieve the ends in view. Those means fall into two categories: internal efforts (moves to increase economic capability, to increase military strength, to develop clever strategies) and external efforts (moves to strengthen and enlarge one's own alliance or to weaken and shrink an opposing one). The external game of alignment and realignment requires three or more players, and it is usually said that balance-of-power systems require at least that number. The statement is false, for in a two-power system the politics of balance continue, but the way to compensate for an incipient external disequilibrium is primarily by intensifying one's internal efforts. To the assumptions of the theory we then add the condition for its operation: that two or more states coexist in a self-help system, one with no superior agent to come to the aid of states that may be weakening or to deny to any of them the use of whatever instruments they think will serve their purposes. The theory, then, is built up from the assumed motivations of states and the actions that correspond to them. It describes the constraints that arise from the system that those actions produce, and it indicates the expected outcome: namely, the formation of balances of power. Balance-of-power theory is microtheory precisely in the economist's sense. The system, like a market in economics, is made by the actions and interactions of its units, and the theory is based on assumptions about their behavior.

A self-help system is one in which those who do not help themselves, or who do so less ef-fectively than others, will fail to prosper, will lay themselves open to dangers, will suffer. Fear of such unwanted consequences stimulates states to behave in ways that tend toward the creation of balances of power. Notice that the theory requires no assumptions of rationality or of constancy of will on the part of all of the actors. The theory says simply that if some do relatively well, others will emulate them or fall by the wayside. Obviously, the system won't work if all states lose interest in preserving themselves. It will, however, continue to work if some states do, while others do not, choose to lose their political identities, say, through amalgamation. Nor need it be assumed that all of the competing states are striving relentlessly to increase their power. The possibility that force may be used by some states to weaken or destroy others does, however, make it difficult for them to break out of the competitive system.

The meaning and importance of the theory are made clear by examining prevalent misconceptions of it. Recall our first proposition about theory. A theory contains assumptions that are theoretical, not factual. One of the most common misunderstandings of balance-of-power theory centers on this point. The theory is criticized because its assumptions are erroneous. . . . From previous discussion, we know that assumptions are neither true nor false and that they are essential for the construction of theory. We can freely admit that states are in fact not unitary, purposive actors. States pursue many goals, which are often vaguely formulated and inconsistent. They fluctuate with the changing currents of domestic politics, are prey to the vagaries of a shifting cast of political leaders, and are influenced by the outcomes of bureaucratic struggles. But all of this has always been known, and it tells us nothing about the merits of balance-of-power theory.

A further confusion relates to our second proposition about theory. Balance-of-power theory claims to explain a result (the recurrent formation of balances of power), which may not accord with the intentions of any of the units whose actions combine to produce that result. To contrive and maintain a balance may be the aim of one or more states, but then again it may not be. According to the theory, balances of power tend to form whether some or all states consciously aim to establish and maintain a balance, or whether some or all states aim for universal domination. Yet many, and perhaps most, statements of balance-of-power theory attribute the maintenance of a balance to the separate states as a motive. David Hume, in his classic essay "Of the Balance of Power," offers "the maxim of preserving the balance of power" as a constant rule of prudent politics. So it may be, but it has proved to be an unfortunately short step from the belief that a high regard for preserving a balance is at the heart of wise statesmanship to the belief that states must follow the maxim if a balance of power is to be maintained. . . .

The closely related errors that fall under our second proposition about theory are, as we have seen, twin traits of the field of international politics: namely, to assume a necessary correspondence of motive and result and to infer rules for the actors from the observed results of their action. What has gone wrong can be made clear by recalling the economic analogy. In a purely competitive economy, everyone's striving to make a profit drives the profit rate downward. Let the competition continue long enough under static conditions, and everyone's profit will be zero. To infer from that result that everyone, or anyone, is seeking to minimize profit, and that the competitors must adopt that goal as a rule in order for the system to work, would be absurd. And yet in international politics one frequently finds that rules inferred from the results of the interactions of states are prescribed to the actors and are said to be a condition of the system's maintenance. Such errors, often made, are also often pointed out, though seemingly to no avail. S. F. Nadel has put the matter simply: "an orderliness abstracted from behaviour cannot guide behaviour" (Nadel 1957, p. 148).

Analytic reasoning applied where a systems approach is needed leads to the laying down of all sorts of conditions as prerequisites to balances of power forming and tending toward equilibrium and as general precondi-

tions of world stability and peace. Some require that the number of great powers exceed two; others that a major power be willing to play the role of balancer. Some require that military technology not change radically or rapidly; others that the major states abide by arbitrarily specified rules. But balances of power form in the absence of the "necessary" conditions, and since 1945 the world has been stable, and the world of major powers remarkably peaceful, even though international conditions have not conformed to theorists' stipulations. Balance-of-power politics prevail wherever two, and only two, requirements are met: that the order be anarchic and that it be populated by units wishing to survive. . . .

Finally, and related to our third proposition about theory in general; balance-of-power theory is often criticized because it does not explain the particular policies of states. True, the theory does not tell us why state X made a certain move last Tuesday. To expect it to do so would be like expecting the theory of universal gravitation to explain the wayward path of a falling leaf. A theory at one level of generality cannot answer questions about matters at a different level of generality. . . .

Any theory covers some matters and leaves other matters aside. Balance-of-power theory is a theory about the results produced by the uncoordinated actions of states. The theory makes assumptions about the interests and motive of states, rather than explaining them. What it does explain are the constraints that confine all states. The clear perception of constraints provides many clues to the expected reactions of states, but by itself the theory cannot explain those reactions. They depend not only on international constraints but also on the characteristics of states. How will a particular state react? To answer that question we need not only a theory of the market, so to speak, but also a theory about the firms that compose it. What will a state have to react to? Balance-of-power theory can give general and useful answers to that question. The theory explains why a certain similarity of behavior is expected from similarly situated states. The expected behavior is similar, not identical. To explain the expected differences in national responses, a theory would have to show how the different internal structures of states affect their external policies and actions. A theory of foreign policy would not predict the detailed content of policy but instead would lead to different expectations about the tendencies and styles of different countries' policies. Because the national and the international levels are linked, theories of both types, if they are any good, tell us some things, but not the same things, about behavior and outcomes at both levels.

REFERENCES

ALLISON, GRAHAM T. (1971). *Essence of Decision.* Boston: Little, Brown.

FOX, WILLIAM T. R. (1959). "The Uses of International Relations Theory," in William T. R. Fox, ed., *Theoretical Aspects of International Relations.* Notre Dame: University of Notre Dame Press.

HAAS, ERNST B. (1953). The Balance of Power: Prescription, Concept, or Propaganda? *World Politics* 5 (July):442–477.

MORGENTHAU, HANS J. (1973). *Politics Among Nations,* 5th ed. New York: Knopf.

NADEL, S. F. (1957). *The Theory of Social Structure.* Glencoe, Ill.: Free Press.

ORGANSKI, A. F. K. (1968). *World Politics,* 2nd ed. New York: Knopf.

WIGHT, MARTIN. (1966). "The Balance of Power," in H. Butterfield and Martin Wight, eds. *Diplomatic Investigations: Essays in the Theory of International Politics.* London: Allen and Unwin.

Chapter 11

Politico-Military Strategy and Nuclear Deterrence

40. On the Nature of War

KARL VON CLAUSEWITZ

WHAT IS WAR?

1. Introduction

We propose to consider first the single elements of our subject, then each branch or part, and, last of all, the whole, in all its relations—therefore to advance from the simple to the complex. But it is necessary for us to commence with a glance at the nature of the whole, because it is particularly necessary that in the consideration of any of the parts their relation to the whole should be kept constantly in view.

2. Definition

We shall not enter into any of the abstruse definitions of War used by publicists. We shall keep to the element of the thing itself, to a duel. War is nothing but a duel on an extensive scale. If we would conceive as a unit the countless number of duels which make up a War, we shall do so best by supposing to ourselves two wrestlers. Each strives by physical force to compel the other to submit to his will: each endeavours to throw his adversary, and thus render him incapable of further resistance.

War therefore is an act of violence intended to compel our opponent to fulfil our will.

From *On War*, Book I, Chap. 1, the J. J. Graham translation of 1874, republished in London in 1909.

Violence arms itself with the inventions of Art and Science in order to contend against violence. Self-imposed restrictions, almost imperceptible and hardly worth mentioning, termed usages of International Law, accompany it without essentially impairing its power. Violence, that is to say, physical force (for there is no moral force without the conception of States and Law), is therefore the *means*; the compulsory submission of the enemy to our will is the ultimate *object*. In order to attain this object fully, the enemy must be disarmed, and disarmament becomes therefore the immediate object of hostilities in theory. It takes the place of the final object, and puts it aside as something we can eliminated from our calculations.

3. Utmost Use of Force

Now, philanthropists may easily imagine there is a skillful method of disarming and overcoming an enemy without causing great bloodshed, and that this is the proper tendency of the Art of War. However plausible this may appear, still it is an error which must be extirpated; for in such dangerous things as War, the errors which proceed from a spirit of benevolence are the worst. As the use of physical power to the utmost extent by no means excludes the co-operation of the intelligence, it follows that he who uses force unsparingly, without reference to the bloodshed involved, must obtain a superiority if his adversary uses less vigour in its application. The former then dictates the law to the latter, and both proceed to extremities to which the only limitations are those imposed by the amount of counteracting force on each side.

This is the way in which the matter must be viewed and it is to no purpose, it is even against one's own interest, to turn away from the consideration of the real nature of the affair because the horror of its elements excites repugnance. . . .

Therefore, if we find civilised nations do not put their prisoners to death, do not devastate towns and countries, this is because their intelligence exercises greater influence on their mode of carrying on War, and has taught them more effectual means of applying force than these rude acts of mere instinct. The invention of gunpowder, the constant progress of improvements in the construction of firearms, are sufficient proofs that the tendency to destroy the adversary which lies at the bottom of the conception of War is in no way changed or modified through the progress of civilisation.

We therefore repeat our proposition, that War is an act of violence pushed to its utmost bounds[1]; as one side dictates the law to the other, there arises a sort of reciprocal action, which logically must lead to an extreme. This is the first reciprocal action, and the first extreme with which we meet.

4. The Aim Is to Disarm the Enemy

We have already said that the aim of all actions in War is to disarm the enemy, and we shall now show that this, theoretically at least, is indispensable.

If our opponent is to be made to comply with our will, we must place him in a situation which is more oppressive to him than the sacrifice which we demand; but the disadvantages of this position must naturally not be of a transitory nature, at least in appearance, otherwise the enemy, instead of yielding, will hold out, in the prospect of a change for the better. Every

change in this position which is produced by a continuation of the War should therefore be a change for the worse. The worst condition in which a belligerent can be placed is that of being completely disarmed. . . .

. . . As long as the enemy is not defeated, he may defeat me; then I shall be no longer my own master; he will dictate the law to me as I did to him. This is the second reciprocal action, and leads to a second extreme.

5. Utmost Exertion of Powers

If we desire to defeat the enemy, we must proportion our efforts to his powers of resistance. This is expressed by the product of two factors which cannot be separated, namely, *the sum of available means* and *the strength of the Will*. The sum of the available means may be estimated in a measure, as it depends (although not entirely) upon numbers; but the strength of volition is more difficult to determine, and can only be estimated to a certain extent by the strength of the motives. Granted we have obtained in this way an approximation to the strength of the power to be contended with, we can then take a review of our own means, and either increase them so as to obtain a preponderance, or, in case we have not the resources to effect his, then do our best by increasing our means as far as possible. But the adversary does the same; therefore, there is a new mutual enhancement, which, in pure conception, must create a fresh effort towards an extreme. This is the third case of reciprocal action, and a third extreme with which we meet.

6. Modification in the Reality

Thus reasoning in the abstract, the mind cannot stop short of an extreme, because it has to deal with an extreme, with a conflict of forces left to themselves, and obeying no other but their own inner laws. If we should seek to deduce from the pure conception of War an absolute point for the aim which we shall propose and for the means which we shall apply, this constant reciprocal action would involve us in extremes, which would be nothing but a

---

[1]By this Clausewitz means that there is no limit to the use of force.—ED.

play of ideas produced by an almost invisible train of logical subtleties. . . . But everything takes a different shape when we pass from abstractions to reality. . . .

7. War Is Never an Isolated Act

With regard to the first point, neither of the two opponents is an abstract person to the other, not even as regards that factor in the sum of resistance which does not depend on objective things, viz., the Will. This Will is not an entirely unknown quantity; it indicates what it will be tomorrow by what it is today. War does not spring up quite suddenly, it does not spread to the full in a moment, each of the two opponents can, therefore, form an opinion of the other, in a great measure, from what he is and what he does, instead of judging of him according to what he, strictly speaking, should be or should do. . . . thus these deficiencies, having an influence on both sides, become a modifying principle.

8. War Does Not Consist of a Single Instantaneous Blow

The second point gives rise to the following considerations:

If War ended in a single solution, or a number of simultaneous ones, then naturally all the preparations for the same would have a tendency to the extreme, for an omission could not in any way be repaired; the utmost, then, that the world of reality could furnish as a guide for us would be the preparations of the enemy, as far as they are known to us; all the rest would fall into the domain of the abstract. But if the result is made up from several successive acts, then naturally that which precedes with all its phases may be taken as a measure for that which will follow, and in this manner the world of reality again takes the place of the abstract, and thus modifies the effort towards the extreme. . . .

. . . the possibility of gaining a later result causes men to take refuge in that expectation, owing to the repugnance in the human mind to making excessive efforts; and therefore forces are not concentrated and measures are not taken for the first decision with that energy which would otherwise be used. Whatever one belligerent omits from weakness, becomes to the other a real objective ground for limiting his own efforts, and thus again, through this reciprocal action, extreme tendencies are brought down to efforts on a limited scale.

9. The Result in War Is Never Absolute

Lastly, even the final decision of a whole War is not always to be regarded as absolute. The conquered State often sees in it only a passing evil, which may be repaired in after times by means of political combinations. How much this must modify the degree of tension, and the vigour of the efforts made, is evident in itself.

10. The Probabilities of Real Life Take the Place of the Conceptions of the Extreme and the Absolute

In this manner, the whole act of War is removed from the rigorous law of forces exerted to the utmost. If the extreme is no longer to be apprehended, and no longer to be sought for, it is left to the judgment to determine the limits for the efforts to be made in place of it, and this can only be done on the data furnished by the facts of the real world by the *laws of probability*. Once the belligerents are no longer mere conceptions, but individual States and Govern-ments, once the War is no longer an ideal, but a definite substantial procedure, then the reality will furnish the data to compute the unknown quantities which are required to be found.

From the character, the measures, the situation of the adversary, and the relations with which he is surrounded, each side will draw conclusions by the law of probability as to the designs of the other, and act accordingly.

11. The Political Object Now Reappears

Here the question which we had laid aside forces itself again into consideration (*see* No. 2), viz., *the political object of the War.* The law of the extreme, the view to disarm the adversary, to overthrow him, has hitherto to a certain extent usurped the place of this end or object. Just as this law loses its force, the political object must again come forward. If the whole consideration is a calculation of probability based on definite persons and relations, then the political object, being the original motive, must be an essential factor in the product. The smaller the sacrifice we demand from our opponent, the smaller, it may be expected, will be the means of resistance which he will employ; but the smaller his preparation, the smaller will ours require to be. Further, the smaller our political object, the less value shall we set upon it, and the more easily shall we be induced to give it up altogether.

Thus, therefore, the political object, as the original motive of the War, will be the standard for determining both the aim of the military force and also the amount of effort to be made. This it cannot be in itself, but is so in relation to both the belligerent States, because we are concerned with realities, not with mere abstractions. One and the same political object may produce totally different effects upon different people, or even upon the same people at different times; . . .

23. War Is Always a Serious Means for a Serious Object. Its More Particular Definition

. . . The War of a community—of whole Nations, and particularly of civilised Nations—always starts from a political condition, and is called forth by a political motive. It is, therefore, a political act. Now if it was a perfect, unrestrained, and absolute expression of force, as we had to deduce it from its mere conception, then the moment it is called forth by policy it would step into the place of policy, and as something quite independent of it would set it aside, and only follow its own laws, just as a mine at the moment of explosion cannot be guided into any other direction than that which has been given to it by preparatory arrangements. This is how the thing has really been viewed hitherto, whenever a want of har-

mony between policy and the conduct of a War has led to theoretical distinctions of the kind. But it is not so, and the idea is radically false. War in the real world, as we have already seen, is not an extreme thing which expends itself at one single discharge; it is the operation of powers which do not develop themselves completely in the same manner and in the same measure, but which at one time expand sufficiently to overcome the resistance opposed by inertia or friction, while at another they are too weak to produce an effect; it is therefore, in a certain measure, a pulsation of violent force more or less vehement, consequently making its discharges and exhausting its powers more or less quickly—in other words, conducting more or less quickly to the aim, but always lasting long enough to admit of influence being exerted on it in its course, so as to give it this or that direction, in short, to be subject to the will of a guiding intelligence. Now, if we reflect that War has its root in a political object, then naturally this original motive which called it into existence should also continue the first and highest consideration in its conduct. Still, the political object is no despotic lawgiver on that account; it must accommodate itself to the nature of the means, and though changes in these means may involve modification in the political objective, the latter always retains a prior right to consideration. Policy, therefore, is interwoven with the whole action of War, and must exercise a continuous influence upon it, as far as the nature of the forces liberated by it will permit.

24. War Is a Mere Continuation of Policy by Other Means

We see, therefore, that War is not merely a political act, but also a real political instrument, a continuation of political commerce, a carrying out of the same by other means. All beyond this which is strictly peculiar to War relates merely to the peculiar nature of the means which it uses. That the tendencies and views of policy shall not be incompatible with these means, the Art of War in general and the Commander in each particular case may demand, and this claim is truly not a trifling one. But however powerfully this may react on political views in particular cases, still it must always be regarded as only a modification of them; for the political view is the object, War is the means, and the means must always include the object in our conception.

25. Diversity in the Nature of Wars

The greater and the more powerful the motives of a War, the more it affects the whole existence of a people. The more violent the excitement which precedes the War, by so much the nearer will the War approach to its abstract form, so much the more will it be directed to the destruction of the enemy, so much the nearer will the military and political ends coincide, so much the more purely military and less political the War appears to be; but the weaker the motives and the tensions, so much the less will the natural direction of the military element—that is, force—be coin-

cident with the direction which the political element indicates; so much the more must, therefore, the War become diverted from its natural direction, the political object diverge from the aim of an ideal War, and the War appear to become political. . . .

27. Influence of this View on the Right Understanding of Military History, and on the Foundations of Theory

We see, therefore, in the first place, that under all circumstances War is to be regarded not as an independent thing, but as a political instrument; and it is only by taking this point of view that we can avoid finding ourselves in opposition to all military history. This is the only means of unlocking the great book and making it intelligible. Secondly, this view shows us how Wars must differ in character according to the nature of the motives and circumstances from which they proceed. . . .

41. The Three Types of Deterrence

HERMAN KAHN

TYPE I DETERRENCE (DETERRENCE AGAINST A DIRECT ATTACK)

It is important to distinguish three types of deterrence. The first of these is: Type I Deterrence, or deterrence against a direct attack.

Most experts today argue that we must make this type of deterrence work, that we simply cannot face the possibility of a failure. Never have the stakes on success or failure of prevention been so high. Although the extreme view, that deterrence is everything and that alleviation is hopeless, is questionable, clearly Type I Deterrence must have first priority.

Typically, discussions of the capability of the United States to deter a direct attack compare the pre-attack inventory of the Russian forces—that is, the number of planes, missiles, army divisions, and submarines of the two countries are directly compared. This is a World War I and World War II approach.

The really essential numbers, however, are estimates of the damage that the retaliatory forces can inflict after being hit. Evaluation must take into account that the Russians could

strike *at a time and with tactics of their choosing.* We strike back with a *damaged* and perhaps *un-co-ordinated* force which must conduct its operations in the *post-attack environment.* The Soviets may use *blackmail* threats to intimidate our response. The Russian defense is completely *alerted.* If the strike has been preceded by a tense period, their active defense forces have been *augmented* and their cities have been at least partially *evacuated.* Any of the emphasized words can be very important, but almost all of them are ignored in most discussions of Type I Deterrence.

The first step in this calculation—analysis of the effects of the Russian strike on U.S. retaliatory ability—depends critically on the enemy's tactics and capabilities. The question of warning is generally uppermost. Analyses of the effect of the enemy's first strike often neglect the most important part of the problem by assuming that warning will be effective and that our forces get off the ground and are sent on their way to their targets. Actually, without effective warning, attrition on the ground can be much more important than attrition in the air. The enemy may not only use tactics that limit our warning but he may do other things to counter our defensive measures, such as interfering with command and control arrangements. Thus it is important in evaluating enemy capabilities to look not only at the tactics that past history and standard assumptions

Excerpted from "The Nature and Feasibility of War and Deterrence," by Herman Kahn, in Walter Hahn and John Neff, eds., *American Strategy in the Nuclear Age* (Garden City, N.Y.: Anchor, 1960), pp. 225–229, 233–237. Reprinted by permission of the author.

lead us to expect but also at any other tactics that a clever enemy might use. . . .

The second part of the calculation—consequences of the lack of co-ordination of the surviving U.S. forces—depends greatly on our tactics and the flexibility of our plans. If, for example, our offensive force is assigned a large target system, so that it is spread thinly, and if because of a large or successful Russian attack the Russians have succeeded in destroying much of our force, many important Russian targets would go unattacked. If, on the other hand, to avoid this we double to triple the assignment to important targets, we might overdestroy many targets, especially if the Soviets had not struck us successfully. For this and other reasons, it would be wise to evaluate the damage and then retarget the surviving forces. Whether this can be done depends critically on the timing of the attack, the nature of the targeting process, and our post-attack capability for evaluation, command, and control. . . .

Another point that may be of great importance is that modern nuclear weapons are so powerful that even if they don't destroy their target, they may change the environment so as to cause the retaliating weapons to be inoperable. The various effects of nuclear weapons include blast, thermal and electromagnetic radiation, ground shock, debris, dust, and ionizing radiation—any of which may affect people, equipment, propagation of electromagnetic signals, and so on. One might say that the problem of operating in a post-attack environment after training in the peacetime environment is similar to training at the Equator and then moving a major but incomplete part (that is, a damaged system) to the Arctic and expecting this incomplete system to work efficiently the first time it is tried. This is particularly implausible if, as is often true, the intact system is barely operable at the Equator (that is, in peacetime).

In addition to attacking the system, the enemy may attempt to attack our resolve. Imagine, for example, that we had a pure Polaris system invulnerable to an all-out simultaneous enemy attack (invulnerable by assumption and not by analysis) and the enemy started to destroy our submarines one at a time at sea. Suppose an American President were told that if we started an all-out war in retaliation, the Soviets could and would destroy every American because of limitations in our offense and our active and passive defenses. Now if the President has a chance to think about the problem, he simply cannot initiate this kind of war even with such provocation.

One of the most important and yet the most neglected elements of the retaliatory calculation is the effect of the Russian civil-defense measures. The Russians are seldom credited with even modest preparedness in civil defense. A much more reasonable alternative that would apply in many situations—that the Russians might at some point evacuate their city population to places affording existing or improvisable fallout protection—is almost never realistically examined. If the Russians should take steps to evacuate their cities, the vulnerability of their population would be dramatically reduced.

The Soviets also know that they can take an enormous amount of economic damage and be set back only a few years in their development. Not only did they do something like this after World War II, but, what is even more impressive, they fought a war *after* the Germans had destroyed most of their existing military power and occupied an area that contained about 40 percent of the pre-war Soviet population—the most industrialized 40 percent.

The difficulties of Type I Deterrence arise mainly from the fact that the deterring nation must strike second. These difficulties are compounded by the rapidity with which the technology of war changes and the special difficulty the defender has in reacting quickly and adequately to changes in the offense. . . .

TYPE II DETERRENCE (DETERRENCE OF EXTREME PROVOCATION)

A quite different calculation is relevant to U.S. Type II Deterrence, although it is still a Soviet calculation (but this time a Soviet calculation of an American calculation). Type II Deterrence is defined as using strategic threats to deter an enemy from engaging in very provocative acts other than a direct attack on the United States itself. The Soviet planner asks himself: If I make this very provocative move, will the Americans strike us? Whether the Soviets then proceed with the contemplated provocation will be influenced by their estimate of the American calculation as to what happens if the tables are reversed. That is, what happens if the Americans strike and damage the Russian strategic air force and the Russians strike back un-co-ordinated in the teeth of an alerted U.S. air defense and possibly against an evacuated U.S. population? If this possibility is to be credible to the Soviets, it must be because they recognize that their own Type I Deterrence can fail. If Khrushchev is a convinced adherent of the balance-of-terror theory and does not believe that his Type I Deterrence can fail, then he may just go ahead with the provocative action.

It is important to realize that the operation of Type II Deterrence will involve the possibility that the United States will obtain the first strategic strike or some temporizing move, such as evacuation. Many people talk about the importance of having adequate civil and air defense to back our foreign policy. However, calculations made in evaluating the performance of a proposed civil- and air-defense program invariably assume a Russian surprise attack and—to make the problem even harder—a surprise attack directed mostly against civilians. This is unnecessarily pessimistic. The calculations in which one looks at a U.S. first strike in retaliation for a Russian provocation is probably more relevant in trying to evaluate the role that the offense and defense play in affecting some important aspects of foreign policy.

Under this assumption, if we have even a moderate nonmilitary defense program, its performance is likely to look impressive to the Russians and probably to most Europeans. For example, the crucial problem of obtaining adequate warning will have been greatly lessened, at least in the eyes of the Soviets. They are also likely to think that we have more freedom than we will have. The Soviets may believe that we are not worried by the possibility that they will get strategic or premature tactical warning. This could be true in spite of the fact that in actual practice such an attack would probably involve a considerable risk that the Soviets would get some warning. Any planning would have to be tempered by the sobering realization that a disclosure or mistake could bring a pre-emptive Russian attack.

The possibility of augmenting our active and passive defense is very important. That is, rather than striking the Russians if they do something very provocative, we might prefer to evacuate our city population to fallout protection, "beef up" our air defense and air offense, and then tell the Russians that we had put ourselves into a much stronger position to initiate hostilities. After we had put ourselves in a position in which the Russian retaliatory strike would inflict much less than a total catastrophe, the Russians would have just three broad classes of alternatives:

1. To initiate some kind of strike.
2. To prolong the crisis, even though it would then be very credible that we would strike if they continued to provoke us.
3. To back down or compromise the crisis satisfactorily.

Hopefully the Soviets would end up preferring the third alternative, because our Type I Deterrence would make the first choice sufficiently unattractive and our Type II Deterrence would do the same for the second.

TYPE III DETERRENCE (DETERRENCE OF MODERATE PROVOCATION)

Type III Deterrence might be called *"tit-for-tat* deterrence." It refers to those acts that are deterred because the potential aggressor is afraid that the defender or others will then take limited actions, military or nonmilitary, that will make the aggression unprofitable.

The most obvious threat that we could muster under Type III Deterrence would be the capability to fight a limited war of some sort. Because this subject is complicated and space is limited, I will not discuss this particular Type III Deterrence capability—although it is important and necessary. Instead, I shall consider some of the nonmilitary gambits open to us. . . .

What deters the Russians from a series of Koreas and Indochinas? It is probably less the fear of a direct U.S. attack with its current forces than the probability that the United States and her allies would greatly increase both their military strength and their resolve in response to such crises. The deterrent effect of this possibility can be increased by making explicit preparations so that we can increase our strength very rapidly whenever the other side provokes us. For example, in June 1950 the United States was engaged in a great debate on whether the defense budget should be 14, 15, or 16 billion dollars. Along came Korea. Congress quickly authorized 60 billion dollars, an increase by a factor of four!

No matter what successes the Communist cause had in Korea, that authorization represents an enormous military defeat for the Soviets. However, it was almost three years before that authorization was fully translated into increased expenditures and corresponding military power. It is very valuable to be able to increase our defense expenditures, but this ability becomes many times more valuable if authorizations can be translated into military strength in a year or so. If the Russians know that deterioration in international relations will push us into a crash program, they may be much less willing to let international relations deteriorate. The problem is: Would we have time to put in a useful program? After all, the basic military posture (including installations) must be of the proper sort if it is to be possible to expand it within a year or so to the point where it is prepared to fight a war in addition to being able to deter one. Our current posture (1960) is probably far from optimal for doing this.

If preparations like these were at least moderately expensive and very explicit, the Russians might find it credible that the United States would initiate and carry through such a program if they were provocative even, say, on the scale of Korea or less. The Russians would then be presented with the following three alternatives:

1. They could strike the United States before build-up got very far. This might look very unattractive, especially since the build-up would almost certainly be accompanied by an increased alert and other measures to reduce the vulnerability of SAC.
2. They could try to match the U.S. program. This would be very expensive.
3. They could accept a position of inferiority. Such an acceptance would be serious, since the United States would now have a "fight the war" capability as well as a "deter the war" capability.

In each case the costs and risks of their provocation would have been increased, and it is likely that the Soviets would take these extra costs and risks into account before attempting any provocation. If they were not deterred, we could launch the crash program. Then we would be in a position to correct the results of their past provocation or at least to deter them in the future from exploiting these results.

It might be particularly valuable to have credible and explicit plans to institute crash programs for civil defense and limited-war capabilities. It seems to be particularly feasible to maintain inexpensive and effective mobilization bases in these two fields, and the institution of a crash program would make it very credible to the Russians, our allies, and neutrals that we would go to war at an appropriate level if we were provoked again.

This is one of the major threats we can bring to bear on the Russians. If we are not aware that we have this threat, if we believe that doubling the budget would really mean immediate bankruptcy or other financial catastrophe, then the Russians can present us with alternatives that may in the end result in their winning the diplomatic, political, and foreign-policy victory. It is important that we understand our own strengths as well as our possible weaknesses.

42. The Gap Between Deterrence Theory and Deterrence Policy

ALEXANDER L. GEORGE AND RICHARD SMOKE

Much of Part One of this study revolved around the theme that the contemporary abstract, deductivistic theory of deterrence is inadequate for policy application, notwithstanding its having been offered in a normative-prescriptive mode. The eleven cases we have now examined indicate the kinds of complexities which arise when the United States makes actual deterrence attempts, complexities which in many respects are not addressed by the abstract theory of deterrence.

To be sure, deterrence theorists have always acknowledged that like any other theory theirs, too, simplifies reality. It does not suffice, however, to stop with such a caveat. In addition, there is an obligation, recognized by most deterrence theorists, to go further and identify those aspects of deterrence phenomena in real-life settings which may be critical for determining deterrence outcomes but which are not encompassed by the simplifying assumptions of the theory in its present form. This difficult task, all the more necessary since deterrence theory has offered guidelines for policy-making, has not been satisfactorily accomplished. At the same time, it must be rec-

ognized that prudent and successful application of deterrence strategy to real-life situations is highly problematic without a clear grasp of precisely those complexities which deterrence theory simplifies or ignores.

It is not surprising, therefore, that the simplifying assumptions of prescriptive deterrence theory should have seriously restricted its relevance and usefulness for foreign policy-making. The inability of deterrence theorists to make an adequate analysis of the gap between the assumptions of their theory and the complexities of deterrence behavior in real life has necessarily left that important task in the hands of policy-makers. Left to their own devices, American policy-makers have filled this gap as best they could in their own way, and the results have often been unfortunate. Moreover, deterrence *strategy*, as applied by policy-makers, bears only a loose resemblance to the primitive, abstract, only partly developed deterrence *theory*. Hence neither the successes nor the failures of deterrence strategy in American foreign policy can be attributed to the influence of formal deterrence theory, which has stopped well short of the level of detail required of a policy-relevant theory and therefore has had only modest influence.

As a prescriptive theory, deterrence theory remains incomplete and unsatisfactory. It has become increasingly clear that initial state-

Reprinted from *Deterrence in American Foreign Policy* by Alexander L. George and Richard Smoke (New York: Columbia University Press, 1974), pp. 503–508. Reprinted by permission of the publisher. Footnotes deleted.

ments of the theory merely adumbrated a starting point and that the necessary development and refinement of the theory did not follow. It is instructive to reflect on this experience and what it implies more broadly for the goal of developing policy-relevant theory for different aspects of international politics. . . .

Let us briefly recall seven simplifying assumptions of abstract deterrence theory . . . ;

Assumption 1: Each side in the deterrence situation is a unitary, purposive actor. (This assumption overlooks the fact that the policy behavior of governments is affected by the dynamics of organizational behavior and internal governmental politics.)

Assumption 2: The payoffs and choices of action by the actors in the deterrence situation can be deduced by assuming a single general "rationality."

Assumption 3: General deterrence theory can be useful to policy-makers, even though it does not define the scope or relevance of deterrence strategy as an instrument of foreign policy.

Assumption 4: The major threat to the defending power's interests lies in its opponents' capacity for launching military attacks.

Assumption 5: Deterrence commitments are always a simple "either-or" matter, i.e., either the defending power commits itself or it does not; if it does, then the commitment is strong, unequivocal, unqualified, and of indefinite duration.

Assumption 6: The deterring power can rely upon threats to persuade the opponent not to alter the status quo.

Assumption 7: The critical and only problematical task of deterrence strategy is to achieve credibility of commitment.

The assumptions of prescriptive deterrence theory have often had to be discarded or modified by the policy-maker in diagnosing specific situations. A few examples will suffice to indicate the poor or even misleading quality of formal deterrence theory for the situational diagnoses needed in policy-making. Against the second assumption just listed, we noted in Part Two the chronic difficulty American policy-makers experienced in trying to estimate

how the opponent calculated the risks of his options. In all three Berlin cases, the Korean War, and the Cuban missile crisis, American policy-makers were surprised by the action the opponent took. In each case American officials had thought the opponent would not act as he did because such action would entail high risks. In fact, there is reason to believe that in each of these cases the opponent regarded his initiative as a low risk strategy through which he was confident of controlling and avoiding unwanted risks of greater magnitude. It is evident that to make the diagnoses needed in assessing situations, the policy-maker cannot work on the assumption that all actors operate with the same kind of "rationality." Rather, the policy-maker needs more discriminating theoretical models of how particular opponents behave in conflict situations.

With respect to the third assumption, our case studies suggest, to the contrary, that the scope and relevance of deterrence strategy for foreign policy needs to be strictly and carefully defined. Our case histories of the Eisenhower Doctrine for the Middle East and the Communist Chinese intervention in Korea both illustrate the risks of U.S. over-reliance on deterrence strategy. The deterrence commitment embodied in the Eisenhower Doctrine paradoxically increased internal political instability in some of the Middle Eastern countries which it was designed to help. Our study of Chinese intervention in Korea emphasizes that deterrence strategy cannot be a reliable substitute for a sensible foreign policy or be used, as Truman and Acheson did in that case, to avoid the consequences of a dangerously provocative foreign policy error. Only a timely abandonment of the policy of trying to unify Korea by force could have reliably reduced the danger of war with Communist China by removing or substantially reducing its motivation to intervene.

More broadly, the American policy of containment during the Cold War suffered badly from a *failure to define limits to the scope and relevance of deterrence strategy.* While containment logically required some use of deterrence strategy, the need for selective, discriminating use of deterrence to uphold containment gave way to a rigid attempt to exclude loss of any territory, even the off-shore islands lying a few miles off mainland China. The deformation of containment led to a proliferation of American deterrence commitments throughout the world and, as George Kennan was to complain, also to a "militarization" of containment. As we noted in our account of the Taiwan Strait crisis of 1954–1955, the American effort to extend containment from Europe to Asia invited serious new risks because of the different structure of the situation, which was dangerously fluid and not neatly structured, as Europe was, for a classical *defensive* application of deterrence strategy. Because the Chinese civil war remained unresolved, the American effort to employ deterrence strategy on behalf of the Nationalist regime on Taiwan resulted in a confusion of containment with "liberation," thereby increasing tensions and inviting crisis.

Finally, as our account of the origins of the Cuban missile crisis stressed, the risks and untoward consequences of too heavy a reliance by both sides on deterrence strategy and strategic power during the Cold War to achieve a broad range of foreign policy objectives contributed to bringing about the most dangerous confrontation of the two nuclear superpowers.

In contrast to the fifth assumption, regarding the "either-or" character of commitments, our case studies indicate that policy-makers need a much more complex understanding of the nature of commitments both in order to convey their own commitments more effectively and to diagnose better the commitments other actors are making. . . .

As for the sixth assumption, which concerns the central role of threats in deterrence strategy, we argue to the contrary that the policy-maker would be better served in the conduct of foreign policy by a broader influence theory. A variety of policy means should be considered for reducing, rechanneling, accommodating, deterring, or frustrating challenges to different kinds of interests, not just deterrent threats. The need for threatening sanctions cannot be properly judged by the policy-maker on the basis of a prescriptive theory that confines itself to indicating that such threats are likely to be necessary to deter encroachments on one's interests. A policy-maker who diagnoses conflict situations solely from the standpoint of how to make more effective use of threats will find that threats are often irrelevant or dysfunctional. This irrelevance of deterrence threats was evident in the Middle East crises of 1957–1958. Some of their harmful consequences are suggested by the Berlin crisis of 1961; after it was over President Kennedy wondered whether some of the moves he had taken to signal resolution had not aggravated the crisis by forcing Khrushchev to undertake similar moves.

In certain situations, moreover, threats may be provocative. The threats the United States and its allies made in 1941 to deter Japan from further encroachments against Asian countries were all too potent and credible to Japanese leaders. They decided they had no choice but to resort to a still more ambitious strategy and attack the United States. But the fact that deterrent threats against a highly motivated opponent are sometimes ineffectual or may boomerang does not permit us to conclude that deterrent threats will surely be more effective against a cautious opponent who confines himself to low-risk and controlled-risk options. In the Quemoy and the Cuban missile crises, threats did not deter the controlled low-risk strategies the opponents were engaged in.

A policy-maker who invariably relies upon threats to deter encroachments on his interests is likely in some situations to pay a high price for temporary deterrence successes which do not really remove the sources of the conflict. We called attention to this in our accounts of the Taiwan Strait and Quemoy crises of 1954–1955 and 1958. A deterrence success of this kind buys time for efforts to restructure the situation after the crisis subsides, in order to defuse its conflict potential. Failure to utilize a temporary deterrence success to alter the situation invites a repetition of the crisis in the future, perhaps under new circumstances in which resort to deterrence strategy may be even more costly and ineffectual.

Viewed from a broader perspective on international relations, therefore, controlled crises of the kind we have seen in Berlin and the Taiwan Strait often have a *catalytic* function for bringing about changes that are necessary if war is to be avoided in the longer run. While deterrence may be necessary to avoid the dangers of "appeasement" under pressure, a deterrence success in such crises creates dangers of another kind if it encourages the defending power to ignore the need for utilizing other policy approaches in the ensuing non-crisis period to find more viable, mutually acceptable solutions to the conflict of interests.

43. Sex and Death in the Rational World of Defense Intellectuals

CAROL COHN

My close encounter with nuclear strategic analysis started in the summer of 1984. I was one of forty-eight college teachers (one of ten women) attending a summer workshop on nuclear weapons, nuclear strategic doctrine, and arms control, taught by distinguished "defense intellectuals." Defense intellectuals are men (and indeed, they are virtually all men) "who use the concept of deterrence to explain why it is safe to have weapons of a kind and number it is not safe to use." They are civilians who move in and out of government, working sometimes as administrative officials or consultants, sometimes at universities and think tanks. They formulate what they call "rational" systems for dealing with the problems created by nuclear weapons: how to manage the arms race; how to deter the use of nuclear weapons; how to fight a nuclear war if deterrence fails. It is their calculations that are used to explain the necessity of having nuclear destructive capability at what George Kennan has called "levels of such grotesque dimensions as to defy rational understanding." At the same time, it is their reasoning that is used to explain why it is not safe to live without nuclear weapons. In short, they

create the theory that informs and legitimates American nuclear strategic practice.

For two weeks, I listened to men engage in dispassionate discussion of nuclear war. I found myself aghast, but morbidly fascinated—not by nuclear weaponry, or by images of nuclear destruction, but by the extraordinary abstraction and removal from what I knew as reality that characterized the professional discourse. I became obsessed by the question. How can they think this way? At the end of the summer program, when I was offered the opportunity to stay on at the university's center on defense technology and arms control (hereafter known as "the Center"), I jumped at the chance to find out how they could think "this" way.

I spent the next year of my life immersed in the world of defense intellectuals. As a participant observer, I attended lectures, listened to arguments, conversed with defense analysts, and interviewed graduate students at the beginning, middle, and end of their training. I learned their specialized language, and I tried to understand what they thought and how they thought. I sifted through their logic for its internal inconsistencies and its unspoken assumptions. But as I learned their language, as I became more and more engaged with their information and their arguments. I found that my own thinking was changing. Soon, I could

From *Signs, Journal of Women in Culture and Society* (1987) Vol. 12, No. 4; 687–718. © 1987 by The University of Chicago. Reprinted by permission of the publisher and author. All footnotes suppressed.

no longer cling to the comfort of studying an external and objectified "them." I had to confront a new question: How can *I* think this way? How can any of us?

Throughout my time in the world of strategic analysis, it was hard not to notice the ubiquitous weight of gender, both in social relations and in the language itself; it is an almost entirely male world (with the exception of the secretaries), and the language contains many rather arresting metaphors. There is, of course, an important and growing body of feminist theory about gender and language. In addition, there is a rich and increasingly vast body of theoretical work exploring the gendered aspects of war and militarism, which examines such issues as men's and women's different relations to militarism and pacifism, and the ways in which gender ideology is used in the service of militarization. Some of the feminist work on gender and war is also part of an emerging, powerful feminist critique of ideas of rationality as they have developed in Western culture. While I am indebted to all of these bodies of work, my own project is most closely linked to the development of feminist critiques of dominant Western concepts of reason. My goal is to discuss the nature of nuclear strategic thinking; in particular, my emphasis is on the role of its specialized language, a language that I call "technostrategic." I have come to believe that this language both reflects and shapes the nature of the American nuclear strategic project, that it plays a central role in allowing defense intellectuals to think and act as they do, and that feminists who are concerned about nuclear weaponry and nuclear war must give careful attention to the language we choose to use—whom it allows us to communicate with and what it allows us to think as well as say.

STATE I: LISTENING

Clean Bombs and Clean Language

Entering the world of defense intellectuals was a bizarre experience—bizarre because it is a world where men spend their days calmly and matter-of-factly discussing nuclear weapons, nuclear strategy, and nuclear war. The discussions are carefully and intricately reasoned, occurring seemingly without any sense of horror, urgency, or moral outrage—in fact, there seems to be no graphic reality behind the words, as they speak of "first strikes," "counterforce exchanges," and "limited nuclear war," or as they debate the comparative values of a "minimum deterrent posture" versus a "nuclear war–fighting capability."

Yet what is striking about the men themselves is not, as the content of their conversations might suggest, their cold-bloodedness. Rather, it is that they are a group of men unusually endowed with charm, humor, intelligence, concern, and decency. Reader, I liked them. At least, I liked many of them. The attempt to understand how such men could contribute to an endeavor that I see as so fundamentally destructive became a continuing obsession for me, a lens through which I came to examine all of my experiences in their world.

In this early stage, I was gripped by the extraordinary language used to discuss nuclear war. What hit me first was the elaborate use of abstraction and euphemism, of words so bland that they never forced the speaker or enabled the listener to touch the realities of nuclear holocaust that lay behind the words.

Anyone who has seen pictures of Hiroshima burn victims or tried to imagine the pain of hundreds of glass shards blasted into flesh may find it perverse beyond imagination to hear a class of nuclear devices matter-of-factly referred to as "clean bombs." "Clean bombs" are nuclear devices that are largely fusion rather than fission and they release a somewhat higher proportion of their energy as prompt radiation, but produce less radioactive fallout than fission bombs of the same yield.

"Clean bombs" may provide the perfect metaphor for the language of defense analysts and arms controllers. This language has enormous destructive power, but without emotional fallout; without the emotional fallout that would result if it were clear one was talking about plans for mass murder, mangled bodies, human suffering. Defense analysts don't talk about incinerating cities: they talk about "countervalue attacks." Human death, in nuclear parlance, is most often referred to as "collateral damage"; for, as one defense analyst said, with just the right touch of irony in his voice and twinkle in his eye, "the Air Force doesn't target people, it targets shoe factories."

Some phrases carry this cleaning up so far as to invert meaning. The MX missile will carry ten warheads, each with the explosive power of 300 to 475 kilotons of TNT: *one* missile the bearer of destruction approximately *250* to *400* times that of the Hiroshima bombing. Ronald Reagan has christened the MX missile "the Peacekeeper." While this renaming was the object of considerable scorn in the community of defense analysts, some of these very same analysts refer to the MX as a "damage limitation weapon."

Such phrases exemplify the astounding chasm between image and reality that characterizes techno-strategic language. They also hint at the terrifying way in which the existence of nuclear devices has distorted our perceptions and redefined the world. "Clean bombs" as a phrase tells us that radioactivity is the only "dirty" part of killing people.

To take this one step further, such phrases can even seem healthful/curative/corrective. So that we not only have "clean bombs" but also "surgically clean strikes" ("counterforce" attacks that can purportedly "take out"—i.e., accurately destroy—an opponent's weapons or command centers without causing significant injury to anything else). The image of excision of the offending weapon is unspeakably ludicrous when the surgical tool is not a delicately controlled scalpel but a nuclear warhead. And somehow it seems to be forgotten that even scalpels spill blood.

White Men in Ties Discussing Missile Size

Feminists have often suggested that an important aspect of the arms race is phallic worship, that "missile envy" is a significant

motivating force in the nuclear build-up. I have always found this an uncomfortably reductionist explanation and hoped that my research at the Center would yield a more complex analysis. But still, I was curious about the extent to which I might find a sexual subtext in the defense professionals' discourse. I was not prepared for what I found.

I think I had naively imagined myself as a feminist spy in the house of death—that I would need to sneak around and eavesdrop on what men said in unguarded moments, using all my subtlety and cunning to unearth whatever sexual imagery might be underneath how they thought and spoke. I had naively believed that these men, at least in public, would appear to be aware of feminist critiques. If they had not changed their language, I thought that at least at some point in a long talk about "penetration aids," someone would suddenly look up, slightly embarrassed to be caught in such blatant confirmation of feminist analyses of What's Going On Here.

Of course, I was wrong. There was no evidence that any feminist critiques had ever reached the ears, much less the minds, of these men. American military dependence on nuclear weapons was explained as "irresistible, because you get more bang for the buck." Another lecturer solemnly and scientifically announced "to disarm is to get rid of all your stuff." (This may, in turn, explain why they see serious talk of nuclear disarmament as perfectly resistable, not to mention foolish. If disarmament is emasculation, how could any real man even consider it?) A professor's explanation of why the MX missile is to be placed in the silos of the newest Minuteman missiles, instead of replacing the older, less accurate ones, was "because they're in the nicest hole—you're not going to take the nicest missile you have and put it in a crummy hole." Other lectures were filled with discussion of vertical erector launchers, thrust-to-weight ratios, soft lay downs, deep penetration, and the comparative advantages of protracted versus spasm attacks—or what one military adviser to the National Security Council has called "releasing 70 to 80 percent of our megatonnage in one orgasmic whump." There was serious concern about the need to harden our missiles and the need to "face it, the Russians are a little harder than we are." Disbelieving glances would occasionally pass between me and my one ally in the summer program, another woman, but no one else seemed to notice.

If the imagery is transparent, its significance may be less so. The temptation is to draw some conclusions about the defense intellectuals themselves—about what they are *really* talking about, or their motivations; but the temptation is worth resisting. Individual motivations cannot necessarily be read directly from imagery; the imagery itself does not originate in these particular individuals but in a broader cultural context.

Sexual imagery has, of course, been a part of the world of warfare since long before nuclear weapons were even a gleam in a physicist's eye. The history of the atomic bomb project itself is rife with overt images of competitive male sexuality, as is the discourse of the early nuclear physicists, strategists, and SAC commanders. Both the military itself and the arms manufacturers are constantly exploiting the phallic imagery and promise of sexual domination that their weapons so conveniently suggest. . . .

Given the degree to which it suffuses their world, that defense intellectuals themselves use a lot of sexual imagery does not seem especially surprising. Nor does it, by itself, constitute grounds for imputing motivation. For me, the interesting issue is not so much the imagery's psychodynamic origins, as how it functions. How does it serve to make it possible for strategic planners and other defense intellectuals to do their macabre work? How does it function in their construction of a work world that feels tenable? Several stories illustrate the complexity.

During the summer program, a group of us visited the New London Navy base where nuclear submarines are homeported and the General Dynamics Electric Boat boatyards where a new Trident submarine was being constructed. At one point during the trip we took a tour of a nuclear powered submarine. When we reached the part of the sub where the missiles are housed, the officer accompanying us turned with a grin and asked if we wanted to stick our hands through a hole to "pat the missile." *Pat the missile?*

The image reappeared the next week, when a lecturer scornfully declared that the only real reason for deploying cruise and Pershing II missiles in Western Europe was "so that our allies can pat them." Some months later, another group of us went to be briefed at NORAD (the North American Aerospace Defense Command). On the way back, our plane went to refuel at Offut Air Force Base, the Strategic Air Command headquarters near Omaha, Nebraska. When word leaked out that our landing would be delayed because the new B-1 bomber was in the area, the plane became charged with a tangible excitement that built as we flew in our holding pattern, people craning their necks to try to catch a glimpse of the B-1 in the skies, and climaxed as we touched down on the runway and hurtled past it. Later, when I returned to the Center I encountered a man who, unable to go on the trip, said to me enviously, "I hear you got to pat a B-1."

What is all this "patting"? What are men doing when they "pat" these high-tech phalluses? Patting is an assertion of intimacy, sexual possession, affectionate domination. The thrill and pleasure of "patting the missile" is the proximity of all that phallic power, the possibility of vicariously appropriating it as one's own.

But if the predilection for patting phallic objects indicates something of the homoerotic excitement suggested by the language, it also has another side. For patting is not only an act of sexual intimacy. It is also what one does to babies, small children, the pet dog. One pats that which is small, cute, and harmless—not terrifyingly destructive. Pat it, and its lethality disappears.

Much of the sexual imagery I heard was rife with the sort of ambiguity suggested by "patting the missiles." The imagery can be construed as a deadly serious display of the connections between masculine sexuality and the arms race. At the same time, it can also be heard as a way of minimizing the seriousness of militarist endeavors, of denying their deadly consequences. A former Pentagon target analyst, in telling me why he thought plans for "limited nuclear war" were ridiculous, said, "Look, you gotta understand that it's a pissing contest—you gotta expect them to use everything they've got." What does this image say? Most obviously, that this is all about competition for manhood, and thus there is tremendous danger. But at the same time, the image diminishes the contest and its outcomes, by representing it as an act of boyish mischief. . . .

Domestic Bliss

Sanitized abstraction and sexual and patriarchal imagery, even if disturbing, seemed to fit easily into the masculinist world of nuclear war planning. What did not fit, what surprised and puzzled me most when I first heard it, was the set of metaphors that evoked images that can only be called domestic.

Nuclear missiles are based in "silos." On a Trident submarine, which carries twenty-four multiple warhead nuclear missiles, crew members call the part of the submarine where the missiles are lined up in their silos ready for launching "the Christmas tree farm." What could be more bucolic—farms, silos, Christmas trees?

In the ever-friendly, even romantic world of nuclear weaponry, enemies "exchange" warheads; one missile "takes out" another; weapons systems can "marry up"; "coupling" is sometimes used to refer to the wiring between mechanisms of warning and response, or to the psychopolitical links between strategic (intercontinental) and theater (European-based) weapons. The patterns in which a MIRVed missile's nuclear warheads land is known as a "footprint." These nuclear explosives are not dropped; a "bus" "delivers" them. In addition, nuclear bombs are not referred to as bombs or even warheads; they are referred to as "reentry vehicles," a term far more bland and benign, which is then shortened to "RVs," a term not only totally abstract and removed from the reality of a bomb but also resonant with the image of the recreational vehicles of the ideal family vacation.

These domestic images must be more than simply one more form of distancing, one more way to remove oneself from the grisly reality behind the words; ordinary abstraction is adequate to that task. Something else, something very peculiar, is going on here. Calling the pattern in which bombs fall a "footprint" almost seems a willful distorting process, a playful, perverse refusal of accountability—because to be accountable to reality is to be unable to do this work.

These words may also serve to domesticate, to *tame* the wild and uncontrollable forces of nuclear destruction. The metaphors minimize; they are a way to make phenomena that are beyond what the mind can encompass smaller and safer, and thus they are a way of gaining mastery over the unmasterable. The fire-breathing dragon under the bed, the one who threatens to incinerate your family, your town, your planet, becomes a pet you can pat.

Using language evocative of everyday experiences also may simply serve to make the nuclear strategic community more comfortable with what they are doing. "PAL" (permissive action links) is the carefully constructed, friendly acronym for the electronic system designed to prevent the unauthorized firing of nuclear warheads. "BAMBI" was the acronym developed for an early version of an antiballistic missile system (for Ballistic Missile Boost Intercept). The president's Annual Nuclear Weapons Stockpile Memorandum, which outlines both short- and long-range plans for production of new nuclear weapons, is benignly referred to as "the shopping list." The National Command Authorities choose from a "menu of options" when deciding among different targeting plans. The "cookie cutter" is a phrase used to describe a particular model of nuclear attack. Apparently it is also used at the Department of Defense to refer to the neutron bomb.

The imagery that domesticates, that humanizes insentient weapons, may also serve, paradoxically, to make it all right to ignore sentient human bodies, human lives. Perhaps it is possible to spend one's time thinking about scenarios for the use of destructive technology and to have human bodies remain invisible in that technological world precisely because that world itself now *includes* the domestic, the human, the warm, and playful—the Christmas trees, the RVs, the affectionate pats. It is a world that is in some sense complete unto itself; it even includes death and loss. But it is weapons, not humans, that get "killed." "Fratricide" occurs when one of your warheads "kills" another of your own warheads. There is much discussion of "vulnerability" and "survivability," but it is about the vulnerability and survival of weapons systems, not people. . . .

God and the Nuclear Priesthood

The possibility that the language reveals an attempt to appropriate ultimate creative power is evident in a. . . striking aspect of the language of nuclear weaponry and doctrine—the religious imagery. In a subculture of hard-nosed realism and hyper-rationality, in a world that claims as a sign of its superiority its vigilant purging of all nonrational elements, and in which people carefully excise from their discourse every possible trace of soft sentimentality, as though purging dangerous nonsterile elements from a lab, the last thing one might expect to find is religious imagery—imagery of the forces that science has been defined in *opposition to*. For surely, given that science's identity was forged by its separation from, by its struggle for freedom from, the constraints of religion, the only thing as unscientific as the female, the subjective, the emotional, would be the religious. And yet, religious imagery permeates the nuclear past and present. The first atomic bomb test was called Trinity—the unity of the Father, the Son, and the Holy Spirit, the male forces of Creation. The imagery is echoed in the language of the physicists who worked on the bomb and witnessed the test: "It was as though we stood at the first day of creation." Robert Oppenheimer thought of Krishna's words to Arjuna in the *Bhagavad Gita*: "I am become Death, the Shatterer of Worlds."

Perhaps most astonishing of all is the fact that the creators of strategic doctrine actually refer to members of their community as "the

nuclear priesthood." It is hard to decide what is most extraordinary about this: the easy arrogance of their claim to the virtues and supernatural power of the priesthood; the tacit admission (*never* spoken directly) that rather than being unflinching, hard-nosed, objective, empirically minded scientific describers of reality, they are really the creators of dogma; or the extraordinary implicit statement about who, or rather what, has become god. . . .

STAGE 2: LEARNING TO SPEAK THE LANGUAGE

Although I was startled by the combination of dry abstraction and counter-intuitive imagery that characterizes the language of defense intellectuals, my attention and energy were quickly focused on decoding and learning to speak it. The first task was training the tongue in the articulation of acronyms.

Several years of reading the literature of nuclear weaponry and strategy had not prepared me for the degree to which acronyms littered all conversations, nor for the way in which they are used. Formerly, I had thought of them mainly as utilitarian. They allow you to write or speak faster. They act as a form of abstraction, removing you from the reality behind the words. They restrict communication to the initiated, leaving all others both uncomprehending and voiceless in the debate.

But, being at the Center, hearing the defense analysts use the acronyms, and then watching as I and others in the group started to fling acronyms around in our conversation revealed some additional, unexpected dimensions.

First, in speaking and hearing, a lot of these terms can be very sexy. A small supersonic rocket "designed to penetrate any Soviet air defense" is called a SRAM (for short-range attack missile). Submarine-launched cruise missiles are not referred to as SLCMs, but "slick'ems." Ground-launched cruise missiles are "glick'ems." Air-launched cruise missiles are not sexy but magical—"alchems" (ALCMs) replete with the illusion of turning base metals into gold. . . .

In other words, what I learned at the program is that talking about nuclear weapons is fun. I am serious. The words are fun to say; they are racy, sexy, snappy. You can throw them around in rapid-fire succession. They are quick, clean, light; they trip off the tongue. You can reel off dozens of them in seconds, forgetting about how one might just interfere with the next, not to mention with the lives beneath them.

I am not describing a phenomenon experienced only by the perverse, although the phenomenon itself may be perverse indeed. Nearly everyone I observed clearly took pleasure in using the words. It mattered little whether we were lecturers or students, hawks or doves, men or women—we all learned it, and we all spoke it. Some of us may have spoken with a self-consciously ironic edge, but the pleasure was there nonetheless.

Part of the appeal was the thrill of being able to manipulate an arcane language, the power of entering the secret kingdom, being someone in the know. It is a glow that is a significant part of learning about nuclear weaponry. Few know, and those who do are powerful. You can rub elbows with them, perhaps even be one yourself.

That feeling, of course, does not come solely from the language. The whole set-up of the summer program itself, for example, communicated the allures of power and the benefits of white male privileges. We were provided with luxurious accommodations, complete with young black women who came in to clean up after us each day; generous funding paid not only our transportation and food but also a large honorarium for attending; we met in lavishly appointed classrooms and lounges. Access to excellent athletic facilities was guaranteed by a "Temporary Privilege Card," which seemed to me to sum up the essence of the experience. Perhaps most important of all were the endless allusions by our lecturers to "what I told John [Kennedy]" and "and then Henry [Kissinger] said," or the lunches where we could sit next to a prominent political figure and listen to Washington gossip.

A more subtle, but perhaps more important, element of learning the language is that, when you speak it, you feel in control. The experience of mastering the words infuses your relation to the material. You can get so good at manipulating the words that it almost feels as though the whole thing is under control. Learning the language gives a sense of what I would call cognitive mastery; the feeling of mastery of technology that is finally *not* controllable but is instead powerful beyond human comprehension, powerful in a way that stretches and even thrills the imagination.

The more conversations I participated in using this language, the less frightened I was of nuclear war. How can learning to speak a language have such a powerful effect? One answer, I believe, is that the *process* of learning the language is itself a part of what removes you from the reality of nuclear war.

I entered a world where people spoke what amounted to a foreign language, a language I had to learn if we were to communicate with one another. So I became engaged in the challenge of it—of decoding the acronyms and figuring out which were the proper verbs to use. My focus was on the task of solving the puzzles, developing language competency—not on the weapons and wars behind the words. Although my interest was in thinking about nuclear war and its prevention, my energy was elsewhere.

By the time I was through, I had learned far more than a set of abstract words that refers to grisly subjects, for even when the subjects of a standard English and nukespeak description seem to be the same, they are, in fact, about utterly different phenomena. Consider the following descriptions, in each of which the subject is the aftermath of a nuclear attack:

Everything was black, had vanished into the black dust, was destroyed. Only the flames that were beginning to lick their way up had any color. From the dust that was like a fog, figures began to loom up, black, hairless, faceless. They screamed with voices that were no longer human. Their screams drowned out the groans rising everywhere from the rubble, groans that seemed to rise from the very earth itself. [Hisako Matsubara, *Cranes at Dusk*].

[You have to have ways to maintain communications in a] nuclear environment, a situation bound to include EMP blackout, brute force damage to systems, a heavy jamming environment, and so on. [General Robert Rosenberg, 1980].

There are no ways to describe the phenomena represented in the first with the language of the second. Learning to speak the language of defense analysts is not a conscious, cold-blooded decision to ignore the effects of nuclear weapons on real live human beings, to ignore the sensory, the emotional experience, the human impact. It is simply learning a new language, but by the time you are through, the content of what you can talk about is monumentally different, as is the perspective from which you speak.

In the example above, the differences in the two descriptions of a "nuclear environment" stem partly from a difference in the vividness of the words themselves—the words of the first intensely immediate and evocative, the words of the second abstract and distancing. The passages also differ in their content; the first describes the effects of a nuclear blast on human beings, the second describes the impact of a nuclear blast on technical systems designed to assure the "command and control" of nuclear weapons. Both of these differences may stem from the difference of perspective: the speaker in the first is a victim of nuclear weapons, the speaker in the second is a user. The speaker in the first is using words to try to name and contain the horror of human suffering all around her; the speaker in the second is using words to ensure the possibility of launching the next nuclear attack. Technostrategic language can be used only to articulate the perspective of the users of nuclear weapons, not that of the victims.

Thus, speaking the expert language not only offers distance, a feeling of control, and an alternative focus for one's energies; it also offers escape—escape from thinking of oneself as a victim of nuclear war. I do not mean this on the level of individual consciousness; it is not that defense analysts somehow convince themselves that they would not be among the victims of nuclear war, should it occur. But I do mean it in terms of the structural position the speakers of the language occupy and the perspective they get from that position. *Structurally*, speaking technostrategic language removes them from the position of victim and puts them in the position of the planner, the user, the actor. From that position, there is neither need nor way to see oneself as a victim; no matter what one deeply knows or believes about the likelihood of nuclear war, and no matter what sort of terror or despair the knowledge of nuclear war's reality might inspire, the speakers of technostrategic language are positionally allowed, even forced, to escape that awareness, to escape viewing nuclear war from the position of the victim, by virtue of their linguistic stance as users, rather than victims, of nuclear weaponry.

Finally, then, I suspect that much of the reduced anxiety about nuclear war commonly experienced by both new speakers of the language and long-time experts comes from characteristics of the language itself: the distance afforded by its abstraction; the sense of control afforded by mastering it; and the fact that its content and concerns are that of the users rather than the victims of nuclear weapons. In learning the language, one goes from being the passive, powerless victim to the competent, wily, powerful purveyor of nuclear threats and nuclear explosive power. The enormous destructive effects of nuclear weapons systems become extensions of the self, rather than threats to it.

STAGE 3: DIALOGUE

It did not take very long to learn the language of nuclear war and much of the specialized information it contained. My focus quickly changed from mastering technical information and doctrinal arcana to attempting to understand more about how the dogma was rationalized. Instead of trying, for example, to find out why submarines are so hard to detect or why, prior to the Trident II, submarine-based ballistic missiles were not considered counterforce weapons, I now wanted to know why we really "need" a strategic triad, given submarines' "invulnerability." I also wanted to know why it is considered reasonable to base U.S. military planning on the Soviet Union's military capabilities rather than seriously attempting to gauge what their intentions might be. This standard practice is one I found particularly troubling. Military analysts say that since we cannot know for certain what Soviet intentions are, we must plan our military forces and strategies as if we knew that the Soviets planned to use all of their weapons. While this might appear to have the benefit of prudence, it leads to a major problem. When we ask only what the Soviets *can* do, we quickly come to assume that that is what they *intend* to do. We base our planning on "worst-case scenarios" and then come to believe that we live in a world where vast resources must he committed to "prevent" them from happening.

Since underlying rationales are rarely discussed in the everyday business of defense planning, I had to start asking more questions. At first, although I was tempted to use my newly acquired proficiency in technostrategic jargon, I vowed to speak English. I had long believed that one of the most important functions of an expert language is exclusion—the denial of a voice to those outside the professional community. I wanted to see whether a well-informed person could speak English and still carry on a knowledgeable conversation.

What I found was that no matter how well-informed or complex my questions were, if I spoke English rather than expert jargon, the men responded to me as though I were ignorant, simpleminded, or both. It did not appear to occur to anyone that I might actually be choosing not to speak their language.

A strong distaste for being patronized and dismissed made my experiment in English short-lived. I adapted my everyday speech to the vocabulary of strategic analysis. I spoke of "escalation dominance," "preemptive strikes," and, one of my favorites, "subholocaust engagements." Using the right phrases opened my way into long, elaborate discussions that taught me a lot about technostrategic reasoning and how to manipulate it.

I found, however, that the better I got at engaging in this discourse, the more impossible it became for me to express my own ideas, my own values. I could adopt the language and gain a wealth of new concepts and reasoning strategies—but at the same time as the language gave me access to things I had been unable to speak about before, it radically excluded others. I could not use the language to express my concerns because it was physically impossible. This language does not allow certain questions to be asked or certain values to be expressed.

To pick a bald example: the word "peace" is not a part of this discourse. As close as one can come is "strategic stability," a term that refers to a balance of numbers and types of weapons systems—not the political, social, economic, and psychological conditions implied by the word "peace". Not only is there no word signifying peace in this discourse, but the word "peace" itself cannot be used. To speak it is immediately to brand oneself as a soft-headed activist instead of an expert, a professional to be taken seriously.

If I was unable to speak my concerns in this language, more disturbing still was that I found it hard even to keep them in my own head. I had begun my research expecting abstract and sanitized discussions of nuclear war and had readied myself to replace my words for theirs, to be ever vigilant against slipping into the never-never land of abstraction. But no matter how prepared I was, no matter how firm my commitment to staying aware of the reality behind the words, over and over I found that I could not stay connected, could not keep human lives as my reference point. I found I could go for days speaking about nuclear weapons without once thinking about the people who would be incinerated by them.

It is tempting to attribute this problem to qualities of the language, the words themselves—the abstractness, the euphemisms, the sanitized, friendly, sexy acronyms. Then all we would need to do is change the words, make them more vivid; get the military planners to say "mass murder" instead of "collateral damage" and their thinking would change.

The problem, however, is not only that defense intellectuals use abstract terminology that removes them from the realities of which they speak. There is no reality of which they speak. Or, rather, the "reality" of which they speak is itself a world of abstractions. Deterrence theory, and much of strategic doctrine altogether, was invented largely by mathematicians, economists, and a few political scientists. It was invented to hold together abstractly, its validity judged by its internal logic. Questions of the correspondence to observable reality were not the issue. These abstract systems were developed as a way to make it possible to "think about the unthinkable"— not as a way to describe or codify relations on the ground. . . .

To use more descriptive language would not, by itself, change that. In fact, I am tempted to say that the abstractness of the entire conceptual system makes descriptive language nearly beside the point. In a discussion of "limited nuclear war," for example, it might make some difference if in place of saying "In a counter-force attack against hard targets collateral damage could be limited," a strategic analyst had to use words that were less abstract—if he had to say, for instance. "If we launch the missiles we have aimed at their missile silos, the explosions would cause the immediate mass murder of 10 million women, men, and children, as well as the extended illness, suffering, and eventual death of many millions more." It is true that the second sentence does not roll off the tongue or slide across one's consciousness quite as easily. But it is also true, I believe, that the ability to speak about "limited nuclear war" stems as much, if not more, from the fact that the term "limited nuclear war" refers to an abstract conceptual system rather than to events that might take place in the real world. As such, there is no need to think about the concrete human realities behind the model; what counts is the internal logic of the system.

This realization that the abstraction was not just in the words but also characterized the entire conceptual system itself helped me make sense of my difficulty in staying connected to human lives. But there was still a piece missing. How is it possible, for example, to make sense of the following paragraph? It is taken from a discussion of a scenario ("regime A") in which the United States and the USSR have revised their offensive weaponry, banned MIRVs, and gone to a regime of single warhead (Midgetman) missiles, with no "defensive shield" (or what is familiarly known as "Star Wars" or SDI):

The strategic stability of regime A is based on the fact that both sides are deprived of any incentive ever to strike first. Since it takes roughly two warheads to destroy one enemy silo, an attacker must expend two of his missiles to destroy one of the enemy's. A first strike disarms the attacker. The aggressor ends up worse off than the aggressed.

"The aggressor ends up worse off than the aggressed"? The homeland of "the aggressed" has just been devastated by the explosions of, say, a thousand nuclear bombs, each likely to be ten to one hundred times more powerful than the bomb dropped on Hiroshima, and the aggressor, whose homeland is still untouched, "ends up worse off"? How is it possible to think this? Even abstract language and abstract thinking do not seem to be a sufficient explanation.

I was only able to "make sense of it" when I finally asked myself the question that feminists have been asking about theories in every discipline: What is the reference point? Who (or what) is the *subject* here?

In other disciplines, we have frequently found that the reference point for theories about "universal human phenomena" has actually been white men. In technostrategic discourse, the reference point is not white men, it is not human beings at all; it is the weapons themselves. The aggressor thus ends up worse off than the aggressed because he has fewer weapons left; human factors are irrelevant to the calculus of gain and loss.

. . . if human lives are not the reference point, then it is not only impossible to talk about humans in this language, it also becomes in some sense illegitimate to ask the paradigm to reflect human concerns. Hence, questions that break through the numbing language of strategic analysis and raise issues in human terms can be dismissed easily. No one will claim that the questions are unimportant, but they are inexpert, unprofessional, irrelevant to the business at hand to ask. The discourse among the experts remains hermetically sealed.

The problem, then, is not only that the language is narrow but also that it is seen by its speakers as complete or whole unto itself—as representing a body of truths that exist independently of any other truth or knowledge. . . .

STAGE 4: THE TERROR

As a newcomer to the world of defense analysts, I was continually startled by likeable and admirable men, by their gallows humor, by the bloodcurdling casualness with which they regularly blew up the world while standing and chatting over the coffee pot. I also *heard* the language they spoke—heard the acronyms and euphemisms, and abstractions, heard the imagery, heard the pleasure with which they used it.

Within a few weeks, what had once been remarkable became unnoticeable. As I learned to speak, my perspective changed. I no longer stood outside the impermeable wall of technostrategic language and, once inside, I could no longer see it. Speaking the language, I could no longer really hear it. And once inside its protective walls, I began to find it difficult to get out. The impermeability worked both ways.

I had not only learned to speak a language: I had started to think in it. Its questions became my questions, its concepts shaped my responses to new ideas. Its definitions of the parameters of reality became mine. Like the White Queen [in *Alice in Wonderland*], I began to believe six impossible things before breakfast. Not because I consciously believed, for instance, that a "surgically clean counterforce strike" was really possible, but instead because some elaborate piece of doctrinal reasoning I

used was already predicated on the possibility of those strikes, as well as on a host of other impossible things.

My grasp on what *I* knew as reality seemed to slip. I might get very excited, for example, about a new strategic justification for a "no first use" policy and spend time discussing the ways in which its implications for our force structure in Western Europe were superior to the older version. And after a day or two I would suddenly step back, aghast that I was so involved with the military justifications for not using nuclear weapons—as though the moral ones were not enough. What I was actually talking about—the mass incineration caused by a nuclear attack—was no longer in my head. . . .

CONCLUSIONS

Suffice it to say that the issues about language do not disappear after you have mastered technostrategic discourse. The seductions remain great. You can find all sorts of ways to seemingly beat the boys at their own game; you can show how even within their own definitions of rationality, most of what is happening in the development and deployment of nuclear forces is wildly irrational. You can also impress your friends and colleagues with sickly humorous stories about the way things really happen on the inside. There is tremendous pleasure in it, especially for those of us who have been closed out, who have been told that it is really all beyond us and we should just leave it to the benevolently paternal men in charge.

But as the pleasures deepen, so do the dangers. The activity of trying to out-reason defense intellectuals in their own games gets you thinking inside their rules, tacitly accepting all the unspoken assumptions of their paradigms. You become subject to the tyranny of concepts. The language shapes your categories of thought (e.g., here it becomes "good nukes" or "bad nukes," not, nukes or no nukes) and defines the boundaries of imagination (as you try to imagine a "minimally destabilizing basing mode" rather than a way to prevent the weapon from being deployed at all).

Yet, the issues of language have now become somewhat less vivid and central to me. . . . My own move away from a focus on the language is quite typical. Other recent entrants into this world have commented to me that, while it is the cold-blooded, abstract discussions that are most striking at first, within a short time "you get past it—you stop hearing it, it stops bothering you, it becomes normal—and you come to see that the language, itself, is not the problem."

However, I think it would be a mistake to dismiss these early impressions. They can help us learn something about the militarization of the mind, and they have, I believe, important implications for feminist scholars and activists who seek to create a more just and peaceful world. . . .

Listening to the discourse of nuclear experts reveals a series of culturally grounded and culturally acceptable mechanisms that serve this purpose and that make it possible to "think about the unthinkable," to work in institutions that foster the proliferation of nuclear weapons, to plan mass incinerations of millions of human beings for a living. Language that is abstract, sanitized, full of euphemisms; language that is sexy and fun to use; paradigms whose referent is weapons; imagery that domesticates and deflates the forces of mass destruction; imagery that reverses sentient and nonsentient matter, that conflates birth and death, destruction and creation—all of these are part of what makes it possible to be radically removed from the reality of what one is talking about and from the realities one is creating through the discourse.

Learning to speak the language reveals something about how thinking can become more abstract, more focused on parts disembedded from their context, more attentive to the survival of weapons than the survival of human beings. That is, it reveals something about the process of militarization—and the way in which that process may be undergone by man or woman, hawk or dove.

Most often, the act of learning technostrategic language is conceived of as an additive process: you add a new set of vocabulary words;

you add the reflex ability to decode and use endless numbers of acronyms; you add some new information that the specialized language contains; you add the conceptual tools that will allow you to "think strategically." This additive view appears to be held by defense intellectuals themselves; as one said to me, "Much of the debate is in technical terms—learn it, and decide whether it's relevant later." This view also appears to be held by many who think of themselves as antinuclear, be they scholars and professionals attempting to change the field from within, or public interest lobbyists and educational organizations, or some feminist antimilitarists. Some believe that our nuclear policies are so riddled with irrationality that there is a lot of room for well-reasoned, well-informed arguments to make a difference; others, even if they do not believe that the technical information is very important, see it as necessary to master the language simply because it is too difficult to attain public legitimacy without it. In either case, the idea is that you add the expert language and information and proceed from there.

However, I have been arguing throughout this paper that learning the language is a transformative, rather than an additive, process. When you choose to learn it you enter a new mode of thinking—a mode of thinking not only about nuclear weapons but also, de facto, about military and political power and about the relationship between human ends and technological means.

Thus, those of us who find U.S. nuclear policy desperately misguided appear to face a serious quandary. If we refuse to learn the language, we are virtually guaranteed that our voices will remain outside the "politically relevant" spectrum of opinion. Yet, if we do learn and speak it, we not only severely limit what we can say but we also invite the transformation, the militarization, of our own thinking.

I have no solutions to this dilemma, but I would like to offer a few thoughts in an effort to reformulate its terms. First, it is important to recognize an assumption implicit in adopting the strategy of learning the language. When we assume that learning and speaking the language will give us a voice recognized as legitimate and will give us greater political influence, *we are assuming that the language itself actually articulates the criteria and reasoning strategies upon which nuclear weapons development and deployment decisions are made.* I believe that this is largely an illusion. Instead, I want to suggest that technostrategic discourse functions more as a gloss, as an ideological curtain behind which the actual reasons for these decisions hide. That rather than informing and shaping decisions, it far more often functions as a legitimation for political outcomes that have occurred for utterly different reasons. If this is true, it raises some serious questions about the extent of the political returns we might get from using technostrategic discourse, and whether they can ever balance out the potential problems and inherent costs.

I do not, however want to suggest that none of us should learn the language. . . . One of the most intriguing options opened by learning the language is that it suggests a basis upon which to challenge the legitimacy of the defense intellectuals dominance of the discourse on nuclear issues. When defense intellectuals are criticized for the cold-blooded inhumanity of the scenarios they plan, their response is to claim the high ground of rationality; they are the only ones whose response to the existence of nuclear weapons is objective and realistic. They portray those who are radically opposed to the nuclear status quo as irrational, unrealistic, too emotional. "Idealistic activists" is the pejorative they set against their own hardnosed professionalism.

Much of their claim to legitimacy, then, is a claim to objectivity born of technical expertise and to the disciplined purging of the emotional valences that might threaten their objectivity. But if the surface of their discourse—its abstraction and technical jargon—

appears at first to support these claims, a look just below the surface does not. There we find currents of homoerotic excitement, heterosexual domination, the drive toward competency and mastery, the pleasures of membership in an elite and privileged group, the ultimate importance and meaning of membership in the priesthood, and the thrilling power of becoming Death, shatterer of worlds. How is it possible to hold this up as a paragon of cool-headed objectivity?

I do not wish here to discuss or judge the holding of "objectivity" as an epistemological goal. I would simply point out that, as defense intellectuals rest their claims to legitimacy on the untainted rationality of their discourse, their project fails according to its own criteria. Deconstructing strategic discourse's claims to rationality is, then, in and of itself, an important way to challenge its hegemony as the sole legitimate language for public debate about nuclear policy.

I believe that feminists, and others who seek a more just and peaceful world, have a dual task before us—a deconstructive project and a reconstructive project that are intimately linked. Our deconstructive task requires close attention to, and the dismantling of, technostrategic discourse. The dominant voice of militarized masculinity and decontextualized rationality speaks so loudly in our culture, it will remain difficult for any other voices to be heard until that voice loses some of its power to define what we hear and how we name the world—until that voice is delegitimated.

Our reconstructive task is a task of creating compelling alternative visions of possible futures, a task of recognizing and developing alternative conceptions of rationality, a task of creating rich and imaginative alternative voices—diverse voices whose conversations with each other will invent those futures.

Chapter 12
Global Leadership, World Order, and the World Political Economy

44. A New Concert of Powers

RICHARD ROSECRANCE

I

The world does not need to be reminded that it exists in a formal state of anarchy. There is no international government. Nor is there sufficient interdependence or division of labor among states to transform international relations into a social system akin to domestic affairs. Under prevailing circumstances there are only three methods by which that anarchic system can be regulated or prevented from lapsing into chaos: the traditional balance of power; nuclear deterrence; and rule by a central coalition. Each system has been employed at different times during the last two hundred years.

The balance of power held sway during most of the nineteenth and the first part of the twentieth century. It was an inefficient mechanism at best, providing no automatic equilibration of power relationships. It also gave rise to both world wars this century. Under this system nations found it difficult to respond credibly to an aggressor state. While the balancing system aimed to restrain conflict, it did not fully control the aggressive policies of major nations.

Deterrence, used during the period of bipolarity from 1945 to 1989, was more successful. Through the threat of nuclear retaliation the

From *Foreign Affairs* 71 (Spring), 1992:64–82. Reprinted by permission of the author. All footnotes suppressed.

system constrained the behavior of the two superpowers. With forces stationed in other countries the great powers largely solved the chronic problem of credibility of engagement that had beset the nineteenth-century balance. But deterrence was an expensive and tension-laden system. Major wars were prevented only through recurrent crises of resolve, such as Berlin, Cuba and the Yom Kippur War. Nuclear weapons were never used in anger, but the world veered uncomfortably close to the brink from time to time.

The arms race also involved the expenditure of about $500 billion per year by the Soviet Union and United States alone. The opportunity costs of such staggering sums prevented the so-called superpowers from dealing effectively with domestic social problems, as well as denying them rapid and continuous economic growth. Like seventeenth-century Spain, the U.S.S.R. and the United States armed themselves into virtual economic stasis, while other powers proceeded to make unparalleled gains.

The third organizing method, rule by a central coalition, has existed only briefly and episodically in the past two centuries, but it is by far the most efficient peacekeeping device. In the nineteenth century the Concert of Europe functioned effectively from 1815 to 1822, and desultorily thereafter. Post-Napoleonic France was allowed to rejoin Britain, Russia, Austria and Prussia, and agreement among the five great powers provided a short period of direction for domestic as well as foreign affairs. After World War I the League of Nations Council briefly received international attention and obedience. But hampered from the outset by the absence of the United States, after 1924 it was no longer able to guide national or international policy.

Today the breakup of the Soviet Union, the liberation of eastern Europe, the Gulf War and the rapprochement between the United States and Russia have lent the world a new concert of powers. Five great bases of power again control the organization of the world order: the United States, Russia, the European Community, Japan and China. The U.N. Security Council is one manifestation of this new central coalition, which reaches its decisions in great power diplomatic consultations and only then expresses these in the United Nations and other forums.

The present-day situation is both urgent and precarious. While past concerts lingered on for some years, they failed to control events after about a decade. If the new post-Cold War system began in 1989, with the collapse of the Iron Curtain, the world now has about seven to ten years to make it workable and lasting. If this new system is not firmly established within that period, the world order may again lapse into a balance of power or an unworkable multipolar deterrence by the year 2000.

The critical question, therefore, is how long this coalition will last. Its longevity is a matter of greatest consequence: a relapse into a balance of power system, or even a proliferate deterrence, could produce a reversion to violence and the threat of force as chronic components of international relations. Such an outcome would represent a defeat of the most profound hopes aroused in Europe, America and the world since 1945.

II

Much of the traditional writing on the balance of power glorifies an institution that was phlegmatic and unpredictable at best. Contrary to conventional wisdom, the aggressive French Emperor Napoleon was not brought to heel by a rapidly organized and powerful counter-coalition. Rather he defeated one opponent at a time and then (with the exception of Great Britain) co-opted each into the French system of empire.

In 1812 Napoleon decided to attack Russia. An effective coalition began to form against him only after his first defeats in that campaign. In fact the European powers leaned toward his side, or at least toward that of the apparent victor. Such a response was not surprising: in the balance of power system, European nations each waited for the other to take the lead against a disruptive state. Despite celebrations of the balance of power system at the 1815 Congress of Vienna, most European states had propitiated the disrupter—they did not want to challenge a successful aggressor.

When Italy and Germany were unified, the balance was equally somnolent and unresponsive. Italian unification was bound to contribute to the glory of France; it could only come at the humiliation of Austria—Italy's imperial overlord, France's premier foe and the major upholder of the Vienna settlement. France defeated Austria in 1859 and then seized Nice: the European powers did nothing.

Stunning Prussian-German gains were also neglected as Germany was unified. Prussia and Austria defeated Denmark while Britain, despite historical commitments to Copenhagen, sat on its hands. Prussia then took on Austria, and again the European powers failed to act. More egregious, Prussia defeated France in 1870–71 without opposition. The powers were languidly considering what they might do in July 1870 when news came of the Prussian victory at Sedan; they quickly and pusillanimously decided to support the winner.

For the next twenty years the European states continued to sustain an overbalance of power under the leadership of German Chancellor Prince Otto von Bismarck. It was not until Kaiser Wilhelm II ascended to the imperial throne in 1890 that a real balance began to form. This was not the result of an overweening reaction against Germany but rather Wilhelm's own inept casting-off of clients. When in 1890 Germany refused to renew its Reinsurance Treaty with Russia, the tsar turned to France for help against Austria, the traditional Balkan enemy. But even the Franco-Russian alliance of 1894 did not represent a "balance" against Germany, any more than against England. Both France and Russia were eager to expand their colonies at Britain's expense, and Russia, at least, still eyed the prospect of reconciliation with Berlin. As did Britain: between 1899 and 1901 England repeatedly asked Germany for an alliance and only settled for an arrangement with Paris in 1904 because Berlin was unavailable.

The consolidation of the Triple Entente against the Triple Alliance, therefore, did not make for a solid balance against Germany. The Kaiser and his advisers, like other nineteenth-century military expansionists, adhered to the view that opponents would cave in once Germany made startling new gains. France, then, might be defeated quickly in 1914, as it had been in 1870. Germany thus did not hesitate to force the issue, and the surprise was that Britain did not yield or compromise. Russia also took an unwontedly strong stand against Berlin and was itself responsible for early actions toward partial and general mobilization.

Thus the balance in 1914 did not prevent war; it fomented it. The alliances were neither strong nor credible enough to face down resolute action by the adversary; they were just strong enough to drag reluctant participants into military conflict. Instead of deterring war *ex ante*, they actually brought it on *ex post*.

The same result occurred in 1939. Britain and France could not save Poland or Romania when they guaranteed them against German aggression that spring. They could only enforce a guarantee through the military power of Russia—the only nation that could provide defense on the spot. Neither Paris nor London thought they could succeed in a military offensive that would have to bridge the Rhine and smash the German westwall. The *Wehrmacht* would be too strong. Thus Hitler understandably believed that Britain and France would back down once he reached agreement with Stalin.

There was thus no effective "balance" against Germany that August. It was surprising that Britain and France went to war at all: they could do little unless Hitler decided to attack them. Nor did either have an agreement with the United States, despite President Roosevelt's occasional musings about how he would save England. Military guarantees and alliances in 1939 did not deter war; again, they merely dragged unwilling participants into it.

In all these major wars it is interesting to note that the aggressor forged the decisive balance against himself, a balance that would not otherwise have been created. Napoleon resolved on the campaign against Russia in 1812; it was not St. Petersburg. Imperial Germany decided in 1917 to wage unrestricted submarine warfare against the United States, and it was Hitler who made the colossal mistake (after inexplicably waiting three days to decide) of declaring war on December 11, 1941, against the world's strongest power, the United States, thereby sealing his own fate.

The international economic system of the late nineteenth century also made the balance of power function ineffectively. The world economy did not create an interdependence that prohibited war. Links among the major powers (except perhaps those between France and Russia) were tenuous and did not cement relations. For most necessary food and raw materials, trade was directed to less developed areas and colonies. Britain wanted to make its empire a unit largely independent of trade with the rest of the world. Economic relations forged few necessary links among industrial states themselves. Although there was a great deal of trade among Britain, France and Germany, little of it was strategic. Important political leaders in each country instead wished to reorient trade to perpetuate an "imperial federation" or, in the German case, a *Mitteleuropa* that would exclude or substitute for past economic dependence on other European powers.

In sum, the history of the so-called balance of power is one of either weakness or misperceived strength—of attempts to divert the attention of the aggressor and focus it on another state. It is only occasionally redeemed by strong but vainglorious stands against aggression. As a method of regulating international behavior and conflict, it either did too little or too much, but it did not generally deter hostile political or military action.

III

Bipolar nuclear deterrence was a more effective but risky and expensive system of conflict control. It remedied some of the deficiencies of the balance of power. Credibility of response to aggression was far greater, partly because the system was bipolar. But its greater effectiveness was also due to ideological differences that created an antagonism not fully sustained in power terms. Given the ideological rift, each power would respond immediately to the actions of the other. In such circumstances the Soviet Union would be opposed even though it was much weaker.

Nuclear weapons added another element of stability. They were employed in the last phase of the Pacific War against Japan, and doctrine held that they would be used again in the event of a Soviet attack on Europe. Perhaps more important, the United States placed forces in the territories of its allies, thereby committing itself in advance to resist. That commitment became very important when the range of Soviet nuclear weapons was extended to include the continental United States.

In contrast nineteenth-century alliances did not station forces in other nations; forces got there only after war began. One wonders whether the Kaiser, Bethmann-Hollweg and the younger Moltke would have been so anxious to begin war at the end of July 1914 had a British expeditionary force already been based on the Marne. Would the Austrian leaders, Conrad and Berchtold, have moved so quickly if Russian forces had been stationed in Serbia?

While the nuclear deterrent system guaranteed some response to aggression, it was not self-operating. Truman and his advisers worried so much about the advent of Soviet nuclear weapons that they spent huge amounts on conventional forces, all in the name of creating credibility. Credibility problems, however, surfaced once again in the Kennedy administration, when it appeared that nuclear weapons might not be employed against certain types of targets or in response to limited Soviet probes. The Defense Department occasionally contended that a Russian conventional attack could be parried by Western conventional forces alone. In this respect the credibility of U.S. nuclear deterrence declined with time and as Soviet forces grew both qualitatively and quantitatively.

It thus sometimes appeared useful for the United States (as well as the Soviet Union) to engage in military ventures to enhance overall credibility. The Soviets thus invaded Hungary and Czechoslovakia and threatened Poland. The United States demonstrated its military resolve by responding to the attack on South Korea and fighting in Vietnam. In 1962 the United States also threatened to intervene in Cuba and in 1973 in the Yom Kippur War. The Soviet Union sent its own forces into Afghanistan and proxy forces to Angola, Mozambique and Ethiopia.

Fortunately U.S. and Soviet forces rarely encountered one another, but there was the episodic possibility that nuclear weapons might be used. Each new American administration was pressed to take a tough line with the Soviets at the outset of its term, to pave the way for later agreements. These early periods could be quite tense. War did not occur, but the world may have emerged unscathed from the machinations of deterrence through a not negligible quantity of good fortune.

Economically the deterrent system paid the public-goods costs of creating an international economy to sustain the Western half of the bipolar order. There was a structural link between the American, European and Japanese economies; the resumption of European and Japanese growth was sustained by sales in the

United States. World markets were opened to Japanese and European goods. The Soviet bloc reciprocated and created its own "hothouse" Eastern economy. Sales of poorly manufactured east European wares went to the Soviet Union in return for Soviet exports of raw materials and oil.

Although economic frontiers reinforced military ones and therefore added to unity and credibility, the nuclear deterrent system was beset by high opportunity costs. These, of course, were not reflected merely in excess military spending. The United States sought to organize the Western world politically and economically—as well as militarily—in order to sustain its chain of commitments to allies. It paid the public-goods costs of keeping an open Western and democratic trading system; it encouraged associates to sell their products in the American market.

In that effort the United States fostered European unity and revived the Japanese automotive industry, never considering whether it might be creating a "third force" or opponent among its erstwhile allies. In investing and loaning money overseas, America did not fully realize that eventually it would have to allow foreigners to discharge their debts and finance U.S. investments by selling goods in the United States. All too soon such policy created export surpluses for presumably dependent allies and friends. . . .

This problem was no doubt exacerbated by Americans' own unwillingness to allow their government to save, even if they would not. The government's failure to save had much to do with continuing $200 billion to $300 billion defense budgets: it was not only social programs that broke the U.S. bank. If economic growth is a function of high productivity, and if productivity results from investment, and if investment only comes from savings (private or public), then high military "dissavings" directly impinged on U.S. growth. Nuclear deterrence, more than forty allies to support and spending on conventional weaponry represented high opportunity costs for the continuing progress and prosperity of the American economy.

Deterrence in short was relatively effective, but also a risky and costly endeavor. Over the long term it probably represented a recipe for American and Soviet decline relative to other nations. And even over the short term it contained manifold contradictions. Only a well-fed, well-housed and well-insured populace would support the free and democratic system against Eastern totalitarianism. But prosperity for U.S. allies was sometimes bought at the expense of economic progress at home.

IV

The operation of a central coalition was fundamentally different from that of the balance of power and deterrence. Members of the Concert of Powers, brought together at the Vienna Congress in 1815 by common interests in the aftermath of a victorious war, sought to enforce and perpetuate their notions of war prevention. They did so successfully for approximately the next thirty years.

Agreement on war causation and prevention welded the great powers together, at least for a time. The European powers fundamentally concluded that the revolutionary social system in Europe (extended to other countries by the military victories of Napoleonic France) had caused war. If they could contain those liberal sentiments and revolutions, they could prevent war. They also reasoned that war itself created the conditions for social dissolution; hence if they could prevent war, they could regulate social change. Performance of the two tasks was self-reinforcing.

The great powers also concurred that the task of war prevention was more important than gains for any one player. Russia thus limited its ambitions in the Near East; a reformed France gave up a policy of military expansion; and Austria under Metternich sought no particular national ambition, only the repose of the system as a whole. As a result there did not have to be a balance of power *within* the concert; agreement among the major powers made that unnecessary. Moreover the strength of the central coalition attracted strength from outside. Smaller powers could not balance against the great and instead joined them.

Three factors eventually led to the breakup of the central coalition. The first was the abstention and partial isolation of Great Britain, withdrawing from participation in the affairs of the continent and concert. Britain was ready to act against a renewal of aggression from France, but it was not willing to endorse a policy of wholesale concert intervention in the domestic lives of European nations. Conservative though he was, even Lord Castlereagh would not have admitted a foreign right to intervene to change England's political constitution; he could therefore not agree to intervention in Italy or Greece. His successor, George Canning, was even more isolationist. With the British withdrawal the concert no longer retained the legitimacy or the power to direct political affairs on the continent.

Second, new ideological divisions arose to separate members of the concert. In 1815 the victors were united by a moderate conservatism that harked back to eighteenth-century social and political institutions. With the revolutions of 1830, however, France was once again transformed into a more liberal polity, and the 1832 Reform Act in Great Britain produced far greater middle-class influence in British politics. Thus in the early 1830s, the liberal two (Britain and France) increasingly came to oppose the conservative three (Russia, Prussia and Austria). This alignment was supported by the pattern of the Industrial Revolution—it moved from west to east across the continent, initially separating the two halves of Europe. The resumption of ideological conflict broke the agreement that had united Europe and the concert.

The final quietus of the concert occurred when the revolutions of 1848 and their aftermath proved that war was no longer the automatic result of revolution. More important, in the 1850s nations appeared able to stave off revolution by a policy of quick and efficient use of military force. In the 1860s it became clear that war could actually protect unreformed domestic institutions. Bismarck and the Prussian-German conservatives won a new lease on life through a policy of "blood and iron" enforced against weaker nations. Hence war was no longer the greatest social evil; it could even be therapeutic.

With those three shifts the concert gave way to the balance of power.

The world economic system also failed to hold the political system together. After the onset of the "Great Depression" in 1873, tariffs began to rise and the growth of international trade declined. European colonization resumed with a vengeance, and Britain tried to cultivate its colonies' markets for industrial products. Vertical trade moved to the forefront; intra-industrial (horizontal) trade, while continuing, had less significance.

After the First World War when the time came to construct a new concert (in the League of Nations), the same three problems had to be overcome. First, war prevention had to be buttressed as a paramount goal, superior to the sectarian national interests of any great power. Second, there could be no breakdown into ideological conflict; this would create a rift among the major powers and reinstitute the balance of power. Finally, no crucial great power could return to a policy of isolation. If so, whatever its moral legitimacy, a concert decision could not be effectively enforced.

All three principles were, of course, rapidly challenged and then overthrown. While war avoidance remained a firm guiding rule for France and Britain, it was not so for fascist Italy or National Socialist Germany. They promptly rearmed and eyed their coveted territorial prizes to the east. Virulent ideological disagreements emerged at the same time, undermining the League Council's domestic consensus. These transformations were partly the result of the disastrous depression of 1929–39. The economic crisis forced desperation upon hard-pressed but still liberal governments in the 1920s, making them vulnerable to the appeals of either fascism or socialism.

The dissensus was increased by communist control of Russia. It was not just that ideological solidarity was shattered: it was sundered in a way that led to an epic misunderstanding of the policies of the fascist states. America and Britain had been anti-Soviet since 1917, and they expected Russia's communism to forge a link between Western states and the Italian and German dictators. Even Chamberlain's appeasement policy was supposed to have the sturdy foundation of common interests with Germany *vis-à-vis* Bolshevik Russia. The ideological conflict thus misled the Western powers about the identity of the true enemy, and they temporized far too long. The United States did not help.

Finally the absence of America from the still-born League of Nations underscored its impotence. Articles 10 and 16 of the League Covenant could only have been made effective by strong international leadership. If powerful states had been willing to act when one nation violated its covenants, others would have followed. Instead there was no leadership, and the United States nullified its own influence through isolation and then neutrality. The international consensus that seemed to have been forged in 1918 was dissipated as early as 1924. The balance of power was reinstituted, and Britain and France were left on their own.

V

As in past ages today's concert rests on acceptance by the major powers of the same three principles: involvement of all; ideological agreement; and renunciation of war and territorial expansion, giving liberal democratic and economic development first priority.

Can the three problems of a concert be solved? One danger is that in the next five years or so three major centers of power may return to a de facto condition of isolation: the United States, Russia and the European Community.

In the United States there is palpable revulsion against further international heroics, not because of failure abroad, as was the case with Vietnam, but because domestic priorities have been so chronically underserved. Homeless people are beginning to populate even suburban streets; the twin problems of

crime and drugs have yet to be solved; American education remains ineffective, despite large expenditures. Infrastructure, inner-cities and family solidarity have eroded under the treble impact of luxurious private consumption, foreign imports and a reversal of public spending priorities.

. . . The temptation to put American domestic priorities first may well become overwhelming, as it did in the 1920s. It may be accompanied by a disastrous reconcentration on the American umbilicus.

Russia, Ukraine, Belarus and Kazakhstan face far graver domestic and economic crises than the United States. It now appears that Russia may be too hobbled to become the center of a unified economic space of 12 independent republics. There is also the question of whether a single international policy can be maintained at all; the rivalry between Russia and Ukraine poses important economic, military and territorial issues.

Russia will almost certainly seek to dispose of some financial burdens by cutting international commitments, dropping red regimes in Afghanistan and Cuba, and pink ones in Africa. But even so, Russia will not solve the new confederation's economic difficulties. These will continue to be linked to the need for true privatization and supply-side revolutions in societies long dominated by government ministries and monopolies. . . .

Russian economic reform will be so onerous and absorbing that a stable and active foreign policy may be precluded in the coming years. Like Tokyo after World War II, Moscow may need a period of freedom from international responsibilities in order to reestablish a growing economy. Such internal stresses could almost entirely suppress Russian activity in international relations. Isolationism could occur *de facto*, if not *de jure*.

Finally, the European Community may become so preoccupied with its own growing pains—the debates over widening and deepening of EC integration—that it will neglect problems and conflicts beyond its sphere. . . .

It is possible that the EC is entering a stage, not unlike that of the federal United States in the early nineteenth century, in which questions of the accession of new states and territories largely overshadowed foreign policy. America's "manifest destiny" of westward expansion rested on the suppression of foreign entanglements. Europe's manifest destiny is eastward expansion. The Community could become so embroiled in the problems of integrating new nations that broader foreign policy is neglected. A move toward greater political unity may paradoxically worsen that outcome: the more concentrated their political and economic union, the less authority member states retain. National foreign policies would lose power and momentum; supranational policy would remain focused inward.

VI

The prospective reanimation of ideological conflict cannot be dismissed either. Under bipolarity and deterrence, sectarian and ethnic nationalism yielded to power imperatives. Ideological conflict only reaffirmed an already existent bipolar split in power terms. With the collapse of that conflict new ideological flowers will bloom, from irredentism in the former Soviet empire to Islamic fundamentalism in the Middle East. Perhaps the dangerous portents of such conflicts have been overstressed, however, because they imbue smaller and less powerful nations. But ideological conflict among the great powers could still occur as well.

The most potent future antagonism the world could witness is a radical division between the United States and Japan. The Westernization of contemporary Japan is as yet incomplete. Beneath the external policy of a Japanese trading state boil nationalist resentments directed at a half century of American tutelage and Western neglect. Japanese nationalism and militarism are bubbling up against the MacArthur-written constitution; contempt for an economically inept America resonates throughout Japanese culture and institutions.

Especially galling to the Japanese has been America's tendency to consult Japan last among major allies, while Washington insists that Tokyo pay for or participate in American-dictated endeavors. Japanese believe that, while having achieved economic equality or superiority, they are still relegated to second or third place politically. Such U.S. policy may lead Japan to seek the independent military and strategic strength needed to establish a new political identity. A Japanese nuclear deterrent would be directed against no one, but it could be designed to earn the respect and attention chronically lacking from the rest of the world.

If current trends continue, it may not be too long before ideological rationalizations of Confucian strength and vitality are propounded by Japan as antidotes to supposed Western decadence and lethargy.

VII

Under such circumstances maintenance of the territorial status quo could again come into question. Isolation of key participants—the United States, Russia and Europe—could pave the way for a renaissance of expansionist ambitions in other quarters of the globe.

Japan's past vocation in southeast Asia might again become tempting as economic conflict with the United States intensifies. Burgeoning economic ties in the Asian-Pacific region might tempt Tokyo to forge another "co-prosperity sphere." Japanese economic influence would be stretched into a form of political tutelage or even imperialism.

While such a renewed endeavor would appear quixotic, Japan's history demonstrates that the nation is sometimes willing to attempt the improbable. Such policy becomes the more credible if partially masked by financial and economic controls that merely "induce" dependent parties to yield resources and territorial demands. The United States once ruled Latin America through its own "dollar diplomacy." It did not always have to employ military force, and Japan would have much less need for overt intervention today.

VIII

If not addressed these three problems—isolationism, ideology and pacification—could erode the edifice of a modern concert. With its breakup no coalition would exist to pay the public-goods costs to maintain an open global trading system or to assist developing nations. Greater regionalism would prevail and give rise to a looser, disconnected international system. The great powers would no longer seek to resolve problems on the basis of fundamentally similar ideological and political orientations. Economic differences could widen to political fissures, instead of serving to transcend them. An introverted America would no longer provide essential global leadership. The recrudescence of isolation, the renaissance of ideological conflict and the resumption of territorial expansionism could together end the most hopeful period in the history of modern interstate relations.

All three international systems required the presence of a "threat" to make them cohere. This was most obvious in the balance of power and deterrence systems, but is equally necessary in a concert. Nations need to cooperate *against* something as well as *for* something. In the early nineteenth century, it was against the progress of liberalism. During the early period of the League of Nations, it was against nations that violated their covenants. Today, it must be against the threat of global economic breakdown.

It would be ideal if all major powers were in favor of the progress of democracy and liberalism, but that is not the case for mainland China. Still, the threat of a collapse of the international economy would represent a decisive check to the forward progress of all powers, as much to China as Japan. China is today as much resolved on a course of "export-led" growth as was Victorian Britain in the 1840s. In many respects Japan's dependence on international trade is equally great. Its industrial edifice is twice as large as needed to serve the domestic market.

Even Americans have found that the world economy is critical. . . . Europe's foreign direct investment, to say nothing of its powerful exports, also depend on an open and progressive world economy. Nor are trading blocs the answer. To be successful they would have to include all the markets, raw materials, energy and technology that powers previously required for their development and growth. History teaches that an open world economy is better, but the 1930s show that it cannot always be guaranteed.

This does not mean that any of these malign evolutions need occur, but they are within the realm of political possibility. The violation of these three principles has operated twice before to limit the scope of a world concert of powers. History does not necessarily repeat, but precedent suggests that a costly, inefficient and conflict-ridden balance of power reasserts itself just when the world's great powers assume it has been abolished.

The end of the Cold War is in this sense like the end of a military war: it injects relief from international endeavors and renewed internal introspection into the domestic lives of the great powers. In the past nations have lost their sense of prudence and proportion: they have abruptly reversed course time and again. Excesses of international conflict were followed by excesses of domestic introversion; the cooperative necessities of redressing power conflicts yielded to nationalistic and egoistic indulgence. This must not happen again.

Today the most propitious element uniting the world and facilitating the cooperation of a concert is its high degree of ideological agreement. That agreement can only be sustained in liberal, democratic and free-market terms if the world economy permits it to prosper. A world recession or depression breaks the ideological links that have knit nations together. . . .

Ultimately what is necessary is a new sense of proportion in the allocation of international and domestic tasks and benefits. Governments and peoples must decide to continue to work on foreign problems, while devoting greater attention to neglected domestic issues. In one sense the two represent competing priorities, but for many purposes they are complementary. The United States cannot ultimately continue to play a large international role if its savings rates and economic growth remain low. Japan cannot continue to export without importing if its foreign customers (because of low growth) cannot afford to buy Japanese goods.

Increases in Japanese consumption of imported goods are therefore not only a key to the solution of other nations' problems, but also their own. Integrating Russia and its former republics into the world economy is necessary not only to achieve economic growth in Moscow, St. Petersburg and Kiev, but also because only a vibrant Eastern economy can buy Western consumer products. Ideological agreement thus continues to ride not only on a rising, but also more balanced, tide of economic growth for the world economy as a whole.

It is of course possible that this will not occur. It may be easier, politically speaking, for overburdened governments to respect popular wishes and focus largely on domestic tasks. The funds needed to sustain and restructure the Russian economy are, after all, very large. Not only domestic publics but also the Third World will resent the necessary diversion of capital to the East. But ultimately the choice is between offering help or foisting social barbarism on a weakened Russia. If this help succeeds, it will build trust upon which a heightened ideological agreement can be based. If Europe and Japan are drawn in to this historic effort (as they must be), it will forge a linkage between four major centers of power in world politics.

If such cooperation occurs, the balance of power begins to operate in reverse: once a strong central group has been consolidated, others will not try to balance against it; they will be drawn to its core. In this way even China, in time, will become a member of the Concert of Powers, with the Third World next in train. Despite historic precedents, this time the central coalition does not have to collapse.

A central coalition would be a much cheaper international regulatory device than either an inefficient and dilatory balance of power or an expensive deterrence. This is important. It now appears that while American leaders are still willing for the nation to exert itself abroad, intervene in foreign conflicts and give large amounts of foreign assistance, the American public is more reluctant. Only a relatively efficient and cost-effective international order is likely to have U.S. public support over the long term. History may tell little about the future, but it seems to indicate that a central coalition—united by economic interest in an open and growing world economy—is not doomed to fail.

45. A Critique of Collective Security

INIS L. CLAUDE, JR.

. . . Collective security assumes the *lonely* aggressor; the violator of the world's peace may be allowed an accomplice or two, but in principle the evil-doer is supposed to find himself virtually isolated in confrontation with the massive forces of the international *posse comitatus*. . . .

The doctrine of collective security also postulates the *obvious* aggressor, and the *clear-cut* case of aggression. A state sends its armed forces across the frontier; an invasion has occurred, launched by State A, aggressor, against State B, victim of aggression. The duty of all loyal members of the community of states is evident: They must rally to the defense of State B against State A. It must be conceded that the founders of the League of Nations and the United Nations did not take such a simple view of things. They did not attempt an explicit definition of aggression, and this omission probably reflected an awareness that aggression is too complex a concept to be readily defined, rather than a belief that it is so simple that its meaning must be obvious. Nevertheless, the theory of collective security, with its promise of prompt and dependable collective measures to frustrate aggression, does rest heavily

upon the assumption that the fact of aggression and the identity of the aggressor can be established without great difficulty. In so far as this assumption may prove invalid, the certainty of a prompt international decision that an occasion for collective action has arisen and of the virtually unanimous collaboration of the members of the system in such action is sharply diminished, with the result that the system's capability of fulfilling its promise becomes questionable. The theoretical merit of collective security depends largely upon the element of certainty; unless both the potential aggressor and the potential victim are firmly convinced that collective action will be forthcoming, the objects of deterring the former and reassuring the latter cannot be achieved.

The possibility of an effective collective security system in today's world is limited by the fact that ambiguity has attained an unprecedented lead over clarity in the realm of aggression. It has probably never been true that one could expect normally to make a simple identification of "guilty" and "innocent" parties in international conflicts; it is certainly not the case in recent international relations that most conflict situations lend themselves to such an analysis. For a number of reasons, the unambiguous invasion of one state's territory by the forces of another state has become a rather unlikely phenomenon. This old-fashioned manner of aggression has probably not

Excerpted from *Power and International Relations* by Inis L. Claude, Jr., pp. 196–204. Copyright © 1962 by Random House, Inc. Reprinted by permission of Random House, Inc.

been wholly or definitively supplanted, but it has been markedly supplemented by a considerable variety of techniques of indirect aggression. . . .

These are clearly not circumstances conducive to the ideal realization of the promise of collective security. When even the most dispassionate observer might have difficulty in deciding for himself whether aggression has occurred and, if so, what state is the aggressor, one must recognize the improbability that an international organ comprising representatives of governments could be relied upon to reach a quick consensus on the facts of the case and the appropriate international response, or to obtain the vigorous and unquestioning support of all or most states in the conduct of the collective action which it might determine to be necessary. In this respect as in the others that we have noted, collective security appears to be obsolete—to refer to a picture of the world which has steadily become less true to life in the years since World War I. . . .

From another standpoint, it appears that it is *too early* for the realization of the collective security ideal. Considering the subjective requirements of collective security, the doctrine is premature; neither statesmen nor their peoples have undergone the transformations in attitude and outlook, in loyalty and commitment, which are demanded by the theory of collective security. In this sense, the failure to create an operative system of collective security derives not from statesmen's awareness of changes in the objective context within which the system would have to operate, but from the lack of change in their own subjective patterns.

Fundamentally, collective security requires statesmen who will lead, and peoples who will follow, in the development of a community consciousness which overrides the divisiveness of national interests. It requires a conception of national interest which identifies the destiny of the state so closely with the order of the global community as to make participation in the safeguarding of that order a virtually automatic response to any disturbance. It requires a belief that "what is good for the world is good for the state," so profoundly rooted that the question of the compatibility of the national interest with the obligations of collective security does not seriously arise. This is not a matter of repudiating the national interest, or of neglecting it, but of defining it in terms of, and identifying it with, the international interest in peace and order. Collective security requires the relinquishment of the sovereign free hand in the most vital issues of foreign policy, the abandonment of national biases for and against other states, and a consequent willingness to follow the lead of organs of the community in taking action in opposition to any aggressor, on behalf of any victim of attack. It is clear that these subjective prerequisites of a workable collective security system are very far from having been fulfilled, and it is doubtful that a meaningful trend in that direction can be discerned in contemporary world politics. . . .

In any case, the doctrine of collective security requires a more thoroughgoing renunciation of the free hand in foreign policy, a more nearly complete acceptance of advance commitment to participate in sanctions against any aggressor, on behalf of any victim, under any circumstances, than leaders of states are prepared to acknowledge as either necessary or desirable or permissible, given their obligations to the states which they represent.

This situation, I submit, is not attributable to the moral deficiency of the world's statesmen. It is simply a fact that statesmen and peoples in today's world find it impossible to believe that either world order or national interest can be safeguarded by following the formula of collective security. Should every state rally to the defense of any state which is subjected to attack, regardless of the possibility that the aggressor may be feinting with a view to striking elsewhere when the defenders of order have been pulled out of position? Should every state join in collective action against any aggressor, regardless of the possibility that this may precipitate a global war which might otherwise still be avoided? Should every state be encouraged and permitted to become involved in collective sanctions in a given case, regardless of the danger that such intervention might be abused by some states for the promotion of their own selfish purposes? Most statesmen, I believe, would answer these and other questions relating to the prescription offered by collective security in the negative. In so doing, they would not so much betray inadequate concern for the general interest of mankind, or excessive devotion to their vested interest in their professional roles, or inordinate pride in their professional capacity to play the game of international politics, as give evidence of their conviction that the effort to be prudent cannot be abandoned in favor of the urge to conform to an abstract principle. Statesmen are not prepared to abandon the function of judging each international crisis in terms of the context of events and possibilities within which it occurs, weighing the implications, so far as they can discern them, of various alternative responses, and determining policy in the light of these considerations. It would appear that the peoples for whom statesmen act generally share this conception of the proper role of their representatives. This basic rejection of the commitments required by the theory of collective security is ultimately an expression of the judgment that the pursuit of peace and security requires a pragmatic rather than a doctrinaire approach to international relations.

It is in this connection that I would regard the epithet *unrealistic* as fairly applicable to the theory of collective security. As I have argued, collective security is not unrealistic about *power*; it is unrealistic about *policy*. From Wilson's day to our own, advocates of collective security have entertained unrealistic hopes or expectations concerning the transformation of the foreign policies of states; states are not prepared to do, or convinced that they should do, the things that an operative system of collective security would require them to do.

This is not to say that the persistent ideological popularity of collective security is wholly meaningless, or that recurrent endorsements of the doctrine by statesmen can be explained away as exercises in hypocrisy. While the urge to create a *system* of collective security has been discarded, the *doctrine* has left a considerable deposit. The proposition that international aggression is legally and morally reprehensible, the idea that any aggression is everybody's business, the view that a general international organization should concern itself with all disturbances of the peace, the notion that potential aggressors should be forewarned of the solidarities with which they may be confronted—such basic propositions as these, attributable in large part to the doctrinal impact of collective security, have become embedded in twentieth-century thinking about international relations. In this limited but important sense, collective security has been "adopted."

46. From *After Hegemony*

ROBERT O. KEOHANE

REALISM, INSTITUTIONALISM, AND COOPERATION

Impressed with the difficulties of cooperation, observers have often compared world politics to a "state of war." In this conception, international politics is "a competition of units in the kind of state of nature that knows no restraints other than those which the changing necessities of the game and the shallow conveniences of the players impose" (Hoffmann, 1965, p. vii). It is anarchic in the sense that it lacks an authoritative government that can enact and enforce rules of behavior. States must rely on "the means they can generate and the arrangements they can make for themselves" (Waltz, 1979, p. 111). Conflict and war result, since each state is judge in its own cause and can use force to carry out its judgments (Waltz, 1959, p. 159). The discord that prevails is accounted for by fundamental conflicts of interest (Waltz, 1959).

Were this portrayal of world politics correct, any cooperation that occurs would be derivative from overall patterns of conflict. Alliance cooperation would be easy to explain as a result of the operation of a balance of power, but

From *After Hegemony* by Robert O. Keohane, pp. 7–10, 31–35, 39, 136–139, 244–247. Copyright © 1984 by Princeton University Press. Reprinted by permission of Princeton University Press and the author. Footnotes and selected citations deleted.

system-wide patterns of cooperation that benefit many countries without being tied to an alliance system directed against an adversary would not. If international politics were a state of war, institutionalized patterns of cooperation on the basis of shared purposes should not exist except as part of a larger struggle for power. The extensive patterns of international agreement that we observe on issues as diverse as trade, financial relations, health, telecommunications, and environmental protection would be absent.

At the other extreme from these "Realists" are writers who see cooperation as essential in a world of economic interdependence, and who argue that shared economic interests create a demand for international institutions and rules (Mitrany, 1975). Such an approach, which I refer to as "Institutionalist" because of its adherents' emphasis on the functions performed by international institutions, runs the risk of being naive about power and conflict. Too often its proponents incorporate in their theories excessively optimistic assumptions about the role of ideals in world politics, or about the ability of statesmen to learn what the theorist considers the "right lessons." But sophisticated students of institutions and rules have a good deal to teach us. They view institutions not simply as formal organizations with headquarters buildings and specialized staffs, but more broadly as "recognized patterns of practice around which expectations converge" (Young, 1980, p. 337). They regard these patterns of practice as significant because they affect state behavior. Sophisticated institutionalists do not expect cooperation always to prevail, but they are aware of the malleability of interests and they argue that interdependence creates interests in cooperation.

During the first twenty years or so after World War II, these views, though very different in their intellectual origins and their broader implications about human society, made similar predictions about the world political economy, and particularly about the subject of this book, the political economy of the advanced market-economy countries. Institutionalists expected successful cooperation in one field to "spill over" into others (Haas, 1958). Realists anticipated a relatively stable international economic order as a result of the dominance of the United States. Neither set of observers was surprised by what happened, although they interpreted events differently.

Institutionalists could interpret the liberal international arrangements for trade and international finance as responses to the need for policy coordination created by the fact of interdependence. These arrangements, which we will call "international regimes," contained rules, norms, principles, and decisionmaking procedures. Realists could reply that these regimes were constructed on the basis of principles espoused by the United States, and that American power was essential for their construction and maintenance. For Realists, in other words, the early postwar regimes rested on the *political hegemony* of the United States. Thus Realists and Institutionalists could both regard early postwar developments as supporting their theories.

After the mid-1960s, however, U.S. dominance in the world political economy was challenged by the economic recovery and increasing unity of Europe and by the rapid economic growth of Japan. Yet economic interdependence continued to grow, and the pace of increased U.S. involvement in the world economy even accelerated after 1970. At this point, therefore, the Institutionalist and Realist predictions began to diverge. From a strict Institutionalist standpoint, the increasing need for coordination of policy, created by interdependence, should have led to more cooperation. From a Realist perspective, by contrast, the diffusion of power should have undermined the ability of anyone to create order.

On the surface, the Realists would seem to have made the better forecast. Since the late 1960s there have been signs of decline in the extent and efficacy of efforts to cooperate in the world political economy. As American power eroded, so did international regimes. The erosion of these regimes after World War II certainly refutes a naive version of the Institutionalist faith in interdependence as a solvent of conflict and a creator of cooperation. But it does not prove that only the Realist emphasis on power as a creator of order is valid. It might be possible, after the decline of hegemonic regimes, for more symmetrical patterns of cooperation to evolve after a transitional period of discord. Indeed, the persistence of attempts at cooperation during the 1970s suggests that the decline of hegemony does not necessarily sound cooperation's death knell.

International cooperation and discord thus remain puzzling. Under what conditions can independent countries cooperate in the world political economy? In particular, can cooperation take place without hegemony and, if so, how? This book is designed to help us find answers to these questions. I begin with Realist insights about the role of power and the effects of hegemony. But my central arguments draw more on the Institutionalist tradition, arguing that cooperation can under some conditions develop on the basis of complementary interests, and that institutions, broadly defined, affect the patterns of cooperation that emerge.

Hegemonic leadership is unlikely to be revived in this century for the United States or any other country. Hegemonic powers have historically only emerged after world wars; during peacetime, weaker countries have tended to gain on the hegemon rather than vice versa (Gilpin, 1981). It is difficult to believe that world civilization, much less a complex international economy, would survive such a war in the nuclear age. Certainly no prosperous hegemonic power is likely to emerge from such a cataclysm. As long as a world political economy persists, therefore, its central political dilemma will be how to organize cooperation without hegemony. . . .

HEGEMONY IN THE WORLD POLITICAL ECONOMY

It is common today for troubled supporters of liberal capitalism to look back with nostalgia on British preponderance in the nineteenth century and American dominance after World War II. Those eras are imagined to be simpler ones in which a single power, possessing superiority of economic and military resources, implemented a plan for international order based on its interests and its vision of the world. As Robert Gilpin has expressed it, "The *Pax Britannica* and *Pax Americana*, like the *Pax Romana*, ensured an international system of relative peace and security. Great Britain and the United States created and enforced the rules of a liberal international economic order" (1981, p. 144).

Underlying this statement is one of the two central propositions of the theory of hegemonic stability: that order in world politics is typically created by a single dominant power. Since regimes constitute elements of an international order, this implies that the formation of international regimes normally depends on hegemony. The other major tenet of the theory of hegemonic stability is that the maintenance of order requires continued hegemony. As Charles P. Kindleberger has said, "for the world economy to be stabilized, there has to be a stabilizer, one stabilizer" (1973, p. 305). This implies that cooperation, which we define . . . as mutual adjustment of state policies to one another, also depends on the perpetuation of hegemony.

I discuss hegemony before elaborating my definitions of cooperation and regimes because my emphasis on how international institutions such as regimes facilitate cooperation only makes sense if cooperation and discord are not determined simply by interests and power. . . . I argue that a deterministic version of the theory of hegemonic stability, relying only on the Realist concepts of interests and power, is indeed incorrect. There is some validity in a modest version of the first proposition of the theory of hegemonic stability—that hegemony can facilitate a certain type of cooperation—but there is little reason to believe that hegemony is either a necessary or a sufficient condition for the emergence of cooperative relationships. Furthermore, and even more important for the argument presented here, the second major proposition of the theory is erroneous: cooperation does not necessarily require the existence of a hegemonic leader after international regimes have been established. Post-hegemonic cooperation is also possible. . . .

Evaluating the Theory of Hegemonic Stability

The theory of hegemonic stability, as applied to the world political economy, defines hegemony as preponderance of material resources. Four sets of resources are especially important. . . . To be considered hegemonic in the world political economy . . . a country must have access to crucial raw materials, control major sources of capital, maintain a large market for imports, and hold comparative advantages in goods with high value added, yielding relatively high wages and profits. It must also be stronger, on these dimensions taken as a whole, than any other country. The theory of hegemonic stability predicts that the more one such power dominates the world political economy, the more cooperative will interstate relations be. This is a parsimonious theory that relies on . . . a "basic force model," in which outcomes reflect the tangible capabilities of actors.

Yet, like many such basic force models, this crude theory of hegemonic stability makes imperfect predictions. In the twentieth century it correctly anticipates the relative cooperativeness of the twenty years after World War II. It is at least partially mistaken, however, about trends of cooperation when hegemony erodes. Between 1900 and 1913 a decline in British power coincided with a decrease rather than an increase in conflict over commercial issues. . . . Recent changes in international regimes can only partially be attributed to a decline in American power. How to interpret the prevalence of discord in the interwar years is difficult, since it is not clear whether any country was hegemonic in material terms during those two decades. The United States, though considerably ahead in productivity, did not replace Britain as the most important financial center and lagged behind in volume of trade. Although American domestic oil production was more than sufficient for domestic needs during these years, Britain still controlled the bulk of major Middle Eastern oil fields. Nevertheless, what prevented American leadership of a cooperative world political economy in these years was less lack of economic resources than an absence of political willingness to make and enforce rules for the system. Britain, despite its efforts, was too weak to do so effectively (Kindleberger, 1973). The crucial factor in producing discord lay in American politics, not in the material factors to which the theory points.

Unlike the crude basic force model, a refined version of hegemonic stability theory does not assert an automatic link between power and leadership. Hegemony is defined as a situation in which "one state is powerful enough to maintain the essential rules governing interstate relations, and willing to do so" (Keohane and Nye, 1977, p. 44). This interpretive framework retains an emphasis on power but looks more seriously than the crude power theory at the internal characteristics of the strong state. It does not assume that strength automatically creates incentives to project one's power abroad. Domestic attitudes, political structures, and decision making processes are also important.

This argument's reliance on state decisions as well as power capabilities puts it into the category of what [James] March calls "force activation models." Decisions to exercise leadership are necessary to "activate" the posited relationship between power capabilities and outcomes. Force activation models are essentially *post hoc* rather than *a priori*, since one can always "save" such a theory after the fact by thinking of reasons why an actor would not have wanted to use all of its available potential power. In effect, this modification of the theory declares that states with preponderant resources will be hegemonic except when they decide not to commit the necessary effort to the tasks of leadership, yet it does not tell us what will determine the latter decision. As a causal theory this is not very helpful, since whether a given configuration of power will lead the potential hegemon to maintain a set of rules remains indeterminate unless we know a great deal about its domestic politics.

Only the cruder theory generates predictions. When I refer without qualification to the theory of hegemonic stability, therefore, I will be referring to this basic force model. We have seen that the most striking contention of this theory—that hegemony is both a necessary and a sufficient condition for cooperation—is not strongly supported by the experience of this century. Taking a longer period of about 150 years, the record remains ambiguous. International economic relations were relatively cooperative both in the era of British hegemony during the mid-to-late nineteenth century and in the two decades of American dominance after World War II. But only in the second of these periods was there a trend toward the predicted disruption of established rules and increased discord. And a closer examination of the British experience casts doubt on the causal role of British hegemony in producing cooperation in the nineteenth century. . . .

The crude theory of hegemonic stability establishes a useful, if somewhat simplistic, starting-point for an analysis of changes in international cooperation and discord. Its refined version raises a looser but suggestive set of interpretive questions for the analysis of some eras in the history of the international political economy. Such an interpretive framework does not constitute an explanatory systemic theory, but it can help us think of hegemony in another way—less as a concept that helps to explain outcomes in terms of power than as a way of describing an international system in which leadership is exercised by a single state. Rather than being a component of a scientific generalization—that power is a necessary or sufficient condition for co-operation—the concept of hegemony, defined in terms of willingness as well as ability to lead, helps us think about the incentives facing the potential hegemon. Under what conditions, domestic and international, will such a country decide to invest in the construction of rules and institutions? . . .

HEGEMONIC COOPERATION IN THE POSTWAR ERA

Powerful states seek to construct international political economies that suit their interests and their ideologies. But as we have noted, converting resources into outcomes is far from automatic in world politics. Even the highly qualified neo-Realist position, . . . that hegemony can facilitate cooperation, therefore requires an answer to the question of how hegemons translate their resources, both material and ideological, into rules for the system. How does the hegemon construct international regimes that facilitate the "right kind" of cooperation from the standpoint of the hegemon itself? That is, how does hegemonic leadership operate?

This question is posed by Realism's emphasis on power, so I begin my analysis there. But in explaining changes in the world political economy, I emphasize the economic sources of power. . . . rather than military force. Sufficient military power to protect an international political economy from incursions by hostile powers is indeed a necessary condition for successful hegemony. Since World War II the United States has maintained such power,

pursuing a strategy of "containment" of the Soviet Union. In the shelter of its military strength, the United States constructed a liberal-capitalist world political economy based on multilateral principles and embodying rules that the United States approved. . . . American military power served as a shield protecting the international political economy that it dominated, and it remained an important factor in the background of bargaining on economic issues; but it did not frequently impinge directly on such bargaining. Thus, . . . it is justifiable to focus principally on the political economy of the advanced industrialized countries without continually taking into account the politics of international security. . . .

We explore in detail the characteristics of economic power resources in the postwar world, and how their distribution and use changed over time. But to answer our questions about the operation of hegemonic co-operation, we must also think about interests and institutions. Hegemonic leadership does not begin with a *tabula rasa*, but rather builds on the interests of states. The hegemon seeks to persuade others to conform to its vision of world order and to defer to its leadership. American hegemonic leadership in the postwar period presupposed a rough consensus in the North Atlantic area, and later with Japan, on the maintenance of international capitalism, as opposed to socialism or a pattern of semi-autocratic national capitalisms. This consensus can be viewed, in Gramscian terms, as the acceptance by its partners of the ideological hegemony of the United States. Such acceptance rested, in turn, on the belief of leaders of secondary states that they were benefiting from the structure of order that was being created. There was thus a high degree of perceived complementarity between the United States and its partners. The United States sought to reinforce this sense of complementarity by creating international regimes that would provide specific benefits to its partners as well as reduce uncertainty and otherwise encourage cooperation.

Hegemonic power and the international regimes established under conditions of hegemony combine to facilitate cooperation. Hegemony itself reduces transaction costs and mitigates uncertainty, since each ally can deal with the hegemon and expect it to ensure consistency for the system as a whole. The formation of international regimes can ensure legitimacy for the standards of behavior that the hegemon plays a key role in maintaining. In the areas of money and trade, where their allies' cooperation was necessary, American leaders therefore invested resources in building stable international arrangements with known rules. It made sense for the United States to bind itself, as well as others, in order to induce weaker states to agree to follow the American lead.

American leaders did not construct hegemonic regimes simply by commanding their weaker partners to behave in prescribed ways. On the contrary, they had to search for mutual interests with their partners, and they had to make some adjustments themselves in addition to demanding that others conform to their design. They had to invest some of their power resources in the building of institutions. In so doing, they encountered numerous frustrations. As William Diebold has reminded us, "we have no memoirs called 'my days as a happy hegemon.' " It is important not to exaggerate the ease with which the United States could make and enforce the rules. Yet the United States ultimately succeeded in attaining its crucial objectives, if not by one expedient, then by another. Frustrations on particular issues melded into a rewarding overall pattern of hegemonic cooperation. Simplistic notions of hegemony as either complete dominance or selfless, dedicated leadership hinder rather than promote historical understanding.

Although Henry Luce foresaw an American Century, the period of hegemonic cooperation premised on a common commitment to openness and nondiscrimination lasted only about twenty years. This era began in 1947, the year of the Truman Doctrine and the Marshall Plan. It was already fading on some issues by 1963, the year of the Interest Equalization Tax, the first attempt by the United States to protect the status of the dollar against the consequences of the open world economy that it had struggled to create. In oil and trade, the first signs of new selective protectionist initiatives had already appeared. Mandatory oil import quotas were imposed in 1959, and in 1961 the United States secured a Short-Term Agreement on Cotton Textiles, which led eventually to a series of restrictive agreements on textile fibers. On some issues, such as tariff reductions, the 1960s witnessed further liberalization. But by 1971, when the United States broke the link between the dollar and gold, it was clear that something fundamental had changed. Exact dating is arbitrary. . . . We focus on the twenty years or so after 1947, and especially on the 1950s, to discover how hegemonic cooperation operated. Whichever date between 1963 and 1971 were chosen, it would still be clear that one of the most important features of American hegemony was its brevity.

At the end of World War II the United States was clearly the leading power in the world political economy, with respect to each of the resources . . . essential to hegemony: productivity in manufacturing and control over capital, markets, and raw materials. The United States used many of these resources after the war to gain what Albert Hirschman has referred to as an "influence effect" of supplying something valuable to another country. Specifically, American influence rested on three major sets of benefits that its partners received from joining American-centered regimes and deferring to U.S. leadership:

1. *A stable international monetary system,* designed to facilitate liberal international trade and payments. This implied that the United States would manage the monetary system in a responsible way, providing sufficient but not excessive international liquidity.

2. *Provision of open markets for goods.* The United States actively worked to reduce tariffs and took the lead in pressing for the removal of discriminatory restrictions, although it tolerated regional discrimination by European countries and permitted the Europeans to maintain temporary postwar barriers during the period of dollar shortage.

3. *Access to oil at stable prices.* The United States, and American companies, provided oil to Europe and Japan from the Middle East, where U.S. oil corporations held sway, and in emergencies such as 1956–57 from the United States itself.

CONCLUSION: THE VALUE OF INSTITUTIONS

. . . [T]he ability and willingness of the United States to devote substantial resources to maintaining international economic regimes have both declined since the mid-1960s. . . . It seems unlikely that the United States will reassume the dominant position that it had during the 1950s. . . . If we are to have cooperation, therefore, it will be cooperation without hegemony.

Nonhegemonic cooperation is difficult, since it must take place among independent states that are motivated more by their own conceptions of self-interest than by a devotion to the common good. Nothing in this book denies this difficulty, nor do I forecast a marvelous new era of smooth mutual policy adjustment, much less one of harmony. But despite the persistence of discord, world politics is not a state of war. States do have complementary interests, which make certain forms of cooperation potentially beneficial. As hegemony erodes, the demand for international regimes may even increase, as the lack of a formal intergovernmental oil regime in the 1950s, and the institution of one in 1974, suggest. Furthermore, the legacy of American hegemony persists, in the form of a number of international regimes. These regimes create a more favorable institutional environment for cooperation than would otherwise exist; it is easier to maintain them than it would be to create new ones. Such regimes are important not because they constitute centralized quasi-governments, but because they can facilitate agreements, and decentralized enforcement of agreements, among governments. They enhance the likelihood of cooperation by reducing the costs of making transactions that are consistent with the principles of the regime. They create the conditions for orderly multilateral negotiations, legitimate and delegitimate different types of state action, and facilitate linkages among issues within regimes and between regimes. They increase the symmetry and improve the quality of the information that governments receive. By clustering issues together in the same forums over a long period of time, they help to bring governments into continuing interaction with one another, reducing incentives to cheat and enhancing the value of reputation. By establishing legitimate standards of behavior for states to follow and by providing ways to monitor compliance, they create the basis for decentralized enforcement founded on the principle of reciprocity. The network of international regimes bequeathed to the contemporary international political economy by American hegemony provides a valuable foundation for constructing post-hegemonic patterns of cooperation, which can be used by policy-makers interested in achieving their objectives through multilateral action.

The importance of regimes for cooperation supports the Institutionalist claim . . . that international institutions help to realize common interests in world politics. An argument for this view has been made here not by smuggling in cosmopolitan preferences under the rubric of "world welfare" or "global interests," but by relying on Realist assumptions that states are egoistic, rational actors operating on the basis of their own conceptions of self-interest. Institutions are necessary, even on these restrictive premises, in order to achieve *state* purposes.

Realism provides a good starting-point for the analysis of cooperation and discord, since its taut logical structure and its pessimistic assumptions about individual and state behavior serve as barriers against wishful thinking. Furthermore, it suggests valuable insights that help us interpret the evolution of the world political economy since the end of World War II. Yet it is in need of revision, because it fails to take into account that states' conceptions of their interests, and of how their objectives should be pursued, depend not merely on national interests and the distribution of world power, but on the quantity, quality, and distribution of information. Agreements that are impossible to make under conditions of high uncertainty may become feasible when uncertainty has been reduced. Human beings, and governments, behave differently in information-rich environments than in information-poor ones. Information, as well as power, is a significant systemic variable in world politics. International systems containing institutions that generate a great deal of high-quality information and make it available on a reasonably even basis to the major actors are likely to experience more cooperation than systems that do not contain such institutions, even if fundamental state interests and the distribution of power are the same in each system. Realism should not be discarded, since its insights are fundamental to an understanding of world politics, but it does need to be reformulated to reflect the impact of information-providing institutions on state behavior, even when rational egoism persists.

Thus when we think about cooperation after hegemony, we need to think about institutions. Theories that dismiss international institutions as insignificant fail to help us understand the conditions under which states' attempts at cooperation, *in their own interests*, will be successful. This is especially true in the contemporary world political economy, since it is endowed with a number of important international regimes, created under conditions of American hegemony but facilitating cooperation even after the erosion of U.S. dominance. We seem now to be in a period of potential transition between the hegemonic cooperation of the two decades after World War II and a new state of affairs, either one of prevailing discord or of post-hegemonic cooperation. Whether discord or cooperation prevails will depend in considerable measure on how well governments take advantage of established international regimes to make new agreements and ensure compliance with old ones.

Yet an awareness of the importance of institutions—defined broadly as sets of practices and expectations rather than in terms of for-

mal organizations with imposing headquarters buildings—must not lead us to lapse into old habits of thought. It is not particularly helpful to think about institutions in terms of "peace through law" or world government. Institutions that facilitate cooperation do not mandate what governments must do; rather, they help governments pursue their own interests through cooperation. Regimes provide information and reduce the costs of transactions that are consistent with their injunctions, thus facilitating interstate agreements and their decentralized enforcement. It is misleading, therefore, to evaluate regimes on the basis of whether they effectively centralize authority. Nor do institutions that promote cooperation need to be universal. Indeed, since regimes depend on shared interests, and on conditions that permit problems of collective action to be overcome, they are often most useful when relatively few like-minded countries are responsible for both making the essential rules and maintaining them. Finally, international institutions do not need to be integrated into one coherent network. Cooperation is almost always fragmentary in world politics: not all the pieces of the puzzle will fit together.

Building institutions in world politics is a frustrating and difficult business. Common interests are often hard to discover or to maintain. Furthermore, collective action invites myopic behavior: as in Rousseau's well-known tale, the hunters may chase individually after rabbits rather than cooperate to capture the deer. Yet institutions are often worth constructing, because their presence or absence may determine whether governments can cooperate effectively for common ends. It is even more important to seek to maintain the valuable international institutions that continue to exist, since the effort required to maintain them is less than would be needed to construct new ones, and if they did not exist, many of them would have to be invented. Information-rich institutions that reduce uncertainty may make agreement possible in a future crisis. Since they may facilitate cooperation on issues that were not thought about at the time of their creation, international regimes have potential value beyond their concrete purposes. Such institutions cannot, therefore, be evaluated merely on the basis of how well they serve the perceived national interest at a given time; on the contrary, an adequate judgment of their worth depends on an estimate of the contribution they are likely to make, in the future, to the solution of problems that cannot yet be precisely defined. Such estimates should reflect an awareness that, in world politics, unexpected events—whether assassinations, coups, or defaults on debts—are likely, and that we need to insure against them.

The significance of information and institutions is not limited to political-economic relations among the advanced industrialized countries, although that is the substantive focus of this book. The theory presented here is relevant to any situation in world politics in which states have common or complementary interests that can only be realized through mutual agreement. As we have seen, there are almost always conflictual elements in these relationships as well. Like Prisoners' Dilemma, most of these situations will be "mixed-motive games," characterized by a combination of conflicting and complementary interests. Building information-rich institutions is as important in relations among the superpowers, where confidence is a key variable, and in arms control negotiations, in which monitoring and verification are of great importance, as in managing political-economic relations among the advanced industrialized countries. Institution-building may be more difficult where security issues are concerned, but is equally essential if cooperation is to be achieved.

REFERENCES

GILPIN, ROBERT. 1981. *War and Change in World Politics.* Cambridge: Cambridge University Press.

HAAS, ERNST B. 1958. *The Uniting of Europe.* Stanford: Stanford University Press.

HOFFMANN, STANLEY. 1965. *The State of War: Essays on the Theory and Practice of International Politics.* New York: Praeger.

KEOHANE, ROBERT O., AND JOSEPH S. NYE. 1977. *Power and Interdependence: World Politics in Transition.* Boston: Little, Brown.

KINDLEBERGER, CHARLES P. 1973. *The World in Depression, 1929–1939.* Berkeley: University of California Press.

MITRANY, DAVID. 1975. *The Functional Theory of Politics.* London: St. Martin's Press for the London School of Economics and Political Science.

YOUNG, ORAN R. 1980. International Regimes: Problems of Concept Formation. *World Politics* 32, no. 3 (April): 331–356.

WALTZ, KENNETH. 1959. *Man, the State and War.* New York: Columbia University Press.

———. 1979. *Theory of World Politics.* Reading, MA.: Addison-Wesley.

47. The Rise and Future Demise
of the World Capitalist System: Concepts
for Comparative Analysis

IMMANUEL WALLERSTEIN

... Leaving aside the now defunct mini-systems [e.g., hunter and gathering societies—ED.], the only kind of social system is a world-system, which we define quite simply as a unit with a single division of labor and multiple cultural systems. It follows logically that there can, however, be two varieties of such world-systems, one with a common political system and one without. We shall designate these respectively as world-empires and world-economies. . . .

What was happening in Europe from the sixteenth to the eighteenth centuries is that over a large geographical area going from Poland in the northeast westwards and southwards throughout Europe and including large parts of the Western Hemisphere as well, there grew up a world-economy with a single division of labor within which there was a world market, for which men produced largely agricultural products for sale and profit. I would think the simplest thing to do would be to call this agricultural capitalism. . . .

By a series of accidents—historical, ecological, geographic—northwest Europe was bet-

ter situated in the sixteenth century to diversify its agricultural specialization and add to it certain industries (such as textiles, shipbuilding, and metal wares) than were other parts of Europe. Northwest Europe emerged as the core area of this world-economy, specializing in agricultural production of higher skill levels, which favored (again for reasons too complex to develop) tenancy and wage-labor as the modes of labor control. Eastern Europe and the Western Hemisphere became peripheral areas specializing in export of grains, bullion, wood, cotton, sugar—all of which favored the use of slavery and coerced cash-crop labor as the modes of labor control. Mediterranean Europe emerged as the semi-peripheral area of this world-economy specializing in high-cost industrial products (for example, silks) and credit and specie transactions, which had as a consequence in the agricultural arena sharecropping as the mode of labor control and little export to other areas.

The three structural positions in a world-economy—core, periphery, and semi-periphery—had become stabilized by about 1640. . . . One cannot reasonably explain the strength of various state-machineries at specific moments of the history of the modern world-system primarily in terms of a genetic-cultural line of argumentation, but rather in terms of the

From *Comparative Studies in Society and History* 16/4 (September 1974), pp. 390, 399–403, 406–415. Reprinted with the permission of Cambridge University Press and the author. Footnotes deleted.

structural role a country plays in the world-economy at that moment in time. . . .

We are now in a position to look at the historical evolution of this capitalist world-economy itself and analyze the degree to which it is fruitful to talk of distinct stages in its evolution as a system. The emergence of the European world-economy in the "long" sixteenth century (1450–1640) was made possible by an historical conjuncture: on those long-term trends which were the culmination of what has been sometimes described as the "crisis of feudalism" was superimposed a more immediate cyclical crisis plus climatic changes, all of which created a dilemma that could only be resolved by a geographic expansion of the division of labor. Furthermore, the balance of inter-system forces was such as to make this realizable. Thus a geographic expansion did take place in conjunction with a demographic expansion and an upward price rise.

The remarkable thing was not that a European world-economy was thereby created, but that it survived the Hapsburg attempt to transform it into a world-empire, an attempt seriously pursued by Charles V. The Spanish attempt to absorb the whole failed because the rapid economic-demographic-technological burst forward of the preceding century made the whole enterprise too expensive for the imperial base to sustain, especially given many structural insufficiencies in Castilian economic development. Spain could afford neither the bureaucracy nor the army that was necessary to the enterprise, and in the event went bankrupt, as did the French monarchs making a similar albeit even less plausible attempt.

Once the Hapsburg dream of world-empire was over—and in 1557 it was over forever—the capitalist world-economy was an established system that became almost impossible to unbalance. It quickly reached an equilibrium point in its relations with other world-systems: the Ottoman and Russian world-empires, the Indian Ocean protoworld-economy. Each of the states or potential states within the European world-economy was quickly in the race to bureaucratize, to raise a standing army, to homogenize its culture, to diversify its economic activities. By 1640, those in northwest Europe had succeeded in establishing themselves as the core-states; Spain and the northern Italian city-states declined into being semi-peripheral; northeastern Europe and Iberian America had become the periphery. At this point, those in semi-peripheral status had reached it by virtue of decline from a former more pre-eminent status.

It was the system-wide recession of 1650—1730 that consolidated the European world-economy and opened stage two of the modern world-economy. For the recession forced retrenchment, and the decline in relative surplus allowed room for only one core-state to survive. The mode of struggle was mercantilism, which was a device of partial insulation and withdrawal from the world market of *large* areas themselves hierarchically constructed—that is, empires within the world-economy (which is quite different from world-empires). In this struggle England first ousted the Netherlands from its commercial primacy and then resisted successfully France's attempt to catch up. As England began to speed up the process of industrialization after 1760, there was one last attempt of those capitalist forces located in France to break the imminent British hegemony. This attempt was expressed first in the French Revolution's replacement of the cadres of the regime and then in Napoleon's continental blockade. But it failed.

Stage three of the capitalist world-economy begins then, a stage of industrial rather than of agricultural capitalism. Henceforth, industrial production is no longer a minor aspect of the world market but comprises an ever larger percentage of world gross production—and even more important, of world gross surplus. This involves a whole series of consequences for the world-system.

First of all, it led to the further geographic expansion of the European world-economy to include now the whole of the globe. This was in part the result of its technological feasibility both in terms of improved military firepower and improved shipping facilities which made regular trade sufficiently inexpensive to be viable. But, in addition, industrial production *required* access to raw materials of a nature and in a quantity such that the needs could not be supplied within the former boundaries. At first, however, the search for new markets was not a primary consideration in the geographic expansion since the new markets were more readily available within the old boundaries, as we shall see.

The geographic expansion of the European world-economy meant the elimination of other world-systems as well as the absorption of the remaining mini-systems. The most important world-system up to then outside of the European world-economy, Russia, entered in semi-peripheral status, the consequence of the strength of its state-machinery (including its army) and the degree of industrialization already achieved in the eighteenth century. The independences in the Latin American countries did nothing to change their peripheral status. They merely eliminated the last vestiges of Spain's semi-peripheral role and ended pockets of non-involvement in the world-economy in the interior of Latin America. Asia and Africa were absorbed into the periphery in the nineteenth century, although Japan, because of the combination of the strength of its state-machinery, the poverty of its resource base (which led to a certain disinterest on the part of world capitalist forces), and its geographic remoteness from the core areas, was able quickly to graduate into semi-peripheral status.

The absorption of Africa as part of the periphery meant the end of slavery worldwide for two reasons. First of all, the manpower that was used as slaves was now needed for cash-crop production in Africa itself, whereas in the eighteenth century Europeans had sought to *discourage* just such cash-crop production. In the second place, once Africa was part of the periphery and not the external area, slavery was no longer economic. To understand this, we must appreciate the economics of slavery. Slaves receiving the lowest conceivable reward for their labor are the least productive form of labor and have the shortest life span, both because of undernourishment and maltreatment

and because of lowered psychic resistance to death. Furthermore, if recruited from areas surrounding their workplace the escape rate is too high. Hence, there must be a high transport cost for a product of low productivity. This makes economic sense only if the purchase price is virtually nil. In capitalist market trade, purchase always has a real cost. It is only in long-distance trade, the exchange of preciosities, that the purchase price can be in the social system of the purchaser virtually nil. Such was the slave-trade. Slaves were bought at low immediate cost (the production cost of the items actually exchanged) and none of the usual invisible costs. That is to say, the fact that removing a man from West Africa lowered the productive potential of the region was of *zero* cost to the European world-economy since these areas were not part of the division of labor. Of course, had the slave trade totally denuded Africa of all possibilities of furnishing further slaves, then a real cost to Europe would have commenced. But that point was never historically reached. Once, however, Africa was part of the periphery, then the real cost of a slave in terms of the production of surplus in the world-economy went up to such a point that it became far more economical to use wage-labor even on sugar or cotton plantations, which is precisely what transpired in the nineteenth-century Caribbean and other slave-labor regions.

The creation of vast new areas as the periphery of the expanded world-economy made possible a shift in the role of some other areas. Specifically, both the United States and Germany (as it came into being) combined formerly peripheral and semi-peripheral regions. The manufacturing sector in each was able to gain political ascendancy, as the peripheral subregions became less economically crucial to the world-economy. Mercantilism now became the major tool of semi-peripheral countries seeking to become core countries, thus still performing a function analogous to that of the mercantilist drives of the late seventeenth and eighteenth centuries in England and France. To be sure, the struggle of semi-peripheral countries to "industrialize" varied in the degree to which it succeeded in the period before the First World War: all the way in the United States, only partially in Germany, not at all in Russia.

The internal structure of core-states also changed fundamentally under industrial capitalism. For a core area, industrialism involved divesting itself of substantially all agricultural activities (except that in the twentieth century further mechanization was to create a new form of working the land that was so highly mechanized as to warrant the appellation industrial). Thus whereas, in the period 1700–40, England not only was Europe's leading industrial exporter but was also Europe's leading agricultural exporter—this was at a high point in the economy-wide recession—by 1900, less than 10 percent of England's population were engaged in agricultural pursuits.

At first under industrial capitalism, the core exchanged manufactured products against the periphery's agricultural products—hence, Britain from 1815 to 1873 as the "workshop of the world." Even to those semi-peripheral countries that had some manufacture (France, Germany, Belgium, the U.S.), Britain in this period supplied about half their needs in manufactured goods. As, however, the mercantilist practices of this latter group both cut Britain off from outlets and even created competition for Britain in sales to peripheral areas, a competition which led to the late nineteenth-century "scramble for Africa," the world division of labor was reallocated to ensure a new special role for the core: less the provision of the manufactures, more the provision of the machines to make the manufactures as well as the provision of infra-structure (especially, in this period, railroads).

The rise of manufacturing created for the first time under capitalism a large-scale urban proletariat. And in consequence for the first time there arose what Michels has called the "anti-capitalist mass spirit," which was translated into concrete organizational forms (trade-unions, socialist parties). This development intruded a new factor as threatening to the stability of the states and of the capitalist forces now so securely in control of them as

the earlier centrifugal thrusts of regional anti-capitalist landed elements had been in the seventeenth century.

At the same time that the bourgeoisies of the core countries were faced by this threat to the internal stability of their state structures, they were simultaneously faced with the economic crisis of the latter third of the nineteenth century resulting from the more rapid increase of agricultural production (and indeed of light manufactures) than the expansion of a potential market for these goods. Some of the surplus would have to be redistributed to someone to allow these goods to be bought and the economic machinery to return to smooth operation. By expanding the purchasing power of the industrial proletariat of the core countries, the world-economy was unburdened simultaneously of two problems: the bottleneck of demand and the unsettling "class conflict" of the core states—hence, the social liberalism or welfare-state ideology that arose just at that point in time.

The first World War was, as men of the time observed, the end of an era; and the Russian Revolution of October 1917 the beginning of a new one—our stage four. This stage was to be sure a stage of revolutionary turmoil but it also was, in a seeming paradox, the stage of the *consolidation* of the industrial capitalist world-economy. The Russian Revolution was essentially that of a semi-peripheral country whose internal balance of forces had been such that as of the late nineteenth century it began on a decline towards a peripheral status. This was the result of the marked penetration of foreign capital into the industrial sector which was on its way to eliminating all indigenous capitalist forces, the resistance to the mechanization of the agricultural sector, the decline of relative military power (as evidenced by the defeat by the Japanese in 1905). The Revolution brought to power a group of state-managers who reversed each one of these trends by using the classic technique of mercantilist semi-withdrawal from the world-economy. In the process of doing this, the now U.S.S.R. mobilized considerable popular support, especially in the urban sector. At the end of the Second World

War, Russia was reinstated as a very strong member of the semi-periphery and could begin to seek full core status.

Meanwhile, the decline of Britain which dates from 1873 was confirmed and its hegemonic role was assumed by the United States. While the U.S. thus rose, Germany fell further behind as a result of its military defeat. Various German attempts in the 1920s to find new industrial outlets in the Middle East and South America were unsuccessful in the face of the U.S. thrust combined with Britain's continuing relative strength. Germany's thrust of desperation to recoup lost ground took the noxious and unsuccessful form of Nazism.

It was the Second World War that enabled the United States for a brief period (1945—65) to attain the same level of primacy as Britain had in the first part of the nineteenth century. United States growth in this period was spectacular and created a great need for expanded market outlets. The Cold War closure denied not only the U.S.S.R. but Eastern Europe to U.S. exports. And the Chinese Revolution meant that this region, which had been destined for much exploitative activity, was also cut off. Three alternative areas were available and each was pursued with assiduity. First, Western Europe had to be rapidly "reconstructed," and it was the Marshall Plan which thus allowed this area to play a primary role in the expansion of world productivity. Secondly, Latin America became the reserve of U.S. investment from which now Britain and Germany were completely cut off. Thirdly, Southern Asia, the Middle East and Africa had to be decolonized. On the one hand, this was necessary in order to reduce the share of the surplus taken by the Western European intermediaries, as Canning covertly supported the Latin American revolutionaries against Spain in the 1820s. But also these countries had to be decolonized in order to mobilize productive potential in a way that had never been achieved in the colonial era. Colonial rule after all had been an *inferior* mode of relationship of core and periphery, one occasioned by the strenuous late-nineteenth-century conflict among industrial states but one no longer desirable from the point of view of the new hegemonic power.

But a world capitalist economy does not permit true imperium. Charles V could not succeed in his dream of world-empire. The Pax Britannica stimulated its own demise. So too did the Pax Americana. In each case, the cost of *political* imperium was too high economically, and in a capitalist system, over the middle run when profits decline, new *political* formulae are sought. In this case the costs mounted along several fronts. The efforts of the U.S.S.R. to further its own industrialization, protect a privileged market area (eastern Europe), and force entry into other market areas led to an immense spiralling of military expenditure, which on the Soviet side promised long-run returns whereas for the U.S. it was merely a question of running very fast to stand still. The economic resurgence of western Europe, made necessary both to provide markets for U.S. sales and investments and to counter the U.S.S.R. military thrust, meant over time that the west European state structures collectively became as strong as that of the U.S., which led in the late 1960s to the "dollar and gold crisis" and the retreat of Nixon from the free-trade stance which is the definitive mark of the self-confident leader in a capitalist market system. When the cumulated Third World pressures, most notably Vietnam, were added on, a restructuring of the world division of labor was inevitable, involving probably in the 1970s a quadripartite division of the larger part of the world surplus by the U.S., the European Common Market, Japan, and the U.S.S.R.

Such a decline in U.S. state hegemony has actually *increased* the freedom of action of capitalist enterprises, the larger of which have now taken the form of multinational corporations which are able to maneuver against state bureaucracies whenever the national politicians become too responsive to internal worker pressures. Whether some effective links can be established between multinational corporations, presently limited to operating in certain areas, and the U.S.S.R. remains to be seen, but it is by no means impossible.

. . . We thus come to projections about the future, which has always been man's great game, his true *hybris*, the most convincing argument for the dogma of original sin. Having read Dante, I will therefore be brief.

There are two fundamental contradictions, it seems to me, involved in the workings of the capitalist world-system. In the first place, there is the contradiction to which the nineteenth-century Marxian corpus pointed, which I would phrase as follows: whereas in the short-run the maximization of profit requires maximizing the withdrawal of surplus from immediate consumption of the majority, in the long-run the continued production of surplus requires a mass demand which can only be created by redistributing the surplus withdrawn. Since these two considerations move in opposite directions (a "contradiction"), the system has constant crises which in the long-run both weaken it and make the game for those with privilege less worth playing.

The second fundamental contradiction, to which Mao's concept of socialism as process points, is the following: whenever the tenants of privilege seek to co-opt an oppositional movement by including them in a minor share of the privilege, they may no doubt eliminate opponents in the short-run; but they also up the ante for the next oppositional movement created in the next crisis of the world-economy. Thus the cost of "co-option" rises ever higher and the advantages of co-option seem ever less worthwhile.

There are today no socialist systems in the world-economy any more than there are feudal systems because there is only *one* world-system. It is a world-economy and it is by definition capitalist in form. Socialism involves the creation of a new kind of *world*-system, neither a redistributive world-empire nor a capitalist world-economy but a socialist world-government. I don't see this projection as being in the least utopian but I also don't feel its institution is imminent. It will be the outcome of a long struggle in forms that may be familiar and perhaps in very new forms, that will take place in *all* the areas of the world-economy (Mao's continual "class struggle"). Governments may be in the hands of persons, groups or movements sympathetic to this transformation but *states* as such are neither progressive nor reactionary. It is movements and forces that deserve such evaluative judgments.

Having gone as far as I care to in projecting the future, let me return to the present and to the scholarly enterprise which is never neutral but does have its own logic and to some extent its own priorities. We have adumbrated as our basic unit of observation a concept of world-systems that have structural parts and evolving stages. It is within such a framework, I am arguing, that we can fruitfully make comparative analyses—of the wholes and of parts of the whole. Conceptions precede and govern measurements. I am all for minute and sophisticated quantitative indicators. I am all for minute and diligent archival work that will trace a concrete historical series of events in terms of all its immediate complexities. But the point of either is to enable us to see better what has happened and what is happening. For that we need glasses with which to discern the dimensions of difference, we need models with which to weigh significance, we need summarizing concepts with which to create the knowledge which we then seek to communicate to each other. And all this because we are men with hybris and original sin and therefore seek the good, the true, and the beautiful.

Chapter 13

The Democratic Security Community

48. Perpetual Peace: A Philosophical Sketch

IMMANUEL KANT

'THE PERPETUAL PEACE'

A Dutch innkeeper once put this satirical inscription on his signboard, along with the picture of a graveyard. We shall not trouble to ask whether it applies to men in general, or particularly to heads of state (who can never have enough of war), or only to the philosophers who blissfully dream of perpetual peace. . . .

FIRST SECTION

Which Contains the Preliminary Articles of a Perpetual Peace Between States

1. 'No conclusion of peace shall be considered valid . . . if it was made with a secret reservation . . . for a future war.'

For if this were the case, it would be a mere truce, a suspension of hostilities, not a *peace*. Peace means an end to all hostilities, and to attach the adjective 'perpetual' to it is already suspiciously close to pleonasm. A conclusion of peace nullifies all existing reasons for a future war, even if these are not yet known to the

contracting parties, and no matter how acutely and carefully they may later be pieced together out of old documents. . . .

2. 'No independently existing state, whether it be large or small, may be acquired by another state by inheritance, exchange, purchase or gift.'

For a state, unlike the ground on which it is based, is not a possession (*patrimonium*). It is a society of men, which no-one other than itself can command or dispose of. Like a tree, it has its own roots, and to graft it on to another state as if it were a shoot is to terminate its existence as a moral personality and make it into a commodity. . . .

3. 'Standing armies (*miles perpetuus*) will gradually be abolished altogether.'

For they constantly threaten other states with war by the very fact that they are always prepared for it. They spur on the states to outdo one another in arming unlimited numbers of soldiers, and since the resultant costs eventually make peace more oppressive than a short war, the armies are themselves the cause of wars of aggression which set out to end burdensome military expenditure. Furthermore, the hiring of men to kill or to be killed seems to mean using them as mere machines and instruments in the hands of someone else (the state), which cannot eas-

From *Kant: Political Writings* ed. by Hans Reiss. Translated by H. B. Nisbet. © Cambridge University Press, 2nd enlarged ed., 1991:93–114. Reprinted with the permission of Cambridge University Press.

ily be reconciled with the rights of man in one's own person. It is quite a different matter if the citizens undertake voluntary military training from time to time in order to secure themselves and their fatherland against attacks from outside. But it would be just the same if wealth rather than soldiers were accumulated, for it would be seen by other states as a military threat; it might compel them to mount preventive attacks, for of the three powers within a state—the *power of the army*, the *power of alliance* and the *power of money*—the third is probably the most reliable instrument of war. It would lead more often to wars if it were not so difficult to discover the amount of wealth which another state possesses.

4. 'No national debt shall be contracted in connection with the external affairs of the state.'

There is no cause for suspicion if help for the national economy is sought inside or outside the state (e.g., for improvements to roads, new settlements, storage of foodstuffs for years of famine, etc.). But a credit system, if used by the powers as an instrument of aggression against one another, shows the power of money in its most dangerous form. . . . This ingenious system, invented by a commercial people [the British—Ed.] in the present century, provides a military fund which may exceed the resources of all the other states put together. It can only be exhausted by an eventual tax-deficit, which may be postponed for a considerable time by the commercial stimulus which industry and trade receive through the credit system. This ease in making war, coupled with the warlike inclination of those in power (which seems to be an integral feature of human nature), is thus a great obstacle in the way of perpetual peace. Foreign debts must therefore be prohibited by a preliminary article of such a peace, otherwise national bankruptcy, inevitable in the long run, would necessarily involve various other states in the resultant loss without their having deserved it, thus inflicting upon them a public injury. Other

states are therefore justified in allying themselves against such a state and its pretensions.

5. 'No state shall forcibly interfere in the constitution and government of another state.'

For what could justify such interference? Surely not any sense of scandal or offence which a state arouses in the subjects of another state. . . . And a bad example which one free person gives to another is not the same as an injury to the latter. But it would be a different matter if a state, through internal discord, were to split into two parts, . . . [Nevertheless,] as long as this internal conflict is not yet decided, the interference of external powers would be a violation of the rights of an independent people which is merely struggling with its internal ills. Such interference would be an active offence and would make the autonomy of all other states insecure.

6. 'No state at war with another shall permit such acts of hostility as would make mutual confidence impossible during a future time of peace. Such acts would include the employment of *assassins* (*percussores*) or *poisoners* (*venefici*), *breach of agreements, the instigation of treason* (*perduellio*) within the enemy state, etc.'

These are dishonourable stratagems. For it must still remain possible, even in wartime, to have some sort of trust in the attitude of the enemy, otherwise peace could not be concluded and the hostilities would turn into a war of extermination (*bellum internecinum*). After all, war is only a regrettable expedient for asserting one's rights by force within a state of nature, where no court of justice is available to judge with legal authority. . . .

All of the articles listed above, when regarded objectively or in relation to the intentions of those in power, are *prohibitive laws* (*leges prohibitivae*). Yet some of them are of the *strictest* sort (*leges strictae*), being valid irrespective of differing circumstances, and they require that the abuses they prohibit should be abolished *immediately* (Nos. 1, 5, and 6). Others (Nos. 2, 3, and 4), although they are not exceptions to the rule of justice, allow some *subjective* latitude according to the circumstances in which they are applied (*leges latae*). The latter need not necessarily be executed at once, so long as their ultimate purpose (e.g., the *restoration* of freedom to certain states in accordance with the second article) is not lost sight of. But their execution may not be *put off* to a non-existent date (*ad calendas graecas*, as Augustus used to promise). . . .

SECOND SECTION

Which Contains the Definitive Articles of a Perpetual Peace Between States

A state of peace among men living together is not the same as the state of nature, which is rather a state of war. For even if it does not involve active hostilities, it involves a constant threat of their breaking out. Thus the state of peace must be *formally instituted*, for a suspension of hostilities is not in itself a guarantee of peace. And unless one neighbour gives a guarantee to the other at his request (which can happen only in a *lawful* state), the latter may treat him as an enemy.

First Definitive Article of a Perpetual Peace: The Civil Constitution of Every State Shall Be Republican

A *republican constitution* is founded upon three principles: firstly, the principle of *freedom* for all members of a society (as men); secondly, the principle of the *dependence* of everyone upon a single common legislation (as subjects); and thirdly, the principle of legal *equality* for everyone (as citizens). It is the only constitution which can be derived from the idea of an original contract, upon which all rightful legislation of a people must be founded. Thus as far as right is concerned, republicanism is in itself the original basis of every kind of civil constitution, and it only remains to ask whether it is the only constitution which can lead to a perpetual peace.

The republican constitution is not only pure in its origin (since it springs from the pure concept of right); it also offers a prospect of attaining the desired result, i.e., a perpetual peace, and the reason for this is as follows.—If, as is inevitably the case under this constitution, the consent of the citizens is required to decide whether or not war is to be declared, it is very natural that they will have great hesitation in embarking on so dangerous an enterprise. For this would mean calling down on themselves all the miseries of war, such as doing the fighting themselves, supplying the costs of the war from their own resources, painfully making good the ensuing devastation, and, as the crowning evil, having to take upon themselves a burden of debt which will embitter peace itself and which can never be paid off on account of the constant threat of new wars. But under a constitution where the subject is not a citizen, and which is therefore not republican, it is the simplest thing in the world to go to war. For the head of state is not a fellow citizen, but the owner of the state, and a war will not force him to make the slightest sacrifice so far as his banquets, hunts, pleasure palaces and court festivals are concerned. He can thus decide on war, without any significant reason, as a kind of amusement, and unconcernedly leave it to the diplomatic corps (who are always ready for such purposes) to justify the war for the sake of propriety.

The following remarks are necessary to prevent the republican constitution from being confused with the democratic one, as commonly happens. The various forms of state (*civitas*) may be classified either according to the different persons who exercise supreme authority or according to the way in which the nation is governed by its ruler, whoever he may be. The first classification goes by the form of sovereignty (*forma imperii*), and only three such forms are possible, depending on whether the ruling power is in the hands of an *individual*, of *several persons* in association, or of *all* those who together constitute civil society (i.e., *autocracy*, *aristocracy* and *democracy*—the power of a prince, the power of a nobility, and the power of the people). The second classification depends on the form of government (*forma regiminis*), and relates to the way in which the state, setting out from its constitution (i.e., an act of the general will whereby the mass becomes a people), makes use of its plenary power. The form of government, in this case, will be either *republican* or *despotic*. *Republicanism* is that political principle whereby the executive power (the government) is separated from the legislative power. Despotism prevails in a state if the laws are made and arbitrarily executed by one and the same power, and it reflects the will of the people only in so far as the ruler treats the will of the people as his own private will. Of the three forms of sovereignty, *democracy*, in the truest sense of the word, is necessarily a *despotism*, because it establishes an executive power through which all the citizens may make decisions about (and indeed against) the single individual without his consent, so that decisions are made by all the people and yet not by all the people; and this means that the general will is in contradiction with itself, and thus also with freedom. . . .

. . . [I]f the mode of government is to accord with the concept of right, it must be based on the representative system. This system alone makes possible a republican state, and without it, despotism and violence will result, no matter what kind of constitution is in force. . . .

Second Definitive Article of a Perpetual Peace: The Right of Nations Shall Be Based on a Federation of Free States

Peoples who have grouped themselves into nation states may be judged in the same way as individual men living in a state of nature, independent of external laws; for they are a standing offence to one another by the very fact that they are neighbours. Each nation, for the sake of its own security, can and ought to demand of the others that they should enter along with it into a constitution, similar to the civil one, within which the rights of each could be secured. This would mean es-

tablishing a *federation of peoples*. But a federation of this sort would not be the same thing as an international state. . . .

We look with profound contempt upon the way in which savages cling to their lawless freedom. They would rather engage in incessant strife than submit to a legal constraint which they might impose upon themselves, for they prefer the freedom of folly to the freedom of reason. We regard this as barbarism, coarseness, and brutish debasement of humanity. We might thus expect that civilised peoples, each united within itself as a state, would hasten to abandon so degrading a condition as soon as possible. But instead of doing so, each *state* sees its own majesty precisely in not having to submit to any external legal constraint, and the glory of its ruler consists in his power to order thousands of people to immolate themselves for a cause which does not truly concern them, while he need not himself incur any danger whatsoever.* . . .

Although it is largely concealed by governmental constraints in law-governed civil society, the depravity of human nature is displayed without disguise in the unrestricted relations which obtain between the various nations. It is therefore to be wondered at that the word *right* has not been completely banished from military politics as superfluous pedantry, and that no state has been bold enough to declare itself publicly in favour of doing so. For Hugo Grotius, Pufendorf, Vattel and the rest (sorry comforters as they are) are still dutifully quoted in *justification* of military aggression, although their philosophically or diplomatically formulated codes do not and cannot have the slightest *legal* force, since states as such are not subject to a common external constraint. Yet there is no instance of a state ever having been moved to desist from its purpose by arguments supported by the testimonies of

---

*Thus a Bulgarian prince, replying to the Greek Emperor who had kindly offered to settle his dispute with him by a duel, declared: 'A smith who possesses tongs will not lift the glowing iron out of the coals with his own hands.'

such notable men. This homage which every state pays (in words at least) to the concept of right proves that man possesses a greater moral capacity, still dormant at present, to overcome eventually the evil principle within him (for he cannot deny that it exists), and to hope that others will do likewise. Otherwise the word *right* would never be used by states which intend to make war on one another. . . .

The way in which states seek their rights can only be by war, since there is no external tribunal to put their claims to trial. But rights cannot be decided by military victory, and a *peace treaty* may put an end to the current war, but not to that general warlike condition within which pretexts can always be for a new war. . . .

On the other hand, reason, as the highest legislative moral power, absolutely condemns war as a test of rights and sets up peace as an immediate duty. But peace can neither be inaugurated nor secured without a general agreement between the nations; thus a particular kind of league, which we might call a *pacific federation* (*foedus pacificum*), is required. It would differ from a *peace treaty* (*pactum pacis*) in that the latter terminates *one* war, whereas the former would seek to end *all* wars for good. This federation does not aim to acquire any power like that of a state, but merely to preserve and secure the *freedom* of each state in itself, along with that of the other confederated states, although this does not mean that they need to submit to public laws and to a coercive power which enforces them, as do men in a state of nature. It can be shown that this idea of *federalism*, extending gradually to encompass all states and thus leading to perpetual peace, is practicable and has objective reality. For if by good fortune one powerful and enlightened nation can form a republic (which is by its nature inclined to seek perpetual peace), this will provide a focal point for federal association among other states. These will join up with the first one, thus securing the freedom of each state in accordance with the idea of international right, and the whole will grad-

ually spread further and further by a series of alliances of this kind.

It would be understandable for a people to say: 'There shall be no war among us; for we will form ourselves into a state, appointing for ourselves a supreme legislative, executive and juridical power to resolve our conflicts by peaceful means.' But if this state says: 'There shall be no war between myself and other states, although I do not recognise any supreme legislative power which could secure my rights and whose rights I should in turn secure,' it is impossible to understand what justification I can have for placing any confidence in my rights, unless I can rely on some substitute for the union of civil society, i.e., on a free federation. If the concept of international right is to retain any meaning at all, reason must necessarily couple it with a federation of this kind.

The concept of international right becomes meaningless if interpreted as a right to go to war. For this would make it a right to determine what is lawful not by means of universally valid external laws, but by means of one-sided maxims backed up by physical force. It could be taken to mean that it is perfectly just for men who adopt this attitude to destroy one another, and thus to find perpetual peace in the vast grave where all the horrors of violence and those responsible for them would be buried. There is only one rational way in which states coexisting with other states can emerge from the lawless condition of pure warfare. Just like individual men, they must renounce their savage and lawless freedom, adapt themselves to public coercive laws, and thus form an *international state* (*civitas gentium*), which would necessarily continue to grow until it embraced all the peoples of the earth. But since this is not the will of the nations, according to their present conception of international right (so that they reject *in hypothesi* what is true *in thesi*), the positive idea of a *world republic* cannot be realised. If all is not to be lost, this can at best find a negative substitute in the shape of an enduring and gradually expanding *federation* likely to prevent war. The latter may check the current of man's inclination to defy the law and antagonise his fellows, although there will always be a risk of it bursting forth anew. *Furor impius intus—fremit horridus ore cruento* (Wicked frenzy rages savagely with blood-stained mouth.—Virgil).*

Third Definitive Article of a Perpetual Peace: Cosmopolitan Right Shall Be Limited to Conditions of Universal Hospitality

As in the foregoing articles, we are here concerned not with philanthropy, but with *right*. In this context, *hospitality* means the right of a stranger not to be treated with hostility when he arrives on someone else's territory. He can indeed be turned away, if this can be done without causing his death, but he must not be treated with hostility, so long as he behaves in a peaceable manner in the place he happens to be in. The stranger cannot claim the *right of a guest* to be entertained, for this would require a special friendly agreement whereby he might become a member of the native household for a certain time. He may only claim a *right of resort*, for all men are entitled to present themselves in the society of others by virtue of their right to communal possession of the earth's surface. . . . And no-one originally has any greater right than anyone else to occupy any particular portion of the earth. . . . But this natural right of hospitality, i.e., the right of strangers, does not extend beyond those conditions which make it possible for them to *attempt* to enter into relations with the native inhabitants. In this way, continents distant from each other can enter into peaceful mutual relations which may eventually be regulated by public laws, thus bringing the human race nearer and nearer to a cosmopolitan constitution.

If we compare with this ultimate end the *inhospitable* conduct of the civilised states of our continent, especially the commercial states, the injustice which they display in *visiting* foreign countries and peoples (which in their case is the same as *conquering* them) seems appallingly great. America, the negro countries, the Spice Islands, the Cape, etc. were looked upon at the time of their discovery as ownerless territories; for the native inhabitants were counted as nothing. In East India (Hindustan), foreign troops were brought in under the pretext of merely setting up trading posts. This led to oppression of the natives, incitement of the various Indian states to widespread wars, famine, insurrection, treachery and that whole litany of evils which can afflict the human race. . . .

The peoples of the earth have thus entered in varying degrees into a universal community, and it has developed to the point where a violation of rights in *one* part of the world is felt *everywhere*. The idea of a cosmopolitan right is therefore not fantastic and overstrained; it is a necessary complement to the unwritten code of political and international right, transforming it into a universal right of humanity. Only under this condition can we flatter ourselves that we are continually advancing towards a perpetual peace.

FIRST SUPPLEMENT: ON THE GUARANTEE OF A PERPETUAL PEACE

Perpetual peace is *guaranteed* by no less an authority than the great artist *Nature* herself (*natura daedala rerum*) (Nature the contriver of things—Lucretius). The mechanical pro-

---

*At the end of a war, when peace is concluded, it would not be inappropriate for a people to appoint a day of atonement after the festival of thanksgiving. Heaven would be invoked in the name of the state to forgive the human race for the great sin of which it continues to be guilty, since it will not accommodate itself to a lawful constitution in international relations. Proud of its independence, each state prefers to employ the barbarous expedient of war, although war cannot produce the desired decision on the rights of particular states. The thanksgivings for individual victories during a war, the hymns which are sung (in the style of the Israelites) to the *Lord of Hosts*, contrast no less markedly with the moral conception of a father of mankind. For besides displaying indifference to the way in which nations pursue their mutual rights (deplorable though it is), they actually rejoice at having annihilated numerous human beings or their happiness.

cess of nature visibly exhibits the purposive plan of producing concord among men, even against their will and indeed by means of their very discord. . . . But before we define this guarantee more precisely, we must first examine the situation in which nature has placed the actors in her great spectacle, for it is this situation which ultimately demands the guarantee of peace. We may next enquire in what manner the guarantee is provided.

Nature's provisional arrangement is as follows. Firstly, she has taken care that human beings are able to live in all the areas where they are settled. Secondly, she has driven them in all directions by means of *war*, so that they inhabit even the most inhospitable regions. And thirdly, she has compelled them by the same means to enter into more or less legal relationships. . . .

In seeing to it that men *could* live everywhere on earth, nature has at the same time despotically willed that they *should* live everywhere, even against their own inclinations. And this obligation does not rest upon any concept of duty which might bind them to fulfil it in accordance with a moral law; on the contrary, nature has chosen war as a means of attaining this end. . . . [w]hat else but war, nature's means of peopling the whole earth, can have driven the Eskimos so far North—for they are quite distinct from all other American races, and are perhaps descended from European adventurers of ancient times; the Pesherae have been driven South into Tierra del Fuego in the same manner. War itself, however, does not require any particular kind of motivation, for it seems to be ingrained in human nature, and even to be regarded as something noble to which man is inspired by his love of honour, without selfish motives. Thus warlike courage, with the American savages as with their European counterparts in medieval times, is held to be of great and immediate value—and not just *in times of* war (as might be expected), but also *in order that* there may be war. Thus wars are often started merely to display this quality, so that war itself is invested with an inherent *dignity*; for even philosophers have eulogised it as a kind of ennobling influence on man, forgetting the

Greek saying that 'war is bad in that it produces more evil people than it destroys.' So much, then, for what nature does to further *her own end* with respect to the human race as an animal species.

We now come to the essential question regarding the prospect of perpetual peace. What does nature do in relation to the end which man's own reason prescribes to him as a duty, i.e., how does nature help to promote his *moral purpose*? And how does nature guarantee that what man *ought* to do by the laws of his freedom (but does not do) will in fact be done through nature's compulsion, without prejudice to the free agency of man? This question arises, moreover, in all three areas of public right—in *political, international* and *cosmopolitan right*. For if I say that nature *wills* that this or that should happen, this does not mean that nature imposes on us a *duty* to do it, for duties can only be imposed by practical reason, acting without any external constraint. On the contrary, nature does it herself, whether we are willing or not: *fata volentem ducunt, nolentem trahunt* (The fates lend him who is willing, but drag him who is unwilling.—Seneca).

1. Even if people were not compelled by internal dissent to submit to the coercion of public laws, war would produce the same effect from outside. For in accordance with the natural arrangement described above, each people would find itself confronted by another neighbouring people pressing in upon it, thus forcing it to form itself internally into a *state* in order to encounter the other as an armed *power*. Now the *republican* constitution is the only one which does complete justice to the rights of man. But it is also the most difficult to establish, and even more so to preserve, so that many maintain that it would only be possible within a state of *angels*, since men, with their self-seeking inclinations, would be incapable of adhering to a constitution of so sublime a nature. But in fact, nature comes to the aid of the universal and rational human will, so admirable in itself but so impotent in practice, and makes use of precisely those self-seeking inclinations in order to do so. It only remains for men to create a good organisation

for the state, a task which is well within their capability, and to arrange it in such a way that their self-seeking energies are opposed to one another, each thereby neutralising or eliminating the destructive effects of the rest. And as far as reason is concerned, the result is the same as if man's selfish tendencies were non-existent, so that man, even if he is not morally good in himself, is nevertheless compelled to be a good citizen. As hard as it may sound, the problem of setting up a state can be solved even by a nation of devils (so long as they possess understanding). It may be stated as follows: 'In order to organise a group of rational beings who together require universal laws for their survival, but of whom each separate individual is secretly inclined to exempt himself from them, the constitution must be so designed that, although the citizens are opposed to one another in their private attitudes, these opposing views may inhibit one another in such a way that the public conduct of the citizens will be the same as if they did not have such evil attitudes.' A problem of this kind must be soluble. For such a task does not involve the moral improvement of man; it only means finding out how the mechanism of nature can be applied to men in such a manner that the antagonism of their hostile attitudes will make them compel one another to submit to coercive laws, thereby producing a condition of peace within which the laws can be enforced. . . . Thus that mechanism of nature by which selfish inclinations are naturally opposed to one another in their external relations can be used by reason to facilitate the attainment of its own end, the reign of established right. Internal and external peace are thereby furthered and assured, so far as it lies within the power of the state itself to do so. We may therefore say that nature *irresistibly wills* that right should eventually gain the upper hand. What men have neglected to do will ultimately happen of its own accord, albeit with much inconvenience. As Bouterwek puts it: 'If the reed is bent too far, it breaks; and he who wants too much gets nothing.'

2. The idea of international right presupposes the separate existence of many independent adjoining states. And such a state of affairs is essentially a state of war, unless there is a federal union to prevent hostilities breaking out. But in the light of the idea of reason, this state is still to be preferred to an amalgamation of the separate nations under a single power which has overruled the rest and created a universal monarchy. For the laws progressively lose their impact as the government increases its range, and a soulless despotism, after crushing the germs of goodness, will finally lapse into anarchy. It is nonetheless the desire of every state (or its ruler) to achieve lasting peace by thus dominating the whole world, if at all possible. But *nature* wills it otherwise, and uses two means to separate the nations and prevent them from intermingling—*linguistic* and *religious* differences. These may certainly occasion mutual hatred and provide pretexts for wars, but as culture grows and men gradually move towards greater agreement over their principles, they lead to mutual understanding and peace. And unlike that universal despotism which saps all man's energies and ends in the graveyard of freedom, this peace is created and guaranteed by an equilibrium of forces and a most vigorous rivalry.

3. Thus nature wisely separates the nations, although the will of each individual state, even basing its arguments on international right, would gladly unite them under its own sway by force or by cunning. On the other hand, nature also unites nations which the concept of cosmopolitan right would not have protected from violence and war, and does so by means of their mutual self-interest. For the *spirit of commerce* sooner or later takes hold of every people, and it cannot exist side by side with war. And of all the powers (or means) at the disposal of the power of the state, *financial power* can probably be relied on most. Thus states find themselves compelled to promote the noble cause of peace, though not exactly from motives of morality. And wherever in the world there is a threat of war breaking out, they will try to prevent it by mediation, just as if they had entered into a permanent league for this purpose; for by the very nature of things, large

military alliances can only rarely be formed, and will even more rarely be successful.

In this way, nature guarantees perpetual peace by the actual mechanism of human inclinations. And while the likelihood of its being attained is not sufficient to enable us to *prophesy* the future theoretically, it is enough for practical purposes. It makes it our duty to work our way towards this goal, which is more than an empty chimera.

49. From *Political Community and the North Atlantic Area*

KARL W. DEUTSCH ET AL.

THE PROBLEM

We undertook this inquiry as a contribution to the study of possible ways in which men some day might abolish war. From the outset, we realized the complexity of the problem. It is difficult to relate "peace" clearly to other prime values such as "justice" and "freedom." There is little common agreement on acceptable alternatives to war and there is much ambiguity in the use of the terms "war" and "peace." Yet we can start with the assumption that war is now so dangerous that mankind must eliminate it, must put it beyond serious possibility. The attempt to do this may fail. But in a civilization that wishes to survive, the central problem in the study of international organization is this: How can men learn to act together to eliminate war as a social institution?

. . . We are seeking new light with which to look at the conditions and processes of long-range or permanent peace, applying our findings to one contemporary problem which, though not so difficult as the East-West problem, is by no means simple: peace *within* the North-Atlantic area.

From *Political Community and the North Atlantic Area* by Karl W. Deutsch et al., pp. 3–9. Copyright © 1957 by Princeton University Press. Reprinted by permission of Princeton University Press.

Whenever a difficult political problem arises, men turn to history for clues to its solution. They do this knowing they will not find the whole answer there. Every political problem is unique, of course, for history does not "repeat itself." But often the reflective mind will discover situations in the past that are essentially similar to the one being considered. Usually, with these rough parallels or suggestive analogies, the problem is not so much to find the facts as it is to decide what is essentially the same and what is essentially different between the historical facts and those of the present.

When most people discuss war and history in the same breath, they are likely to adopt one of two extreme positions. Some say that because history shows a continuous record of war, it indicates nothing but more of the same for the future. Others say that history shows a persistent growth in the size of the communities into which men organize themselves, and that this trend will continue until the world is living peacefully in a single community. Neither of these conclusions seems warranted on its face, though both contain some truth.

There is plenty of room between such extreme interpretations of history. Yet we know of no thorough investigation into the ways in which certain areas of the world have, in the past, "permanently" eliminated war.

Historians, especially diplomatic historians, have covered a great deal of ground in explaining how wars were avoided for long and short periods of time, but they have not gone into detail in explaining how and why certain groups have permanently stopped warring. Those who believe that international war is here to stay may be correct. But we may point out that war *has* been eliminated permanently, for all practical purposes, over large areas. If we could be sure of results, we would find it worth our while to spend many millions of man-hours and many millions of dollars in studying how this condition came about and how it might be extended over larger and larger areas of the globe. Thus far no such effort has been made, and no techniques for it have been perfected. In the course of our study, therefore, we had to develop our own techniques. This book is the first result of a limited but somewhat novel inquiry.

We are dealing here with political communities. These we regard as social groups with a process of political communication, some machinery for enforcement, and some popular habits of compliance. A political community is not necessarily able to prevent war within the area it covers: the United States was unable to do so at the time of the Civil War. Some political communities do, however, eliminate war and the expectation of war within their boundaries. It is these that call for intensive study.

We have concentrated, therefore, upon the formation of "security-communities" in certain historical cases. The use of this term starts a chain of definitions, and we must break in here to introduce the other main links needed for a fuller understanding of our findings.

A SECURITY-COMMUNITY is a group of people which has become "integrated."

By INTEGRATION we mean the attainment, within a territory, of a "sense of community" and of institutions and practices strong enough and widespread enough to assure, for a "long" time, dependable expectations of "peaceful change" among its population.

By SENSE OF COMMUNITY we mean a belief on the part of individuals in a group that they have come to

agreement on at least this one point: that common social problems must and can be resolved by processes of "peaceful change."

By PEACEFUL CHANGE we mean the resolution of social problems, normally by institutionalized procedures, without resort to large-scale physical force.

A security-community, therefore, is one in which there is real assurance that the members of that community will not fight each other physically, but will settle their disputes in some other way. If the entire world were integrated as a security-community, wars would be automatically eliminated. But there is apt to be confusion about the term "integration."

In our usage, the term "integration" does not necessarily mean only the merging of peoples or governmental units into a single unit. Rather, we divide security-communities into two types: "amalgamated" and "pluralistic."

By AMALGAMATION we mean the formal merger of two or more previously independent units into a single larger unit, with some type of common government after amalgamation. This common government may be unitary or federal. The United States today is an example of the amalgamated type. It became a single governmental unit by the formal merger of several formerly independent units. It has one supreme decision-making center.

The PLURALISTIC security-community, on the other hand, retains the legal independence of separate governments. The combined territory of the United States and Canada is an example of the pluralistic type. Its two separate governmental units form a security-community without being merged. It has two supreme decision-making centers. Where amalgamation occurs without integration, of course a security-community does not exist.

Since our study deals with the problem of ensuring peace, we shall say that any political community, be it amalgamated or pluralistic, was eventually SUCCESSFUL if it became a security-community—that is, if it achieved integration—and that it was UNSUCCESSFUL if it ended eventually in secession or civil war.

Perhaps we should point out here that both types of integration require, at the international level, some kind of organization, even though it may be very loose. We put no credence in the old aphorism that among friends a constitution is not necessary and among enemies it is of no avail. The area of practicability lies in between.

Integration is a matter of fact, not of time. If people on both sides do not fear war and do not prepare for it, it matters little how long it took them to reach this stage. But once integration has been reached, the length of time over which it persists may contribute to its consolidation.

It should be noted that integration and amalgamation overlap, but not completely. This means that there can be amalgamation without integration, and that there can be integration without amalgamation [see Figure 13.1]. . . .

One of our basic premises is that whatever we can learn about the process of forming security-communities should be helpful in an indirect way not only to planners, but also to existing international organizations. If the way to integration, domestic or international, is through the achievement of a sense of community that undergirds institutions, then it seems likely that an increased sense of community would help to strengthen whatever institutions—supranational or international—are already operating. When

these institutions are agencies for enforcement of the public will, we encounter that ancient and tantalizing puzzle: who polices the police? Can we make certain that agreements, freely entered into, will be reliably enforced or peacefully changed? Until we can do this, war may be called upon to do the job, liquidating the disputing parties instead of the dispute.

Everyone knows that political machinery already exists for reaching international decisions, and that these decisions cannot always be enforced after they are decided upon. Likewise, judicial machinery also exists which could be used for settling any international dispute without force; but states cannot be brought before a court against their will, nor made to abide by its judgment. It is equally true that enforcement or compliance can be achieved for a time without willing acceptance, as in the case of a strong state against a weak one. But without steady acceptance by large numbers of people, compliance is bound to be ineffective or temporary.

A situation of compliance, then, presupposes general agreement about something. Perhaps the "something" has to be the substance of the matter being complied with, or perhaps merely the legitimacy of the enforcing agent, or even the rightfulness of the

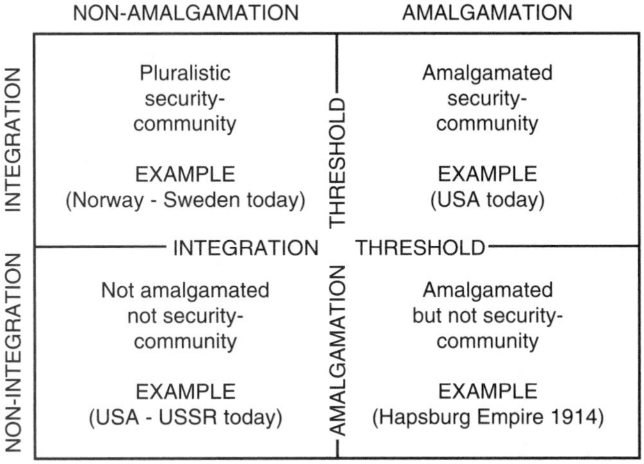

FIGURE 13.1

procedure being used. Once men have attained this condition of agreement with regard to a social institution for enforcement of the public will, and have stabilized this condition, that institution would seem to be reliably supported: the police are effectively policed. This kind of institution—perhaps the most crucial of all—represents the force organized on behalf of the community. In our terms, a sense of community would have been achieved to a high degree—perhaps high enough to be considered as integration.

It is the object of our inquiry to learn as much as possible about how such a condition has been reached under various circumstances at various times. Through this study, we hope to learn how that condition could be approached more closely in the present world.

50. Elective Governments—A Force for Peace*

DEAN V. BABST

In 1961 Congress created the United States Arms Control and Disarmament Agency. One of the goals assigned to it was to carry out research toward achieving a "better understanding of how the basic structure of a lasting peace may be established (1)." One approach to this problem is to inquire whether there are certain types of governments which do not make war against each other.

Purely impressionistically the hypothesis was formulated that these would be freely elected governments of independent countries, the borders of which are firmly established. This is based on the assumption that the general public does not want war, if it can choose. However, the possibility of choice requires independence and the existence of an elective government. The tendencies of such governments to work out international differences by means other than war would be most obvious in their dealings with other such governments.

The purpose of this paper is to provide a preliminary test of this hypothesis. This test was made by asking the question "Have there been any wars fought between independent freely elected governments?" In order to make a systematic test, a search was made for a list of wars and the countries participating in them. One of the best enumerations was found in Quincy Wright's book *A Study of War* (2).

Wright and his associates listed all major wars fought since 1500. They define a major war as one important enough to involve over 50,000 troops or to cause the creation or extinction of states, territorial transfers, or changes in governments.

Using this list, each war was evaluated to determine if any freely elected independent government fought each other. In order to objectively compare governments of various areas for different periods, it was necessary to develop an operational definition of the type of government in which we are interested. The definition used is that a country's government will be considered as freely elected, for the year under consideration, when it has the following four characteristics:

1. Legislation and national finances are controlled by a legislature or parliament whose members are chosen by majority vote from at least two opposing choices, at regular intervals, by the electorate.

2. The administrative control of the government is by an executive chosen by majority vote by a parliament secured in the above manner, or by

The author wishes to express his gratitude to Hugo O. Engelman, John W. Mannering and Paul H. Kusuda for their critical review of an earlier version of the paper.

From *The Wisconsin Sociologist*. (1964), Vol. 3, No. 1:9–14. Complete and unabridged. Reprinted by permission of the publisher.

direct vote of the electorate, from two or more opposing candidates, at regular intervals. If an hereditary ruler, such as a king, can chose the prime minister or president, then the country is not considered to have an elective government unless the monarch's function is primarily ceremonial.

3. There is a secret ballot and some freedom of speech and press; otherwise the opposing choices are not legitimate.

4. Since in a country that is not independent the population cannot exercise a relevant choice, the country must be independent at the start of the war.

The question here is whether any wars occurred between governments meeting the preceding specifications. Quincy Wright's list of wars extends from 1480 to 1941, when his book was published. However, only the wars from 1789 to 1941 were analyzed. 1789 was selected as a starting point for this study, because it was this year the first elective government in our sense, that of the United States, began operating.

James Bryce, shows the recency of popular elective governments in human history (3).

A century ago there was in the Old World only one tiny spot in which the working of democracy could be studied. A few of the ancient rural cantons of Switzerland had recovered their freedom after the fall of Napoleon, and were governing themselves as they had done from the earlier Middle Ages, but they were too small and their conditions too peculiar to furnish instruction to larger communities or throw much light on popular governments in general. Nowhere else in Europe did the people rule. Britain enjoyed far wider freedom than any part of the European Continent, but her local as well as central government was still oligarchic. When the American Republic began its national life with the framing and adoption of the Federal Constitution in 1787–89, the only materials which history furnished to its founders were those which the republics of antiquity had provided, so it was to these materials that both those founders and the men of the first French Revolution constantly recurred for examples to be followed or avoided.

From this shaky beginning, popular elected governments have grown greatly in number and size to become a world force. Despite two world wars and many lesser ones there has been a large growth in the number of elective governments, e.g., United States, Great Britain, Norway, West Germany, Finland, India, Canada, Ireland, Netherlands, Israel, Australia, Switzerland.

Quincy Wright and his associates list 116 major wars from 1789 to 1941 (date of publication), with 438 participating countries. An analysis of this list shows that no wars have been fought between independent nations with elective governments. Such nations have fought many wars against autocratic governments, and even some against their own colonies who wanted to become independent, but these nations have not waged war against each other.

Only the major wars can be considered in this paper. It is hoped that the testing of the hypothesis can be extended to the future. We should also find answers to these further, unresolved questions. For example, why have some of these elective governments occasionally fought a colony or area under their control which also had a freely elected government and was trying to become independent? This appears to be a serious weakness with elective governments but cannot be considered here.

The first war that came close to being a war between independent nations with elective governments was the war of 1812. In this war the United States was independent and had an elective government. Great Britain had an elected parliament but the king still dictated the choice of the prime minister and had considerable power in the operation of the government. It was not until about 1832 that parliament choose the prime minister.

In the Civil War, starting in 1861, the Southern States had an elective government but were not independent. Rather they were fighting to become independent and establish their boundaries. The South African War, starting in 1899, between Great Britain and South Africa was another war of this type.

In the nineteenth century the number of independent nations with freely elected governments was limited. Consequently, while there was the possibility of war between such governments the probability of such occurring at any one time was small. However, the fact that during the entire century no major war occurred between such nations lend support to our hypothesis.

Could the fact that there were no major wars between independent elective governments have occurred by chance? World Wars I and II provide an opportunity to make a more rigorous test of this possibility. These wars had more participants than any of the other wars listed by Wright.

In World War I 38 countries participated (Wright, Table 41). Five of these were not independent at the start of the war; India, Hejaz, Poland, Hungary, and Czechoslovakia. This leaves the 33 independent nations shown in Table 13.1. Of these, ten had elective governments as defined earlier.

Could the fact, that all of the independent elective governments were on the same side, have occurred by chance? One way of statistically testing this relationship is in the following manner. Between the 33 independent nations there were $33!/(33-2)!\,2!$ or 528 possible ways they could have fought one another. There were 72 declarations of war between them. With this many war relationships the probability of war between any two nations was p equals $72/528$ equals .14. Between the 10 elective governments there were $10!/(10-2)!$

2! or 45 different ways they could have fought one another. There were no wars declared between them. The proportion of wars fought to wars possible was p equals $0/45$ equals 0.

Using the test for the **significance of the difference between proportions** it was found that the difference between these proportions was statistically significant on the 1 percent level.

Another intriguing thing about World War I is that before Italy entered the war she was allied with the Central Powers. This meant that Italy, with an elective government at that time, was allied against many other elective governments. However, before she entered the war public sentiment turned so strongly against the alliance that it was broken and eventually Italy entered the war on the side of other elective governments.

Germany and Austria-Hungary prior to World War I had governments with some elective features; however they could not be considered elective governments as specified in this study. Germany had an elective Reichstag but the Emperor, an hereditary ruler, had much authority such as choosing the chancellor. In Austria-Hungary the Emperor had considerable power and used it. Prior to the war he had parliament adjourned, and it remained muzzled for several years thereafter.

World War II provides another opportunity to test whether the lack of wars between inde-

TABLE 13.1   Independent Nations Which Participated in World War I

ALLIES AND ASSOCIATED POWERS			CENTRAL POWERS
Elective Governments	*Non-Elective Governments*		*Non-Elective Governments*
Australia	China	Montenegro	Austria-Hungary
Belgium	Costa Rica	Nicaragua	Bulgaria
Canada	Cuba	Panama	Germany
Great Britain	Greece	Portugal	Turkey
France	Guatemala	Rumania	
Italy	Haiti	Russia	
Brazil	Honduras	San Marino	
New Zealand	Japan	Serbia	
Union of South Africa	Liberia	Siam	
United States	Luxemburg		

pendent nations with elective governments could have occurred by chance. The same procedure was followed as in the case of World War I. Fifty-two nations which participated in the war were independent on Sept 1, 1939, the date the invasion of Poland began. See Table 13.2. Of the 52 nations, 14 had elective governments in our sense. Between the 52 nations there were $52!/(52-2)!\ 2!$ or 1,326 possible ways they could have fought one another.

During the second World War there were 103 war relationships between the independent nations. The only war relationships counted were those that occurred before the nations lost their independence. A declaration of war or an invasion of a country without a declaration of war were counted as war relationship.

With this many war relationships the probability of war between any two nations was p equals $103/1,326$ equals .078.

Between the 14 elective nations involved there were $14!/(14-2)!\ 2!$ or 91 different ways they could have fought one another. Since there were no wars declared between them, the proportion of wars fought to that possible was p equals $0/105$ equals 0. Again testing the difference between these proportions, it was found to be statistically significant on the 1 percent level.

In World War II there was one nation with an elective government, Finland, which fought with the Axis Powers against the other elective governments. This situation provides a very interesting example of the desire for peace between nations with elective governments. Finland frequently expressed a desire not to fight the other nations with elective governments but she had lost her independence prior to December 1941, when she entered the war.

After Hitler took Norway he insisted on the right to transport troops across Finland to face Russia. This was reluctantly granted. He then

TABLE 13.2 Nations Which Were Independent on September 1, 1939, and Which Participated in World War II

ALLIES		*AXIS POWERS*
Nations With Elective Governments	*Nations Without Elective Governments*	
Australia	Argentina Latvia	Bulgaria*
Belgium	Bolivia Liberia	Finland*
Canada	Brazil Lithuania	Germany
Chile	China Luxenburg	Hungary*
Costa Rica	Columbia Mexico	Italy
Denmark	Cuba Nicaragua	Japan
France	Dominican Republic Panama	Rumania
Great Britain	Ecuador Paraguay	Siam*
Netherlands	El Salvador Peru	
New Zealand	Estonia Poland	
Norway	Greece Russia	
Union of South Africa	Guatemala Saudi Arabia	
Uruguay	Haiti Turkey	
United States	Honduras Venezula	
	Iran Yugoslavia	

*These members of the Axis Powers were first occupied by Germany and Japan and then used against the Allies.
Wright's book was published before the end of the war; therefore the source for the data on World War II are his book and the *Statesman's Yearbooks* (4).

disregarded the terms of the transit agreement so that by June 1941 there were two German SS divisions with their entire military equipment moving about North Finland. During the war the Finns were left some independence of action since Hitler wanted their help in fighting Russia. However, an indication of how little this independence amounted to is given by the fact that the Germans were only removed after they had devasted much of Northern Finland in 1945.

No rigorous test of the wars from World War II to 1963 was made. This is another study in itself. However, a general review of the main wars since 1941 appears to be consistent with the findings here reported.

This study suggests that the existence of independent nations with elective governments greatly increases the chances for the maintenance of peace. What is important is the form of government, not national character. Many nations, such as England and France, fought wars against each other before they acquired freely elected governments, but have not done so since. The rapid increase in the number of elective governments since World War II is an encouraging sign. Diplomatic efforts at war prevention might well be directed toward further accelerating this growth.

REFERENCES

(1) *An Act To Establish A United States Arms Control and Disarmament Agency,* Public Law 87–297, September 27, 1961.

(2) WRIGHT, QUINCY: *A Study of War,* Volume 1, Chicago: University of Chicago Press, 1942.

(3) BRYCE, JAMES: *Modern Democracies,* Volume 1, New York: The Macmillan Company, 1929 p. 3.

(4) STEINBERG, S. H. ed. *Statesman's Yearbook,* New York: Saint Martin Press.

51. Normative and Structural Causes of Democratic Peace, 1946–1986

ZEEV MAOZ AND BRUCE RUSSETT

Recognition of the *democratic-peace* result is probably one of the most significant nontrivial products of the scientific study of world politics. It may also be the basis of far more important insights into the workings of the international political world in modern times. This result consists of two parts of equal importance: (1) democratic states are in general about as conflict- and war-prone as nondemocracies; and (2) over the last two centuries, democracies have rarely clashed with one another in violent or potentially violent conflict and (by some reasonable criteria) have virtually never fought one another in a full-scale international war.

Beyond the extraordinary convergence of research results that confirm that "democracies rarely fight each other" (see Maoz and Abdolali 1989 and Russett 1993 for reviews), there is, more importantly, significant evidence that this finding is causally meaningful. There is something in the internal makeup of democratic states that prevents them from fighting one another *despite the fact that they are not less conflict-prone than non-democracies*. Attempts to attribute this result to factors other than the democratic system of the states revealed that the relationship between democracy and peace is probably not a spurious one (Bremer 1992; Maoz and Russett 1992). Disputes between democracies are far less likely than expected when compared with disputes between rich, rapidly growing, noncontiguous, and allied states.

The robustness of this result and its theoretical and practical significance call for a deeper inquiry into the causes of democratic peace. Specifically, a better understanding is required of the causal mechanism explaining simultaneously both the democratic-peace phenomenon and the lack of difference between democracies and non-democracies in terms of their overall conflict proneness. This study continues and extends a number of inquiries on democratic peace by addressing the following questions: (1) Does the degree of democratization of a dyad, in addition to the effort of other factors, reduce its likelihood to engage in conflict? (2) What specific factors in the politics and norms of democratic societies prevent them from fighting one another? (3) Why is it that the same factors that prevent democracies from fighting one another fail to reduce the general rate of conflict involvement of democratic states?

From *American Political Science Review*, Vol. 87, No. 3 (September 1993):624–38. Reprinted by permission of the publisher and the authors. Most footnotes and citations suppressed.

We shall outline two principal explanations that have been invoked to account for the democratic-peace phenomenon, derive the logical and empirical implications of each of these explanations, and test the deduced propositions on the contemporary international system.

THEORETICAL CONSIDERATIONS

. . .We label these two explanations as the normative and structural models of democratic peace.

The Normative Model

Elements of this model can be traced back to political thinkers such as Immanuel Kant and Woodrow Wilson; it is also represented by such modern scholars as Doyle (1986). It is based on two basic assumptions.

NORMATIVE ASSUMPTION 1. *States, to the extent possible, externalize the norms of behavior that are developed within and characterize their domestic political processes and institutions.*

NORMATIVE ASSUMPTION 2. *The anarchic nature of international politics implies that a clash between democratic and nondemocratic norms is dominated by the latter, rather than by the former.*

Assumption 1 suggests that different norms of domestic political conduct will be expressed in terms of different patterns of international behavior. Democratic regimes are based on political norms that emphasize regulated political competition through peaceful means. Winning does not require elimination of the opponent, and losing does not prohibit the loser from trying again. Political conflicts in democracies are resolved through compromise rather than through elimination of opponents. This norm allows for an atmosphere of "live and let live" that results in a fundamental sense of stability at the personal, communal, and national level. We term these *democratic norms.*

In contrast, political competition in nondemocratic regimes is likely to be more zero-sum in terms of the conception of the parties and in its consequences. The winner may take all, denying the loser the power or opportunity to rise again. Political conflicts in nondemocratic regimes are more likely to be conducted and resolved through violence and coercion. This norm creates an atmosphere of mistrust and fear within and outside the government. Stability may be maintained only in the absence of an overt and effective political opposition. This is the essence of *nondemocratic norms.*

Assumption 2 deals with the limits of the ability to apply certain norms in an anarchic international system. In such a system, states put their survival above any other value they seek to promote. If states come to believe that their application of domestically developed democratic norms would endanger their survival, they will act in accordance with the norms established by their rival. Democratic norms could be more easily exploited than could nondemocratic ones. Hence democracies are more likely to shift norms when confronted by a nondemocratic rival than is the nondemocratic rival to shift to democratic norms of international conduct.

It follows that when two democracies confront one another in conflicts of interest, they are able effectively to apply democratic norms in their interaction, thereby preventing most conflicts from escalating to a militarized level, involving the threat, display, or use of military force, and—of course—from going to all-out war. However, when a democratic state confronts a nondemocratic one, it may be forced to adapt to the norms of international conduct of the latter lest it be exploited or eliminated by the nondemocratic state that takes advantage of the inherent moderation of democracies.

A conflict between nondemocracies would be dominated by the norm of forceful conduct and by both parties' efforts to resolve the conflict through a decisive outcome and elimination of the opponent. Thus, conflicts between nondemocracies are more likely to escalate into war than are conflicts between a democratic and nondemocratic state.

In disputes between democracies, however, the expectation that conflicts can be settled peacefully, by compromise, lowers the relative benefit to be achieved from violence. Dependence on democratic norms tips rational cost–benefit calculations toward further support of those norms. Empirically, disputes between democracies are more likely to be settled by third-party conflict management, by agreement or stalemate (rather than an imposed solution), and by strategies of reciprocation.

Political culture and political norms constitute images that a state transmits to its external environment. One of the most important images that a democratic state can communicate to its environment is a sense of political stability. Likewise, instability conveys images linked with nondemocratic states. We elsewhere specify just why instability or the perception of instability may work to encourage the use of force by an unstable regime or to identify an unstable regime as the object for the exercise of the use of force (Maoz and Russett 1992).

Perceptions of instability may be based on the recency and immaturity of experience with democratic processes and norms; a new democracy will not yet have developed wide experience in practices of democratic conflict resolution. Perceptions of instability may also be based on a high degree of violent opposition to the democratic government; a democracy under siege of domestic terrorism, insurgency, or civil war is one in which the ostensible norms of peaceful conflict resolution simply are not working well. To the degree that the practice of democratic forms of government is very recent, subject to violent domestic challenge, or incomplete, it may be imperfectly constrained by the norms of democratic government that are supposed to keep conflict nonviolent. Or uncertainty about the commitment to democratic norms by a state with which one has a conflict of interest may lead to perceptions and expectations that it will practice those norms imperfectly.

The Structural Model

This model was discussed by modern students of international conflict. It rests upon the following assumptions:

STRUCTURAL ASSUMPTION 1. *International challenges require political leaders to mobilize domestic support to their policies. Such support must be mobilized from those groups that provide the leadership the kind of legitimacy that is required for international action.*

STRUCTURAL ASSUMPTION 2. *Shortcuts to political mobilization of relevant political support can be accomplished only in situations that can be appropriately described as emergencies.*

International action in a democratic political system requires the mobilization of both general public opinion and of a variety of institutions that make up the system of government, such as the legislature, the political bureaucracies, and key interest groups. This implies that very few goals could be presented to justify fighting wars in democracies. It also implies that the process of national mobilization for war in democracies is both difficult and cumbersome. On the other hand, in nondemocratic societies, once the support of the key legitimizing groups is secured, the government can launch its policy with little regard to public opinion or for due political process. Because, in many cases, the legitimizing groups may benefit from the use of force in foreign affairs, the leadership may feel little restraint in its dealings with other states.

This set of assumptions implies, therefore, that due to the complexity of the democratic process and the requirement of securing a broad base of support for risky policies, democratic leaders are reluctant to wage wars, except in cases wherein war seems a necessity or when the war aims are seen as justifying the mobilization costs. The time required for a democratic state to prepare for war is far longer than for nondemocracies. Thus, in a conflict between democracies, by the time the two states are militarily ready for war, diplomats have the opportunity to find a nonmilitary solution to the conflict.

Conflicts between a democracy and a nondemocracy, however, are driven by the lack of structural constraints on the mobilization and escalation process of the latter. The democratic state finds itself in a no-choice situation. Leaders are forced to find ways to circumvent the due political process. Thus, in such a conflict, the nondemocracy imposes on the democratic political system emergency conditions enabling the government to rally support rather rapidly.

Conflicts between nondemocratic systems are, by the same token, likely to escalate because both leaderships operate under relatively few structural constraints. The failure of initial efforts to find a peaceful solution may result in a rapid flare-up of the conflict into a violent level.

Comparing the Models

These two explanations are not mutually exclusive. They do emphasize, however, two different facets of democratic politics that are presumably responsible for the democratic-peace phenomenon. The structural model views the constitutional and legal constraints on executive action as a key to understanding how governments act in their international politics. The normative model looks primarily at the effects of norms of domestic political behavior on international politics.

Obviously, it is extremely difficult to distinguish between these models in terms of contradictory predictions. Normative and structural explanations are often not well differentiated conceptually, thus enhancing the difficulties of testing them as alternative hypotheses. For example, both models would claim that the tendency toward conflict decreases with the extent of political participation in a society. The normative model explains this relationship in terms of a correlation between political participation and democratic norms. The structural model explains this relationship in terms of a correlation between political participation and structural constraints on the executive's ability to use force. There may be, however, a number of areas where the models differ in their predictions. Two, in particular, come to mind. First, democratic norms take time to develop. Hence if the normative model is right, then older democracies should be less likely to

clash with one another than would newer ones. The structural model would claim that as long as structural constraints operate on the executive, the age of the political regime should not matter. Second, the structural model implies variations between democracies in terms of their conflict behavior. Presidential systems should be less constrained than parliamentary systems, in which the government is far more dependent on the support it gets from the legislature. Coalition governments or minority cabinets are far more constrained than are governments controlled by a single party. On the other hand, the normative model does not expect variation within democratic political systems; despite different structures, they operate within the same normative system.

Before examining the two models, however, it is important to assess the extent to which democracy, relative to other variables, accounts for the conflict involvement patterns of international dyads. For the purpose of such an analysis, we reiterate briefly the factors that have been variously mentioned as potential causes of democratic peace, outside of the realm of democracy.

OTHER POTENTIAL CAUSES

Three other potential causes of democratic peace should be considered. First, rich states do not fight one another because they have far more to lose than to gain by doing so. Rich states are often engaged in heavy trading with one another. The costs of a war would be enormous and the benefits would be little. Since most democracies in the post–World War II era were economically developed states, it was their economic structure, rather than their type of political system, that prevented them from fighting one another.

Second, rapidly growing states would harm themselves by engaging in conflict against other rapidly growing states—again, because conflict and war would harm the economic benefits associated with growth. Fighting other rapidly growing states is both more costly and risks reversing the positive economic-growth pattern. Most democracies experienced rapid economic growth and for that reason refrained from conflict with each other.

Third, most democracies in the post–World War II era have been in some sort of a direct or indirect alliance with one another. These alliance bonds, rather than their political system, prevented them from fighting one another.

In addition to these factors, we examine the potentially confounding effects of geographic contiguity and military capability ratios on dyadic conflict involvement. These factors are included because they have been found to be highly potent predictors of conflict escalation (Bremer 1992; reprinted herein as selection 32).

RESEARCH DESIGN

The normative–cultural and the structural–institutional models suggest several testable hypotheses. In addition, multivariate statistical analysis allows assessment of how far each of various influences other than type of political system (e.g., contiguity, wealth, economic growth, alliance, and military capability ratio) affects conflict. Critical tests allow for a competitive and simultaneous assessment of the relative power of the two models. We test these hypotheses:

HYPOTHESIS 1. *The more democratic are both members of a pair of states, the less likely it is that militarized disputes break out between them, and the less likely it is that any disputes that do break out will escalate. This effect will operate independently of other dyadic attributes (e.g., wealth, economic growth, contiguity, alliance, capability ratio).*

HYPOTHESIS 2 (NORMATIVE MODEL). *The more deeply rooted are democratic norms in the political processes operating in two states, the lower the likelihood that disputes will break out or that disputes will escalate.*

HYPOTHESIS 3 (STRUCTURAL MODEL) *The higher the political constraints on the executives of the two states, the lower the likelihood that disputes will break out or that disputes will escalate.*

Spatial–Temporal Domain

We look at pairs of independent states in the world during the period 1946–86, in essence, at the Cold War era. This era is appropriate for three reasons. First, although a score or more of democracies existed in the first half of the twentieth century, the number of pairs of democratic states was three times as large in the later era.

Second, as a "nice" generalization at least partly context-dependent, the role of democracy in restraining violent conflict between democratic dyads may have been stronger in the past half-century than earlier. Democratic norms have become deeply entrenched, since many states have been democracies for long periods and principles such as true universal suffrage have been put into practice. Similarly, many countries' democratic institutions have been reinforced over time. Continuity of democracy in a state encourages its partners in foreign affairs to perceive it as stably democratic. The experience of three world "wars" (World War I, World War II, and the Cold War)—each characterized by both rhetoric and some reality as a conflict of democracies against authoritarian states—helped build normative principles that democracies ought not to fight among themselves.

Third, many influences put forward as confounding and contributing to the phenomenon of peace between democratic states were much more prominent after World War II. The post-1945 era brought unprecedented global wealth and growth, and the alliance system was far wider and more durable than any that preceded it. Thus a more complex test of the basic hypothesis becomes possible—a test designed to display the power of competing hypotheses. Moreover, data on economic levels and growth rates are much more reliable and widespread for the past half-century than before.

Our unit of analysis is the dyad-year; we look at each pair of countries in each year to see whether they engaged in any kind of militarized dispute. Over the period 1946–86 the international system averaged about 110 countries per year, which would give us roughly 265,000 dyad-years to study. But the vast majority are nearly irrelevant. The countries comprising them were too far apart and too weak militarily, with few serious interests potentially in conflict, for them plausibly to engage in any militarized diplomatic dispute. Contiguity and major-power involvement are the two most important static factors accounting for the likelihood of war between any pair of states (Bremer 1992). If we limit the analysis to pairs of states that are directly or indirectly contiguous or in which one member is a major power (*contiguity* and *major power* will be defined), we have a total of 36,162 dyad-years, with disputes occurring in 714 of them by the Militarized Interstate Dispute (MID) data set or 448 by the International Crisis Behavior (ICB) data set.*

Some disputes do, of course, arise between "implausible" pairs, as between a minor European power like Belgium or the Netherlands and a former colony or the case of distant collective security action, as in Korea and Vietnam. In dropping all but about 12% of total dyad-years, the list of plausible pairs nevertheless retains 74% of disputes in the MID data set and 80% in the ICB one. In the more comprehensive MID data it picks up 78% of all the disputes that democracies engaged in with anyone and all but one of the 15 disputes between democracies. Thus we are fairly confident that no major case-selection biases exist in favor of the hypothesis, and the refined "universe" of politically relevant dyads is theoretically appropriate.

Data and Measurement

We want to explain patterns of conflict. The conflict data are from two different data sets, compiled for somewhat different analytical purposes and using different definitions. That allows us to establish whether our conclusions remain consistent over different measures of the concepts. The more robust the results are

*In the analysis, the actual number of cases is often much lower due to missing data for some variables and years.

to such changes (in measures of independent variables, as well as conflict), the more confidence we can have in the generalization.

Dependent Variables. One data set is the MID data from the Correlates of War (COW) project. These data were derived from a set developed for the period 1816—1976. They were updated to 1986 by Maoz.... A MID (Militarized Interstate Dispute) is defined as "a set of interactions between or among states involving threats to use military force, displays of military force, or actual uses of force. To be included, these acts must be explicit, overt, nonaccidental, and government sanctioned" (Gochman and Maoz 1984, 586). We use the data in two forms. First, we identify each dyad-year dichotomously as having some kind of dispute or none. In doing so, we include both disputes begun any time in this year and ongoing disputes that continued into this year from a previous one. This variable is labeled *dispute involvement.* Second, we record the highest level of hostility reached by either member of the dyad in that year, using the Gochman–Maoz five-level scale of hostility. This is termed *dispute escalation.*

The other set of conflict data is that collected by the ICB project. Its compilers define an international crisis as "a situational change characterized by an increase in the intensity of disruptive interaction between two or more adversaries, with a high probability of military hostilities. ... The higher-than-normal conflictual interactions destabilize the existing relationships of the adversaries and pose a challenge to the existing structure of an international system—global, dominant, and/or subsystem" (Brecher and Wilkenfeld 1989, p. 5). Levels of hostility for international crises are the same as for disputes.

The two data sets are not strongly related. Due to different definitions and criteria, among politically relevant dyads there are 959 with MID conflicts begun or underway, only 260 (27%) of which were identified by the ICB data set. This is not surprising, given the latter's concern with "a high probability of military hostilities" and the likelihood that many

MIDs neither carried (nor, often as symbolic acts in a bargaining process, were they always intended to carry) great likelihood of escalating to actual violence. It is also true, however, that out of the 359 politically relevant crisis dyads identified by ICB listing, only 260 (72%) are found in the MID data. This is not to imply that either set is inaccurate; rather, there is sufficient variability in case identification to enable us to use the two data sets as a check on the robustness of our results.

Independent Variables: Democracy. Our foremost independent variable is of course form of government, or "regime." Our chief source of data here is developed from the Polity II data by Ted Gurr, Keith Jaggers, and Will Moore.

. . . We defined the type of regime as follows. First, we identified the level of authority of a political system as a combination of (1) competitiveness of political participation, (2) regulation of participation, (3) competitiveness of executive recruitment, (4) openness of executive recruitment, and (5) constraints on the chief executive, following Gurr, Jaggers, and Moore. Their aggregation of these dimensions produced one 11-point scale for the level of democracy (DEM) and another for autocracy (AUT).

Second, because the Eckstein-Gurr conception is not linear, a state can have mixed characteristics; some features may be democratic at the same time that others are highly autocratic. . . . Therefore, we created a *continuous* index taking into account both democratic and autocratic features—and also the level of power concentration, which reflects how far the state authorities exercised effective control over their constituents. . . .

Then, we needed to convert the individual scores into a joint democratization one because our analysis requires a dyadic characterization of regime type. The joint measure (JOINREG) reflect[ed] two things simultaneously, namely, How democratic or undemocratic are the members of the dyad? and How different or similar in their regime types are the two states? . . .

We [also] created an alternative measure from data of Arthur Banks (1986) included in the Polity II data set. We identified democratic states as those in which both legislature and executive were selected in a competitive election and in which the legislature was at least partially effective. This simpler categorization is less fully documented than Gurr's. The two are moderately correlated, suggesting, as with the two conflict data sets, that each measures a similar concept but with enough difference to provide a good test for robustness.

Degree of Institutional Constraints. To distinguish between the two models for explaining the rarity of conflict between democracies, we used several key attributes identified by Gurr and his associates. We constructed a multifaceted measure from related but distinguishable elements, in which an executive is considered to be subject to the least restraint when able to operate by "one-man rule," without institutionalized constraint, in a centralized political system in which the government exerts a wide scope of control over economic and social life.

Degree of "one-man rule" (*monocratism*) ranges on a five-point ordinal scale from states where it prevails to "those in which some kind of assent is required, whether by especially prestigious minorities . . . numerical majorities, or virtually all of them" (Eckstein and Gurr 1975, p. 375). *Degree of executive constraint* represents the extent to which the executive must abide by clear and distinguishable rules—institutionalized constraints—while making policy decisions, whether the chief executive be an individual or collectivity, measured on a seven-point ordinal scale. *Centralization* distinguishes between unitary and federal political systems, on a three-point ordinal scale. . . . *Scope of government actions* refers to the extent to which all levels of government combined—national, regional, and local—attempt to regulate and organize the economic and social life of the citizens and subjects." It is measured on a seven-point scale from *totalitarian*, or those governments that "directly organize and control almost all aspects of social and political life," to *minimal*, or those whose operations are largely or wholly limited to such core functions as maintenance of internal security and administration of justice" (Gurr, Jaggers, and Moore).

These four measures are summed over their categories to produce an overall scale of institutional constraints ranging from 4 (a totalitarian system lacking any form of constraint) to 22 (a highly constrained political system in which the government must go through a long, complex, and uncertain political process to invoke national action). . . . Democracies exhibiting low constraint include the French Fifth Republic under Charles De Gaulle and Georges Pompidou, Venezuela after the 1958 overthrow of the military dictatorship, and Argentina under the elected government of the Perons in 1973–75. Nondemocratic governments operating under rather high constraint include Pakistan shortly after independence, Indonesia into 1956, and several Middle Eastern states in the 1950s (King Hussein's Jordan being the clearest example).

Democratic Norms. The extent to which some norms of democratic behavior have become accepted in a political regime may not be closely related to states' political structures. For example, a system may lack a democratic institutional structure yet be widely regarded by its citizens as politically legitimate; such a regime would require little overt oppression of opposition in ways obviously violating democratic norms. On the other hand, a democratic government undergoing violent insurgency and a fundamental crisis of legitimacy may resort to political and military oppression in the name of maintaining public order and, indeed, of maintaining democratic institutions.

We employ two related but distinct ways of measuring the extent to which democratic or other kinds of norms operate in a society. The first is through the concept of political stability. It is based on the notion that it takes time for norms to develop. A society that undergoes fundamental change requires a considerable period of time to develop norms of political

conduct and for the citizens to internalize those norms and become accustomed to them. The longer a given political system or regime exists in a society without fundamental change, the more likely that norms of political conduct, whether democratic or nondemocratic, will form and influence the foreign policy codes of conduct of the regime.

We can then measure the prevalence of political norms in a society as the persistence of its political regime in years. By this conception, democracies that are highly stable (i.e., have kept their fundamental political structure for a long time) are said to be more influenced by democratic norms than democracies that have existed only a short while. Conflicts between stable democracies should thus be far less common than conflicts between democracies in which one (or, worse, both) are unstable. Note that our stability measure is not fully distinct from structures. It can also be an institutional constraint in the limited sense that an unstable democracy is subject to overthrow, releasing the institutional constraints on leaders. Also, we are measuring the duration of political institutions more directly than the norms that support them. Nonetheless, this measure still seems separable from the indices we introduced to measure the strength and breadth of institutions.

An alternative procedure for measuring democratic norms relies directly on the level of violent internal social and political conflict. All states experience some degree of social conflict. The difference between states where democratic norms prevail and states where they do not, however, is twofold. First, in democracies these conflicts are predominantly nonviolent; both challengers and defenders of the status quo usually find peaceful avenues for expressing their differences. In nondemocratic systems conflicts are likely to take on violent forms because most forms of peaceful protest are forbidden. Second, in a democracy, the government rarely needs to use force to resolve conflicts; order can be maintained without violent suppression. But in nondemocracies, order is often maintained by overt state violence. Democratic norms are tested in times of political unrest and instability.

Therefore, we measure democratic norms by the amount of political violence within a state. Two types of measures are used: deaths from political violence and extent of domestic conflict. . . . Here again, the joint conflict event measure is an average, over both states, of the mean level of net conflict in each state over the last five years.

Wealth. Average levels of income were rising over the period, so we needed a measure of relative rather than absolute wealth. Since the standard economic data are delineated in U.S. dollars, we simply used the cross-national estimates as a baseline for each year. The income data produced a continuous dyadic measure computed in the same way as that for regimes (JOINREG).

Economic Growth. Economic growth is the percentage change in a state's gross domestic product (in constant 1980 prices) from one year to the next, computed as the average growth rate over the three years preceding the first year.

Alliance. Alliance data have been compiled as part of the COW project to which we added a category for indirect alliance with the United States. An indirect alliance occurs where two states which have no direct alliance with each other are each allied individually with another . . . . Some reason that restraints imposed by the "hegemon" may moderate disputes between indirectly linked states. We use a dichotomous break between any direct or indirect alliance and none.

Contiguity. Here too we used a revised version of a COW data set listing several degrees of contiguity, to which we added colonial contiguity for cases where one state bordered another's colony or trusteeship. Conceptually, contiguity is meant to identify states with the capability and possible reason for fighting each other, so our sample also includes all dyads containing a major power with the ability to exert military force beyond immediately contiguous states. We identified the United States, United Kingdom, France, and the

Soviet Union as major powers and (perhaps more arguably) followed the COW designation of China as a major power from 1950 onward. . . . We make a dichotomous break between any kind of contiguity and the noncontiguous dyads including a great power.

Military Capability Ratio. Are two states with similar capabilities more likely to dispute with each other than are states whose economic and military capabilities are very disparate? This question, vigorously debated without dear resolution, may confound this analysis. Power disparity represents one final control variable. We use the widely employed COW military capability index. In effect, that composite index weights about equally (two separate indices for each) military forces in being, economic strength, and demography, suggesting both capacity for winning a short war with existing military forces and long-term capacity for waging a war of attrition. It only imperfectly reflects the perception or reality of military power but is adequate here as an interval measure of the ratio of the capability score of the stronger state to the weaker.

Data Analysis Methods

Data analysis was done in three steps. The first step was designed to perform a multivariate analysis of the various factors that may support the hypothesis that the democratic-peace phenomenon is spurious. This is a replication and extension of earlier analyses we conducted (Maoz and Russett 1992). The second step in the analysis was to examine jointly the structural and normative models of democratic peace. If one of the models were supported consistently while the other were rejected consistently, no critical testing would be required. But since both models received some empirical support, we moved to a third analysis with a critical test. . . .

RESULTS

We start by examining the effect of several variables that potentially confound the relationship between democracy and peace on dyadic conflict involvement and conflict escalation, along with the democracy variable. This test of hypothesis 1 is shown in Table 13.3. Table 13.3 shows the effect of the independent variables, measured in continuous terms (with exception of alliance and contiguity), on the dependent variables. Tests with dichotomized measures of democracy give similar or stronger results and need not be shown. In the upper half, the dependent variable is defined as the presence or absence of a dispute (crisis) between a pair of states at a given year. In the lower half, the dependent variable is defined as a five-point ordinal scale with 0 representing no dispute crisis and 4 representing a full-scale war. The multiple dependent variables and the different measurement scales of the independent variables serve as a way of assessing the stability of the results and their robustness. Analyses performed on the same dependent variables using the Banks measure of democracy yielded consistently similar results.

Hypothesis 1 is—with some exceptions—supported by the data. In the MID data both the continuous version of democracy and the dichotomous one (not shown in Table 1) have a significant effect on conflict involvement. In the ICB data the continuous version of democracy is not significant, but the dichotomous version (not shown) is consistently related to crisis involvement. Among the confounding variables, almost all are related to both the MID measures of conflict and the ICB measures. The results for dispute or crisis escalation are nearly identical to those obtained for conflict involvement. The level of democratization has a significant main effect on dispute escalation, and when dichotomized, on crisis escalation even when we control for potentially

TABLE 13.3 Effects of Joint Democracy and Potentially Confounding Factors on Conflict Involvement and Escalation

Independent Variable	Militarized Disputes[a]	International Crises[b]
	EFFECT ON CONFLICT INVOLVEMENT	
Democracy	−.004 (.002)**	−.002 (.003)
Wealth	−.022 (.008)**	−.040 (.016)*
Growth	−.107 (.021)**	−.133 (.032)**
Alliance	−.517 (.105)**	−.339 (.165)*
Contiguity	1.419 (.108)**	1.964 (.190)**
Capability ratio	−.007 (.001)**	−.002 (.001)**
	EFFECT ON CONFLICT ESCALATION	
Democracy	−.004 (.002)*	−.001 (.003)
Wealth	−.022 (.008)**	−.040 (.016)*
Growth	−.111 (.021)**	−.139 (.031)**
Alliance	−.522 (.105)**	−.336 (.164)*
Contiguity	1.417 (.108)**	1.962 (.190)**
Capability ratio	−.007 (.001)**	−.002 (.001)*

Note: $N = 19{,}020$. Entries are unstandardized parameter estimates in logistic regression equations; standard errors are in parentheses. Gamma is a measure of the difference between the observed and expected values throughout the analysis, appropriate for a priori prediction of monotonic relationships.
[a]Gamma = .54.
[b]Gamma = .59.
*$p < .05$.
**$p < .01$.

confounding variables. Democracies are less likely to escalate disputes against other democracies than are states that have other types of political systems.

Taken together, these findings corroborate our bivariate results (Maoz and Russett 1992). Not surprisingly, power relationships make a big difference. Great disparities in power sharply discourage the expression of diplomatic disputes in any militarized form. Contiguity also matters, with its power-related emphasis on capability, as well as on the possibility of incentive for dispute. But the other variables also make a significant difference in almost every instance. The multivariate analysis also corroborates Bremer's (1992) findings regarding alliance effects on dispute involvement and dispute escalation. It appears that while the bivariate relationship between alliance and conflict is positive (Maoz and Russett 1992), after controlling for other relevant variables, allied parties are less likely to fight each other than would be expected by chance alone.

All the theories competing with that about democracy find solid support. Nevertheless, a strong, independent, and fairly robust role for joint democracy remains evident. In the ICB data democracy in continuous form is not significant, but the dichotomous version (democracy/nondemocracy) is. A strong relationship is apparent in the MID data in both continuous and dichotomous form; the more democratic each member of the dyad, the less likely is conflict. The phenomenon of democratic peace is real, not spurious. . . .

The critical test examines the differences in the probabilities of conflict in the cases denoted by Table 13.4, rows 2–3 (low level of norms with high level of political constraints, vice versa). If the probability of conflict in the case denoted by row 2 is significantly lower than the probability of conflict in the case denoted by row 3, then the structural model is judged superior to the normative one. If the reverse, then the normative model can be said to provide a superior account of the data. Should the difference between them not be statistically significant, then the critical test would be inconclusive. . . .

Tables 13.5 and 13.6 . . . give a sense of how the models perform. The bottoms of the tables also show what happens when the joint regime type for each dyad is controlled for. Columns 1 and 2 in each table represent the occurrence of conflicts and the occurrence of war, respectively. . . .

Table 13.5 shows the differences in the probabilities of conflict involvement in the critical cases, and Table 13.6 does the same for war. They compare the frequency of involvement (both dispute and crisis data) by pairs of states with the combination of low normative constraints and high institutional ones versus high normative and low institutional. They strengthen the previous impression regarding the relative superiority of the normative explanation over the structural-institutional one. In 16 of the 30 separate tests in the two tables, the probability of involvement when the level of democratic norms is high and the level of political constraints is low is significantly below

TABLE 13.4 Critical and Noncritical Cases from the Perspective of the Normative and Structural Models of Democratic Peace

| | DYAD'S | ATTRIBUTES | | | |
Case #	Level of Democratic Norms	Level of Political Constraints	Prediction of Normative Model	Prediction of Structural Model	Type of Case
1	Low	Low	Conflict	Conflict	Noncritical
2	Low	High	Conflict	Low Conflict	Critical
3	High	Low	Low Conflict	Conflict	Critical
4	High	High	No Conflict	No Conflict	Noncritical

TABLE 13.5 Critical Test of the Effects of Democratic Norms, Institutional Constraints, and Regime Type on Conflict Involvement

Measure of Democratic Norms	Combinations of Independent Variables	Probability of Disputes	Probability of Crises
Stability ($N = 26{,}129$)	Low norms, high constr.	2.89%	.95%
	High norms, low constr.	2.11%	.56%
Z-score		−2.07**	−1.87**
Executions ($N = 22{,}870$)	Low norms, high constr.	5.71%	1.95%
	High norms, low constr.	2.27%	.82%
Z-score		−3.76**	−2.08**
Domestic conflict ($N = 16{,}262$)	Low norms, high constr.	3.96%	1.20%
	High norms, low constr.	1.97%	.38%
Z-score		−5.37**	−4.51**
		Controlling for Regime Type	
Stability			
Not both democracies ($N = 22{,}292$)	Low norms, high constr.	3.82%	1.29%
	High norms, low constr.	2.16%	.58%
Z-score		−3.56**	−2.68**
Both democracies ($N = 3{,}837$)	Low norms, high constr.	.95%	.03%
	High norms, low constr.	.00%	.00%
Z-score		−3.32**	−1.73*
Executions			
Not both democracies ($N = 19{,}577$)	Low norms, high constr.	5.91%	2.12%
	High norms, low constr.	2.48%	.89%
Z-score		−3.58**	−2.08**
Both democracies ($N = 3{,}293$)	Low norms, high constr.	.25%	.00%
	High norms, low constr.	.00%	.00%
Z-score		−1.01	—
Domestic conflict			
Not both democracies ($N = 14{,}345$)	Low norms, high constr.	3.31%	.64%
	High norms, low constr.	4.10%	1.24%
Z-score		1.34	2.16**
Both democracies ($N = 1{,}917$)	Low norms, high constr.	.85%	.15%
	High norms, low constr.	.00%	.00%
Z-score		−3.33**	−1.42

Note: Z-scores represent a difference of proportions test. Negative scores imply that the normative model provides a better explanation than does the structural model; positive scores imply that the structural model provides the superior explanation.
*$p < .05$.
**$p < .01$.

TABLE 13.6   Critical Test of the Effects of Democratic Norms, Institutional Constraints, and Regime Type on War Involvement

Measure of Democratic Norms	*Combinations of Independent Variables*	*Probability of Disputes*	*Probability of Crises*
Stability (*N* = 26,129)	Low norms, high constr.	.08%	.14%
	High norms, low constr.	.03%	.15%
Z-score		−.96	.09
Executions (*N* = 22,870)	Low norms, high constr.	.15%	.20%
	High norms, low constr.	.20%	.30%
Z-score		.35	.58
Domestic conflict (*N* = 16,262)	Low norms, high constr.	.56%	.42%
	High norms, low constr.	.00%	.00%
Z-score		−6.18*	−5.30*
		Not Both Democracies	
Stability (*N* = 22,292)	Low norms, high constr.	.12%	.21%
	High norms, low constr.	.03%	.15%
Z-score		−1.21	−.49
Executions (N = 19,577)	Low norms, high constr.	.16%	.00%
	High norms, low constr.	.22%	.00%
Z-score		.38	—
Domestic conflict (N = 14,345)	Low norms, high constr.	.58%	.09%
	High norms, low constr.	.00%	.00%
Z-score		−6.18*	−2.45*

Note: *Z*-scores represent a difference-of-proportions test. Negative scores imply that the normative model provides a better explanation than does the structural model; positive scores imply that the structural model provides the superior explanation. There are no entries for effects on war involvement between democracies because there were no such wars.
*p < .01.

the probability of involvement in the reverse case (with only one test significantly the other way). As before and as expected, the difference almost always appears for conflict involvement in general, much less often for war involvement. The bottom of Table 13.5 controlling for regime type, shows clearly that three different measures of democratic political norms usually significantly reduce the probability of conflict in dyads, even when the institutional constraints on the regimes are low and even when at least one member of the dyad is not democratic?

These results suggest that the normative model provides a more robust and consistent fit to the data than the structural one. The former model has a consistent relationship with both conflict occurrence and war occurrence, almost irrespective of the specific measure of democratic norms used, whereas the latter model sometimes provides a significant relationship, but often not. Moreover, in the critical situations (when one model suggests high levels of conflict and the other suggests low levels of conflict), the predictions of the normative model are more consistent with the data.

CONCLUSIONS

We have offered a comprehensive analysis of potential explanations of the democratic-peace phenomenon. We draw four conclusions:

1. The democratic-peace phenomenon, that is, the relative lack of conflict and complete absence of war between democracies, is probably not a spurious correlation. When controlling for other potentially confounding factors, regime type has a consistent dampening effect on international conflict.
2. These results are robust. They usually hold regardless of the conflict data set used, the definition of the dependent variable, and the scale and type of measure of democracy. This increases our confidence in the substantive results.
3. Both political constraints and democratic norms provide reasonably good explanations of why democracies rarely fight each other.
4. However, the relationship between institutional constraints and measures of dispute and war occurrence is not as robust as the relationship between measures of democratic norms and the dependent variables. This suggests that the normative model may be a better overall account of the democratic-peace phenomenon than the structural model.

Both the fact that the democratic-peace phenomenon is causally meaningful and the fact that we are beginning to move toward a substantive understanding of its causes carry important theoretical implications. First, they suggest that domestic political processes and structures significantly affect state behavior and that these effects are quite generalizable. Second, they provide strong evidence that the strict top–down or outside–in models developed by system theorists are in deep trouble.

In terms of processes operating in the present interstate system, this result suggests that to the extent that norms and institutions take time to develop, newly created democracies in Eastern Europe and elsewhere may still experience some significant amount of interstate conflict while their political systems are in the process of transition to democracy. But the process of global democratization may carry long-term prospects of international stability that arise not out of the missile launchers but out of popular control of governments and of norms of peaceful resolution of political conflicts associated with democratic political systems.

It is possible that major features of the international system can be socially constructed from the bottom up; that is, norms and rules of behavior internationally become extensions of the norms and rules of domestic political behavior. When many states are ruled autocratically (as they were at the Peace of Westphalia and throughout virtually all of history since then), playing by the rules of autocracy may be the only way for any state—democracy or not—to survive in Hobbesian international anarchy. But if enough states become stably democratic—as may be happening in the 1990s—then the possibility emerges of reconstructing the norms and rules of the international system to reflect those of democracies. A system created by autocracies may be recreated by a critical mass of democratic states.

REFERENCES

AZAR, EDWARD E. 1980. The Conflict and Peace Data Bank (COPDAB) Project. *Journal of Conflict Resolution* 24:379–403.

BANKS, ARTHUR. 1986. *Cross-National Time-Series Data File.* Binghamton: State University of New York.

BRECHER, MICHAEL, AND JONATHAN WILKENFELD. 1989. *Crisis in the Twentieth Century.* New York: Pergamon.

BREMER, STUART. 1992. Dangerous Dyads: Conditions Affecting the Likelihood of Interstate War, 1816–1965. *Journal of Conflict Resolution* 36:309–41.

DOYLE, MICHAEL. 1986. Liberalism and World Politics. *American Political Science Review* 80:1151–61.

ECKSTEIN, HARRY S., AND TED ROBERT GURR. 1975. *Patterns of Authority: A Structural Basis for Political Inquiry.* New York: Wiley-Interscience.

GOCHMAN, CHARLES S., AND ZEEY MAOZ. 1984. "Militarized Interstate Disputes, 1816–1976." *Journal of Conflict Resolution* 29:585–615.

MAOZ, ZEEY AND NASRIN ABDOLALI. 1989. Regime Type and International Conflict, 1816–1976. *Journal of Conflict Resolution* 33:3–35.

———— AND BRUCE RUSSETT. 1992. Alliances, Wealth, Contiguity and Political Stability: Is the Lack of Conflict between Democracies a Statistical Artifact? *International Interactions* 17:245–67.

TAYLOR, CHARLES L., AND DAVID A. JODICE. 1983. *World Handbook of Political and Social Indicators.* 3d ed. New Haven: Yale University Press.

Chapter 14
International Law and World Government

52. Prolegomena to *The Law of War and Peace*

HUGO GROTIUS

1. The municipal law of Rome and of other states has been treated by many, who have undertaken to elucidate it by means of commentaries or to reduce it to a convenient digest. That body of law, however, which is concerned with the mutual relations among states or rulers of states, whether derived from nature, or established by divine ordinances, or having its origin in custom and tacit agreement, few have touched upon. Up to the present time no one has treated it in a comprehensive and systematic manner; yet the welfare of mankind demands that this task be accomplished. . . .

3. Such a work is all the more necessary because in our day, as in former times, there is no lack of men who view this branch of law with contempt as having no reality outside of an empty name. On the lips of men quite generally is the saying of Euphemus, which Thucydides quotes, that in the case of a king or imperial city nothing is unjust which is expedient. Of like implication is the statement that for those whom fortune favours might makes right, and that the administration of a state cannot be carried on without injustice.

Furthermore, the controversies which arise between peoples or kings generally have Mars as their arbiter. That war is irreconcilable with all law is a view held not alone by the ignorant populace; expressions are often let slip by well-informed and thoughtful men which lend countenance to such a view. Nothing is more common than the assertion of antagonism between law and arms. . . .

5. Since our discussion concerning law will have been undertaken in vain if there is no law, in order to open the way for a favourable reception of our work and at the same time to fortify it against attacks, this very serious error must be briefly refuted. In order that we may not be obliged to deal with a crowd of opponents, let us assign to them a pleader. And whom should we choose in preference to Carneades? . . .

Carneades, then, having undertaken to hold a brief against justice, in particular against that phase of justice with which we are concerned, was able to muster no argument stronger than this, that, for reasons of expediency, men imposed upon themselves laws, which vary according to customs, and among the same peoples often undergo changes as times change; moreover that there is no law of nature, because all creatures, men as well as animals, are impelled by nature toward ends advantageous to themselves; that, consequently, there is no justice, or, if such there be,

Excerpted from *The Law of War and Peace*, by Hugo Grotius. Translated by Francis W. Kelsey in 1925 for the Carnegie Endowment for International Peace. Reprinted by permission of the publisher. Footnotes deleted.

it is supreme folly, since one does violence to his own interests if he consults the advantage of others.

6. . . . Man is, to be sure, an animal, but an animal of a superior kind, much farther removed from all other animals than the different kinds of animals are from one another; evidence on this point may be found in the many traits peculiar to the human species. But among the traits characteristic of man is an impelling desire for society, that is, for the social life—not of any and every sort, but peaceful, and organized according to the measure of his intelligence, with those who are of his own kind; this social trend the Stoics called "sociableness." Stated as a universal truth, therefore, the assertion that every animal is impelled by nature to seek only its own good cannot be conceded. . . .

8. This maintenance of the social order, which we have roughly sketched, and which is consonant with human intelligence, is the source of law properly so called. To this sphere of law belong the abstaining from that which is another's, the restoration to another of anything of his which we may have, together with any gain which we may have received from it; the obligation to fulfil promises, the making good of a loss incurred through our fault, and the inflicting of penalties upon men according to their deserts.

9. From this signification of the word "law" there has flowed another and more extended meaning. Since over other animals man has the advantage of possessing not only a strong bent towards social life, of which we have spoken, but also a power of discrimination which enables him to decide what things are agreeable or harmful (as to both things present and things to come), and what can lead to either alternative: in such things it is meant for the nature of man, within the limitations of human intelligence, to follow the direction of a well-tempered judgement, being neither led astray by fear or the allurement of immediate pleasure, nor carried away by rash impulse. Whatever is clearly at variance with such judgement is understood to be contrary also to the law of nature, that is, to the nature of man. ·

10. To this exercise of judgement belongs moreover the rational allotment to each man, or to each social group, of those things which are properly theirs, in such a way as to give the preference now to him who is more wise over the less wise, now to a kinsman rather than to a stranger, now to a poor man rather than to a man of means, as the conduct of each or the nature of the thing suggests. Long ago the view came to be held by many, that this discriminating allotment is a part of law, properly and strictly so called; nevertheless law, properly defined, has a far different nature, because its essence lies in leaving to another that which belongs to him, or in fulfilling our obligation to him.

11. What we have been saying would have a degree of validity even if we should concede that which cannot be conceded without the utmost wickedness, that there is no God, or that the affairs of men are of no concern to Him. . . .

15. Again, since it is a rule of the law of nature to abide by pacts (for it was necessary that among men there be some method of obligating themselves one to another, and no other natural method can be imagined), out of this source the bodies of municipal law have arisen. For those who had associated themselves with some group, or had subjected themselves to a man or to men, had either expressly promised, or from the nature of the transaction must be understood impliedly to have promised, that they would conform to that which should have been determined, in the one case by the majority, in the other by those upon whom authority had been conferred.

16. What is said, therefore, in accordance with the view not only of Carneades but also of others, that

Expediency is, as it were, the mother
Of what is just and fair,

is not true, if we wish to speak accurately. For the very nature of man, which even if we had no lack of anything would lead us into the mutual relations of society, is the mother of the law of nature. But the mother of municipal law is that obligation which arises from mutual consent; and since this obligation derives its force from the law of nature, nature may be considered, so to say, the great-grandmother of municipal law.

The law of nature nevertheless has the reinforcement of expediency; for the Author of nature willed that as individuals we should be weak, and should lack many things needed in order to live properly, to the end that we might be the more constrained to cultivate the social life. But expediency afforded an opportunity also for municipal law, since that kind of association of which we have spoken, and subjection to authority, have their roots in expediency. From this it follows that those who prescribe laws for others in so doing are accustomed to have, or ought to have, some advantage in view.

17. But just as the laws of each state have in view the advantage of that state, so by mutual consent it has become possible that certain laws should originate as between all states, or a great many states; and it is apparent that the laws thus originating had in view the advantage, not of particular states, but of the great society of states. And this is what is called the law of nations, whenever we distinguish that term from the law of nature. . . .

For since, by his own admission, the national who in his own country obeys its laws is not foolish, even though, out of regard for that law, he may be obliged to forgo certain things advantageous for himself, so that nation is not foolish which does not press its own advantage to the point of disregarding the laws common to nations. The reason in either case is the same. For just as the national, who violates the law of his country in order to obtain an immediate advantage, breaks down that by which the advantages of himself and his posterity are for all future time assured, so the state which transgresses the laws of nature and of nations cuts away also the bulwarks which safeguard its own future peace. Even if no advantage were to be contemplated from the keeping of the law, it would be a mark of wisdom, not of folly, to allow ourselves to be drawn towards that to which we feel that our nature leads.

19. Wherefore, in general, it is by no means true that

You must confess that laws were framed
From fear of the unjust,

a thought which in Plato some one explains thus, that laws were invented from fear of receiving injury, and that men are constrained by a kind of force to cultivate justice. . . .

53. From *World Peace Through World Law*

GRENVILLE CLARK AND LOUIS B. SOHN

INTRODUCTION
By Grenville Clark

This book sets forth a comprehensive and detailed plan for the maintenance of world peace in the form of a proposed revision of the United Nations Charter. The purpose is to contribute material for the world-wide discussions which must precede the adoption of universal and complete disarmament and the establishment of truly effective institutions for the prevention of war.

At the outset, it may be helpful to explain: *first*, the underlying conceptions of this plan for peace; and *second*, the main features of the plan whereby these conceptions would be carried out.

The fundamental premise of the book is identical with the pronouncement of the President of the United States on October 31, 1956: "There can be no peace without law." In this context the word "law" necessarily implies the law of a world authority, i.e., law which would be uniformly applicable to all nations and all individuals in the world and which would definitely forbid violence or the threat

of it as a means for dealing with any international dispute. This world law must also be law in the sense of law which is capable of enforcement as distinguished from a mere set of exhortations or injunctions which it is desirable to observe but for the enforcement of which there is no effective machinery.

The proposition "no peace without law" also embodies the conception that peace cannot be ensured by a continued arms race, nor by an indefinite "balance of terror," nor by diplomatic maneuver, but only by universal and complete national disarmament together with the establishment of institutions corresponding in the world field to those which maintain law and order within local communities and nations.

A prime motive for this book is that the world is far more likely to make progress toward genuine peace, as distinguished from a precarious armed truce, when a *detailed* plan adequate to the purpose is available, so that the structure and functions of the requisite world institutions may be fully discussed on a world-wide basis. Consequently, this book comprises a set of definite and interrelated proposals to carry out complete and universal disarmament and to strengthen the United Nations through the establishment of such leg-

Reprinted by permission of the publishers from *World Peace Through World Law*, third edition, by Grenville Clark and Louis B. Sohn (Cambridge, Mass.: Harvard University Press, 1966), pp. xv–xvii. Copyright © 1958, 1960, 1966 by the President and Fellows of Harvard College.

islative, executive and judicial institutions as are necessary to maintain world order.

UNDERLYING PRINCIPLES

The following are the basic principles by which Professor Sohn and I have been governed.

First: It is futile to expect genuine peace until there is put into effect an effective system of *enforceable* world law in the limited field of war prevention. This implies: (a) the complete disarmament, under effective controls, of each and every nation, and (b) the simultaneous adoption on a world-wide basis of the measures and institutions which the experience of centuries has shown to be essential for the maintenance of law and order, namely, clearly stated law against violence, courts to interpret and apply that law and police to enforce it. All else, we conceive, depends upon the acceptance of this approach.

Second: The world law against international violence must be explicitly stated in constitutional and statutory form. It must, under appropriate penalties, forbid the use of force by any nation against any other for any cause whatever, save only in self-defense; and must be applicable to all individuals as well as to all nations.

Third: World judicial tribunals to interpret and apply the world law against international violence must be established and maintained, and also organs of mediation and conciliation—so as to substitute peaceful means of adjudication and adjustment in place of violence, or the threat of it, as the means for dealing with all international disputes.

Fourth: A permanent world police force must be created and maintained which, while safeguarded with utmost care against misuse, would be fully adequate to forestall or suppress any violation of the world law against international violence.

Fifth: The complete disarmament of all the nations (rather than the mere "reduction" or "limitation" of armaments) is essential for any solid and lasting peace, this disarmament to be accomplished in a simultaneous and proportionate manner by carefully verified stages and subject to a well-organized system of inspection. It is now generally accepted that disarmament must be universal and enforceable. That it must also be complete is no less necessary, since: (a) in the nuclear age no mere reduction in the new means of mass destruction could be effective to remove fear and tension; and (b) if any substantial national armaments were to remain, even if only ten percent of the armaments of 1960, it would be impracticable to maintain a sufficiently strong world police force to deal with any possible aggression or revolt against the authority of the world organization. We should face the fact that until there is *complete* disarmament of every nation without exception there can be no assurance of genuine peace.

Sixth: Effective world machinery must be created to mitigate the vast disparities in the economic condition of various regions of the world, the continuance of which tends to instability and conflict.

The following supplementary principles have also guided us:

Active participation in the world peace authority must be universal, or virtually so; and although a few nations may be permitted to decline active membership, any such nonmember nations must be equally bound by the obligation to abolish their armed forces and to abide by all the laws and regulations of the world organization with relation to the prevention of war. It follows that ratification of the constitutional document creating the world peace organization (whether in the form of a revised United Nations Charter or otherwise) must be by a preponderant majority of all the nations and people of the world.

The world law, in the limited field of war prevention to which it would be restricted, should apply to all individual persons in the world as well as to all the nations—to the end that in case of violations by individuals without the support of their governments, the world law could be invoked directly against them without the necessity of indicting a whole nation or group of nations.

The basic rights and duties of all nations in respect of the maintenance of peace should be clearly defined not in laws enacted by a world legislature but in the constitutional document itself. That document should also carefully set forth not only the structure but also the most important powers of the various world institutions established or authorized by it: and the constitutional document should also define the limits of those powers and provide specific safeguards to guarantee the observance of those limits and the protection of individual rights against abuse of power. By this method of "constitutional legislation" the nations and peoples would know in advance within close limits what obligations they would assume by acceptance of the new world system, and only a restricted field of discretion would be left to the legislative branch of the world authority.

The powers of the world organization should be restricted to matters directly related to the maintenance of peace. All other powers should be reserved to the nations and their peoples. This definition and reservation of powers is advisable not only to avoid opposition based upon fear of possible interference in the domestic affairs of the nations, but also because it is wise for this generation to limit itself to the single task of preventing international violence or the threat of it. If we can accomplish that, we should feel satisfied and could well leave to later generations any enlargement of the powers of the world organization that they might find desirable.

While any plan to prevent war through total disarmament and the substitution of world law for international violence must be fully adequate to the end in view, it must also be *acceptable* to this generation. To propose a plan lacking in the basic essentials for the prevention of war would be futile. On the other hand, a plan which, however ideal in conception, is so far ahead of the times as to raise insuperable opposition would be equally futile. Therefore, we have tried hard to strike a sound balance by setting forth a plan which, while really adequate to prevent war, would, at the same time, be so carefully safeguarded that it *ought* to be acceptable to all nations.

It is not out of the question to carry out universal and complete disarmament and to establish the necessary new world institutions through an entirely new world authority, but it seems more normal and sensible to make the necessary revisions of the present United Nations Charter.

54. World Government

INIS L. CLAUDE, JR.

THE ANALOGY OF NATIONAL STATE AND WORLD STATE

The theory of world government is essentially analogical; it proposes to reproduce the national state on an international scale, and it looks to the operation of government as an instrument of order within national society for clues as to the means by which global order might be achieved. This clearly means that the preliminary problem for the designer of global institutions and processes is to develop an understanding of national institutions and processes. How does government function within the national state? How then might government function within the world state?

It should be acknowledged that government might not function in the same manner, or with the same degree of success, in the larger as in the smaller setting, and that devices and techniques quite different from those normally associated with government might be found appropriate for international order-keeping. Champions of world government frequently seem too much concerned

Excerpted from *Power and International Relations* by Inis L. Claude, Jr. (New York: Random House, 1962), pp. 255–271. Copyright © 1962 by Random House, Inc. Reprinted by permission of Random House, Inc. and the author. Footnotes deleted.

about the persuasiveness of advocacy to make these acknowledgements. Such dogmatic assurance that effective global institutions can be simply defined as national government writ large is as regrettable in intellectual terms as it may be satisfying in emotional terms, and one might reasonably ask for less dedication and more qualification. However, it must be stressed that this sort of ideological exuberance is not inherent in the position itself. One can legitimately ask what can be learned from national government experience that *might* usefully be adopted or adapted for the purpose of building a system of world order, without indulging in the illusion that the national and international problems are perfectly comparable or that solutions are perfectly transferable from the one level to the other. Indeed, I should argue that one *must* do so, for we are not so well supplied with promising ideas for solving the problem of war that we can afford to neglect the possibility of that decisively valuable insights might be gained in this way. Whatever its defects, the world government school of thought has to its credit the achievement of directing attention to this important question.

It is a striking fact that most commentators, whether they are numbered among the dedicated promoters of the world government movement or among those who look more dispassionately upon the theory of world government, tend to visualize national government as an instrumentality for dealing with individuals when they consider the question of the transferability of governmental techniques to the global level. Asking "What, if anything, can we learn from domestic government that might be relevant to the problem of world order?", they begin by noting that states have judges and policemen who undertake to cope with individual criminals. There is little difference on this score between those who conceive world government as dealing exclusively with individual law-breakers and those who contemplate a world organization concerned with enforcing orderly conduct upon states instead of, or in addition to, individuals; the ideal presumably is to enable a world government to relate itself to the objects of its regulatory action, whether individuals, states, or both, as an effective national government relates itself to individuals. . . .

It is strange that those who have been most devoted to the idea that the solution of the problem of relations among states is to be found in the creation of a global version of the national state have displayed so little interest in the peace-among-groups aspect of domestic government. It would seem to be almost self-evident that national societies are most comparable to the international society when they are viewed as pluralistic rather than atomistic communities, and that the problem of civil war is the closest domestic analogue of the problem of international war. If one is concerned about preventing an aggressive state from disrupting world peace, it would be more natural, I suggest, to turn one's thoughts to the prevention of large-scale rebellion against the public order in a federal system than to the prevention of armed robbery in a well-governed city. How, then, is one to explain the concentration of attention upon the analogy of domestic government as a regulator of individual behavior?

To some degree, this peculiar focus appears to be the product of an utterly unsophisticated conception of government. In schoolboyish fashion, one sees government as a legislature, a code of law, a policeman, a judge, and a jail; those who misbehave are arrested and punished. The social discipline of government is located essentially at the end of the night stick wielded by the cop on the corner. If this works in Kalamazoo, why should it not work on a world-wide scale? . . .

This explanation ought not to be pushed too far. Many prominent advocates of world government are thoroughly cognizant of the complexity of the modern governmental process; . . . How is it that men such as these consider the problem of world government as if it were a large-scale reproduction of the problem of domestic law-enforcement against individuals?

A clue may perhaps be found in the intimate association between the idea of world government and the fashionable theme of a world rule of law. *Law* is a key word in the vocabulary of world government. One reacts against anarchy—disorder, insecurity, violence, injustice visited by the strong upon the weak. In contrast, one postulates law—the symbol of the happy opposites to those distasteful and dangerous evils. Law suggests properly constituted authority and effectively implemented control; it symbolizes the supreme will of the community, the will to maintain justice and public order. This abstract concept is all too readily transformed, by worshipful contemplation, from one of the devices by which societies seek to order internal relationships, into a symbolic key to the good society. As this transformation takes place, law becomes a magic word for those who advocate world government and those who share with them the ideological bond of dedication to the rule of law. . . . Most significantly, it leads them to forget about *politics,* to play down the role of the political process in the management of human affairs, and to imagine that somehow *law,* in all its purity, can displace the soiled devices of politics.

Inexorably, the emphasis upon law which is characteristic of advocates of world government carries with it a tendency to focus upon the relationship of individuals to government; thinking in legal terms, one visualizes the individual apprehended by the police and brought before the judge. The rejection, or the brushing aside, of politics involves the neglect of the pluralistic aspect of the state, for the political process is preeminently concerned with the ordering of relationships among the groups which constitute a society. In short, it would appear to be the legal orientation of world government theory which produces its characteristic bias against treating government as an instrument for dealing with groups.

The effect of the *rule of law* stress in discouraging attention to politics, with its pluralistic implications, is illustrated by the contention of Clark and Sohn that the representatives constituting the General Assembly of their projected world organization would, after a transitional period of voting largely along national lines, "more and more tend to vote in accordance with their individual judgment as to the best interests of all the people of the world, as in the case of national parliaments where the interests of the whole nation are usually regarded as of no less importance than the interests of a particular section or group." One cannot deny that legislators sometimes exercise individual judgment or that they sometimes show great devotion to the general interest, but one would expect commentary on this subject to reflect awareness of the phenomenon of political parties. . . .

The political process by which governments attempt to manage the relationships of segments of society with each other and with the society as a whole, with all the pulling and hauling, haggling and cajoling that it involves, is not so neat and orderly, so dignified and awe-inspiring, as the law-enforcement process by which they assert authority over individuals. But it is a vitally important aspect of the role of government, and the one which bears the closest relation to the problem of establishing order in international affairs. It is ironical that those who have done most to stimulate consideration of the possible applicability of the lessons of domestic governmental experience to the problem of world order have been so enamored of the concept of law that they have neglected and discouraged consideration of the relevant aspect of that experience. . . .

Looking specifically at the United States, I suggest that the tributes which are regularly paid to the "rule of law" should more realistically be paid to the "rule of politics." In a society of contending groups, law is *not* the only effective way of preventing violence, or even the most important method; instead, politics is the device which has proved most useful. The American Civil War was the result of a failure of political adjustment among sectional forces, not of a breakdown of law enforcement against individuals. . . .

Americans today regard civil war as unthinkable; the threat and reality of such internal disorder has become a historical memory. This fundamental change of outlook does not derive from conviction that the United States Government is vastly more capable of enforcing law against individuals or segments of society in the 1960s than it was in the 1860s. Rather, it seems to me to be based upon confidence in the adequacy of our political process for working out compromises and promoting accommodations of interest among the diverse and overlapping groups which constitute American society. . . .

One of the lessons of governmental experience is that coercion can seldom be usefully invoked against significant collectivities which exhibit a determination to defend their interests, as they conceive them, against the public authority. The order-keeping function of government is not fulfilled by the winning of a civil war, but by its prevention. If groups cannot be coerced without the disruption of the order which government exists to maintain, it does not follow that the alternative tactic of coercing individuals should be adopted. What follows is rather that the difficult task of ordering group relationships by political means should be attempted. . . .

I would conclude that theorists of world government are not mistaken in their insistence that one should look to domestic governmental experience for clues as to the most promising means for achieving world order, but that they tend to misread the lessons of that experience. In some instances, they treat the domestic problem of crime prevention as comparable to the international problem of war, and draw from national experience the conclusion that the central function of a world government would be to maintain order by enforcing legal restrictions upon individual behavior. In other instances, they note the domestic problem of coping with dissident groups, acknowledge its comparability to the problem of dealing with aggressive states, and suggest that the governmental pattern requires that a central authority be equipped with adequate military force to coerce any possible rebellion within the larger society.

In contrast, I would argue that the prevention of civil war is the function of national government most relevant to the problem of ordering international relations, that governments cannot and do not perform this function by relying primarily upon either police action against individuals or military action against significant segments of their societies, and that governments succeed in this vitally important task only when they are able to operate an effective system of political accommodation. . . .

This conception treats government not as a monopoly of power which effectuates a rule of law, but as the focal point of a political process. If the history of national government tells us anything about the problem of achieving international order, it seems to me to be this: There is no substitute for political adjustment as a means of managing relationships among the units which constitute complex human societies, and there is no magic formula for producing either the kind of society which lends itself to ordering in this manner or the kind of institutional system which can effectively preside over the process of adjustment.

I do not contend that this analysis demonstrates the invalidity of the concept, or that it disproves the desirability of a system of world government. It does, I think, call into question the assumption that the task of devising an adequate theoretical scheme for world order has been completed—that we know the answer to the problem, and now face only the issue of whether, and how, the answer can be translated from theory into reality. To say that the insti-

tution of government in international affairs would transform that realm from a world of politics into a world of law seems to me to deny the lessons of experience with governed national societies, and to lead to false expectations regarding the means by which relations among states may be regulated. To say that the management of power in international relations cannot be achieved except by concentrating an effective monopoly of power in a central agency, which thus becomes capable of maintaining order by the threat of bringing overwhelming coercion to bear against any and all dissident elements, seems to me to misstate the position which governments occupy in national societies and to overstate both the requirements and the possibilities of the centralization of coercive capacity in the global society. To say that governments succeed, if they do and when they do, in maintaining order by sensitive and skillful operation of the mechanisms of political adjustment seems to me to be correct—but it does not point the way to a revolutionary new system of international relations, or promise a dramatic escape from the perils of international conflict. The idealized concept of government which advocates of world government expound exists primarily in their own minds; few actual governments are very government-like in their terms. The more mundane version of government which I have described is not wholly missing even in the international sphere; in my terms, the United Nations is not entirely "un-government-like." Government, defined in terms of the function of promoting order through political management of inter-group relations, is a matter of degree. Looking at it in this way, we can say that British society enjoys a high degree of government, that Indonesian society suffers from having achieved only a precarious minimum of government, and that the international society is in dire peril because of the manifest inadequacy of the level of government which it has thus far reached.

In the final analysis, it appears that the theory of world government does not *answer* the question of how the world can be saved from catastrophic international conflict. Rather, it helps us to *restate* the question: How can the world achieve the degree of assurance that inter-group conflicts will be resolved or contained by political rather than violent means that has been achieved in the most effectively governed states? This is a valuable and provocative restatement of the question—but it ought not to be mistaken for a definitive answer.